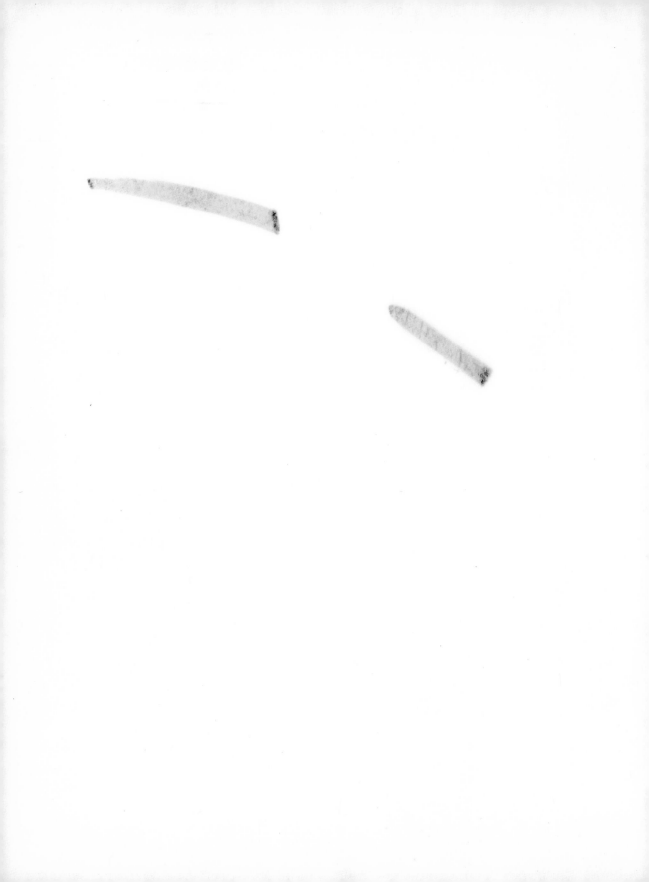

Marketing Management

The Irwin Series in Marketing
Consulting Editor Gilbert A. Churchill, Jr., University of Wisconsin, Madison

Marketing Management

David W. Cravens
Texas Christian University

Gerald E. Hills
University of Illinois at Chicago

Robert B. Woodruff
University of Tennessee

1987

IRWIN

Homewood, Illinois 60430

Cover: Computer Graphic Image by Ron Scott © 1986

© RICHARD D. IRWIN, INC., 1987

ISBN 0-256-05547-5

Library of Congress Catalog Card No. 86-82594

Printed in the United States of America

1 2 3 4 5 6 7 8 9 0 DO 4 3 2 1 0 9 8 7

This book is dedicated to
Karen Cravens
Douglas and Renee Hills
Christopher Woodruff

Preface

As the practice of marketing nears the 1990s, its role in business practice is clearly critical. Rapid change and intense global competition exist in many markets. Deregulation in key industries such as transportation, communications, and financial services has led to the need for market-driven strategies. Nonprofit organizations have discovered the importance of marketing in attaining goals. Buyers of consumer and business goods and services increasingly demand products that meet their specific needs. Finally, survival and growth in a turbulent environment are more and more difficult to achieve without professional marketing practices.

Because markets and market opportunity are greatly affected by worldwide environmental forces, marketing plays a leading role in designing and implementing strategic business plans. Marketing management should be viewed as an enterprise-spanning activity, not restricted to the marketing or sales department. Broadly defined, marketing is a responsibility of the entire organization. Key strategic marketing decisions include determining which target markets to serve, choosing the product or service to offer and setting its price, designing a channel of distribution, and planning advertising and selling programs. These all require in-depth analyses of environmental, market, and competitive conditions, the stock-in-trade of marketing professionals.

Substantial progress is occurring in advancing the state of the art of marketing management practice. Strategic marketing concepts, behavioral and analytical techniques, and systematic approaches to marketing decision making are dramatically increasing the impact of marketing in business and nonbusiness organizations. Different types of organizations, from banks to hospitals to charities to governments, are integrating marketing management into their operations. Increasing organizational effectiveness demands that managers understand the fundamentals of marketing practice. Education is crucial for managers who specialize in marketing functions and for those who interact with marketing personnel in the integration of marketing into the organizational mission.

This book is built upon a solid core that existed within a previously published book, *Marketing Decision Making: Concepts and Strategy.* That book was consistently used in well over one hundred universities. It ranked second among the marketing MBA textbooks for many years and was widely adopted for junior and senior classes. Nevertheless, we decided to start anew, to take a fresh look at the needs and interests of professors and students in these markets and to develop a high-quality book that would fit today's marketplace. The result was this book.

The book has several strengths:

■ *Active Writing Style.* Special attention has been given to making the writing as clear, concise, and action oriented as the ideas and concepts themselves.

■ *Strategic Orientation.* Reflecting the reality of a competitive marketplace has forced business managers to think longer term, in the context of organizational strengths, weaknesses, and positioning.

■ *Implementation Focus.* Through examples and a special chapter section, emphasis has been given to the importance of successfully implementing strategic plans through marketing practices at the lowest level of the organization.

■ *Competitive Positioning.* Reflecting the heightened realization that increasingly intense competition often spells success or failure, a full chapter covers this topic analytically and practically.

■ *International/Global Focus.* Through examples and a special chapter, considerable attention has been given to the world marketplace.

■ *Environmental Scanning.* Market and competitive situations often change because of broader, macroenvironmental changes. A chapter highlights a process for strategically monitoring basic shifts in the macroenvironment.

■ *Market Opportunity Analysis.* Extensive conceptual and practical coverage has been given to the identification and evaluation of market opportunities.

■ *Services and Nonprofit Focus.* There is no longer a dominance of goods marketing, and the examples provided in this book reflect that reality of modern economies. Special sections have also been devoted to the uniquenesses of services and nonprofit marketing.

■ *Current and Classic Examples.* A special effort has been made to provide numerous examples of effective marketing practices that are interesting and relevant to our readers.

Developing marketing strategies is a systematic process requiring information and analysis as the basis for decisions and action. This process is operationalized in this book by viewing marketing decision making as three major, largely sequential activities:

■ Managerial analysis of the marketing environment.
■ Market opportunity analysis.
■ Design, implementation, and control of marketing strategy.

This highly practical framework combines information, analysis, and action into an integrated approach to marketing management. These sequential activities are adaptable to any type of organization that is faced with attracting support from external publics or constituencies.

Integration of this practical approach is seen across chapters and sections. The chapter sequence emphasizes the importance of basing the formulation of marketing strategy on a foundation of well-developed information. Chapters are organized around a decision-making framework, so that the factors relevant to each marketing activity are systematically integrated. The intent is to construct a "picture" of marketing management that readers can supplement and apply to any organization. Extensive use of examples illustrates how strategy is formulated and implemented.

There is a clear emphasis on how marketing management decisions should be made. The reader will find a useful approach for analyzing marketing situations rather than just descriptions of business practice. The objective is not only to impart an understanding of marketing management but also to offer an approach to marketing management that will contribute to organizational performance. The role of analytical models and techniques is discussed in a readily understandable fashion.

Another significant feature of this book is the extensive attention it gives to the role of information in marketing decision making. Marketing's unique contribution to organization management lies in developing and using information about the environment, markets, and competitors as a basis for sound marketing practice. Practical information-gathering methods for analyzing markets are presented. The approach integrates procedures into an overall process that shows how to carry out needed analyses. The presentation goes well beyond a mere discussion of buyer behavior and marketing research to providing operational approaches to gathering, interpreting, and using information for marketing decisions. Managers who develop and implement marketing strategy can use these approaches to tap market opportunities.

This book is organized into six parts. In Part 1, marketing planning in the organization is examined and linked to the corporate mission and strategy. Part 2 is concerned with analyzing the marketing situation. Understanding the environment, buyer behavior, markets, and competition is critical to sales forecasting and marketing strategy development. An operational approach to market analysis is presented, utilizing an increasingly specific process that ranges from broad consideration of product markets to selecting the target markets that best correspond with the corporate mission. Part 3 examines several important aspects of marketing strategy development, including marketing planning, strategic situation screening, target marketing and positioning, and new product development. In Part 4, the marketing decision areas are considered, including the product or service, the channel of distribution, physical distribution, pricing, advertising, and sales force management decisions. Strategies in each of these areas are integrated to seek favorable responses from the organization's target markets. In Part 5, guidelines for effectively implementing the marketing program are presented, with attention to effectively organizing the effort, analyzing performance, and gathering market research and feedback. Finally, in Part 6, expanding international and global marketing activity is highlighted, the importance of marketing in nonprofit organizations is discussed, and major legal and social issues that pertain to marketing are examined.

A comprehensive instructors' manual is available, containing suggestions for course design, teaching-learning objectives, and teaching approaches for each chapter. Several student projects are suggested, and guidelines are provided for the end-of-chapter exercises. Cases are suggested, and a large bank of objective test questions is included. An expanded set of transparency masters covering each chapter is available in a separate package to facilitate the preparation of class presentation materials.

David W. Cravens
Gerald E. Hills
Robert B. Woodruff

Acknowledgments

No book is written in a vacuum. Numerous professional and personal relationships contributed to the development of this product.

At Texas Christian University, the encouragement and support of Dean Edward Johnson and Department Chairman Charles W. Lamb, Jr., are sincerely appreciated. The assistance and suggestions of many graduate assistants and students provided an important student perspective in the development of the book and supporting package. Finally, a special thank you is given to Sue Cravens and Nancy Robbins for their efforts in typing the manuscript and assisting on various other aspects of the project.

At the University of Illinois at Chicago, thanks go to Deans Marcus Alexis and Ralph L. Westfall, to Dr. Chem L. Narayana, Head of the Department of Marketing, and to Professors Lawrence Feldman, Albert L. Page, and Robert E. Weigand for their valuable suggestions regarding chapter content. Special thanks go to Mary Ann Koch, Maria Lowers, Gerri Shehorn, and Paul Ragas for converting rough script into legible chapters and to Beverly J. Parker, James W. Powers, David B. Vaughn, and Wendy Kabaker for indispensable research assistance throughout the process. Thanks also go to Dr. Charles Davis at the University of Missouri, Kansas City, for his insightful reviews and to the Coleman/Fannie May Candies Foundation for their support and assistance. Finally, the highest thank you must go to Michele Hills and to Douglas and Renee for their patience, understanding, and assistance.

At the University of Tennessee, Knoxville, appreciation is extended to Dean C. Warren Neel and to Dr. David J. Barnaby, Chairman of the Department of Marketing and Transportation, for helping to create an environment in which contributions to the profession are clearly encouraged. Meeting deadlines is always tough in a long developmental process, and so thanks are in order to those that helped me prepare and deliver manuscript on time— Sally Bullard, Coleen Thomason, and Rich Morrison. Finally, I could not have accomplished all that was expected without that special patience and understanding that only a family can give. So a heartfelt thank you is extended to Dorothy and Chris Woodruff.

The following reviewers contributed to the development of this book:

Gilbert A. Churchill, Jr.,
University of Wisconsin, Madison

Benny Barak
CUNY—Bernard M. Baruch

Delores A. Barsellotti
California State Polytechnic

Alan J. Bush
Louisiana State University

David K. Chowdhury
British Columbia Institute of Technology

Eddie V. Easley
Drake University

Gary M. Erickson
University of Washington

J. Robert Foster
University of Texas at El Paso

Deborah Roedder John
University of Wisconsin, Madison

Michael Menasco
University of California—Los Angeles

Philip Rosson
Dalhousie University

John Schlacter
Arizona State University

and Donald L. Shawver
University of Missouri—Columbia

Thanks also go to our professional peers who granted us permission to use their materials, although we accept all responsibility for any errors or omissions. Finally, and importantly, we thank our students from whom we learn as well as teach.

Contents

Part 3 Marketing Strategy Development

Part 4   Marketing Program Design

Decisions: *Sales Force Role and Objectives. Deployment Decisions. Management of the Sales Force. Evaluation and Control.*

Part 5 Implementing the Marketing Program

What Is an Organization? Designing the Marketing Organization. Organizational Decisions within Marketing: *Functionally-Based Organization. Product-Based Organization. Customer-Based Organization. Geographically Based Organization. Combination of Bases. Organizational Patterns. Implementation and Marketing Organization. Marketing within the Corporate Organization.* Intercorporate Linkages.

The Marketing Control Process: *Controlling Activity Centers. The Control Process.* Monitoring Marketing Performance: *Specifying Performance and Setting Standards. Data for Monitoring Performance.* Comparing Performance to Standards: *Control Requires Standards for Performance. Finding Problems with Static Comparisons. Finding Problems with Time-Oriented Comparisons.* Searching for Causes of Problems: *Examining Marketing Effort in Activity Centers. Searching for External Causes. The Marketing Audit.* Action to Correct Problems.

Strategies for Obtaining Information: *Deciding What Information Is Needed. Collect Existing Information. Use Standarized Research Services. Conduct Research Study.* Evaluating Costs and Benefits of Alternative Information Strategies: *Coping with Uncertain Benefits. Decision Models.* Designing the Research Study: *Problem Formulation. Research Design. Data Collection Methods. Sampling Design. Data Collection. Analysis and Results.* Evaluating Research Suppliers: *Supplier Services. Evaluation Guidelines.* Building a Marketing Information System: *Uses of an MIS. Components of an MIS. Decision Support Systems.*

Part 6 Marketing's Broadening Role

International Marketing: *Analyze the Macro and Task Environments. Determine Which Markets to Enter. Select Entry Strategies. Designing the Marketing Program.* Nonprofit Marketing: *The Uniquenesses of Nonbusiness Marketing. Social and Nonbusiness Marketing.*

Marketing Management

PART

1

*S*ophisticated marketing management practices are increasingly used by profit and nonprofit organizations serving domestic as well as international markets. Organizations achieve their objectives better when they develop marketing strategies to serve carefully defined target markets. In today's economy, marketing is a basic factor in the success of both profit and nonprofit organizations, an understanding important for all functional specialists, whether accountants, engineers, or marketers.

Chapter 1 outlines the nature of marketing and the perspective of organizations serving customers and markets. This perspective permeates every chapter—and virtually every successful business as well. Marketing management is a process that includes monitoring the macroenvironment, identifying and understanding market opportunities, developing marketing strategies, and then implementing and controlling the outcomes.

Marketing is playing an increasing role within corporate strategy. Chapter 2 examines the strategic planning process used in many companies and shows how marketing contributes to such a process. We discuss developing a company mission and objectives and deciding on the units that should comprise a business. The strategic analysis of business units is illustrated and the selection of a business unit strategy shown. Finally, the role of marketing in an overall business strategy is highlighted.

The six sections of this book show how marketing works: they cover marketing planning, analyzing the situation, developing marketing strategy, marketing program design, implementation, and finally, coping with social and legal forces as well as nonprofit and international markets ∎

CHAPTER 1

Marketing Management

*E*ntrepreneur R. David Thomas opened the first Wendy's restaurant because he saw an unfilled need in the marketplace. Thus, he started with a market orientation.[1] Realizing that many consumers wanted more choice and a fresher hamburger than they received at McDonald's, he decided to sell his four Kentucky Fried Chicken franchises and open Wendy's (his daughter's nickname was Wendy.) Thomas said, "I like a hamburger with mustard, pickle, and onion, and you didn't have a choice at a McDonald's or Burger King. I thought the other ones were . . . just giving you what they wanted to and not what you really wanted." This kind of customer orientation is the foundation for modern marketing. "No one else was doing a very good job, and I wanted a hamburger that was different, made to order so you could choose whatever you wanted to put on it and get out of the heat-lamp and heat-bin syndrome." Thomas did not use frozen patties but made his hamburger fresh daily, and he let the customers select their own condiments. That provided customers with 256 choices. The market perceived Wendy's products to be of higher quality and better taste than those of the competition, and Thomas grabbed a piece of the market not exploited by McDonald's and Burger King. Wendy's went on to successfully offer the restaurant industry's first drive-up windows.

When Thomas started, McDonald's had 1,298 restaurants. Two years after he started, he had two restaurants. He opened 2 more the year after that, then 4 more, then 12 more. In 1973, he sold his first franchise for $5,000 (they now sell for $25,000); in 1976, there were 300 Wendy's restaurants and the company went public. By the mid-1980s, nearly 3,500 Wendy's were operating in the United States and 19 other countries. McDonald's had grown to 8,900 units and Burger King to 4,600. In the early days, Thomas joked with others about becoming as big as McDonald's. But now people no longer laugh when

EXHIBIT 1-1

All types of organizations use marketing.

Courtesy Civic Center for Performing Arts.

he says, "We will be as big as McDonald's." R. David Thomas, along with a talented, professional management team, has once again shown what can be done with entrepreneurial spirit and sound marketing fundamentals.

Marketing has long been a major strength in many companies. The strategic importance of marketing is widely accepted by top executives, and they are moving toward greater **marketing** professionalism. A study by Coopers & Lybrand, the accounting firm, indicates that in 1983 only 29 percent of executives believed that marketing was the most important management area, but by 1986, when the study was released, 64 percent held that opinion. The report, titled "Business Planning in the Eighties: The New Marketing Shape of American Corporations," concluded that strategic marketing, marketing strategies, and market plans that help corporations develop and hold a competitive advantage were paramount management issues. It stated:

Customers needs, wants, and desires long have been management concerns at consumer goods firms, and that same marketing focus is becoming the standard at

Marketing
is the process of planning and executing the conception, pricing, promotion, and distribution of ideas, goods, and services to create exchanges that satisfy individual and organizational objectives.[2]

high-tech, industrial, and services firms as well . . . . CEOs intend to get closer to their customers by forging a closer link between marketing and strategic planning, elevating marketing to equal status with other corporate functions in the process.[3]

The Wendy's operation illustrates the definition of marketing. Through convenient distribution of quality goods and services at the right price, Wendy's has created millions of mutually beneficial exchanges that satisfy individuals and attain company objectives. With blockbuster promotion, including Clara Peller and the "Where's the Beef?" commercials, the number of exchanges and the amount of profits continue skyward.

This chapter begins by defining marketing and discussing the marketing concept, the foundation of contemporary marketing management. Then, it compares market-oriented companies with companies that tend to be driven by technology, manufacturing, or sales. Next, it provides an overview of effective marketing management, which includes monitoring macroenvironmental trends, conducting market opportunity analyses, developing marketing strategies, and implementing and controlling the results. Finally, the marketing management process is applied in an actual marketing situation.

Marketing today is widely used by both profit and nonprofit organizations to attain their objectives. Whether what is being marketed is hamburgers, industrial toxic gas detectors in India, the idea that high salt consumption is bad, or the Joffrey Ballet (Exhibit 1-1), marketing is basically the same. This book shows how to carry out marketing activities and how to understand and relate to those activities. We have defined marketing; now we will define a related but different term—the marketing concept.

Marketing Concept

Marketing concept is a customer-oriented philosophy that is implemented and integrated throughout an organization to serve customers better than competitors and achieve specified goals.

The foundation for contemporary marketing management is the **marketing concept**, which provides an orientation for conducting business, a way of thinking, and a basic approach to business problems. Although the marketing concept seems obvious, a surprising number of firms still fail to grasp its far-reaching implications.

Marketing itself is, of course, a specific function in the enterprise, as are finance and accounting. But the *marketing concept* is fundamental to the overall rationale and conduct of the enterprise.

Marketing requires separate work and a distinct group of activities. But it is, first, a central dimension of the entire business. It is the whole business seen from the point of view of its final result, that is, from the customer's point of view.[4]

As Exhibit 1-2 shows, the marketing concept is made up of three components. Starting with customer needs and wants, a firm must develop an organizationally integrated marketing strategy and thereby accomplish its organizational goals. Let us look now at each of the three components.

EXHIBIT 1-2 The Marketing Concept

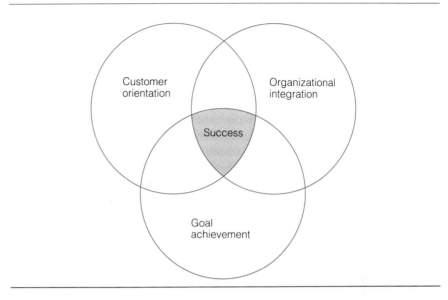

Customer Orientation

Over three decades ago, General Electric pioneered in developing the marketing concept. As expressed by a GE executive, the concept begins with the customer: "The principal task of the marketing function in a management concept is not so much to be skillful in making the customer do what suits the interests of the business as to be skillful in conceiving and then making the business do what suits the interests of the customer."[5]

A host of firms followed General Electric's lead. Well before deregulation, John D. deButts, then chairman of American Telephone & Telegraph, entered millions of households via television advertising. His message: "We're redesigning our marketing approach to serve customer needs." The shift represented a major commitment to managing AT&T within the guidelines provided by the marketing concept. Historically a product-oriented company, this corporate giant rapidly shifted to a customer focus. The role of the customer in AT&T's new management philosophy is described as follows:

> More than technology, however, it is our customers' needs that shape our services. Accordingly, our marketing organization has undertaken comprehensive surveys of the operations of the nation's principal industries and the role that communications play in improving their effectiveness and profitability. Our aim is to design service offerings that meet or—better—anticipate these needs.[6]

This management philosophy ultimately helped smooth AT&T's mid-1980s transition to fully confronting competitive market forces. Moreover, in contributing to the company's admirable record of offering high-quality, cus-

EXHIBIT 1–3 More Firms Use 800 Numbers To Keep Consumers Satisfied

When gizzards and livers were dropped from the Kentucky Fried Chicken menu, disappointed customers in Louisville didn't have to stew in silence. They could air their gripes on a toll-free telephone hot line that the chicken chain is testing there.

Dishwasher on the fritz? Phone General Electric, whose customer service staff can also answer questions about GE jet engines or the composers of music in GE television commercials.

Kentucky Fried Chicken and General Electric are among the latest companies to join a growing list of marketers with 800 phone lines for their customers. Pioneered several years ago by Whirlpool, Polaroid, Clairol, and Procter & Gamble, the toll-free services have spread rapidly.

"Major companies, including GE, have become somewhat faceless," says Powell Taylor, manager of GE's Answer Center, which expects 1.5 million calls this year.

Answering a complaint or an inquiry costs roughly $3 for a three-minute phone conversation. Often that's more than the cost of the product itself and several times the profit that the manufacturer makes from the sale. But "companies no longer are looking at complaints as just a nuisance," says John Goodman, president of Technical Assistance Research Programs, Inc., a customer service consultant. "By aggressively soliciting them, you can improve brand loyalty."

Many companies have overlooked the cost of alienating consumers, says Mr. Goodman. His company's studies show that only about 4 percent of dissatisfied customers complain to a manufacturer. Instead, they usually stop buying the product and also bad-mouth it to 9 or 10 other people.

In contrast, quickly resolved complaints lead to repeat purchases in 95 percent of the cases involving inexpensive items and 82 percent of those involving products that cost at least $100.

Surprisingly, only a minority of calls are actual complaints. P&G classifies one third of its calls as such; Clairol, 15 percent; and GE, 8 percent. Even irate customers frequently compliment the companies for providing human contact.

Source: Abstracted from Bill Abrams, "More Firms Use '800' Numbers To Keep Customers Satisfied," *The Wall Street Journal*, April 7, 1983, p. 31. Reprinted by permission of *The Wall Street Journal*, © Dow Jones & Company, Inc., 1983. All rights reserved.

tomer-oriented telephone services to diverse markets, it illustrates the benefits of the controversial breakup of Ma Bell.

Since no businesses have the skills and resources to be all things to all people, management must identify which customer preferences can and should be met. Deciding which preferences and potential customers to serve is crucial, given any firm's limited resources and competitive strengths. Selectively choosing **target markets** is an integral part of the philosophy suggested by the marketing concept. The alternative is to try to serve all potential customers in a mediocre fashion and thus to fall short in providing customer satisfaction and achieving organizational goals. A specific implementation of the marketing concept is the use of 800 telephone numbers, as reported in Exhibit 1–3.

Target market is a group of existing or potential customers within a particular product market toward which an organization directs its marketing efforts.

Organizational Integration

For many managers, beginning with the customer's needs and wants when planning the organization's marketing efforts, is nothing more than common sense. By necessity, this managerial approach has been prevalent in successful firms for decades. Although the marketing concept is simple and logical, its significance and the difficulty of implementing it should not be underestimated. The marketing concept offers key guidelines for planning, organizing, integrating, and managing the entire enterprise—not just marketing. Its philosophy should span the entire organization because marketing and nonmarketing functions in a company together determine whether the company as a whole is customer oriented. Consider these other parts of the organization and some ways in which they can undermine the implementation of the marketing concept:

- Credit: A conservative financial administrator grants credit only to firms with the very highest credit rating and thereby alienates potential customers.
- Research and development: A product is developed with components of the highest quality, but the market rejects the added cost of such components.
- Production: Employees are not motivated to produce a quality product with resulting quality control problems and customer dissatisfaction.
- Personnel: Secretarial personnel are not trained to deal with incoming customer calls pleasantly and tactfully.

Although marketing by definition links the firm and its customers, most departments and employees in a company affect how customers perceive the firm. Only through leadership at the top, with related organizational structures, policies, and procedures, can the marketing concept be integrated throughout the firm. This requires that executives answer the question, "What business are we in?" with the answer "that of deciding which customers to serve and then satisfying them." The marketing concept is not marketing as a business function but marketing as a philosophy for doing business. It applies to accounting, finance, personnel, production, and all other business functions. Without satisfied customers who return again and again, *all* of these functions cease to exist! A customer-oriented, integrated organization is exemplified by Whirlpool (Exhibit 1-4).

Typical organizational structures are shown in Exhibit 1-5. The "Before" portion makes no reference to marketing—only to sales, advertising, and service. The "After" portion discloses several changes concerned with marketing. A high-level executive is responsible for organizing and managing all of the firm's marketing activities. The functions associated with the marketing program are grouped together to facilitate the development of an integrated marketing strategy. The new organizational arrangements also facilitate the coordination of marketing activities with other business functions in the enterprise. Despite these improvements, the marketing concept remains difficult to implement due to the extensive coordination that is required.

Goal Achievement

In most companies, the marketing function was once viewed as responsible for achieving only sales objectives, not broader organizational goals. The marketing concept changed this view. An objective in GE's original statement of its marketing concept was "obtaining profitable sales," not just high-volume sales. Although organizations vary in what they want to accomplish,

EXHIBIT 1-4

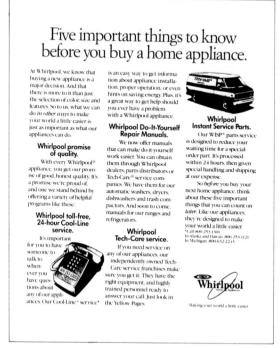

Whirlpool pledges not only a quality product but also a customer-oriented, integrated service organization.

Courtesy D'Arcy Masius Benton & Bowles, Inc.

they are all concerned with more than meeting sales goals. Not-for-profit organizations such as the U.S. Postal Service are concerned with costs as well as revenues. The dangers of an excessive emphasis on sales are illustrated by the experience of the W. T. Grant general merchandise chain, an American institution for nearly a century, which went bankrupt despite a very high sales level.

Another call for attention to profitable sales, not just sales volume, was made in the 1980s by Robert A. Fox, president of Del Monte Corporation.

Profitability in the decades ahead may depend importantly on our ability to put marketing on a more businesslike basis, to go beyond traditional or volume-oriented marketing practices and achieve a much more selective, profit-oriented approach.

The first third of this century might best be characterized as "The Age of the Salesman." Markets were young, products were new, and there seemed to be no limit to the number of potential customers. A company's greatest asset was the champion salesman, with the loyalty of Willie Loman and the flair of Professor

EXHIBIT 1-5 Organizational Integration of the Marketing Concept

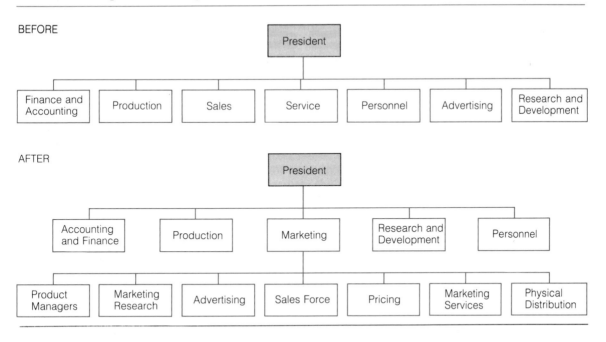

Harold Hill, traveling the land with a smile and a shoeshine, outtalking the competition.

The middle third of the century might best be characterized as "The Age of the Branded Product." Dozens of brand names became household words from Maine to California; America's evenings were spent with the Chase and Sanborn Hour, the Kraft Music Hall, the Voice of Firestone, or the Camel Caravan. Advertising slogans and company logos became as familiar to Americans as the folks next door. Brand marketing had become a nationwide phenomenon.

For the past [two decades], however, the marketplace has been changing. . . . What we have been witnessing, I believe, is the start of a new era. One of "slow" or "no" growth, of even more intense competition; the age, not of the salesman or the brand, but of the total business manager. Good salespeople and good products, while still essential, are not enough. In the future, the emphasis must be on total business management—on our ability to take a much more critical approach to products, to costs, to markets, even to volume, than we have in the past.[7]

But a further update of the marketing concept requires recognizing the role of marketing in achieving goals other than profits. Such goals may include altering a firm's image or increasing its market share. Nonprofit organizations seek a variety of goals. The American Cancer Society strives to reduce the sale of cigarettes. A community zoo works toward educational objectives. Marketing thus plays a broader role than increasing sales (and even profit), and the third pillar of the marketing concept, goal achievement, reflects this fact. The underlying goal of all marketing activity is customer satisfaction, whether that satisfaction is achieved by visiting the zoo, giving up cigarettes, or using a newly purchased personal computer.

Variations exist in the extent to which organizations have adopted the marketing concept. Such variations have been related to firm size, channel level (manufacturers, middlemen, retailers), and type of customer (consumer or industrial). Consumer goods firms have implemented the marketing concept more extensively than industrial producers, and larger firms (over $150 million annual sales) tend to adopt and implement the concept more extensively than small and medium-sized firms. But the differences are diminishing.

Is the Marketing Concept Adequate?

Some critics have viewed the marketing concept as hype rather than actual management philosophy. In reality, however, the marketing concept simply underscores the fact that few businesses survive over the long term if they take an "us versus them" approach. For a profit or nonprofit organization to remain viable, its marketing exchanges must be perceived as mutually beneficial (see the marketing definition).

It has been said, however, that the perception of mutual benefit is not enough, that the marketing concept is faltering in today's environment because, even though organizations respond to customer groups, they are not sufficiently responsive to society. Providing narrowly defined customer groups with what they want leads to the sale of knives, guns, fireworks, high-speed automobiles, junk food, and many other potentially harmful products. Customer satisfaction may be high, but the overall societal impact may be negative.

Critics who hold such views have called for a *societal marketing concept*. This would require company managements to "include the consideration of social implications in their decision processes and their management control procedures."[8] Although social responsibility is perhaps implied in the marketing concept, consumerism and related social concerns accentuate its importance. Increasingly, firms such as McDonald's and Xerox include a strong commitment to social responsibility in their corporate objectives and recognize that customer satisfaction must take into account the societal impact of a product's use.

Technology, Manufacturing, and Sales Orientation

The previous section focused on customer- or market-oriented organizations but made little mention of other basic management orientations that may exist in organizations. Companies that are not market oriented are often technology or product oriented, manufacturing (production) oriented, or selling oriented.

Technology and Product Orientation

A technology or product orientation often exists in firms that have had a highly successful product. Where such an orientation exists, management implicitly believes that if "you build a better mousetrap, the world will beat a path to your door." It is true that, given enough publicity, a glamorous technological innovation may for a time seem to create its own market. Yet competition inevitably grows and product obsolescence eventually sets in. Texas Instruments has been accused of being a technology-oriented company because when it was founded, its high-tech products seemed almost to sell themselves. In recent years, however, competition and the company's failure to adapt spelled trouble for its entry into the home computer market. The personal computer industry in general has come under criticism for its product orientation:

> The industry's enthusiastic marketing staffs have rushed to tell the world about the technical wizardry of their new computers—but typically haven't stopped to explain why the world needs their products. . . . these ads risk losing computer illiterates unversed in bits and bytes. Lotus Development Corp., for instance, once talked about the superior features of its 1-2-3 spreadsheet program, but now, sensing confusion among shoppers, simply stresses the security factor of buying the industry's best selling program.[9]

Entrepreneurs with nontechnical products also often exclude the market side of their business. Their total commitment to a product often impedes its market success. Management in product-oriented firms thinks in terms of the product itself rather than of the needs and wants it must serve. Communicating the reasons to buy a product requires adopting the role of a buyer, not that of an engineer, inventor, or developer. A product orientation, somewhat ironically, is sometimes evident in nonprofit organizations as well. On the assumption that a service or cause fulfills a need or want, it sometimes becomes the entire rationale for an organization. But the organization may fill a need for a time and then fade away as needs change.

There is, obviously, a very real need for the development of quality technology, products, and services. But these should not be developed for their own sake. For an organization to be successful, its products must respond to needs. The continuing high failure rate of new products provides ongoing evidence that a product orientation exists in many firms. Although the product is a critically important part of a marketing strategy, the value of the marketing concept as a guiding philosophy for corporate and marketing strategies cannot be overemphasized. Peter Drucker captured the essential difference between a product orientation and a customer orientation:

> True marketing starts . . . with the customer. . . . It asks, "What does the customer want to buy?" It does not say, "This is what our product or service does." It says, "These are the satisfactions the customer looks for, values, and needs."[10]

Manufacturing Orientation

The manufacturing or production orientation arose when there was a scarcity of basic goods, because at that time the firms with the most efficient production processes were often the most successful. Demand exceeded supply, and companies could be primarily producers, with limited market sensitivity. In the highly competitive business environment of industrialized countries today, production-oriented firms often have difficulty. With intense import competition, the U.S. auto industry has been struggling to better balance a marketing and manufacturing orientation. But critics still charge that Detroit is production oriented rather than market oriented. With massive investments in production, plant, and equipment, as well as related human resources, auto executives are understandably tempted to orient themselves toward the production processes that control much of their companies' day-to-day activity. Yet the record of the past two decades provides clear evidence of that orientation's pitfalls.

By the mid-1980s, another challenge confronted U.S. carmakers. Following the onslaught of Japanese competition, European cars were capturing a growing share of the U.S. luxury auto market:

> In 1970, U.S. sales of all European luxury cars amounted to only 68,000 units. But this had changed by the mid-1980s. European "imports have become our number 1 competitor," said L. B. Pryor, general sales manager of General Motors Corporation's Cadillac Division.
>
> European models, which are often higher priced, produced in limited quantities, and considered better values than U.S. luxury cars, also confer prestige.
>
> From 1975 to 1983, foreign makes doubled their share of the U.S. luxury car market to 38 percent, or 363,000 units, according to figures from Chase Econometrics. More importantly, the Chase figures indicated that luxury imports were capturing the most lucrative part of the market: young people.
>
> Selling cars to those affluent families became increasingly difficult for the Big Three U.S. makers as the once-obscure European models became popular status symbols.
>
> Besides looks, import buyers prefer the performance and handling of foreign models.[11]

Success requires good products, good production, good marketing, and a well-coordinated team effort. The philosophy that an organization exists to create satisfied customers is more viable than the philosophy that an organization's existence is justified by the creation of superior production processes. An organization that exists to serve the larger community and society has a sound foundation for long-term success.

EXHIBIT 1–6 Management Orientations Compared

	Manufacturing Oriented	Sales Oriented	Technology Oriented	Marketing Oriented
Typical strategy	Lower cost	Increase volume	Push research	Build Share and profitability
Key systems	Plant P&Ls Budgets	Sales forecasts Results versus plan	Performance tests R&D plans	Marketing plans
Traditional skills	Engineering	Sales	Science and engineering	Market analysis
Normal focus	Internal efficiencies	Distribution channels Short-term sales results	Product performance	Consumers and market share
Typical response to competitive pressure	Cut costs	Cut price Sell harder	Improve product	Consumer research, planning, testing, refining
Overall mental set	"What we need to do in this company is get our costs down and our quality up."	"Where can I sell what we make?"	"The best product wins the day."	"What will the consumer buy that we can profitably make?"

Source: Adapted from Edward G. Michaels, "Marketing Muscle," *Business Horizons*, May–June 1982, p. 72. Copyright 1982 by the Foundation for the School of Business at Indiana University. Reprinted by permission.

Sales Orientation

Finally, an organization with a sales orientation is one that assumes that effective selling can push its output into the hands of customers. Even professional personal selling, however, is at most one element in an overall marketing program. A selling orientation is an orientation geared toward converting an existing product into cash rather than an orientation that begins with customer needs and responds to those needs before the product rolls off the production line. Pushing products is less necessary if an organization's products are better able to fill needs than the products offered by competitors. An office furniture producer learned this truth. The furniture, prices, and distribution channels of his firm were like those of most other firms in the industry. He believed that his key to success was a better group of furniture brokers and more company salespeople. The firm went bankrupt within a year. This producer had fallen victim to a sales orientation.

The different management orientations are detailed in Exhibit 1–6. The differences between a manufacturing, sales, or technology/product orientation and a market orientation are clear. Marketing is oriented toward market share and profitability, not toward lower production costs, higher sales at all costs, or more glamorous technical achievements. Marketing is committed to well-designed and organizationally integrated plans rather than to a narrow focus on production plant, sales forecasts, or R&D efforts. Marketing is oriented toward creating satisfied customers rather than toward internal efficiencies, short-term sales results, or product performance. All of the latter are necessary, but they are not sufficient to create satisfied customers. Marketing develops strategies based on analysis of the market rather than responding to troubles by cutting costs, selling harder, or assuming that an improved product is always essential for success. And, most important, marketing begins with the customer, not with production costs, sales, or technological landmarks.

Marketing Management

Marketing
management
is the process of scanning the environment, analyzing market opportunities, designing marketing strategies, and then effectively implementing and controlling marketing practices.

Marketing management involves several activities, including environmental scanning, market opportunity analysis, marketing strategy programming, and implementation and control. This entire book is devoted to discussing these subjects, shown in Exhibit 1-7, which presents an overview of the basic components of marketing management and their interrelationships. The organization's mission provides the priorities for scanning the broader environment and identifying and analyzing market opportunities. Understanding the changing marketing environment and the organization's markets, in turn, provides a basis for developing effective marketing strategies. Then, specific target markets are defined, marketing objectives delineated for each target market, and the numerous marketing program decisions made (prices, advertising, distribution, etc.). Together, these activities make up a marketing strategy, which is then implemented and controlled. Implementation is often the most difficult stage. It is important to realize that marketing management usually involves this sequential process. Implementation occurs only after programming decisions are made; programming decisions are based on target market decisions and realistic objectives; target market decisions and realistic objectives hinge on in-depth market opportunity analyses; all of these stages benefit from keeping a keen eye on the shifting environment; and, together, these stages make a major contribution toward achieving the corporate mission. But before considering the components of marketing management, let us consider how the organizational mission shapes marketing management.

Organizational Mission

The mission of an organization defines the organization's basic purpose and what the organization wants to accomplish. In the mid-1970s, Sara Lee Corporation was restructured around a core business concept—emphasizing major businesses with strong leadership positions in major markets. Sara Lee divested itself of some businesses and added others. Other than the Sara Lee brand itself, its brands included Popsicle, Rudy's Farm, Shasta Beverages, Slenderalls, Underalls, Electrolux, and Fuller Brush as well as lesser known brands. By the mid-1980s, it formalized a management priorities process providing flexible guidelines for managing change. The Sara Lee mission statement provided fundamental direction:

EXHIBIT 1-7 Marketing Management in Action

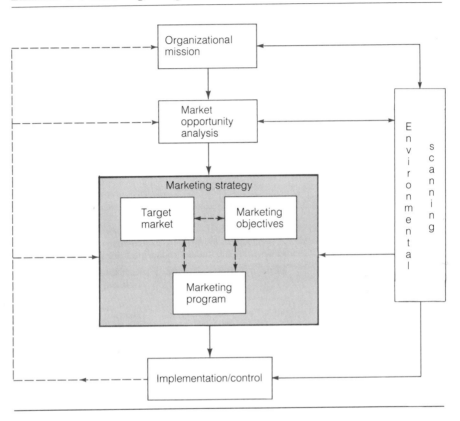

Sara Lee Corporation's mission is to be a leading consumer marketing company in the United States and internationally by manufacturing, marketing and distributing:

Food and consumer packaged goods products through retail outlets;

Products and services for the foodservice industry; and

Consumer products through distribution channels that are direct to the consumer.[12]

Sara Lee's primary goal is to consistently maximize the corporation's long-term financial performance so as to better serve its employees, stockholders, customers, and the communities where it does business. To accomplish this, Sara Lee:

■ Focuses on products and services that are particularly sensitive to marketing and responsive to emerging consumer trends.

■ Ensures an exceptionally high level of quality for all products and services offered.

■ Uses a decentralized management approach so that product and market knowledge, expertise, and innovation can be effectively applied.

Mission statements are by definition broad in scope, but each word in such statements is important. For example, the word *internationally* in Sara Lee's mission statement is used with serious intent. The company's operating income from non-U.S. operations from 1975 to 1985 rose from 11 to 25 percent, and it is seeking to achieve a similar growth rate until 1990. The mission statement sets the priorities for scanning the marketing environment.

Environmental Scanning

Environmental scanning
is information collection and interpretation concerning outside forces, events, and relationships as they affect or may affect the future of the organization.

Environmental scanning helps identify market opportunities and threats and provides guidelines for the design of marketing strategy. Environmental analysis concentrates on the macroenvironment—the economic, governmental, technological, social, and natural environments.

The environment can create opportunities for some companies and threats for others, as seen in the $3 billion market for automated building heating and air conditioning controls. Technological change meant a shift from electromechanical to electronic controls in the middle to late 1960s. Then, in the 1970s, global governmental forces contributed to the acceleration of energy prices, making it more economical for building owners to install systems that reduced utility bills.

In 1972, Johnson Controls, Inc. introduced the first minicomputer-based system to regulate a commercial building. By the mid-1980s the firm had sales of well over $1 billion and a 30 percent market share. While other fine old Milwaukee companies such as Rexnord and Allis-Chalmers coped with troubled times, 97-year-old Johnson Controls, Inc. had relatively few worries about the future.[13]

Johnson Controls' management anticipated the changing technological and industry environment and developed a strategy to cope with it. Global forces affecting the energy industry provided even greater opportunities. Identifying and evaluating relevant environmental change are essential means for capitalizing on new opportunities and circumventing threats to markets and marketing strategies.

It is tempting to simply project current environmental trends into the future, but history tells us that such projections are fraught with pitfalls. It is easy for management to ignore an organization's broader environment, especially given day-to-day operating pressures. Yet to look outside the company only to competition and markets is to ignore the macroenvironment— the source of many changes.—As Sara Lee stated in its *1985 Annual Report,* "What's different these days is the *accelerating pace* at which change confronts companies. . . . The daily papers overflow with reports of demographic shifts, technological innovations and altered lifestyles. Trends spill into each other, and the ripples reach every corner of society." The key is to anticipate important **environmental forces** and adapt in time.

Environmental forces are changes emanating from the environment with the potential of impacting organizations' market opportunities and strategies.

Building adaptive strategies requires an understanding of both the nature and the rate of change. And extremely few environmental forces are easy to predict. In the 1970s, two recreational vehicle (RV) retailers opened their doors within a mile of each other. Only one of them is still operating. The successful retailer, anticipating substantial gasoline price hikes and consumer uncertainty, minimized the initial investment in facilities and inventory. The unsuccessful retailer, ignoring the signals from external forces, purchased land, constructed a building, and offered a large RV inventory and a full array of services. The changing environment reduced consumer demand for RVs, and the second retailer was forced to liquidate. One could argue that with the high level of environmental uncertainty at that time, neither retailer should have started.

Market Opportunity Analysis

A product-market is comprised of individual and institutional end users (ultimate consumers) who are able and willing to purchase a particular product or service.

Market opportunity analysis (MOA) is the step-by-step process of defining, describing, and estimating the size and characteristics of each product-market of interest to a company, as well as the way and the extent to which each product-market is served by competition.

Market opportunity analysis can be used to investigate a potential market opportunity or better understand a market already served. A precise description of the size and characteristics of a target market can show how a firm's marketing approach can be improved.

Wendy's International entered a mature and competitive fast-food market in the 1970s. Firms such as Wendy's need three kinds of information about their market.

■ *Market definition and customer profiles* provide market descriptions used by marketing management in evaluating market opportunities and designing marketing programs to serve target markets. For example, Wendy's end users (consumers of its services) represent a key population group: young adults over 25 years of age. This group had not received emphasis in the marketing efforts of McDonald's or Burger King. Customer profiles also include information on buyer perceptions, attitudes, shopping patterns, and so forth. Adopting a customer viewpoint of the marketplace is an essential basis for developing realistic strategies.

■ *Market size estimation* builds on a clear definition of an organization's target market. Wendy's had to estimate how many prospective customers existed in various geographic markets, what share of each market it could capture, what the average dollar purchase would be, and what the repeat purchase rate would be.

■ *Industry and competitor analysis* identifies probable trends and operating practices in the industry of which the firm is a part as well as the strengths and weaknesses of each key competitor. For Wendy's, the industry includes all national and regional fast-food chains. Industry analysis includes an investigation of how an industry is reaching its markets through its channels of distribution (e.g., manufacturer-wholesaler-retailer-consumer). Competitor analysis concentrates on the key firms with which a company competes. Thus, McDonald's and Burger King represent competing firms, whereas Taco Bell is probably not a key competitor for the Wendy's target market.

Knowledge of markets and competitors is essential in designing and managing marketing strategy.

Marketing Strategy

Marketing strategy is the set of guidelines and policies used for effectively matching marketing programs (products, prices, promotion, and distribution) with target market opportunities in order to achieve organizational objectives.

Marketing cannot fulfill its managerial (or societal) role unless customer needs and wants are understood and satisfied. The development of an overall **marketing strategy** helps ensure that mutually beneficial exchanges occur (part of the definition of marketing). It is oriented toward the long run, comprised of fundamental decisions (not day-to-day adjustments), and developed with an eye to competition as well as markets. Developing marketing strategy includes deciding which customers to target and how to position products (and the organization) relative to competitors in the minds of existing and potential customers.

Developing marketing programs involves identifying alternative combinations of marketing variables (for example, higher-quality, higher-priced hamburgers) and then judging how well these combinations match the market opportunity. The core of such matching is forecasting potential customer response to the mix of marketing variables. Then, the program with the greatest potential is implemented.

Let us consider the luxury car market. The guidelines and policies that constitute a strategy for the luxury car market must be oriented toward creating the highest quality image possible. They include:

■ A high, narrow pricing range that conveys an image of price exclusiveness.

■ New models that offer high technical quality, few repairs, and excellent warranty coverage.

■ Advertising media and messages that impart an exclusive, high-quality image.

These illustrative guidelines and policies (marketing strategy) narrow the range of marketing actions that are appropriate given the overall marketing objectives (e.g., quality image). Basically, a marketing strategy outlines how marketing objectives will be achieved.

Target Market Selection A target market may consist of all end users or one or more subgroups in a product-market. Making decisions about target markets is one of management's most important tasks. Wendy's decision to go after a subgroup of the population, young adults, with a particular service offering was a target market decision.

Strategic decisions involving target markets include:

■ *Deciding whether to go after an entire product-market by using a mass-marketing approach or to concentrate marketing strategy on only a portion of the market.* The highly successful B. Dalton Bookseller subsidiary of Dayton-Hudson Corporation typically stocks 25,000 books per store and serves the mass market. Yet its president says, "we think there is a new level of the market out there, made up in part of people intimidated by a full-selection bookstore."[14]

■ *Determining when to modify an existing target market strategy.* The top management of Sherwin-Williams decided to shift from the firm's traditional orientation as a paint store for contractors and to appeal instead to consumers. A completely redesigned marketing approach was implemented with home decorating centers that offer paints, floor and wall coverings, and related products.

■ *Deciding to stop serving a particular target market.* Increasingly, managements are confronted by the question of whether to withdraw from a market. Maturing products, slow growth rates, competition, and environmental changes gradually alter the attractiveness of target markets.

Target market selection is guided by an organization's mission and objectives, so target market decisions must be properly positioned within this larger context and their strategic implications assessed. Once selected, the target market provides the focus for setting marketing objectives and designing the marketing program.

Marketing Objectives. Marketing objectives should be consistent with corporate objectives and should be stated for each target market in terms of sales, market share, profit contribution, and other qualitative aims, such as strengthening a brand image. Objectives are sometimes divided into two groups: market *performance* objectives and market *support* objectives. The former are specific outcomes such as sales and profits. The latter pertain to tasks that precede the final performance outcome and may include building customer awareness, engaging in educational efforts, and creating a brand image.

Objectives help shape the marketing mix for each target market. A firm seeking to increase sales in a target market by 6 percent for the coming year would probably make only limited changes in the existing marketing program. Alternatively, striving for a substantial sales increase, say 20 percent, could require major changes in the composition of the marketing program, including increases in the marketing budget for elements of the program (e.g., size of the sales force).

Objectives must, at least to some degree, be measurable; otherwise, identifying progress toward their achievement is impossible. In marketing, measurability is no easy order. A support objective could include changing a brand image in the minds of potential customers—and progress toward that objective could be measured by surveying customer perceptions. This is often done. Objectives should be worded very carefully, with the intention of developing measurable and attainable *standards*. The following marketing performance and support objectives were used in a personal computer education business:

- To increase (over last year) the number of student/class hours by 36 percent.

- To increase class size to an average of 28 (despite a 6 percent price increase) and thereby to increase profits by 20 percent.

- To increase awareness of our services to at least 50 percent of our targeted customers.

- To develop over the next year three new class offerings, with high-quality instructors, to serve the personal computer user.

- To develop a targeted, systematic, and coordinated advertising program.

The first two objectives are oriented toward market performance, whereas the last three are market support objectives.

Marketing Program.   A firm's marketing must consist of an integrated strategy aimed at providing customer satisfaction. To develop such a strategy, a firm uses demand-influencing variables that together constitute the marketing mix. The marketing mix, like a puzzle, has numerous pieces that must be appropriately combined for a successful end result (Exhibit 1–8). It includes the product (or service) offered by the firm, the distribution channels it uses (wholesalers, distributors, retailers) to make the product available to customers, the price it charges for the product, and promotion (advertising, personal selling, sales promotion and publicity). Other terms often used to describe the components of the marketing mix are the marketing program, the marketing offer, and the 4-Ps (product, place, price, and promotion).[15] These variables must be consistent with one another, and ideally, they complement one another for a synergistic result. Building a quality, prestige product and combining it with inconsistent mix ingredients such as heavy price discounting would yield a poorly integrated, internally inconsistent marketing program. The mix ingredients would conflict with one another in the minds of customers.

EXHIBIT 1–8 Marketing Mix Variables

Product	Distribution	Price	Promotion
Features	Types of channels/ middlemen	List price	Promotion blend Advertising Media
Quality		Credit terms	Copy Timing
	Store/distributor location		
Packaging		Discounts	
	Storage		Personal selling Selection and
Branding		Allowances	training Motivation
	Transportation and logistics		Allocation
Services		Flexibility	
			Sales promotion
Guarantees	Service levels		
Assortment			Publicity

The creative role that management must play in moving from knowledge of the market to the formulation of marketing programs is both a major challenge and an opportunity. Mallard's clothing specialty stores for men (Chicago) provide an excellent example of the development and implementation of an appropriate marketing mix for a firm's target market. Starting with one store in 1984, entrepreneur G. Phillip Kelly now has three stores and plans for rapid expansion. He offers updated versions of classic Ivy League and sportswear-oriented clothing for men, which, because of its traditional styling, avoids quick outdating. The target market is ambitious and active career-oriented individuals, 25–45-year-old college graduates, mostly professionals, with above-average incomes. Yet Mallard's customers still value a good buy. The clothing is mostly private label, obtained directly from high-quality producers. This departure from traditional industry practices enables the firm to offer reasonable prices for the quality it provides. The store locations project a quality image and are convenient for the targeted customers. The company engages in limited advertising, relying primarily on location, window displays, and a quality reputation to attract customers. All Mallard's employees also project a quality image. They are fully trained in selling techniques, fitting, garment care, fabrics, and styles, allowing them to deal with discriminating buyers. Retail clothing stores in general experience high failure rates, but it is clear that Mallard's offers an appealing blend of marketing mix elements.

Building a marketing program for a target market consists of determining how large the marketing budget should be, allocating the budget to the marketing mix variables of the firm and determining the best use of the resources for each marketing mix variable. Over time, organizations make many important decisions about the marketing mix, including:

1. The development of new products or services, the improvement of product, and the elimination of products.

2. The choice of channel intermediaries (agents, brokers, wholesalers, distributors, and retailers) or the use of direct distribution for reaching target markets.

3. The setting of pricing objectives and strategies that are consistent with the target markets and with the other elements of the marketing program.

4. The development of advertising, sales promotion, and publicity programs to accomplish the communication objectives assigned to the promotion function.

5. The formulation of personal selling goals; the determination of the type, number, and location of salespeople; and the adoption of policies for managing salespeople (such as compensation policies).

Given the myriad of possible marketing programs that could be developed and the difficulty of estimating the likely revenue and cost results of each alternative program, these are complex decisions. Management must determine the level and combination of marketing variables that will yield the most favorable profit contribution, net of marketing costs. *Estimating the responsiveness of target markets to alternative marketing mixes is perhaps the key uncertainty in all of marketing management.*

Finally, the terms *strategy* and *tactics* are often used in management discussions. Strategy (or strategic) decisions provide a broad, long-term framework (a year or usually more) for marketing action. They are fundamental decisions that guide day-to-day actions. Tactical decisions determine how marketing strategies are to be carried out on a day-to-day basis. For Mallard's, strategy included placing an emphasis on quality, private brands, and reasonable prices. The strategy of a company is implemented by day-to-day tactical decisions, such as setting the exact prices, deciding whether or not to include prices in advertising copy, deciding how frequently to offer sale prices and on which items, and opening new locations.

Implementation and Control of Marketing Strategy

Marketing implementation
is the execution of marketing practices, consistent with marketing programs and strategies.

Good marketing strategies too often fail due to poor **marketing implementation**.[16] Poor implementation can also make it difficult to judge whether or not a marketing strategy is itself appropriate. For this reason, if performance is poor, it is usually best to first consider making adjustments in marketing implementation. Marketing implementation brings us to the lowest level of marketing, the actual day-to-day execution of marketing tactics and practices. The finest marketing strategies will fail unless the implementation link that makes the contact with customers is strong.

Personal execution skills are critically important in marketing. By its nature, the marketing job is one of influencing people inside and outside the company to carry out functions that implement a marketing strategy and program. Those who have empathy with the feelings of others and good bargaining skills are often the best implementers. Personal execution skills also carry over to how one creates an informal network and organization, parcels out employees' time and assignments, and ensures an information flow that is not burdensome, yet is sufficient for monitoring day-to-day programs. Being tough but fair with employees may well be better than being egalitarian. The best personal chemistry and leadership formula varies from situation to situation. Yet it is clear that leadership, a partially indefinable talent, is often critical to success in the marketplace.

Implementation, however, requires far more than leadership talent. At the policy level, it is important that all of the key managers have a shared understanding of the company's marketing purpose. Having key managers write a single sentence describing the essence of that purpose can be very revealing. Contradictory understandings among managers can lead to havoc in a sales force or among distributors. A common understanding can be engendered and reinforced through compensation, training programs, and the like. There should be a clarity of theme and vision.

The marketing culture also deserves attention. The unspoken social web of management powerfully channels managers into comfortable ruts. The role assigned to marketing in the company directly affects the boldness of talented managers in implementing programs.

Finally, effective implementation often requires individuals to creatively do whatever is required to "make it happen" or accomplish a key task, even at the expense of overcoming the formal organization structure. Bureaucratic obstacles can challenge the finest execution efforts, but successful companies provide managers with latitude, flexibility, and authority for carrying out important tasks.

Monitoring and controlling results provides a feedback loop that is essential for making strategy and implementation adjustments. The company-wide reappraisal of operations launched by Toro Company during the early 1980s illustrates the ongoing control of marketing strategy.

In 1979, Toro had 33,000 new chain store outlets and was rolling out new products.

The snowless winters of 1979–80 and 1980–81 ended Toro's dreams of grandeur. Snow removal equipment clogged the warehouses of dealers, distributors, and Toro. Toro came perilously close to going under. Thousands of dealers gave up the account; many were furious that Toro let stores like J. C. Penney Company and K-Mart Corporation discount the machines without servicing them.

A new president in 1981 quickly slashed costs and smoothed dealer relations. He also improved Toro's inventory support program.

By the mid-1980s, observers agreed Toro had narrowly survived.[17]

Although the changes made by Toro were more drastic than those typically involved in controlling a marketing strategy, Toro's experience underscores the need for regular monitoring of marketing actions and results. An earlier response to the mounting problems could have reduced the trauma level.

The purpose of evaluation and control is to bring the results of the firm's marketing efforts as close as possible to its marketing objectives. Control accounts for a large portion of the marketing manager's daily activities in most companies, whereas planning is more demanding during the early stages of a new business venture. Control determines whether modifications are needed in marketing strategies. **Marketing control** consists of:

Marketing control is the setting of standards and the monitoring of marketing performance to keep performance in line with objectives.

1. Deciding which aspects of marketing strategy to monitor (e.g., the total marketing program, the sales force, the advertising program).

2. Setting standards (based on objectives) for use in gauging performance—these may include sales targets, market share, and profit contribution—as well as market-support and behavioral standards (e.g., level of customer awareness).

3. Designing feedback mechanisms so that useful and timely information is available to evaluate the effectiveness of marketing activities (e.g., Toro's dealer inventory situation).

4. Interpreting results to identify gaps between objectives and performance.

5. Implementing changes in strategy and tactics to eliminate or reduce performance gaps.

Control is an integral part of marketing management.

Application

The Marketing Management Process

Huffy Corporation has used both principles and experience in tackling one of the most difficult marketing management tasks—that of changing an established image. It is usually best to "start anew," and that is what Huffy Corporation did to reach the adult market for bicycles.

Huffy Corporation sells more bikes than any other U.S. bicycle maker. But most of them are for children. Status-conscious adults would no more ride a Huffy 10-speed than wear a polyester leisure suit. Huffy has an image problem that prevents it from appealing to "sophisticated adults."

Huffy lacks status because it sells its inexpensive bikes in discount and department stores. But Huffy wants to sell in bike shops too. These shops account for only 25 percent of the 6.7 million bikes sold, but because they sell adult bikes costing $200 or more, they account for nearly 40 percent of dollar sales. However, bike shops won't stock Huffy bikes, partly because of their name and their lower quality, but also because dealers fear that their prices will be undercut by high-volume stores.

So Huffy developed a grand strategy. It bought the exclusive U.S. rights to the Raleigh trademark from the British bike maker, TI Raleigh Industries, Inc. Although Raleigh had slipped in market share to less than 3 percent before Huffy bought the name, its bikes have the image, specifications, and acceptance that Huffy bikes lack, says a Raleigh executive. "We realize name is important," he says. "That's why we think we found the vehicle to get to the adult market."

Huffy will keep the two brands distinct. Raleigh will be the company's high-quality bike, featuring the alloy frames, lugged joints, and imported parts that serious cyclists look for. To improve its image with adults, Huffy hired a team to ride Huffy and Raleigh bikes in prestigious races.

The feedback from bike store managers is not all positive. One said, "People come in to look at Raleighs, and the first thing they ask is, 'Is this one of the Raleighs that Huffy makes?'"

Keeping the Huffy and Raleigh names distinct in the eyes of consumers might work, some competitors say. But Huffy has another problem. Independent bike shop dealers fear that Raleigh bikes will be sold by discount and department stores, even though the company tells dealers over and over that that won't happen.[18]

Although the information is limited, we can easily conclude that Huffy's top-priority organizational objective was to successfully capture a share of the adult bike market. The marketing environment encompassed a population that had a growing leisure orientation and was health and exercise conscious as well. In analyzing the market opportunity, Huffy Corporation concluded that use of the Huffy name would engender major barriers among potential buyers. It also concluded that even a new name on a bike produced by Huffy would be less effective than riding on the coattails of Raleigh's brand image. This conclusion was based on recognition that the target market consisted of status-conscious, sophisticated, and serious adult bicyclists who perceived Huffy as a lower-quality, inexpensive toy for children that did not meet their needs and wants.

Huffy's key competitor was Schwinn, which had 23 percent of the market, but bicycle makers from Japan and Taiwan had an additional 56 percent. Names such as Trek, Gitane, Fuji, and Puch were the competition. The market opportunity was a share of the 6.7 million units sold to adults, comprising 40 percent of total dollar sales. Market opportunity analysis, leading to a precise definition of the target market, included attention to market size, competition, customer demographics, and, perhaps most important, the subtleties of potential buyers' perceptions of Huffy and Raleigh.

Huffy undoubtedly stated its marketing objectives in terms of sales, market share, dealer acceptance, and other measures. The marketing program, although not reviewed in detail above, included a product with the essential attributes preferred by those in the target market (e.g., alloy frames). Just as the quality was higher, so was the price. Indeed, one might easily argue that underpricing in this situation could have provided a fatal signal concerning quality. The promotion included entering racing teams in prestigious races, specialty magazine advertising, dealer-oriented promotions, personal selling, and other efforts. Finally, distribution through independent bike shops was essential. And although the end user is the primary focus in a market opportunity analysis, it is clear that an understanding of the dealer's perceptions and predispositions was also essential. Exhibit 1–A provides an overview of the dual-brand strategy developed by Huffy.

Implementation and control were particularly needed for Huffy's bold, new strategy. In addition to sales information, continuous feedback from dealers and the marketplace was critically

EXHIBIT 1-A Two Marketing Programs for Two Target Markets: Huffy's Dual-Brand Strategy

	Huffy	**Raleigh**
Target market	Children	Status-conscious and sophisticated adults
Product	Huffy brand bicycles	Raleigh brand bicycles—high quality with a good quality image
Distribution channels	Discount and department stores	Independent bike shops
Price	Inexpensive	Expensive
Promotion	BMX magazines Children's TV BMX races	Prestigious races Dealer advertising and selling

important as the basis for making tactical adjustments. Understanding and coping with customers are what surrounds marketing with so much uncertainty and gives marketing its exciting, entrepreneurial character ▪

Summary

The decision-making areas that constitute marketing management are linked together in Exhibit 1-7. The process shown plays an essential integrating role throughout the book, so you may want to refer to this chapter when reading later ones. The management process is a guide to action, regardless of the size or type of organization involved, and it is applicable to both business and nonbusiness organizations. The basic steps of marketing management are similar for all kinds of organizations, though the importance of each step varies from situation to situation, along with the external influences operating on the firm. As a result, marketing is more effective when intuition, judgment, and experience are combined with marketing principles and concepts.

The remainder of this book examines the marketing management process. With a clear understanding of the organizational mission, marketing management engages in environmental scanning, market opportunity analysis, marketing program design, and ongoing implementation and control.

Marketing is the process of planning and executing the conception, pricing, promotion, and distribution of ideas, goods, and services to create exchanges that satisfy individual and organizational objectives. Marketing strategy is the set of guidelines and policies used for effectively matching marketing programs (products, prices, promotion, and distribution) with target market opportunities to achieve organizational objectives.

The foundation for contemporary marketing management is the marketing concept. It is a customer-oriented philosophy implemented and integrated throughout an organization so as to serve customers better than competitors and thereby to achieve specified goals. Systematic implementation of the marketing concept can revolutionize an otherwise stagnant organization, whether business or nonbusiness.

Companies are often built on a technology, manufacturing, or sales orientation, but with increasing competition, they find that a market orientation is essential.

Marketing management is the process of

scanning the environment, analyzing market opportunities, designing marketing strategies, and then effectively implementing and controlling marketing practices. It begins with understanding the organizational mission and its implications for marketing. Then, attention must be given to the macroenvironment. Environmental scanning is collecting and interpreting information on outside forces, events, and relationships as they affect or may affect the future of the organization. With a full awareness of environmental trends and forces, product-markets offering opportunities for the firm are identified. Market opportunity analysis (MOA) is the step-by-step process of defining, describing, and estimating the size and characteristics of each product-market of interest to a company, as well as the way and the extent to which each product-market is served by the company's competitors. Then, marketing strategies are developed, specific target markets are selected, marketing objectives are set, the elements of the marketing program are decided upon, and implementation and control begin.

The most time-consuming day-to-day marketing activity is control. Did all of our planning and strategizing work? Based on the monitoring of performance versus standards, do adjustments have to be made? If our marketing objectives are not achieved, the process shown in Exhibit 1–7 is recycled.

Exercises for Review and Discussion

1. You have decided to start your own business. You are planning to open a fast-food restaurant that specializes in nutritional, low-calorie meals. What types of market information do you need? Based on what you know from experience, what would be some likely elements in a marketing strategy for this business?

2. Discuss the similarities and the differences in the marketing strategy of companies such as Ethan Allen, a furniture manufacturer, and Reliance Electric, an industrial equipment manufacturer.

3. Based on your observations, discuss the marketing strategies of recently deregulated industries (e.g., airlines, financial services, telecommuniations). How has the orientation of these industries changed since deregulation?

4. The marketing concept advocates starting with customer needs and wants and developing an integrated marketing strategy to achieve customer satisfaction. Magnavox and RCA reportedly spent huge amounts of money in the 1970s to develop videodisc players for playing records on TV sets. RCA dropped the product in the 1980s after having suffered losses in the hundreds of millions of dollars. Was it practicing the marketing concept?

5. You have just invented a machine that can attend classes and take notes for you. What might be included in a marketing program for the "substitute student"? Include discussion of the marketing mix in the context of the market opportunity and the environment.

6. Assume that you have been asked by the president of J. C. Penney to review and evaluate the firm's marketing activities and to make appropriate recommendations for improvement. What are the major areas that you would assess, and why?

7. How would you explain marketing concepts to a government official who is interested in applying them to mass transit systems in urban communities?

8. "Marketing management is a decision-making process that is primarily useful for firms involved in the manufacture and distribution of consumer goods (e.g., television sets, clothing, processed foods, and beer)." Comment on this statement.

Notes

1. This discussion is based on John Gorman, "Wendy's: A Made to Order Hamburger Empire," *Chicago Tribune*, Business Section, March 10, 1986, pp. 1, 5, 6.

2. "AMA Board Approves New Marketing Definition," *Marketing News*, March 1, 1986, p. 1. Published by the American Marketing Association.

3. "Strategic Marketing Top Priority of Chief Execs," *Marketing News*, January 31, 1986, p. 1. Published by the American Marketing Association.

4. Peter F. Drucker, *Management: Tasks, Responsibilities, Practices* (New York: Harper & Row, 1974), p. 63.

5. Reprinted from J. B. McKitterick, "What Is the Marketing Management Concept?" in *The Frontiers of Marketing Thought and Science*, ed. Frank M. Bass (Chicago: American Marketing Association, 1957), p. 78.

6. "To Market, to Market," *Newsweek*, January 9, 1984, p. 71.

7. Robert A. Fox, "Putting Marketing on a 'Business' Basis," The Conference Board's 1982 Marketing Conference. Copyright 1983 by The Conference Board, Inc. Reprinted with permission.

8. Martin L. Bell and C. William Emery, "The Faltering Marketing Concept," *Journal of Marketing*, October 1971, p. 42; and Philip Kotler, *Marketing Management* (Englewood Cliffs, N.J.: Prentice-Hall, 1980), p. 35.

9. John Marcom, Jr., "Computer Firms Confused on How to Advertise to Changing Market," *The Wall Street Journal*, September 19, 1985, p. 29.

10. Drucker, *Management: Tasks, Responsibilities, Practices*, p. 64.

11. Adapted from Charles W. Stevens, "European Luxury Cars Capturing a Growing Share of the U.S. Market," *The Wall Street Journal*, May 6, 1983, p. 36. Reprinted by permission of *The Wall Street Journal*, © Dow Jones & Company, Inc., 1983. All rights reserved.

12. Sara Lee Corporation, *1985 Annual Report*, p. 6.

13. Kathleen K. Wiegner, "Bright Spot," *Forbes*, July 5, 1982, pp. 175-76.

14. Jeff Blyskal, "Dalton, Walden, and the Amazing Money Machine," *Forbes*, January 18, 1982, p. 48.

15. E. Jerome McCarthy and William D. Perreault, Jr., *Basic Marketing*, 8th ed. (Homewood, Ill.: Richard D. Irwin, 1984), pp. 46.

16. The discussion of implementation here is largely based on Thomas V. Bonoma, "Making Your Marketing Strategy Work," *Harvard Business Review*, March–April 1984, pp. 69–76.

17. "Toro: Coming to Life after Warm Weather Wilted Its Big Plans," adapted from *Business Week*, October 10, 1983, p. 118.

18. Abstracted from Damon Darlin, *The Wall Street Journal*, April 8, 1983, pp. 25–28. Reprinted by permission of *The Wall Street Journal*, © Dow Jones & Company, Inc., 1983. All rights reserved.

CHAPTER 2

Strategic Marketing Planning

*T*he Gillette Company is diversifying because of the projections of a flat domestic market for shaving products through the mid-1990s and the intense competition in toiletries, the firm's two major contributors to sales and profits.[1] Gillette's top management is evaluating opportunities for investing in low-capital, fast-growth companies that offer potential long-range profits for the company. It plans to invest in companies with less than $5 million in sales that can grow to the $50–100 million range in 5 to 10 years. Gillette is also eliminating business units that are not doing well and for which the costs versus returns of turning them around are unfavorable. Acquisitions have been made or are under consideration. In 1984, Gillette acquired Oral-B Laboratories, with products in the ethical over-the-counter market, including toothpastes, toothbrushes, fluorides, and dental flosses. Other acquisitions that can benefit from Gillette's distribution and marketing strengths may be added to the firm's portfolio of businesses. A stated corporate objective is to double sales by 1995. Aggressive emphasis on razors and blades will continue to be important, since these products contribute two thirds of the company's total profits and one third of its total sales. Given Gillette's strong position in the shaving and personal care markets, some industry observers suggest that moving into new investments and acquisitions may dilute its efforts and resources in its primary markets. Managing the company's expanding portfolio of businesses will present a variety of strategic issues, including evaluating a variety of market and competitive situations, setting objectives, developing a strategy for each unit, allocating resources, and tracking performance. Top management's responsibilities will increase with the addition of each business activity.

Marketing strategy is inevitably shaped by the mission and the strategic plans that top management develops for the organization. It is therefore important in marketing strategy development to understand how companies like Gillette develop their corporate and business area strategies. When business purpose shifts over time, marketing strategy must be altered to meet the needs of new target markets. Since the nature and scope of the corporation are built around the markets in which top management wants to compete, several corporate strategy issues have a direct impact on marketing strategy. Moreover, marketing management plays an important role in selecting appropriate markets for a company and in deciding how to serve them. The term often used to describe marketing's strategic role in the corporation is *strategic marketing planning.*

This chapter examines the corporate and business area strategic planning process used in many businesses, highlighting marketing management's expanding role in corporate strategy. First, the strategic planning process is described and the corporate situation analysis is discussed and illustrated. Next, the development of the corporate mission and objectives and the determination of its business composition are considered. Then, the strategic analysis of business units, including a comparison of analysis methods, is discussed. Consideration of the selection of business unit strategy follows. Finally, marketing's role in business strategy is highlighted.

Strategic Planning Process

Until the 1970s, the involvement of marketing executives in corporate strategic planning was limited. The situation changed in the early 1980s as company strategies became more market driven (influenced by the market). Today, marketing management is being asked to fulfill an expanded strategic role in many firms.

An overview of strategic planning is shown in Exhibit 2-1.[2] Strategic planning is a continuing process that begins with an assessment of the situation faced by the corporation. This leads to an examination of the corporation's mission and objectives, which may, over time, be changed to respond to the situation assessment. Strategies are required to accomplish the mission and objectives. These strategies are developed for the product and market areas that determine the composition of the business. An important part of planning in a firm that serves more than one product-market is regular evaluation of the different business units, such as Gillette's Oral-B Laboratories. These units often have different objectives and strategies, creating for top management the task of managing a portfolio of businesses. The plan for each unit spells out its assigned role in the corporation and the strategy it will follow to fulfill that role. Underlying the unit's strategic plan are functional plans for marketing, finance, operations, and other supporting areas. Strategies are then implemented and managed. Regular evaluation via the situation assessment completes the cycle shown.

EXHIBIT 2-1 Corporate Strategic Planning Process

Analyze the Situation

Situation analysis consists of identifying and evaluating uncontrollable external influences, customers, competition, as well as company capabilities to determine opportunities, threats, strengths, and weaknesses.

The **situation analysis** involves assessing uncontrollable influences such as economic conditions, customers, competitors, and corporate capabilities and limitations. It should delineate the opportunities and threats facing the corporation. This information is then used in preparing and implementing strategic plans. Richard J. Mahoney, president and chief executive officer of Monsanto Company, comments on the importance of analyzing the corporate situation:

Hundreds of U.S. companies, including my own, have engaged in strategic analysis in recent years. In general, despite the trauma, they have found the exercise valuable, particularly when it was done carefully and without mindless adherence to technique. Companies gained a better understanding of what they do well, what they can do better, and what they will never do well. As a result, in the past few years we have seen perhaps the greatest corporate repositioning in recent industrial history—the culmination of the "era of portfolio analysis."[3]

Consider the experience of Berkey Photo, Inc., a photofinishing and distribution company in need of a strategic plan to counter several environmental and industry influences that were adversely affecting its business opportunities.[4] Fierce competition from one-hour photo processing companies and other low-rate, fast-service developers drastically altered the nature of the photo processing industry in the early 1980s. From 1980 to 1984, the number of quick-service, minilab processors expanded from 600 to 5,600. Mass merchants such as K mart and Target also became formidable competitors. In 1984, Berkey's top executives began developing a strategic plan for redirecting the company. Management's assessment of the situation was that Berkey's organizational strengths were not in research and development or in manufacturing but in marketing and service. A wholesale distribution business, a large New York retail store, the photofinishing operation, and two new marketing acquisitions made up the firm's portfolio of businesses. Management considered two strategic options to counter the threat to the company's survival resulting from the situation assessment. Either expand the photofinishing business through acquisition to gain scale economies and lower costs, or sell the business. A suitable acquisition could not be found. The photofinishing business was therefore sold even though it accounted for 58 percent of Berkey's $216 million in sales and two thirds of its profits. Berkey, the leading independent U.S. distributor of cameras and accessories, then expanded its product mix to include distribution of General Electric Company video products as well as video accessories, binoculars, and telescopes. In this instance, the situation assessment led to a major shift in corporate mission and strategy, based on management's assessment of Berkey's opportunities and threats and of its strengths and weaknesses. Part 2 of this book is totally devoted to situation analysis.

Corporate Mission and Objectives

Management must decide the nature and scope of the organization's operations and then make whatever adjustments are necessary over time. These choices about where the firm is going, taking into account company capabilities, resources, opportunities, and problems, establish the mission of the enterprise, as was shown by Sara Lee Corporation in Chapter 1.

Corporate Mission

Corporate mission is the purpose and scope of the organization, its responsibilities to its various stakeholders, its areas of product and market involvement, and management's performance expectations.

Early in the organizational planning process, the **corporate mission** should be examined and a statement of mission either developed or reviewed and updated. The corporate mission—what management wants the company to be—establishes several important guidelines for planning, including:

■ The company's reason for existence and its responsibilities to stockholders, employees, society, and various other stakeholders.

■ The customer needs and wants that are to be served by the company's product or service (areas of product and market involvement).

■ The extent of specialization within each product-market area.

■ The amount and types of diversification of product-markets desired by management.

- Management's performance expectations for the company.
- Other general guidelines for overall business strategy, such as the role of research and development in the company.

Even considering the constraints of company capabilities, resources, opportunities, and threats, management has a lot of flexibility in making and changing the mission decision. Uncontrollable influences may necessitate altering the mission, as illustrated by Berkey Photo's movement out of photofinishing. Management must decide how to solve problems or capitalize on opportunities. Consider how the chairman of NCH Corporation, a specialty chemical producer, describes its mission:

> NCH is well positioned in the maintenance specialty market and the plans for internal and external growth are built upon that strength. The "mission" of NCH has been defined as "Meeting Maintenance Needs Worldwide."
>
> To carry out that mission, marketing, research, and selling strategies are targeting customer maintenance needs to help the customer perform maintenance tasks more efficiently. Your company views marketing as understanding our customers "from the inside out." To accomplish this, we have initiated a number of research studies of various customer segments that concentrate on gaining an in-depth knowledge of the customers' needs and problems. Input from the sales force is a vital part of these studies.
>
> NCH has grown through internal development in the past, and we intend for internal growth to provide future expansion. In addition, selective acquisitions have been made and will continue to be sought in related markets where internal development would be either too costly or too slow.[5]

Understanding Corporate Objectives

In addition to developing a mission statement, an enterprise should formulate long-range objectives against which its performance can be gauged. Peter Drucker argues convincingly for establishing objectives in eight key areas:

> A business must first be able to create a customer. There is, therefore, need for a *marketing objective*. Businesses must be able to innovate or else their competitors will make them obsolescent. There is need for an *innovation objective*. All businesses depend on the three factors of production of the economist, that is, on the *human resource*, the *capital resource*, and *physical resources*. There must be objectives for their supply, their employment, and their development. The resources must be employed productively, and their productivity has to grow if the business is to survive. There is need, therefore, for *productivity objectives*. Business exists in society and community and, therefore, has to discharge social responsibilities, at least to the point where it takes responsibility for its impact upon the environment. Therefore objectives in respect to the *social dimensions* of business are needed.
>
> Finally, there is need for *profit*—otherwise none of the objectives can be attained. They all require effort, that is, cost. And they can be financed only out of the profits of a business. They all entail risks; they all, therefore, require a profit to cover the risk of potential losses. Profit is not an objective, but it is a requirement that has to

be objectively determined in respect to the individual business, its strategy, its needs, and its risks.[6]

Drucker brings profit into its proper perspective, pointing out that it is essential to the survival of the enterprise and provides the means for meeting the expectations of stakeholders.

Among possible corporate objectives are growth and market share, human resources training and development, number of new products, return on invested capital, earning growth rates, debt limits, energy reduction, and pollution standards. When corporate objectives are general, it is important that they be made more specific at lower levels in the organization. Moreover, each major business unit of a corporation should have its own objectives. Objectives should be realistic and specific so that management can measure progress toward their achievement.

Objectives help translate the organizational mission into desired results. When accomplished, objectives will move the enterprise forward on the course charted by management. Objectives establish priorities and show what corporate and marketing strategy must achieve (Exhibit 2-2).

Business Composition

Business composition is the different types of business activities that make up the total operations of a corporation.

Understanding the composition of a business is essential in developing both corporate and marketing strategy. In single-product firms such as Tootsie Roll Industries or Tampax, Inc., determining **business composition** is relatively easy. In many corporations, the business must be divided into similar parts to facilitate analysis and planning. And when a company is serving multiple markets with different products, grouping similar business areas together facilitates planning. However, before we discuss the establishment of business boundaries, we must identify some of the alternative ways to determine business composition.

Business Development Alternatives

Most companies start operations in some core business area. Success often leads to expansion into related areas and sometimes into an entirely new product-market. The major options in corporate development are shown in Exhibit 2-3. There are, of course, many combinations of the major options. Each option is examined to gain a better understanding of corporate expansion activities.

Core business is the product and market activity in which an enterprise first engages.

Core Business. Many firms start out serving one product market with a single product or a line of products. The initial venture is called the **core business,** as sewing machines were when the Singer Company was founded. This option, when it involves a single product-market, offers the advantages

EXHIBIT 2-2

Governments develop and implement organizational and marketing strategies to achieve their objectives. This state is aggressively marketing its advantages to corporations that are expanding and relocating their operations.

Courtesy Beber Silverstein & Partners Advertising, Inc.

of specialization but entails the risks of being dependent on one set of customer needs. Consequently, as a corporation grows and prospers, management often decides to move into one or more product and market areas.

Tootsie Roll Industries, founded in 1896, is one company that has stayed close to the core business. "Fully 93 percent of its sales still come from the basic Tootsie Roll and its permutations such as Tootsie Pops, Flavor Rolls, Caramel Pops, and Tootsie Squares."[7] This single-product business continues to prosper, although management recognizes the risks of having all its eggs in the Tootsie Roll basket.

Rarely do successful firms stay with the original business. Instead, management decides at some point to pursue one or more alternatives. Less dependence on the core business is a major factor in corporate development. Of course, financial resources are necessary to expand into new areas. In some situations, selling the business may offer management an attractive oppor-

EXHIBIT 2-3 Business Development Options

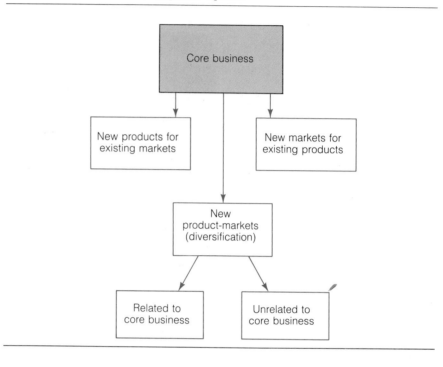

tunity for expansion. Entemann's, Inc., a small but highly successful bakery in the Northeast and Florida, lacked the capital needed to expand at the rate desired by its owner-managers. Consequently, the owners sold the company to Warner-Lambert, remaining with the company to move it toward national status. Subsequently, Warner-Lambert sold Entemann's to a food products firm.

New Markets for Existing Products.   One way to expand from the core business is to serve other needs and wants using the same or a similar product. The Maytag Company expanded from home laundry equipment to also produce commercial units. Responding to the trend of consolidation of home appliance lines, Maytag acquired Magic Chef in 1986. This acquisition transformed the firm into a dominant supplier of home appliances. A. T. Cross markets its line of writing instruments to consumers. Management has also expanded into marketing Cross products to organizational buyers for such purposes as sales incentives and employee recognition. For many companies, using the same product in new markets is a natural line of development. This strategy reduces the risks of depending on a single market, yet allows the use of existing technical and production capabilities. The major demands arising from this alternative are adequate resources for expansion and the capability for developing a new marketing strategy. Since it may be difficult to acquire marketing capability or to turn marketing over to an intermediary, the requirements for developing an internal marketing strategy should be recognized when this alternative is adopted. The primary caution is to be sure that the feasibility and attractiveness of the new market opportunity is carefully evaluated.

New Products for Existing Markets.   Another strategy for shifting away from dependence on one product is to expand the product mix offered to the firm's target market. Before its consolidation with Maytag, Magic Chef, originally only a range and oven manufacturer, had acquired lines of washers, dryers, refrigerators, and freezers. The possible advantages of this strategy include the use of common distribution channels, promotional support, and research and development. New products can also be developed internally, although acquisition is faster. Resources are necessary to support either method. A disadvantage of this strategy is continued dependence on a particular market area.

Diversification.   Finally, diversification is a popular option for corporate development among firms. Diversification involves movement into a *new product and market*, through either internal development or acquisition. Often the riskiest and costliest alternative, diversification, may be attractive because of slow growth in existing product market areas, if the necessary resources are available and good choices are made. Once diversification has been successfully implemented, it offers the advantage of spreading business risks over two or more segments. It may follow one of two avenues:

■ Movement into different, yet *related* product-market areas—Dayton-Hudson's branching out from traditional department stores into B. Dalton bookstores and Target discount stores.

■ Building the corporation into a conglomerate of *unrelated* product-market areas—Singer's diversification into business machines and the aerospace industry.

Analysis of successful diversification strategies suggests that the following factors are often important:

■ Top management has the capabilities, including a proven record of sound strategic planning, to manage a portfolio of businesses. (Adequate cash for diversification is also essential.)

■ The new areas are in attractive (fast-growing) product markets, and business strength is greater than that of the competition.

■ Each business area offers the company one or more key advantages over competing firms—low production costs, strong acceptance by customers, proprietary products, marketing strengths, or technical strengths.

- The new business area has good internal management and technical people who are strongly committed to the success of the business.

- The acquisition prospects have had a strong financial performance record over several years.

- The costs of internal development or acquisition are not so high as to jeopardize the profitable operation of the new business area.

Clearly, satisfying all of the above criteria is difficult, if not impossible. Nevertheless, if a new business area does not offer some distinct advantages in terms of these and other situation-specific factors, success is doubtful. Of course, each situation must be assessed in terms of its unique characteristics. Movement into entirely new fields is often riskier than expanding into business areas related to a company's existing business activities. This is illustrated by the experiences of California's Lucky Stores, Inc., the nation's third-largest supermarket chain:

> So successful was Lucky in supermarkets, in fact, that in 1973 it decided to extend its retailing skills beyond food. Diversifying by acquisition, Lucky bought restaurants, drugstores, family department stores, fabric, automotive supply, and women's apparel stores. On its own, Lucky opened specialty sporting goods and discount department stores. Today it is the nation's seventh-largest retailer, getting 47 percent of its earnings and 35 percent of its sales from nonfood businesses.[8]

A decade after diversification, in 1983, Lucky's top management began to reappraise the strategy. Financial performance during the decade had been mixed. Some of the firm's acquisitions did not work out, including the Sirloin Stockade restaurant chain, which was sold in 1982. Lucky's management continued to be cautiously optimistic concerning diversification.[9]

Establishing Business Boundaries

Strategic business unit (SBU) is an organizational unit within a corporation that performs all (or most) of the basic business functions in meeting the needs of a particular market with a product, a product line, or a mix of related lines.

Within each company, there may be one or more business areas or **strategic business units (SBU).** Southwestern Bell Corporation, for example, is organized into four major business areas: telephone services (the core business), mobile phone services and products, publications, and telecommunications equipment, as shown in Exhibit 2-4. An SBU such as cellular mobile phone services operates much like an independent business, performing the various basic functions, such as operations, marketing, finance, and human resources. Typically, the SBU serves a specific market with one product or service or a line of similar products or services. A corporation does not need to be a manufacturer in order to have SBUs. A retailer or wholesaler operating in two or more business areas may divide the firm into SBUs.

While delineating the areas of a corporation's business involvement is useful, it is also necessary to establish boundaries between these areas. Traditionally, product or industry designations have been used to identify the nature and scope of business operations. A company might be described as a

EXHIBIT 2-4 Business Composition of Southwestern Bell Corporation

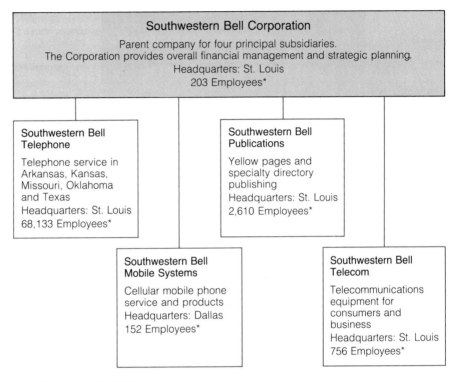

Southwestern Bell Corporation

Parent company for four principal subsidiaries.
The Corporation provides overall financial management and strategic planning.
Headquarters: St. Louis
203 Employees*

Southwestern Bell Telephone

Telephone service in Arkansas, Kansas, Missouri, Oklahoma and Texas
Headquarters: St. Louis
68,133 Employees*

Southwestern Bell Publications

Yellow pages and specialty directory publishing
Headquarters: St. Louis
2,610 Employees*

Southwestern Bell Mobile Systems

Cellular mobile phone service and products
Headquarters: Dallas
152 Employees*

Southwestern Bell Telecom

Telecommunications equipment for consumers and business
Headquarters: St. Louis
756 Employees*

*As of December 31, 1984

Source: Southwestern Bell Corporation, *1984 Annual Report*, p. 4.

steel producer, a candy maker, or a heavy equipment manufacturer. However, using only the product or service to establish boundaries between areas of business activity is incomplete because this excludes the end user. Thus, three important dimensions should be considered in defining the boundaries of a business.

■ What need or want is the business attempting to meet?

■ Which end users does the business want to serve?

■ What product or service offering will be used to meet the needs of customers.[10]

An example will help illustrate each dimension. Suppose that there is a need to photograph action scenes such as swimming races for later viewing. Look at the three dimensions shown in Exhibit 2-5. Notice that the type of need varies, that different end users are involved, and that the need can be met using two different product offerings. The three dimensions provide useful

EXHIBIT 2-5 Dimensions in Analyzing Business Activities

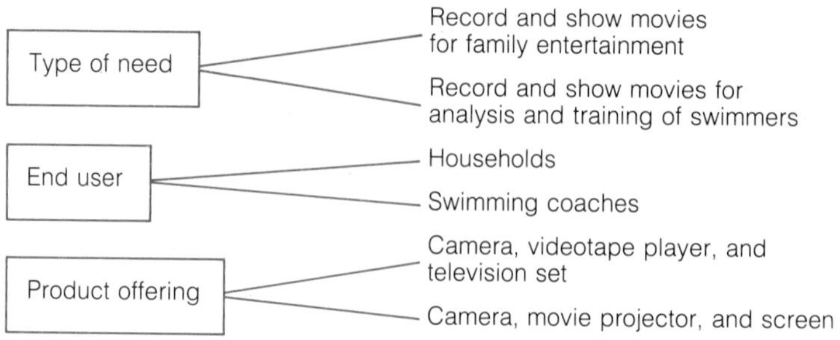

bases in establishing business boundaries for firms serving a range of needs with several products or services. Even in a company serving a single product-market, the three dimensions add considerable direction to strategic planning by showing how other product-market categories (and the firms that serve them) must be considered in developing strategies.

As a company attempts to satisfy more and more needs by offering various products and services, it becomes more diversified. Meeting the needs of different user groups with the same product or service may position a firm in more than one product-market, each requiring a different marketing strategy. So all three dimensions should be considered in defining a business and in grouping together similar product-market activities.

Forming Strategic Business Units

The SBU is being used increasingly to determine the composition of a corporation. An example will illustrate how this is done. General Foods Corporation, a leading producer of packaged foods, regrouped its divisional structure into strategic business units. James L. Ferguson describes repositioning the firm's products into menu segments:

> We started out with four divisions: Kool-Aid, Bird's Eye, Jell-O, and Post. Among the products in those four divisions, we saw five basic menu segments in addition to coffee: dessert, main meal, breakfast, beverage, and pet food. We combined these five strategic business units—SBUs—into three new divisions: main meal and dessert SBUs became the food products division; beverage and breakfast SBUs were combined into one division; and pet foods—which we considered a major growth opportunity—were put into a third division.[11]

The General Foods approach to SBU formation involves a group of brands that are linked together by their natural interrelationship on the consumer's menu rather than by the fact that they share a common manufacturing

EXHIBIT 2-6 Guidelines for Forming Strategic Business Units

Inventory the products offered by the corporation to identify specific products, product lines, and mixes of product lines. Determine end-user needs that each product is intended to satisfy.

Identify which products satisfy similar needs (foods for main meals). Also determine which products satisfy needs of more than one user group.

Form units composed of one or more products or product lines that satisfy similar needs (food preparation appliances). The products that form a planning unit should have in com-

mon major strategic features such as distribution channels, target markets, technology, or advertising and sales force strategies.

Determine whether there are management, market, operating, or other advantages to combining two or more planning units into a division, group, or business segment.

Review the proposed scheme to determine whether it offers both operational and strategic advantages. Do the potential benefits of the scheme exceed the costs?

---

process or method of distribution. Thus, the need being satisfied is an essential factor in defining SBUs. The company's main meal SBU includes frozen vegetables, instant rice, seasoned coating mix, and salad dressing mixes. While all of these are foods, different manufacturing processes are involved.

Several guidelines for forming SBUs are shown in Exhibit 2-6. Management, of course, has some flexibility in deciding how to divide the business into strategic units. Building up from specific product-market categories is more useful than starting from the top and breaking categories down. It is important to avoid forming too many units. A large number of units will require the use of a correspondingly large number of strategies and management structures, which is expensive and probably not cost effective.

Strategic Analysis of Business Units

Analysis of a business unit essentially involves gauging its past performance, determining its present strategic situation, and forecasting the future attractiveness of the product-markets in which it participates. Using this information, management must determine the business unit's future strategy, considering the unit's *opportunities, threats, strengths,* and *weaknesses* and taking into account its position relative to other units in the corporation.

Several methods of analysis have been developed. The two most popular approaches are:

■ *Product-market grids.* Each business unit or specific product-market is positioned on a two-way grid according to the attractiveness of the product-market and the unit's business strength compared to that of the competition. Depending on where a unit is located on the grid, alternative strategies will be indicated. Several versions of grid analysis exist, the most popular being the Boston Consulting Group's (BCG) *portfolio analysis* and General Electric's (GE) *screening grid.*

■ *Profit impact of marketing strategy (PIMS).* Using a large data bank, the Strategic Planning Institute in Cambridge, Massachusetts, can analyze various strategic factors (e.g., market share) that are related to profit performance and can compare a company or business unit with other firms and units in the data bank. These computerized analyses provide various diagnostic comparisons and indicate promising strategic actions based on the results of the analyses.

Product Market Grid Analysis

A firm's SBUs can be managed as a *portfolio* of varying opportunities and risks. Based on the extent of the opportunities, the anticipated risks, market position, profitability, and other considerations, each business unit in the portfolio presents management with a specific strategic situation. Management must develop, implement, and oversee a set of strategies designed to accomplish the firm's mission and objectives, considering the market opportunity, the competition, and other important influences on strategy. These portfolio analyses commonly use a grid on which SBUs or products are positioned so that each can be examined in terms of its strategic strengths and limitations (Exhibit 2-7).

Industry Attractiveness.
Corporate strategists have found that analyzing specific product-markets is often more effective than attempting to evaluate an entire industry, such as steel, paper, or electronics. Products from one industry, such as aluminum, may be competing against products from a second industry, such as plastics, and a particular product or service may meet different needs in different markets. The fine writing instruments of A. T. Cross are regarded by many customers as gifts. The attractiveness of both the gift and writing instrument market should be evaluated. One perplexing problem in gauging market attractiveness is defining the strategic product-market to be analyzed. Considerable direction in defining product-market boundaries is provided in Chapter 4.

One of two approaches to assessing product-market attractiveness is typically employed. The first, using the Boston Consulting Group's portfolio analysis, entails an estimate of the average annual growth rate over some time period, recognizing that a product-market typically has a life cycle encompassing introduction and the growth, maturity, and possible decline of sales.[12] The rate of growth slows down as the product matures. In this approach, a product-market is assigned to a high-, medium-, or low-growth category that reflects its general attractiveness. An estimated annual rate of growth ranging from less than 6 percent up to 12 percent would signify medium attractiveness, and a growth rate of 12 percent or more would signify high attractiveness. Implicit in the assessment of industry attractiveness is consideration of market size. In highly specialized product-markets, total sales volume may be low because of limited end-user need for the product.

EXHIBIT 2-7 GE's Screening Grid

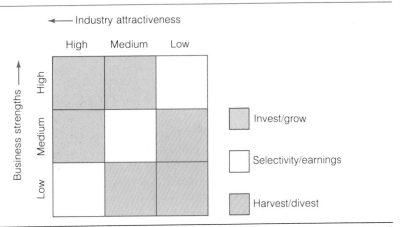

Sources: Adapted from "Market-Share-ROI Corporate Strategy Approach Can Be an 'Oversimplistic Snare.'" *Marketing News*, December 15, 1978, pp. 6–7; and "General Electric's 'Stoplight Strategy' for Planning," *Business Week*, April 28, 1974, p. 49.

The second approach (screening grid), developed nearly two decades ago at General Electric, takes into account several variables in addition to size and growth rate in assessing industry attractiveness.[13] These include the characteristics of the market (e.g., size, growth, market requirements, changes in market composition, and market locations), industry trends and structure, key competitors servicing the product-market, and environmental influences (shifts in population age groups), all of which may affect the attractiveness of the market over time. The screening grid approach combines various factors into two major criteria for gauging each SBU. As shown in Exhibit 2-7, a strategic unit is positioned on the grid in terms of industry attractiveness and business strengths. The end result is a description of the product-market opportunity that utilizes those factors identified by management as proper measures of attractiveness.

An SBU falling into the low/low category may be a candidate for divestment unless management can find a way to move it to a more favorable position. Alternatively, business units in the high/high category are prime candidates for investment and growth. Those in the intermediate range call for selective use of resources and emphasis on earnings.

Business Strength. Approaches to measuring competitive position fall into single-factor or multiple-factor categories, depending on whether the BCG portfolio analysis or the GE screening grid is used.[14] Market share (actual or relative) serves as a composite for positioning a firm against its competition when single-factor portfolio analysis is used. Market share can be used as a proxy for how well the firm is doing in a product-market. Although the measure is not universally accepted, there is evidence that market position indicates business strength. The multiple-factor measure of business strength used for the GE screening grid evaluates several aspects of business strength, including technical, management, marketing, and financial capabilities; sales position in the product-market; profitability; margins; and other factors considered important by management.

PIMS

As an alternative in analyzing business units, the Strategic Planning Institute (SPI) in Cambridge, Massachusetts, built an extensive data bank that contains information about business performance and various factors found to be related to performance. SPI's research program, called PIMS (profit impact of marketing strategy), involves data collected and analyzed over a period of nearly two decades by Sidney Schoeffler and his colleagues. The PIMS data bank currently contains information from over 2,000 companies or units within companies.

The data obtained from each participating company consist of about 100 items, including descriptive characteristics of the *market environment*, the state of *competition*, the *strategy* pursued by the business, and the *operating results* obtained. As a part of its input, each company must supply its assumptions about the "most likely" future rates of change in sales, prices, materials costs, wage rates, and equipment costs. This is done for short-term (1–4-year) and long-term (5–10-year) periods.

A business area serves as the unit of analysis in the PIMS studies:

> Each business is a division, product line, or other profit center within its parent company, selling a distinct set of products and/or services to an identifiable group of customers, in competition with a well-defined set of competitors, and for which meaningful separation can be made of revenues, operating costs, investments, and strategic plans.[15]

Thus, one company may choose to submit data on an entire division with several products, whereas another may select a particular product category. The requirement of meaningful separation of revenues, operating costs, investments, and strategic plans is likely to result in reporting by division or business unit rather than by specific product-market categories.

Examples of the information included in the PIMS data base are given in Exhibit 2–8. Nine major strategic influences on profitability and net cash flow, accounting for 80 percent of business success or failure, have been identified. These influences, in approximate order of importance, are:

1. *Investment intensity.* Technology and the chosen way of doing business govern how much fixed capital and working capital are required to produce a dollar of sales or a dollar of value added in the business. Investment intensity

EXHIBIT 2-8 Business Information in the PIMS Data Base

Characteristics of the business environment	Structure of the production process
Long-run growth rate of the market	Capital intensity (degree of automation, etc.)
Short-run growth rate of the market	Degree of vertical integration
Rate of inflation of selling price levels	Capacity utilization
Number and size of customers	Productivity of capital equipment
Purchase frequency and magnitude	Productivity of people
	Inventory levels
Competitive position of the business	
Share of the served market	Discretionary budget allocations
Share relative to that of largest competitors	R&D budgets
Product quality relative to that of competitors	Advertising and promotion budgets
Prices relative to those of competitors	Sales force expenditures
Pay scales relative to those of competitors	
Marketing efforts relative to those of competitors	Strategic moves
Pattern of market segmentation	Patterns of change in the controllable elements above
Rate of new product introductions	
	Operating results
	Profitability results
	Cash flow results
	Growth results

Source: Strategic Planning Institute, Cambridge, Massachusetts.

generally has a *negative* impact on percentage measures of profitability or net cash flow; this means that mechanized, automated, or inventory-intensive businesses generally show lower returns on investment and sales.

2. *Productivity.* Businesses with high value added per employee are *more* profitable than those with low value added per employee. (Value added is the amount by which the business increases the market value of the raw materials and components it buys.)

3. *Market position.* A business's share of its served market (both absolute and relative to that of its three largest competitors) has a *positive* impact on profit and net cash flow. (The served market is the specific segment of the total potential market—defined in terms of products, customers, or areas—in which the business actually competes.)

4. *Growth of the served market.* Growth is generally *favorable* to *dollar* measures of profit, *indifferent* to *percentage* measures of profit, and *negative* to all measures of net cash flow.

5. *Quality of the products or services offered.* Quality, defined as the customers' evaluation of the business's product/service package as compared to that of competitors, has a generally *favorable* impact on all measures of financial performance.

6. *Innovation/differentiation.* Extensive actions taken by a business in the areas of new product introduction, R&D, marketing effort, and so on, generally have a *positive* effect on performance *if* that business has a strong market position to begin with. Otherwise, the reverse is true.

7. *Vertical integration.* For businesses located in mature and stable markets, vertical integration (make rather than buy) generally affects perform-

ance *favorably*. In markets that are rapidly growing, declining, or otherwise changing, the opposite is true.

8. *Cost push.* The rates of increase in wages, salaries, and raw material prices and the presence of a labor union have *complex* impacts on profit and cash flow, depending on how the business is positioned to pass along the cost increases to its customers or to absorb the higher costs.

9. *Current strategic effort.* The current direction of change of any of the above factors has effects on profit and cash flow that are *frequently* opposite to the direction of the factor itself. For example, *having* strong market share tends to *increase* net cash flow, but *getting* market share *drains* cash while the business is making that effort.

There is also a good or a poor "operator." A good operator can improve the profitability of a strong strategic position or minimize the damage of a weak one; a poor operator does the opposite. The presence of a management team that functions as a good operator is therefore a *favorable* element of a business and produces a financial result greater than would be expected from the strategic position of the business alone.[16]

One of the major strengths of PIMS is that through empirical analysis it has shown several strategic factors to be related to profitability (return on investment) and cash flow. The PIMS approach is historical, however, so there is no way to be sure that past relationships will hold in the future. Regression analysis indicates which factors are closely related to perform- ance but not why. Finally, since PIMS data are supplied by the firm, they can be inaccurate or incorrectly reported. But assuming that the relationships in the model will hold in the future, PIMS can be used to analyze the impact of alternative strategies, thus helping identify promising future strategies.

Comparison of the Analysis Methods

Several kinds of analyses may be useful in determining future strategies. A major difference between the grid method and the PIMS approach is that the grid method can be used to examine several business units at the same time and to establish priorities for each unit, whereas the PIMS approach looks at one unit or product at a time, comparing it to the firms in the PIMS data bank. Thus, the grid places more emphasis on relative position, whereas PIMS focuses on absolute position.

With the portfolio analysis and screening grid methods, the major outputs are guidelines for resource allocation. These methods also indicate the rela- tive attractiveness of different business units. The most extensive output is provided by PIMS, which supplies several reports and analyses. In this regard, the screening grid ranks second and portfolio analysis third.

The portfolio, screening grid, and PIMS methods are compared in Exhibit 2-9. All three are generally most useful in showing where problems or

EXHIBIT 2-9 Comparison of Strategic Analysis Methods for Various Planning Activities

Planning Activity	Portfolio Analysis	Screening Grid	PIMS
Comparison of business unit* with:			
Other internal units	Position of the growth rate category is the basis of comparison, with cash flow serving as the performance criterion.	Position on the screening grid is the basis of comparison, with ROI serving as the performance criterion.	The PIMS output provides no direct basis of comparison.
Competition	Competing units (or products) can be plotted on the grid if market share data are available.	Placing competitive units (or products) on the screen is very difficult due to the information needed on business strength.	Two reports indicate comparative data for *groups* of firms with similar characteristics.
Present situation analysis:			
Corporation	None of the three methods is suitable on a direct basis for this purpose unless the corporation is a single-unit or single-product business. Management can form a composite assessment using the information obtained from the business unit analyses.		
Business unit	Desirability of present situation is based on position on the grid.	Same as portfolio analysis.	Extensive diagnostic information is provided by the various PIMS reports.
Functional areas	Not useful for this purpose.	Screening analyses for the various factors may provide some indication of functional strengths and limitations.	Some of the diagnostic information can be used to compare the unit with the data base.
Determining future strategies:			
Corporation	Provides resource allocation guidelines based on cash flow growth prospects.	Provides resource allocation guidelines based on ROI considerations.	Management can use the business unit analyses as a basis for considering overall corporate strategy.
Business unit	Indicates cash flow strategy but provides no specific indication of other strategic guidelines.	Strengths and weaknesses of various screening factors may suggest possible future business strategies.	The PIMS reports indicate the projected effect of several possible strategic moves and nominate an optimal strategy.
Functional areas	Not useful.	Of only limited value.	The reports are of general value in certain functional areas because they highlight strategic actions that are related to functions (e.g., product quality, market share).

* Or other appropriate units of analysis.

Source: Portions of this exhibit are based on Derek F. Abell and John S. Hammond, *Strategic Market Planning* (Englewood Cliffs, N.J.: Prentice-Hall, 1979), p. 380.

opportunities exist rather than in indicating which strategies should be adopted. And whichever method is selected, it should generate information that management can use in making decisions. The methods themselves are not intended to make decisions. Some firms are using all three methods, thus enjoying the strengths of each in various analysis activities. In fact, it is quite possible that the three methods may eventually merge into one. Interestingly, both screening and PIMS got their start at General Electric.

Business Unit Objectives and Strategy

Strategic analysis provides guidelines for determining objectives and strategies for individual business units. In evaluating a business unit, management must decide whether to:

- Maintain or strengthen its position.
- Attempt to shift it into a more desirable position.
- Exit from the business unit.

Management must develop a strategic plan for each business unit, taking into account its strategic situation, available resources, forecasts of future competitive and market conditions, and the relative attractiveness of available opportunities.

Marketing strategy will depend on how a business unit is positioned with regard to product-market attractiveness and business strengths and on top management's priorities for that unit. If the business unit is in a high-growth category and the company is more favorably positioned than the competition, then marketing strategy should take advantage of this opportunity. Alternatively, if the business unit is a candidate for withdrawal, marketing strategy should work toward that objective. Marketing should be matched to the unit's strategic position and to management's plans for the unit's business area. Growth, building market position, drawing cash from a mature business, and withdrawal or repositioning call for different marketing strategies.

The real advantage in using one or more of the strategic analysis methods lies in raising such questions as how to strengthen a weak business unit or how to capitalize on a strong one. Raising such questions will help management decide what actions to take to reposition the business unit.

Finding a Competitive Advantage

The essence of both corporate and marketing strategy is finding an advantage over competition. Companies can gain competitive advantage in various ways, such as:

- Establishing market power through market share dominance—General Motors holds this position in the U.S. automobile market.

- Developing new products—Xerox pioneered a new industry using this strategy, as did U.S. Surgical with its line of surgical staplers.

- Finding a specialized niche in a product-market that can be dominated—this strategy has been adopted by Nucor in steel joists and by J. L. Clark in specialized containers.

- Establishing strong distribution channels—Snap-on Tools, by concentrating on professional mechanics who are served by independent dealers in a van, dominates the professional market for socket wrenches and other tools.

- Obtaining manufacturing or operating cost advantages due to geographic location, process innovation, or other operating improvements—low-cost air carriers are using this strategy.

- Developing a strong financial position for growth—Delta Air Lines' very low debt compared to that of other carriers illustrates this advantage in the troubled airline industry.

- Building a powerful consumer franchise with highly advertised brands—Gillette has done this with its shaving products.

These are but a few of the many ways in which firms establish strong positions in product-markets. As is obvious from the examples, differential advantage is gained by deciding what customer needs and wants to serve and by developing appropriate plans for meeting the needs of target customers.

Strategies for a Low-Market-Share Business. Are companies with low market share faced with mediocre profit prospects? This has been one of the hottest issues debated by corporate strategists in the past decade. Research findings such as the PIMS studies indicate a strong relationship between market share and profitability. Based on a study of 57 companies, researchers found that, on average, a difference of 10 percentage points in market share is accompanied by a difference of about 5 percentage points in pretax return on investment.[17] Although such research results are convincing, it is inappropriate to conclude that strategic decisions should be based only on share in a product-market. This conclusion implies that each business and industry has one "winner" and several "losers." Moreover, it suggests that a company's only strategic options are to go after market share or withdraw from the industry. Such inferences are dangerous: "These prescriptions completely overlook the fact that, in many industries, companies having a low market share consistently outperform their larger rivals and show very little inclination to expand their share or withdraw from the fight."[18]

Clearly, many firms with low market shares are in excellent shape. Burroughs, Crown Cork & Seal, and Union Camp, for example, have low-market-share positions in both rapidly growing and mature markets, yet their profitability records compare favorably with those of the market leaders. One key factor in their success has been their ability to find a product-market niche in which their strengths are great compared to those of the competition. And that niche has not been actively pursued by large competitors. Research results suggest that market segmentation, the establishment of priorities for the use of resources, and strong top management are essential in companies with low market share.[19] This amounts to finding a differential advantage over competing firms.

Gaining Competitive Advantage. Differential advantage can be gained in various ways, including market segmentation, strong distribution channels, product or service offerings, selling approach, geographic location, and manufacturing expertise. Finding a differential advantage in the marketplace is a major management challenge, requiring both creative and analytic skills (Exhibit 2–10). Consider the business strategy used by a successful furniture manufacturer. Ethan Allen, Inc., designs, builds, and markets furniture and furnishings for the home. Although ranking only fifth in size among furniture manufacturers, the firm has established itself in the number one sales position in American traditional furnitures. By specializing in this product-market and catering to the medium- to high-quality sector of the consumer market, Ethan Allen has established a strong competitive position in its product-market niche. It uses a selective distribution strategy built around 330 independent and 20 company-owned "Ethan Allen Showcase Galleries." A wide range of designs and styles is available, supplemented by specially designed home furnishings from other manufacturers. Strong consumer acceptance and cost control have allowed the firm to achieve higher than typical margins in its industry. Ethan Allen's advertising emphasizes the excellent value and scope of its product offerings and decorating services. The company uses both network television and a broad base of national shelter and women's service magazines. Recognizing the key role of its retailers in effectively serving the end-user market, Ethan Allen supplies them with a complete range of merchandising services, including the "Treasury of Ethan Allen American Traditional Interiors," an impressive 400-page color catalog and decorating guide; site selection assistance; and sales, product, and design seminars. Sales and profits have advanced steadily during the past decade.

Notice that Ethan Allen's management has not relied on only one factor to gain an impressive position in the furniture industry. The firm's corporate and marketing strategies have been designed to fill a special market segment in the product-market. Attention has been given to customer needs, product design, distribution approaches, the marketing program, and manufacturing efficiency. Ethan Allen's strategy illustrates the importance and the rewards of attaining a differential advantage.

The strategy of each SBU must be developed in line with the resources that top management assigns to the unit and with the needs and structure of a particular organization. Within the unit, priorities are often allocated according to customer importance, geographic area, product line, and other units for planning.

EXHIBIT 2-10

Direct marketers like Lands' End must coordinate their business and marketing strategies to attract and service customers. The coordination of ordering goods, inventory, order processing, and other business functions is essential to provide rapid and accurate response to customers' needs.

Courtesy Lands' End Corp.

Marketing's Role in Corporate Strategy

The Ethan Allen illustration shows the close relationship between corporate and marketing strategy. Marketing management's role is to help define and evaluate strategic product-market areas. Once this has been accomplished and objectives have been established, marketing management must evaluate alternative ways of serving each product-market of interest. This results in the selection of a target market strategy for which objectives are set and cost-effective programs to meet end-user needs are developed.

Strategic business units often compete in several product-markets. As a result, such units are often too broad to use in designing operational marketing strategies. Thus, it is essential that the composition of the SBU be analyzed from a marketing strategy point of view. Market opportunity analysis (MOA), discussed in Part 2, provides direction in developing marketing strategy. Definition of the product-market, coupled with information about demand, industry, and competition, offers an operational scheme for use in analyzing and selecting strategies. Defining and assessing a strategic product-market area are essential both for firms competing in only one area, such as Ethan Allen, and for firms with several SBUs, such as General Electric. Deciding the best way to select customer targets in a market offers both large and small firms a means of establishing a differential advantage over the competition. Corporate and marketing strategies must be managed over time and modified where necessary to respond to new opportunities and to counter impending threats caused by competition and such environmental influences as technological and social change. Changes that affect specific product-markets (such as microwave ovens) occur more frequently than do changes that significantly alter an entire strategic product-market area (such as home appliances). Responses to opportunities and threats include developing new products to compete in product-markets of interest, moving out of particular markets, and eliminating products.

Coordination with Other Functional Areas

It is important to identify and recognize marketing's interrelationship with and dependence on other areas of the organization. Marketing is only one of several functional areas that carry out the corporate mission. As noted in Chapter 1, the marketing manager and staff encounter many situations that require coordination with other functional areas of the firm, such as accounting and finance, engineering and production, personnel, and transportation. Many of the actions taken by marketing management to favorably influence customers require assistance from individuals and groups outside the marketing organization.

The success of the marketing effort can be greatly facilitated by a corporate team effort aimed at providing customer satisfaction. As an example of the necessary coordination, consider the planning required for developing and marketing a new antiperspirant. Marketing identifies the opportunity for a new product from ongoing consumer research studies. To evaluate the new product, a team consisting of representatives from several of the functional areas is appointed by top management. If after comprehensive evaluation the team is convinced of the product's potential, the team leader asks marketing to test several possible product concepts with consumers. The most promising concept, a dry roll-on, is turned over to research, which is told to develop a superior product. And so the activities and coordination continue as the product is developed, tested, and placed on the market.

Regardless of the organizational approaches used to encourage coordination among functional areas, conflicts sometimes occur. The politics of marketing management may consume a substantial portion of the chief marketing executive's time unless relationships are carefully developed and strengthened. There can be various areas of conflict among functional areas such as:

- Competition for scarce resources (a new machine for production versus an expanded advertising budget for marketing).
- Differences in goal priorities (manufacturing may seek to minimize inventory carrying costs, whereas marketing may wish to minimize sales losses and customer dissatisfaction).
- Power struggles among executives in functional areas who are competing for top-management opportunities.

The power of various functional areas tends to vary in different organizations. In high-technology firms, the engineering function wields considerable influence over organizational strategy. In consumer goods companies, marketing people often occupy positions of power.

Application

Changing the Mission of Daimler-Benz AG

Daimler-Benz AG, the conservative and very successful West German world-class automaker, is diversifying from its core auto and truck business by acquiring three high-technology companies. These acquisitions will transform Daimler from a narrowly focused automotive company into a complex industrial conglomerate with a wide mix of products. Management has altered the company's mission of maintaining a technological and competitive edge over its rivals. A key objective of the acquisitions is to obtain important auto-related technology for controlling such functions as brakes, suspension, steering, and air conditioning. General Motors has made similar moves by acquiring Hughes Aircraft Corporation and Electronic Data Systems.

The strategic fit of the new businesses is being questioned by some industry experts, since much of the product and market activities of the acquired firms is not auto related. These experts acknowledge that Daimler's management has the capability to successfully operate the new conglomerate, but they question the linkage between automobiles and such acquired products as vacuum cleaners, typewriters, refrigerators, and radar. Daimler will become the largest company in West Germany, with 300,000 employees and sales in excess of $22 billion.

Daimler's management has been very successful in developing and implementing business and marketing strategies in the very competitive automobile industry. For example, Baby Benz, the innovative Model 190, has been able to take market share away from BMW and Audi. The new challenge of managing a portfolio of businesses will confront Daimler's management with such strategic issues as establishing priorities for resource allocation, evaluating SBU strategies and results, and adjusting the composition of the corporate business portfolio to take advantage of opportunities and threats. For example, Daimler's management must contend with the fact that the acquired companies are operating in several product areas whose outlook for growth is poor or uncertain[20]

Summary

This chapter examines the corporate and business unit strategic planning process used by many businesses, highlighting marketing management's expanding role in corporate strategy. The strategic planning process consists of the situation analysis, development of the mission statement and objectives, determination of the composition of the business, strategic analysis of business units, selection of business unit objectives and strategy, and formulation of the business unit strategic plan.

The situation analysis indicates the organization's strengths and weaknesses and the opportunities and threats facing the organization. The mission indicates the purpose and scope of the organization and its responsibilities to various stakeholders. Companies begin with the core business and then follow various paths of development. Some companies remain in the core business. Others expand into new markets and new products. Diversification into totally new product-market areas may also occur. A large corporation may encompass one or more divisions, and each of these divisions may include one or more strategic business units (SBUs).

Strategic analysis of the corporation's portfolio of SBUs seeks to determine the best total portfolio strategy, taking into account the strategic situation of each SBU. Methods used to evaluate SBUs include the product-market grid and PIMS analyses. These methods are primarily useful in diagnosis rather than in strategy determination. The analyses provide guidelines for determining objectives and strategies for each SBU. Management must decide whether to maintain or strengthen an SBU's position, to shift its position, or to exit from the business.

Which marketing strategy is selected depends on how a business unit is positioned with regard to product-market attractiveness and business strengths and on top management's priorities for that business area. The essence of both corporate and marketing strategy is finding an advantage over competition. Differential advantage can be gained in various ways, including market segmentation, strong distribution channels, product offerings, selling approach, geographic location, and manufacturing expertise. The success of marketing strategy depends importantly on the contributions of other functional areas of the corporation.

Exercises for Review and Discussion

1. Since there is a close relationship between corporate and marketing strategy, identify and discuss the decision areas in which coordination is essential in developing corporate and marketing plans.

2. Colgate-Palmolive produces and markets a broad line of consumer packaged goods (soaps, detergents, toiletries, drugs, cosmetics, etc.), whereas the William Wrigley, Jr. Company produces and markets primarily chewing gum. Discuss the influence of corporate mission on the marketing management function in each of these firms.

3. Suppose that you are responsible for defining the corporate mission of a diversified international company such as Avco Corporation, City Investing, or IU International. Develop a set of questions to which you will need answers in describing the business purpose of the firm you have selected. Review of the company annual report will help you answer the question.

4. You have been given the responsibility for strategic corporate and marketing planning in a company organized around manufacturing centers. Prepare a brief memorandum (maximum of three pages) that will acquaint the board of directors with the purpose of and need for dividing a business into product-market groups.

5. Strategic planning draws from all the functional areas of an organization. What specific contributions are needed from marketing management in developing a company's strategic plan?

6. Suppose that you are the marketing manager for a company that falls into the low/low category with regard to market attractiveness and business strengths. What alternatives should be investigated as possible ways of attaining a more favorable business position?

7. Below are five companies that have achieved differential advantages over their competition in various ways. Select one, and indicate how it has done so.

Winn-Dixie Stores (retail supermarkets)
Nucor Corporation (steel)
Measurex Corporation (process control systems)
Snap-on Tools (hand tools)
A. T. Cross (writing instruments)

8. Discuss the major limitations of grid analysis for use in deciding what future strategies a firm should follow.

9. Select a diversified company and then outline an approach that could be used by management to divide the company into strategic planning units (SBUs).

Notes

1. This illustration is based on Gay Jervey, "Gillette Sharpens Edge with New Ventures," *Advertising Age*, June 24, 1985, pp. 4, 94.

2. David W. Cravens, *Strategic Marketing* (Homewood, Ill.: Richard D. Irwin, 1982), p. 30.

3. Richard J. Mahoney, "What to Do after the Consultants Go Home," *Business Week*, February 13, 1984, p. 17.

4. Elaine Johnson, "Berkey Photo Refocuses Its Business: Firm Seeks to Grow as Marketer and Distributor," *The Wall Street Journal*, August 1, 1985, p. 5.

5. NCH Corporation, *1983 Report to Shareholders*, p. 2.

6. Peter F. Drucker, *Management: Tasks, Responsibilities, Practices* (New York: Harper & Row, 1974), p. 100.

7. John Brimelow, "Toot, Toot Tootsie Roll," *Barron's*, September 17, 1979, p. 9.

8. Ellen Paris, "Know Your Real Strength," *Forbes*, May 9, 1983, p. 71.

9. Ibid.

10. These are similar to the customer group, function, and technology dimensions recommended by Derek F. Abell and John S. Hammond, *Strategic Market Planning* (Englewood Cliffs, N.J.: Prentice-Hall, 1979), p. 392.

11. "James L. Ferguson, General Food's Super-Marketer," *MBA Executive*, March–April 1980, p. 6.

12. Cravens, *Strategic Marketing*, pp. 64–72.

13. Ibid., pp. 72–79.

14. Ibid., pp. 64–79.

15. *The PIMS Program* (Cambridge, Mass.: Strategic Planning Institute, 1980), p. 8.

16. *THE PIMSLETTER on Business Strategy*, no. 1 (Cambridge, Mass.: Strategic Planning Institute, 1977), pp. 3–5.

17. Robert D. Buzzell, Bradley T. Gale, and Ralph G. M. Sultan, "Market Share—A Key to Profitability," *Harvard Business Review*, January–February 1975, p. 97.

18. R. G. Hammermesh, M. J. Anderson, Jr., and J. E. Harris, "Strategies for Low Market Share Businesses," *Harvard Business Review*, May–June 1978, p. 95.

19. Ibid., p. 98.

20. Peter Gumbel, "Daimler-Benz Seeks Technological Edge over Rivals with Its Takeover of AEG," *The Wall Street Journal*, October 21, 1985, p. 26.

PART

2

Marketing Planning

Analyzing the Situation

Marketing Strategy Development

Marketing Program Design

Implementing the Marketing Program

Marketing's Broadening Role

*T*he essence of planning marketing strategy is matching the capabilities of a company with the external forces that determine market opportunity. Management must understand the dynamic interplay among markets, competition, and the macroenvironmental forces affecting them. Thus, an important planning step is to examine the situation existing outside the company through analyzing the environment and market opportunities. The six chapters in Part II examine the nature of this analysis activity.

Chapter 3, "The Marketing Environment," shows the importance of understanding the macroenvironment as a foundation for analyzing markets. The nature and relevance of the environment are explored, and an operational way to scan the environment is illustrated.

Chapter 4, "Defining and Analyzing Product Markets," provides an overview of a market opportunity analysis. The determinants of market opportunity are examined, and a framework is established to guide the analysis of such opportunities.

At the heart of a market opportunity analysis is learning about the behavior of buyers in markets. Chapter 5, "Consumer Markets and Buyer Behavior," is concerned with the concepts and theories that provide the foundation for analyzing consumer behavior. Some companies sell not to consumers, but to other organizations. Chapter 6, "Industrial Markets and Buyer Behavior," examines the behavior of these industrial buyers.

A major part of a market opportunity analysis assesses the effect of competition on markets. Chapter 7, "Analyzing Competition," presents an analytic approach for evaluating competition's impact on market opportunity. Finally, a market opportunity analysis must quantify the amount of sales opportunity in markets. Chapter 8, "Market Measurement and Forecasting," is concerned with the sales forecasting activity.

Analyses of the situation underlie all marketing strategy decisions, from selecting target markets to designing marketing programs. Only after understanding the forces affecting the market opportunity for a company's products or services can management effectively plan how best to meet customer needs and position against competition ■

CHAPTER 3

The Marketing Environment

*S*ome of the most dramatic examples of the link between marketing and environmental change arose from the energy shortages of the 1970s and 1980s. In the first major energy crisis, environmental forces severely hit oil companies, automakers, independent auto dealers, and such fuel-dependent industries as plastics. This crisis was precipitated by a combination of the infamous 1973 oil embargo, which was clearly a product of the governmental environment, and overestimates of the availability of U.S. resources. It was argued that U.S. oil companies underinvested in refining capacity, in part because of the increased capital investment required by environmental legislation. One thing certain about the crisis was its impact. Nearly 60,000 auto production workers were unemployed at one point; 16 of the 44 auto plants in the nation were either closed or partially shut down; and major plans of the automakers, such as expanding General Motors' Oldsmobile Division, were scrapped.[1]

The impact of the crisis was sharply felt by the 25,000 independent dealerships for U.S.-made autos. Shortages and higher gasoline prices caused consumers to postpone car purchases and buy smaller, more economical cars. Dealers offering inventories of smaller cars clobbered dealers that were stocked up with larger, gas-guzzling autos. The slump in big-car sales became an unprecedented rout, with sales running more than 50 percent behind sales for the previous year. The sudden collapse of the big-car market forced many dealers into bankruptcy.

Five years later, after a period of readjustment and reduced concern, history repeated itself. With the 1980s approaching, gas prices again skyrocketed and gas rationing was actively discussed. The auto industry debated how to interpret the change:

> Auto industry experts confess they don't know how serious the wave of concern is, or how long it might last. Some see it as aberrant buying behavior born of something like panic, and they note the fickleness of auto buyers in times past.
>
> But some hardened industry veterans are surmising with amazement that the rush toward economy may really be serious this time.[2]

By this time, the auto companies had new lines of smaller cars and stood a better chance of weathering the storm. Yet the changes created major challenges for all firms in the industry. The survival of Chrysler Corporation hung by a thread.

By the mid-1980s, Chrysler had fully recovered and had increased its line of smaller, fuel-efficient cars, but due to the lower prices and greater supply of gasoline, the sale of larger cars was on the rise. Fuel efficiency had become a way of life, yet Detroit was still struggling. The lesser productivity, higher wage rates, and questionable product quality of the U.S. automakers as compared with the Japanese automakers continued to spell trouble.[3] A healthier economy in the middle to late 1980s eased the pressure, but the long-term prospects of the U.S. auto industry remained uncertain.

What does this example show us? First, and most obviously, it demonstrates the dependence of organizations on uncontrollable environmental change. And forecasters warn that uncontrollable disruptions of various types will probably increase. Second, it shows that governmental, natural, and economic forces affect customers, competitors, and marketing.

Environmental scanning is an essential part of marketing management (Chapter 1). This chapter underscores the importance of understanding environmental change in order to make good marketing decisions. First, the growing importance of the environment is discussed. Then, the characteristics of the environment are defined and an overview is provided of the social, technological, economic, governmental, and natural environments as they relate to marketing. A step-by-step way to scan the environment is presented. The steps include *identifying* threats and opportunities, *monitoring* and *forecasting* these potential forces, and *developing strategic responses*.

Environmental Importance

Marketing environment is that which is external to the marketing management function, largely uncontrollable, potentially relevant to marketing decision making, and changing and/or constraining in nature.

The **marketing environment** is more important to management today than ever before. This is both because the *rate* of environmental change has increased and because there are more *types* of important environmental changes.

First, consider the rate of environmental change. It should be remembered that all of the development experienced by humankind has occurred within a mere moment of history. If we were to equate the earth's history to the distance around the world, the last 50 years, the period of most rapid development, would equal only one foot. Yet an unprecedented acceleration in environmental change occurred during that brief period and people today are experiencing a unique chapter in human history.

In addition, new *types* of environmental change have come to the forefront. Economic factors go to the core of business activity, and historically they have always been important to marketing management. Until around 1900,

EXHIBIT 3-1 Deregulation Rekindles Marketing Activity

Deregulation has forced entire new categories of business into marketing. Banks, railroads, and AT&T have begun to use market research, product development, and other classic marketing tools in order to fend off competition. Banks have come to rely heavily on marketing during the last few years, as restrictions on their industry have been removed. Citibank and the Bank of America, among others, have begun to sell stocks and insurance and to offer other special services to keep the market from being gobbled up by Merrill Lynch, Sears, and other new rivals.

Railroads came up against a similar predicament as restrictive regulations disappeared. The Burlington Northern, Union Pacific, and other railroads restructured their systems. Marketing research found that if the container service was tailored to fit the needs of each customer—special

shapes for coal, refrigeration for perishable goods, timetables that meshed with grain harvest schedules—the railroads could eventually run away with some of the trucking industry's share of the freight business. Backed by extensive advertising and promotional campaigns, the investment paid off.

AT&T used to develop new products based on its latest technological advances, ignoring the needs of its customers. It would even delay the introduction of some products, reluctant to cut short the selling life of similar established items. But since the breakup of Ma Bell, admits Victor Pelson, executive vice president of planning and administration, "we have to give the customer what he wants, how he wants it, and when he wants it. From now on, it's the customer that's going to call the shots."

Source: Adapted from "To Market, to Market," *Newsweek*, January 9, 1984, p. 71.

such factors effectively represented the firm's entire macroenvironment. At the turn of the century, however, governmental and legal forces became more significant, as evidenced by antitrust legislation. The significance of government has grown greatly over the past few decades. Even the recent deregulation of selected industries has meant turbulent times for the companies involved (see Exhibit 3-1).

During the 1930s, the growth of labor organizations further affected the decision realm of management. More recently, consumer groups have used tactics similar to those of labor. Labor and consumer groups highlight a movement toward a pluralistic and interdependent society of interest groups, with business no longer the dominant element. Demands on businesses also arise from their stockholders and from citizens in the communities where they are located. The net result of these developments is several more types of important external changes than existed a few decades ago. This has forced management to invest more time and energy in monitoring the environment.

Some of the more important current environmental changes are what John Naisbitt refers to as "megatrends." Among the most important for marketers is the transition from an industrial society to an information society and from a national economy to a global economy. Of today's occupations, 62 percent are information based, an increase from 17 percent in 1950. Since such occupations require little capital and have few restrictions on their location decisions (no need for transportation, water, etc.), Naisbitt foresees an entrepreneurial revolution, with companies (and markets) springing up where the quality of life is high, particularly in the Southwest.[4]

What implications do such changes have for strategic marketing planning? And how should line marketers cope with the environment? These questions reflect a growing recognition by both corporate strategic planners and line marketers that ignoring the threats and opportunities posed by uncontrollable environmental change is nothing short of folly. Although environmental analysis by itself is no panacea, the penalty for not monitoring the environment can be severe, if not fatal. Consistent with this theme, a study conducted for a Big Eight accounting firm concluded that corporate strategic planning had become more closely geared to marketing. In the results, Terrence D. Daniels, an executive vice president of W. R. Grace & Co., contended that a broad viewpoint was essential because today's corporate planners must consider the environment and social demographics.[5]

Characteristics of the Marketing Environment

The environment of anything is as large or small, and as simple or complex, as one's definition of it. Changing consumer incomes, technological innovation, changing government agencies, and shifting consumer values are examples of the marketing environment. This environment includes those things that are external, largely uncontrollable, changing, constraining, and potentially relevant. The marketing environment includes nonmarketing departments within the firm, as well as markets, competitors, and the macroenvironment.

Marketers are primarily adapters. They adapt their products, prices, promotion, and distribution to fit the marketplace, as was true for the auto industry during the energy crisis. Certain environmental forces are partially controllable, but most are largely uncontrollable. Some *changes* in environmental factors, such as shifting population characteristics, represent a key source of uncertainty. Other changes *constrain* management to the extent of defining a straight and narrow path for it. The Flammable Fabrics Act, for example, imposes constraints on the product decisions of apparel marketers. The marketing environment must be *potentially relevant* to marketing decision making in the organization. The potentially relevant environment for an electronic calculator firm is very different from that for a soap producer.

A snapshot of the environment surrounding most organizations is shown in Exhibit 3-2. It is the view of a marketing vice president looking outward from the home turf. The first visible part of the environment comprises surrounding offices and personnel within the company, the *intraorganizational environment*. Within each company, there may be environmental forces that must be dealt with.

Perhaps the most important aspect of the intraorganizational environment is the internal corporate culture, or "the collection of beliefs, expectations, and values shared by the corporation members and transmitted from one generation of employees to another."[6] Leading companies seem to exhibit a relatively open, creative, and adaptive corporate culture. A more entrepreneurial corporate culture, popularized by the best seller *In Search of Excellence*, has been fostered by such companies as General Electric. Achiev-

EXHIBIT 3–2 The Marketing Environment

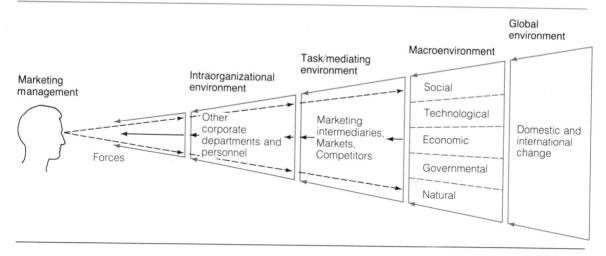

ing such a culture is a delicate and difficult task. AT&T Information Systems, in contrast, shuffled an innovative vice president for marketing into a staff position, despite the VP's impressive sales and profit record. His "style" was apparently too radical for the entrenched culture.[7]

Exhibit 3–2 also shows the environment outside the corporation in layers representing both the immediacy of the factors to marketing management (the closer, the more immediate) as well as the frequency with which management has to deal with such factors. However, to focus only on the inner layer, or task environment, is to ignore changes in the macroenvironment that cause the task environment to change. It is critical to understand these macro changes to better anticipate changes in markets and competitive relationships.

Looking just beyond the corporate wall, marketers work with independent parties that require constant attention; these include such marketing intermediaries as distributors, advertising agencies, and marketing research firms. This task environment includes markets and competitors. The task environment should be thought of as mediating between the macroenvironment and management; changes in markets and competitors often result from macroenvironmental changes, as was illustrated by the effects of the energy crisis on the auto industry.

The macroenvironment, to which the bulk of this chapter is devoted, comprises the social, technological, economic, governmental, and natural environments. Subsequent chapters cover the intraorganizational and task environments. The final portion of the marketing environment consists of global, international change, and this is covered in Chapter 23.

Understanding the Marketing Macroenvironment

What is the nature of the macroenvironment, and what are some current trends of importance to marketers? The sections that follow provide a definition and a descriptive overview of each macroenvironmental sector.

The Social Environment

The social environment affects the functioning of virtually everything in a democratic society, and it implicitly sets the priorities and the directions for change. Some **social changes** of special interest to marketers include:

Social change is the occurrence of an alteration in the form or functioning of a significant group, institution, or social order.[8]

- Changing population characteristics (demographic and socioeconomic)
- Changing consumer values and lifestyles
- Social issues, such as consumerism

Because these broad social changes affect consumer markets, such firms as Whirlpool Corporation commit significant resources to anticipating social trends. As customers change, marketing must adapt. In a sense, social change is simply changing people.

Demographic change is change in such population characteristics as geographic distribution and growth, as well as income, education, and age levels. These characteristics may or may not be related to a company's specific product markets. Geritol is targeted to the old and Clearasil to the young due to concern about health among older people and concern about skin blemishes among teenagers. In both cases, there is a tie between consumers' perceived needs and a particular age category. Demographic traits are closely linked to the sales of many products, and the investigation of these traits is a natural first step in searching for market opportunities, if such a link exists.

The first step in a population analysis is to tentatively observe and confirm relationships between population characteristics and the sales of products. Some relationships seem self-evident, such as targeting Mennen's aftershave products to males. Yet hair spray, which was once "obviously" targeted to women, is now a big seller with men.

Subsequent steps in a population analysis include monitoring, forecasting, and interpreting. Demographers may be reasonably certain when they describe existing conditions, but they "have a forecasting accuracy which just rates marginally better than the meteorologists . . . [making demography a] very nervous way to earn a living."[9] For example, it is very difficult to forecast the disposition of women to have or not have babies.

Demographic change is not just a matter of population growth rates. It is related to such exciting changes as the continuing effects of the post–World War II baby boom (1947–57). A Harvard demographer referred to the baby boom as a population bulge passing through American life like a watermelon

EXHIBIT 3-3 Demographic Trends and Marketing

Not all consumer dollars are slipping to the Sun Belt. In a five-year projection to identify the 50 most affluent U.S. metropolitan markets, 38 were in the Frost Belt and only 2 of the top 10 were in the Sun Belt. Similarly, close analysis of the Sun Belt shows that many areas within it are experiencing below average growth.

American Express Company estimated that it was capturing only about 20 percent of the women who met its financial, occupational, and lifestyle criteria. Male cardholders outnumbered female cardholders four to one. This led to a major advertising campaign targeted toward upscale women. The early results were overwhelmingly successful.

Kids "R" Us, a national children's wear retailer (owned by Toys "R" Us, Inc.), is stirring the industry with a price-discounting strategy. The baby boom generation is having children of its own, and with small families there are few hand-me-downs. A two-paycheck family that saved while waiting to have children has ample resources. With divorces and remarriages, there are more grandparents to buy as well.

Fuddruckers Inc., a Texas-based fast-food restaurant chain, is catering to people in their mid-30s, the first generation to grow up on fast food and America's fastest-growing age group. A shift in tastes within this group has led to new restaurants with more nutritious, more varied, fresher, and higher-quality food. Fuddruckers sells its hamburger as "gourmet" food, visibly grinding raw slabs of meat, and bakes its own buns.

Frozen TV dinners are also changing. Consumers have become wealthier, half of all U.S. mothers work, and a record number of single people don't want to cook. "There's never been a greater need for high-quality convenience food," says Steven A. McNeil, frozen food manager at Campbell, which owns Swanson Frozen Foods. Campbell has introduced Le Menu, a line of quality frozen dinners, and is testing lobster thermidor, chicken cordon bleu, and other items.

Mary Kay Cosmetics, Inc. became a major cosmetic distributor through the use of party plan direct selling. But it has encountered problems in attracting new recruits for its 200,000-member sales force. The declining availability of housewives with their market networks of friends and relatives is a major challenge to Tupperware and other direct marketers as well.

Sources: Robin Peterson, "Overreaction to Consumer Trends Can Prove a Dangerous Practice," *Marketing News*, January 17, 1986, p. 2; Bill Abrams, "American Express Is Gearing New Ad Campaign to Women," *The Wall Street Journal*, August 4, 1983, p. 19; Claude Ricci, "Children's Wear Retailers Brace for Competition from Toys R Us," *The Wall Street Journal*, August 25, 1983, p. 17.; Sue Shellenbarger and J. Zaslow, "Fast Food Chains Improve Menus to Tap Big Change in Public Tastes," *The Wall Street Journal*, October 27, 1983, p. 33.; Paul A. Engelmayer, "Food Concerns Rush to Serve More Quality Frozen Dinners," *The Wall Street Journal*, October 20, 1983, p. 35.; Dean Rotbart and Laurie P. Cohen, "The Party at Mary Kay Isn't So Lively, as Recruiting Falls Off," *The Wall Street Journal*, October 28, 1983, pp. 1, 18; Eugene Carlson, "Affluent Buyers Seen Staying in Suburbs of the Frost Belt," *The Wall Street Journal*, November 22, 1983, p. 35; and "U.S. Population Trends Defy Neat Classification by Experts," *The Wall Street Journal*, October 18, 1983, p. 37.

passing through a boa constrictor. This "watermelon" continues to affect marketing. Furniture industry analysts project bleak conditions after 1990, but radical expansion of the age group from 35 to 44 (the aging babies) has made the 1980s exceptionally good years for that industry. This age group buys 50 percent more furniture than the average household. The baby boom bulge constitutes 46 million consumers, the largest reservoir of buyers provided by any such age span, and these buyers are within the age group that generates the highest income and saving levels.[10] Some other demographic trends and related market strategies are shown in Exhibit 3-3.

Marketers must be cautious of reacting to demographic trends without careful market analysis, however. Although yuppies represent an important market for some products, it could be a mistake to exclude other, somewhat less upwardly mobile professionals. Specific product market analysis is usually required in addition to trend analysis.[11]

Value change is a second and more fundamental type of social change. If we assume that cultural values shape what consumers value, their relevance to marketing is clear. Value change is so pervasive in its effects on business

EXHIBIT 3-4 Important Value-Related Trends

More individualized lifestyles and self-concepts

More informed, cosmopolitan, world oriented

Greater acceptance of multiple lifestyles, fashions, etc.

More natural, informal lifestyles

Blending of male/female roles: less traditional roles

More "live for today" versus live for the long term

Pleasure orientation

Different family structures: smaller families, more divorces, more remarriages, more single parents, less grandparent influence, more two-career households

More demanding consumers

Greater sexual freedom

Increased value placed on conservation ethic

Increased perception of time as a scarce resource

---

that a General Electric analyst once cited shifts in people's basic values as the single most important element in forecasting the business environment. There is considerable agreement among several U.S. studies as to the prevalence of the value-related trends shown in Exhibit 3-4, although these trends are occurring more rapidly in some population groups than in others. Although values do not change rapidly, some observers believe that we are now experiencing as great a change in values in 7 or 8 years as used to occur in 20 years.

Value trends are considered not only as a source of general input into the planning process but as a factor in marketing strategies. Understanding creativity and fulfillment values led to positioning do-it-yourself home improvement products as creativity outlets rather than as cheaper substitutes for more professional services. What important class of values is appealed to in the *Wall Street Journal* advertisement in Exhibit 3-5?

The designers of the *Yankelovich Monitor*, a subscription source of data on values, indicate that forecasts based on values trends have been validated "time and time again," despite earlier skepticism concerning such forecasts. The designers claim greater success than their counterparts in economic forecasting.[12] Yet they caution against using generalized value trends and clusters as market segments, holding that specific analysis of the product-market involved is essential. This was an important point for *Playboy* magazine's management, which debated whether *Playboy* was out of touch with social changes. Although still the country's best-selling men's magazine, its circulation, ad pages, revenues, and earnings were declining in the mid-1980s. Critics said that *Playboy* was slipping because society and the publishing climate had changed, while the magazine had not.[13] In 1985, it was announced that *Playboy* would become more of a lifestyle magazine with greater relevance to the times.

A third important type of social change encompasses *social issues* and the possible formalization of social pressure into law. Social or consumer issues typically result from a gap between consumer perceptions of the marketplace and their expectations, and may concern *product* quality and safety, planned obsolescence, wasteful and deceptive packaging, product differentiation, and

EXHIBIT 3-5

Advertising matches the message to the values held by the target market.

Courtesy Fallon McElligott Rice. Reprinted with permission of Dow Jones & Company, © 1986.

warranties. *Promotion* is affected by such social issues as questionable personal selling techniques, deceptive advertising, the cost of advertising, promotion directed to vulnerable groups (children and less-educated consumers), and the use of advertising to foster "unreal" perceived differences between products. *Distribution* decisions raise issues about the cost of distribution itself, the level of service in economically disadvantaged areas, and the impact of large shopping centers on communities. *Pricing* decisions, although historically circumscribed by laws dealing with collusion and unfair price discrimination, continue to be an area of abuse. Finally, *marketing research* is sometimes challenged as an invasion of privacy.

In sum, the social environment encompasses people's characteristics, their culture and values, and their specific concerns. Social changes pose threats as well as untold opportunities for astute marketers.

The Technological Environment

The technological environment is important in several ways, the most obvious of which is its relationship to the marketing of new or modified products. The manifestation of technology may be a physical entity such as a computer, yet the essence of technology is new understanding. Technology, broadly viewed, is the means for extending human capability, encompassing tools, techniques, products, processes, and methods. Technology forged the success of the horseless carriage, solid-state color television, and laser applications. Entire industries emerged from such technological advances as photocopiers and air conditioning. An equally important product to serious golfers is their golf ball! In 1968, Spaulding developed a two-piece ball that would come off the tee at a higher angle and fly higher and farther than the wound-rubber, balata-covered ball. Sales of this improved ball now account for most of the $250 million annual market. Yet professionals have continued to use the balata ball because of its greater control and accuracy. Now, after years of research by chemists and technicians, Spaulding has a new ball (Tour Edition) that it says offers the advantages but avoids the disadvantages of the balata ball. Acushnet, producer of the Titlist balata ball, claims that golfers are not adopting the Tour Edition ball. Spaulding insists, "We'll make balata-covered balls obsolete."[14]

Technology
is the application of knowledge, encompassing the related concepts of science, innovation, invention, and discovery.

The impact of **technology** on marketing goes far beyond new product decisions because it fundamentally alters the social and economic environment for doing business. The changing role of women in the United States is one of the most significant social and market developments in U.S. history, and technology facilitated that development. In kitchen cupboards are now found instant potatoes, cake mixes, and dinner mixes. And consider the wide array of timesaving and laborsaving appliances, such as the microwave oven. Is it any wonder that the role of the housewife was revolutionized and that in recent decades more and more women have entered the labor force?

Technology also directly affects companies through new methods and techniques for use by marketing management, and it affects such marketing decision areas as new products, pricing, distribution, and promotion (Exhibit 3-6). Marketing and technology must be bridged by the customer orientation dictated by the marketing concept. Given that the role of marketing is to channel want-satisfying products and services to customers, management must continually engage in the "creative destruction" of existing products by seeking new and better ways to meet market demands.[15]

Most technological innovations (potential products) are visible long before their use becomes widespread. This means that management should place attention on monitoring developing competitive technologies rather than on totally new ones. A young IBM marketing man noted Chester Carlson's patent on xerography in the *New York Times* in 1940, but he failed to interest IBM management. The xerography patent was also abstracted in an Eastman Kodak publication in 1943, but the abstract was ignored by management.

EXHIBIT 3-6 Marketing Mix Decisions and Technology

Marketing Mix	*Technology/Markets*	*Examples*
Product/service	Source of new products	Personal computer
	Improvement in product performance	Transistors
	Response to consumer lifestyles	Microwave oven
Channels of distribution	Increased speed of distribution	Airfreight
	Increased capacity of distribution	Super oil tankers
	Logistical control of distribution	Computers
Pricing	Lower production cost	Synthetic fabrics
	Price comparisons	Airline information systems
	Coded price scanning	Computerized laser reader
Promotion	Improved communications capabilities	Communication satellites
	Scheduling of advertising media	Management science models
	Computerized word processing	Direct mail

Monitoring often begins after the point of *innovation*—after the first acceptance and use of an idea or invention. Marketing then assumes the job of increasing the rate of adoption and diffusion (Exhibit 3-7).

$$\text{Science} \rightarrow \frac{\text{Invention/}}{\text{discovery}} \rightarrow \text{Innovation} \rightarrow \frac{\text{Adoption and}}{\text{diffusion}}$$

Current technological trends of interest to marketers include:

■ Product life cycles have become shorter and shorter in recent decades. Companies must therefore seek a faster payback from new product investments. This, combined with generally increasing costs and the risks of government intervention (by such agencies as the Food and Drug Administration), makes new product development an even greater risk.

■ Fine-tuning innovations versus seeking invention breakthroughs has become a priority for much of U.S. industry. Refining existing technologies has taken precedence over the long-term expenditures required to generate basic scientific developments. The result has been more milking of existing products and a dearth of the breakthroughs required to build new industries. Also, the number of patents granted to U.S. citizens has declined in recent years, while other industrialized countries have increased their number of patent filings.

Technological advancements will continue, however, to present opportunities as well as competitive threats to marketing management.

The Economic Environment

The most severe recession since the Great Depression hit in 1982–83, leaving many organizations struggling to survive. Measures of consumer confidence declined, and a different "mood" surrounded markets. Instead of buying

EXHIBIT 3-7

The marketing of innovative technology increases the rate of acceptance by making the technology user friendly.

Courtesy Bozell, Jacobs, Kenyon & Eckhardt, Inc.

luxuries, consumers shifted toward basics. By the end of the recession, discount outlets had become a major retailing phenomenon. It was not until the upswing in late 1983 and 1984 that consumer optimism began to rise. By 1986, the economic expansion was into its fourth year. The Gallup Organization reported, "Most consumers are still very optimistic about the economic outlook—and why shouldn't they be? The job market is strong, inflation remains relatively low, and interest rates are down. . . . Can you imagine some guy walking into a car dealership and worrying, 'Should I buy this car with the federal budget deficit as high as it is?' "[16]

The economic environment is of critical importance to marketers because economic cycles (prosperity, recession, recovery) and other economic factors (inflation, productivity, shortages, the value of the dollar) have a tremendous impact on prices and incomes. This affects consumers' real purchasing power as well as their confidence in purchasing. Economic changes require substantial marketplace adaptation within the same organization over time. For example, Sears, Roebuck & Co. began as a catalog sales operation for rural America, but it has survived and prospered during decades of phenomenal environmental change, including consumer affluence, suburbanization, increased consumer mobility, and changed values and tastes. During the 1970s, Sears continued to improve its service and the quality of its merchandise and to raise prices in response to rising consumer affluence. However, Sears moved somewhat ahead of consumer price preferences, particularly when recession and inflation hit the family pocketbook during the mid-1970s. Sears felt this economic impact more strongly than the second- and third-largest retailers, K mart and J. C. Penney, and the management of Sears realized its mistake. The economic environment had led Sears customers to shift toward price- and inflation-conscious buying and a back-to-basics orientation. Sears responded with more low-end merchandise and pricing cuts, and its new advertising concentrated on special sale items with larger markdowns and longer sales periods. Sears corporate sales once again rose to record levels by the late 1970s, but the company had outdone itself: profits plummeted.

During the 1980s, Sears made further adjustments and increased its profits through efforts to reestablish itself as a price and quality leader in the minds of consumers. By the mid-1980s, it was again upgrading its apparel components with more fashion and quality.[17] The objective was to take advantage of more favorable economic trends. Sears was also well along toward building its financial services business to reduce its dependence on merchandising. Throughout its history, Sears has done an admirable job in adapting to changing economic conditions, although its merchandising business continued to struggle into the latter half of the 1980s.

Economic changes can affect different organizations in unequal ways. Recession, for example, crippled a 40-year-old major appliance distributor, so a feasibility study was conducted to determine whether or not to add an appliance parts business. On the basis of that study, the distributor entered the parts business, due largely to its countercyclical nature. The parts business flourished, while new major appliance sales remained stagnant.

Another disruptive force in the economic environment for marketers has been shortages. Shortages occurred in petroleum-based products, sugar, coffee, and other products during the 1970s, and despite surpluses in the 1980s, they will undoubtedly occur in the future. Few environmental factors disrupt marketers as much as not having products to sell! During shortages, demand shifts to substitute products or is simply reduced. Shortages, of course, also lead to higher prices. Monitoring the possibility of shortages, although difficult, deserves attention in today's interdependent world economy.

Despite the many uncertainties of the economic environment, it is one of the best-understood sectors of the macroenvironment. It is clear that economic cycles, inflation, productivity, recession, shortages, the value of the dollar, and many other factors make this environmental sector critically important to markets. Students of business will study this sector extensively in other coursework.

The Governmental Environment

Legislation enacted at the beginning of this century to curb business abuses has mushroomed into a myriad of complex laws and enforcement mechanisms impinging on every marketing decision area. Marketing management cannot afford to ignore the governmental environment—whether this be legislative activities, regulatory trends, interpretations by the courts, or the actions of government executive offices. At least 87 federal entities regulate U.S. business. To complete the 4,000 different forms they dispense requires an estimated 140 million hours of executive and clerical effort each year.

Fully legitimate government objectives include:

- The maintenance of healthy, workable competition within the business system.

- The prevention of deceptive, fraudulent, or unsafe marketing practices.

The limits of legality for marketing activity are specified by antitrust laws and by laws that address specific consumer problems.

Antitrust Law.   Several legislative pillars have been passed over the years to maintain and promote healthy, workable competition. Most significant in this regard are the antitrust laws. In essence, these regulate the structure of the marketplace. Federal statutes pertaining to interstate commerce are reviewed in Exhibit 3–8; most of the states have similar intrastate antitrust laws.

The frequency of antitrust charges and more severe penalties have spurred more companies to initiate in-house educational campaigns to sensitize employees to the dos and don'ts of antitrust. Criminal felony charges may now be made against individual executives, on whom prison sentences and fines may be imposed. Of special importance to marketers, salespeople are probably the employees who are most likely to slip inadvertently into antitrust hot water, but company education programs often cover personnel in all areas. Educational programs emphasize the necessity of avoiding price discussions at trade association meetings, even to the point of leaving meetings or resigning from an association if its activities are questionable.

Consumer Legislation.   This type of legislation regulates corporate behavior within the marketplace, but the antitrust laws probably do more to assist consumers through promoting competition and determining the structure of the marketplace. Major examples of consumer legislation are listed in Exhibit 3–9. Other consumer-related laws not listed in Exhibit 3–9 involve numerous environmental protection laws, such as the 1970 Clean Air Act

EXHIBIT 3–8 Major Antitrust Laws

Act	Provision	Act	Provision
Sherman Act (1890)	Sec. 1: "Every contract, combination, . . . or conspiracy, in restraint of trade or commerce among the several States, or with foreign nations, is hereby declared to be illegal. Every person who shall make any such contract or engage in any such combination or conspiracy, shall be deemed guilty of a misdemeanor." Sec. 2: "Every person who shall monopolize, or attempt to monopolize, or combine or conspire with any other person or persons, or monopolize any part of the trade or commerce among the several states, or with foreign nations, shall be deemed guilty of a misdemeanor."		granted in "good faith" to meet competition. (Amended by the Robinson-Patman Act.) Sec. 3: Forbids sellers to lease, sell, or make a contract for the sale of goods on the condition that the purchaser or lessee agree not to use or sell the goods of a competitor (tying contract) where the effect of such an agreement is substantially less competition or a tendency toward monopoly in any line of commerce. Sec. 7: Forbids any corporation engaged in commerce to acquire the stock of a corporation or of two or more competing corporations where the effect is substantially less competition or a tendency toward monopoly. (Amended by the Celler-Kefauver Act.) Sec. 8: Forbids the same persons from serving on the boards of directors of two or more competing corporations when one of the corporations has assets of more than $1 million and where the elimination of competition between them would violate any of the provisions of the antitrust laws (i.e., interlocking directorates.)
Clayton Act (1914)	Specifically outlawed price discrimination, tying contracts, exclusive dealing, and intercorporate stockholdings and interlocking directorates in directly competing companies, where the effect is to "substantially lessen competition or tend to create a monopoly." Sec. 2: Forbids sellers to discriminate in the price charged purchasers of commodities of like grade, quantity, or quality where such discrimination results in a substantial lessening of competition or tends to create a monopoly in any line of commerce. Price discrimination is permitted where there are differences in costs incident to serving different customers or where lower prices are	*Federal Trade Commission Act (1914)*	Established the Federal Trade Commission to enforce the provisions of the Clayton Act. Sec. 5: Forbids "unfair methods" of competition as defined by the FTC and gives the FTC the power to prosecute. (Amended by the Wheeler-Lea Act.)

amendments and the 1972 Clean Water amendments, both of which give the Environmental Protection Agency standards for environmental improvement.

Marketing Impact. What is the rationale for government influence over marketing? In a democracy, the government acts at the discretion of its citizens. Despite lags and imperfections, the government interprets the needs of the people, directly satisfying certain collective needs (e.g., for schools and roads) and determining the appropriate *means* for satisfying other needs. The "means" in the United States is a mixed economy with reliance on the market system.

For this market system to function effectively, customers must:

■ Have different product/brand choices available from independent sources (competitors).

EXHIBIT 3–8 (*concluded*)

Act	Provision
Robinson-Patman Act (1936)	Sec. 2(a): Prohibits the granting of different prices to different buyers of commodities of like grade and quality where the effect of such discrimination would be a reduction in competition between the seller and his competitors, between a buyer and the buyer's competitors, or between the customers of a buyer. Price differences for different customers are permitted if they do not exceed the differences in the costs of serving the customers. The FTC was given the power to establish maximum limits on quantity discounts granted to any customer or class of customers, regardless of the differences in the costs of serving them.
	Sec. 2(b): The "good faith defense" in the Clayton Act was to continue to apply.
	Sec. 2(c): Prohibits the granting of brokerage allowances by a seller to a buyer or a brokerage firm owned by the buyer.
	Sec. 2(d and e): Sellers must make any supplementary services or allowances to all purchasers on a proportionately equal basis.
	Sec. 2(f): It is illegal for a buyer to knowingly obtain a discriminatory price from a seller.

Act	Provision
Celler-Kefauver Antimerger Act of 1950	Amended Section 7 of the Clayton Act to include the purchase of assets.
Wheeler-Lea Act (1938)	Broadened Section 5 of the FTC Act to include the prohibition of practices that might injure the public without affecting competition. Also extended the FTC's authority over the false advertising of food, drugs, cosmetics, and therapeutic devices.
Fair Trade Laws	The Consumer Goods Pricing Act of 1975 ended state laws that provided for vertical price-fixing in channels of distribution. A "nonsigners clause" provided that once a manufacturer obtained the agreement of one dealer in a state to resell its product at a given price, no other competitors in that state could sell the product at a lower price. The Miller-Tydings Act (1937) exempted interstate resale price-fixing contracts from the antitrust laws when both of the states involved recognized the legality of such contracts. The McGuire Act (1952) established the legality of the nonsigners clause for interstate commerce. These were actually exemptions from the antitrust laws that were terminated in all interstate commerce in 1975.

Source: Partially based on Louis W. Stern and John R. Grabner, Jr., *Competition in the Marketplace* (Glenview, Ill.: Scott, Foresman, 1970), pp. 69–78.

■ Have freedom of choice and financial resources.

■ Have a sufficient amount of reliable, timely information for decision making.

■ Be capable decision makers.

Poorly informed or uneducated consumers thwart the functioning of the market system. Deceptive advertising contributes to misallocating consumers' incomes, sustains undeserving marketers, and places the legitimate competitor at a disadvantage. Collusive actions among firms restrict consumer choice and support artificially high prices. Therefore, most government activity with regard to the market system is targeted to create workable competition ensuring that these four customer requirements are met.

The laws listed in Exhibits 3–8 and 3–9 have numerous implications for marketing management because they affect pricing, distribution, products, promotion, and marketing research. Although large companies often have in-house legal counsel, management must be sensitive to possible legal prob-

EXHIBIT 3-9 Selected Consumer Legislation

Act	Provision	Act	Provision
Food and Drugs Act (1906):	Guarded against unsafe and adulterated food and drug products.	*Textile Fiber Products Identification Act (1958):*	Required identification of the fiber content of clothing and textile fiber products.
Meat Inspection Act (1906):	Required that meat shipped in interstate commerce be processed and packed under wholesome and sanitary conditions.	*Food Additives (Delaney) Amendment (1958):*	Amended the Food, Drug, and Cosmetic Act (1938) to require that only food additives that do not cause cancer in man or animals be generally recognized as safe for human consumption.
Federal Trade Commission Act (1914):	Established the Federal Trade Commission. Declared "unfair methods of competition" to be illegal (see Exhibit 3-8).		
Food, Drug, and Cosmetic Act (1938):	Amended Food and Drugs Act (1906), expanding the jurisdiction of the Food and Drug Administration to include cosmetics and therapeutic devices, and established standards of identity for food products.	*Kefauver-Harris Amendment (1962):*	Amended the Food, Drug, and Cosmetic Act (1938) by requiring that all drugs be tested for safety and efficacy.
Wheeler-Lea Act (1938):	Expanded the consumer protection activities of the Federal Trade Commission by amending the FTC Act to include "unfair or deceptive acts or practices."	*Fair Packaging and Labeling Act (1966):*	Regulated the packaging and labeling of consumer goods. Provided for the voluntary adoption, by industry, of uniform packaging standards.
Wool Products Labeling Act (1939):	Made fiber content labeling by percentages mandatory in products containing wool.	*National Traffic and Motor Vehicle Safety Act (1966):*	Authorized the establishment of compulsory safety standards for automobiles and new and used tires.
Fur Products Labeling Act (1951):	Established mandatory labeling requirements for fur products.	*Child Protection Act of 1966:*	Amended the Hazardous Substances Labeling Act (1960) to become the Hazardous Substances Act. Permitted the banning of hazardous substances from the market and prevented the marketing of potentially harmful toys and other articles used by children.
Flammable Fabrics Act (1953):	Outlawed the manufacture or sale of wearing apparel or fabrics so highly flammable as to be dangerous.	*Cigarette Labeling Act (1966):*	Required health warning labels on cigarette packaging.

lems and know when to seek counsel. We will return to legislation and regulation that apply to marketing in Chapter 24.

The Natural Environment

For marketing, the natural environment has long been considered an uncontrollable force. Sweltering summers increase sales for soft-drink distributors; cold winters and higher energy costs create demand for wood stoves. Although it is common sense to advertise cold medicine more in the winter and beer more in the summer, the entrepreneurs who founded Advertiming use computer models to match product usage with weather conditions. They say that weather can change people's habits and taste preferences enough to boost consumption of a product by 50 to 100 percent. And Campbell Soup Company boosted its "winter storm ad budget" for 1985 to about $750,000.[18]

Natural resources, climate, physical barriers, and terrain are factors of the natural environment that affect marketing decisions, sometimes greatly. For most companies, the uncertainties of such factors are recognized and the

EXHIBIT 3–9 (*concluded*)

Act	Provision	Act	Provision
Flammable Fabrics Act Amendments (1967):	Broadened federal authority to set safety standards for flammable fabrics.	*Magnuson-Moss Warranty/Federal Trade Commission Improvement Act (1975):*	Empowered the FTC specifically to make rules for consumer product warranties. Provided for consumer redress, including class action. Expanded the FTC's jurisdiction to matters "affecting commerce" and increased its general rule-making powers with respect to unfair or deceptive acts or practices.
Consumer Credit Protection Act (Truth in Lending) (1968):	Required full disclosure of terms and conditions of finance charges in consumer credit transactions.		
Child Protection and Toy Safety Act of 1969:	Amended the Hazardous Substances Act (1966) by broadening coverage to provide for a ban on toys and other articles used by children that posed electrical, mechanical, or thermal hazards.	*Fair Credit Billing Act (1975):*	Provided consumers with an opportunity to dispute errors in billing statements. Required creditors to make efforts to correct such errors.
Fair Credit Reporting Act of 1970:	Amended the Consumer Credit Protection Act (1968). Stated conditions for the maintenance and dissemination of consumer credit records.	*FTC Improvements Act (1980):*	Placed several limitations and restraints on the commission's activities. Every six months, the FTC must list the trade regulation rules it intends to propose and the related justification, and projected costs and benefits. This act also gave Congress veto power over such rules.
Poison Prevention Packaging Act (1970):	Authorized the establishment of standards for child-resistant packaging of hazardous substances.		
Consumer Product Safety Act (1972):	Established the Consumer Product Safety Commission, which assumed responsibility for many FDA product safety programs. Empowered the commission to set safety standards for a broad range of consumer products and to levy penalties for failure to meet the standards.		

Source: Reprinted by permission from *Consumer Protection: Problems and Prospects*, 2nd ed., by Laurence P. Feldman; copyright 1980 by West Publishing Company. All rights reserved.

adaptive responses are known, although not necessarily pleasant, as was shown by the responses of the auto industry to the energy crisis.

The primary *threat* of the natural environment to marketers is that of resource shortages for existing and new products. The silver lining within these threatening clouds is the creation of market *opportunities*. Auto companies introduced newly designed, energy-efficient vans to recapture customers lost by the gas-guzzling vans of the past. Appliance manufacturers promote new, energy-efficient products, and new companies have sprung up to capitalize on the energy conservation needs of both businesses and homes.

Environmental Scanning

Environmental scanning within a company can be organized in various ways. Yet the leading advocate of environmental scanning must be the chief executive officer, who ensures line management involvement through example and incentives; otherwise, subordinates will continue to put out fires with a short time horizon.

Executives, managers, and employees under the CEO must all be trained, sensitized, and made alert to external changes, and they must be given incentives to pass information forward. Identifying, monitoring, forecasting, and interpreting environmental change must be tackled in part by *line* managers from marketing for several reasons:

- Line management's knowledge of operations is necessary for identifying potentially relevant environmental change and for interpreting its meaning and implications.
- Directly engaging in environmental scanning helps develop managerial sensitivity to new types of information, including from nonbusiness sources.
- Line management involvement contributes to a comprehension of *why* environmental changes are occurring, providing valuable insight for interpreting and anticipating the future.

Line management involvement increases the chances that the most important questions will be raised.

The complete process of environmental scanning and analysis (see Exhibit 3-10) requires a significant commitment of executive time. So the potential payoff must be weighed against the costs; in the early phases, management should delete the third stage, select only some of the most relevant changes for study, and limit the resources invested until potential benefits become evident. Now let us examine each of the stages.

Identify Relevant Change

Although the word *scanning* may bring to mind a rotating radar detection unit, attention in marketing is focused on movement in markets, on movement by competitors, and on changes in the macroenvironment that precipitate this movement. An almost infinite variety of changes may be somewhat relevant to the firm, so it is essential to assess their importance in view of the costs of scanning. The changes normally selected for attention include:

- Highly probable changes that are most likely to impact the company.
- Lower-probability changes that could have major consequences.

One of two basic approaches to identifying potentially relevant change is to begin with significant macroenvironmental changes in society and then to assess their potential future relevance to the organization—for example, annually identifying and monitoring the 20 most significant societal changes and then interpreting their potential threats and opportunities to the company's markets, competitive relationships, and marketing strategy. This external to internal (EX→IN) approach has the advantage of providing a

EXHIBIT 3-10 Environmental Scanning in Action: An Overview

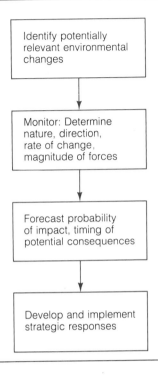

candidate list of potential changes that might be missed in a more narrowly focused search.

The second and more common approach, ideally combined with the first, starts with internal parameters of relevance. The most common parameter is the product-market that a company serves. Division and project managers familiar with specific product-markets pose questions to the environmental scanning staff and have the staff maintain profiles and information of interest to the division or project. This internal to external (IN→EX) search approach offers the advantage of giving in-depth attention to previously identified areas of relevance.

An extensive approach for identifying change forces is SPIRE (Systematic Procedure for Identifying the Relevant Environments).[19] SPIRE was constructed in the belief that significant external forces are often not identified, and that decision makers often disregard the forecasts made. Although the process is too elaborate to review in detail, it centers on a matrix with likely external changes on one axis and possible strategic decisions or assumptions on the other axis. The impact linkages in the cells are studied, screened, and clustered. In one use of SPIRE by an oil company, 250 environmental changes were considered and then distilled into the constellations of greatest relevance. Central to SPIRE is the involvement of line management in the creative grouping processes that help ensure relevance and later acceptance.

Management must also decide on the frequency of scanning—from continuous to irregular. Few corporate systems today use continuous scanning. Where the rate of an environmental change is consistently slow, this may be outright wasteful.

Erratic or rapid environmental change, however, may require continuous attention. Irregular and infrequent attention to identifying environmental factors is usually a crisis-related response tied to specific, immediate decisions, with little orientation to the future. The regular frequency model in Exhibit 3–11 is more comprehensive and systematic, but it still involves only an annual attempt to identify important changes. It is proactive or future oriented in the sense that it studies the environment to determine the possibility of future impact on current issues or decisions, but it is retrospective in that it is tied to current decisions. The continuous model is distinctively different because it is not oriented toward specific decisions or events and because it is often built into the firm's existing information collection and processing activities. It is oriented to the future and to long-term decisions. The primary advantage of continuous scanning is that it increases the chances of identifying emerging threats and opportunities, not just those that already exist.

Monitor Change

Once a potentially relevant change has been identified, an organization must decide whether to keep tabs on it—first by learning more about its nature and direction and then by learning more about its current rate of change and magnitude.

An abundance of valuable monitoring information is readily available from government and trade sources. These include the Department of Commerce, the Bureau of Labor Statistics, and the Data Resources, Inc. economic forecasting service. Considerable amounts are also spent by major companies for services that monitor social trends and issues. Daniel Yankelovich, Inc. was among the first to respond to the opportunity, and a number of companies purchase its Social Trends Monitor, an extensive data collection program that periodically measures 35 social/value trends—such as materialism, sexual freedom, hypocrisy, religion, hedonism, and personalization. Other outside subscription services include Arthur D. Little's Impact Service, Future's Group Scout Service, the Stanford Research Institute's Business Intelligence Program, Predicasts, and the National Planning Association's Economic Projections series.

Some corporations are working in-house to analyze and predict social changes. General Motors' Societal Analysis Department combines talents

EXHIBIT 3-11 Scanning Model Framework

	Scanning models		
	Irregular	**Regular**	**Continuous**
Media for scanning	Ad hoc studies	Periodically updated studies	Structured data collection and processing system
Scope of scanning	Specific events	Selected events	Broad range of environmental systems
Motivation for activity	Crisis initiated	Decision and issue oriented	Planning process oriented
Time frame for decision impact	Current and near term	Near term	Long term

Source: Adapted from Liam Fahey and William R. King, "Environmental Scanning for Corporate Planning," *Business Horizons* 9 (August 1977), p. 63. Copyright, ©1977, by the Foundation for the School of Business at Indiana University. Reprinted by permission.

from several disciplines to work on projects dealing with change in public attitude, the modeling and simulation of social systems, and the quantification of social costs. Legislative and regulatory information services have also been developed, as have newsletters on technology transfer and new product patents.

Most environmental information, however, is inexpensively gathered from readily available data sources, such as business and nonbusiness magazines (*The Futurist, Futures, Harper's,* the *Journal of Social and Technological Forecasting*), the Conference Board, and trade association publications, and from systematic but informal discussions with industry executives and peers.

Forecast Impact, Timing, Consequences

Because the future is by definition unknown, any forecast relies on intuitively or explicitly seeking past and present relationships that help in anticipating it. This includes projecting historical trends, forecasting the future from related current events, or basing forecasts on variables that are thought to cause future events. Effective monitoring provides a good basis for forecasting. Indeed, it may be difficult to separate the monitoring and forecasting tasks when gathering industry information.

The relative sophistication of forecasting varies by environmental sector. Environmental forecasting for much of the social, governmental, and technological environment is intuitive and judgmental, and compared to forecasting of the economic environment, it is relatively unsophisticated. The level of sophistication depends on the degree to which the processes of change are understood. The methods used include extrapolation, models (including descriptive, predictive, and normative models), and subjective/judgmental techniques. Descriptive (as opposed to predictive) modeling tends to dominate in all environmental sectors but the economic, with forecasting attempts for the other sectors dominated by extrapolation and subjective methods.

An overriding objective of environment forecasting is estimating the timing of environmental forces and the likelihood of their impact.[20] There are several methods for doing this.

Individual Judgment.   When understanding of the actual causes of change is not sufficient to allow for causal modeling, individual judgment is typically used to provide the "best guess." However, the validity and reliability of individual judgments cannot be evaluated, and their replication is impossible. Consequently, several methods have been developed that utilize judgment in a more structured fashion.

The Delphi Method.   Developed several years ago at the Rand Corporation, the Delphi method involves questioning each member of a panel of experts concerning some future event or trend. Each expert is independently questioned without group discussion, and then anonymous responses from all of the panel members are combined, summarized, and returned to the participants. This process continues until an acceptable degree of consensus is achieved or until the responses stabilize.

Trend Extrapolation.   The main objection to Delphi forecasts is their intuitive nature. This has undoubtedly contributed to the continued use of extrapolation, a so-called black box approach because it makes no attempt to identify the causes of change but instead projects historical trends forward on the assumption that the factors causing change in the future will be similar to those that caused it in the past. There is some evidence that trend extrapolation has been successful. It may be the best available approach when the true nature of change is not well understood.

Cross-Impact Matrices.   Forecasts derived by means of various methods may be combined into a well-integrated and internally consistent description of the future. To ensure internal consistency in these forecasts, cross-impact matrices are used to search for important interactions among them.

To carefully search for important interactions, forecasted events within different environmental sectors are arrayed on both axes of a matrix. This ensures that no potential interactions are overlooked. The events are arrayed in chronological order, and each cell (except the overlapping diagonal) is inspected to determine whether the occurrence or nonoccurrence of a forecast event would, in turn:

1. Alter the likelihood of another event.
2. Advance or delay another event.
3. Have a strong or weak influence on another event.

Cross-impact matrices are simple in concept, but they can be extremely complex, especially if a large number of discrete events are entered.[21]

Scenarios. A scenario is a composite verbal picture of the future that often includes an account of the events or conditions that contributed to the situation described. Multiple scenarios are usually developed, and then alternative corporate strategic directions are evaluated in terms of each scenario. How many scenarios to develop, who should develop them, which themes to emphasize, and what time span to cover must be decided in advance.

Modeling. When underlying causes and correlates can be specified in equation form, as in econometric models, hundreds of simultaneous regression equations are used to forecast economic changes. As conditions and assumptions change, forecasts based on such models must be carefully tempered by judgment. Each of the above methods may be studied in other coursework by interested students.

Develop Strategic Responses

Once important environment changes have been identified and monitored and their future state has been forecast, marketing management should have the necessary information to cope with external change. But a major step remains. That step is judicious and creative interpretation and response in light of the organization's resources and limitations. Marketing management must decide not only what to do but when to do it. Strategic marketing decisions rest on two related premises.[22]

■ The objective is to effectively match changing markets with a company's strengths—its special marketing, financial, engineering, and managerial resources.

■ The firm's strengths and resources are difficult to change in the short term, even if this would be advantageous.

We can therefore conclude that there are usually only defined periods during which a good fit or a "strategic window" exists for a given company. The requirements of a market optimally match a firm's particular competencies only for a time. During that time, the strategic window is open. So timing is critical.

Several guidelines may be used to help organizations cope with change.

Focus on Probabilities, Consequences, and Timing. Those who are familiar with decision tree analysis and the use of expected values are acquainted with procedures for balancing probabilities against consequences in evaluating alternative strategies. Potentially disastrous consequences (or fantastic opportunities) must receive attention even though the probability of their occurrence may be low. Similarly, highly probable events should be considered even if their related consequences are limited (although significant). Also, erratic and rapidly changing forces with significant potential consequences should receive continuing attention, whereas slower and/or more consistent changes may be treated as lower in priority.

Stay Flexible.   Forecasts are probabilistic, so maintaining flexibility has to be a paramount consideration. If a particular advertising strategy, for example, is appropriate within two future scenarios rather than one, the added flexibility should be positively weighed in selecting the strategy. However, the potential return might be lower for the flexible strategy. Thus, potential return must be traded off against the risk of reduced flexibility.

Develop Counterforces.   Responses to environmental forces are of two types—*modify the forces*, or *make adaptive strategy changes*. These types may be combined. Attempts to modify forces are often unsuccessful or clearly impossible. Nevertheless, in recent years there has been a growing acceptance of a proactive, entrepreneurial management style that often attempts to change the environment rather than just passively adapting to it.[23]

Strategies: Join Them or Reposition.   A more common response is for the organization to alter its marketing strategies to reduce the potential impact of the environmental force. It can reposition itself off the force's projected path, or it can move in the same direction as the force to reduce the force's impact.

Application

Environmental Scanning for Levi Strauss & Co.

How does Levi Strauss & Co. cope with environmental change? In an internal report titled "Environmental Outlook," several environmental factors were identified, as summarized in Exhibit 3-A.[24] Prepared by a small corporate planning group that relied heavily on outside information and forecasts, the report identified economic, social, and governmental factors at the industry, national, and international levels. The social factors included fashion trends, the changing age and geographic distribution of the U.S. population, and the changing role of women in the family and the work force. The governmental factors were regulations concerning flame-retardant fabric qualities in the United States, use of the metric system, tariffs that could affect competition, and California legal actions to end suggested retail prices. The economic factors varied from world, national, and industry growth and inflation, to foreign and domestic competition, to U.S. consumer spending in apparel and department stores. Implicit in each factor identified was a relevance dimension—for example, "the number of teenagers will decline in future years and, *ceteris paribus*, negatively affect jean sales"; or "fashion trends indicate a declining U.S. demand for basic jeans with potential negative effects on future jean sales"; or "department store sales will decline, with negative implications for our department

EXHIBIT 3-A Identification of Selected Environmental Factors of Importance to Levi Strauss & Co.

	Factor		
Level	**Social**	**Governmental**	**Economic**
Global	Fashion trends in European markets	Tariffs and imports	World GNP and inflation Share of domestic market given foreign competition

National	Population shifts
	  Age
	  Geographic
	Female participation in work force
	Family size and income
	Leisure-time recreation
		FTC consent decree ending retail price maintenance
		Metrication
			U.S. economy
			  Growth
			  Inflation
			  Taxes
			  Wages

Industry	Natural fabric preferences by consumers Fashion jeans	Flame-retardant standards	Clothing spending Apparel store and department store growth

store channel of distribution." Each change was a potential environmental force, quite possibly requiring strategic marketing adjustments.

Monitoring and Forecasting at LS & Co.

Levi Strauss & Co. was affected by many trends, including technological trends. Only the changes most relevant to marketing and to LS & Co. markets were monitored, such as developments in fibers, chemicals, and production processes that could affect the appearance, comfort, durability, and required care of LS & Co.'s apparel. Improvements in synthetic fiber technology and improved fabric stretch capability were important changes that could lead to competitive threats.

Social and population changes were also monitored. Because the blue jeans business is targeted toward young groups, Levi Strauss & Co. analysts concluded:

It is anticipated that the birthrate will increase slightly over the next several years, increasing the population in the 0 to 2 range. This will be a modest increase, and not anywhere near the postwar baby boom which radically influenced marketing strategies at the time. During the same period, the age groups 3 to 13 and 14 to 17 (LS & Co.'s historical

target market) will show declines. The 18 to 24 group (a primary target market) will only slightly increase, and the 24 to 35 group [and over] will show the greatest growth.

One important implication of these trends at the time was the decline in the teenager market after several years of growth.

Levi Strauss & Co. also monitored regional population trends and purchasing power within the United States. The analysts concluded:

A shift in population to southern and western states . . . began several years ago and accelerated in more recent times. . . . The northeastern regions, particularly the Middle Atlantic region, showed the slowest growth rate of income. . . . The southern and western regions, particularly the South Atlantic and the Mountain region in the West, showed the largest increase in the growth rate of income. . . . This regional shift in aggregate income is expected to continue over the next several years.

Levi Strauss & Co. was following regional population movements in part because of their implications for the firm's geographic distribution strategies.

The company also monitored relevant governmental developments at the state and federal levels. One concern, for example, was the possibility of new flammability standards involving the Consumer Product Safety Commission (CPSC) and the National Bureau of Standards (NBS).

Economic monitoring, familiar terrain for business students, comprised over one third of LS & Co.'s environmental outlook report, with a focus on growth trends, inflation rates, unemployment, and the value of the dollar. Analyses were presented that showed the relationship between clothing spending and family income levels, the consumer price index (inflation) for clothing and specific types of apparel as compared to the consumer price index for other types of goods, and apparel store and department store growth trends.

Import competition was seen as a growing force (task environment), with imports taking an increasing share of Levi Strauss's domestic market. Oversupply caused by imports had already cut into the growth of the market for LS & Co.'s blue jeans.

Strategies and Implementation at Levi Strauss & Co.

The shifting U.S. age distribution could not be changed by Levi Strauss & Co. Yet, as noted earlier, it is sometimes possible to develop a counterforce to modify the nature, rate, or direction of some changes. By drastically increasing advertising expenditures and emphasizing the quality of its brand, Levi Strauss & Co. could hope to slow the competitive inroads of importers. Exhibit 3–B shows such counterforces with regard to import competition.

As for developing strategies (join them or reposition), Levi Strauss & Co. did both. Skirting U.S. population changes led to reduction of the company's dependence on the male teenage group in the United States by diversifying into other product lines (e.g., forming a Women's Wear Division) and by increasing Levi Strauss &

Co.'s jeans market share internationally. Levi Strauss & Co. also moved in the same direction as the forces of import competition by importing goods itself and selling the imported merchandise under its brand.

Entrepreneurial Implementation

Environmental change requires change in the management and structure of business itself. As the U.S. moves into the postindustrial era, its organizations *and its people* must adapt. During the mid-1980s, the top management of Levi Strauss & Co. decided that more was required than environmental scanning per se. It added more line management involvement in the process and more strategic focus. Special attention was given to the company's fit within its environment, and related attention was given to identifying LS & Co. "leverages and vulnerabilities." In a presentation by the president of the company, an overview of changes in the process was provided:

"We knew that things were not going right in our long-range planning process. The plans were cumbersome, with lengthy documents emphasizing numbers projections and operational activities with very little sense of any strategizing. Former plans were evaluated by their weight, not their content. Management felt they knew the projections that senior management wanted to see—and so they submitted them.

We hit upon several important "firsts" in this past year in our approach to planning processes. The net results were significant and included:

1. Management involvement at all levels which paid out in enhanced communications.
2. A logical, strategic focus, simplistic actually, and readily assimilated, but one which netted a very strong sense of commitment.

What did we do?

EXHIBIT 3–B Strategic Responses to Environmental Change: Levi Strauss & Co.

	U.S. Demographics	Import Competition
Modify force	Not possible Totally uncontrollable	Counterforce: Increase advertising expenditures
Modify strategies	Reposition: Reduce relevance of force Move to serve other demographic groups Reduce dependence on domestic demographics—build international distribution	Join them: Move in same direction Import apparel for resale under Levi Strauss & Co. brand

1. We started with a mega-meeting which we called LS USA's Strategic Direction for the 80s.
    a. We assembled some 150 key managers from the company and the divisions. We did not limit the audience to marketing.
    b. We had the top corporate executives . . . state their thoughts relative to:
        (1) The corporate mission.
        (2) The corporate culture.
        (3) The overall corporate financial/growth objectives and then those same objectives specified for the LS USA company.
        (4) Business direction and trends.
        (5) Key issues regarding quality, channels of distribution, private label, etc.
    c. I talked about my perception of:
        (1) The current business environment.
        (2) The factors critical to the success of the company.
        (3) Most importantly, perceptions of each major business in our portfolio, what strengths we should be capitalizing upon, what weaknesses we should be addressing, what we thought each business's strategic direction ought to be.
    d. We had various staff executives also in the "act":
        (1) Our chief market researcher presented the more specific retail environment trends for the 80s.

        (2) Our marketing VP covered brand management guidelines.
        (3) Our planning director capsulized what was to be perceived as a "new" process.

    This mega-meeting was then followed up in the ensuing two weeks by each division holding its own mini-mega-meeting, spreading the word to even lower levels of management in the divisions.

2. We trained the divisional planners, who, in turn, trained their divisional personnel in a new approach. We call it shirt-sleeves planning. . . . it has about it a sense of organization in its various steps of building a plan which is logical, palatable, and readily assimilated.[25]

It essentially provides for the following:
    a. An examination of the current business environment. . . . it asks each business to consider its positioning in that environment and arrive at a most likely scenario for the business.
    b. It provides a framework to review current resources, compare resources to needs, provide control, and allow for an identification of key issues. It also takes into consideration probable alternatives to the most likely scenario.
    c. It promotes a methodology which encourages building a plan based on logic—logic founded in business experi-

d. It downplays numbers; financial estimations, which are only submitted at the very end of the process, grow out of strategic direction and are based on a historical perspective.

e. It results in clear, succinct mission statements; concise, measurable (for the most part) objectives; and strategies and action plans which grow out of cap-italizing upon one's leverages and addressing one's vulnerabilities."

Levi Strauss & Co. found that identifying, monitoring, and forecasting alone do not work. Successful scanning and planning require top-level leadership, line management involvement, and an intense commitment to translating environmental changes into action-oriented goals. Without these elements, nicely packaged plans collect dust on corporate bookshelves ∎

Summary

The marketing environment encompasses more types of relevant change than it did only a few decades ago, and the rate of change has accelerated. This makes managerial tasks more complex and highlights management's dependence on uncontrollable, external factors. Pressing day-to-day problems plague the manager and impede meaningful environmental analysis. But the day of reckoning will arrive. Effective managers recognize the value of preparing for the future.

As more types of environmental change have moved more rapidly in and around organizations, it has become critical to put up antennas and develop a sensitivity to environmental information. Whether domestic or international; whether social, technological, governmental, economic, or natural; whether affecting markets, competitors, or marketing intermediaries—marketing strategies flower or die depending on their match with the changing scene.

The marketing environment is comprised of largely uncontrollable forces (changing or constraining) that are external, yet potentially relevant to the organization's marketing management function. These forces include the intraorganizational environment of the firm, the task or mediating environment, the macroenvironment, and the global environment.

Change in the social environment involves an alteration in the form or functioning of a significant group, institution, or social order. Alterations of interest to marketers include changes in population characteristics, consumer values and lifestyles, and social issues.

Technology is the application of knowledge, encompassing science, innovation, invention, and discovery. Technology leads to new and modified products, and it also directly affects marketing management through the development of new methods and techniques. Most technological innovations are visible long before their use becomes widespread, so monitoring developing technologies can be useful.

The economic environment is critically important to marketers, whether the factor is economic growth, recession, inflation, shortages, or the value of the dollar. The challenge for marketers is to interpret such changes in the context of specific product markets.

Government, in striving to maintain healthy, workable competition and prevent deceptive, fraudulent, or unsafe marketing practices, has become a major sector of the macroenvironment. Monitoring changes in governmental legislation and regulation, whether antitrust or consumer, is important to ensure compliance with legal standards.

The natural environment—natural resources,

climate, physical barriers, and terrain—affects marketing as well.

Identifying potentially relevant forces, monitoring them to determine their nature and direction, forecasting their rate of change and the likelihood of their impact, and interpreting and strategically responding to them—this is the essence of environmental scanning. Identifying change involves an EX → IN approach or an IN → EX approach—beginning with either external or internal relevance parameters. Scanning may be conducted on an irregular, regular (annual), or continuous basis. Monitoring involves learning about the nature and direction of relevant environmental changes and then studying their current rate of change and magnitude. Numerous sources of information are available. Forecasting is a difficult task, and the appropriate techniques and their sophistication vary by environmental sector. Forecasting techniques include the Delphi method, trend extrapolation, cross-impact matrices, scenarios, and modeling. Developing strategic responses to environmental change requires attention to the probabilities of its occurrence, the likely consequences, and timing. Maintaining decision option flexibility is a desirable objective, but the actual responses to environmental change are of two types—modify the force, or make adaptive strategic changes. The former is usually difficult, at least in the short run.

As shown by the management of Levi Strauss, the way in which environmental scanning and planning are implemented is critically important to their ultimate usefulness and success.

Exercises for Review and Discussion

1. Videophones (visual display and voice) employ a technology that has been commercially available for the past several years. Assume that this mode of communication gains widespread acceptance by both commercial and residential telephone users, and then identify and discuss several potential effects that this product could have on marketing promotion, pricing, and distribution practices.

2. Chrysler Corporation represents a classic case of an old, entrenched company that faced a drastically changing environment and, under crisis conditions, adapted successfully. At the end of the 1970s, the picture for Chrysler was one of solid gloom. At a time of high gasoline prices, double-digit inflation, and pending recession, the company had huge inventories of large automobiles. Based on your knowledge of environmental analysis from this chapter, develop an argument for either (*a*) supporting the inability of Chrysler's management to forecast relevant environmental changes, or (*b*) showing how the firm's problems could have been avoided or at least reduced in impact.

3. The birth control pill has clearly had a pervasive impact on contemporary society. A technological innovation, the pill has stimulated a variety of environmental changes, thus illustrating the close relationship between social and technological change. Identify and discuss the nature and scope of related impacts on the various levels of the environment, and identify several tentative implications for marketers.

4. It is possible to overconcentrate on a firm's products and thus to lose sight of the market needs that they fulfill. But it is also possible to understand shifting market needs without comprehending the different technologies required to meet them—that is, to suffer from "technological myopia." Discuss with examples.

5. You have been assigned responsibility for planning and implementing a technology scanning program for a manufacturer of laser discs (compact discs) and other high-technology au-

dio equipment. Outline an approach to this task, including in your discussion: (*a*) relevant factors to be assessed, (*b*) specific types of information needs, (*c*) potential sources of information, and (*d*) major problem areas that you anticipate in carrying out your assignment.

6. Look to each stage of the environmental scanning process, and identify basic differences that would arise in implementing these stages

across different industries, such as (*a*) a producer of men's toiletry items, (*b*) the automobile industry, (*c*) a real estate development company, and (*d*) an electric utility.

7. Select either inflation or shortages, and identify several effects that this condition could have on marketing activity generally. Consider markets, competition, and product, pricing, promotion, and distribution decisions.

Notes

1. This example is partly adapted from Charles B. Camp, "Plunge in Big-Car Sales Leaves Some Dealers with Serious Problems," *The Wall Street Journal*, January 30, 1974, p. 1.

2. Amanda Bennett, "Small Cars and Diesels Get Rush from Buyers amid Gas Price Fears," *The Wall Street Journal*, March 12, 1979, pp. 1, 30.

3. Amal Nag, "U.S. Car Industry Has Full-Sized Problems in Subcompact Market," *The Wall Street Journal*, January 7, 1983, pp. 1, 4.

4. John Naisbitt, "Restructuring of America—When, Where, How, and Why," *U.S. News and World Report*, December 27, 1982, pp. 49-50.

5. Elizabeth M. Fowler, "A Need for Strategic Planners," *New York Times*, October 12, 1983, p. 45.

6. Thomas L. Wheelen and J. David Hunger, *Strategic Management and Business Policy*, (Reading, Mass.: Addison-Wesley Publishing 1983), p. 95.

7. Monica Langley, "AT&T Manager Finds His Effort to Galvanize Sales Meets Resistance," *The Wall Street Journal*, December 16, 1983, pp. 1, 9.

8. Philip Kotler, "The Elements of Social Action," in *Processes and Phenomena of Social Change*, ed. Gerald Zaltman et al. (New York: John Wiley & Sons, 1973), p. 171.

9. James C. Hyatt, "Demographers Finally Come into Their Own in Firms, Government," *The Wall Street Journal*, July 19, 1978, p. 30.

10. William D. Wells, "Marketers Should Scrutinize Needs and Preferences of the Class of '74," *Marketing News*, March 4, 1983, p. 3.

11. Robin Peterson, "Overreaction to Consumer Trends Can Prove a Dangerous Practice," *Marketing News*, January 17, 1986, p. 2.

12. Florence R. Skelly, "Using Social Trend Data to Shape Marketing Policy: Some Do's and a Don't," *Journal of Consumer Marketing* 1 (Summer 1983), pp. 15, 17.

13. Robert Reed, "Why *Playboy* Magazine Is Stumbling," *Crain's Chicago Business*, August 8, 1983, p. 15.

14. Jerry E. Bishop, "Spaulding's New Golf Ball Aims for Improved Slice of Market," *The Wall Street Journal*, January 31, 1986, p. 17.

15. Theodore Levitt, "Marketing Myopia," *Harvard Business Review*, July-August 1960, pp. 45-56.

16. L. Clark, Jr., and A. Malabre, Jr., "Consumers Continue Fast Spending Pace despite Steep Debts," *The Wall Street Journal*, January 31, 1986, p. 1.

17. Partially based on David M. Elsner, "Back to Basics: Recession Spurs Sears to Cut Prices, Return to Past Sales Strategy," *The Wall Street Journal*, February 10, 1975, pp. 1, 14. Lewis Lazare, "Sears Heads Upscale on New Apparel Lines," *Crain's Chicago Business*, January 3, 1983, p. 4.

18. Ronald Alsop, "Companies Look to Weather to Find Best Climate for Ads," *The Wall Street Journal*, January 10, 1985, p. 27.

19. Harold E. Klein and William H. Neuman, "How to Use SPIRE: A Systematic Procedure for Identifying Relevant Environments for Strategic Planning," *Journal of Business Strategy* 1 (Summer 1980), pp. 327-45.

20. Reprinted by permission from *Business* magazine. "Environmental Forecasting: Key to Strategic Management," by John A. Pearce II and Richard B. Robinson, Jr., July–September 1983. Copyright © 1983 by the College of Business Administration, Georgia State University, Atlanta.

21. Joseph P. Martino, *Technological Forecasting for Decision Making* (New York: American Elsevier, 1972), pp. 271-81.

22. The remainder of this paragraph is based on Derek F. Abell, "Strategic Windows," *Journal of Marketing*, July 1978, pp. 21, 24. Used with permission of the American Marketing Association.

23. Carl P. Zeithaml and Valarie A. Zeithaml, "Environmental Management: Revising the Marketing Perspective," *Journal of Marketing*, Spring 1984, pp. 46-50.

24. The authors wish to express their gratitude to Levi Strauss & Co. officials for their assistance and cooperation in providing information for this section.

25. Robert E. Linneman and John D. Kennell, "Shirt-Sleeve Approach to Long-Range Plans," *Harvard Business Review*, March-April 1977, pp. 141-50.

CHAPTER 4

Defining and Analyzing Product-Markets

*F*or Worlds of Wonder (WOW) and other companies in the toy manufacturing industry, the latter part of the 1980s holds considerable promise. The U.S. birthrate has started to increase, and forecasts predict that this trend will continue. There has been a hefty increase in the number of children under nine years of age, which is expected to reach 40 million by 1990. More than 40 percent of new births are expected to be the first child in the family. The toy companies regard this as a promising development because parents tend to spend more on the first child. Add to this the trend toward families with two adults working and more money to spend, and the present and prospective market for toys looks very attractive.[1]

When people think of the toy industry, the larger companies—Mattel, Hasbro, Tonka Toys, and Coleco—generally come to mind. But most of the industry is made up of much smaller companies, such as WOW and The Little Tikes Company, many of which are growing very fast. There has been relatively little competition from foreign toy companies. Thus far, these companies have been content to remain suppliers to U.S. manufacturers.

Not surprisingly, new technologies have helped speed the growth in toy sales. In the early 1980s, electronics seemed to be taking over the industry. Video and electronic games brought several firms to new highs in sales. More recently, a wider variety of toys have been selling very well. Talking bears— teddy bears that tell stories—helped WOW get started. Coleco's Cabbage Patch Kids, Hasbro's G. I. Joe (reintroduced to fight terrorists), and Tonka Toys' GoBots are other toys that have not had to rely on sophisticated electronics to win sales. Further, all of these new toys are being sold as part of whole lines of toy items centered on the same idea, a marketing strategy that is catching hold in the entire industry.

As the toy business illustrates, market opportunity depends on many factors that affect market demand. Managers who understand these factors are in the best position to take advantage of such opportunity. Clearly, having the right kinds of information is crucial to planning the marketing strategy needed to compete in target markets. According to one executive, the game has become, "Get the right information to the right guy at the right time to make the right decision to beat the other guy out in the marketplace."[2]

In today's corporation, marketing managers are expected to know what the "right information" is. They are responsible for bringing an understanding of market forces not only to marketing strategy decisions but also to business strategy decisions. As a result, marketing is playing a more important role in decisions regarding new product development, acquisitions, new ventures, and distribution—decisions that span the organization.[3] The ability of marketing managers to use market opportunity analyses for planning effective marketing strategies is at the heart of the expanding contribution of marketing to business decision making.

This chapter examines the coverage and application of market opportunity analysis (MOA). The next section takes up the basic notions of markets and market opportunity. Building on these ideas, a framework for understanding the coverage of an MOA is then introduced. Guided by this framework, the final sections of the chapter discuss each of the major components of an MOA.

Understanding Market Opportunity

Market opportunity refers to a situation in which a combination of factors creates the potential for sales of the company's product or service.

Market opportunity is created by many factors in the macroenvironment and task environment of a company. Yet opportunity remains only potential until the company plans and implements marketing strategy to generate sales. The extent to which a particular company can turn potential into real sales depends on its strengths and weaknesses. This explains why several companies going after essentially the same market can have different success in generating sales and market share. Gerber Products Company has achieved impressive performance with products aimed at families with babies. It has capitalized on its marketing expertise to capture and maintain over a 70 percent share of the U.S. market. H. J. Heinz and Beech-Nut, on the other hand, have not done as well in this market, though they have been more formidable competitors overseas.[4]

Marketing planning should start with an assessment of the company's capabilities; we assume that this has already been done. Here, we are concerned with the factors outside the company that affect market opportunity and that management must understand. It is here that an MOA makes a powerful contribution to planning marketing strategy. While many factors can determine a particular market's opportunity, four major categories usually prove to be pivotal for strategy decisions:

- Structure of a market
- Customers' market requirements
- Competition for sales
- Market size

EXHIBIT 4-1 Determinants of Market Opportunity

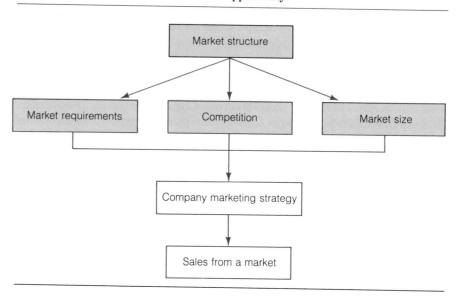

These external determinants of market opportunity combine with company marketing strategy to yield sales, as shown in Exhibit 4-1.

Market Structure

Since not everyone in an entire population would be in a market for a company's product, managers must identify those who are most likely to buy and must distinguish them from those who will not be buyers. Managers of housing construction companies know that housing buyers are typically adults over 18 years of age, usually with at least moderate income. Even among a group of prospective buyers, not everyone will have the same preferences for products that satisfy a particular need or want. Thus, the market is further subdivided into different buyer groups, often called segments. The housing market contains distinct segments. The housing preferences of people who are married and have young children at home are different from those of young, single people. The housing preferences of older adults whose children have left the home are different from the preferences of either of these two groups. In this fashion, a **market structure** is described that delineates the particular set of these market groups or segments.

Companies that sell similar products may see market structure differently. This can happen when companies see only part of a market structure or when they find new ways to describe market structure. How management sees market structure influences its choice of marketing strategies. Com-

Market structure is the particular arrangement of market groups or segments from which a company's management selects target markets.

panies installing artificial turf for sports use traditionally saw their markets as comprised of owners of large playing fields—municipal school systems, colleges, universities, municipal stadiums. OmniTurf is one such company that saw the market structure differently. Recognizing that only a few sports—football, soccer, baseball—are played on large fields with reasonably uniform dimensions but that such other sports as golf and tennis require sport surfaces, its management expanded market structure to include owners of golf greens, golf courses, and tennis courts. Consequently, OmniTurf developed marketing strategies to tap potential sales in golf and tennis market segments.

Market Requirements.   All buyers, whether consumer or industrial, have certain expectations that they want to be met by purchasing and using products.[5] These expectations may involve particular product benefits, convenience in obtaining or servicing products, value for dollars spent, or information and know-how concerning product uses. Such expectations are evident in the baby food market. Mothers develop expectations for nutritional benefits from baby food. They may also develop such expectations as ease of feeding, freshness, opportunities for the selection of different foods, reasonable price, information about preparation, and awareness of dietary restrictions. Expectations of this kind are **market requirements** that sellers must satisfy to capture sales from markets.

Market requirements refer to the expectations that customers want fulfilled by the purchase and use of products.

The success of a marketing strategy depends on the extent to which buyers believe that a company's marketing offer meets their requirements. Thus, management must carefully tailor each component of its marketing mix to satisfy specific requirements. Gerber has worked hard to build a reputation for quality baby foods. The company's nutritious foods, broad product line, value prices, convenience through wide distribution, informative promotion, and after-the-sale services account in large part for its impressive sales performance. These marketing mix components meet customers' requirements, and customers respond by buying more Gerber products than products of competing brands.

Competition.   Surprisingly, competition can have simultaneous advantageous and detrimental effects on a company's market opportunity. On the one hand, competition can cause an entire market to grow through **market development.** This occurs when marketing by companies in an industry causes more people to be aware of a product and to understand what the product can do for them. As a result, more people buy or buy more of the product, increasing total sales for the entire industry. Recently, market development has been at work in the U.S. baby foods industry. By educating mothers to the benefits of combining breast feeding with formula feeding, the industry has enjoyed expanded sales. Here, the increase of sales for a type of product through market development—in this case, formula food products—has led to greater sales for all of the companies serving the baby food market.

Market development is the expansion of sales caused by companies in an industry using marketing programs to make buyers aware of a product and to understand the benefits of using it.

Competitive position refers to the extent to which a company's use of marketing strategy has enabled it to stand out from competitors in the minds of customers with regard to how well it will satisfy their market requirements.

At the same time, competition limits market opportunity for individual companies. Sales flow to the firms in an industry according to how well each jockeys for **competitive position** in the market. When one firm is quite successful at building a greater percentage or share of the market, other firms necessarily get a smaller share. This jockeying for position is ongoing, as evidenced by the battle for market share in the baby food industry. Gerber's ability to maintain its 70 percent market share throughout the 1980s will depend on how successfully it appeals to markets as compared to Heinz, Beech-Nut, and other baby food manufacturers.[6]

Market Size. The most direct measure of market opportunity is the amount of sales coming from a market. *Market size* refers to this sales volume. Market size is more than just how many people are in a market. It is based both on the number of customers and on the quantity or frequency at which each customer buys during a time period:

$$MS = N \times R$$

where:

MS = Total sales from a market

N = Number of customers in the market

R = Rate or frequency of a product purchase

The dependence of market size on both N and R has important implications for MOAs. The market segment with the most customers is not necessarily the one that offers the most market opportunity. Fewer customers, each of whom buys a lot more of the product, can yield greater market size. American Express, Visa U.S.A., MasterCard International, and other credit card companies recognize this important characteristic of market size by placing priority on the premium card segment:

> The reasons behind the new marketing efforts go beyond mere body count. Most of the premium cards generate more revenue from annual customer fees, which tend to be $20 to $30 higher than on regular cards. More important, people with prestige cards—which offer bigger lines of credit and more services—use them 150 percent more than traditional credit-card customers.[7]

Markets, the Source of Opportunity

An MOA identifies markets and evaluates the factors that determine demand in those markets. But exactly what is a market? In practice, the term *market* is used rather loosely, as suggested by the following: super*market*, stock *market*, elderly *market*, youth *market*, the Canadian *market*, and *mar-ket*place. Unfortunately, each of these terms has a somewhat different meaning and none of them is adequate for understanding the nature of an MOA. Let us examine the market concept more closely.

People, whether in organizations or households, make buying decisions that lead to sales. Because marketing strategy is intended to influence buying decisions, the notion of a market should center on these people. However, only certain people in a population decide to buy any particular product. These people comprise a **market** because they have the key characteristics that create demand: ability to buy, willingness to buy, and an end-use purpose.

Market
is a group of people with demand—with both the ability and the willingness to buy a product or service for end-use purposes.

Ability to Buy.   No matter how much certain people would like to have a product, some of them may not be able to buy it. Lack of resources keeps them from being part of a market. Consider the purchase of microcomputers by primary schools. Even though computer companies have special programs to lower the price of microcomputers sold to schools, some school systems do not have the funds to buy them. These schools are not part of the educational market for microcomputers.

Other factors may also prevent some people from buying. Not having access to a product causes inability to buy. People living in rural areas are typically not included in a market for a city's bus service. Charters often legally restrict the area served by such a service, preventing routes from being established to and from rural locations. In addition, physical disabilities keep some people from buying. Severely handicapped citizens who cannot get on or off a bus are not part of the market for a regular bus service, regardless of how much they may want to use the service.

Willingness to Buy.   Even if people are able to buy a product, they may not want to do so. To be in a market, people must have a desire to buy. This fact was forcibly demonstrated in analyzing market opportunity for wine sales in a southeastern city. A survey showed that people who opposed the consumption of alcoholic beverages on religious grounds and people who had recovered from alcohol abuse had strong desires *not* to buy wine. Most of these people could afford to buy wine but chose not to.

Willingness to buy is a state of mind. Usually, MOAs must delve into values, opinions, attitudes, experiences, and lifestyles to find out who has the desire to buy. Further, many of these factors are susceptible to change, causing market demand to be dynamic over time. Thus, MOAs must be repeated to keep up with the changes that are taking place.

End-Users, Not Resellers.   Suppose that a manufacturer sells a consumer product directly to retailers. Which buyers make up that manufacturer's market—the consumers who buy from the retailers or the retailers? Many managers would argue that their market comprises the buyers to whom they sell directly. Yet this point of view is short sided. If resellers (the retailers in this case) are the market, then an MOA may never get around to assessing the ultimate source of sales—end users. End users are customers, in either households or organizations, who buy to satisfy the need or want for which the product was designed. Purchases by end users determine the market opportunity enjoyed by all firms—manufacturers and resellers. Therefore, all companies in a channel should be involved in planning and coordinating marketing strategies to generate sales from end users. Considering end users as markets is the best way to ensure this involvement.

Markets Are for Products

There is no market unless there is a product available for customers to buy. Of course, people have needs and wants regardless of whether products exist to satisfy them. But the presence of people with needs and wants is not a sufficient condition to form a market. For a market to exist, there must be needs or wants, buying power, and ways of satisfying the needs or wants. Since television first appeared in the United States, viewers have wanted to watch programming at their convenience, which often is not at the scheduled airtime. However, until videocassette recorders (VCRs) were invented, there was no market for an MOA to analyze. Who has ability and willingness to buy cannot be determined without knowing the specific benefits and costs offered by a product. The early VCRs possessed limited benefits and were very expensive ($2,000 or more), so the corresponding market was relatively small. However, as the prices of VCRs dropped to less than $400 and new capabilities were added, the market for VCRs grew dramatically. Clearly, the makeup and size of a market depend on the product and its marketing offer. To emphasize this relationship between product and market, we use the term **product-market.**

Product-market
is the combination of a product or products and the groups of people who have demand for that product or products.

The dependence of market on product has an important implication. How the product is defined will affect the nature and extent of the opportunity in markets eventually evaluated by an MOA. For instance, the market for housing is not quite the same as the market for condominiums. Condominiums are a more narrowly defined product than housing because condominiums represent only one form or type of housing. Similarly, Watergate condominiums are an even more narrowly defined product than condominiums because Watergate is a particular building complex in Washington, D.C. Correspondingly, the market for Watergate is not the same as the market for all condominiums, even in the same city. Thus, we can think of product as a generic class (housing), a product type (condominiums), or a brand (Watergate).

Generic class
is a category or grouping of all products that people view as competing to satisfy the same need or want.

Generic-Class Product Markets. A buyer's purchase decision begins when priority is placed on satisfying a particular need or want. Demand first appears at this point, since both willingness and ability to buy some product to satisfy that need or want are now present. Because more than one product may be able to satisfy the need or want, these products can be grouped together into a **generic class** of products. For every generic class, there is a corresponding generic-class product-market that includes people with the ability and willingness to satisfy a want by purchasing a product in the class.

Because people cannot satisfy all their needs and wants simultaneously and are therefore forced to prioritize them, whole generic classes can compete with each other for sales. This form of competition occurs when one purchase is postponed to make another. If a couple is deciding whether to buy a new car or to take an overseas vacation, automobiles are in competition with travel services even though these products are intended to satisfy different wants. Competition between generic classes is easily overlooked and difficult to analyze, yet over time it may account for changes in the sales of seemingly unrelated products.

Product-Type Product-Markets. Buyers in a generic-class product-market may not all satisfy a particular want in the same way. They must decide what particular benefits and cost will best satisfy the want. Suppose the couple decides on the overseas vacation. The next consideration might be whether to buy a packaged group tour or to arrange their own travel itinerary. Businesses recognize this characteristic of demand by offering different **product types** to market segments within generic-class product-markets. Exhibit 4–2 shows product types that are grouped into generic classes for selected customer wants.

Product type is a unique combination of product benefits and cost designed to satisfy a need or want in a particular way.

Alternative, competing product types offer buyers a choice. All can satisfy the want, but each offers both benefits and limitations not found in the others. The electric typewriter is a product type that has been an effective word processor for decades. This product type is relatively inexpensive, provides interchangeable type styles, and is easy to use. A microcomputer can also be used as a word processor, making it a competing product type. It is more expensive and more difficult to learn to use than an electric typewriter. But it provides extensive editing and storage functions that are well beyond the capabilities of a typewriter. Not surprisingly, the rapid growth in microcomputer sales has been achieved at the expense of electric typewriter sales.

When buyers choose among product types, market demand is created for each type. In this way, generic-class demand breaks down into different product-type product-markets. The relative advantages and disadvantages of each product type determine the sizes of corresponding markets. However, market demand may shift from one product-type product-market to another, since each product type is capable of satisfying the same want. Any of a number of factors may cause such shifts—e.g., higher interest rates can make renting an apartment more popular than buying a condominium. For this reason, product types within the same generic class are vying for sales and represent a second kind of competition for market demand.

Brand is a company's unique offering of a particular product type.

Brand Markets. After selecting one product type over others in a class, a buyer then decides which **brand** or company to buy from. Only brands of the desired product type are in the running at this point. Bayer, St. Joseph, and Ascriptin are similar brands of the same product type—aspirin. Through creative use of its marketing mix, each brand tries to win a share of sales

EXHIBIT 4–2 Product Types within Selected Generic Classes for Specific Customer Wants

Customer Want	Generic Class	Product Types
Move about in a city	Urban transportation	Bus service, private autos, taxi service, limousine service, car pooling
Measure temperature	Temperature measurement instruments	Mercury and glass thermometer, RTD instrument
Prevent headaches	Headache remedies	Aspirin, acetaminophen
Avoid home meal preparation	Restaurants	Fast-food restaurant, family restaurant, atmosphere/specialty restaurant
Produce manuscripts	Word processing equipment	Typewriters, printers, microcomputers, dedicated word processors

from the aspirin product-type product-market. The result is a third kind of competition, that between similar brands.

The generic class, product type, and brand classification of products has two important implications for the analysis of market opportunities. First, company brands are vying for sales in larger product-markets created by customer wants and by customer preferences for alternative ways of satisfying those wants. An MOA must help managers understand the dimensions of these generic-class and product-type product-markets. Second, there are different forms of competition with which each brand must contend. Wants compete, product types compete, and similar brands compete. A successful marketing strategy must consider all of the threats from these different forms of competition.

An Approach to Analyzing Market Opportunity

In some ways, conducting an MOA is similar to putting together a jigsaw puzzle. An analyst gathers pieces of information from many sources. Each piece describes some aspect of the customers, the competition, or the environmental forces influencing them. The challenge lies in putting all of the information together to form a picture of the nature and extent of market opportunity. This picture becomes the foundation for building a marketing strategy to tap that opportunity.

Before doing an MOA, we do not know what the picture of market opportunity will show. (In this respect, doing an MOA differs from putting together the typical jigsaw puzzle.) In fact, our reason for seeking and analyzing information is to discover what market opportunity is like. We need an approach for conducting an MOA that can be used to guide the analysis, particularly in situations where we start with little or no advance understanding of product-markets. Exhibit 4-3 provides such an approach.

EXHIBIT 4-3 The MOA Process

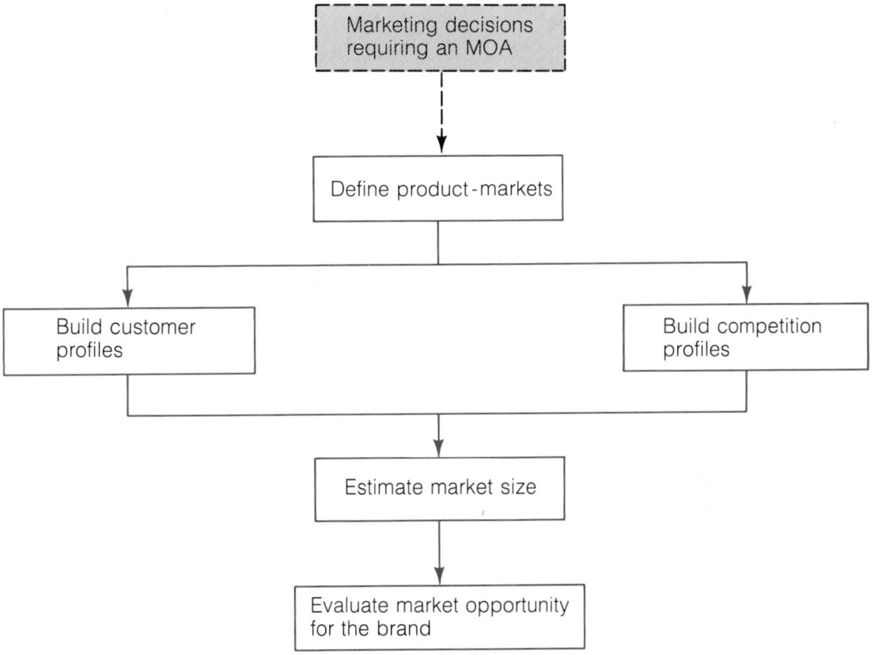

```
        ┌─────────────────────────┐
        ┊  Marketing decisions    ┊
        ┊  requiring an MOA       ┊
        └─────────────────────────┘
                    ┊
                    ▼
        ┌─────────────────────────┐
        │  Define product-markets │
        └─────────────────────────┘
         │                       │
         ▼                       ▼
┌──────────────────┐   ┌──────────────────────┐
│ Build customer   │   │  Build competition   │
│ profiles         │   │  profiles            │
└──────────────────┘   └──────────────────────┘
         │                       │
         └──────────┬────────────┘
                    ▼
        ┌─────────────────────────┐
        │  Estimate market size   │
        └─────────────────────────┘
                    │
                    ▼
        ┌─────────────────────────────┐
        │ Evaluate market opportunity │
        │ for the brand               │
        └─────────────────────────────┘
```

Overview of the MOA Process

The entire MOA assesses sales opportunity in markets for a product or service. The marketing decisions to be based on the MOA establish the product of interest. The first phase of the MOA defines the product-markets in which opportunity lies. Managers need information that helps them understand the structure of the market in terms of:

1. How the generic-class product-market is broken down into product-type markets.

2. Which product-type product-markets can be served by the company's brand.

Next, the MOA branches into two important analyses. One analysis describes the people (or organizations) in product-markets. Customer profiles are constructed to learn more about the characteristics of customers and how and why they are expected to buy and use the product. This information enables managers to discover market segments within product-markets and to understand market requirements so that marketing offers can be tailored to meet them. The other analysis is of the competition serving the defined product-markets. Profiles of the competition are constructed to learn about the strategies and tactics used to tap the opportunity. Managers need this information to assess how well their company's brand can match up with the competition.

The MOA can now be used to estimate the size of markets. Before a strategy for markets is planned, the size of generic-class and product-type markets can be estimated. Then, all of the information from the MOA is used to evaluate the best strategy for the brand in the product-market. Only after the marketing strategy has been determined in the form of a marketing plan can sales for the brand be forecast.

Sources of Information

Exhibit 4–4 shows typical sources of information for MOAs. Published sources are the place to start because they are easily accessible and relatively inexpensive. Interviews with experts, personal observation, and primary marketing research are used to fill in the gaps with information not found in published sources. The costs and time required for an analysis rise dramatically when primary marketing research is used, so other sources are usually exhausted before a decision is made on whether to conduct such research. Interestingly, the personal computer is causing some companies to pay more attention to accumulating MOA information from many sources:

> Now, though, managers can manipulate data themselves on personal computers, and they are hungry for more and better information. The most forward-thinking companies have come up with ways to give it to them. The information can come from sources as diverse as portable computers for salespersons in the field, external data bases that provide intelligence on competitors and markets, and inventory management systems. General Electric Co. found that by creating a toll-free hotline for customer complaints and questions, it could generate a wealth of information that helped it improve old products and develop new ones.[8]

Defining Product Markets

Because markets only exist for particular products, MOAs and marketing planning should be done on a product-by-product, market-by-market basis.[9] This means that an MOA can begin only after management decides on the product for which markets are to be analyzed. The product choice is typically determined by a product-related marketing decision situation.

Product-Related Decisions and MOAs.

Two kinds of product-related situations call for MOAs. First, there may be an idea for a new product. Management analyzes market opportunity to plan a marketing strategy and to evaluate whether profitability and other performance objectives can be met. In this case, a verbal description of a product concept is enough to initiate an MOA.

EXHIBIT 4–4 Sources of Information for MOAs

Published sources
  Periodicals and newspapers
  Trade association reports
  Standardized information service reports
  Government documents
  Company reports

Interviews with experts
  Managers of suppliers
  Managers of trade companies
  Managers of trade associations
  Consultants
  Salespersons

Personal observation
  Of customers
  Of competitors
  Of macroenvironmental influences

Primary marketing research
  Cross-sectional surveys
  Longitudinal panels
  Experiments

Second, a wide variety of marketing decisions concerning existing products may require MOAs. In fact, marketing managers at any level in a company may use an MOA to help plan for the particular unit of business they are responsible for. A salesperson assigned to a new territory needs an MOA to determine a sales plan. A product manager analyzes market opportunity before deciding whether to change target markets, advertising, or distribution for one of the company's brands. A chief marketing executive wants to chart new strategy for an existing line of products. All of these decisions concern marketing strategy for a company's products and provide the necessary direction for the MOA.

Classifying Product Structure. Product-market definition begins with analyzing relationships among products from a buyer's point of view. An important way to start is to find out which product types customers believe are substitutable for the same need or want. All of these product types form a generic product class.

Product structure
is an arrangement of product types in a generic class that describes the substitute product choices that customers consider when buying to satisfy a need or want.

The products that consumers believe are competitive form a **product structure.** There are degrees of substitutability among individual product types in a generic product class. Some product types may be perceived as being very close substitutes and are therefore directly competitive for essentially the same uses. Other product types may be used in different situations and are therefore less directly competitive. Financial services demonstrate this characteristic, and reveal the marketing strategy significance of product structure (see Exhibit 4-5).

A study was conducted by collecting data from buyers concerning the financial services that they regarded as competitive for selected uses. Twenty-four types of financial services were examined. Interestingly, the extent of competition among them differed even though all of them were ways of satisfying wants for financial services. Customers, for instance, saw credit services that offered a convenience benefit (overdraft protection and cash advances on credit card) as more competitive with credit card checking

EXHIBIT 4–5 Product Classification for Financial Services

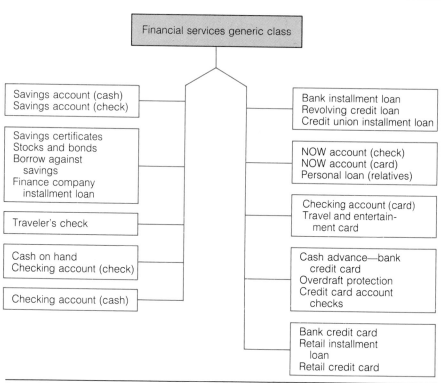

Source: Adapted with permission from Rajendra K. Srivastava, Robert P. Leone, and Allan D. Shocker, "Market Structure Analysis: Hierarchical Clustering of Products Based on Substitution-in-Use," *Journal of Marketing* 45 (Summer 1981), p. 45.

accounts than with other credit accounts (bank installment loans, revolving credit loans, and credit union installment loans).[10]

The situations in which products are used are very important in determining which products customers regard as competitive. The study of financial services revealed that three aspects of use situations were particularly crucial to customers' views of the competitiveness of different bank services:

- The dollar amount required for payment
- The location of payment (local versus out of town)
- The availability of retail credit for payment

Different combinations of the three characteristics define a use situation and largely determine which financial services people will consider using in that situation. As shown in Exhibit 4–5, bank credit cards, retail installment loans, and retail credit cards are generally more competitive with one another than with other product types in the class. However, further analysis revealed that bank credit cards are not as strongly competitive with the other two types of financial services when consumers are making payments for local retail purchases. Bank credit cards do better for out-of-town retail purchases.[11]

Methods for Defining Product Structure. Marketing research methods for uncovering product structure are developing.[12] Although many techniques have been tried, there are two general approaches:

- Analyze data describing purchase behavior.
- Analyze consumer opinion data.

Each of these approaches has its proponents.

Data describing the purchasing behavior of end users come from diaries, checkout scanners, and surveys. From diary data (customers' records of their purchases of brands within a class of products), researchers look for switching among brands over sequential purchases. The brands among which buyers switch most frequently are considered highly competitive with one another for the same need. The brands that are not part of the switching pattern are thought to be less competitive or as simply not part of the generic class. Since individual brands represent product types, inferences can be drawn about product-type competition. If soft-drink buyers switch regularly between cola brands (Coke, Pepsi) and noncola brands (7UP, Sprite), management may conclude that colas and noncolas are closely competing product types.

The other general approach requires collecting data describing end users' opinions about the substitutability of product types. Again, many techniques are available. In one of them, a sample of buyers is asked to list those product types that they regard as being suitable for a given need or want or as falling within a stated generic class. Ratings may also be obtained on the degree to which these product types are competitive for the same use. By looking across different use situations, the analyst can assess the degree of competitiveness in those situations by seeing how the ratings differ.

Product-market structure is an invaluable aid in planning marketing strategy. Among its more important applications are:

- Allowing management to see which product types customers see as competing for the same use. This information may help management to reorganize products in a mix according to the markets they serve.

- Helping management to see new product opportunities. By comparing existing brands in the company's product mix with other competing product types, management can assess the strengths and weaknesses of the company's brands. Product modifications or new products may result from such an assessment.

- Alerting management to the fact that some products in a mix may be taking sales away from other products. On the basis of this information, management can make appropriate changes in marketing strategy.

■ Helping management to evaluate the market impact of a new product by allowing it to see where customers place the product in a competitive structure.[13]

Defining Product-Market Boundaries.   In some industrial markets, customers can be listed individually by name. More typically, customers must be classified by various characteristics to give managers insight into who makes up product-markets. Product structure provides a framework within which the kinds of people comprised by product-markets can be described.

Beginning with product types in a generic class, an MOA must sort from the population those people who are most likely to buy and use the products (see Exhibit 4-6). Then, the analysis can look for specific segments.[14] Many characteristics of people have been used to define the makeup of markets. Among the more frequently used characteristics are demographic characteristics, lifestyles, importance of product benefits, rate of product use, and product preferences.

Frequently, demographic characteristics are among the first characteristics tried when defining product-markets. Age, sex, income, occupation, marital status, family size, employment status, educational attainment, residence location, and the like are applicable to consumer markets. For industrial markets, demographic-like characteristics include organization size, geographic location, products produced and sold, breadth of product line, and type of business. These characteristics are easily measured. More important, they allow the use of population analyses to evaluate the potential of markets. Of course, other characteristics—lifestyle, attitudes, preferred benefits, etc.—may also be tried to see which works best. (Further discussion of this idea is in Chapter 11.)

Market definition for credit cards, a product type within the financial services generic class, benefited significantly from demographic descriptions of consumer users (review Exhibit 4-5). Important demographic characteristics that help management understand what people make up the market for credit cards include:

■ *Age:* Credit card users are concentrated among 18–49-year-olds, with the largest percentage among 25–34-year-olds; the use of credit cards drops off significantly among persons of retirement age.

■ *Education:* The overwhelming majority of credit card users have graduated from high school.

■ *Marital status:* About three quarters of all credit card users are married.

■ *Income:* Credit card users are usually in upper-income groups, with over half of them having household income of $25,000 or more.

■ *Residence:* About three fourths of credit card users own their homes.[15]

These data can help management assess where the best potential for sales lies in a geographic area such as a country, region, or city. Using population

EXHIBIT 4-6 Sorting Product-Markets from a Population

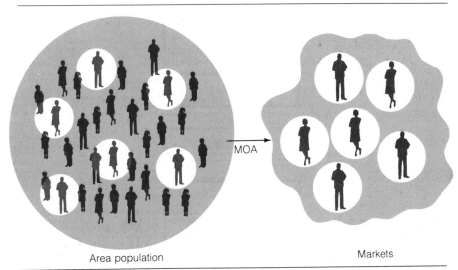

Area population   Markets

data, managers can look for heavy residential concentrations of people who have the above characteristics. Suppose advertising managers for American Express want to allocate their advertising media budget to different metropolitan areas in the United States. They can assess the market potential in these areas by examining the proportions of people in each area with these characteristics. The company's resources would then be allocated to the areas according to the size of their potential.

Profiling Generic-Class and Product-Type Markets

Whatever the characteristics used to define markets, these characteristics provide only a glimpse into the real people. The next task is to build customer profiles to help managers understand customers well enough to anticipate their market requirements. These profiles are intended to describe what these customers are like as people, how they decide what product/brand to buy, and what outside influences affect their buying decisions.

What Customers Are Like. In practice, managers seldom meet and get to know end users. Customer profiles substitute for personal contact by describing the makeup of buyers. Many characteristics are used for this purpose, including activities, interests, attitudes, experiences with the product, personal tastes, values, and personality. Which ones are best depends on the product and market being analyzed.

Learning more about the makeup of customers helps managers visualize how a product fits into lifestyles (or work styles) and how customers might react to brand strategies and tactics. Already knowing the important benefits

EXHIBIT 4–7 A Profile of Credit Card Customers

1. What are customers like as people?

Needs and wants: Source of revolving credit for purchases; source of short-term free credit for purchases; substitute for cash when purchasing; prestige in being among an elite group allowed to use cards; record of purchases; security of never being short of cash for a desired purchase.

Use situations: When shopping in town; when shopping out of town; when entertaining outside the home.

Activities and interests: credit card users are more likely than others to belong to organizations (e.g., book and bridge clubs, churches, social and community groups) and to spend more time in such leisure activities as attending plays, tennis, gardening, and entertaining guests.

Opinions: There is prestige in having certain kinds of credit cards; credit card users prefer shopping in stores with wide varieties of merchandise but like to shop in many different types of stores; they generally have favorable attitudes toward the use of credit; they have increasing time consciousness and are convenience oriented.

2. How do customers decide what to buy?

Problem recognition: Anticipate purchase where convenient-to-use alternative to cash is needed; often the problem is recognized only at the time use (e.g., taking a trip) is anticipated; sometimes receipt of an application triggers problem recognition.

Information search: Rely on advertisements, friends' opinions, banker's advice, and personal experience as sources of information.

Evaluation of alternatives: Important criteria for evaluating credit cards are convenience in using in many places, liberal spending limits, low membership fee, interest rates for credit, option of revolving credit, cash advance option, ease of replacement, record of transactions, prestige, low minimum payments, and repayment procedures.

Purchase: Commonly, more than one card is issued per account so that more than one household member can use the services.

3. What outside, uncontrollable influences are there on buying decisions?

Economic: Continuing high interest rates cause lower use of credit; higher interest rates for other financial service sources of credit cause people to shift to using credit cards; lower inflation rates may ease the pressure to buy now to avoid later higher prices.

Legal: Relaxation of state usury laws will lead to higher interest rates and less use of credit card revolving credit.

Technological: Increasing use of electronic funds transfer capability such as through the debit card may draw customers away from credit cards.

Social: Increasing number of dual-income families, expansion of the 35–44 age group, and greater use of mail order, catalog, and telephone shopping will help expand credit card use.

Source: David Bain, Kevin Broyles, Barbara Fuller, Harold Hassall, Thomas Pinch, and Colette Rittenhouse, "American Express Company Market Opportunity Analysis: Expansion of American Express into Retail Markets" (class project, University of Tennessee, 1982), pp. 18–28.

of the company's brand, managers search profiles for clues to requirements that the brand can best meet. The credit card customer profile information under question 1 in Exhibit 4–7 extends our understanding of buyers considerably beyond that provided by their demographic characteristics. Note that because customers shop in a wide variety of stores and want the security of never being short of cash, having a credit card accepted in many retail establishments is very important to them. Such services as interest-free periods, cash advances, and revolving credit are also important.

How Customers Decide What to Buy. Learning how people make choices among products reveals key market requirements that a company's marketing offer must meet. The decision processes that people go through help them determine how product benefits match their requirements for purchase. The profile information under question 2 in Exhibit 4–7 suggests numerous requirements of credit card users. The most obvious clues are provided by the criteria used to evaluate credit cards (spending limits, membership fee, interest rates, and so forth). Each criterion represents an expectation or market requirement to be met. Further, another requirement is revealed by the fact that for the convenience of family members users want more than one card. Only a careful search through entire customer profiles will reveal all market requirements.

What Outside Influences Affect Buying Decisions. Influences on buying called **demand factors** come from outside the market and the industry. These influences are largely uncontrollable by either customers or competitors. Exhibit 4–7 shows that several demand factors influence credit card use. Each demand factor has been identified and its impact on product demand described. Important categories of demand factors that show up in many MOAs are economic, legal, technological, natural, and social influences coming from the macroenvironment.

Demand factors are influences on customer buying decisions that come from outside the market and the industry serving the market and are largely uncontrolled by customers or competitors.

Since changes in demand factors influence demand in markets, they must be predicted. Analyzing historical trends is the usual way to make such predictions. Trend analysis was the primary basis for many widely predicted demand factor changes in the U.S. population, including the predictions of an increase in the number of dual-income families, the growth of the 35–44 year-old age group, and the increasing frequency of nonstore shopping.

Building Customer Profiles. The generic class/product type product-market structure guides the building of customer profiles. The first step in this process is learning about generic-class customers. Essentially, customer profiling concentrates on learning why demand exists by describing the underlying needs and wants that create the generic-class market. The information in Exhibit 4–7 describing wants, use situations, and problem recognition for credit card users came from an analysis of generic-class financial service markets.

The next step involves narrowing the profiles to markets for the particular product types of interest. Here, profile information helps management understand which generic-class customers are likely to buy a product type. Activities, interests, opinions, decision processes, and demand factors affecting preference for one product type over others are described.

Generic-class and product-type customer profiles provide a picture of the overall markets within which brands must compete. The challenge for management is to create a marketing program that effectively appeals to customers targeted from these product-markets. The marketing program must demonstrate to customers how the company's brand marketing mix meets both product- and non-product-related market requirements. By starting with the generic class and then proceeding to product-type markets, the MOA has the best chance of presenting a complete, in-depth picture of candidate target markets for a brand. This provides the best basis for discovering all of the potential opportunity.

Profiling Generic-Class and Product-Type Industry and Key Competitors

Opportunity in product-markets is influenced as much by competition as by customer characteristics and demand factors. Gaining an advantage over the competition is crucial to successful marketing planning.[16] As one marketing authority says,

> Increased attention to formal strategy planning has highlighted questions that have long been of concern to managers: What is driving competition in my industry or in industries I am thinking of entering? What actions are competitors likely to take, and what is the best way to respond? How will my industry evolve? How can the firm be best positioned to compete in the long run?[17]

To assist managers in determining what the advantage over the competition should be, an MOA profiles and evaluates the capabilities and actions of other organizations serving the product-markets.

When competition comes from only a very few firms, analyzing each of these firms is practical. Typically, however, there are many competitors in the industry, so that analyzing each of them is unnecessarily time-consuming and expensive. As a compromise, analysts can use a step-by-step procedure to obtain the needed information. Again, the product structure provides the guidelines. First, all of the generic-class and product-type industries are analyzed. Then, key competitors are singled out for in-depth evaluation.

Industry
is a group of firms serving the same defined product-market(s) and competing with one another for sales.

Industry Analyses.   Competitors serving the same market can be grouped together into an **industry,** so that conclusions can be drawn about the similarities and differences in the way in which that market is served. Because management is concerned with the most direct competition, an industry can be restricted to those firms that:

1. Sell the same product (either generic class or product type).

2. Operate at the same level in a channel of distribution.

3. Sell in the same geographic area.

Applying these criteria, a wholesale wine distributor serving eastern Tennessee considers its industry to be all of the wine distributors serving the same area. In contrast, a national wine producer such as Gallo views its industry as all the wine producers selling to the nation's markets.

An industry analysis begins with accumulating an information base, or profile. First, the size, growth, and structure of the industry are described. This information helps managers see how closely the industry's size matches the market size. Next, information is obtained on the marketing practices of the industry, including target market coverage, key marketing objectives, and marketing mix strategy and tactics. Exhibit 4–8 illustrates selected results from an industry analysis for the credit card issuers serving U.S. markets. The

EXHIBIT 4–8 An Industry Profile for Credit Card Issuers

---

1. What is the industry's size, growth, and structure?

Number of firms: The credit card industry includes hundreds of U.S. firms; among these firms are retail chains, bank-affiliated organizations, and independent credit card companies.

Industry sales: Estimated annual sales of $141 billion; in 1980, Americans held 585 million cards and engaged in 6.8 billion transactions; sales growth has been very attractive—over 12 percent annually since 1967; the rate of growth varies with economic conditions and particularly with interest rates.

Industry structure: This is best described as monopolistic competition; companies in the industry can be divided into two-party card issuers and three-party issuers; the two-party issuers (retailer-issued card for use only with that retailer) are far more numerous than the three-party issuers.

2. What are typical industry marketing practices?

Market targets: Both mass market and market segmentation approaches are common; the mass market approaches target all adults with minimum income levels; the segmentation approaches have been based on use situations, such as travel, entertainment, and business purchasing.

Marketing objectives: Educational objectives are aimed at helping customers learn about newer services such as cash advances, toll-free hot lines, faster lost card replacement, and quick credit approvals; another major objective is aimed at building and maintaining brand images based on prestige.

Marketing mix: The industry, led by the three-party card issuers, has an innovative track record of adding services to its product offer—cash advances, emergency card replacement, travel insurance, assured reservations, and others; pricing covers a variety of income sources, including membership fees (0 to $50), interest charges (typically 18 percent), and transaction fees; three-party cards also charge a percentage of retail merchant receivables; distribution varies according to industry structure—two-party cards are limited to the issuing retailer, and three-party cards have worldwide coverage; promotion typically includes both media advertising and extensive point-of-purchase displays and is aimed at building brand awareness and prestige for the cards and at stimulating applications.

3. What changes in the industry are anticipated?

Possible payment of interest to cardholders for credit balances and overpayments; merger through acquisition of three-party issuers by financial organizations; use of floating interest rates on revolving credit; greater use of transaction fees; tightening of minimum requirements for issuance of new cards; federal standardization of usury laws; computerized credit cards; three-party issuers' greater use of premium cards targeted at select market groups.

4. What are the strengths and weaknesses of the industry?

Strengths: Coverage of traveler market segments is extensive; the industry is particularly good at providing convenience in using cards, readily available credit, 30-day interest-free credit, revolving credit, and high prestige.

Weaknesses: Coverage of female market segments is weak; at many places, more widespread acceptance of credit cards is needed; credit limits are moderately restrictive.

Source: David Bain, Kevin Broyles, Barbara Fuller, Harold Hassall, Thomas Pinch, and Colette Rittenhouse, "American Express Company Market Opportunity Analysis: Expansion of American Express into Retail Markets" (class project, University of Tennessee, 1982), pp. 46–68.

narrative answers to questions 1 and 2 provide selected profile information about the competition.

Two very important analyses of this information base can be seen under questions 3 and 4. First, managers use the industry information to draw conclusions about probable changes in industry size, structure, and marketing practices. Managers must be forewarned of new directions in an industry so that they can make adjustments in marketing strategy. Note the credit card industry's probable future payment of interest on card users' overpayments, a new practice. A credit card issuer must work out a marketing response to this impending industry practice.

Second, managers evaluate industry marketing practices to look for weaknesses or problem areas that can be exploited. Question 4 shows relatively

EXHIBIT 4–9

The American Express Card.
It's part of a lot of interesting lives.

Call 800-528-8000 for an application.

American Express uses an interesting lives campaign to target to women.

Courtesy Ogilvy & Mather Advertising.

few weaknesses in the credit card issuer industry. However, it is important to be aware of those that exist. One weakness is that a segment of the market (women) has not been adequately reached, and others involve specific marketing practices that do not fully meet customers' market requirements. If a company can develop cost-effective marketing mix tactics to counter these weaknesses, it can build an advantage over its competitors in the eyes of customers (Exhibit 4–9).

Many of the credit card industry's marketing practices are sound because they reach the volume of demand in market segments or because they effectively meet market requirements. Such practices are the industry's strengths. For a company to compete well within the industry, these strengths must usually be matched in some way. Exhibit 4–8 suggests that a card issuer must offer 30-day free credit through float to match similar offers by competitors.

Key competitors
are those companies in,
or predicted to enter,
an industry that are
expected to have the
most effect on the suc-
cess of a company's
marketing strategy.

Key Competitor Analyses.　In many industries, only a few companies demonstrate successful performance in markets as indicated by dominant market share, higher than average growth in market share, higher than average profitability, or leadership in product innovation. Such a company, or a company with the potential for these kinds of performance and that is poised to enter a market and compete for demand, is a **key competitor** because it is expected to be the most serious threat to exploiting sales opportunity. Analysis of competition must single out companies of this kind from the product-type industries of interest.

Key competitor analyses begin with the construction of a profile describing the size, growth, objectives, management, technical capabilities, and market-ing practices of each key competitor. This information is used to predict future changes in the competitor's marketing actions in markets and to evaluate how well the competitor is meeting market requirements. Essen-tially, the questions shown in Exhibit 4–8 are answered for each key com-petitor.

An illustration of this analysis is provided by American Express's assess-ment of market opportunity for consumer credit purchases in retail stores. Its key competitors were the third-party card issuers that already held a strong position in these markets—VISA and MasterCard. American Express had to carefully develop a competitive position against these powerful companies to succeed in the new target market. Key competitor analyses were needed to help managers anticipate changes in current practices and to uncover strengths and weaknesses in the marketing approaches of VISA and Master-Card.

Conducting Industry/Key Competitor Analyses.　Applying the prod-uct-market idea suggests a procedure for analyzing competition that parallels the way in which markets are structured. From the standpoint of American Express, financial service issuers constitute a generic-class industry. An industry analysis begins by analyzing the industry at this level.

The next step is to narrow the analysis to one or more product-type industries. Those organizations not selling the product type are excluded so that management can concentrate on the most direct competition for market demand. Issuers of credit cards, for example, constitute a product-type indus-try in the larger financial services industry. The final step is to select key competitors from one or more product-type industries for special analysis.

Beginning broadly with the generic-class industry and narrowing down to key competitors has several advantages. First, this encourages managers to assess competition coming from sellers of other product types as well as sellers of the same product type. Managers for a third-party credit card issuer might be tempted to consider only competition from other third-party card issuers. Yet significant competition might come from other types of financial services such as retail credit cards—the two-party cards—and retail installment loans. Competition from different product types is often the kind of competition that managers are most likely to overlook.

Second, evaluating the strengths and weaknesses of generic-class and product-type industries may suggest new marketing strategies and tactics. The success of different product types underscores the fact that more than one marketing strategy can satisfy essentially the same needs and wants. If analysis showed that third-party cards were used less for local buying than for out-of-town buying, ideas for promotion might come from analyzing the marketing practices that retail installment loan and two-party card issuers aimed at local buying.

Finally, the analysis of generic-class and product-type industries may help in identifying key competitors. With too narrow a view of competition, managers may regard only similar brands of the same product type as key competitors. Yet a brand of a different product type in the generic class may be a key competitor. For instance, VISA should probably view such two-party card issuers as Sears and Penny's (brands of another product type) as key competitors.

Market Size Estimation

Recall that an important factor in gauging market opportunity is the size of the market. Market size is best measured by the number of unit or dollar sales that are obtained from a defined market within a specified time period. That period may be a month, a quarter, a year, two years, or any other amount of time designated by management. A glance at Exhibit 4–10 shows aspects of market size that are important for analyzing market opportunity. Let us briefly consider each dimension.

Product-Market Levels of Demand. Each product-market level has a corresponding market size. Applying this idea means starting broadly with generic-class estimation and then narrowing down to predictions for the company's brand. *Aggregate* estimates measure the size of generic-class markets. The volume of financial service sales expected in U.S. markets for a given time period is an aggregate estimate. *Market* estimates measure the size of a product-type market within a generic-class market. Sales of third-party credit cards in the U.S. market are an illustration. Finally, *sales* estimates show the return from target markets for a company's brand. An example is VISA's estimate of its sales for the next year.

Potentials versus Forecasts. Market size estimates should distinguish between potentials and forecasts. *Potential* is the upper limit on sales, the amount of sales that would occur if all of the people who preferred a product (or brand) bought it in the quantity that would fully satisfy their wants. Potential would be achieved only if no problems occurred in the implementation of a best marketing strategy for the industry (or company). Note that

EXHIBIT 4-10 Types of Market Size Estimates

Product-market Level	Potentials	Forecasts
Generic-class market	Aggregate potential	Aggregate forecast
Product-type market	Market potential	Market forecast
Brand target markets	Sales potential	Sales forecast

potential can be estimated for a generic class, a product type, or a company brand.

Forecasts estimate the amount of sales that can realistically be achieved in a market given the expected marketing effort by the industry (or company). In essence, forecasts measure how much of potential is likely to be converted into actual sales. Like potential, forecasts can be estimated at each product-market level.

Market Size and Market Opportunity. Comparison of different market size estimates offers clues to market opportunity. Consider the relationship between a market forecast and an aggregate forecast:

Product-type share = Product-type forecast / Aggregate forecast

Product-type share measures the percentage of generic-class sales that is expected to be captured by one product type. It is a measure of the competitive effectiveness of one product type relative to the other product types in the generic class. This measure is important because all of these product types are serving the same underlying customer need or want. Sales of credit cards as a percentage of all financial service sales illustrate this relationship. The percentage shows the expected success of credit cards against product-type competition in the generic class.

Similarly, a sales forecast can be compared to a product-type forecast:

Market share = Sales Forecast / Product-type forecast

Market share can be interpreted as the competitive effectiveness of a brand when compared to all similar brands appealing to the same product-type markets. Thus, market share shows how well the brand is expected to perform against its most direct competition. VISA's management applies this notion of market share if it compares its sales to the sales of all third-party credit cards.

Another indication of market opportunity comes from comparing potentials with forecasts. Consider the product-type level. Subtracting a market forecast from a market potential yields a measure of untapped product-type demand:

$$\text{Untapped demand} = \text{Market potential} - \text{Market forecast}$$

Large untapped demand means a particularly attractive market opportunity, assuming that there are no barriers to serving the market. This indicates that a company's sales growth can come from further penetration into the market and that management does not have to rely as much on taking sales away from competitors to meet future sales growth objectives.

Evaluating Market Opportunity

The payoff from an MOA comes when managers evaluate opportunity for the company's brand in preparation for marketing planning. Information on product-markets (generic class and product type) provides an understanding of the markets in which a brand competes. The challenge is to use that understanding to select target markets and to decide how the brand can best be positioned. To accomplish this, evaluation of market opportunity should include:

- Delineation of target market options

- Listing of important market requirements

- Review of future key competitive strengths and weaknesses for building a differential advantage,

- Forecast of the sales expected from a brand strategy

Target Market Options.   One of the most important applications of an MOA is in identifying target market options. These options are generated from the product-market structure, which can vary from simple to complex. The simplest product-market structure comprises one market, either a generic-class or product-type market. The market is described by highlighting the "typical" buyer, as VISA might do to identify the typical buyer of financial services or credit cards.

More complex market structures are often developed from MOAs. Market groups or segments in which buyers have similar market requirements are identified and are separated from segments in which buyers have different requirements. Each segment becomes a target market option. One study structured financial service markets on the basis of differences in the use situation—where a purchase is made, the size of the payment required, the availability of retail credit for the purchase, and so forth.[18] In Exhibit 4–11, each cell represents a different segment. One segment comprises buyers who make a local purchase of less than $400 at a retail store offering its own credit. Other segments in the market structure are arrived at by considering other combinations of use situation possibilities.

EXHIBIT 4-11 A Product-Market Structure for Financial Services

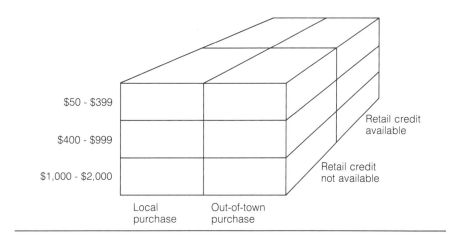

Market Requirements. The sales generated by a marketing strategy depend to a great extent on how well buyers' expectations are met. Matching company strengths (and not exposing weaknesses) to market demand requires understanding exactly what customers want—their market requirements. A major challenge in the evaluation of market opportunity is describing these requirements.

Customer profile information must be examined to develop a list of requirements reflecting the benefits and services desired. The relative importance of each of these requirements should be rated. Exhibit 4-12 shows market requirements and relative importance ratings for two different credit card segments. Notice the variety of expectations uncovered. The analysis found that some market requirements—convenient medium of exchange, widespread acceptance of the card by retail organizations, high prestige/status of the card, liberal credit limits, easy replacement of lost card, and detailed records of purchases—were more important than others. The ratings efficiently describe the relative importance of the various market requirements.

A market structure containing segments must reveal significant differences in the market requirements of the segments. Otherwise, management cannot use the structure to select target markets. Some segments may have market requirements that are entirely different from those of other segments. Exhibit 4-12 illustrates another way in which market requirements may differ. Customers in each market group may attach somewhat different importance to the various market requirements. The two credit card market segments attach quite different importance to "credit revolves over time," "availability

EXHIBIT 4-12 Market Requirements and Ratings for Two Credit Card
Target Markets*

Market Requirements	Importance to Target Market 1	Importance to Target Market 2
Convenient medium of exchange	10	10
Source of credit	5	8
Widespread acceptance	9	9
Liberal credit limits	8	6
Minimal membership fee	3	4
Favorable interest rates	2	3
Low minimum payment on balance due	1	3
Credit revolves over time	2	7
Easy replacement of lost card	8	5
Availability of other financial services	7	2
Flexible timing method of payment	4	2
Detailed records of purchases	8	4
Thirty-day float	7	7
High prestige/status	9	6

* Scale 1-10: 1 = least important; 10 = most important

Source: David Bain, Kevin Broyles, Barbara Fuller, Harold Hassall, Thomas Pinch, and Colette Rittenhouse, "American Express Company Market Opportunity Analysis: Expansion of American Express into Retail Markets" (class project, University of Tennessee, 1982), pp. 46–68.

of other financial services," and "detailed records of purchases." Incurring the high cost of an elaborate revolving credit service is not important for serving buyers in target market 1, but it is very important for serving buyers in target market 2. On the other hand, having a variety of financial services is quite important for target market 1, but not for target market 2.

Competitive Strengths and Weaknesses. Management must periodically assess how well the competition is serving each target market option. Entering or staying too long in a product-market saturated with strong competition is a strategic error. Before deciding that Carte Blanche, a predominantly travel and entertainment credit card, should enter the markets for retail store purchases, its management would have to determine whether VISA, MasterCard, American Express and the multitude of two-party cards presented too much competition for this market.

For those target markets in which management believes that a strong position can be developed or maintained, the company must position itself against the strengths and weaknesses of the competition. Ultimately, success in markets comes from finding a unique advantage over key competitors.[19] If Carte Blanche's management decided to move into a segment of the retail purchases market, a major objective should be to match the strengths of competition on (see Exhibit 4–8, question 4):

1. Convenience as a medium of exchange.

2. Readily available source of credit.

3. Interest-free short-term credit.

EXHIBIT 4–13 Sequence of Market Size Estimates and the Marketing Plan

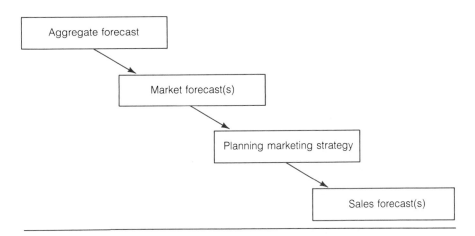

4. High prestige/status.

5. Revolving credit.

At the same time, management would have to find some way to stand out from the competition by addressing competitive weaknesses on important market requirements. Meeting the "widespread acceptance" market requirement, though difficult, would be one essential way to counter competition. Less restrictive credit limits might also be considered.

Forecasting Sales. The final step in evaluating market opportunity is estimation of the sales return for the planned marketing strategy. Look again at Exhibit 4–10. A company's management is highly interested in the sales forecast because it shows how many brand sales are expected from one or more target markets. However, the other estimates also play a role in selecting the target market, as is suggested by the sequence in which estimates are made (see Exhibit 4–13).

Aggregate and market forecasts provide a starting point for the evaluation of sales opportunity in the target markets. Aggregate forecasts can be used to compare entirely different opportunities, such as financial services versus home entertainment products. Using market forecasts, management can compare the size of alternative product-type markets to see where the greatest sources of sales lie.

Having selected markets as candidate targets, management plans a marketing program to tap sales from these markets. The plan will show the extent to which company strengths can be brought to bear on meeting market requirements and providing an advantage over the competition. Only then can a sales forecast be made to estimate the sales return from that marketing program. The sales forecast is used, in turn, to estimate profits, return on investment, cash flow, and other financial indicators of the worth of alternative target markets. Target markets are finally selected based on all of these indicators as well as other considerations, such as consistency with company mission, legal constraints, and available resources. Notice that the final choice of target markets means that the marketing program is also accepted.

Summary

The approach to market opportunity analysis (MOA) presented in this chapter is a practical guide to the kinds of information and analyses that are needed for marketing planning. The matrix in Exhibit 4–14 summarizes the framework for understanding market opportunity. This matrix also serves as a worksheet for organizing information and analyses. Two ideas underlying the framework are particularly important. One concerns the coverage of an MOA. Across the top of the matrix are listed the four different types of analysis activities that an MOA comprises. The column under each activity shows the information and analyses that result from that activity. Each analysis activity focuses on one of the four determinants of market opportunity: market structure, market requirements, competition, and market size.

The other important idea underlying the framework concerns how an analyst should procede through an MOA. The row headings in Exhibit 4–14 suggest a top-to-bottom, narrowing-down procedure for conducting each of the four analysis activities. In essence, an MOA starts by describing the arena in which brands compete for sales. This arena comprises generic-class and product-type product-markets. Starting broadly and narrowing down to target markets for a brand gives management the best chance of uncovering all of the important factors influencing market opportunity. Doing this will give management the background information about product-markets that it needs to determine how best to position a brand in those markets.

EXHIBIT 4–14 Summary of an MOA

	Product/market definition	Market composition	Competitive composition	Market size
Generic-class Product-market	Product class and market identification	Customer profile	Industry profile	Aggregate potential and forecast
Product-type Product-market	Product type and market identification	Customer profile	Industry and key competitor profiles	Market potential and forecasts
Brand Product-market	Target market options	Market requirements	Competitive strengths and weaknesses	Sales potential and forecasts

Exercises for Review and Discussion

1. Product managers at Shutter Manufacturing decided to add a new 35-mm camera to its camera line. The new model was designed for the amateur photographer who wanted a simple-to-use camera for taking home pictures. Before developing a marketing plan for the camera, the managers wanted to have a market opportunity analysis done. One of the managers said, "The market for the camera is all retail camera stores and retail chains with camera departments. This is the market we should have analyzed." Do you agree with this product manager? Why or why not?

2. The president of Real Estate Development Corporation read in the local newspaper that in the United States people over age 60, were enjoying rising buying power. The article in which this was stated convincingly argued that older people were becoming a more important market because of better retirement income and fewer fixed expenses. The president asked whether people over 60 were a market for real estate sales. How would you answer the president's question? Discuss your answer.

3. Sockum Sporting Goods, Inc. manufactures private brand sports equipment for several national retailers. The company's mission has limited the product mix to baseball, football, soccer, and basketball equipment. Sockum's management wants to move into other sports. A proposal has been developed to manufacture tennis rackets, and a market opportunity analysis has been requested. Should this MOA include a generic-class analysis? Why or why not?

4. Having just finished Procter & Gamble's sales training program, you are about to be assigned to a sales territory. Should you conduct a market opportunity analysis for your sales territory? Why or why not? If you did do an MOA, how would you set it up?

5. Choose one of the following products: wine, tennis rackets, personal computers, running shoes, microwave ovens, or fast-food restaurants. Gather information on three major competitors in the product's industry. Use this information to (a) describe the most important market requirements that these competitors are trying to meet and (b) describe the brand positioning strategies that each company is using to compete in markets.

6. Suppose you sell consumer cameras and photography equipment for Kodak. At a sales meeting, you mention that a population analysis would help you develop a more effective plan for your territory. Your boss, the district sales manager, says, "That would take too much time. Anyway, I don't see why you want that information." How would you respond?

7. At a recent meeting of the board of directors of a large, full-service county hospital, the administrator said, "The only competition we have in the health care market is from the three other full-service hospitals serving patients in the county. There isn't room in the market for another hospital like these, so we can rest assured that no more competition is coming into the county." How would you respond to these comments? Discuss your answer.

8. "Analyzing market opportunity for a product is no different from forecasting the product's sales. If you know one, you know the other." Do you agree with this statement? Why or why not?

Notes

1. Information for the toy industry illustration was obtained from Penny Gill, "The Joy in Toymaking," *Nation's Business*, December 1985, pp. 22–25, 28.

2. Catherine L. Harris, "Information Power," *Business Week*, October 14, 1985, p. 111.

3. A discussion of the contributions of market opportunity analysis and marketing strategy to business decisions is found in Yoram Wind and Thomas S. Robertson, "Marketing Strategy: New Directions for Theory and Research," *Journal of Marketing* 47 (Spring 1983), pp. 12-25.

4. "Gerber: Concentrating on Babies Again for Slow, Steady Growth," *Business Week*, August 22, 1980, p. 80.

5. Throughout this chapter, the term *product* will be used in a broad sense to refer to anything that a customer purchases or uses—a physical product, a service, a store, and so forth.

6. "Gerber: Concentrating on Babies Again."

7. Christine Dugas, "Plastic Prestige: Credit Cards that Make You Somebody," *Business Week*, November 11, 1985, p. 62.

8. Harris, "Information Power," p. 110.

9. Bruce J. Hoesman, "Identifying New Competitive Opportunities," in *Product-Line Strategies*, ed. Earl L. Bailey (New York: Conference Board, 1982), p. 64; and Wind and Robertson, "Marketing Strategy," p. 15.

10. Rajendra K. Srivastava, Robert P. Leone, and Allan D. Shocker, "Market Structure Analysis: Hierarchical Clustering of Products Based on Substitution-in-Use," *Journal of Marketing* 45 (Summer 1981), pp. 44-45.

11. Ibid.

12. This discussion of methods for identifying product markets is based on the classification in George S. Day, Allan D. Shocker, and Rajendra K. Srivastava, "Identifying Competitive Product Markets: A Review of Customer-Oriented Approaches," *Journal of Marketing* 43 (Fall 1979), pp. 8-19.

13. These applications are discussed more fully in Day, Shocker, and Srivastava, "Identifying Competitive Product Markets," pp. 44, 46.

14. For an excellent review of segmentation research, see Yoram Wind, "Issues and Advances in Segmentation Research," *Journal of Marketing Research* 15 (August 1978), pp. 317-37.

15. David Bain, Kevin Broyles, Barbara Fuller, Harold Hassall, Thomas Pinch, and Colette Rittenhouse, "American Express Company Market Opportunity Analysis: Expansion of American Express into Retail Markets" (class project, University of Tennessee, 1982), pp. 18-19.

16. For an interesting discussion of planning for competitive advantage, see Victor J. Cook, Jr., "Marketing Strategy and Differential Advantage," *Journal of Marketing* 47 (Spring 1983), pp. 68-75.

17. Michael E. Porter, *Competitive Strategy* (New York: Free Press, 1980), p. xiii.

18. Srivastava, Leone, and Shocker, "Market Structure Analysis," p. 43.

19. Bruce D. Henderson, "The Anatomy of Competition," *Journal of Marketing* 47 (Spring 1983), p. 8.

CHAPTER 5

Consumer Markets and Buyer Behavior

C ompanies with managements that listen to their customers and understand what they want have an essential ingredient for market success. The Stouffer's Lean Cuisine preprepared low-calorie entrées demonstrate the rewards that accrue to such companies. Major lifestyle trends in the United States revolving around concern for fitness and health opened the door to new food products. At the same time, many consumers wanted low-calorie, nutritional meals that did not sacrifice taste. The Stouffer's Lean Cuisine product line entered the under 300-calorie entrée food class with a marketing strategy in tune with these lifestyle trends and consumer requirements. The sales of these entrées quickly reached the $300 million level, an impressive achievement.[1] Not surprisingly, other food companies followed the lead taken by Stouffer's. As one expert notes:

> The under 300-calorie entrée business is a perfect example of responding to the consumer of today. The products satisfy the need for fitness by offering a relatively low-calorie content. They are offered in gourmet recipes to satisfy the needs of more sophisticated, younger consumers. Most can be prepared quickly in a microwave or toaster oven, which is a boon to time-pressed working people. All offer six or more varieties so they can be consumed more than once a week. All are relatively inexpensive vs. comparable food.[2]

This chapter and the next one expand on important ideas for understanding the activities and actions of the people and organizations that purchase and use economic goods and services. The discussion concentrates on the aspects of buyer behavior that managers are most likely to encounter when analyzing markets for opportunity. The first section of this chapter reviews the two key kinds of applications of buyer behavior analyses. Then, a closer look is taken at the behavior of one important kind of buyer—consumers. Consumer behavior is described, and the factors that influence consumer behavior are discussed. Chapter 6 continues this treatment of buyer behavior by examining industrial buyers of products and services.

A Buyer Behavior Perspective

Buyer behavior
is concerned with the
activities and actions of
people and organiza-
tions that purchase and
use economic goods
and services, including
the influences on these
activities and actions.[3]

Information on **buyer behavior** is generally used to predict or diagnose buyers' actions in markets. Because managers are responsible for the outcome of their decisions, they ought to be sure that buyer behavior information is relevant to the decision situation. No one else understands the risks and uncertainties as well as they do. However, participating in the process of gathering and analyzing information, whether for prediction or diagnosis, is not easy. To begin with, managers must know the ways in which buyer behavior information can help them.

Prediction involves anticipating what buyers will do at some future time. Probably the most common kind of buyer behavior prediction is the sales forecast which estimates purchase choices of buyers in markets. Consider the management of a contractor/land development company that agonized over whether to build condominium units on a very expensive tract of land. One factor on which the decision hinged was the anticipated number of units that could be sold to customers. An MOA was conducted to predict condominium unit sales. The MOA helped management see that the likelihood of getting the required level of sales was not high enough, so the planned condominium project was scrapped. Predictions of this kind are needed by managers to evaluate alternative decision options.

Buyer behavior diagnosis seeks explanations for buyer behavior. An administrator for a county hospital reviewed five years of data on hospitals used by patients living in the county. The results showed a steadily declining market share for the hospital. A study conducted to find out why an increasing number of patients were using other hospitals yielded these findings:

- Many patients believed that other hospitals were superior for selected specialty treatments, such as treatments for cancer, heart ailments, and mental illness.

- Patients were going to doctors outside the county for specialty care, and those doctors were affiliated with other hospitals.

- The county hospital's prices were believed to have increased more than the prices of other hospitals.

- Many patients were not aware of the improvements that had been made in the county hospital's facilities and services.

These findings helped the hospital's administrator diagnose why its market share was declining and provided crucial guidelines for developing a marketing plan to stop the decline. Note that prediction and diagnosis can be used in combination, though diagnosis usually precedes prediction. The hospital administrator, after diagnosing the reasons for the market share problem and developing a marketing strategy, had to predict how county citizens would react to the planned strategy. These predictions were needed to justify the strategy.

EXHIBIT 5-1 A Model of Consumer Behavior

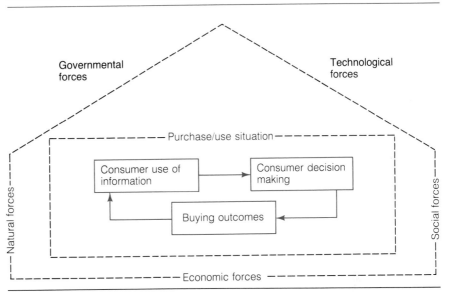

Time and resource limitations dictate being selective in choosing which of the almost unlimited number of aspects of buyer behavior in markets to study. Management can only justify examining those aspects that are most likely to yield insight helpful to the marketing decisions at stake. Fortunately, a relatively few fundamental perspectives provide the foundation for most analyses of buyer behavior, particularly diagnosis. These perspectives provide essential guides to managers faced with deciding which aspects of buyer behavior to focus on. Three especially important perspectives form the basis for the discussion in the remainder of the chapter:

- Buyer behavior is influenced by the buyer's environment.
- Buyer behavior involves people reacting to and interacting with their environment by seeking, receiving, and using information.
- Buyer behavior is generally a purposive, decision-making process.

These perspectives fit nicely together in a model of buyer behavior that serves as a framework for understanding its nature. Such a model, however, must distinguish between **consumers** and industrial buyers. There are enough differences between these two kinds of buyers to justify treating them separately. A simple model of consumer behavior is shown in Exhibit 5-1, and the remainder of the chapter focuses on this type of buyer.

Not all consumer buying is the same. The way people buy cars differs substantially from the way they buy chewing gum. However, certain types of factors are most likely to show up in market opportunity analyses (Exhibit

Consumers
are people in families and other kinds of households who buy and use products and services in order to satisfy their personal needs and wants.

5-1). Macroenvironmental forces affect consumer buying. Ever-present governmental, economic, natural, technological, and social forces affect what each consumer can buy and is willing to buy. For example, high interest rates, an economic force, influence purchases made on credit. The marketing offers of competing companies are also part of the consumer's environment. Within these larger environments is the use situation—the more immediate situation surrounding each particular purchase and use of a product or service.

Consumers interact with and learn about both the macroenvironment and use situations through information. Personal experience, conversations with family and friends, and marketing provide much of this information and influence the buying decisions made by consumers. Needs and wants are also a factor because consumers generally buy to satisfy these needs and wants. The outcomes of buying decisions, such as satisfaction and intentions to buy again, help to build experience that affects future buying decisions.

The model in Exhibit 5-1 helps organize the categories of factors that combine to determine consumer behavior in markets and the ability of managers to achieve sales, profit, and other company objectives dependent on what customers do. Let us examine each component of this model.

The Consumer's Environment

The many environmental influences combine to form a total life setting for consumers. Purchasing and using products and services are among the ways in which people respond to and interact with the world about them. Marketing managers must understand the life setting of consumers to fully appreciate what consumers are trying to accomplish with a particular purchase. Only then can a company demonstrate the relevance of its marketing offer to customers by showing how it will help them deal with their life setting. Ultimately, convincing customers of the product offer's relevance is crucial to sales growth in markets. Many environmental influences on consumers have already been discussed in Chapter 3. Here, the discussion illustrates the important role of the environment by examining social and use situation influences.

Social Interaction

Culture
is shared ideas, beliefs, values, and ways of behaving among large groups of people living in a defined geographic area.

People living in an area interact with and are influenced by one another. The impact of this social interaction on buying can best be visualized by breaking out different kinds of social influences (see Exhibit 5-2). Each has a unique impact on buyers.

Cultural Values.   When conducting market opportunity analyses, managers may consider populations within countries as a **culture**. But culture frequently extends beyond such political boundaries and can vary within a

EXHIBIT 5-2 Social Environmental Influences on Buying

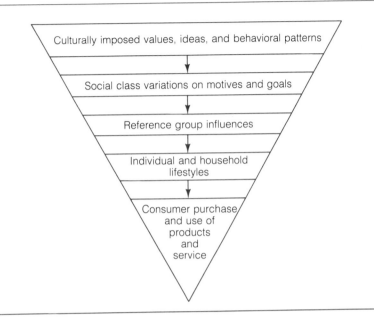

country. Philadelphia, like many large cities, poses an interesting marketing challenge because it has a section populated by Italian immigrants and their decendants. Social interaction within this section is so confined that many values of Italian culture survive. Stores that import many products directly from Italy—olive oil, grapes for wine making, and pasta-making machines—are successful here. They help residents maintain their Italian culture and its values.

Culture exerts powerful influences on people by providing guides and rules concerning what is and what is not acceptable. Comparing the values of people in different countries shows culture at work. In the United States, values related to showing men and women in intimate settings have become more relaxed. Marketing managers have taken advantage of this cultural trend by portraying intimate scenes in advertisements (Exhibit 5-3). This advertisement would not be accepted by people in countries, such as several in the Middle East, where corresponding values are much more restrictive.

Marketing managers must guard against conflicting with established cultural values, because values will win over marketing offers most every time. Studying values before launching a marketing offer is essential, particularly when entering an unfamiliar country. Otherwise, mistakes are easily made. A manufacturer of mouthwash learned this lesson the hard way. In Thailand, there is a strong cultural value against public display of physical contact between a male and a female. Management should not have been surprised

EXHIBIT 5–3

This Slumber Rest advertisement, placed in a popular lifestyle magazine, displays an intimacy that is consistent with cultural values in the United States but not in many other countries.

Courtesy Burton-Campbell, Inc.

that its ad campaign, which showed a man and a woman holding hands, was not successful. Only when the manufacturer's advertisements were changed to show two women were they deemed acceptable.[4]

Social class
is a large group of people in a culture who share similar values, interests, lifestyles, and behaviors. People of different social classes are accorded different status and esteem in the culture.

Social Class. Within a culture are **social classes.** Social classes exist because people tend to see themselves and others in terms of self-esteem and status. Differences in status and self-esteem lead to a hierarchy of social groups such as the one shown in Exhibit 5–4.

Social class is a powerful influence on people's lifestyles. This explains why there are important differences in the buying behavior of the various social classes in a culture. Many companies must take these differences into consideration when planning marketing strategy. Sometimes, target markets may be defined by concentrating on particular social classes. One study showed that the upper classes in America value quality products and services, prestige brands, the theater, books, club memberships, and travel far

EXHIBIT 5–4 Social Classes in the United States

Social Class	Description	Social Class	Description
Upper Americans:	About one sixth of the population, these people are college educated, are in managerial and professional positions of leadership, have above-average income and/or inherited wealth, lead varied lifestyles that include country and service club involvement, and spend their spare time on cultural and athletic activities.	*Working class:*	Numbering about one third of the population, working-class Americans are in middle-level blue-collar jobs, have slightly below-average educational attainment, have somewhat below-average income, lead lifestyles that reflect a very local orientation (they look to relatives for economic help in bad times, are close to relatives for socializing, and do not tend to travel very far from home), maintain traditional sex roles, value possessions as opposed to experiences, and have had little change in lifestyles over the years.
Middle class:	Making up about one third of the population, middle-class Americans typically are educated beyond high school, are in middle-level white-collar occupations or upper-level blue-collar occupations where supervision of others is part of their responsibility, have incomes that range from somewhat above to just below the national average, lead lifestyles that involve providing experiences for themselves and their children, want their children to be college educated, are interested in physical activity that is fun, and are influenced by and emulate upper Americans.	*Lower Americans:*	About one sixth of the population are in nonskilled occupations, may not be regularly employed, have less than a high school education, hover around the poverty level in income, and vary in their lifestyles, with some seeking instant gratification, while others resist such behavior.

Source: Based on Richard P. Coleman, "The Continuing Significance of Social Class to Marketing," *Journal of Consumer Research* 10 (December 1983), pp. 270–72.

away from home. The other social classes do not share this same set of preferences.[5] High-fashion clothing specialty stores, prestige-image automobile brands, haute cuisine restaurants, and many other enterprises recognize this class difference by targeting toward the upper classes with high-quality, high-price, and prestige marketing offers.

Reference group
is a relatively small social group to which a consumer belongs or aspires to belong and that provide guides to acceptable beliefs, values, attitudes, and behavior.

Family
is two or more people who live in the same household and are related by blood, marriage, or adoption.

Reference Group Influence. Within a culture and social class, people belong to or aspire to belong to a wide variety of **reference groups.** Any group with a degree of permanence and the opportunity to influence people is a reference group—a college fraternity or sorority, an office staff at work, a local union, a softball team, and so forth. Such groups can be a potent force in determining the outcome of purchase decisions.

One important reference group for consumer marketing applications is the **family.** Families are the most numerous kind of household, and there is very intimate and frequent interaction among their members. This interaction creates many opportunities for influence. Marketing managers in consumer goods companies often study families rather than individual consumers because more than one person in a family may be involved in the purchase decision process. Some products, such as furniture, many food items, automobiles, and appliances are used by all family members, so that both spouses (and even children) have a stake in their purchase. Other products may be purchased by one family member but used by others as well. Among such products are cereal, toothpaste, men's cologne, and children's clothing.

When several people in a family are involved in purchasing, they may not agree on exactly what to purchase or when. The way in which disagreements are resolved may influence the outcome of a purchase decision. A family faces **conflict,** for instance, if the husband wants to purchase a new Japanese-brand television set that has cable and VCR (videocassette recorder) hookups, and the wife wants a lower-priced brand because she hopes to save money now for a microwave oven purchase later. To resolve conflict, husbands and wives rely on influence strategies to reach some kind of accommodation with each other. These strategies include:

Conflict refers to disagreements among those involved in buying decisions over purchase goals, the attractiveness of purchase alternatives, the timing of the purchase, or other aspects of a purchase decision.

- *Expert:* Influence is exercised by referring to specific information demonstrating more knowledge about the alternatives.
- *Legitimate:* Influence is derived from the defined roles of the spouses. The husband may say, "This is a man's product, so I should decide."
- *Bargaining:* Influence is exercised by granting some kind of concession in return for making the decision. "You let me buy the sofa I want, and you can have the say on where we go on our vacation."
- *Reward/referent:* Influence is exercised by offering some kind of reward in return for being able to make the purchase decision. "Let's buy the green car, and I will take you out to dinner tonight."
- *Emotional:* Influence is attempted by displaying emotion—anger, joy— during the discussion of the purchase.
- *Impression management:* Influence is based on selectively using information to create an impression of outside pressures to make the preferred decision—for example, withholding some information about an alternative to make it appear more or less desirable.[6]

Finding out who has influence in the purchase decision may be important when managers decide which family members to target and what to offer them. The management of a jeans store chain, such as ITS stores, is faced with an interesting family buying situation. Wives are very influential in buying jeans for their children, at least until the children reach the age of 9 or 10. After that age, the children are much more likely to buy for themselves. Wives also buy for their husbands or influence the husbands' choices. And wives buy for themselves. Promotion, in-store selling, and merchandise selection must take these various roles into consideration. For instance, some promotion for men's jeans should be aimed at women.

Lifestyle.   Social influences lead people to adopt certain lifestyles. People follow a living pattern that includes the goals they want to achieve (to be successful, educated, happy, wealthy), the activities they engage in regularly

EXHIBIT 5-5 Profiles of Persons Spending $11 or More Annually on Shotgun Ammunition

Demographic profile:	Lifestyle profile:
Younger (18 to 44); lower income (under $15,000); lower education (less than high school graduate); more likely to be in blue-collar occupations (craftsman); more likely to live in rural areas, particularly in the South, or in moderately sized cities.	Likes many outdoor activities: interested in hunting, fishing, camping, spending a vacation in a cabin by a lake, working outdoors.
	Is a do-it-yourselfer: has a feeling of competence at fixing mechanical things, often works on car.
	Attracted to violent, high-risk situations: likes war stories, feels he would do well in a fistfight, would like to be a professional football player or a policeman, is less likely than others to feel there is too much violence on television, more likely to believe there should be a gun in every home, more likely to like risk such as flying his own airplane or playing poker.
	More self-indulgent: feels he smokes too much, loves to eat, is more likely than others to feel he spends money on himself that should be spent on the family, less likely to read the newspaper, and believes most men would cheat on their wives.

Source: William D. Wells, "Psychographics: A Critical Review," *Journal of Marketing Research* 12 (May 1975), p. 198. Reprinted from the *Journal of Marketing Research*, published by the American Marketing Association.

(school, job, recreation, leisure), and their interests and opinions. Lifestyle analyses have gained in popularity in marketing because lifestyles influence consumers' choices on how to spend time, energy, and money. Lifestyle is at work in families that lead a social, entertainment-oriented lifestyle causing them to be heavy users of snack foods, soft drinks, party napkins, and cassette tapes.

Many marketing managers are accustomed to examining the demographic characteristics of their customers. But this information, by itself, is often insufficient. Studying consumer lifestyles can help marketing managers learn what customers are like as flesh and blood people and why they are buying. One practitioner puts it this way:

> Demographics alone, useful as they are, simply are not enough to define consumer buying patterns in sufficient detail to compete in today's marketplace. Marketing professionals traditionally have defined their markets by demographics and usage habits. But to make the best decisions, we really need more information about how our potential customers think and feel; in short, the kinds of people they are inside.[7]

Exhibit 5-5 contains demographic and lifestyle information describing buyers of shotgun ammunition. Little can be done to plan marketing strategy with the demographic information alone, but the combination of demographics and lifestyle information offers many guides. An experienced marketing manager can identify ways to communicate with shotgun ammunition buyers; advertising themes and layouts might tie shotgun ammunition to many outdoor activities rather than just to hunting; joint promotions with manufacturers of other outdoor products may be possible; and shotgun

EXHIBIT 5-6 Use Situations Affecting Restaurant Choices

Use Situation	Restaurant Types Preferred	Use Situation	Restaurant Types Preferred
"I am taking my wife out for our 25th wedding anniversary, and our closest friends will be there."	Atmosphere/specialty restaurants	"My husband's birthday is next week. He likes to try different types of food. I will surprise him by taking him out to eat somewhere where they don't serve American food."	Ethnic food restaurants
"We are taking our kids out to eat. I hope they don't act up."	Family-style restaurants	"I have 45 minutes to eat lunch in between appointments with customers. I can't be late."	Fast-food restaurants

ammunition might be distributed more widely by selling it through a variety of retail stores handling products for outdoor activities.[8]

Use Situations

Use situation
is the characteristics of the immediate time and place in which a consumer uses a product or service, including all the factors that influence its purchase and use other than those inherent in the marketing of the product or service.

Culture, social class, reference group, and lifestyle influences tend to be slow to change. There is a more transient part of the consumer's environment—the time and place where a product is used. This immediate environment is the consumer's **use situation**.[9] Interestingly, consumers can anticipate a use situation and then purchase a product or service to deal with that situation. When choosing a restaurant, a couple may want to impress other people who will accompany them. If the other people are relatives from out of town, or special friends, only atmosphere/specialty restaurants will be considered. But if the couple's children are being taken out for a meal, then restaurants that specialize in family dining are more likely to be selected.

Because use situations differ, consumers buy different product types within the same class of products (Exhibit 5-6).[10] In fact, marketing managers can sometimes segment markets according to the anticipated use situation. Different kinds of restaurants appeal to people in different situations. Similarly, a drink like Gator-Aid, whose promotion emphasizes its thirst-quenching qualities, appeals to consumers who are in an active, athletic situation such as coming off the tennis courts, whereas 7UP can appeal to consumers who want a mixer when at a social gathering where alcoholic beverages are being served.

Consumer Information Processing

The astute marketing manager realizes that the company's marketing offers are only a small part of all the information vying for the consumer's attention. Only some of this information is used at any given time. From studies of

EXHIBIT 5-7 Steps in Consumer Information Processing

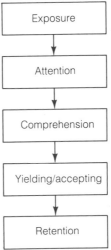

buyer behavior, a consistent picture has emerged of consumers actively receiving and using information in a very selective way (Exhibit 5-7). Creatively designing and implementing marketing to reach and influence target markets requires understanding and coping with this selectivity.

Exposure

Exposure occurs when consumers are in such close proximity to information that it has the potential to reach one or more of their senses. A consumer turning on a radio becomes exposed to a station's advertising and programming. Turning off the radio is one way in which consumers selectively decide not to be exposed to that information source.

Exposure is affected by people's everyday living patterns. The routes that consumers routinely take to work or shop dictate exposure to information from signs and stores along the way. Television programs viewed, radio stations regularly heard, and newspapers and magazines read all influence exposure to advertisements in these media. Further, the stores in which people shop regularly determine exposure to salespeople, brands, and sales promotions. Studying these living patterns allows managers to select information delivery vehicles that reach customers in target markets.

Attention

People are attentive to information when they focus their senses on it. The difference between exposure and attention is apparent if you watch shoppers walking down an aisle in a supermarket. A shopper looking straight ahead is exposed to signs and package information on both sides of the aisle, but only when the shopper glances at a sign or a product or picks up a package to read the label has this information gained the shopper's attention.

Consumers are very selective in determining what they will pay attention to. This selectivity is based in part on their needs, wants, problems, and interests at the moment. They are more likley to attend to information that is currently relevant. When thumbing through a magazine, a hungry person is more likely to notice food-related communications. Advertisers have long applied this knowledge with advertisements featuring attention-getting scenes in which the consumer is very interested. For years, ads for soft drinks have shown social situations. These ads gain attention because many soft-drink users like to go to parties, attend family outings, or otherwise be with others.

People are also attentive toward novel, unusual, or exceptional information. Creative specialists dream up unusual and novel ways to get the attention of potential customers. A Hertz advertisement showing O. J. Simpson flying through the air to his rental car is a novel way of demonstrating Hertz's efficiency in assigning cars to customers. Marketing managers go to such lengths because it is difficult to gain attention in consumers' information-packed world.

Comprehension

Encoding
is interpreting the meaning of incoming information by matching it with previous knowledge stored in memory.

People comprehend new information by **encoding,** or interpreting, incoming information.[11] Some encoding may occur unconsciously. A consumer at an automobile dealership may be drawn to a particular car because of its silver color. From past experience, this consumer has formed the impression that silver connotes elegance, a desirable characteristic in a car. The color is a bit of information that attracts the consumer's attention and conveys the impression that the car is elegant.

Encoding can be done quite consciously. According to one view, bits of knowledge are organized in memory as a network of propositions about the relationships between concepts or thoughts.[12] Additional comprehensions are also influenced by previous knowledge in such networks. One interesting illustration of memory networks is shown in Exhibit 5–8. Suppose our consumer decides to inspect the silver car, a Ford Fiesta, more closely. From previous experience, a relationship has been formed between the central concept "Ford Fiesta" and the associated concept "fun to drive." The silver car in the showroom will now be perceived as fun to drive.

The network model suggests that our knowledge is organized into "packets" of related concepts.[13] All of the concepts related to Ford Fiesta are one packet that organizes a consumer's knowledge about that brand. Retrieving information from a packet is the result of an activation process. An information cue activates a concept in the packet, as when our consumer notices that the silver car is a Ford Fiesta. Other related concepts are retrieved as they become activated. This process spreads through the packet, with the more strongly related concepts more likely to be retrieved.[14]

EXHIBIT 5-8 An Associative Network Model

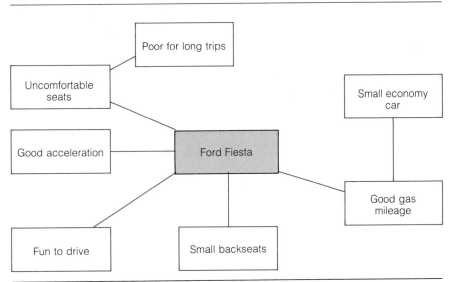

Source: Terrence R. Smith, Andrew A. Mitchell, and Robert Meyer, "A Computational Process Model of Evaluation Based on the Cognitive Structuring of Episodic Knowledge," *Advances in Consumer Research,* ed. Andrew A. Mitchell (Ann Arbor, Mich.: Association For Consumer Research, 1981), p. 138.

These fundamental ideas—encoding, memory, networks, and retrieval through activation—help explain why comprehension is selective. People interpret new information in a very personal way, relying on what has been learned previously. Miscomprehension by consumers sometimes occurs, and when it concerns marketing offers, the consequences can be unpleasant. Campbell Soup Company suffered from this phenomenon when it attempted to sell condensed soup in Great Britain. On a per serving basis, the price was comparable to that of local brands. But the British were not familiar with condensed soup and interpreted the package/price combination to mean that the Campbell's soups cost twice as much as local competitive brands.[15]

Marketing managers must be aware of the potential for miscomprehension. Tests of marketing offers are their best hope of uncovering unfavorable miscomprehensions before these do serious damage to product sales. Automobile manufacturers regularly conduct tests in which consumers are shown a model design and asked to give their impressions of it. The results are used to discover whether consumers perceive the design shapes in any negative way—as slow, bulky, or difficult to handle.

Yielding/Acceptance

Even if marketing information gets attention and is comprehended correctly, its effectiveness is still not assured. That information must also get target consumers to accept or yield to the point of view expressed. American

Express's promotional "Don't leave home without it" campaign has gained consumer acceptance. The campaign has convinced many consumers that the American Express card can help them buy products and services away from home, places where they are not known.

Acceptance seems to depend on what kinds of thoughts people have concerning the information imparted. Consider American Express's advertising message. Some consumers may develop a counterargument to the message. Perhaps they think that they can leave home without the American Express card because they usually carry enough cash. Or they may think poorly of the source of the ad: "Of course, American Express wants me to carry its card. It makes money off me if I do." Such thoughts may cause consumers to not yield to or accept American Express's advertisement. Another kind of thought, a support argument, may lead to accepting the message. Fortunately for American Express, many people apparently believe that the card is accepted by many retail businesses throughout the country and so they should not "leave home without it."[16]

Marketing managers should not assume that consumers are always actively and consciously thinking about the persuasive arguments of marketing offer information. Sometimes they are, but more often they are not. Only when consumers see the message as very relevant to them will they think about the message's arguments. In this case, yielding or acceptance is influenced by how powerful or convincing the arguments are. On the other hand, many messages are seen as not very relevant. Here, more peripheral factors, such as how much the source is liked or how pleasant the consumer felt when listening to the message, are more likely to determine acceptance. The implication is clear. Marketing managers must know how relevant and involving the product, service, or topic of the messages is likely to be before deciding how to persuade target consumers.[17]

Retention

People may attend to, comprehend, and accept information now but not make a related purchase decision until later. A football fan may see an advertisement for Michelob Light on "Monday Night Football" but not buy beer until the following Saturday. Whether this fan remembers the information will influence the ad's effectiveness.

Remembering is a form of learning. Exhibit 5-9 shows the ways in which people learn. Each way of learning is different enough to suggest alternative marketing approaches to help consumers learn brand appeals. Spending to deliver an ad over and over again is necessary for repetitive learning, while offering consumers some kind of reward aids in reinforcement.

Learning involves one of two kinds of memory tasks. Recall is one, and it occurs when a consumer must remember some specific information. When buying videotape, the buyer might have to recall whether the videocassette recorder at home uses the Beta or the VHS format. In contrast, only recogni-

EXHIBIT 5–9 Three Ways in Which People Learn

Type of Learning	Explanation	Illustration
Repetition	People learn by receiving the same information over and over again.	A buyer may readily recall an advertising message for low-price, high-value wine after seeing the ad a number of times.
Reinforcement	People learn by being rewarded for holding a certain point of view or for acting in a certain way.	A buyer may learn to like and to shop in a particular department store because of the help received in the past from salespeople.
Reasoning	People learn by gaining insight from similar but not identical experiences.	A buyer may learn that higher-priced tennis rackets are also better in quality because high-priced skis purchased previously have proved to be long lasting.

tion may be required where a consumer must discriminate one item from another. A shopper buying cereal may have to determine the difference in value of two different package sizes of the same brand.[18]

Opportunities for practical application of these learning ideas abound. Marketing tactics may help consumers accomplish both recall and recognition tasks. However, the approaches must be tailored to the particular task involved. Recognition is often necessary when a consumer shops in a store. When choosing between brands of frozen pizzas, a shopper may try to recognize a brand that was featured in a magazine advertisement seen several days before. The ad facilitates this task by showing the package and its usual location in a store; a promotional display in the store may show the scene from the ad. Aiding recall involves helping consumers store information in an easily retrievable form. Simple information in an advertisement, presented in a novel and interesting way, will be more easily recalled.[19]

Consumer Decision Making

Consumer decision making
is the process by which a consumer judges whether a product will meet a need or want well enough to warrant purchasing and using it; decides when, where, and how to make the purchase; and determines satisfaction with the purchase.

The last of our three important perspectives on consumer behavior is that buying products and services involves a decision-making process. Strict definitions of this process say that true decision making occurs only when consumers do extensive search for information in order to carefully evaluate two or more alternatives. Yet considerable evidence shows that this kind of decision making is not common.[20] A broader definition, more descriptive of what actually takes place, is that purchase decision making is the process that consumers use to match products with needs and wants. The most important idea in these definitions is that **consumer decision making** is purposive. Purchase decisions are made to satisfy needs and wants. Whether or not extensive information search or evaluation of more than one alternative takes place depends on a host of factors, including the buyer, the product, and the situation.

EXHIBIT 5–10 A Classification of Consumer Decision Making

| | Extent of involvement | |
	High	Low
High	Limited decision making	Habit decision making
Low	Extensive decision making	Very limited decision making

Familiarity with product (rows: High / Low)

A similar classification may be found in Henry Assael, *Marketing Management* (Boston: Kent Publishing, 1985), pp. 126–28.

Consistent with this view, there are different types of decision-making processes. A shopper in a store may purchase a brand of cereal with little or no forethought. Yet decision making has occurred if the shopper bought that brand for some purpose—as a taste treat, as a low-calorie breakfast food, or as a way of finding out how it tasted. On the other hand, a consumer's two-month search for the best 35-mm camera is also decision making.

A useful way of classifying types of decision making concerns the extent of involvement in the use situation and product choices and the degree of familiarity with product alternatives. Exhibit 5–10 shows this classification. Originally intended to explain persuasive communication's impact on audiences,[21] the involvement idea has been more recently applied to consumer purchasing. With *high involvement*, people feel that the purchase has great personal significance in their lives.[22] Purchases of cars, houses, fashion clothing, gifts, jewelry, furniture, computers, and videocassette recorders are but a few illustrations. When consumers are unfamiliar with products in a high-involvement purchase, an *extensive decision-making* process, including much search and evaluation, is likely to ensue. But if a consumer is familiar with purchase alternatives, much less search and evaluation are needed and *limited decision making* occurs.

Low involvement occurs when the purchase does not have much significance to a consumer. Products falling into the low-involvement category might include pencils, salt, adhesive tape, chewing gum, fast-food restaurants, and toothbrushes. Since people differ, a high-involvement product for one person may be a low-involvement product for another.

When consumers are familiar with a low involvement product, as might be the case with chewing gum, its purchase may take place by *habit*. A preferred brand is purchased with no search for or evaluation of other alternatives. Even when a consumer is not familiar with a product, only very limited

EXHIBIT 5–11 Consumer High-Involvement Decision-Making Process

decision making is likely. Price may be checked or package information read, but the feeling of low involvement prevents a more extensive process.

High-Involvement Decision Making

For high-involvement, unfamiliar purchases, consumers are most likely to use extensive information processing to reach a purchase decision. Exhibit 5-11 shows the steps in this kind of decision process. Managers can learn a lot about market opportunity by studying what consumers do at each step.

Need Recognition.   Given their various lifestyles, consumers are in many different use situations. Consequently, finding out which use situations will lead to needs or wants for a particular product may seem overwhelming. However, classifications of use situations can help marketing managers sort out the types in which their products' benefits are most likely to be wanted. An interesting classification is shown in Exhibit 5-12. It provides a useful perspective on the kinds of situations that lead to product needs and therefore to problem recognition.

Managers must also learn what needs stem from particular use situations. Then, the marketing offer can be tailored to meet those needs. A study of restaurant-related needs demonstrated that the dining situation played an important role in determining the desire to go to a restaurant and the specific restaurant preferred. Special occasions, such as entertaining an out-of-town

EXHIBIT 5–12 A General Classification of Use Situations

Customer Perception of Product Use Situations	Illustrative Problems, Wants, and Product Solutions	Customer Perception of Product Use Situations	Illustrative Problems, Wants, and Product Solutions
1. *Current problem*—people may be in some state or situation that is unpleasant, that they want to get out of.	a. Dry skin problems—soaps and creams. b. Oily hair—shampoos and rinses.	5. *Sensory pleasure opportunity*—a situation may offer an opportunity to feel sensory pleasure where the feeling is the end being sought.	a. Taste pleasure—ice cream, gourmet foods, fruits. b. Scent pleasure—perfumed soaps, wine, flowers.
2. *Potential problem*—people may anticipate that if something is not done now, a problem will arise later.	a. Bad breath—toothpaste and mouthwashes. b. Lack of social approval—prestige products such as fashion clothes.	6. *Product-related problem*—one of the first five situations, with the added conflict over whether to use a product in a use situation.	a. Side effects from product use—buffered aspirin, hypoallergenic toiletries, ecologically safe laundry detergent. b. Undesirable product characteristic—bad-tasting mouthwash, low-lead gasoline.
3. *Normal depletion*—a product may be gradually used up in the normal course of living. The use situation is not highly important, but more routine in nature.	a. Low on fuel—gasoline, fuel oil. b. Low on cleaners—dishwashing soaps, paper towels, napkins.	7. *Satisfaction-frustration*—a complex situation involving one of the first five situations plus the added dimension of having no satisfactory brand available for the situation.	a. Dog owners may dislike the appearance/odor of dog food but cannot find a brand that solves this problem. b. Overweight people may feel that no foods are tasty, filling, and low calorie at the same time.
4. *Interest opportunity*—a situation may provide a buyer with an opportunity to have fun, experience novelty, or acquire a feeling of being an expert.	a. Feeling of expertise—wine, stereos, perfumes. b. Desire for diversion—sports equipment, autos. c. Desire for fun—sports events, shows, movies.		

Source: Geraldine Fennell, "Consumers' Perceptions of the Product-Use Situation," *Journal of Marketing* 42 (April 1978), pp. 40–43. Reprinted from the *Journal of Marketing*, published by the American Marketing Association.

guest or celebrating an anniversary, were one kind of use situation. The needs in such a use situation included having a taste treat, an atmosphere in which quiet conversation could take place, and fine service to enhance the celebration. Atmosphere/specialty restaurants aim their marketing strategies at this combination of situation and needs.

Search for Information.   Consumers may seek information to identify and assess which products or brands will satisfy a need. How much searching is done depends on prior familiarity with products. Thus, search may be no more than recalling past experiences. Very limited decision making—buying a previously purchased brand again without considering other alternatives— is probably common even for high-involvement products. Returning to a favorite restaurant for a celebration is an illustration. Previous favorable experience with a product can be enough to convince a consumer to buy again.

When past experience is not adequate to make a choice, more extended decision making involving information search from outside sources is more likely to occur. Consumers use various sources for different purposes. Information from marketing-controlled sources—advertising, in-store signs and displays, packages, salespersons—tends to be used to learn about product availability, benefits, prices, and services. But to help decide which alternative product or brand is best, consumers often turn to more personal sources—the opinions of friends, relatives, and others not connected with selling the product.

The extent to which consumers search for information has important implications for marketing. Longer time spent in searching gives companies more time to reach customers with appeals. Further, consumers in this situation are more willing to actively seek information from companies. On the other hand, a less thorough search places more burden on a company to reach people quickly after the need has been recognized.

How might these differences affect advertising or distribution? Consider the challenge of selling radios, a product for which search is quite limited. Distribution will have to be through many outlets because people are not doing much to seek out brand alternatives. The brand has to be placed wherever people might look for radios. Local advertising that promotes brand availability, prices, and store location is more important than national advertising that communicates product benefits. Different marketing tactics are necessary to sell personal computers because most of the prospective buyers are likely to use a more extensive information search.

People apparently consider both the costs and the benefits of having more information when deciding how extensively to search.[23] The costs of searching include time, money, the opportunity cost of delaying the purchase decision, and frustration over trying to find and use relevant information. The counterbalancing benefits stem largely from the extent to which a consumer

EXHIBIT 5–13 A High-Involvement Alternative Evaluation Process

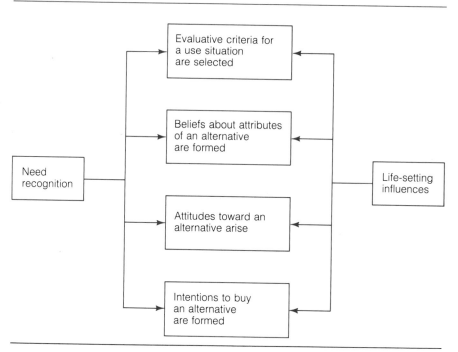

believes that new information will reduce the risk of making a bad purchase. A shopper may ask the druggist about an untried brand of aspirin, fearing an upset stomach from taking the wrong kind and feeling that the cost of talking with the druggist is low.

Influencing the perceived benefits and costs of information is a way of encouraging people to learn more about a company's brand. A manager who wants to draw more people into a store where consumers search for information about alternative products will make many marketing decisions that affect the perceived costs and benefits of conducting such a search at the store. Convenient location, plenty of free parking, and convenient aisle arrangements should lower the costs of search in the store, while an easy return policy, knowledgeable salespeople, and wide assortments should increase the benefits.

Alternative Evaluation. Learning what a product has to offer when it is used in a particular situation is the essence of the alternative evaluation step. Exhibit 5–13 shows the process. From a consumer's point of view, products are bundles of attributes providing benefits. A consumer might see a personal computer in terms of the amount of data storage, the ease of using the keyboard, the clarity and size of the screen, and the variety of compatible

EXHIBIT 5-14 Illustrative Evaluative Criteria for Two Restaurant Use Situations

Criteria Importance	Celebration Use Situation	Time Pressure Use Situation
More important	Atmosphere/decor	Fast service
	Menu specialties	Convenient location
	Reputation for fine cuisine	Tasty food
	Efficient table service	Low price
	Friendly personnel	Friendly personnel
Less important	Price	Decor

software. Consumers must determine which benefits are best for their uses—word processing, home finance, record keeping, games, and so forth.

Evaluative Criteria.   Evaluation is closely tied to need recognition through *evaluative criteria*—attributes or functions that a product must have to satisfy consumers needs. Since needs stem from use situations, these situations will influence which criteria are most important.

Exhibit 5-14 suggests criteria that are important in two different use situations affecting the choice of a restaurant—dining to celebrate an anniversary and eating a meal in a limited amount of time. In the former situation, decor, menu specialties, and efficiency of service are very important; in the latter situation, speed of service is a major consideration.

Beliefs.   Product attributes and evaluative criteria are closely related. People form *beliefs* about the extent to which a product provides benefits that match each evaluative criterion. When evaluating a restaurant for a celebration use, people will rely on beliefs about the restaurant to determine whether it has the atmosphere/decor they seek, the menu specialties they want, and so forth. Previous dining experiences, comments from friends, advertisements, and other sources of information are instrumental in the process of developing beliefs.

Attitude
is a feeling of like or dislike of a purchase alternative that is determined by individual beliefs about product attributes.

Attitude-Based Evaluations.   Consumers form overall **attitudes**—feelings of like or dislike of a purchase alternative—that may reflect evaluations of alternatives. To see how attitudes arise, consider the following attitude model:

$$A_j = \sum_{i=1}^{n} B_{ij} \times I_i$$

where:

A_j = An attitude toward product alternative j.

B_{ij} = The belief about the extent to which alternative j's attributes meets evaluative criterion i.

I_i = The importance of the ith evaluative criterion in determining how well an alternative meets needs.

n = The number of evaluative criteria used to assess how well a product will meet needs in a use situation.

Attitudes are formed from beliefs about a product. In other words, whether a consumer likes or dislikes the product depends on what he or she knows about it. Notice that beliefs about more important attributes will contribute more to determining a consumer's feelings than will beliefs about less important attributes.

The attitude model provides a very practical framework for understanding attitude-based evaluations of alternatives. First, a product may rate poorly on one evaluative criterion but compensate with strong ratings on other criteria. A restaurant may be able to charge very high prices if its atmosphere/decor, menu specialties, and reputation for fine cuisine are believed to be outstanding.

Second, the model shows that changes in evaluative criteria, the relative importance of criteria, or beliefs can lead to a change in overall attitude toward a product. Consider the rejuvenation of television sales in the 1980s. The industry repositioned the television as a "home entertainment and communications center."[24] Product modifications in sets gave television the ability to receive many cable channels and pay-TV programming. Moreover, plug-in features were added to make televisions more compatible with personal computers and videocassette recorders. At the same time, promotion sought to persuade consumers to use a new evaluative criterion—compatibility with other products. Thus, marketing was used both to stimulate problem recognition and to improve attitudes toward the television.

Non-Attitude-Based Evaluations.   Even in high-involvement decision making, alternative evaluation is not always based on overall attitudes.[25] Forming attribute-based beliefs for different alternatives requires a considerable amount of effort. If a consumer trying to decide which camera to buy wants to evaluate four brands of two types of cameras on seven evaluative criteria, a total of 56 beliefs (2 types × 4 brands × 7 criteria) is involved. Few of us could keep so many beliefs in mind at the same time.

Other models explain how consumers might simplify the evaluation task. Exhibit 5–15 presents simplifying procedures used by consumers. A consumer may try to eliminate some brands from further consideration based on how they stack up on a key criterion such as price: all brands that cost more than $120 will not be considered further, no matter what else they have to offer. If after this elimination process only one brand is left and the consumer buys it, no overall attitudinal evaluation has been used to make the purchase decision. Other ways in which consumers simplify the evaluation task also involve screening out alternatives without having to form overall attitudes. The implication of these screening processes is clear: unless a brand is perceived well on the screening criterion, further evaluation will never occur.

EXHIBIT 5-15 Simplifying Approaches to Alternative Evaluation

Lexicographic approach: The consumer decides on the relative importance of evaluative criteria and then compares alternatives on the most important criterion, first. All of the alternatives that do not meet this criterion are eliminated. Only the alternatives that remain after considering this criterion will be evaluated on the next most important criterion. This process continues until one alternative is left.

Conjunctive approach: The consumer sets minimum cutoffs for each evaluative criterion and then compares product alternatives with the cutoffs. If an alternative is below the cutoff on any criterion, it is rejected. The consumer may go through this process beginning with the most important criterion and proceed until an acceptable alternative has been found.

Disjunctive approach: This approach is similar to the conjunctive approach, except that an alternative above the cutoff on any criterion is accepted. Again, the criteria may be considered in sequence rather than all at once until an acceptable alternative has been found.

For more discussion of these models, see Peter Wright, "Consumer Choice Strategies: Simplifying vs. Optimizing," *Journal of Marketing Research* 12 (February 1975), pp. 60-67.

Intentions. An *intention* is a consumer's felt likelihood of buying a product. When evaluations are attitude-based, consumers usually express higher intentions to buy what they like best than what they do not like as well. When evaluations are not attitude-based, more positive beliefs concerning the crucial evaluative criteria will lead to higher intentions to purchase that product. However, two qualifications must be kept in mind (refer to Exhibit 5-13). First, intentions to buy are relevant only when a need has been recognized. Second, influences from a consumer's life setting—social influences—may override product-specific beliefs and attitudes. Thus, a businessman may decide not to buy a Cadillac even though that brand is the one he likes best, because he does not want his business associates, customers, or friends to see him driving an expensive car.

Purchase Decision. We know that consumers do not always follow through on their intentions. Developments at the purchase stage may cause the consumer to make a less preferred choice or not buy at all. A consumer who intends to buy a particular tennis racket at her favorite store may settle for another racket if that store does not carry the one she wants. On the other hand, if she feels strongly enough about the racket, she may go to other stores until she finds one that carries it.

Circumstances at the time of sale may also influence purchase decisions. The shopper's preferred brand may be out of stock, leading to no sale. Or talking with a salesperson may cause a shift in preference to a brand that the shopper had not intended to buy when he or she entered the store.

For inexpensive, frequently purchased products, a consumer's decision to try the company's brand once is less significant than a decision to buy it repeatedly. Managers at Wilson Sporting Goods Company know that repeat buying of its tennis balls by frequent tennis players is crucial to this product's success. However, for infrequently purchased and expensive items—cars, boats, houses, and major appliances—an initial or onetime purchase is very important.

Purchase/Use Outcomes.   Increasingly, managers realize the importance of understanding what happens after a purchase. Consumers who are dissatisfied with a product may complain about it to friends, relatives, or even the seller. In contrast, a favorable experience with a product may lead to testimonials to others, compliments to the seller, and possibly repurchase the next time the need arises.

Satisfaction or *dissatisfaction* is a consumer's emotional feeling about the experience of using a product or service. Based on their past experience, the marketing efforts of companies, and interaction with others, consumers learn performance standards for a product. These standards are either expectations (predictions of the chosen brand's performance) or norms (the performance that a brand should be able to deliver). Consumers will notice how the chosen brand performed in a use situation. To evaluate that performance, they will compare it to the standard. If they believe that the chosen brand's performance matches or exceeds the standard, they will feel satisfied. If not, they will feel dissatisfied.[26]

This view of satisfaction and dissatisfaction has several interesting implications. A consumer does not have to believe that a product performed at a high level to be satisfied. If a meal at a fast-food restaurant lives up to the consumer's standard for that restaurant, the consumer may be quite satisfied with the meal even though he or she does not believe that the food was particularly nutritious or exceptionally tasty. That consumer would probably be dissatisfied if the same meal were served in a haute cuisine restaurant, because the consumer's standards for the haute cuisine restaurant would no doubt be different.

Further, the standard for a product's performance may be influenced by a consumer's experience with other brands or products. Norms as standards may be based on the typical performance of all brands in a product class or on the usual performance received from a highly regarded brand. A consumer's satisfaction with the dining experience at a new specialty restaurant in town may be based on how that experience stacks up against previous experiences at another specialty restaurant, perhaps the consumer's favorite.

Finally, consumers' standards can change even though the performance of a particular brand remains very consistent. As consumers gain experience with different brands, satisfaction may increase or decrease simply because new standards are set. The new specialty restaurant in town may be so good that it becomes the favorite restaurant for many diners. Now all other specialty restaurants are evaluated against the dining experiences with the new favorite.

Satisfaction and dissatisfaction motivate consumers. Surprisingly, their relationship to actual behavior—e.g., complaining directly to the seller about an unfavorable experience—is not as strong as we might expect. Apparently, other factors also play a significant role in determining what people do. However, consumers are more likely to think that they will buy a product again or to tell others about it if they feel satisfied with its performance.[27]

Low-Involvement Decision Making

Many products are purchased with much less enthusiasm and effort than is typical for high-involvement decision making. Nonetheless, even for low-involvement purchases, the decision-making process holds with a few modifications. Low-involvement buying is generally a need-satisfying process, so the need recognition and purchase choice stages occur. However, the need is not particularly significant, as when a consumer has a spur-of-the-moment desire for something sweet and buys a candy bar.

The major difference between low- and high-involvement decision making lies in the search for information and the evaluation of alternatives. First, there is likely to be little or no information search. Our consumer with the sweet tooth may make an immediate purchase if she is familiar with the candy bar. At the most, if the candy bar is new to her, she may read the label, but she will probably do little more. In fact, the purchase may be a way of learning more about the product.

The evaluation of alternatives will also be simple. The consumer may have no attitude toward the alternative selected, basing the choice only on the benefits that the consumer believes the alternative has. And no other alternatives may have been considered. Choosing a new candy bar may be based only on the beliefs that it contains chocolate and that the package looks nice. Only after eating the candy bar will the consumer decide whether she likes it or not. Further, the whole process may happen so quickly and with so little effort that the consumer may be unaware that a decision-making process has taken place.[28]

Reaching consumers who engage in low-involvement decision-making processes is a challenge for marketing. So little time and effort are spent on the purchase choice that information aimed at convincing consumers of the benefits of the product is likely to be selectively ignored. Getting consumers to try the product on the spur of the moment is crucial. Free samples, coupons, and prominent display in stores are tactics that encourage consumers to try a low-involvement product. Further, building an overall positive feeling toward the product among consumers, as opposed to emphasizing specific attributes, is an important objective for the entire marketing offer.

— *Application* —

The Consumer Behavior Model

Marketing managers cannot expect to learn everything there is to know about consumers. There is not enough time or money to do it all. Thus, marketing managers must be selective when requesting buyer behavior information for a particular application. A consumer behavior study for a large department store illustrates this idea. The store's marketing strategy for its clothing departments centered on maintaining an image of fashion leadership and quality merchandise. The store's managers were pleased with the success of this strategy in the primary target markets. However, a secondary target market, students attending the state university, had not been reached nearly as well.

Management felt that these students offered considerable potential for fashion clothing sales. Yet, for unknown reasons, they did not patronize the store very much. Management decided to gather survey data on students' buying behavior to find out why (i.e., a diagnosis purpose). The objective of the study was to determine how the store's marketing offer might be tailored to better match the fashion clothing needs of students. Questionnaires were completed by a sample of university students.

Demographic Characteristics

To classify respondents, data on demographic characteristics were collected (Exhibit 5–A). More than 30 percent of the students in the sample were 22 or older. This surprised management, which had thought that nearly all of the university students were younger than 22. The percentage of students who did not belong to fraternities or sororities was more than three times as large as the percentage who did belong. The Greek organizations were apparently not as important as reference groups for fashion clothing purchases as had been believed.

The Decision-Making Process

A major portion of the study concentrated on store choice decisions. To a retailer, the most important buyer behavior decision is the selection of a store in which to shop. Because of the significance of fashion clothing to students' lifestyles, management assumed that high-involvement decision processes were being used.

Beginning with need recognition, the results showed that a particular use situation, going

EXHIBIT 5–A Student Demographic Characteristics

Characteristic	Percent of Student Sample
Age:	
17–19	38.3
20–21	31.0
22–24	16.4
Over 24	14.3
Sex:	
Male	44.5
Female	55.5
Marital status:	
Married	16.8
Single	83.2
Sorority/fraternity membership:	
Member	23.7
Nonmember	76.3

back to school in the fall, typically caused students to recognize a need for clothing. Students were anticipating the upcoming situation several weeks ahead of time. Particularly significant was the fact that students were still in their hometowns when they began thinking about buying clothing.

To learn about the information search process, students were asked to rank the importance of several sources of fashion clothing information. Management wanted to know how much each source influenced students' purchase decisions. Advertising and store displays were ranked as only slightly less important than information provided by friends, classmates, and personal preference (Exhibit 5–B). Sales personnel and fashion shows were rated much less important. These findings were very enlightening to management. For years, fashion shows had been used as the primary tool for drawing students into the store. Once customers were in the store, management depended heavily on its sales personnel to help students select the most appropriate fashions. Almost no advertising was aimed directly at students.

For evaluation of alternatives, the study measured students' store selection criteria and stu-

EXHIBIT 5-B Importance Rating of Buyer Information Sources

Fashion Information Source	Average Rating*
Personal preference	1.88
Friends/classmates	2.26
Advertising	2.75
Store displays	2.81
Sales personnel	4.26
Fashion shows	4.59

* (1 = very important; 7 = unimportant)

dents' beliefs about the department store and a major competitor (Exhibit 5-C). After examining the findings, management was very pleased with students' beliefs about the store's merchandise offerings. Notice that the department store was rated better than the competition on merchandise-related evaluative criteria. Moreover, the ratings were very good in an absolute sense.

Advertising appeared to be far more effective with students than management had expected.

EXHIBIT 5-C Students' Beliefs about the Department Store and a Major Competitor

Store Dimension	Average Rating: Department Store*	Average Rating: Competitive Store*
Selection of different types of clothing	2.00	2.30
Quality of merchandise	1.96	2.05
Number of brands carried	2.35	2.42
Appealing, informative advertising	2.41	2.57
Frequency with which advertising is seen	2.56	2.63
Prices compared to other stores	3.85	3.71
Value for dollars spent	3.14	3.08
Friendly, courteous sales personnel	2.66	2.85

* A 1-to-5 scale was used to measure students' beliefs, where 1 = the most positive belief on a criterion and 5 = the least positive belief.

Many students were being reached by the store's advertising. Equally important, students generally believed that the advertising was appealing and informative.

Data on the remaining beliefs suggested reasons for lack of strong patronage. First, students believed that the store was charging relatively high prices for its merchandise. To make matters worse, "value received for dollars spent" was apparently not being communicated effectively. Sales personnel were not perceived as particularly friendly or courteous. Since management considered the helpfulness of personnel on the floor to be a critical part of selling, this result was very disturbing. Interestingly, the competitive store was apparently having similar difficulty.

Data on the purchase stage provided several insights into student shopping for fashion clothing. By far, students preferred shopping in a department store; however, over half of the students bought their clothing outside the city (Exhibit 5-D). These students arrived on campus in the fall and after vacations with most of their clothing purchases already made.

Decisions Based on the Study's Findings

The survey of students was instrumental in guiding management's subsequent marketing decisions. The buying power of students was

EXHIBIT 5-D Preference for Type of Store and Location

Type of Store	Percent Preferring
Department store	51
Specialty shop	28
Discount store	21

Location of Purchases	Percent Buying
Outside the city	52
In the city	
Downtown	20
Shopping centers	21
Shops near campus	07

attractive, and their beliefs about the department store's merchandise were more favorable than was expected. Even though many students were buying elsewhere, the opportunity to increase sales among them was considered sufficiently attractive. Management decided to allocate more resources to the student target market.

A portion of the advertising budget was aimed at increasing student patronage. Media having high readership among students were added to the schedule. Messages provided information on specific fashions and emphasized the store's theme of fashion leadership. Communication was changed by using words and phrases familiar to students and a generally irreverent tone and by stressing fashion as an expression of individuality.

Sales promotion decisions were a response to several uncovered weaknesses. The store's fashion shows had been quite elaborate and expensive, using models, varieties of fashions, and considerable lighting and sound equipment. Based on the survey and informal discussions with students, management switched to much less expensive mini-fashion shows. Emphasis

was placed on providing fashion knowledge rather than on showing a wide range of fashions.

During student registration in the fall, a booth was set up to provide refreshments and information on current fashions, the location of the store, and store merchandise. Management wanted to demonstrate the store's interest in students as customers. Finally, the store's sales training program was reevaluated. The program was modified to place more emphasis on fashion knowledge and on how to show an interest in students' fashion needs.

The application of buyer behavior information to a department store's marketing program is an example of diagnosis at work. It demonstrates the importance of having an overall perspective on buyer behavior when determining what information is needed and when analyzing the data. Evident throughout was management's view of students as information processing, need-satisfying consumers reacting to a life setting use situation for fashion clothing. Marketing strategy and tactical decisions were an outgrowth of management's attempt to better match the department store's appeals to students' purchase decision processes ▪

Summary

Studying buyer behavior, whether that of consumers or industrial buyers, is an integral part of market opportunity analyses. Results help managers diagnose buyers' behavior or predict their future behavior. Both purposes are essential for marketing decision making that is intended to influence buyers. Thus, marketing managers must become accustomed to applying buyer behavior information and also to being involved in determining what information is needed for a particular decision.

Application begins with a basic understanding of the nature of buyer behavior. Our current view is based on three key perspectives: (1) buyer behavior is influenced by the buyer's environment; (2) buyer behavior involves people reacting to and interacting with their environment by seeking, receiving, and using information; and (3) buyer behavior is generally a purposive, decision-making process. These perspectives can be combined into an overall model that serves as a framework.

Because there are important differences between consumer and industrial buying behavior, a separate model is needed to describe each of these kinds of buying behavior. The consumer behavior model describes information and decision-making processes in the context of a consumer's macroenvironment and immediate use situation.

Five categories of macroenvironmental forces that affect consumer behavior were discussed in Chapter 3. While all of these forces can influence consumer behavior, many studies concentrate on the social forces arising from interaction with others. Cultural values, social class, reference groups such as the family, and lifestyles all exert powerful influences on consumers that affect buying. Understanding these social forces can be important in selecting target markets and in designing marketing offers. A more transient influence comes from use situations for a product. Consumers can anticipate these situations and then buy products that they feel will best help them deal with the situations.

Consumer buying behavior is generally a purposive, decision-making process that begins with recognizing a problem and proceeds to purchase and subsequent satisfaction or dissatisfaction. There are different kinds of decision processes depending on the degree of involvement felt by the consumer. High involvement with a product or a situation is most likely to lead to limited or extensive decision making, depending on a consumer's familiarity with product alternatives. On the other hand, low involvement encourages only very limited or habitual decision making. The differences lie in the extent of search for information and evaluation of alternatives that a consumer is willing to undertake before making a purchase.

A model of consumer behavior suggests guidelines for selecting important information to gather for an application. The perspectives contained in such a model are particularly important for diagnostic purposes. Marketing managers must be able to specify the kinds of information they need for a decision, and the model helps with this task.

Exercises for Review and Discussion

1. Several government agencies are charged with protecting consumer welfare. For instance, the Federal Trade Commission (FTC) periodically considers proposed regulations that affect both consumer welfare and the marketing decisions of business firms. Illustrations include unit pricing, truth in lending, and restrictions on advertising to children. Suppose that you are an adviser to the FTC. Would you advocate incorporating analyses of consumer decision making into the evaluation of and debate over these proposals? Why or why not?

2. A national fast-food restaurant chain has recently experienced a leveling off of growth in both sales and market share. Management is concerned that important changes in the market have occurred that have not been taken into consideration by either corporate managers or the managers of individual restaurants. Other than tracking sales over the past few years, little market opportunity analysis has been done.

Management has decided to approve a marketing research project to learn more about buyer behavior in its markets. Research objectives are the first consideration. How would you go about determining the most important objectives for this study? How could a buyer behavior model help you with this task?

3. The consumer behavior model presented in this chapter is descriptive. That is, it describes the essence of the way consumers go about making purchase decisions and evaluating how well the purchases turned out. Is there a need for normative models of consumer behavior that describe how consumers *should* go about making purchase decisions? Discuss your answer.

4. An important feature of the buyer behavior model presented in this chapter is the view that buying is a decision process with several steps. What is the significance of this view for planning and controlling marketing strategy? Discuss your answer.

5. Use the consumer behavior model presented in the chapter to describe the probable similarities and differences among consumer purchasing of automobiles, videocassette recorders, toothpaste, and soft drinks.

6. Suppose that you were appointed to the board of directors of a nonprofit charity in your community. The charity has not been able to generate the gifts it needs to support planned activities. Adapt the model of consumer behavior to fit the charity's situation (e.g., the charity's supporters are the "buyers"), and then discuss how studies of buying behavior applying this model can help the board of directors.

7. Weston's Department Store in Jackson, Ohio, is one of two major department stores serving local markets. The advertising manager received a report of a survey of shoppers conducted on selected days of the week and selected weeks of the year. The manager scanned the data and immediately noticed that there were very few shoppers between 18 and 30, even though this age group is a large one in the

community. She wondered what could be done to attract more 18–30-year-olds to the store. Does the advertising manager need information for diagnosis? For prediction? Discuss your answer.

8. The owner of a construction company that specializes in remodeling homes was talking with an account representative for a local advertising agency. The construction company had never advertised before, but the owner wanted to try out an advertising campaign to see whether it would spur sales. The account representative suggested conducting a study of consumers in remodeling markets to "find out about consumers' lifestyles, attitudes, values, and family decision making." The study would be used to help design the advertising campaign. But the owner said, "I don't see how spending money on that study would help. We already know that consumers want a better-looking home." How would you respond to the owner's objection if you were the account representative? Discuss your answer.

Notes

1. The Lean Cuisine story is discussed in "Manufacturers Undaunted by Failures in Quest for New Product Successes," *Marketing News*, November 22, 1985, p. 17.

2. Ibid.

3. This definition of buyer behavior is similar to that in James F. Engel, Roger D. Blackwell, and Paul W. Miniard, *Consumer Behavior* (Hinsdale, Ill.: Dryden Press, 1986), p. 5.

4. David A. Ricks, *Big Business Blunders* (Homewood, Ill.: Richard D. Irwin, 1983), p. 63.

5. Richard P. Coleman, "The Continuing Significance of Social Class to Marketing," *Journal of Consumer Research* 10 (December 1983), p. 271.

6. Rosann L. Spiro, "Persuasion in Family Decision-Making," *Journal of Consumer Research* 9 (March 1983), p. 394.

7. John H. Mather, "No Reason to Fear 'Frightening' Reality of VALS," *Marketing News*, September 13, 1985, p. 15.

8. William D. Wells, "Psychographics: A Critical Review," *Journal of Marketing Research* 12 (May 1975), p. 198.

9. For a discussion of definitions and research on use situation, see James H. Leigh and Claude R. Martin, Jr., "A Review of Situational Influence Paradigms and Research," in *Review of Marketing*, ed. Ben M. Enis and Kenneth J. Roering (Chicago: American Marketing Association, 1981), pp. 57-74.

10. Rajendra K. Srivastava, "Usage-Situational Influences on Perceptions of Product-Markets: Theoretical and Empirical Issues," in *Advances in Consumer Research*, ed. Kent B. Monroe (Ann Arbor, Mich.: Asssociation for Consumer Research, 1980), p. 109.

11. For a review of this research stream, see Robert W. Chestnut and Jacob Jacoby, "Consumer Information Processing: Emerging Theory and Findings," in *Consumer and Industrial Buying Behavior*, ed. Arch Woodside, Jagdeth Sheth, and Peter Bennett (New York: Elsevier-North Holland, 1977), pp. 119–33.

12. Terrence R. Smith, Andrew A. Mitchell, and Robert Meyer, "A Computational Process Model of Evaluation Based on the Cognitive Structuring of Episodic Knowledge," in *Advances in Consumer Research*, ed. Andrew A. Mitchell (Ann Arbor, Mich.: Association for Consumer Research, 1981), p. 138.

13. Andrew A. Mitchell, "Models of Memory: Implications for Measuring Knowledge Structures," in *Advances in Consumer Research*, ed. Andrew A. Mitchell (Ann Arbor, Mich.: Association for Consumer Research, 1981), p. 46.

14. Ibid., p. 47.

15. Ricks, *Big Business Blunders*, p. 24.

16. Engel, Blackwell, and Miniard, *Consumer Behavior*, pp. 226–28.

17. Richard E. Petty, John T. Cacioppo, and David Schumann, "Central and Peripheral Routes to Advertising Effectiveness: The Moderating Role of Involvement," *Journal of Consumer Research* 10 (September 1983), pp. 135–46.

18. The concepts of recall and recognition are discussed at length in James R. Bettman, "Memory Factors in Consumer Choice: A Review," *Journal of Marketing* 43 (Spring 1979), pp. 37–53.

19. These and other implications for marketing are discussed in Bettman, "Memory Factors," pp. 49–51.

20. Richard W. Olshavsky and Donald H. Granbois, "Consumer Decision Making—Fact or Fiction?" *Journal of Consumer Research* 6 (September 1979), pp. 93–100.

21. Clark Leavitt, Anthony G. Greenwald, and Carl Obermiller, "What Is Low Involvement Low In?" in *Advances in Consumer Research*, ed. Kent R. Monroe (Ann Arbor, Mich.: Association for Consumer Research, 1980), p. 15.

22. Harold H. Kassarjian, "Low Involvement: A Second Look," in *Advances in Consumer Research*, ed. Kent R. Monroe (Ann Arbor, Mich.: Association for Consumer Research, 1980), p. 31.

23. For a thorough discussion of this idea, see Joseph W. Newman, "Consumer External Search: Amount and Determinants," in *Consumer and Industrial Buying Behavior*, ed. Arch Woodside, Jagdeth Sheth, and Peter Bennett (New York: Elsevier-North Holland, 1977), pp. 79–94.

24. "TV: A Growth Industry," *Business Week*, February 23, 1981, p. 88.

25. James R. Bettman, "A Functional Analysis of the Role of Overall Evaluation of Alternatives in Choice Processes," in *Advances in Consumer Research*, ed. Andrew A. Mitchell (Ann Arbor, Mich.: Association for Consumer Research, 1981), pp. 88–90.

26. For an in-depth discussion of this view of consumer satisfaction processes, see Robert B. Woodruff, Ernest R. Cadotte, and Roger L. Jenkins, "Modeling Consumer Satisfaction Processes Using Experience-Based Norms," *Journal of Marketing Research* 20 (August 1983), pp. 296–304.

27. Ernest R. Cadotte, Robert B. Woodruff, and Roger L. Jenkins, "The Relationship between Standards of Performance, Disconfirmation, and Satisfaction: A Test of Theory" (working paper, University of Tennessee, 1984).

28. Flemming Hansen, "Hemispheral Lateralization: Implications for Understanding Consumer Behavior," *Journal of Consumer Research* 8 (June 1981), p. 32.

CHAPTER 6

Industrial Markets and Buying Behavior

Borg-Warner, a longtime manufacturer of industrial and consumer products, found a "silver lining" in the trouble it had with its Norge appliance division. In an attempt to keep distributors and dealers from leaving the Norge distribution network, the company set up the Borg-Warner Acceptance Corporation (B-WAC), which offered distributors and dealers financial assistance for inventories, a service not offered by competitors. When Borg-Warner's management decided to get out of the appliance business, it also wanted to stop offering the financial assistance service. Strong reaction from customers caused it to reconsider the latter move.

Borg-Warner found that appliance distributors and dealers wanted to continue using the financial assistance service to finance inventories purchased from other manufacturers. Success in this endeavor encouraged B-WAC to branch out into such related services as accounts receivable financing, personal credit and insurance, and equipment leasing. Today, service businesses are as important to Borg-Warner's total earnings as are its manufacturing operations.[1]

As Borg-Warner's move into services illustrates, organizations purchase products and services for use in their operations. These organizations are end users, and the management of selling firms must plan marketing strategy to meet their needs. This chapter examines the buying behavior of organizations. The first section looks at the nature of organizational buying. Then, organizational and consumer buying are compared. The third section examines the makeup of organizational markets, concentrating on the market opportunity analysis task of identifying the firms comprising markets for the seller's product. This is followed by a discussion of purchase decision making by buying organizations. The chapter concludes by considering the many influences that affect the outcome of organizations' buying decisions.

EXHIBIT 6-1 Classification of U.S. Organizations (1977-1978)

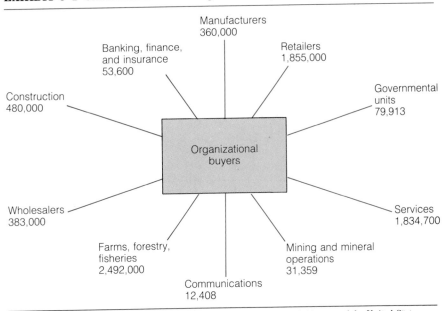

Manufacturers
360,000

Banking, finance,
and insurance
53,600

Retailers
1,855,000

Construction
480,000

Governmental
units
79,913

Organizational
buyers

Wholesalers
383,000

Services
1,834,700

Farms, forestry,
fisheries
2,492,000

Mining and mineral
operations
31,359

Communications
12,408

Source: U.S. Department of Commerce, Bureau of the Census, *Statistical Abstract of the United States: 1984* (Washington, D.C : U.S. Government Printing Office, 1983).

The Nature of Organizational Buyer Behavior

Industrial buying refers to the buying activities of organizations that purchase products and services for end-use purposes.

Not all of the organizations that buy goods and services are alike. Some of the differences among them are apparent in the U.S. government's classification of organizations. Exhibit 6-1 shows the number of establishments in each of several categories of organizations that buy products and services. Although not all of these organizations are private, for-profit companies, we refer to their purchasing as **industrial buying.**

The overwhelming majority of organizations in the United States and around the world are small. Exhibit 6-2 shows a distribution of U.S. manufacturing firms across five size categories. Most of these firms are in the less than 20 employees category, while the smallest percentage of firms is in the category with 1,000 employees or more. On the other hand, the exhibit demonstrates that the largest manufacturing firms provide most of the value added and most of the product sales (shipments). These patterns also characterize other types of industrial buyers.

Organizations buy buildings, plant and office equipment, furniture, supplies, raw materials, packaging, products for resale, and such services as insurance, financing, consulting, and transportation. Most of these industrial purchases are indirectly linked to the economy's purpose of satisfying consumer demand. Consider consumers' demand for ice cream which creates

EXHIBIT 6–2 Size of U.S. Manufacturers as Indicated by Number of
Employees (1977)

	Number of Employees				
	Less than 20	20–29	100–249	250–999	More than 999
Percent of all establishments	67.5%	22.3%	6.1%	3.4%	0.6%
Percent of all employees	6.5	18.8	18.0	29.1	27.5
Percent of all shipments	2.2	15.6	16.2	29.8	34.2
Percent of all value added	5.1	15.4	15.8	29.5	34.2

Source: U.S. Department of Commerce, Bureau of the Census, *Statistical Abstract of the United States:
1984,* (Washington, D.C.: U.S. Government Printing Office, 1983), p. 775.

many industrial markets—paper cartons, milk and cream, business insurance, distribution services and so forth. (Exhibit 6–3).

Industrial buyers purchase a larger volume of products and services than do all consumers. The ice cream illustration shows why. Many transactions go on between companies so that manufacturers can produce the ice cream and get it to where consumers can buy it. Thus, many industrial purchases precede each consumer purchase.

Comparing Industrial and Consumer Buying Behavior

Industrial buying behavior refers to the actions of persons employed by an organization to purchase products or services for the organization, including the communication and decision processes that determine the selection of products and suppliers as well as satisfaction or dissatisfaction with the purchases.

Many of the factors that apply to consumer buying behavior also apply to **industrial buying behavior.** In general, the similarities between the two types of behavior outweigh the differences.[2] Both consumers and industrial buyers look for specific benefits from products being considered, establish criteria for evaluating alternatives, form beliefs and attitudes about sellers and their offers, and buy products intended to satisfy needs.

The differences between consumer and industrial buying are differences more of degree than of kind. In general, many of the same factors are operating, but not necessarily in the same way or to the same extent. In comparing the two kinds of buying, some differences of interest are:

- The organizational setting for buying.
- The product knowledge of buyers.
- The goals established to guide buying.
- The amount and quality of contact with suppliers.
- The number of people who influence and make the purchase decision.
- The factors determining buyer demand.

EXHIBIT 6-3 Industrial Markets Created by Consumer Demand for Ice Cream

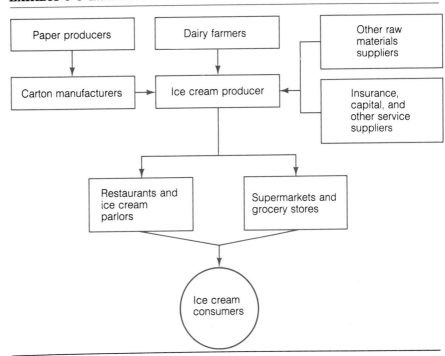

Organizational Setting

The people who make buying decisions are part of some buying unit. The household is often the relevant unit for consumer buying. The majority of households include more than one member, each of whom has a voice in many consumer buying decisions. Industrial buying, in contrast, is done by people who work for organizations, which typically have a formal chain of command and assigned responsibilities for their employees. Yet in both multiperson households and organizations, people interact in well-defined ways. This interaction is a major influence on who contributes to buying decisions and on the way in which buying activities are carried out.

The impact of the overall organization on buying is apparent in the process that a large pharmaceutical manufacturer used to purchase a quality control instrument. The process began when the plant manager decided whether the instrument had priority over other needs. This decision was formalized in the plant's capital budget, a plan listing expenditures for equipment and other investment purchases. After the purchase was authorized, quality control engineers took over the buying process. With help from purchasing managers, the engineers evaluated how well various types of instruments would work in the intended application. Together, engineers and a purchasing manager decided on the supplier from whom to purchase the instrument. As you can see, this process is more formal and involves more people than is typical for even very expensive consumer purchases.

Selling to industrial purchasers can be more difficult than selling to consumers as a result of the organization's influence. In selling the quality control instrument, identifying the employees in the pharmaceutical manufacturer's plant to hear a sales presentation may take considerable effort. A presentation to someone in the purchasing department, the most obvious organizational point of contact, may not get the information to those who most influence the purchase decision.

Many industrial buying decisions are not as complex as this decision of the pharmaceutical manufacturer. The number of people involved in some industrial buying decisions can be quite small. In a small construction firm, the owner may be the sole decision maker involved in the purchase of a computer to help with record-keeping. The firm's accountant and a secretary might give advice on the features needed and the brand to buy. This interaction is more similar to the interaction that goes on in many household purchase decisions than to the interaction that would take place if the same product were purchased by a large firm such as General Mills.

Product Knowledge

Because of their training and their job-related experience, industrial purchasers typically have more product knowledge than do consumers. And the product knowledge of industrial purchasers can be spread among different people in an organization. In the pharmaceutical manufacturer's purchase of a quality control instrument, the formal training of engineers helps them understand how this product works, and their job-related experiences add to that understanding. As a result, they already know or can quickly learn how the quality control instrument works. Similarly, purchasing managers develop technical knowledge from past experience, from working with other employees, from reading product literature, from talking with salespeople, and from observing the use of products in the plant. Consumers can also learn about products, but they generally do not acquire the training and experience needed to become highly knowledgeable about the products they are buying.

When selling to industrial buyers, marketing managers must be able to communicate with the knowledgeable buyer. Industrial promotion must often provide more technical information than is generally contained in promotion to consumers. That is why a salesperson for a drug manufacturer is trained extensively to discuss the medical benefits of a drug. In addition,

EXHIBIT 6-4

Industrial product advertisements, such as this one for Wang computer networking, provide more technical information than is typical of many consumer product advertisements.

Courtesy Hill, Holliday, Conners, Cosmopulus, Inc.

industrial advertisements typically present more technical information on product performance than is found in consumer advertisements (Exhibit 6-4).

Industrial buyers are not always well informed about the products they buy. Industrial salespeople may work with organizational buyers who know very little about the products they want to purchase. Computer manufacturers face this situation in the sale of personal computers. Many of these computers are bought by owners of small businesses and managers in various departments of larger organizations who do not understand what computers can do or how to get the full benefit of their capabilities (Exhibit 6-5). The marketing strategies of computer manufacturers have been helping to build product knowledge among such industrial buyers.

On the consumer side, many markets have segments that comprise con-

EXHIBIT 6–5 Making Sure Computers Earn Their Keep

How do you make computers into truly competitive weapons and not just fancy typewriters or calculators? That's a headscratcher for many businesses. Imperial Oil Ltd., Exxon Corporation's Canadian affiliate, is one company that's slowing the pace of computer purchasing until it comes up with some answers.

After four straight years of 18 percent spending increases, this year it will lay out $88 million (U.S.) for computer expenses. That's 9 percent more than in 1984. "Everyone is trying to position technology more effectively than in the past," explains Timothy J. Hearn, manager of Imperial's systems and computer services department. Hearn calls it "integrating computer plans with business plans." He says Imperial's initial use of computers was to automate simple tasks. Now the company is trying to decide how to make broader use of computers, for instance to do research or design sophisticated marketing plans.

Over the years, Imperial has accumulated seven mainframes, a handful of minicomputers, and 3,000 terminals. Individual managers initiated the purchases of an additional 1,000 IBM personal computers. Now upper management is reining in this expansion. For the first time, data processing managers, as well as their counterparts in other departments, have to explain how their purchases would advance

Imperial's strategic plans. Says James C. Hamilton, manager of the company's Planning and Technology Division: "You find a super product coming next month. But now there's no way you're going to buy it" without such justification.

At the same time, Imperial has halted the steady staff increases that expanded its data processing department from 400 people in 1980 to 500 now. And computer budgets that used to be determined largely by how much the machines cost are subjected to tougher criteria. What's more, data processing managers have to take account of external factors, such as how much competitors spend on processing—the same test that Imperial applies to other spending.

To make sure computers are used effectively, Imperial has put its systems managers on the management committees of business units. That way, they can better understand the problems their computers must solve. Conversely, the company has put a marketing man, Hearn, in charge of data processing.

Hearn interprets his appointment as proof of Imperial's determination to make its computer operation more effective. That job should test his mettle plenty. And it could keep Imperial's computer suppliers waiting for more than a few months.

Source: Bill Javetski, "Making Sure Computers Earn Their Keep," *Business Week*, June 24, 1985, p. 78.

noisseurs with extensive product knowledge. Though relatively few in number, connoisseurs are important because they typically buy products of the highest quality and account for an impressively high percentage of all products purchased. Sports enthusiasts, wine and stereo buffs, computer hackers, hobbyists, and do-it-yourselfers are but a few of the many kinds of consumers who know a lot about certain products.

Purchasing Goals. Consumers buy for their own use or for use by people close to them. Personal goals are important to consumers when deciding what to buy. Industrial buyers buy for their organizations, not just for themselves. But since people are doing the buying in organizations, both personal and organizational goals play a role in industrial buying.[3] This dualism of goals can complicate the marketing task. Salespersons for a supplier may have difficulty in knowing whether personal or organizational goals are more important to the buyer. A buyer of metal cans, a product that does not differ much from supplier to supplier, considers such organizational goals as cost control, package safety, and delivery time when choosing a supplier. At the same time, that buyer may like to be entertained and let this very personal goal influence the size of orders given to different suppliers. An industrial supplier has little choice but to respond to both goals. Exhibit 6–6 compares personal and organizational goals.

EXHIBIT 6-6 Goals Influencing Industrial Buying Decisions

Personal Goals	*Organizational Goals*
Want a feeling of power	Control cost in product use situation
Seek personal pleasure	Few breakdowns of product
Desire job security	Dependable delivery for repeat purchases
Want to be well liked	Adequate supply of product
Want respect	Cost within budget limit

Buyer Contact with Suppliers

When selling to consumers, a company must plan a marketing strategy that is effective for many buyers, sometimes numbering in the millions. Marketing managers do not have the opportunity to deal directly with each and every one of these buyers. On the other hand, an industrial seller usually has a much smaller number of buyers in its target markets. A manufacturer of artificial turf for sports applications has to sell to only the handful of companies that are in the business of installing these surfaces for municipalities, universities, colleges, and school systems. Similarly, a regional distributor of appliances has only a few hundred retailers as customers.

Industrial markets are typically more centralized geographically than consumer markets. Industry buyers often concentrate in certain areas due to their favorable labor supply conditions or their proximity to raw materials or markets. The geographic concentration of markets must be considered by marketing managers in planning many parts of the marketing mix, including sales promotion, distribution, and pricing.

Smaller target markets and greater geographic concentration of buyers also have an important impact on personal selling. There can be much more direct selling to industrial markets than is typically feasible in consumer markets. Salespeople can interact face-to-face with buyers, and middle- and upper-level managers are often able to meet with buyers. Managers of consumer product companies rarely have that opportunity.

Who Makes the Buying Decision?

For each buying unit in a consumer market, there can only be a relatively small number of people who are important to the purchase decision. Household size is the limiting factor, and households are very small. Because industrial buying is done by organizations, a buying unit may include several people who have a say in a purchase. Of course, in a small business such as a home building and remodeling company, the owner and very few others may do the purchasing. However, even in organizations of moderate size, the number of people affecting a buying decision may be much larger.

One study of purchasing in the chemical industry found that an average of five people influenced the purchase decision but that in a few cases the figure was as high as 50. In only 13 percent of the purchases covered by the study did the purchasing agent make the decision alone.[4] In the industrial setting, not only is the number of people who have a say in purchasing relatively large, but personnel from top management as well as from different departments—production, purchasing, engineering—are involved. Each of these people brings a different point of view to the purchasing situation.

Buyer Demand

Derived demand refers to the fact that purchases by industrial buyers are affected by the demand for their products or services.

Reciprocal demand occurs when two companies are purchasing products or services from each other.

A factor that industrial buyers consider in many of their purchase decisions is the outlook for sales in their target markets. When sales forecasts are favorable, industrial buyers tend to purchase more products and services. Thus, industrial purchasing is a **derived demand.**

Industrial buying is also complicated by the fact that buying and selling among firms may be interconnected. Some sellers may also be buyers of their customers' products. While the buying and selling activities should be independent, often they are not. If a large steel company purchases a fleet of cars from an automobile manufacturer that just happens to be a major customer for its steel products, the steel and automobile companies have **reciprocal demand** for each other's products, introducing another influence on purchase decisions in both companies.

Analyzing Industrial Markets

Because consumer and industrial buying behavior are not the same, market opportunity analyses for industrial markets differ in important respects from those for consumer markets. While the general MOA framework applies equally well to both types of markets, obtaining certain kinds of information about industrial buyers is more complicated than obtaining comparable information about consumers. Identifying which personnel in a buying organization influence a purchase decision is usually more difficult than discovering who is making the buying decisions in a household.

At the same time, the general questions that marketing managers want answered about buying behavior are essentially the same for both industrial and consumer markets. These questions are:

- Who makes up the markets?
- How do the buyers make purchase decisions?
- What kinds of influences affect their purchase decisions?

The Makeup of Industrial Markets

The first step in a market opportunity analysis is to identify who is in the market for the seller's product or service. When analyzing industrial markets, marketing managers begin by classifying types of organizations in markets. Then, information is needed to determine who inside these organizations is likely to influence and make purchase decisions.

Classifying Organizations. Marketing managers for consumer goods companies often use demographic/socioeconomic characteristics to classify their end users. Industrial sellers rely on similar characteristics for the same purpose. Industrial buyers can be grouped by such factors as sales volume, number of employees, amount of repeat sales, geographic location, order size, and products produced and sold.[5]

Many industrial sellers are particularly interested in classifying buyers by products produced and sold. The product(s) a company produces and sells determines many of the kinds of products and services it must buy. Pharmaceutical companies that sell sterilized drugs must buy equipment that enables them to meet sterilization standards. A sterilization equipment manufacturer can classify these industrial buyers into one market category. Other markets can be found by looking for other types of companies that need sterilization in their operations because of the products they produce—food companies, product testing laboratories, chemical companies, and so forth.

Additional characteristics may be used to further subdivide each major market category. These finer classifications help marketing managers spot the most important organizations in a category. Market categories are often broken down by size of buyer, such as large-, medium-, and small-volume firms. Very often, a relatively few buyers account for most of the purchases within a market category. These are typically the larger firms whose size of operations makes them heavy users of a product. Classification by size helps marketing managers concentrate on these most important buyers.

Who Influences, Makes the Decision? Marketing strategy planning can benefit from knowing which people in buying organizations are involved in a purchase decision. A marketing program is aimed at these people. Further, industrial salespeople attempt to make their presentations to the influential persons in each buying organization.

Many organizations have a purchasing department. Purchasing agents or managers from this department are the most obvious people to include in a description of buyers. Purchasing agents have many responsibilities, among which are identifying suppliers of a product, collecting information on suppliers and their products, negotiating price for a purchase order, and working with suppliers' salespersons. Surprisingly, the purchasing agent is quite often a lower-level manager who is more likely to implement a purchase order than to make or even seriously influence purchase decisions. At the same time, there is a trend toward upgrading the purchasing agent's position. Such companies as Du Pont, Sperry-Rand, and Kaiser Aluminum have gone as far as creating a position of vice president of purchasing. In these companies and others, managers are recognizing how important purchasing can be in reducing costs. One source estimated that purchasing expenditures are as high as 50 to 60 percent of a company's sales dollars, so there is considerable incentive for seeking these savings.[6]

Recent studies of industrial buying show that formal lines of authority in an organization are not necessarily good clues as to who is involved in a purchasing decision. Industrial purchasing may be influenced by persons who are not members of the organization units that have been assigned buying responsibility. An organization's **buying center** includes all of the people who have some say in a purchase decision. Since the involvement of people changes for different buying decisions, the buying center changes from purchase to purchase. Not everyone in the center plays the same role, of course. In fact, a number of different roles have been identified, as Exhibit 6–7 illustrates with a purchase decision for telecommunications equipment.

The existence of buying centers suggests that joint decision making is characteristic of many industrial purchases. This interaction is crucial in determining the outcomes of decisions. Before planning marketing strategy, marketing managers must understand not only what persons are involved but also their different needs. One executive puts it this way:

> In other words, we must know who is the champion and who could have veto power. Specific people who assume these roles can be end-users, engineering specifiers, senior administration managers, purchasing agents, and unrelated influencers such as "someone you trust." They can also be people outside the organization, such as industry consultants. Each participant in the decision-making process brings a different perspective to the role, depending on background and degree of involvement. And they have different needs. For example, the purchasing agent who is working with engineering on specifications will have different information needs than the buyer who is ready to review bids.[7]

To learn about buying center interaction, the seller must first identify who is in the buying center, a difficult task. Even more difficult is the task of finding out where the power lies in the buying center. In some firms, power may correspond to a formal job title, as when a purchasing agent is given authority to make purchase decisions. Other firms may have more informal ways of determining who has control. The relationship between a person's department and the power to make buying decisions is not always consistent. Consequently, the selling company must use other clues to discover to whom it should direct its marketing programs. An industrial salesperson may have to carefully observe communications among people in the buying organization to see where the power is.[8]

Buying center comprises all of the persons inside or outside an organization who are involved in making a purchase decision, including the persons who influence that decision in some way.

EXHIBIT 6-7 Buying Center Roles for a Telecommunications Purchase

Initiator	Division general manager proposes to replace the company's telecommunications system.
Decider	Vice president of administration selects, with influence from others, the vendor the company will deal with and the system it will buy.
Influencers	Corporate telecommunications department and the vice president of data processing have important say about which system and vendor the company will deal with.
Purchaser	Corporate purchasing department completes the purchase according to predetermined specifications by negotiating or receiving bids from suppliers.
Gatekeeper	Corporate purchasing and corporate telecommunications departments analyze the company's needs and recommend likely matches with potential vendors.
Users	All division employees who use the telecommunications equipment.

Source: Thomas V. Bonoma, "Major Sales: Who *Really* Does the Buying?" *Harvard Business Review,* May–June 1982, p. 113.

Purchase Decisions by Industrial Buyers

Since marketing programs are intended to influence industrial buying decisions, marketing managers should try to understand how industrial buyers make these decisions before planning a program. The experience of Fokker, a Dutch airplane manufacturer, illustrates the value of doing this. Fokker designed a new airplane that could seat up to 100 passengers for short trips. When submitting bids for purchases by airlines, Fokker had to compete with Boeing, McDonnell Douglas, and British Aerospace. One potential customer was Swiss Air Transport Company. To have any chance of getting the Swiss Air order, Fokker's management had to find out how the choice between competitors would be made. Knowing that Swiss Air buyers considered fuel economy, efficiency of the cockpit instrumentation (particularly for operating in heavy fog, a common problem in Switzerland), and price enabled Fokker to make important design decisions and thus improved its chances for getting the sale.[9]

Most experts on industrial buying behavior see this kind of situation as involving a purchase decision process.[10] This simply means that industrial buyers go through a series of steps in determining what products or services to buy and from which sellers. Of course, the steps used and their sequence can vary from one purchase to another.

Industrial Buying Situations.

How industrial buyers decide what to buy seems to depend on the type of situation at hand. In part, situations differ according to how "new" the purchase is to the organization and how much information is needed to make a choice. Three types of situations have been identified:

- New task

EXHIBIT 6–8 Industrial Buying Situations

New task: The purchase decision concerns a product or service with which the members of the buying center have practically no relevant purchasing experience; considerable information is sought, and extensive effort is made to evaluate several alternatives. An illustration would be a manufacturer buying a fleet of delivery trucks for the first time.

Modified rebuy: The purchase decision concerns a product or service that is intended to replace one currently being used by the company; the buying center is considering products or services other than the one now being used, so information is gathered on these alternatives. An example would be the replacement of an industrial robot with a superior model.

Straight rebuy: The purchase decision concerns a product or service that has already been purchased frequently; the buying center has considerable experience with the product and needs little or no additional information; the buying center reorders the product or service from the same supplier. A construction firm that is reordering lumber would be in this situation.

- Modified rebuy
- Straight rebuy.[11]

Exhibit 6–8 provides a brief description of each type.

These types of situations are affected by two additional characteristics. The first is the complexity of the purchase decision. This characteristic covers a number of factors, including how much information has to be collected, how many people are involved in the decision, the amount of training needed to use the product, and the impact of the product on organizational procedures. Many of these factors are evident in the first-time purchase of a computer by an appliance distributor that wanted to computerize its record-keeping system and provide better information for management decisions. Computerizing a record-keeping system will affect many people in the organization—from those that gather and input data to those that use the computer's output. Further, computers are complex and new to the company and its personnel. For these reasons, the computer purchase will be more complicated than, say, the routine purchases of office supplies. The other characteristic is the importance of the purchase to the organization, where importance might be measured by the effect of the purchase on productivity or financial performance.[12]

New tasks and modified rebuys present the greatest challenges to industrial buyers, and they should expect to spend more time and to exert more effort in these situations. Larger buying centers, including people from different departments, are needed for such decisions. Straight rebuys are much more routine and are most likely to be handled by the purchasing department. In fact, straight rebuys can become so systematized that some companies let a computer take them over.

Types of Industrial Buying Decisions. Industrial buying includes several kinds of decisions. Three particularly important purchase decisions are:

EXHIBIT 6-9 Important Decision Influences by Decision Phase

Decision	Primary Influence	Secondary Influence
Initial	Engineering	Purchasing
Determine type	Engineering	Production
Draw up specs	Engineering	Production
Evaluate sources	Purchasing	Production
Select supplier	Purchasing	Corporate management
Determine Amount	Corporate management	Purchasing and production
Final authority	Corporate management	Purchasing

Source: Gary L. Lilien and M. Anthony Wong, "An Exploratory Investigation of the Structure of the Buying Center in the Metalworking Industry," *Journal of Marketing Research* 21 (February 1984), p. 6.

- Authorization to purchase the product or service.
- Determining product specifications.
- Choosing a supplier.

Each of these decisions is quite likely to be made by different people, at least in the larger organizations. Thus, the makeup of the buying center can change for each decision.[13] To illustrate the involvement of people from different functions, Exhibit 6-9 shows typical buying center participation in the metalworking industry.

Selling to industrial buyers is complicated by buying center changes. Marketing managers must determine how marketing programs can influence a favorable decision at each step. A sale is not going to take place, no matter how good the seller's product is, unless the industrial buyer specifies desired product characteristics offered by that seller. A small instrument manufacturer ran into this situation in trying to sell its product to large pharmaceutical companies. The product's major performance benefits were extremely high accuracy in measuring temperature and a very competitive price. For this manufacturer to be included in the list of acceptable suppliers, its sales personnel had to convince engineers and quality control personnel (users) that "high accuracy" should be included in the product specifications for instrument purchases. Only then could the company provide information showing competitive superiority.

Buying Decision Process. While industrial buying is best viewed as a decision process, the steps that make up the process differ across companies and products.[14] Steps needed in a new task or modified rebuy decision may not be necessary in straight rebuy decisions. Over time, each organization evolves its own procedures for making purchase decisions. However, steps common to many decisions provide a model of industrial buying:

1. Recognizing a need.
2. Identifying suppliers.
3. Determining product specifications.
4. Searching for information and evaluating suppliers.
5. Negotiating a purchase order.
6. Evaluating performance of the product/supplier.

A substantial part of profiling customers, a key activity in market opportunity analysis, should be devoted to helping marketing managers understand from a purchaser's point of view how this process is used by the company's customers.

Recognizing a Need.   Industrial purchasing starts with a need for a product or service. While there are many different kinds of needs, most needs arise out of situations related to the operation of the business. In the purchase of an instrument for measuring temperature by a food processing company, need for a new instrument arises when any of the following situations occurs:

■ A temperature measurement instrument currently on line breaks down.

■ New temperature instruments are needed as part of a plant expansion.

■ New temperature instruments are needed to meet a more stringent accuracy requirement for quality control.

■ A quality control engineer comes back from a trade show with information on a new instrument that can save the plant money.

■ Research and development is testing a new product and wants a temperature instrument for laboratory work.

All of these situations have one thing in common: Industrial buyers make purchase decisions to solve problems related to operating the business or to take advantage of new business opportunities. Sellers learn about the various reasons for industrial buyers' purchase decisions to seek guidelines for planning marketing programs. Suppose the seller of sterilization equipment learns that instrument breakdown is a common reason for problem recognition and that when an instrument breaks down, the sterilization process stops until the instrument is repaired or replaced. Guided by that information, the seller includes in its marketing program a guarantee of a temporary replacement instrument if the instrument purchased breaks down. Understanding the industrial buyer's need-recognition situation helps the seller see how important this service is to subsequent purchase.

Need recognition is not always as complicated or involved as it is in new task and modified rebuy decisions. It can be very routine, particularly in straight rebuy situations. A large construction company may negotiate a contract with a steel beam supplier to replenish inventory on demand. Purchase orders are automatically written and sent to the supplier when the inventory reaches a prespecified level. Such routine buying situations offer the best opportunities to use computer reordering.

Identifying Suppliers. When a need for a product arises, the industrial purchaser must decide whether to make the product or to buy it from a supplier. The make or buy decision may be reassessed periodically. After years of buying cans from outside suppliers, several soft-drink and beer manufacturers decided that the advantages of making their own cans outweighed the disadvantages. While cost savings are an important factor in the make or buy decision, management also considers such other factors as dependability of supply and improved quality control.

If the decision is to buy from an outside supplier, then alternative sources of supply must be found. A list of acceptable suppliers from which bids can be solicited is developed. Typically, the purchasing agent is responsible for putting together this list.

For straight and modified rebuys, the purchasing agent probably already has acceptable suppliers in mind from previous experience. In new task situations, the purchasing agent may check with technical people and managers in other departments to identify suppliers. In addition, the purchasing agent scans direct mail or trade journal advertisements and may even talk with purchasing agents from other companies.

Once a list of suppliers has been compiled, preliminary information is collected from each supplier, including financial reports, product brochures, product samples, and data on facility size and location, number of employees, and existing customers.[15] At this point, the suppliers' facilities may be visited to learn about their capabilities.

If there are many suppliers on the list, a screening procedure is needed that bases decisions on criteria. The information gathered enables the industrial buyer to quickly look for suppliers that do not meet minimum requirements. These requirements might be delivery time, capacity to meet the buyer's quantity needs, and breadth of the product line. Failure to meet a minimum requirement usually means that a supplier will not be included on the list of acceptable suppliers no matter how well that supplier stacks up on other criteria. For special reasons, however, a rule may be bent. Because of good past service to the company, a purchasing agent may, for example, put on the list a supplier that does not meet the minimum requirements.

The result of this initial screen is a list of suppliers to evaluate further. The length of the list varies depending on the trade-off between the risk of including too few sources of supply and the difficulty of extensively evaluating many suppliers' bids. Typically, at least three suppliers are included.

Determining Specifications. Before asking suppliers for additional information, members of the buying center must specify product performance characteristics, quantity needed, delivery and installation requirements, and price limits. For the pharmaceutical firm's purchase of a temperature measuring instrument, the product specifications would include:

- Accuracy range of the instrument.
- Ability of the instrument to handle a given number of sterilizer units.
- Ability of the instrument to maintain an accuracy level under specified conditions.
- Paper readouts of temperature.
- Easily movable from one place to another.
- Per unit price of under $6,000.
- Twenty-four-hour repair service for broken instruments.

Well-developed specifications come from studying anticipated uses of a product. Input from primary users may be obtained at this point. The final set of specifications is written by technical experts with help from interested users. Such collaboration worked well for a college of business at a large state university. The college allocated money for a large number of microcomputers that were to be used by both faculty and students. A committee was formed of people from the university's computer center and faculty who had had extensive experience with microcomputers. The committee took several months to study the ways in which the microcomputers would be used. One of its findings was that faculty and students wanted to be able to interface the microcomputers with the university's main computer. As a result, a specification was written that required compatible equipment and programs.

Information Search and Supplier Evaluation. New task and modified rebuy purchases require additional information to evaluate alternative products and suppliers. Purchasing department personnel play an important role by gathering relevant information for buying center members. A wide variety of information sources are available to the skilled purchasing manager. Direct requests for specific information from the supplier company are also common.

A buying center may have to evaluate several product types for a particular use before suppliers can be selected. If products are complicated, technically trained people sort through the alternatives to recommend those that meet previously developed product specifications. For instance, many companies deal with the rapidly changing technology of computer products (both hardware and software) by creating task forces that keep current on product developments. A task force recommends product types that are suitable for particular applications.[16]

Suppliers of a desired product are further evaluated. The procedures are very similar to those used for evaluating products. The criteria selected describe the performance expected from chosen suppliers. Each supplier is evaluated by comparing anticipated performance against these criteria.

EXHIBIT 6-10 Supplier Choice Model

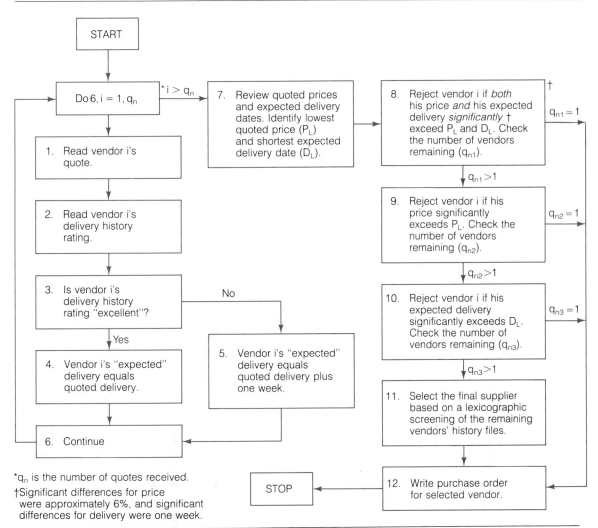

*q_n is the number of quotes received.

†Significant differences for price were approximately 6%, and significant differences for delivery were one week.

Source: Lowell E. Crow, Richard W. Olshavsky, and John O. Summers, "Industrial Buyers' Choice Strategies: A Protocol Analysis," *Journal of Marketing Research* 17 (February 1980), p. 41.

The initial screening processes used to narrow the list of suppliers typically apply very few criteria. Smaller suppliers may be eliminated from further consideration simply because they cannot provide the selection of products, volume, or range of services wanted. Size is an easy criterion to apply when judging which suppliers can meet these performance needs.

In a study of how buying centers choose a supplier, a model of the process used by the majority of firms was developed (Exhibit 6-10).[17] Essentially, steps 1 through 6 describe information-gathering activities, with delivery as a key buying criterion. Steps 7 through 12 represent the evaluation process, which relies heavily on information on file for each supplier. Price and delivery are used as criteria for screening out unacceptable suppliers. Only suppliers that meet these criteria are evaluated further. The "lexicographic screening" in step 11 includes additional criteria that are evaluated, one at a time, until only one supplier is left. This supplier gets the order.

Value analysis
is a procedure used by buyer organizations to evaluate the worth of a product to be purchased; it is based on assessing the functions of the product in the situation in which it will be used and the value of those functions.

Value analysis is a tool used by some industrial buyers to determine which criteria are most important for evaluating products and suppliers. Such analysis predicts the value of a product to the company. It begins by determining the functions that a product is to perform. These functions are stated simply: "to measure temperature within the desired accuracy range," "to support a weight load of 10,000 pounds," and so forth. The prices and costs of using alternative products are assessed to determine the value of each alternative to the industrial buyer. A summary criterion is the maximum value that can be obtained. This value is provided by the product that performs the required functions at the desired level for the lowest cost.[18] Sellers must understand how buyers apply value analyses (see Exhibit 6–11). As one marketing manager argues:

> Industrial selling demands emphasis on quantifying and documenting costs and benefits of the product to the prospect. Closing a sale often hinges on proving the product's advantages relative to the competition, particularly when the sale is made to interdepartmental committees. To develop such a sales tool, management must identify, examine, and document the range of customer situations into which the product will sell.[19]

Negotiation of Purchase Orders. When industrial buyers are considering more than one supplier, they receive formal offers from each of the suppliers being considered. Some industrial purchasers require each supplier to submit a *bid*—a listing of the products to be supplied and their quantity, any other support services, and price. In the purchase of microcomputers by the college of business of a large state university, a list of specifications for the order was sent to several suppliers with an invitation to bid. The specifications covered:

1. The brand of the computer.
2. Memory.
3. Hardware peripherals such as printers and modems.
4. Software.
5. Quantities of all hardware and software.
6. Miscellaneous hookup components.

Suppliers were asked to submit bids showing how they would fill the order and at what price. These bids were compared to find the one that met the specifications at the lowest price.

EXHIBIT 6-11

Control Data Business Centers advertises the value of its human resources and payroll services system to potential buyers.

Courtesy Hicks & Greist, Inc.

A similar procedure, commonly used when purchasing the services provided by such professionals as attorneys, consultants, architects, accountants, and marketing researchers, is a *request for proposal* (RFP). The purchasing company requests proposals from preselected suppliers or makes a general announcement inviting proposals. Suppliers develop written offers that explain how the desired services will be provided and state the price charged.

Finally, an industrial buyer may negotiate a *contractual agreement* with a supplier. An agreement of this kind can cover a single purchase of a product or repurchases of the product over a period of time. Contracts are commonly used in straight rebuy situations. The buying center of a large supermarket chain enters into contracts for purchases of frequently sold products—soap, toothpaste, peanut butter—over a period of a year or more.

In new task and modified rebuy situations, and even in some straight rebuy situations, purchasing managers try to ensure that several quotes are received. These quotes are evaluated to select a supplier for further negotiation. If a large number of quotes are received, the buying center may use *noncompensating evaluation strategies* to quickly eliminate the weaker suppliers from further consideration. Suppliers are evaluated on one or a few criteria at a time, usually product quality, support services, delivery terms, and price.[20] For example, suppliers that cannot meet required delivery dates may be dropped from the list.

When the number of suppliers is very small, *compensating evaluation strategies* are more likely to be used. Here, the buying center sifts through information to see how suppliers stack up on all or most criteria, considering trade-offs among the criteria. A supplier with a higher price, for instance, may be accepted if product quality or support services warrant the extra expense. The result of this process is that the buyer selects one or a combination of suppliers. A purchase order may simply be written to these suppliers, or, if the buying center thinks that more favorable terms can be obtained, a purchasing agent may negotiate with them.

Because there is much direct selling to industrial markets, the interaction between buyers and suppliers can be a major factor influencing purchases. Interaction may be limited to talking with a supplier's sales personnel. But for large purchases, managers who are very high in the management of a supplier company may become involved with customer management. In one company, a manufacturer of precision instruments, the president makes calls along with sales personnel when a particularly big order is on the line. The president is able to answer questions and make commitments that the salesperson cannot.

When negotiating with a supplier, the purchasing agent is under pressure to meet the diverse requirements of the buying center. This pressure can make the purchasing agent less flexible and less willing to compromise. For this reason, negotiations may break down even when the seller thinks that a fair quote has been submitted.[21]

Two approaches are available to purchasers and sellers when trying to win concessions in a negotiation. One is *competitive bargaining*, which uses threats, persuasive arguments, promises, and other such means to gain an advantage. The other is the *coordinative approach*, which relies on problem solving, cooperation, and trust to reach an agreement. Studies indicate that the seller's approach has an important influence on what the buyer will do. If the seller is cooperative, provides requested information, and works with the buyer, the buyer is more likely to respond with the coordinative approach.[22]

Many industrial buyers prefer to have more than one supplier of a product. This reduces the risk of supply being interrupted for such reasons as a strike at the sole supplier's plants. Further, the purchaser's bargaining position is stronger when it is not totally dependent on one supplier. General Motors' supplier selection decisions apply this logic. The company determines in advance the percentage of orders for various types of steel that it will award each steel producer. GM's management does not want to become dependent on any one supplier.[23]

Evaluation of Supplier Performance. Industrial buyers usually want to know how well suppliers comply with the purchase agreement. Thus, an important part of industrial purchasing is evaluation of suppliers after purchase. This task is typically assigned to the purchasing department. The criteria used for supplier selection become performance standards for this evaluation.

Information is collected on the performance of the product or service in use. A questionnaire may be sent to users of the product to obtain their input. Other, more technical measures of performance may also be devised. A manufacturer that purchases aerosol packaging, for instance, may select a sample of its packaging and test it for pressure and evenness of application.

Other terms of the purchase are also evaluated. One of the more important terms is the delivery agreement. Because purchased products and services are used in the buyer's own operations, on-time delivery is often necessary to keep these operations running smoothly. A soft-drink manufacturer must have aluminum cans on hand to meet its production schedule. For a single purchase order, a onetime evaluation may be made. If periodic deliveries are required, delivery times are monitored to regularly evaluate how well the supplier is meeting delivery commitments.

How a supplier's actual performance matches the standards is crucial to the degree of satisfaction felt by the industrial purchaser. Dissatisfaction may lead to demands on the supplier for the correction of problems or the improvement of performance. Even worse, dissatisfaction may cause choosing a different supplier. On the other hand, a high degree of satisfaction with the way the supplier has complied with a purchase agreement may generate goodwill that will help secure future orders. Thus, the incentive is typically very strong for suppliers to fulfill purchase agreements.

Influences on Organizational Buying Behavior

Economic factors are not the only influences on industrial buying decisions. Many other factors must be analyzed to understand why industrial buyers make the choices they do. These factors fall into four categories:[24]

- Environmental influences
- Organizational characteristics
- Buying center interaction
- Individual buyer characteristics

Influences from the Environment. Many conditions in the environment in which a buying company operates affect its purchasing. Governmental regulations, changes in demand for the buyer's products, technological innovations, the cost of funds, and shortages of supplies are among the factors that buyers must contend with. Buying centers react to these factors by adjusting their purchases of products and services. Thus, suppliers must be ready to change their marketing strategy to keep up with buyers' changing purchase needs.

Suppliers study how various environmental influences affect their customers. Understanding which factors are most important to their customers' purchasing decisions is a start. Then, suppliers look for changes in these factors to predict how buyers will adjust their purchases. An illustration is provided by industrial toolmakers' analysis of their markets. The customers of industrial toolmakers are manufacturers that use tools in production processes. These manufacturers' need for tools is closely tied to market demand, rising when it grows and declining when it shrinks. Recently, U.S. agricultural and construction equipment manufacturers have been hard hit by lessening demand for their products, so this market for industrial tools has been depressed. On the other hand, the markets of automakers and defense contractors have been growing, making these customers more attractive to industrial toolmakers. Forecasting such shifts in customers' markets is essential for marketing planning.

Organizational Characteristics. Every organization has certain goals and objectives, accepted procedures for purchasing, and an organizational structure, all of which influence its purchase decisions. These organizational characteristics provide clues for determining how one industrial buyer might be different from another and how purchase decisions are likely to be made. The goals and objectives of an organization influence the types of products it needs and the criteria by which it evaluates suppliers. Procter & Gamble strives to have products of higher quality and better performance than those of the competition. As a result, various aspects of quality receive very high priority in its purchase decisions.

Over time, companies develop procedures for making purchase decisions. By law, many governmental organizations must use bidding when making a purchase. Specifications for a purchase are established, and suppliers must submit bids as described in the bid request or general notice. Because the specifications allow little room for varying the product, delivery, or other nonprice terms, the supplier with the lowest bid is often selected. Other industrial purchasers with different procedures are likely to have criteria that reflect more nonprice considerations. Suppliers can use their understanding of these procedural differences to adjust marketing programs aimed at different buyers.

Organizational structure assigns responsibilities and authority for decision making to job positions across a company. The formal structure can influence buying by determining who should make purchase decisions. Some companies assign high-level authority for purchasing decisions to purchasing managers, while others do not. Informal relations among people in different job positions in a purchasing organization can also affect buying decisions. This is particularly important in determining who is in an industrial buyer's buying center. Informal power centered in office management and secretarial positions, for instance, can affect purchases of office equipment.

A marketing manager should not automatically look at organizational factors as just constraints. The challenge is to find ways of turning them into opportunities. Returning to the toolmaker illustration, manufacturers of industrial tools are joining with major customers such as General Motors to develop tools and to support such products as sensors. This effort should generate new purchases as the toolmakers help their customers achieve the goal of completely automated factories.[25]

Buying Center Interaction.   The buying center is an especially important influence because interaction among the members of a buying center affects purchase decisions. One aspect of such interaction is the possibility of *conflict* among members in making a buying decision.[26] A purchasing manager and a product user may have quite different opinions about how important price is relative to product quality and specific product features. The purchasing manager is evaluated in terms of the price savings attributed to the purchasing department's efforts, so he or she sees price as very important. In contrast, the product user is more concerned with how well the product performs and may therefore see product features as more important than a low price.

Suppliers need to know about such conflicts and how they will probably be resolved so that a marketing program can be adjusted accordingly. If the purchasing manager can win out over the product user, a logical tactic is to direct most of the selling effort toward the purchasing manager and emphasize the product's competitive price. On the other hand, the purchasing manager and the product user may resolve the conflict through compromise by weighing price, product features, and delivery equally. Here, the supplier should allocate its selling effort more evenly among buying center participants.

Finding out about buying center conflict is not easy. Buying center participants may not want to talk about such conflict to outsiders. However, salespeople and others having direct contact with buying center members should watch carefully for indications of conflict and how it is resolved. Even during a product presentation, a salesperson can listen to the conversation among individuals from the buying organization for clues to conflict.

Individual Buyer Characteristics.   Clearly, individuals make buying decisions for organizations. Thus, the makeup of these individuals is a major factor influencing purchasing decisions. Characteristics that are particularly important for sellers are personal goals, personality traits, opinions and attitudes, job-related experience, values, and lifestyles. These are very similar to the relevant characteristics of consumer buyers. A supplier's challenge is to learn about these characteristics so that selling appeals can be tailored to the individual nature of buyers. As one marketing manager notes:

Sales and marketing managers should encourage reps to adjust their sales initiatives by observing precisely what type of prospects they are talking to. Reps then should classify the prospect's behavior, determine the priorities associated with that behavior, and respond to them. The conventional approach to instructing sales reps about prospects—"this is how you approach steel buyers, computer manufacturers, or bankers"—is much too limiting.[27]

A supplier's sales representatives can learn to spot and keep records of important characteristics of industrial buyers. Market research may also be needed to find out more about the people the supplier is selling to. This information can help in the planning of selling approaches that take into consideration differences among buyers. A buyer who has an assertive personality will probably want to be in charge and direct the interchange during a sales call. Further, the buyer is not likely to want to waste time with idle conversation. The supplier's sales representative should make a very efficient presentation to this buyer and quickly discuss the benefits of the product. Another buyer may have a much more amiable personality. Here, the sales representative should develop a more relaxed and low-key sales presentation.[28]

In general, analyzing industrial buyer behavior is a challenge for any marketing professional. A supplier must learn about the individuals in the buying center and how they go about selecting products and suppliers. Only then can a marketing plan be designed to appeal effectively to those who will make the purchase.

Summary

Consumer buying helps create demand for many products and services in organizations. Industrial buying behavior occurs as these organizations buy what they need to maintain and expand their operations. Manufacturers, wholesalers, retailers, governments, and other organizations make up markets for industrial sellers.

Whether in households or in organizations, people make buying decisions. For this reason, industrial buying behavior is similar in many ways to consumer buying behavior. Characteristics of the individuals doing the buying influence both kinds of buying. Moreover, both kinds of buying are the result of decision making, so the steps in the purchase decision process provide an important model for analyzing

both consumer and industrial buyer behavior. These and other similarities are apparent from a comparison of Chapters 5 and 6. At the same time, there are significant differences between consumer and industrial buying. The steps in the decision process, the criteria for making purchase decisions, the influence of the organization, and the size of and interaction among the members of buying units are among these differences.

Marketing managers, whether for sellers of consumer or industrial products, have basically the same needs for buyer behavior information. Thus, industrial marketing managers want to know who industrial buyers are, how they make buying decisions, and what influences those buying decisions. While these questions are the same as those asked of consumer buyers, the answers are different.

Identifying industrial buyers is a classification activity that involves grouping organizations into markets. A supplier must also determine which persons in a buying organization are involved in the purchase. These people constitute a buying center. Typical buying center members are purchasing managers, engineers, product users, and top management.

Not all industrial purchasing is the same. The different purchasing situations include new task, modified rebuy, and straight rebuy purchases. These situations indicate that past experience with a purchase decision and the novelty of the alternative products considered affect how purchasing decisions are made. The complexity of the purchase and the importance of the product to the organization are other factors that affect the handling of purchasing decisions. Further, purchasers make different kinds of decisions during a purchase. Authorization for a purchase is one kind. Other kinds are product specifications, quantity ordered, delivery terms, and choice of suppliers.

Need recognition initiates a buying process. Unless a straight rebuy is indicated, product specifications must be determined. If more than one supplier is considered, information is needed to evaluate each of these suppliers. There are many different sources of such information, and the purchasing manager plays an important role in getting it. A selection process based on preset criteria such as product quality, service, delivery, and price must be implemented.

During the buying process, there may be considerable interaction between the supplier and buying organizations. Usually, some negotiation is necessary before a purchase order is made.

Industrial buyers are concerned with how well the supplier met the commitments it made when the purchase order was accepted. Managers apply the same criteria that were used in supplier selection to evaluate suppliers after the purchase has been made. Future purchases are affected by how satisfied the buying organization is, so the supplier has a great incentive to perform well.

Finally, many kinds of influences affect a buying center's purchase decision. These influences can be grouped into four major categories: environmental influences, organizational characteristics, buying center interaction and conflict, and personal characteristics. Learning about the influences in these categories can provide important clues to planning effective marketing programs.

Exercises for Review and Discussion

1. "Because prices are higher at retail than at other levels in channels of distribution, the dollar volume of sales to consumers is larger than the dollar volume of industrial sales." Do you agree with this statement? Why or why not?

2. Jack Labaron worked in the marketing research department of Procter & Gamble. He was responsible for studies conducted for brand managers planning marketing strategy for the various P&G consumer brands. Then, Jack went to work in the marketing research department of AT&T. The studies he worked on were intended to generate information about the company's industrial buyers of telecommunications equipment and services. Would Jack's understanding of consumer buying developed from his work at P&G be of any use in his work at AT&T? Discuss reasons for your answer.

3. Joyce Donovan was having trouble selling to several of her customer companies. She worked for a manufacturer of specialty instruments used in quality control and R&D. The customer companies were new accounts, and she had been making sales presentations to their purchasing managers. Even though she was sure that she had convinced these managers of her company's product quality, excellent delivery, and competitive price, she kept losing most orders to competitors. What are the possible reasons for her lost sales? Discuss reasons for your answer.

4. A large construction company bought the following three products: its first mainframe computer, a new truck to expand its fleet of trucks, and concrete. Would the same steps be used in the buying decision for all three products? Why or why not?

5. While 10 to 15 suppliers of personal computers usually try to obtain orders for personal computers from major corporate customers, only a very few seem to be in the running by the time the purchase decision draws near. Suppose that as an industrial salesperson for Apple Computer you learn that these industrial buyers use noncompensating evaluation strategies to screen suppliers down to a list of two or three that will be seriously considered. What implications would this fact have on planning strategy

to sell your company's personal computers to these customers? Discuss reasons for your answer.

6. You have just been hired as a product manager with profit responsibility for your company's brand of industrial robot. In preparation for developing a marketing plan, you decide to learn more about the buying behavior of industrial buyers in your markets. How would you go about setting objectives for this study? Discuss your answer.

7. As the marketing manager for a company that manufactures machinery for production lines, you are reviewing the information that is being used for marketing planning. Your assistant suggests that studies be conducted to assess the outlook in the markets served by your customers. Would these studies be helpful for your marketing planning? Why or why not?

8. You are trying to win a purchase order for telecommunications equipment from a major customer. You find that several members of the customer's buying center are in conflict over the purchase decision. What would you want to know about the conflict? How would this information help you in planning subsequent selling efforts aimed at this customer?

Notes

1. Irving D. Canton, "Learning to Love the Service Economy," *Harvard Business Review*, May–June 1984, p. 89.

2. Edward F. Fern and James R. Brown, "The Industrial/Consumer Marketing Dichotomy: A Case of Insufficient Justification," *Journal of Marketing* 48 (Spring 1984), pp. 68–77.

3. Thomas V. Bonoma, "Major Sales: Who *Really* Does the Buying?" *Harvard Business Review*, May–June 1982, p. 116.

4. From a study by *Purchasing* magazine as reported in Gary L. Lilien and M. Anthony Wong, "An Exploratory Investigation of the Structure of the Buy-

ing Center in the Metalworking Industry," *Journal of Marketing Research* 21 (February 1984), p. 1.

5. "Measures Exist for Segmenting Industrial Markets," *Marketing News*, April 1, 1983, p. 11.

6. Gregory D. Upah and Monroe M. Bird, "Changes in Industrial Buying: Implications for Industrial Marketers," *Industrial Marketing Management*, April 1980, pp. 117-18.

7. "Communicating 'Differential Advantage' Is Essential," *Marketing News*, October 25, 1985, p. 26.

8. Bonoma, "Major Sales," p. 116.

9. "Fokker's 'Right Plane at the Right Time' Is Taking Off," *Business Week*, July 23, 1984, p. 84.

10. The decision process is evident in widely cited models of industrial buying behavior, including those discussed in Frederick E. Webster and Yoram Wind, "A General Model for Understanding Organizational Buying Behavior," *Journal of Marketing* 36 (April 1972), pp. 12–19; Jagdish N. Sheth, "A Model of Industrial Buyer Behavior," *Journal of Marketing* 37 (October 1973), pp. 50–56; and Jean-Marie Choffray and Gary L. Lilien, "Assessing Response to Industrial Marketing Strategy," *Journal of Marketing* 42 (April 1978), pp. 20–31.

11. P. J. Robinson, C. W. Faris, and Y. Wind, *Industrial Buying and Creative Marketing* (Boston: Allyn & Bacon, 1967), chap. 2.

12. James F. Engel, Roger D. Blackwell, and Paul W. Miniard, *Consumer Behavior* (Hinsdale, Ill.: Dryden Press, 1986), p. 558.

13. Buying center participation by different personnel is discussed in Choffray and Lilien, "Assessing Response," pp. 27–28; and Wesley J. Johnston and Thomas V. Bonoma, "The Buying Center: Structure and Interaction Patterns," *Journal of Marketing* 45 (Summer 1981), pp. 143–56.

14. Wesley J. Johnston, "Industrial Buying Behavior: A State of the Art Review," in *Review of Marketing*, Ben M. Enis and Kenneth J. Roering, eds. (Chicago: American Marketing Association, 1981), pp. 77–78.

15. Niren Vyas and Arch G. Woodside, "An Inductive Model of Industrial Supplier Choice Processes," *Journal of Marketing* 48 (Winter 1984), pp. 33–34.

16. "The Bewildering Array of Options Facing Users," *Business Week*, July 16, 1984, p. 86.

17. Lowell E. Crow, Richard W. Olshavsky, and John O. Summers, "Industrial Buyers' Choice Strategies: A Protocol Analysis," *Journal of Marketing Research* 17 (February 1980), p. 34.

18. For further discussion of value analysis, see B. Charles Ames and James D. Hlavacek, *Managerial Marketing for Industrial Firms* (New York: Random House, 1984), pp. 42–47.

19. Michael S. Yalowitz, "Cost-Benefit Assessments Help Fill Gaps in Industrial Companies," *Marketing News*, May 27, 1983, p. 5.

20. Crow, Olshavsky, and Summers, "Industrial Buyers' Choice Strategies," p. 34.

21. Stephen W. Clopton, "Seller and Buying Firm Factors Affecting Industrial Buyers' Negotiation Behavior and Outcomes," *Journal of Marketing Research* 21 (February 1984), p. 39.

22. Ibid., pp. 40–41.

23. Steven Flax, "How Detroit Is Reforming the Steelmakers," *Fortune*, May 16, 1984, p. 34.

24. These categories are discussed in Webster and Wind, "General Model for Understanding Organizational Buying Behavior," p. 15.

25. "Machine Tool Makers: Healing, but Still Sickly," *Business Week*, October 1, 1984, p. 117.

26. Michael J. Ryan and Morris B. Holbrook, "Decision-Specific Conflict in Organizational Buyer Behavior," *Journal of Marketing* 46 (Summer 1982), pp. 62–68.

27. Jack R. Snader, "Amiable, Analytical, Driving, or Expressive? Base Marketing Style on Prospect's Behavior," *Marketing News*, March 16, 1984, sec. 2, p. 3.

28. Ibid.

CHAPTER 7

Analyzing Competition

*T*o K mart Corporation, the $65 billion do-it-yourself market looked especially attractive. Maturing baby-boomers, many of whom became involved in home improvement projects, helped the market grow at a healthy 11 percent a year. Further, the do-it-yourself retail industry looked inviting, being made up primarily of mom-and-pop hardware stores, lumberyards, and a few home improvement chains such as Payless Cashways, Inc. and Handy Dan. The time seemed right for entering the fray, and K mart bought a chain of home improvement stores, renaming them Builders Square. At about the same time, two other retail giants, Service Merchandise Company and Home Depot, moved aggressively into the market with retail chain operations, creating intense competition. All three use price-cutting and huge advertising budgets to attract do-it-yourselfers. Moreover, the smaller companies did not fold but learned to fight back more effectively. As a result, K mart's Builders Square stores are losing money. Management is faced with a formidable challenge to use marketing strategy to build an edge against the increasingly fierce competition.[1]

Meeting customers' needs and wants is not always enough to perform well in a market. Other companies are usually competing for the same customers with need-satisfying marketing programs, and their success can affect market opportunity for all of the companies serving the market. Thus, **competition** is often a driving force behind the planning of marketing strategies, as K mart's situation in the do-it-yourself market emphasizes. One marketing expert puts it this way:

> Because substitutes exist for most products and services, firms typically encounter competitors when marketing their offerings. Consequently, the effectiveness of marketing programs usually depends on the reaction of both customers and competitors. . . . it is difficult to imagine a marketing decision that is not affected by competitive activity.[2]

Competition
is the vying for market share among sellers that are targeting a market comprising customers having the same or similar needs or wants.

Industry and key competitor analyses are an integral part of an overall market opportunity analysis (MOA). Such analyses are the source of competitive information for marketing planning. This chapter expands on the coverage and application of competitive analyses. First, the nature of competition and its impact on demand are considered. Then, the task of analyzing an industry serving a market is discussed. Next, the analysis of particular sellers designated as key competitors is examined. The chapter ends with a discussion of the use of competitive analyses to plan marketing strategy.

Markets and Competition

The competition facing a company depends largely on how markets are defined. Dependence on market definition adds considerable risk to the challenge of correctly identifying competition. Recently, Lanier Business Products, Inc. experienced the downside of this risk. By 1980, Lanier had established itself as the leading seller of stand-alone word processors. Then, personal computers (PCs) became one of the hottest growth products of the decade. PCs are clearly capable of meeting word processing needs but have many other uses as well. Lanier saw its market share eroded as buyers realized that they could perform word processing and other tasks for a lower price using PCs rather than specialized word processors. Management had to change its view of markets and competition in developing marketing strategies for the remainder of the decade.[3]

Recall the very important idea underlying approaches to market definition: customers whose similar needs or wants cause them to respond similarly to a marketing offer are grouped into a market. This idea has a powerful implication for the nature of competition. To see the full extent of competition, any and all products (or services) that customers see as solutions to a need or want must be considered a threat. Otherwise, managers will be in the uncomfortable position, as Lanier was, of overlooking potential and powerful competition from unexpected sources.

Brand competition is not the only concern for managers. A major battle is also waged through **product-type competition,** the struggle for share of the larger generic-class market achieved by one product type in competition with other product types that customers believe are solutions for a given need or want. In this sense, personal computers compete with typewriters, glass competes with plastic, houses compete with condominiums, nuclear energy competes with coal, and banks compete with mutual funds. Competition between product types is really competition between brands, but brands that are quite dissimilar in the total configuration of benefits offered. Defining markets around customer needs and wants will help managers see the potential competition from similar brands and, equally important, from dissimilar brands of other product types.

Brand competition is the vying or market share among brands of the same product type serving the same markets.

Product-type competition is the vying for market demand among brands of different product types serving the same markets.

Competition Caused by Need Priorities

Realistically, no person and no organization can buy all of the products and services that are needed or wanted. Given limitations on ability to buy and on time, customers set priorities on different needs that involve trade-offs between seemingly unrelated products. A family might decide to postpone the purchase of a new car in order to travel. Similarly, a company's management may decide to modernize a production line rather than install new quality control equipment.

To some extent, setting priorities on needs suggests that all products and services are ultimately in competition with one another. The practical significance of this fact for many sellers is probably not great. Yet some groups of products may be more likely than others to be involved in priority-setting trade-offs. Consumers may choose between such luxury products and services as a boat, a vacation, large-screen television, and a hot tub. Needs for these products are somewhat related since all of them involve the use of leisure time.

In general, competition among similar brands, product types, and even generic classes of products can affect market opportunity simultaneously. Each type of competition is a threat to the success of a firm's marketing strategy. Some of these forms of competition are more indirect than others, so managers must assess the severity of competition coming from these sources. As a rule, the severity of competition among brands, both similar and dissimilar, depends on how suitable customers believe the brands are for meeting similar needs or wants:

> Competition among firms and brands is a matter of degree. At one extreme, all firms and products compete indirectly against each other for the limited resources of customers. At the other extreme, Coke and Pepsi compete against each other using similar production and marketing technology to satisfy almost identical customer needs. Thus, the degree of similarity in needs satisfied and methods used to satisfy those needs determines the degree to which firms and brands compete against each other.[4]

Competition and the Product Life Cycle

Just as markets change, so too will competition. Consequently, marketing managers can never relax their vigil but must constantly try to anticipate such changes. Only then can marketing strategy be adjusted to respond to new threats and opportunities. Analyzing competition is a never-ending activity.

A very useful concept for understanding competitive change over time is the product life cycle. Products have definite lives and are thought to go through different stages over time.[5] Exhibit 7–1 shows the typical stages of a product life cycle as measured by sales over time. Of most importance is the change in the growth of sales from stage to stage. Upon introduction, a product's sales are low and grow rather slowly. Profits may actually be

EXHIBIT 7-1 Product Life Cycle

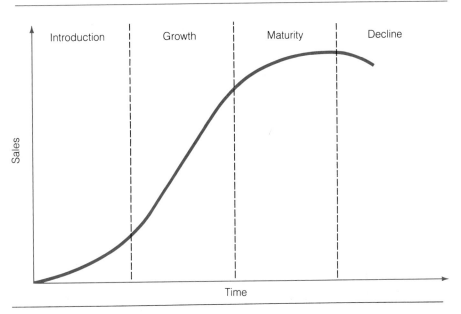

negative due to the often high costs of acquainting the market with the product. At some point, the product will move into a growth stage as more customers become familiar with it and like what it has to offer. The markets for the product grow larger, generating more sales and profits. Eventually, the product will reach most of the potential customers that have a need or want for it, causing sales growth to slow as the product reaches maturity. During this stage, profits may peak and begin to decline. Finally, maturity shifts into decline as improved product substitutes begin to appear.

The product life cycle is a controversial concept in practice.[6] The length and rate of sales growth in the different life-cycle stages vary for different products. In addition, our ability to measure the exact position of a product in its life cycle, much less forecast its movement through a cycle, is not very good.[7] Nevertheless, the product life cycle is a very useful framework for visualizing how competition and marketing strategy change over time. Exhibit 7-2 suggests some of the changes in competition that managers might expect. Three forms of competition are considered across four life-cycle stages for a product type.

Introductory Stage. When a new product type is first introduced, there is a period during which there is little or no competition from similar brands. It may take time for competitors to decide that there is opportunity for selling a similar brand and to enter the market. Prince Manufacturing Company encountered this situation when it introduced the oversized tennis racket, a

EXHIBIT 7–2 Changes in Competition over a Product Life Cycle

| | Forms of competition | | |
	Need priority	Product type	Brand
Introductory	High	High	Low
Growth	Stable	Moderate to low	Growing
Maturity	Stable	Growing	High
Decline	Stable	High	High; Fewer brands

product type representing truly innovative racket design. Other companies needed time to develop and introduce competitive brands of similar design. As a result, many months passed before similar brands began to appear.

Lack of similar-brand competition in the introductory stage does not mean that there is no competition. Typically, the need that the new product is designed to serve is already being met by other product types. Thus, the marketing challenge is to convince customers of the new product's superiority over those product types. This task can be formidable because it involves changing established customer behavior. In spite of Prince's innovative racket design, most tennis players initially saw little reason to switch to a different kind of racket. An aggressive promotion effort was needed over several years to convince players that the over-size racket would significantly improve their enjoyment of the game. The effort was successful, and the innovative racket became the leader in tennis racket sales.

Growth and Maturity Stages.   Marketing strategy for a product typically changes as new competition emerges. As demand for an innovation grows, people become more and more convinced of its superiority over existing product types. Managers may experience a period during which product-type competition lessens and similar-brand competition increases. Other companies, seeing the increasing popularity of the innovation, will try to get on the bandwagon with similar brands. Prince saw this situation develop as other manufacturers flooded the market with their own brands of midsize and oversize rackets. It had to change its strategy to demonstrate superiority over the brands of competitors.

Decline.   No product lasts forever. Several market conditions can cause a product to slide into decline:

- New technology may lead to improved substitute products.
- Markets may shrink due to population changes.
- A key customer group may lose ability to buy.
- Changes in customer lifestyles may lead to changes in needs or tastes.
- Costs of supplies or complementary products may rise.[8]

Competition again changes. Brand competition remains intense, but now it comes from a smaller number of companies that have survived the shakeout of sellers. Low price through cost cutting often characterizes this battle. In addition, the threat of competition from other product types increases as companies search for new ways of satisfying the market's needs. Competition from other need priorities remains as before.

The decline stage creates an enormous strategic challenge for a company. One option is to try to become one of the leading companies in the market. This can be done by:

1. Building sales and market share to take advantage of cost economies.
2. Differentiating the brand from other brands.
3. Specializing in a stable market niche or segment while moving out of less stable and more rapidly declining segments.
4. Leaving the market and putting resources to work in other areas.[9]

Analyzing Competition from Industries

The product-market structure presented in Chapter 4 can be applied to analyzing competition. At the outset, competition should be defined broadly to identify all the forms of competition influencing market opportunity. An important first step is analyzing whole industries that sell products aimed at satisfying a given market need. This approach forces a manager to carefully consider competition from other product types as well as from similar brands. It provides a general understanding of the competition without requiring separate analysis of each and every one of the typically large number of firms in an industry.

Exhibit 7-3 shows the steps in an industry analysis. First, the industry to be analyzed is defined. Then, an information base for describing the industry and its marketing strategies and tactics is accumulated. This information helps marketing managers predict changes in the industry over time and allows managers to evaluate the industry's competitive ability to serve markets. Let us consider each step in more detail.

EXHIBIT 7–3 Analyzing an Industry

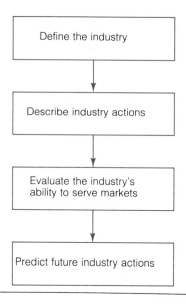

Defining the Industry

Industries comprise organizations that compete for demand in markets of interest. Since the purpose of industry analyses is to help in planning competitive marketing strategy, certain criteria are applied to identify the industry.

Definition Criteria. First, the products that organizations offer for sale must be considered. An industry comprises organizations with competing brands of the same product type (a product-type industry) or organizations offering competing product types (a generic-class industry). Second, the scope of an industry is confined to the most direct competition for end-user demand. This criterion can most easily be applied by restricting the industry to organizations at the same level in a distribution channel for a product or service. A manufacturer will define the industry as made up of manufacturers, but a retailer will see its industry as made up of retailers.

Finally, since markets are defined within geographic boundaries, an industry must be limited to the same geographic area. An organization does not have to be located in the area to be considered part of an industry. All that is necessary is that it be distributing and selling in the geographic area of interest.

Industry Characteristics. When an industry is very small, the organizations that it comprises can simply be listed. A county hospital used this

EXHIBIT 7–4 Illustration of an Industry Definition

Industry Characteristic	*Industry Definition*
Product	Cooking appliances
Level in channel	Manufacturing
Market area	United States
Location	United States, Japan, and Western Europe
Organizational structure	Major divisions of large organizations
Product line	Multiproduct line including gas and electric stoves, conventional ovens, microwave ovens, toaster ovens, etc.

approach in defining its generic class industry. A list of the other hospitals, specialty-care centers, and clinics attracting patients from the market area was developed. However, many industries are too large for a simple listing. An alternative is to describe the characteristics of the types of organizations that make up the industry. At a minimum, the characteristics should correspond to the three definitional criteria (product sold, distribution channel level, and geographic area). But additional characteristics may also be used, such as location, organizational structure (company versus division of company), and extensiveness of product lines. Exhibit 7-4 provides an illustration for the cooking appliance industry.

Describing Industry Marketing

After an industry has been defined, the analyst builds an information base describing important aspects of the industry affecting its serving of market demand. At this point, what is typical for the entire industry is of greatest interest. The description should cover:

- Industry size and growth.
- Industry structure.
- Influence of governmental economic policy.
- Typical marketing strategy and tactics.

Size and Growth. A description of an industry's size and growth helps a marketing manager relate the industry to market demand. Market opportunity is influenced by an industry's ability to meet the volume of demand in markets. Such commonly available indicators as industry sales, profits, number of firms, number of employees, and assets are used to determine how an industry has grown in recent years. These data provide clues on the life-cycle stage of the industry. Comparisons can be made between industry size and market size to assess untapped market opportunity.

Industry structure refers to the nature and degree of competition among firms caused by their number, their relative size, and the differentiation of their marketing offers.

Industry Structure.   Industries, like markets, have structure. One way to examine **industry structure** is to consider the number, size, and degree of marketing offer differentiation of organizations in an industry. As economic analysis has demonstrated, these factors influence the nature of competition, particularly price competition, in markets.

At one extreme is an industry that comprises one organization—a *monopoly*. Its major characteristic is the absence of brand competition. Monopolies are more common in free enterprise systems than might be expected. A utility, a cable TV company, a community's only neurosurgeon, and a distributor that has been granted exclusive territory rights by a supplier are but a few illustrations. Because monopolies do not provide buyers with choices, market forces may have little effect on their response to needs and wants. Often government supervision and regulation must ensure the responsiveness of monopolies to market forces.

At the other extreme is *pure competition.* An industry in which pure competition exists has many organizations, no one of which is large enough to have a significant effect on the total supply of its products. Competition is intense because there is little or no differentiation among offerings. Each organization has little or no control over the price charged. Because no firm in a pure competitive situation has much control over its own performance, there is incentive to break out either by growing larger or by differentiating product offerings in some way. Farming at one time was characterized by pure competition for many agricultural products, but growth and buyouts have created huge farming operations that are not characteristic of pure competition.

Between monopoly and pure competition are oligopolies and monopolistic competition. In *monopolistic competition,* as with pure competition, there are many organizations, each of which is relatively small. But successful differentiation of product offerings allows more freedom to vary the prices charged. Points of difference among firms cause customers to develop brand preferences that allow flexibility in marketing strategy. The restaurant industry in a large community is characterized by monopolistic competition. Through location, menu specialty, decor, or other nonprice means, each restaurant differentiates its marketing offer from that of other restaurants.

With *oligopoly,* an industry is dominated by a relatively small number of very large organizations. Each marketing offer is at least somewhat differentiated from the others. Typically, these few large organizations become leaders for the rest of the industry. In regulated free enterprise economies, such leadership is provided by example rather than by collusion. Oligopolies are a common industry form in more developed countries like the United States, where industries are older. The automobiles, TV, packaging, and computer industries are of this form.

Industry structure can dramatically affect the competitive strategies employed by a company. The number of firms in an industry, the differentiation of marketing strategies among these firms, and the domination of the industry by one or a few firms all affect the marketing options open to a company. Organizations in an oligopoly, in particular, face an interesting competitive choice. Each firm can continue with a basic strategy that leads to a reasonable profit without being overly disruptive to the rest of the industry. But if in its own interest one firm adopts a strategy that is disruptive or detrimental to the rest of the industry, it invites retaliation. The whole industry may become worse off as a result.[10] The calculator manufacturing industry has experienced this fate. A long-term price war, triggered by individual competitors, has taken much of the profit out of the entire industry.

Another way to analyze the structure of an industry is to look for groups of organizations with similar marketing strategies. More than one kind of marketing strategy usually works well in a market. In the retail industry for sports equipment, small specialty stores, large department stores, mail-order establishments, and discount stores place different emphases on price, merchandise assortments, merchandise depth, credit, and other components in their marketing mixes. Yet all of these enterprises have achieved a measure of success. Breaking down an industry into its marketing subdivisions can help reveal the proven competitive strategy options.

Influence of Government Policy.   As markets continue to expand beyond the boundaries of a single country, government economic policy can become intertwined with the marketing strategies of an industry.[11] Governmental policy involves economic decisions aimed at achieving national goals. Such goals might include independence, security, or leadership. Government may provide industry with management assistance, support, financial and other incentives, and sometimes regulation, all of which influence the marketing actions of industries deemed critical to achieving national goals. It is no accident that such Japanese companies as Hitachi, Toshiba, and Mitsubishi are becoming an important part of the nuclear reactor industry competing in world markets. Part of the reason for Japanese leadership in these markets is governmental policy toward expanding the country's nuclear power capabilities.[12]

Marketing Strategies and Tactics.   At the heart of an industry analysis is a description of the marketing strategies and tactics typical for the industry. Information should be gathered on all aspects of marketing strategies. This includes:

- Market target strategies common in the industry.
- Typical marketing objectives.
- Similarities and differences among marketing programs.

Exhibit 7–5 suggests the kinds of questions that need to be answered by the industry analysis.

EXHIBIT 7–5 Information on Industry Marketing Practices

Target markets	Is a mass or segmentation strategy characteristic of the industry? If both strategies are used in the industry, which types of firms use each one? If segmentation strategies are used, which groups are given highest priority?
Marketing objectives	Which marketing support objectives are most important to industry programs? Are there typical objectives that cut across the industry?
Marketing mix	What key product characteristics are typical? What product variety (models, colors, styles, etc.) is offered? What are typical branding strategies? What emphasis is placed on key sources of supply required for production? What is the outlook for the continued supply of key resources for production? What price variation is typical? Is discounting allowed? How are prices stated? What terms are typical? What advertising themes and layouts are used? What terms are commonly used? To what extent are products positioned against substitute products versus similar competing brands? What media are used? How much is spent on advertising? Is public relations a typical activity? What sales promotion approaches are used? How important is personal selling in the promotion mix? What selling approaches are used? How important is service in the salesperson's total responsibility? What channel is used to reach end-user markets? What support is expected by channel organizations? What support is needed from channel organizations? What facilitating services are provided for customers? How important are these services to the total marketing mix?

A historical perspective of where the industry has been over a period of time, say 5 to 10 years or more, should be provided. Industries change, and managers must understand how and why change has caused an industry to move to its present marketing strategies and tactics. Trends that indicate where an industry is headed are likely to be discovered in this way.

Industry Evaluation

After building an industry information base, management can use it to evaluate the industry. Every industry has certain strengths in the way it serves markets; to do well in an industry, these strengths must be matched in some way. At the same time, most industries have weaknesses that can be exploited by a well-designed marketing strategy. An industry evaluation identifies these strengths and weaknesses. Two different kinds of evaluation are essential: industry market coverage and industry ability to meet market requirements.

Industry Market Coverage. One way in which an industry serves markets is through **market coverage**—meeting the quantity or volume of demand. Information on industry size, target market priorities, and other indicators of the quantity of effort committed by an industry to markets helps managers see whether there is untapped demand. Demand larger than an industry's ability to distribute and sell a product is an indication of future growth opportunity. Untapped demand is largely responsible, for instance, for the impressive growth of the high-tech industry in the United States. Untapped demand is usually temporary, however, because it attracts new competition.

Industry supply may meet or even exceed market demand. In that case, competition intensifies as each firm's sales growth becomes increasingly dependent on expanding market share at the expense of other firms. Lack of substantial untapped demand changes the marketing strategies and tactics that will be successful. Building demand for the product type becomes less important; management spends more time in establishing or maintaining an edge over competition from similar brands. The battle of the soft-drink companies, particularly Coke and Pepsi, is characteristic of this situation, as reflected in the comments by a senior vice president of Pepsi-Cola USA:

> Consumers are more demanding. They are shopping around more, so you have to know your competitor and develop products that clearly differentiate your product from theirs.[13]

Industry coverage analysis becomes more complicated when market structure includes segments. Evaluation must include an analysis of the extent to which each segment is being served. Obviously, conclusions about coverage will be heavily dependent on the way in which market structure is defined, as may be seen from the information presented in Exhibit 7-6. Market structure for temperature measurement instruments, the industrial product analyzed in this matrix, was based on recognizing three different use situations for which different levels of accuracy were needed. There are nine possible market segments (three use situations × three levels of accuracy preference), each having a different configuration of market requirements. Evaluation of industry size and target market strategies revealed that the industry was concentrating most of its distribution and marketing on three segments (moderate- and low-accuracy instruments for quality control and moderate-accuracy instruments for calibration).

Industry coverage evaluations must consider market size. Look again at Exhibit 7-6. Three of the nine markets, those with no coverage, were virtually nonexistent (quality control/high accuracy, calibration/low accuracy, and product testing/low accuracy). There was not enough demand there to consider targeting them. The remaining three segments contained significant demand but were still not big enough to attract much competition, particu-

EXHIBIT 7-6 Analysis of Industry Coverage of a Market's Structure

	ACCURACY		
	High	Moderate	Low
Quality control	No market	Extensive	Extensive
Calibration	Very limited	Extensive	No market
Product testing	Very limited	Moderate	No market

USES

larly from the larger firms in the industry. In general, the industry was allocating the quantity of marketing effort in direct relation to market segment size, a very common pattern. This opened holes for smaller firms to enter in the market structure where the smaller segments were not being adequately targeted by the industry.

Industry's Ability to Meet Market Requirements. An evaluation equal in importance to the evaluation of market coverage concerns the quality of the industry's effort to satisfy buyers' needs and wants. Buyers' market requirements provide the crucial focus for this evaluation. Information on the industry's marketing offer strategies and tactics is scrutinized to find out how each market requirement is met. Then, opinions are formed concerning how well (or poorly) the industry is satisfying each requirement. Because the market requirements of segments differ, the analysis must be done for each segment.

Analysis of the temperature measurement instrument industry illustrates this kind of evaluation. Exhibit 7-7 provides a format for conveniently presenting the evaluation for a single market segment. The first column shows market requirements derived from a customer profile for an important market segment. The market requirements indicate what organizational buyers want in high-accuracy instruments, a product type. The second column shows how much importance customers attach to each requirement. The third column is a subjective rating of the marketing practices used by the industry to meet each requirement. The last column shows the analyst's conclusions about how well or poorly the industry is doing on certain requirements.

The numerical ratings used in the evaluation of the temperature measurement industry are subjective and are therefore only as accurate as the information on which they are based and the skill of the analyst. However, ratings are an efficient way of portraying and communicating the results of

EXHIBIT 7-7 An Industry Evaluation for a Market Segment

Market Requirements	Importance Rating*	Industry Effectiveness Rating†	Comment
Variety of models	10	5	Weakness
Value for price	9	5	Weakness
Fast repair service	10	10	Strength
Easy operation	4	6	
Easy installation	6	8	
Ruggedness	8	5	Weakness
Durability	7	8	Strength
Easy movement from place to place	6	6	
Convenience of recording data	5	9	
Stable measurements	8	8	Strength
Understanding how the instrument works	7	9	Strength

* 10 = essential; 1 = not important.

† 10 = perfectly effective; 0 = no practices evident.

evaluation. More important, ratings illustrate two key aspects of this phase of industry evaluation. First, the evaluation of an industry should be done from a market's perspective based on market requirements. Because there are usually several such requirements, an industry will perform better on some market requirements than on others, depending on how well marketing offers are planned and implemented. Thus, the evaluation must be performed on a requirement-by-requirement basis and for each segment.

The second aspect concerns the identification of the industry's strengths and weaknesses. Both the importance of a requirement and the marketing offer components intended to satisfy that requirement should be examined. A high evaluation on a very important market requirement is an **industry strength.** In contrast, a low evaluation on a very important market requirement is an **industry weakness.** A high or low industry evaluation in itself does not necessarily mean that there is a strength or weakness. If the corresponding requirement is not very important, the industry's marketing offer components aimed at that requirement may not have a great influence on customers. Looking back to Exhibit 7-7, easy operation of instruments (rated moderately low with a 6) is not considered a serious weakness because it is not a very important requirement (importance rating of 4).

Evaluating an industry's ability to meet market requirements yields important guidelines for marketing planning. Strengths must be matched. Weaknesses give a company opportunities to build competitive advantages into its offer, assuming that ways can be found to overcome the weaknesses. In the temperature measurement industry, demonstrating value for price, providing depth of product line, and promoting the ruggedness of brands are crucial means for differentiating a company's marketing offer from the marketing offers made by other companies. At the same time, the company must match

Industry strengths refer to those components of marketing offers typical of firms in an industry that are satisfying important market requirements very well.

Industry weaknesses refer to those components of marketing offers typical of firms in an industry that are not satisfying important market requirements very well.

the industry on repair service, durability of instruments, and stability of measurements and in the inputing of information on how the instruments work.

Predicting Industry Actions

Predicting changes in marketing strategies and tactics is probably the most difficult part of an industry analysis. Macroenvironmental shifts, market changes, and competitive pressures will cause competitors to look for new ways to attract market demand. At the same time, companies are secretive about their plans. Yet anticipating changes in marketing strategy and tactics is crucial in planning competitive marketing strategy. Only those managements that regularly scrutinize industry information for clues to competitive moves will have the lead time to plan and implement countermoves.

Since changes in the marketing strategy and tactics of an industry are generally responses to changes in market and competitive conditions, understanding these conditions allows astute managers to anticipate logical competitive reactions. Looking for historical trends and other clues in market opportunity analysis information is an essential means for predicting industry changes.

Historical Trend Analyses.   Trend analysis requires carefully monitoring how an industry typically reacts to market conditions over time. In this way, regular patterns can sometimes be discovered. (This approach applies the technique of trend forecasting, discussed more fully in Chapter 8.) The advertising of the microwave oven industry over the past decade evidences a trend that illustrates the approach. When microwave ovens became very popular in the late 1970s, industry advertising positioned them as complementary to conventional ovens. People were shown using microwaves primarily for special purposes such as defrosting meat or cooking a baked potato quickly. Gradually, as the microwave became more versatile, industry advertising changed to show it as the basic oven for the kitchen. This trend toward a different positioning of the product took place over several years and was therefore easily seen by comparing year-to-year advertising during the early 1980s. Prediction occurs when the trend is projected into the future. Most would predict that the microwave will continue to be improved and positioned as an all-purpose oven in the years to come.

Supplementary Analyses.   Trend analyses should never be the only means for predicting industry marketing strategy and tactical changes. Through supplemental analyses, management may be able to predict an industry change even before a trend becomes fully apparent. More judgment is required to see change near its inception, but certain kinds of information may help. Two kinds are particularly useful:

- Monitoring industry leaders.
- Logically anticipating industry reaction to changing market conditions.

In many industries, there are companies that tend to lead the industry in implementing new marketing strategies and tactics. The actions taken by these companies should be closely monitored for clues as to the direction that an entire industry may take. In the personal computer industry, IBM is generally considered a leader. Its approach to distribution has set the standard for the industry. Personal computers are purchased by many individuals in both companies and households, creating a difficult situation for the distribution system. IBM was a leader in using both a personal sales force and such retail outlets as Computerland stores to reach these markets. Other manufacturers had been using one or the other, but seldom both in combination. Considering the logic of IBM's distribution strategy could provide just the clue needed to predict that the industry would gradually follow IBM's lead.

Information on important changes in market conditions, such as changing demand factors, shifting market structure, and emerging market requirements, should enable experienced managers to make reasonable guesses as to how the industry will respond to these changes. Such guesses are based on familiarity with the industry's responses to similar past changes. Managers in larger companies increasingly want personal computers to serve as office work stations. An understanding of this emerging market condition may help in predicting the industry's response to it. Since work stations are used by many different office personnel, one logical prediction is that the industry will turn to advertising and promotion to reach these users directly, rather than trying to sell solely to data processing managers and purchasing agents. This prediction is coming true (Exhibit 7–8).[14]

Results of an Industry Analysis

Industry analyses provide an overall view of the competitive environment in which individual companies vie for sales. The framework for such analyses that has been developed in this chapter can be applied to generic-class industries as well as product-type industries. The framework identifies the industry competitive factors that affect market opportunity and therefore marketing planning. Exhibit 7-9 summarizes the key forces influencing the marketing strategies and tactics of an industry. The crucial role that industry analyses play in planning marketing strategy is effectively argued by Michael E. Porter, a well-known expert on competitive strategy:

> The essence of formulating competitive strategy is relating a company to its environment. Although the relevant environment is very broad, encompassing social as well as economic forces, the key aspect of the firm's environment is the industry

EXHIBIT 7–8

This IBM ad, which ran in leading business publications, is addressed to the executive who will use the equipment.

Courtesy International Business Machines. Reprinted by permission.

or industries in which it competes. Industry structure has a strong influence in determining the competitive rules of the game as well as the strategies potentially available to the firm.[15]

Industry analyses by themselves are not sufficient. They must be complemented by a careful analysis of individual competitors. However, not all competitive companies in an industry need this kind of scrutiny. Only those that are most likely to affect a company's marketing strategy success, the *key competitors*, should be selected for further analysis. An industry analysis provides the background information necessary for this selection.

EXHIBIT 7-9 Forces Influencing the Marketing Strategies in Industries

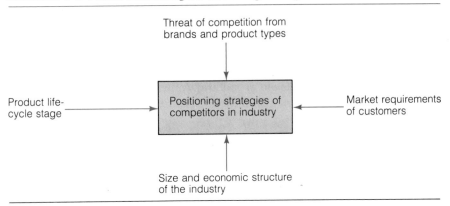

Analyzing Key Competitors

When formulating marketing strategy, some managers may want to consider the actions of each and every competitor in an industry. In most cases, however, the sheer size of industries makes this approach impractical. Moreover, the approach is rarely necessary. Concentrating on key competitors is a viable alternative. To facilitate the comparison of key competitors with the entire industry, a key competitor analysis should apply the same concepts that have been discussed in the previous section.

Identifying Key Competitors

Which are the key competitors in an industry? Answering this question correctly is crucial because marketing strategy will position the company's marketing offer against the marketing offers of these competitors. Setting criteria for the selection of the key competitors is the best way to make a considered choice. Two such criteria are particularly important:

- Companies serving the same markets.
- Companies successful in meeting demand.

Serving Same Markets.　A company can be a key competitor only if it is targeting the same markets or is expected to do so. After all, the essence of competition is vying for the same customers. At first glance, you might think that IBM has long been a key competitor of Digital Equipment Corporation (DEC), because both sell computers. However, IBM became a key competitor of DEC only after both firms decided to move into the personal computer markets. Previously, IBM and DEC did not compete directly, since DEC concentrated on the minicomputer market, which was largely ignored by IBM.[16]

One implication of the same-market criterion is that management must be far enough along in marketing planning to know its target markets before it can confidently select key competitors. When the competition for an established brand in the company's line is being analyzed, the key competitors may be known because the target markets are not new. But to analyze the competition for a new product, management may have to wait until the market opportunity analysis has identified market structure, revealing the probable target markets.

Another implication concerns whether a key competitor must be a company offering a similar brand—a brand of the same product type. For example, must all of Apple's key competitors for personal computer markets be other producers of personal computers? The answer is: Not necessarily.[17] Product types can compete for the same target markets if they are close substitutes. Thus, a key competitor can be a company offering a brand of a substitute product type. Currently, personal computers compete with electronic typewriters, stand-alone word processors, and even minicomputers in business markets and with video games in home markets. Companies selling brands of these different product types could be selected as Apple's key competitors, depending on its target markets.

Successful Companies.   Serving the same markets is a necessary but not sufficient criterion for identifying key competitors. Analyses should also concentrate on those competitors that are likely to have the greatest impact on a company's sales. Successful competitors are most likely to meet this criterion. While success can have different meanings, the "bottom line" kind of success is of most interest. Indicators of size and growth in sales, market share, and profitability are typically used in this context.

Having once identified key competitors, management should not assume that they will remain in that position forever. A major challenge is predicting which companies will be the key competitors of the future. In today's world, new competitors may emerge from a foreign industry. European and U.S. personal computer manufacturers face the possibility of strong competition from Japanese firms. The track record of the Japanese in other product markets, such as automobiles, cameras, television, and video tape recorders, has been very good, and there are indications that personal computers are being developed by several Japanese firms.

Describing Key Competitors' Capabilities

Through published sources, interviews with those familiar with the competitor, and personal observation, a picture can be pieced together of the marketing strategies, tactics, and management styles of each key competitor. The crucial factors that influence the marketing strategies and tactics of key competitors are shown in Exhibit 7-10. The purpose of key competitor analyses is to describe these factors and to evaluate their effect on the marketing decisions of key competitors.

EXHIBIT 7–10 Factors Influencing the Marketing Strategy of Key Competitors

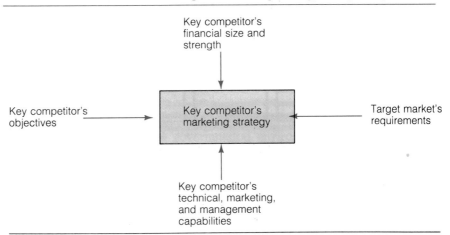

Financial Size and Strength. First, a financial picture of each key competitor is constructed. Typical income statement and balance sheet data are sought for this purpose. In the United States, government disclosure requirements aid this effort tremendously. There are also independent published sources of financial information, such as Value Line, Dun & Bradstreet, Standard & Poor's, Moody's, and others. More creative means may sometimes have to be employed to estimate financial strength—counting the number of advertisements run in a certain time period, examining bond ratings, or keeping track of the number of sales personnel in overlapping sales territories.

The resulting financial profile can be invaluable as an indicator of a key competitor's ability to access supply sources and to sustain a marketing strategy in target markets. Further, the financial profile may give the analyst a rough idea of how resources are allocated to such components of the key competitor's marketing program as advertising, product research and development, and personal selling.

Key Competitors' Objectives and Capabilities. Analyses must help management understand what to expect from the marketing strategies and tactics of key competitors. Only with forewarning can a company develop appropriate offensive or defensive strategies. Specific competitor characteristics that should be profiled are:

- Mission and business objectives
- Market share position and trends
- Management capabilities and limitations
- Technical and operating capabilities
- Target market strategies

- Marketing objectives
- Marketing offer strategies and tactics
- Access to key resources

The profile can then be searched for insights into the potential actions of each competitor. The result is a picture of the way in which a key competitor strives to reach markets and positions itself against competition.

Periodically updating the profile of a key competitor will provide a historical picture of the decision-making style and tendencies of its management. Past decisions show the pattern of changes in marketing strategy and tactics as managers responded to market conditions. Analysis of these decisions includes matching them with specific changes in markets or competition. An experienced marketer can then develop a feel for the management style of a key competitor by looking for patterns or consistencies in these decisions. An interesting illustration comes from Digital Equipment Corporation's entry into personal computer markets. Historical analysis of DEC's marketing decisions shows its goal of concentrating on minicomputers. Thus, a logical prediction is that DEC's personal computers will be compatible with its minicomputers so that users can communicate between both types of systems. And, in fact, that is DEC's strategy.[18]

Evaluating Key Competitors

The information gathered allows an analyst to evaluate a key competitor's strengths and weaknesses. The analyst considers both the competitor's coverage of market segments and its success in meeting market requirements. This analysis parallels the analysis of the corresponding industry, so that comparisons can be made.

Competitor Coverage. Beginning with coverage, managers will want to know what priority a key competitor has placed on each target market. The market's structure is used as a basis for evaluation. This structure is generated from a market opportunity analysis of market composition for a product and is the same structure that is used to evaluate the coverage of the corresponding industry. (For an illustration, review Exhibit 7-6). Extensive coverage is indicated by the placing of high priorities on specific market segments and by correspondingly high allocation of marketing effort to them. In contrast, limited coverage is revealed when viable market segments are found that are not targeted by a key competitor or at least have more demand than is indicated by the competitor's target market priority. For instance, IBM's lack of minicomputers was a weakness in market coverage, allowing DEC to serve that market without directly confronting the more powerful IBM.[19]

Meeting Market Requirements   As important as assessing key competitors' market coverage is the evaluation of key competitors' ability to meet or exceed customers' market requirements. This assessment is concerned with the quality of each key competitor's marketing program. Customer profiles are examined to identify customers' important market requirements. The strategy and tactics used by the key competitor must be scrutinized to see how they meet each market requirement. Judgments can then be formed as to how well or poorly each of these requirements is satisfied.

This analysis helps management uncover the strengths (important market requirements met well) and weaknesses (important market requirements met poorly) of each key competitor's technical and marketing strategy and tactics. Management is alerted to the strengths that must be matched and the weaknesses that offer opportunities to find better ways of satisfying unmet market requirements.[20] DEC's personal computer strategy, for instance, had to match the strengths of IBM and other competitors in distribution, service, and software support. At the same time, DEC was able to exploit its own strength in system compatibility among different computer models, an important market requirement for professional manager markets. Key competitive manufacturers have historically not met this system compatibility requirement very well.[21]

Predicting Key Competitors' Future Marketing Actions

The final step in a key competitor analysis is predicting changes in key competitors' marketing strategy and tactics. Since it takes considerable time to fully implement new strategies and tactics, management should be able to base many such predictions on patterns or trends in the past marketing actions of key competitors. Predictions are made when these trends are extrapolated, or projected into the future. Such extrapolation is based in part on management's belief that given the probable market conditions, continuing the patterns or trends is logical and sound. A historical pattern is evident in DEC's distribution decisions. For several years, DEC has been expanding the number of its retail stores and changing them into one-stop computer centers.[22] An extrapolation prediction is that DEC will continue to do this until it has achieved a national distribution system.

Management should not overrely on trend analysis. Other techniques are needed to complement trend analyses of key competitors' marketing strategies and tactics. These techniques indicate changes that are too new to be spotted by examining historical trends. Here, a competitor intelligence system is needed.[23] Among the important methods of such a system are monitoring key competitors' marketing research; analyzing key competitors' probable response, given their management styles, to anticipated changes in market conditions; interviewing key competitors' suppliers, distributors, and customers; and hiring away key competitors' managers. Equally important is an ongoing, diligent effort by management to derive predictions from the information obtained by the intelligence system. This requires thorough assessment of the information and imaginative conclusions concerning its implications. One expert comments on the efforts of some companies to familiarize themselves with the management styles of key competitors:

EXHIBIT 7-11 Ganging Up on Black & Decker

Black & Decker is halfway through the biggest brand swap in history. The company, known for power tools and its Dustbuster cordless vacuum cleaner, spent $300 million 19 months ago to buy General Electric's small-appliance business; it has until April 1987 to bring all of GE's 150-odd products under its own logo. In renaming the GE appliances, Black & Decker is doing for its competitors something they could not possibly have accomplished themselves—eliminating the best-known name in the small-appliance business.

The other guys aren't showing much gratitude. Sensing confusion in the market and weakness in their competitor, they've fattened their advertising budgets and unleashed a torrent of new products to intercept GE's customers before they get to Black & Decker.

Sunbeam, Rival, Hamilton Beach, Norelco, and several European labels are taking aim at the company, which has had limited experience selling small appliances beyond the Dust-

buster. Sunbeam, a unit of Allegheny International, is leading the assault, spearheaded by the unexpected success of Oskar, its compact food processor. Oskar has opened the door at retail stores for other products from Sunbeam; indeed, Sunbeam executives say that orders of all of its appliances are up 40 percent so far this year.

Black & Decker has orchestrated a new-product blitz of its own and has begun a $100-million advertising and promotion campaign, the largest ever in the small-appliance industry. The company insists that its program to wean consumers off GE's label and onto its own has gone better than expected. But even Black & Decker concedes that it is losing ground in the iron business—which with estimated sales of $275 billion annually is one of the biggest chunks of the $8.3 billion-a-year small-appliance industry. In other big categories, market surveys show Black & Decker slipping in toaster ovens, at least holding its own in coffee makers, and gaining in toasters.

Source: Bill Saporito, "Ganging Up on Black & Decker," *Fortune*, December 23, 1985, pp. 63–64.

What appears to be vital to effective intelligence activities is that the emphasis be focused on anticipating expected behavior by key competitors. . . . Several firms have successfully institutionalized this emphasis on anticipating behavior or responses by key players by assigning to line managers the role of a "shadow" competitor. . . . In strategy meetings, it is expected of these "shadow" executives that they be able to present their best judgment as to how their particular "shadow" will respond to strategic moves being considered.[24]

Competition Analyses and Marketing Planning

Positioning
refers to the use of marketing strategy to match the strengths of competition and to exploit its weaknesses, thereby giving customers a reason to buy from one seller rather than another.

Clearly, to be successful, a company's marketing strategy must meet customers' market requirements. But a marketing strategy must also meet another, often more difficult challenge. A company must effectively position itself against competition within an industry. In fact, the essence of planning marketing strategy is to find ways of effectively **positioning** a company against the competition in the minds of customers. Positioning in action is shown in Exhibit 7-11, which describes Black & Decker's struggle to compete in small appliance markets.

There are many alternative positioning strategies.[25] From a marketing viewpoint, however, most of them revolve around a combination of two basic and complementary approaches (Exhibit 7-12): positioning by target market strategies and positioning marketing programs for differential advantage.

Target Market Strategies

Positioning can be achieved through target market decisions by exploiting competitive weaknesses in market coverage. From the industry and key

EXHIBIT 7–12 Competitive Positioning Strategies

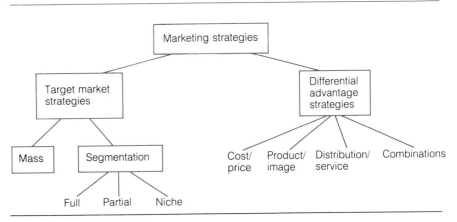

competitor analyses, management looks for "holes" in the competitive coverage across the market's structure. A hole is evident when there is more demand in the market, or in a specific market segment, than is being met by competition. When competition is very limited, as might happen early in a product type's life cycle, a mass strategy may be best. Here, an entire generic-class or product-type market is treated as undifferentiated and served with a single marketing offer. Considerable cost efficiencies are gained from concentrating resources on the one offer.

As competitive coverage improves across a market, a company is more likely to employ a segmentation strategy. In analyzing product-market structure, marketing managers look for segments where a company can effectively compete. The coverage of existing and anticipated competition is deemed not to be so extensive as to completely saturate these segments. Segments in which competition is too extensive may be avoided or given lower priority. A company can elect to cover all or most segments (full segmentation) or some segments (partial segmentation) or to specialize in one or a few segments (niche segmentation). Chapter 11 expands more fully on the target market strategy decision.

The role of competitive coverage in target market decisions is illustrated by the soft-drink industry. Recently, this industry has found segments based on preferences for such products as diet, decaffeinated, and noncola soft drinks in addition to the segment for sugar-based cola drinks. The largest competitor, Coca-Cola Company, has chosen an interesting target market strategy. Coca-Cola waits for competitors to discover a segment and demonstrate its market opportunity before moving in with a competitive brand. Royal Crown was the first to tap the diet cola segment, with its Diet Rite brand. Coke moved in later with Tab and Diet Coke. This strategy has been successful because of Coke's product, promotion, and distribution strengths relative to those of its key competitors.

Smaller soft-drink manufacturers have had to develop different targeting strategies to compete with Coke in the United States. Dr Pepper has chosen to concentrate in the South and Southwest, where it has had market strength; 7UP is focusing on the no-caffeine segment, though it does have a cola drink; and Royal Crown is trying to find new segments.[26]

Target market strategies for positioning depend heavily on the way in which market structure is defined. Market structure can change over time as new segments are uncovered, as is well illustrated by the soft-drink market. Thus, companies that rely on target marketing for positioning must continually reassess existing market structure, searching for market segments that are not well served by competition.

Differential Advantage

Properly selecting target markets is only a start toward effective positioning. The marketing program must also be creatively employed to build a differential advantage over competition in the minds of customers. Being different from the competition is not enough. The difference must represent an advantage to customers by meeting at least some important market requirements better than do other sellers. Although IBM's personal computer was not the first personal computer on the market or the most innovative, it became one of the leading brands rather quickly because IBM built differential advantages in a combination of areas—rapid development of compatible software and peripherals through independent suppliers, extensive distribution to home and business markets, size economies to enable strong price competition, and a corporate reputation for product quality and service. This set of differential advantages, all relating to important market requirements, added up to a huge market success.

Careful analyses both of market requirements and of competitor strengths and weaknesses in meeting those requirements are the cornerstone for differential advantage strategies. In addition, a company has to assess its own capabilities to ensure that the planned strategies can be carried out. Not every personal computer manufacturer, for instance, has the combination of size, marketing know-how, and reputation to pull off the strategy with which IBM supported its personal computers. But the ability to effectively use whatever capabilities a company has is clearly dependent on understanding competitive strengths and weaknesses.

Summary

Analysis of competition has a crucial role in planning marketing strategy. A significant part of any marketing plan must be devoted to spec- ifying how a company intends to position itself against the competition. The success of a planned position depends on the soundness of management's understanding of the competition's strengths and weaknesses. Careful and imaginative analysis of the competition is instrumental in building such an understanding.

Competition may not be limited to the similar brands of other companies. Management must be alert to different kinds of competition. The most serious competition sometimes comes from other product types—dissimilar brands that are capable of satisfying the same needs or wants. Even needs and wants can compete with each other as customers set buying priorities. Identifying competition begins with market definition. Markets are the arena in which organizations compete for sales. How the management of an organization sees the arena (defines markets) influences which other organizations are or will be competitors. Furthermore, competition changes over a product life cycle. The life-cycle concept serves as a framework for analyzing both the emergence of new competition and the shakeout of existing competition.

Our approach to analyzing competition involves two steps: analyzing entire industries and analyzing individual key competitors. Beginning with the analysis of industries generates a background on product-type and brand competition. Industry analyses encourage management to step back and look at the similarities and differences in the way organizations are reaching markets and developing demand. Analyzing industries also helps management identify the companies that are truly key competitors.

Analyses of industries and of key competitors use parallel procedures. Both require information that is essentially historical and descriptive. Marketing managers want to understand industry structure, industry size and growth, the influence of governmental policy on an industry, and the typical marketing strategies and tactics employed in an industry. Similarly, for key competitors information on financial size and strength and on technical, marketing, and management capabilities is sought. These information profiles are then used to analyze market coverage, strengths and weakness in meeting market requirements, and anticipated changes in marketing strategy both for an industry and for key competitors.

Analyses of competition play a crucial role in marketing planning. Marketing strategy is essentially a way of positioning against the competition when seeking to meet demand in markets. Every company must develop an appeal to markets that matches the strengths of competitors and exploits their weaknesses.

There are many ways to position effectively, all of which involve a combination of two kinds of strategic marketing decisions. First, management must carefully select target markets in which a company can succeed against the competition. Holes in competitive coverage are sought, and markets where the competition is too extensive are avoided. Second, marketing mix components are used to build a differential advantage over the competition. Usually, a company must find a way to be different from its competitors, particularly its key competitors, in the minds of customers. The difference must offer an advantage to customers in meeting one or more important market requirements. Essentially, a differential advantage causes customers to see a company as standing out from the competition.

Exercises for Review and Discussion

1. Your Serve, a tennis shop in a medium-sized city, experienced a leveling off of sales of tennis clothing and equipment. The owner was puzzled as to the reasons because she felt that her store was very competitive with other tennis stores in the city. She decided to do some analysis of competition to see whether her store had lost its edge. What kinds of competition should she analyze? Discuss the reasons for your answer.

2. Stouffer's recently introduced a new frozen

food product type, Lean Cuisine low-calorie gourmet frozen meals. What can the management of Stouffer's expect from competition over the next several years? Discuss the reasons for your answer.

3. Compare the probable competitive impact that would be experienced by a company that decreased its price if the company were in a monopoly, an oligopoly, or a pure competition industry. Would the impact be the same in all three situations? Why or why not?

4. Suppose you have the industry coverage information shown in Exhibit 7-A and are using it to select target markets for your company's brand. The slices of the circle represent market segments, and the words *extensive, moderate,* and *low* indicate the analyst's opinion of the extent to which the industry is targeting and meeting the volume of demand in these market segments. How would you apply this information to the target market decision? Discuss the reasons for your answer.

5. Suppose you were evaluating a key competitor as part of an MOA. A report on the competitor's marketing strategy concludes that it has a high-quality product, a price about the same as the average price for the industry, and creative advertising. Further, the report points out that the competitor has a large sales force, offers few services, and has a distribution system that is typical for the industry. Can you assess the key competitor's strengths and weaknesses from this information? Why or why not?

6. Charlie Jones is a sales manager for a soft-drink manufacturer. He prides himself on knowing the competition in his sales district. He has taken the time to keep track of how competitors

Exhibit 7-A

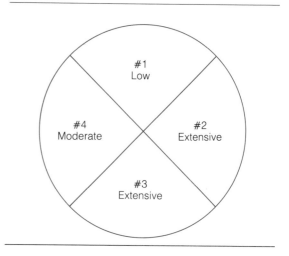

responded in the past to his company's marketing strategy changes and to other changes occurring in markets. Is Charlie safe in feeling that he can predict the moves of his company's competitors? Why or why not?

7. Pick any company that uses advertising extensively. Build a file of the company's advertisements, being sure to consider the various media that may be used. After analyzing the content of these advertisements, discuss the way in which the company is positioning its products in markets.

8. The popular noncola soft drink 7UP has been trying to make inroads in soft-drink markets by increasing market share. Management is trying to position 7UP against key competitors. Should these key competitors be restricted to other noncola soft drinks? Why or why not?

Notes

1. Information for the do-it-yourselfer illustration came from Jo Ellen Davis. "Hardware Wars: The Big Boys Might Lose This One," *Business Week*, October 14, 1985, pp. 84, 89, 91.

2. Barton A. Weitz, "Introduction to Special Issue on Competition in Marketing," *Journal of Marketing Research* 22 (August 1985), p. 229.

3. "Lanier Aims to Win Back its office leadership," *Business Week*, May 16, 1983, p. 133.

4. Weitz, "Introduction to Special Issue," p. 229.

5. George S. Day, *Analysis for Strategic Market Decisions* (St. Paul, Minn.: West Publishing, 1986), p. 59.

6. For a discussion of the product life-cycle concept, see George Day, "The Product Life Cycle: Analysis and Applications Issues," *Journal of Marketing* 45 (Fall 1981), pp. 60–67.

7. David R. Rink and John E. Swan, "Product Life Cycle Research: A Literature Review," *Journal of Business Research* 78 (September 1979), p. 238.

8. These reasons for product decline are discussed in Kathryn Rudie Harrigan and Michael E. Porter, "End-Game Strategies for Declining Industries," *Harvard Business Review*, July–August 1983, pp. 112–13.

9. Strategies for a declining product are more fully discussed in Harrigan and Porter, "End-Game Strategies," pp. 116–20.

10. An interesting and thorough discussion of competitive moves in industries can be found in Michael E. Porter, *Competitive Strategy* (New York: Free Press, 1980), chap. 5.

11. The importance of national policy to competitive analyses is more fully discussed in Philip Wellons, "International Bankers: Size Up Your Competitors," *Harvard Business Review*, November–December 1982, pp. 95–105.

12. "Japan: The Unlikely Nuclear Giant," *Business Week*, September 19, 1983, pp. 66, 71.

13. Paul B. Brown, Barbara Buell, Jo Ellen Davis, and Kenneth Dreyfack, "Forget Satisfying the Consumer—Just Outfox the Other Guy," *Business Week*, October 7, 1985, p. 55.

14. "Suppliers Battle It Out for Space on the Desk," *Business Week*, August 8, 1983, p. 52.

15. Porter, *Competitive Strategy*, p. 3.

16. "A New Strategy for No. 2 in Computers," *Business Week*, May 2, 1983, pp. 66–75.

17. William E. Rothschild, "Competitor Analysis: The Missing Link in Strategy," *Management Review*, July 1979, p. 23.

18. "A New Strategy for No. 2," p. 67.

19. Ibid.

20. Robert E. MacAvoy, "Corporate Strategy and the Power of Competitive Analysis," *Management Review*, July 1983, p. 13.

21. "A New Strategy for No. 2," p. 67.

22. Ibid.

23. Interesting discussions of competitor intelligence systems and sources of information are contained in "Business Sharpens Its Spying Techniques," *Business Week*, August 4, 1975, 60–62; and "How to Snoop on Your Competitors," *Fortune*, May 14, 1984, pp. 29–30.

24. Ian C. MacMillan, "Seizing Competitive Initiative," *Journal of Business Strategy*, Spring 1982, p. 45.

25. More comprehensive discussions of marketing strategy alternatives are found in Porter, *Competitive Strategy*, chap. 2; and Philip Kotler and Ravi Singh, "Marketing Warfare in the 1980s," *Journal of Business Strategy*, Spring 1983, pp. 30–41.

26. Information for the soft-drink example was taken from "Coke's Big Marketing Blitz," *Business Week*, May 30, 1983, pp. 58-64.

CHAPTER 8

Market Measurement and Forecasting

General Electric Company is locked in a battle for supremacy in worldwide sales of industrial robots and machine tool controls. A few years ago, GE bet heavily on forecasts of very attractive sales for these products. Management predicted that world sales would mushroom to a "megamarket" size of some $25 billion a year and that the company's market share would eventually reach 20 percent. Strategy was planned to position GE as the one place to shop for all of the computerized control equipment and consultation that "factories of the future" might need. More than $500 million was sunk into this venture. The forecasts proved to be much too optimistic, and GE lost over $120 million before deciding to rethink its strategy. The company had to revise its forecasts of product sales and market share downward and adjust its scale of operations correspondingly.[1]

Seldom does anyone know exactly what the future holds, as GE's management found out. Nevertheless, managers make plans based on what they anticipate. In any organization, planning in many functional areas requires knowing what sales of products to expect. Building factories, determining appropriate levels of inventory, planning for cash flows, and hiring production workers are just a few of the nonmarketing activities that depend on demand forecasts. In addition, marketing managers must estimate demand in order to plan marketing strategy and tactics. Exhibit 8-1 provides a revealing insight into the use of sales forecasts by various company departments as reported by one study.

The marketing function often has responsibility for predicting sales, because sales are the result of customer buying decisions in markets. Future sales are estimated in the market measurement and forecasting component of a market opportunity analysis. This chapter expands on this component to help you become better users of sales predictions. The first section discusses the nature of demand or sales estimation and the marketing manager's role in forecasting. Then, a forecasting process is examined that applies the product-market concept introduced in Chapter 4. Next, alternative forecasting approaches are presented. An actual forecasting process is reviewed so that the

EXHIBIT 8-1 Company Departments Using Sales Forecasts

Department	Percent of Firms That Said Department Used Sales Forecasts
Finance	80
Executive or administrative	78
Budgeting	63
Manufacturing	61
Inventory control	55
Purchasing	53
Planning	52
Accounting	44
Advertising	34
Personnel	23
Merchandising	22
Research and development	22
Transportation	19

Source: Douglas J. Dalrymple, "Sales Forecasting Methods and Accuracy," *Business Horizons*, December 1975, p. 70.

criteria for selecting a forecasting approach in a real situation can be assessed. Finally, the task of evaluating a company's forecasting system is examined.

Nature of Demand Estimation

Market conditions are all of the factors that influence customer buying decisions and include macroenvironmental demand factors; the physical, attitudinal, and motivational makeup of buyers; and the marketing strategies and tactics of competition.

Forecast scenario is the particular combination of market conditions assumed in a particular forecast.

As is true of any event that can be forecast, demand for a product is not random. It is caused by the particular set of **market conditions** that exist when customers make purchase decisions: macroenvironmental demand factors, the composition of markets, and competition. The implication is that all forecasts of demand are actually conditional predictions. That is, when making a demand estimate, the forecaster is saying, "If all market conditions affect demand as we anticipate they will, then demand is expected to be as estimated." In a way, the forecaster must predict the combination of market conditions, called a **forecast scenario,** before estimating the expected resulting level of sales. Different scenarios will lead to different forecasts.

The conditional nature of demand estimates is clearly evident in Sears' projections for U.S. auto sales for the middle 1980s. Using hindsight, we can see the role played by the scenario. As the largest seller of auto accessories, Sears was very interested in the growth of automobile sales during this period because its sales of accessories were directly dependent on auto sales. The projection, made at the end of 1983, predicted continued growth in automobile sales to a peak of 10.9 million in 1985, when a cyclical decline would occur. The forecasters identified specific market conditions affecting auto sales and made a prediction for each one:

- Slow growth in number of drivers.

- Interest rates going back up, beginning in 1984.

- The probable inability of Congress to deal with large budget deficits.

- A general lack of growth in the number of miles driven by Americans.

The accuracy of the auto sales forecasts depended on the extent to which these predictions were confirmed.[2]

Information for Demand Estimation

Many kinds of data are used in forecasting. Most such data have one characteristic in common: They describe what has happened in markets or what is happening now. Many companies examine their past and present sales for clues to forecasting future sales. Historical and current events are fact, so they can be objectively observed or measured. And they can yield insights into what will happen in the future. John Naisbitt, a well-known trend forecaster, strongly argues for this approach to forecasting:

> The key to understanding what *might* go on is really to understand what *is* going on. What I really do is try to figure out the present.[3]

The ease of collecting historical data is an advantage, but it is not the full reason for their use in forecasting. Future demand for a product is at least partly dependent on what has already occurred in markets. Advertising of product benefits has a carryover effect to future periods. Repeat buying depends in part on how satisfied customers are with past purchases. And there are many other such carryover effects, suggesting that future sales are tied to past events. While market conditions do change, the changes are often evolutionary, rather than complete departures from the past. Evolutionary or trend changes in demand are evident in historical data. Thus, forecasters can often obtain reasonable estimates of future demand by projecting from these historical data into the future.

The Manager's Role in Forecasting

Despite the advantages of historical data, there is a very real danger in using *only* such data for forecasting. Changes in one or more market conditions may be so recent that a trend has not yet developed, and even the present may offer limited clues. This situation is well illustrated by the market explosion that hit the bicycle industry in the early to middle 1970s. Prior to that time, bicycles were typically purchased for children, so growth in demand for bicycles was tied closely to growth in the U.S. population. In 1971, however, demand for bicycles accelerated rapidly, catching the U.S. industry by surprise. The forecasts used by the industry had not predicted that unit sales would more than double during the three-year period from 1971 to 1973. What happened was that an important market condition changed quickly. Adults discovered that bicycling was fun and healthful. The bicycle became a toy for adults as well as children.[4]

To guard against overrelying on past and current events, managers must be willing to examine forecasts in light of their own judgment of future market conditions. Often forecasts may have to be adjusted in light of anticipated events in markets. From our perspective in the 1980s, the change in the bicycle industry's market structure appears more predictable than it did in the early 1970s. Could U.S. bicycle companies have predicted the change when it was happening? Perhaps. Analysis of population trends would have revealed growth in the number of young adults, who later became buyers. Examining emerging lifestyle trends, particularly among these young adults, would have shown an awakening interest in physical fitness and recreation. Managers accustomed to using such supplemental analyses might have predicted a coming change in market structure. Studies could then have been made to see whether the prediction was being confirmed. Without doing the analyses or using judgment, managers had little chance of predicting the change. The implication is that managers who use forecasts should be involved in making them.

A Forecasting Process

Demand estimates can be made at any or all product-market levels: generic product class, product type, and brand. At each level, a potential or a forecast can be estimated. Managers may request all or some subset of these estimates, depending on the marketing decisions at stake.

Building Market Conditions into Forecasting

The forecasting process begins with the construction of a scenario describing important market conditions affecting future demand. (Management may want to construct several scenarios and to forecast future sales under each of them.) Exhibit 8–2 summarizes important market conditions that are likely to be uncovered by a market opportunity analysis. These stem from analyses of market composition, demand factors, and competition. Only after these analyses have been completed can market conditions be systematically incorporated into the forecasting process using data and judgment.

The role of prior analyses of market conditions is aptly illustrated in a market expansion decision made by the management of a small company, Environmental Systems Corporation (ESC). ESC's engineers had developed a very accurate electronic temperature measurement instrument that they used on consulting projects. A few sales of the instrument had been made to

EXHIBIT 8-2 Market Conditions Influence Demand Estimates at All
Product-Market Levels

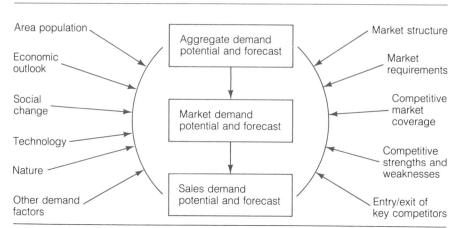

unsolicited customers, suggesting market interest. Management quickly recognized that the product created an opportunity for the company to diversify beyond consulting and into manufacturing. However, it had to find out whether demand was great enough to support the costs of the new venture.

ESC did not have sufficient internal data for forecasting sales of the product. Consequently, secondary sources and telephone interviews were used to analyze market conditions for the generic class, product type, and brand (see Exhibit 8-3). The results led to the assumptions shown in column 2. The estimates in column 3 for U.S. markets over a four-year forecasting period are based on these assumptions. For instance, the estimated $4 million increase in product-type sales was based on an anticipated change in federal regulation of quality control standards in certain industries and on an expected increase in buyer familiarity with the technology characteristic of the product type. The accuracy of the demand estimates depends on the validity of these market condition predictions.

Alternative Forecasting Approaches

Managers may not feel comfortable with demand estimates that are derived by means of an unfamiliar estimation technique. If they do not understand the reasons for a forecast, they are unlikely to accept it. This fact was evident when sales managers for a large appliance manufacturer would not use forecasts generated by a sophisticated computer-based model; they did not

EXHIBIT 8–3 Demand Forecasts for Precision Temperature Instruments

(1) **Product-Market Levels**	(2) **Market Condition Predictions**	(3) **Four-Year Market Demand Increases**
Generic class		
Temperature measurement instruments	Expansion in uses of process control Increasing use of microprocessor technology Industrial growth No major recession	$60 million
Product type		
RTD-type instrument with better than +/− 2° C accuracy	New federal regulation requiring more accurate temperature measurement Increasing familiarity of engineers with microprocessor technology and RTD technology	$4 million
Brand ESC's brand of RTD-type instrument	Pharmaceutical firms to be initial market target Small size of market unattractive to large competitors Implementation of marketing plan	$400,000

understand or trust the technique. To overcome such problems, managers who use demand forecasts must be familiarized with forecasting techniques.

A Classification Scheme

Learning about forecasting is complicated by the fact that no one forecasting technique is best for all situations. This explains why so many different techniques are used. A classification scheme, such as the one shown in Exhibit 8–4, is needed to organize the many available techniques and to provide guidelines for matching them to decision situations. The first branching shows that there are essentially two classes of techniques:

■ Formal modeling techniques, which specify an explicit mathematical model and rely on "hard" data to build and implement the model.

■ Informed judgment techniques, which do not require an explicit model and use "soft" data (opinions).

Each class, in turn, includes three major types. With proper data, all forecasting techniques can be used at every product-market level, from generic class to product type to brand.

EXHIBIT 8–4 A Classification of Alternative Demand Estimation Techniques

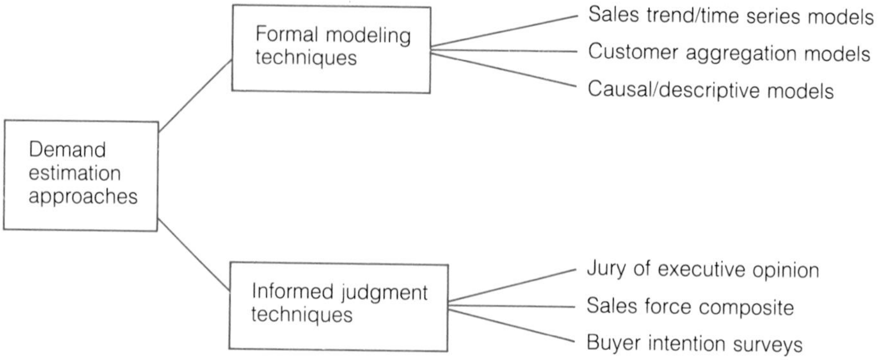

Formal modeling techniques
use hard data and mathematical equations to predict future sales.

Formal Modeling Techniques. **Formal modeling techniques** employ a mathematical model that specifies how a forecast is to be derived from data. The model uses mathematical equations that describe:

■ What data are to be used.

■ The relative importance of different data to the forecast, if data of more than one type are to be used.

■ How the data are to be manipulated mathematically to derive the forecast.

In formal models, "hard" data are used. These data are collected under carefully controlled conditions, and they usually measure objective, observable events or characteristics as opposed to more intangible opinions and attitudes. Information collected from a company's accounting records, sales data from a test market field experiment, and census survey data are examples of hard data.

Forecasting models vary widely. Typically, however, they fall into one of three categories: trend/time series models, customer aggregation models, and causal/descriptive models.

Trend/time series models
search for patterns or regularities of change in a series of historical data, such as past product sales; the patterns are projected into the future to make forecasts.

Trend/time series models. **Trend/time series models** rely on historical data series for forecasting growth. When applied to forecasting sales, the data series is usually past sales. (See Exhibit 8–5, column 2 for an example of a product sales series.) Various procedures are used to search for regularities or patterns of change in the sales series. Once found, that pattern is projected into the future by assuming that the underlying factors causing historical changes from period to period will continue to exert the same or similar influences.

Period-to-period changes in the sales series are analyzed to determine historical growth, which can then be projected into the forecast period.

EXHIBIT 8-5 A Sales Series and Year-to-Year Changes for Microwave Oven Retail Sales in the United States

(1) Year	(2) U.S. Microwave Oven Sales (units)	(3) Year-to-Year Change (units)	(4) Year-to-Year Change (percent)
1970	30,000		
1971	100,000	70,000	233%
1972	325,000	225,000	225
1973	440,000	115,000	35
1974	635,000	195,000	44
1975	840,000	205,000	32
1976	1,661,000	821,000	98
1977	2,175,000	514,000	31
1978	2,422,000	247,000	11
1979	2,815,000	393,000	14
1980	3,585,000	770,000	27
1981	4,575,000	990,000	22
1982	4,201,000	(374,000)	(08)
1983	4,896,000	695,000	17
1984	5,200,000	304,000	6

Sources: *Predicasts Basebook* (Cleveland: Predicasts, Inc., 1983), p. 652; and *Predicasts Forecasts* (Cleveland: Predicasts, Inc., 1984), p. B-114.

Columns 3 and 4 of Exhibit 8-5 show two ways to calculate period-to-period changes in sales: unit change and percentage change. If we are interested in forecasting annual sales over a period of several years, *trend analysis* of the sales series is used to uncover growth trends over a preselected future period of time.

A long-run trend is usually hidden by short-run up-and-down fluctuations in sales. This characteristic of sales series can be seen in columns 3 and 4 of Exhibit 8-5. While sales of microwave ovens have increased in every year except 1982, the amount of growth shows considerable variation. The overall trend can be revealed by smoothing out these short-run fluctuations. There are many techniques for smoothing, too many to review here.[5] However, the logic of the process can be illustrated by a few of the simpler techniques.

Suppose the forecaster believes that the *long-run average* change in units is the best indication of future growth in sales. Calculation of the long-run average is very straightforward:

$$\text{ALRC} = \sum_{i=1}^{n-1} C_i \tag{8-1}$$

where:

ALRC = Average long-run change in unit sales

C_i = Unit change in sales for the ith pair of periods

n − 1 = Number of pairs of periods for which change in sales is calculated

A forecast of the next period's sales would apply this average unit growth to the previous period's sales:

$$Sales_{t+1} = Sales_t + ALRC \qquad (8\text{-}2)$$

Average change may work well for a very stable product-market situation. However, with such products as microwave ovens, for which dramatic changes in market conditions have occurred over immediate past periods, other smoothing approaches are more appropriate. A forecaster may believe, for instance, that only the r most recent periods in the sales series should be used in computing an average change in sales. Periods more distant in time than r may involve market conditions very different from those believed to be important influences on sales during the forecast period. A simple *moving average* technique could be used in this situation.

A moving average calculates average growth using Equation (8-1), except that n − 1 is replaced by r − 1. Equation (8-2) is the forecasting model (assuming that growth is calculated in units rather than as a percentage). The average growth applied in Equation (8-2) changes for each subsequent period forecast since the r − 1 most recent sales changes are always being used, which is why this is called a "moving average" technique.

A forecaster may search for a linear (or nonlinear) trend by applying *curve-fitting* techniques to the sales series. The most common technique of this kind is least squares regression. A straight line is fitted directly to the sales series such that the sum of the squared deviations between the sales data points and the line is minimized. The model is:

$$S_{t+1} = a + b\,(t + 1) \qquad (8\text{-}3)$$

where:

S_{t+1} = Forecast sales

    a = Constant measuring the level of sales that would be predicted without the effect of time

    b = Slope of the regression line showing unit change over time

t + 1 = Forecast time period

The values of a and b are determined by calculating the one line that best fits the historical sales series. To project the line for forecasting, these values are assumed to hold for the forecast period. Forecasts are made by inserting a value for t + 1, the forecast period. Essentially, the calculation extends the line into the forecast period to determine expected sales. Exhibit 8-6 shows a plot of the microwave oven sales series and a line fitted to those data. To determine the forecasts for 1985 and 1986, the forecast periods, the line is extended to these years. Forecast sales are found by projecting from the line for these two years over to the sales axis.

Applications of forecasts may require knowing whether there is any regularity in the short-run fluctuations around the long-run trend. Scheduling

EXHIBIT 8-6 Linear Trend Forecast

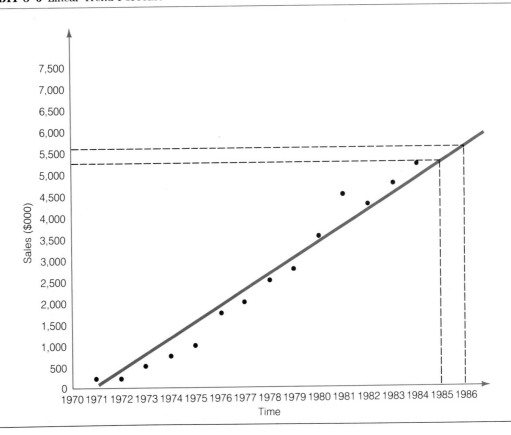

advertising, planning for inventories, and other company decisions may benefit from forecasts of short-run (within one year) variations. *Time series*
techniques are used to uncover regularities in such variations. In the general
model for time series, sales are assumed to be caused by five components:

D = Sales for a product in the forecast period

T = Long-run trend effect on sales

C = Cyclical effects on sales, which are medium-length up-and-down,
wavelike movements around the trend, often but not always tied to a
nation's business cycle

S = Seasonal effects on sales, which are short-run (within one year), up-
and-down variations around the trend due to such very predictable
events as weather (seasons), holidays, and school opening and closing

TD = Trading day effects on sales due to differences in the number of trading days in a time period (e.g., February's 28 days versus March's 31 days)

I = Irregular effects on sales due to such unpredictable, randomly occurring events as storms, fire, and floods.[6]

A sales series is examined to estimate each component separately. Discussion of alternative analytic procedures for analyzing each of these components is beyond the scope of this chapter. However, the concept of smoothing, introduced above, is central to the time series estimation process.[7] Individual forecasts of each component (except I, which is not forecastable) are inserted into a model of prespecified form such as:

$$D = T \times C \times S \times TD \qquad (8\text{-}4)$$

Both trend and time series approaches require a reasonably long historical sales series to identify projectable patterns. Moreover, these approaches make the rather restrictive assumption that the market conditions affecting future sales will be similar to those that generated the sale series. These limitations suggest that trend and time series approaches are best applied to forecasts for established products, such as those in the late growth and maturity stages of a product life cycle.[8]

One of the most challenging aspects of forecasting is predicting *turning points*—when a declining sales pattern levels out and starts to rise, or when an upward pattern turns down. Trend and time series approaches are not very good at predicting turning points, particularly when the turning points are caused by new market conditions, so other approaches may be better here.[9]

Customer Aggregation Models. Generally, when marketing managers need forecasts of sales, some survey work has been done on product demand. Information typically available includes: characteristics of the typical buyers, extent of product use, life of the product, types of use situations, and substitute products. Further, data describing populations in which markets are located are often readily obtainable. **Customer aggregation models** rely on these kinds of data to estimate future demand. The basic model breaks demand down into its components:

- Number of people in a target market.
- Likelihood that these people will buy in the forecast period.
- Quantity purchased.

The calculation is:

$$S = N \times L \times R \qquad (8\text{-}5)$$

where:

S = Estimated future product sales

Customer aggregation models break sales down into their major components, each component is forecast, and the resulting forecasts are multiplied together to get a sales estimate.

N = Number of people (or organizations) in the target market

L = Likelihood that the typical person in N will make a purchase in the forecast time period

R = Quantity purchased during the forecast time period

Demand is estimated by separately forecasting each component. Demographic and socioeconomic characteristics are often used in the estimation of N. Suppose we want to count N, the number of households in markets for day-care centers. Demand for these centers arises because while away from home, working parents need care for their children. Demographics help to describe this market: households with two parents working or with a single working parent in which there is at least one child 12 or under. Population data can be used to count the number of such households in an area.

The estimation of N results from a count of the number of people in each population group. However, some of these people will not buy at all, while others may not buy during the forecast period. Thus, N must be adjusted downward to obtain a more realistic estimate of the number of buyers. The model uses L, a number between 0 and 1, to measure the likelihood of buying. L is influenced by such factors as product life, product availability, the popularity of substitute products, and the use situations requiring the product. It can be quite difficult to estimate. Historical data on product penetration into markets are a starting point. If we know, for instance, that 15 percent of families with working parents use day-care centers, then a reasonable guess is a .15 likelihood that a household in our market will use day-care centers in the future. The forecaster may want to adjust that likelihood to reflect growth (or decline) in market demand. Data from studies, experience with substitute or complementary products, and knowledge of product characteristics and use situations are very useful for this purpose. In this forecast, improving the quality of day-care services may suggest a greater L or, in contrast, scandals involving the abuse of children at day-care centers may suggest a smaller L.

An estimate of purchase quantity, R, completes the forecasting process. This component converts number of buyers into number of unit or dollar sales. Purchases are dependent on product life, product availability, needs or wants, and use situations. Thus, data on these factors are used to make the estimate. The use of day care-centers by working parents is dependent, for example, on the number of working days during the forecast period.

Customer aggregation models can be applied in situations where sales data are not available. Moreover, the procedure encourages managers to examine the impact of key demand determinants on sales. Managers can see whether growth in sales is coming from population changes (e.g., growth in N), greater likelihood of buying as people learn more about the product, expanding uses, or some combination of these sources. The result is usually a greater understanding of market opportunity. Finally, by using data on market needs, use situations, and product life, the forecaster can estimate the maximum sales that a market will support—potential. In contrast, sales trend techniques are limited to estimating forecasts.

Causal/Descriptive Models.   If it is thought that demand is caused by certain identifiable market conditions or factors, **causal/descriptive models** can be used. Forecasters try to uncover such factors through a trial-and-error search process. The search usually involves examining how historical data on selected factors correlate with a historical sales series for the same time periods. We can look at this process at work. Suppose the manager of a bicycle store wanted to forecast next year's sales of bicycles and had seven years data on:

Causal/descriptive models
base demand estimates on forecasts of one or more market conditions shown to influence product sales.

- The store's bicycle sales.
- Population size in the county.
- Retail sales for the county.
- Effective buying income for the county.

By using a modeling technique such as regression analysis, she could evaluate the extent to which population size, retail sales, and effective buying income "explain" the historical variation in sales. If the relationship is strong, she can apply estimates of future population size, retail sales, and effective buying income to the forecast of the store's sales using the regression equation.

A forecasting model for air travel demand illustrates the essential characteristics of descriptive models. Historical data on revenue passenger-miles per capita (a unit measure of airline sales) and on five market conditions were used to build the model:

$$M_{t+1} = (1.12) \, M_t \, (P_{t+1}/P_t)^{-1.2} \, (S_{t+1}/S_t)^{0.2} (I_{t+1}/I_t)^{0.5} \qquad (8\text{-}6)$$
$$(N_{t+1}/N_t)^{1} (D_{t+1}/D_t)^{0.05}$$

where:

t = Time period immediately preceding forecast period

$t + 1$ = Forecast time period

M = U.S. domestic revenue passenger-miles per capita

P = Price of air travel in cents per revenue passenger-mile (in constant dollars)

S = Average miles per hour airborne speed

I = GNP per capita (in constant dollars)

N = U.S. population size

D = Death rate per 100 million revenue passenger-miles[10]

The five market conditions on the right-hand side of Equation (8-6) were selected by trial-and-error regression analyses from a larger number of factors. The factors are described in terms of the data used to measure them. The model also specifies, through the exponents, the way each factor influences demand. For example, the negative exponent for price (-1.2) shows that price has an inverse relationship with air travel demand. Finally, the model specifies how the five factors are to be combined to estimate sales (multiplicatively).

After the model-building steps have been completed, the actual forecast can be made. Sales are not forecast directly; instead, a forecast is first made for each factor in the model. For Equation (8-6), this involves forecasting the numerator of each of the five fractions on the right-hand side. Extrapolations from historical series can be used for this purpose. Each of the factor forecasts is then plugged into the equation to forecast demand.

Descriptive models can be quite difficult and expensive to build, particularly as compared with the other two classes of formal models. Data must be collected on sales and on each of the market conditions that are thought to influence sales. Further, individual forecasts must be made of each of these conditions before sales can be estimated. Obviously, this task increases in difficulty with the number of market conditions that are included in the model. For a descriptive model to be feasible, several criteria must be met:

- Data on the relevant market conditions must be obtainable at a reasonable cost.

- The strength of the relationship between sales and the market conditions included in the model must be great enough to yield the desired accuracy.

- The relationship between sales and the market conditions included in the model must remain stable through the forecasting period.

Descriptive models offer significant advantages over the other forecasting models, particularly over the sales trend/time series models. They allow managers to examine the market conditions affecting sales and thus may enable managers to learn more about the underlying forces operating in a market. In addition, managers can use such models to evaluate strategic or tactical alternatives by asking "what if" questions that disclose how possible changes in market conditions would affect demand. (Airline executives, for example, might use such a model to evaluate the impact of an anticipated recession or anticipated industry reductions in average price.) Managers would then be in a better position to choose those alternatives that have acceptable risk under one or more scenarios. As one expert puts it:

> Test strategies using forecasting models. This is one of the best uses of models. Rather than trying to project the "actual" future, forecasts can be used to produce contingent futures; that is, futures that would result if certain strategies were followed.[11]

Informed judgment techniques
are forecasting techniques that rely on the opinions of preselected, knowledgeable people to estimate sales for future periods.

Informed Judgment Approaches.   Alternatives to formal models are **informed judgment techniques.** These approaches rely on key people who have special knowledge of market conditions affecting sales. All judgment forecasting techniques use the opinions of experts. Usually, control over how these opinions are formed is limited, but some control comes from careful selection of forecasters and from step-by-step procedures for questioning them. Alternative informed judgment techniques differ primarily in terms of these two characteristics.

Jury of Executive Opinion.   One source of expert opinion is management— typically the people heading up the sales, production, finance, purchasing, marketing, and research departments.[12] These people have a wealth of experience gained from working with company products and markets. Rarely is the opinion of only a single executive solicited, however. Combining the opinions of several executives ensures a wider base of experience. If an even broader base is needed, such outside experts as consultants, advertising agency managers, and financial experts may also be involved. The group selected for a forecast is a **panel** or **jury of experts.**

Jury of experts
consists of those managers and outside experts whose opinions will be pooled to provide a forecast of sales.

Because persons with differing experience are included in the jury of experts, their estimates will typically vary. Therefore, a procedure is needed to pool the individual estimates to create a single forecast. An unweighted or simple weighted average of the diverse opinions might be calculated. However, this approach gives no regard to the relative importance of the opinions of the different experts.

An alternative approach is to ask the experts to reach consensus in a face-to-face discussion. In this way, they can present their opinions orally and provide rationales. However, a number of problems can occur in face-to-face discussion, most of which are due to group interaction dynamics.[13] A participant may become very defensive about an estimate if he or she has to take a stand in front of the group. An executive may not want to disagree with a superior. Or, an opinion may receive undue weight because of the participant's communication skills.

The *Delphi technique* has been used by some organizations to overcome these difficulties. It is a procedure for obtaining consensus opinion without having face-to-face interaction among members of the jury. American Hoist & Derrick Company, for instance, has for years used the Delphi technique to estimate industry and company sales of construction equipment. During one period, the company was able, by using this technique, to reduce forecast errors from plus or minus 20 percent to less than 1 percent.[14]

Sales force composite
pools the opinions of the company's sales personnel concerning sales; each salesperson is responsible for estimating sales in his or her sales territory.

Sales Force Composite.   Some companies rely on salespersons' special knowledge of their territories to estimate demand by constructing a **sales force composite.** Sales personnel become familiar with buyers' needs, problems, buying preferences, and requirements and with the selling approaches of competitors. Polling salespeople concerning their opinions of future sales in their territories can bring this knowledge to bear on demand estimates.

Careful analysis of salespersons' opinions and a general awareness of the potential problems they present are essential to the success of this technique. Sales personnel are hired and rewarded primarily for their sales abilities rather than for their forecasting expertise. Some will undoubtedly be poor forecasters—either too optimistic or too pessimistic about the future. Yet analysis may overcome these sources of error. The past accuracy of each salespersons' opinions should be assessed to identify salespersons who tend to be consistently high or low. Their demand estimates can then be adjusted accordingly.

Salespeople typically do not have knowledge of all the factors influencing demand. They may be unaware of coming changes in general economic conditions that affect the buying plans of their customers, or they may be unaware of a planned change in their company's marketing strategy. Sales managers may have to adjust the forecasts of sales personnel to better reflect market conditions of which the sales personnel are unaware.

While the techniques for eliciting the opinions of sales personnel vary, they are typically asked to complete some kind of form. The forms used provide relevant historical sales information, remind sales personnel of basic factors to consider when making their estimates, and ask for observations regarding key market conditions.[15]

The salespeople submit their estimates to sales managers so that composite estimates can be made. The composites are derived by summing the adjusted estimates of each salesperson. A composite sales forecast for one product line for a sales office of a large corporation is shown in Exhibit 8-7. Such sales forecasts can be made for specific geographic areas that correspond to districts or regions, for individual products and customers, or for the entire company, depending on how the salespeople's opinions are combined.

Buyer intention surveys
are marketing research studies that are used to elicit buyers' opinions about their own planned purchases of a product or brand; these opinions are combined into estimates of future sales.

Buyer Intention Surveys. A company may survey customers concerning their **buying intentions** or plans for the forecast period. For this technique to work, buyers must be able to anticipate their needs and be willing to discuss their plans with a seller. These conditions are most likely to be met in situations in which customers are buying such high-involvement products as consumer durables, industrial equipment, and new products.

Surveying customer intentions requires applying marketing research techniques (see Chapter 22 for further discussion). Usually, only a representative sample of customers is surveyed. Customers are briefed about the product so that they understand what it is and how it is used. This task is not difficult when customers have seen or used the product. For new products, however, an elaborate verbal and pictorial description of the product (concept test) or a sample of the product (product use test) is needed.[16]

Once buyers are familiar with the product, a questionnaire is used to ascertain their intentions to buy. These intentions are typically measured by having respondents specify a probability category such as the ones illustrated in Exhibit 8-8. Using probabilities keeps potential buyers from saying that

EXHIBIT 8-7 Composite Sales Forecast for a Sales Office and Product Line

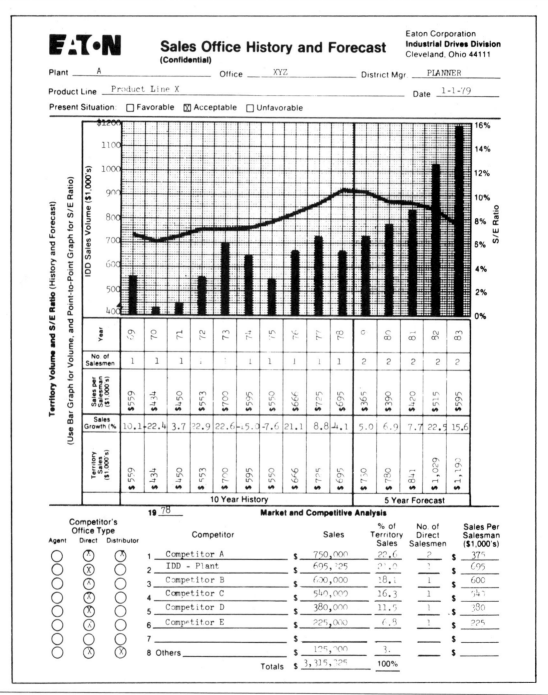

Source: D. L. Harwood, E. S. Grossman, and E. L. Bailey, *Sales Forecasting* (New York: Conference Board, 1978), p. 33.

EXHIBIT 8-8 Customer Survey Intention Likelihood Scale

How likely is it that you will buy a (*Product Name*) in the next six months? (Please check the scale category below that best shows this likelihood.)

_____ 100% chance of buying		_____ 40% chance of buying
_____ 90% chance of buying		_____ 30% chance of buying
_____ 80% chance of buying		_____ 20% chance of buying
_____ 70% chance of buying		_____ 10% chance of buying
_____ 60% chance of buying		_____ 0% chance of buying
_____ 50% chance of buying		

they have no intention of purchasing just because they are not absolutely certain of making a purchase.

Analysis of survey response involves pooling customers' opinions concerning planned purchases and uses some variation of the following equation:

$$S = I \times F \times Q \times P/n \qquad (8\text{-}7)$$

where

S = Sales estimate for product

I = Number of respondents in the sample who say they intend to buy the product

F = Percentage of intenders who will fulfill their intention to buy the product

Q = Average quantity purchased by a buyer in the sample

P = Size of the population from which the sample was drawn

n = Size of sample used in the analysis

The number of intenders, I, is calculated directly from the intention scale responses. Alternative procedures include:

1. Summing the number of responses in predetermined scale categories, such as all of the categories above "40 percent chance of buying."

2. Using the probabilities as weights to determine the expected number of intenders.

3. Maintaining a separate forecasting equation for each intender/probability category.

Because people do not always follow through on their intentions, a percentage fulfillment rate, F, must be determined. It may be estimated from prior studies of a market's tendency to carry out plans to buy the same or similar products. Longitudinal studies are also used for this purpose; in such studies, respondents are tracked over time to see how many intenders actually purchased the product or a similar product. Another possibility is to conduct an independent study to estimate actual purchases of a product and then to correlate the estimate with buying intentions.

The average quantity purchased by buyers, Q, is estimated from data on buying patterns collected along with the intentions data. Finally, P/n is a proportionality index that projects the forecast of product sales in the sample to sales for the entire population from which the sample was drawn.

Application of Informed Judgment Approaches. Informed judgment approaches are intended to complement formal model approaches. They are particularly useful when few or no hard data are available for forecasting, as may be the case when introducing a new product, entering a new market, or assessing the impact of a major new market condition on product sales (entry of a major new competitor). In such situations, a company may have no choice but to use informed judgment approaches.

Even when hard data are available, informed judgment approaches are very useful for adjusting demand estimates derived by means of formal modeling techniques. Adjustments are necessary because the historical data used in formal models never completely describe all future market conditions. A large manufacturer of industrial equipment guards against over-reliance on formal models by using a committee of managers to review short-run time series forecasts of company sales. These managers, who are in sales-related positions, are constantly watching events in the markets. From time to time, they spot materials shortages, distribution bottlenecks, competitor testing of new products, and other events influencing company product sales. The committee then discusses how these events will affect forecasts, so that estimates can be adjusted upward or downward for improved accuracy.

Selecting a Demand Estimation Technique

Because no one technique is always best, forecasters must choose the forecasting technique most suitable for each particular situation. Only by using criteria to evaluate the possible alternative techniques can a logical choice be made.[17]

Selection Criteria. Each forecasting situation can be described by the data available, the intended use of the forecast, the urgency of the need for the forecast, and the product-market circumstances anticipated during the forecast period. Although the selection criteria used to help match forecasting techniques to forecasting situations may differ across companies, the following are typical:

- Required level of accuracy of the estimate.
- Availability of the data required by the technique.
- Cost of implementing the technique.
- Reasonableness of the assumptions made by the technique.

■ Historical accuracy of the technique under similar product-market circumstances.

■ Amount of time allotted to making a forecast before a decision must be made.

■ Users' ability to understand and accept the forecast derived from the technique.

Selecting a Forecasting Technique. No generalizations can be made about which techniques best meet each selection criterion. However, we can get some insight into the application of such criteria by examining the selection of a demand estimation technique in an actual situation. The forecasting of demand for Environmental Systems Corporation (ESC) was previously described to show that forecasts are conditional. This example can now be extended to show how a forecasting technique was selected and implemented.

Application

ESC's Forecast for Market Measurement

ESC's survey of secondary sources contained an acceptable forecast of generic-class demand for temperature measurement instruments. This forecast was not crucial to management's decision on whether to expand ESC's resource commitment to its microprocessor, RTD-type instrument. However, management was pleased to know that such growth in generic demand was expected.

Demand for the product type and expected brand sales over the next four years were key factors in management's expansion decision. For the product type, only the growth trend was important, since management wanted to enter high-growth markets. For brand sales, management had to know whether break-even volumes would be exceeded during this period. The new venture was expected to at least pay for itself within the four-year time frame. Knowing by exactly how much sales would exceed the break-even level was less important to the deci-

sion, because management was interested in seeing whether manufacturing would be a proper avenue for diversification. Consequently, management realized that only ball park accuracy of product and brand sales forecasts was sufficient.

Because the product type (microprocessor-based RTD instruments) was so new, the number of forecasting techniques that could be applied was limited. Since management had very little experience with the marketing of temperature measurement instruments and ESC had no sales force selling instruments, the jury of executive opinion technique and the sales force composite technique were ruled out.

Surveying customer buying plans was a feasible option. Customers' purchase decisions concerning temperature measurement instruments are important enough for prior planning. The persons involved in such decisions could be identified, and management believed that they would discuss their buying plans if interviewed. The major drawbacks were cost and time pressure. A large-scale survey would have cost thousands of dollars, and its results would have been available in no less than two months. ESC's management wanted demand estimates sooner than that and at lower cost. Consequently, a small-scale telephone survey of customer opinions was conducted to provide data supplementing the customer aggregation technique eventually selected. The survey was completed well within management's cost and time limits.

The customer aggregation forecasting model shown in Equation (8-5) was applied. First, the product-markets were defined. Temperature measurement instruments are required in three different use situations: production process quality control, checks of the accuracy of other instruments, and laboratory product testing. For each of these use situations, industrial buyers were identified and grouped according to the type of product they manufactured. One group was chemical firms; another was pharmaceutical firms; a third was food processors; and a fourth was utilities. Equation (8-5) was applied separately for each group. For convenience, the illustration here is confined to demand estimates for the pharmaceutical industry market. The procedure was essentially the same for all groups. Total product-type market potential was determined by summing all estimates over the groups.

To estimate the number of potential pharmaceutical customers, N, the needs of these customers for temperature control were assessed. The survey revealed that certain drugs must be put into sterilized containers before distribution. This use situation suggested that N could be determined by identifying the firms that sold such drugs. A readily available source, *Physicians' Desk Reference*, contained this information. The estimate was complicated by the fact that some companies had multiple plants. An estimate of the average number of plants per company was obtained from *Moody's Industrial*

Manual and from the customer survey. Combining these data, the number of customers was estimated by:

$$N = C \times P$$

where:

N = Number of customers (plants)

C = Number of pharmaceutical companies in the market

P = Average plants per company

The second estimate in Equation (8-5) is L, the likelihood that these plants would buy an RTD instrument. This number was judgmentally estimated by comparing the benefits and costs of this product type with those of competitive product types and by examining the reactions of survey respondents to the product type. Since this estimate was very subjective, a range of estimates that management felt were feasible was tried to see whether differences in the resulting market potentials would influence the expansion decision. The differences did not affect the decision.

The required quantity, R, was determined by analyzing the number of sterilizers in plants and the way in which the RTD instrument would be used. Because of the instrument's high accuracy and its correspondingly high price, its uses would be limited to special measurement situations. The customer survey suggested that for these limited uses, about one RTD instrument would be needed for every 10 sterilizer units. The required quantity was derived from the following relationship:

$$R = (C \times P \times S)/10$$

where:

R = Number of units needed

C = Number of customer companies

P = Average number of plants per company

S = Average number of sterilizers per plant

Combining the three led to an estimate of the

market potential, MP. Selling 100 percent of this amount was unlikely because the market potential was the upper limit on RTD sales to the pharmaceutical industry. Therefore, the estimate was lowered to reflect a more realistic level of sales for the four-year period. Industry marketing effort aimed at the pharmaceutical industry was analyzed to estimate an industry effectiveness index, IEI. (See Chapter 7 for a discussion of industry evaluation procedures.) This index is a number between 0 and 1 that reflects the extent to which an industry is meeting market requirements. Using the following relationship, a market forecast, MF, was derived from the market potential:

$$MF = MP \times IEI$$

The estimate of ESC's unit market share, MS, of all product-type sales was based on a careful evaluation of the competition and on ESC's marketing plan for achieving sales. Competitors' marketing actions aimed at the pharmaceutical market, particularly the marketing actions of key competitors, were described and assessed. A marketing plan was then formulated to show how ESC would distribute and sell to individual pharmaceutical firms. The strengths and weaknesses of the plan when compared to the strengths and weaknesses of the competition provided the basis for estimating a realistic market share. The ESC sales forecast, SF, was derived from the following relationship:

$$SF = MF \times MS$$ ■

Changing Techniques. The ESC illustration shows the application of demand estimation techniques early in a product's life cycle. At later stages, different demand estimation techniques may be selected.[18] Demand estimation techniques may also be changed in one or more of three situations:

■ Different kinds of data become available.

■ Management is faced with different kinds of decisions.

■ Different market condition assumptions are made.

Once ESC introduces the high-accuracy instrument in markets, management must revise plans for the product each subsequent year. Short-run forecasts are needed for production, inventory, and sales planning. At the same time, sales experience is being accumulated for a historical sales series. This combination of changes suggests that times series techniques may become more important in ESC's sales forecasting procedures.

ESC's decision to use a customer aggregation model technique indicates that the situation plays an important role in the selection of forecasting techniques. Exhibit 8-9 considers two characteristics of situations, the newness of products or markets and the time span covered by the forecast, to show circumstances under which each of the forecasting techniques is likely to be used. Because situations change, forecasting procedures must be periodically evaluated to determine whether changes are needed.

Evaluating Forecasting Techniques

At first glance, accuracy, as indicated by how close a forecast came to actual sales for the period, seems to be the best basis for evaluating forecasting

EXHIBIT 8-9 Matching Forecasting Techniques to Situations

		Product and/or market is . . .	
		New	Existing
Forecast is . . .	Short run	Customer opinion survey Test market sales trends Customer aggregation model	Sales trend/ time series models Sales person polling
	Long run	Jury of executive opinion Customer opinion surveys Customer aggregation model	Causal/descriptive models Jury of executive opinion Customer aggregation model

techniques. However, other, more subjective assessments are also necessary. Exhibit 8-10 describes an overall process for evaluating alternative forecasting techniques.[19]

Evaluation begins with examining the historical accuracy of demand estimates. A historical basis is necessary for assessing current estimation errors. A 10 percent forecasting error in the current period may signal problems if the average error was 7 percent or less in the past. On the other hand, the 10 percent error would be a substantial improvement over past errors of 15 percent or more. The historical base provides a standard of what was possible in the past.

Higher accuracy of forecasts is not necessarily desirable. The costs of improving accuracy may be prohibitive, or higher accuracy may not be necessary for the decisions at hand. Based on experience with similar decisions and on the characteristics of the decision situation, managers can assess (1) the costs of making a wrong decision, (2) the critical levels of demand that will lead to the choice of each decision alternative, and (3) the seriousness of over- versus underestimation of demand. These assessments can guide them in determining the degree of accuracy required for a particular decision.

Finally, evaluation must consider the reasons for forecasting error. One possibility is problems with the estimation procedure itself. Poor data, improper use of data by forecasters, or an inadequate technique are problems of

EXHIBIT 8–10 Evaluating Demand Estimate Accuracy

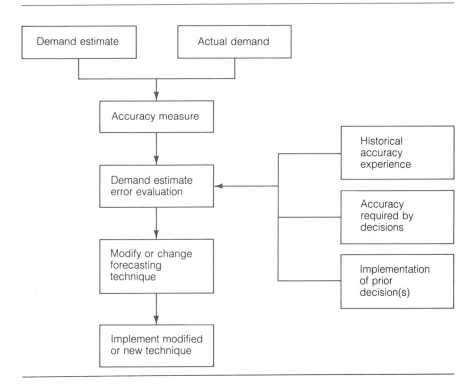

this type. Too often, however, these are the only sources of error examined. Since demand forecasts assume a given level of marketing effort (by an industry or a company, depending on the type of estimate), problems during the implementation of this effort will cause errors. A sales forecast for a company's brand, for example will be in error if an unanticipated number of stockouts occur in key retail outlets. Implementation problems, as well as other matters beyond the control of the forecaster, must be taken into consideration for a full assessment of accuracy.[20]

Improving Demand Estimation Accuracy

To decide whether the forecasting procedure should be modified, errors must be evaluated. Subsequent modifications may include obtaining more data, obtaining better data, employing a more sophisticated technique, incorporating additional techniques into the forecasting system, and/or hiring better forecasters. The management of an industrial products manufacturer found that the sales forecasts obtained by using a time series model were not accurate enough. Improvements were realized when a jury of executive opinion was combined with the time series model, and at a rather low additional cost. Of course, better implementation of marketing plans can also improve sales forecasts.

Summary

An important responsibility of marketing managers is estimating the amount of demand in markets. Demand estimates are needed to fully assess a company's market opportunity and to plan its marketing strategy and tactics. In a larger context, demand forecasts are crucial to the entire budgeting process in organizations because sales are usually the most important source of revenue.[21]

All demand forecasts are dependent on the prediction of market conditions that will influence future demand. Scenarios that describe the expected market conditions must be made explicit. These scenarios are formulated from market opportunity analyses.

Professional marketing managers must become adept at using demand estimates, whether their own or those provided by a company's forecasting staff. Skill in using demand estimates is based on understanding how they were made. There are various forecasting techniques, no single one of which is always best. These techniques generally fall into one of two categories: formal modeling techniques, such as trend/ time series models, customer aggregation models, and causal/descriptive models, or informed judgment approaches such as jury of executive opinion, salesperson polling, and customer intention surveys. Each manager must understand the assumptions about market conditions on which forecast estimates are based, regardless of the technique used.

Managers must have confidence that the proper forecasting technique was used in dealing with the situation at hand. The availability of data, the accuracy required, cost, historical accuracy, time limits, and the ability of managers to understand the techniques used are usually factors in the choice of forecasting techniques. The most important benefit of forecasting is encouraging managers to systematically analyze market conditions and future possibilities.[22] Only by examining scenarios for the future can management be properly prepared to make decisions that concern changes from present practice. Forecasting procedures should be reviewed periodically to determine whether improvements are needed.

Exercises for Review and Discussion

1. The forecasting staff for Continental Savings and Loan Association developed a two-year market forecast for home mortgage loans in Franklin City, Indiana. It also forecast interest rates, income growth in the area, population growth, inflation rates, and new business coming into the community for the same two-year period. Continental's chief loan officer received a report containing these forecasts. She wanted to use the market forecasts in planning but was not sure how the other forecasts should be used. What is the relationship among the forecasts provided by the forecasting staff that explains why they are all in the same report? In what ways can the loan officer use all of these forecasts for planning?

2.   Video Services, Inc. is a new company that has been established to sell videotex services. These services are aimed at providing consumers with information and shopping through their television sets. The services are very new to consumer markets, and sales volume is very low at present. However, increasing familiarity with personal computers is expected to rapidly expand the acceptance of videotex services. Video Services is trying to make long-run forecasts of videotex sales for the next three to five years. What demand forecasting techniques would be best for this situation? Discuss the reasons for your choice.

3.   The national sales manager for Luxuline Carpet Company wants forecasts for carpet sales in the United States for the next two years. He obtained data on retail sales of carpets for the past nine years from a trade association. He also obtained data on U.S. housing starts, the average age of the U.S. housing inventory, the average price per yard of carpeting, total advertising by carpet firms in the United States, and U.S. population size for the same nine-year period. These factors are believed to be important influences on carpet sales. What technique(s) can be used to forecast carpet sales for the next two years? Discuss the reasons for your choice.

4.   The sales manager for a sporting goods distributor was developing a marketing plan for the sale of tennis rackets, a new addition to the company's product mix. He wanted an estimate of the demand for rackets for the next three years in the three-state area served by the distributor. A sales representative for one of his suppliers gave him a market study describing the age and effective buying income of the typical tennis player. From other sources, the sales manager obtained data on the number of people in the three-state area with these characteristics as well as projections of the growth in the number of these people. The supplier's study estimated the percentage of people with these characteristics who played tennis and how

much that percentage would grow in the next three years. The study also showed how frequently players played tennis during a year and how frequently they bought new rackets. What forecasting technique(s) can use these kinds of data to estimate tennis racket sales? Discuss the reasons for your choice.

5.   Sue Brogden, a brand manager for Clean-Rite Soaps, Inc., had a heated discussion with David Ellis, the head of the company's forecasting staff. She complained that the sales forecasts for her brand of hand soap had been consistently overestimating sales each quarter by 10 percent or more. She felt that this error was unacceptably high and that the forecasting staff was at fault. Ellis defended the technique that generated the quarterly forecasts. He pointed out that the same technique provided very accurate forecasts for other company brands and that Brogden ought to look at her own function to see what was wrong. This comment was puzzling to Brogden. How could her function be the cause of the overestimation of sales? Discuss.

6.   For which of the following product or service types would the customer intention survey technique be most applicable in forecasting sales: microwave ovens, videotex service (see question 2 for background), frozen orange juice, aspirin, napkins, automobiles, camera film, and milk? Discuss the reasons for your selection(s).

7.   A sales manager for Office Designs, Inc., an office furniture manufacturer, reviewed the monthly sales forecasts for each of the products in the company's product mix. He noticed that the accuracy of past forecasts, as measured by average error over the past 12 months, differed for each product:

Desks	7.5%
Desk chairs	8.2
Tables	12.4
Area chairs	13.6
Sofas	16.7
Cabinets	19.4
Desk lamps	19.5
Area lamps	20.2

The sales manager did not know how to evaluate these forecasting errors. Were they too high? How would you assess whether or not these errors are acceptable?

8. At a meeting of the district and regional sales managers of Electroline Appliance Company, the vice president of sales announced that sales personnel were going to supply sales forecast information starting in one month. She urged the regional and district sales managers to set up a procedure for getting such information from salespeople and then funneling it up through the districts to the regional offices. The regional offices would then send the information to the forecasting staff. As a district sales manager, you have one month to set up the procedure you will use. Discuss how you would comply with the vice president's request. Be sure to deal with the question of getting accurate forecasts from salespeople.

Notes

1. Peter Petre, "How GE Bobbled the Factory of the Future," *Fortune*, November 11, 1985, p. 52.

2. "Continued Growth Is Seen for Appliance and Auto Segments of Consumer Durables Market," *Marketing News*, January 20, 1984, p. 6.

3. Myron Magnet, "Who Needs a Trend-Spotter?" *Fortune*, December 9, 1985, p. 52.

4. Arthur M. Louis, "How the Customers Thrust Unexpected Prosperity on the Bicycle Industry," *Fortune*, March 1974, p. 117.

5. A good discussion of alternative trend techniques is found in Charles W. Gross and Robin T. Peterson, *Business Forecasting* (Boston: Houghton Mifflin, 1983), chap. 3.

6. Robert L. McLaughlin, *Sales Forecasting Manual* (Rockville, Md.: Institute for Advanced Technology, 1975), pp. 202-3.

7. Alternative time series techniques are discussed in Gross and Peterson, *Business Forecasting*, chaps. 3 and 5.

8. An exception is the use of test markets to generate a sales series for a new brand.

9. John C. Chambers, Satinder K. Mullick, and Donald D. Smith, "How to Choose the Right Forecasting Technique," *Harvard Business Review* July–August 1971, p. 50.

10. J. Scott Armstrong and Michael C. Grohman, "A Comparative Study of Methods for Long-Range Market Forecasting," *Management Science* 19 (October 1972), p. 215.

11. "12 'Prescriptions' for Better Forecast-Strategy-Goal Link," *Marketing News*, March 13, 1983, sec. 1, p. 6.

12. Steven C. Wheelwright and Darral G. Clarke, "Corporate Forecasting: Promise and Reality," *Harvard Business Review* November–December 1976, p. 52.

13. Shankar Basu and Roger G. Schroeder, "Incorporating Judgments in Sales Forecasts: Application of the Delphi Method at American Hoist & Derrick," *Interfaces*, May 1977, p. 27.

14. Ibid., p. 23.

15. D. L. Hurwood, E. S. Grossman, and E. L. Bailey, *Sales Forecasting* (New York: Conference Board, 1978), p. 32.

16. Discussion of new product demand forecasting is provided in Chapter 12.

17. For a more in-depth discussion of this issue, see Spyrol Makridakis and Steven C. Wheelwright, "Forecasting: Issues and Challenges for Marketing Management," *Journal of Marketing*, October 1977, pp. 24–38; and Chambers, Mullick, and Smith, "How to Choose the Right Forecasting Technique," pp. 45–74.

18. For more discussion of this point, see Chambers, Mullick, and Smith, "How to Choose the Right Forecasting Technique," pp. 51–73.

19. An interesting discussion of this idea is found in Douglas G. Brooks, "The Four Key Elements of an Effective Forecasting System," *Journal of Business Forecasting* 1 (Summer 1982), pp. 12-16.

20. Other reasons are discussed in A. Migliaro, "How Managers Can Obtain, Recognize, and Use 'Good' Forecasts," *Journal of Business Forecasting* 1 (Spring 1982), p. 5.

21. Charles W. Gross and Thomas W. Knowles, "How to Cope with Realities, or Why Forecasts Go Awry; Good Old Charlie Holds Key," *Journal of Business Forecasting* 1 (Spring 1982), p. 7.

22. Ibid., p. 9.

PART

3

*T*he marketing planning process (Chapter 9) provides the framework for marketing strategy development. Strategy determination begins with analyzing the marketing situation. Based on this assessment of the marketing environment, market opportunity, and competition, target markets are identified, objectives are determined, and a marketing program positioning strategy is selected. Implementation of the marketing strategy includes organizing to implement and manage the strategy, preparing forecasts and budgets, and implementing and managing the marketing plan to keep the gap between objectives and actual results as narrow as possible.

Understanding the strategic situation confronting an organization is essential in selecting a marketing strategy that corresponds to that situation. Chapter 10 examines the strategic forces affecting marketing strategy, including the organizational situation, product-market situation, competition, and relevant environmental influences. Based on the prevailing strategic situation, the marketing strategy alternatives that correspond to a particular situation are evaluated and a strategy is selected.

Selecting the target market is the focal point in marketing strategy development. Market segmentation, targeting, and marketing program positioning strategy are discussed in Chapter 11. Companies are increasingly incorporating market segmentation analyses into target market determination. The targeting options include using a mass market strategy and targeting one or more market segments within the product market. Positioning strategy combines product, distribution, price, and promotion strategies into an integrated marketing effort aimed at each target market.

New products are part of the marketing strategy development for many organizations. A new product requires the development of a complete marketing strategy. The steps in moving from a new product idea to commercialization are considered in Chapter 12 ∎

CHAPTER 9

The Marketing Planning Process

*M*arketing strategy development for Polaroid's Spectra camera, introduced in 1986, illustrates the nature and scope of marketing planning.[1] This third-generation instant camera is intended to halt the decline in instant cameras sales (from 9.4 million units in 1978 to 3.6 million in 1985). Five years were spent in developing the camera. Spectra is targeted at the young professionals who have been buying 35-mm cameras since the late 1970s. The promotional campaign stresses the "instant experience" that Spectra photographs provide. Retailing at around $150, the camera has picture quality comparable to that of inexpensive 35-mm cameras. Spectra was introduced in Los Angeles with a $1 million promotional event; this was to be followed by a 12-month $40 million advertising campaign beginning in April 1986. Ben Cross, the star of *Chariots of Fire*, was selected as Spectra's ad spokesperson.

Polaroid faces a tough marketing challenge in its effort to revive a market that has been declining for five years.[2] Nevertheless, the Spectra strategy is logical, given the company's current heavy dependence on the instant photography market. A major problem will be convincing buyers that an instant photo is worth twice the cost of a 35-mm print. With Kodak out of the instant market due to its loss of a patent infringement suit, slowing the downturn in instant camera sales will benefit Polaroid.

Marketing planning is the management process that is used to develop a marketing strategy like that used for the Spectra camera. Marketing strategy flows logically from the organization's mission. The decisions necessary to build a marketing strategy begin with target market selection and continue with the setting of objectives for each target market and the planning of a marketing program to serve the needs of each target market. The marketing program positioning strategy comprises product, distribution, price, and promotion strategies. There are many possible marketing strategies that may be selected, depending on the strategic situation faced by the firm, management's objectives, the target market, the available marketing expertise, and management's assessment of the probable effectiveness of the various components of the marketing program.

This chapter presents an important overview of how marketing strategy components are assembled into the marketing plan. The chapter follows a step-by-step approach to marketing planning. First, the nature and scope of marketing planning are described. Next, the steps in developing the marketing plan are identified and illustrated. This is followed by a discussion of several guidelines useful in building the marketing plan. Finally, useful concepts and methods for estimating market response and resource allocation are reviewed.

Marketing Planning

All firms need marketing plans. Consider the experience of a small company producing metal parts that were purchased and assembled by other manufacturers into various types of products, including typewriters, locks, and automotive equipment. The company employed 65 people, and its annual sales were approaching $1 million. The president, who served as the chief marketing executive, had formulated a preliminary marketing plan. His major concern was determining the content of the plan. A marketing consultant was asked to help review and further develop the plan. The following is an abbreviated description of the actual marketing plan, including answers to the consultant's questions:

—Analysis of the firm's business situation covered present and future trends, opportunities, and problem areas. The assessment of the firm's position in the industry (less than 5 percent market share) was realistic. Rapid growth was projected for the industry. An opportunity was seen in metal parts applications in which the firm had an edge over competition due to lower costs, experience, and flexibility in meeting customer needs. Large increases in sales and profits were feasible for the firm over the next 10 years.

—Information identifying prospective customer groups (industries) and establishing priorities for serving them was collected. The four industry groups that were the most promising target markets in terms of growth, company advantages over competition, and feasibility of obtaining business were identified.

—Specific and realistic objectives had been set for sales, market share, and profitability. Since most of the firm's current business came from six customers, expanding the customer base was also an objective. Marketing objectives were related to the corporate mission and corporate objectives.

—A marketing program positioning strategy for achieving the objectives had been considered. Various aspects of product planning, distribution, pricing, advertising, and personal selling needed to be pulled together into an integrated program that was feasible, given the firm's resources and capabilities. For example, how advertising should be used was not clear. Also needed were time schedules and assignment of responsibility for executing the marketing plan.

—The choice of a marketing organization for implementing and managing the marketing plan left several questions. The president knew that as the firm continued to grow, he could not manage the firm, coordinate the marketing function, call on key customers, and supervise the one salesperson employed by the firm. An additional person would be needed to manage the marketing function, half of whose time would be devoted to directing sales and the remainder to selecting manufacturer's representatives to provide sales coverage in certain areas.

—Marketing objectives had been translated into sales forecasts and budgets. The financial plan included pro forma cash flow and income statements for the next year. Monthly individual customer sales over the next 12 months were forecast. Projections for use in planning and control had been made by target market, geographic area, product, and other revenue-cost groupings.

—Finally, consideration had been given to interrelationships with other operating areas responsible for portions of the marketing plan. Product development, manufacturing, finance, and accounting had been involved in several of the planning decisions and were committed to carrying out their responsibilities in areas on which the marketing plan was contingent.

The results of the marketing plan were impressive. Although some details still had to be resolved, the basic structure of the plan was sound. The president and the consultant, working with the managers of other functional areas, were able to finalize the plan. The completed plan was used to monitor progress; during implementation, it was modified where necessary.

The metal parts company highlights several important characteristics of marketing planning. Marketing planning is making decisions about what target markets to go after, what objectives to meet, and what programs will achieve those objectives. A good marketing plan is pragmatic, action oriented, and specific. The design of such a plan requires direct participation by those responsible for carrying it out. Since marketing decisions must be made, the question is not, "Should we prepare a marketing plan?" but rather, "How should this essential activity be accomplished?"

Developing the Marketing Plan

> **Marketing planning** is the process of making a coordinated set of decisions that constitute a marketing strategy for one or more target markets.

Marketing planning is deciding what marketing actions to undertake, why they are necessary, when and where they will be accomplished, who will be responsible for accomplishing them, and how they will be carried out. Marketing planning consists of an interrelated sequence of analytic and decision-making activities.

Content of Marketing Plans.   One of the questions frequently raised by marketing managers is what to include in the marketing plan. Although the contents of company plans will differ, the major areas covered in all marketing plans are quite similar. Typically, the following areas are covered in a marketing plan:

- Situation assessment
- Target market(s)

EXHIBIT 9-1 Marketing Planning Levels

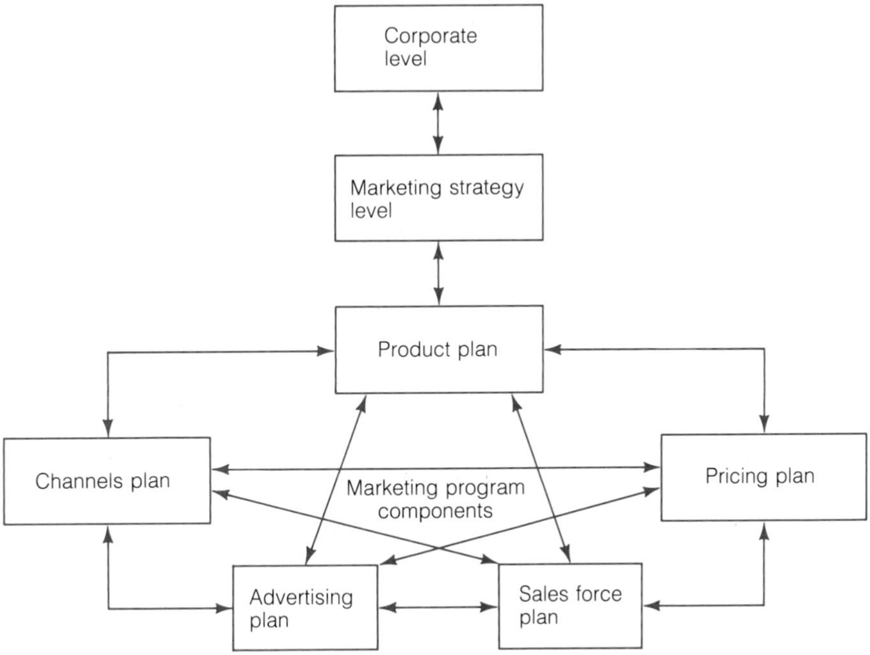

- Objectives
- Marketing program
- Marketing organization
- Sales forecasts and budgets
- Corporate interrelationships

These major planning areas provide a useful guide for developing a marketing plan in any organization and were the basis for the parts manufacturer's marketing plan.

Bottom-Up or Top-Down Planning? Should planning flow upward or downward in the marketing organization? Actually, since various interactions among levels are needed, information flows in both directions. Typically, the marketing planner must determine the proper organizational level at which to focus the planning effort. In smaller firms, a single plan usually covers the entire marketing strategy. In larger firms, planning may occur at three levels: corporate, marketing strategy, and individual program areas, as shown in Exhibit 9-1. General planning guidelines should be communicated to lower planning levels to direct specific planning activities. These guidelines include objectives, resource constraints, and other relevant priorities and constraints. Specific plans are formulated at each level and transmitted upward for analysis, consolidation, and possible revision after discussion among management levels. The marketing strategy plan builds on the specific plans in each of the marketing mix areas and represents a major integrating task for the marketing manager.

Planning Steps

Marketing planning consists of obtaining information, analyzing the situation, and making the decisions necessary to prepare the marketing plan. The major steps in the marketing planning process are shown in Exhibit 9–2. Examination of each step indicates the nature and scope of the planning process.

Situation Assessment

The first step in the marketing planning process is situation assessment. This includes evaluating opportunities and threats in the product-markets of interest to the firm and determining the firm's strengths and weaknesses. Understanding buyers and markets, competition, and environmental forces are central to this activity (Chapters 2 through 8). Recall the Polaroid example in which a major decline in instant camera sales caused management to develop and introduce a new camera. High-quality, inexpensive 35-mm photos and one-hour film-developing services had reduced the advantage of instant photographs.

Target Market Strategy

Deciding what customers to serve is very important in the preparation of the marketing plan. Step 2 in the planning process provides important guidelines for setting objectives, for formulating marketing program positioning strategy, and for taking the other steps required to build the marketing plan. Polaroid's selection of young professionals as the primary target for the new Spectra instant camera and film was an important decision in its attempt to halt the slide in instant camera sales.

Objectives

Deciding what you want to accomplish is basic to marketing strategy, yet a surprising number of firms fail to formulate and quantify marketing objectives (step 3). Such objectives are set at various stages in marketing planning. It is important to establish specific marketing objectives for each target market. Firms also indicate overall marketing objectives for the entire marketing function.

Characteristics of Good Objectives. Marketing objectives must satisfy certain requirements; achieving these objectives should bring about the re-

EXHIBIT 9-2 Steps in Preparing a Marketing Plan

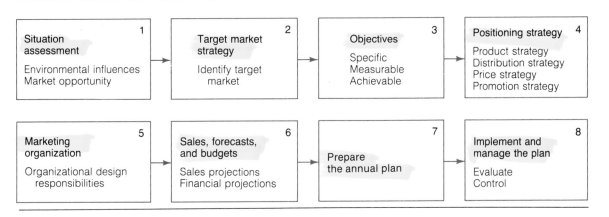

sults desired by management. Choosing correct objectives is essential. The objective of increasing the size of the sales force by 10 percent when the sales force is already too large for the available market opportunity is a bad objective. Suppose the marketing management of a firm is interested in identifying sales prospects for a new industrial product by obtaining inquiries from readers of the firm's trade journal advertisements. Management considers the following objective necessary and achievable, assuming that an effective advertising campaign is developed and implemented:

■ Generate 3,000 qualified sales leads for product X from maintenance supervisors within 12 months beginning April 1, 1987.

Objectives should be specific and measurable. "To increase sales" or "to generate qualified sales leads" is far too general. Targets should be expressed so that progress toward achieving them can be measured. For example: "Our goal for target market B is to increase sales by 15 percent in the year ending December 31, 1987."

Objectives should be achievable, based on management's assessment of market and competitive conditions and company capabilities. Subordinates may not work toward impossible or highly unlikely targets because they find such objectives frustrating. A number of organizations use management by objective (MBO) systems for goal setting and planning. This approach involves participation by superiors and subordinates in developing specific objectives and in specifying the means for accomplishing them.

Hierarchy of Objectives. Marketing objectives are linked to higher-level objectives (Exhibit 9-3). Marketing objectives contribute to corporate objectives. In fact, marketing objectives are often the responsibility of more than one functional area of the firm. For example, both advertising and the sales force are normally assigned sales objectives. If these objectives are to serve

EXHIBIT 9-3 Levels of Marketing Objectives

Level	Objective
Corporate	Achieve a net profit growth rate (in constant dollars) of 18 percent per year for the next five years.
Target market	Increase the number of regular customers served by the company by 12 percent during the next 12 months.
Marketing	Increase market share in the home computer market from 10 percent to 13 percent during the next 24 months.
Advertising	Increase consumer brand awareness in the northwestern region from 35 percent to 45 percent by one year from now.
Salesperson	Increase sales volume by 20 percent in 1986.

as operational targets, they must be translated into specific actions, quantified where possible, and placed on a time schedule.

Program Positioning Strategy

Program positioning strategy is the integrated combination of product, distribution, price, and promotion strategies designed and implemented to meet the needs of the buyers in a firm's target markets.

Marketing **program positioning strategy** is deciding how to combine product (or service), distribution, price, advertising, and personal selling into a mix of strategies to achieve objectives in each target market. Recall how Polaroid's management planned to position the new instant camera based on the concept of the "instant experience." The Spectra name was selected because of its technical sound.[3] Advertisements will feature rushing to take a picture and enjoying its instant creation. Achieving this favorable perception will be essential in convincing buyers that instant photographs are worth double the cost of 35-mm prints. The positioning strategy seeks to have buyers in the target market perceive Spectra as an exciting experience. Product design, features, and promotion are focused on this positioning objective.

The marketing manager must decide how (and when) to deploy available resources to build a marketing program positioning strategy that will yield the best possible results. Contribution to profit over the relevant planning horizon is one criterion that is frequently used to guide such decisions. Objectives may also be specified for increases in market share and sales, mix of products sold, new customers, and other performance criteria for the firm's target markets. In a stable, mature business, the planning horizon is typically from one to a few years, with detailed planning accomplished on an annual basis. In a new venture or a growth situation, some attempt should be made to project future feasible revenue-cost flows to guide short-range marketing mix decisions.

Designing the marketing program consists of three interrelated actions:

- Determining the budget to be used to accomplish marketing objectives. This is the amount that will be spent on the marketing program during the planning period.

■ Allocating dollars to the various parts of the marketing mix (product, channels, price, advertising, and personal selling).

■ Allocating dollars within each element of the marketing mix to achieve the best use of resources. For example, what advertising media should be selected? How will sales personnel be assigned to customers and prospects?

In some firms, the marketing manager is given a fixed annual budget that sets an upper limit on total expenditures. Utilizing recommendations from the marketing staff (sales manager, advertising manager, etc.), the marketing manager decides how to allocate the resources within the assigned budget. The initial recommendations may exceed the available resources. If the marketing manager is unable to obtain additional dollars, then amounts must be trimmed in one or more marketing mix areas. In situations in which the total dollar amount is not fixed, the marketing manager must compete with the other functional areas of the firm for scarce financial resources and must justify requests for increases in the marketing budget.

In practice, top management's frame of reference for expenditures is often what has been done in the past, and the marketing program is often determined by increasing or decreasing the last period's resource allocations to achieve future objectives. Thus, even if the marketing manager is given an opportunity to adjust requests for expenditures substantially above (or below) historical levels, the requests will typically be evaluated against past revenue-cost relationships and future projections.

Factors Affecting the Mix Decision. Three types of variables must be taken into account in building the positioning strategy:[4]

■ Factors controlled by the firm: the various actions that the organization can take to influence its target market—the marketing mix.

■ Factors influenced but not controlled by the firm: markets, competition, and other organizations in the marketing channel and nonmarketing decision-making areas in the firm.

■ Factors neither influenced nor controlled by the firm: external influences in the marketing environment (technology, economic and social change, governmental and legal constraints).

The marketing program is concerned with how the factors controlled by the firm should be assembled into the marketing mix to achieve marketing objectives for each target market, taking into consideration relevant variables that cannot be controlled.

Linkages with Other Business Functions. Coordination with other activities in the company is often required of the marketing manager in developing and managing the marketing program. For example, product planning is a corporate activity shared by various members of the management team. Decisions on new products, product modification, and product elimination

EXHIBIT 9–4

Hartmarx's positioning strategy for the Hart Schaffner & Marx line of men's suits stresses the importance of wearing the Right Suit in achieving business success.

Courtesy Hartmarx.

affect finance, personnel, and operations. The channel of distribution, in addition to involving a long-term decision, often requires coordination with various business functions. In some instances, a marketing decision may be so important that it will be made by top management. Thus, the office of the president of a large television manufacturer conducted a comprehensive review of channel of distribution strategy because the pending decision was considered so critical. Pricing decisions also necessitate careful coordination with the firm. Advertising and sales force decisions are typically the exclusive responsibility of the marketing manager (Exhibit 9–4).

Marketing Organization

Planning step 5 is evaluating the adequacy of the marketing organization. The organization should be consistent with the marketing plan, so steps 1 through 4 must be completed before changes in organizational design are considered. Effective implementation of marketing strategy may require adjustments in the marketing organization. Organizational structure is not changed frequently, so in many annual marketing plans step 5 will not lead to alterations.

A good organizational design has several characteristics:

- The organization should correspond to the marketing plan. If the plan is structured around markets or products, then the structure of the marketing organization should reflect the same emphasis.
- Coordination of activities is essential to successful implementation of plans, both within the marketing function and with other company and business unit functions.
- Specialization of marketing activities will lead to greater efficiency in performing marketing functions and can also provide technical depth.
- Responsibility for results should correspond with a manager's influence on those results. While this objective may be difficult to achieve, it should be a prime consideration in designing the marketing organization.
- The organization should be adaptable to changing conditions; loss of flexibility is a real danger in a highly structured and complex organization.

Some organizational design characteristics conflict with one another. Specialization can be expensive if carried to extremes. The costs of having different sales specialists call on the same account must be weighed against the benefits obtained from the overlapping coverage. Thus, organizational design involves assessing priorities and balancing conflicting consequences.

Sales Forecasts and Budgets

The marketing budget, step 6, is the estimated cost of meeting the sales forecast. This budget is normally prepared on an annual basis. The sales forecast is an estimate of expected sales over the planning period and indicates what management expects to achieve during the planning period. By combining sales forecasts and budgeted expenses for marketing and functional areas, management can prepare pro forma (estimated) income statements and other financial projections. The sales forecast and budget are important planning and control tools for marketing management. Budgets are often prepared for the major marketing departments, such as advertising, sales, product management, and marketing research.

From Strategy to Short-Term Plans

Step 7 in the planning process is writing the plan. The plan should be a working document that can inform all concerned of their implementation responsibilities and that will also serve as a basis for making modifications when needed. The format and length of marketing plans vary widely, though brevity is important in gaining their acceptance and making them usable tools.

EXHIBIT 9–5 Marketing Planning Guide

Marketing objectives

- _____
- _____
- _____
- _____

Influences on marketing strategy

- _____
- _____
- _____
- _____

Priority*	Market/Industry/Customer Targets (description and objectives, including sales targets)	Products/ Services	Channels	Pricing	Advertising and Promotion	Sales Force
		Strategy and tactics	— — — —	Actions Responsibilities Deadlines Estimated costs		

* A, B, C, or D (A: "must"; B: "would be a good thing"; C: "can contribute"; and D: "defer").

A reasonable objective is a plan of less than 20 pages plus such supporting material as forecasts, budgets, and marketing program subplans for advertising and sales. The guide shown in Exhibit 9–5 is useful for building and implementing a company's first attempt at a marketing plan and for managing marketing strategy and tactics. Strategy and tactics for each marketing mix component should be delineated. The plan should note the specific actions to be taken, who is responsible for their implementation, deadline dates, and the estimated costs of each action component.

The guide was followed by the team preparing the first marketing plan for an industrial controls division with sales of $5 million:

■ An initial planning meeting was held to analyze the business situation, formulate objectives, and establish target market priorities. The results of the planning session were recorded on the planning guide by the marketing manager. This information was placed on a 3- by 4-foot sheet that was distributed to team members for discussion at the second meeting, held one week later. Each person was encouraged to use the planning sheet for indicating questions, suggesting changes, and making additions to the plan.

■ During the second session, marketing objectives were finalized, influences on marketing strategy were examined, and priorities were established for each of the firm's three target markets, which were the oil and gas, chemical, and power industry controls markets. Marketing program strategy and tactics were discussed, responsibilities indicated, and tentative deadlines established. Cost estimates were developed, and planning session results were recorded on the worksheet by the marketing manager and distributed to team members for review and preparation for the next meeting.

■ A final planning meeting was held three weeks later. Some changes were made in the marketing program based on a review of cost estimates and estimated sales in each target market. Proposed allocations for trade journal advertising were lowered, and a direct mail program to inform key customer groups of several products that would be available during the next 12 months was added.

■ The marketing manager prepared the marketing plan, using the guide plus some supporting material, including key customer lists, advertising schedules, and sales force deployment changes. The plan was distributed to those responsible for its implementation with the recommendation that the planning guide be placed on each manager's office wall so that it could be used on a day-to-day basis and updated over the planning period.

The planning experience of the controls division illustrates several key ingredients of effective marketing planning. The approach used by the marketing manager encouraged participation. The guide was convenient for organizing work sessions and focusing attention on various planning areas. The large planning sheet was very helpful for recording results, communicating with team members, and revising and updating planning actions. The planning guide also proved to be an essential tool in implementing and managing the plan during the year. Planning for the second year was greatly facilitated by using the first-year plan as a basis.

Implementing and Managing the Plan

Finally, in step 8 the plan is implemented and managed over the planning period. Execution is a critical part of the planning process. Analysis of the experience of Sherwin-Williams will illustrate the importance of implementing and managing the marketing plan. In 1977, after an unsuccessful attempt of several years' duration to launch a new strategic marketing plan, the giant paint company appeared to be on the brink of disaster. The problem was a combination of incomplete planning and faulty implementation.[5] By 1985, recovery was apparent, with both sales and earnings reflecting impressive gains. Let us examine the firm's marketing strategy, its implementation of that strategy, and the subsequent adjustments that were made to move the company toward profitable performance.

■ *The Strategic Plan.* In the late 1960s, the management of Sherwin-Williams decided to shift away from contractors and professional painters and to go after the do-it-yourself home decorating market as a primary target. This required an ambitious and costly store expansion program. The decision offered management an opportunity to reposition the paint segment of the business into the rapidly growing do-it-yourself market that other retail chains had found very attractive. Management reasoned that the main ingredient of the new strategy was a change in image to appeal to consumers interested in home decorating and remodeling.

■ *Implementation.* Launching the strategy involved far more than was anticipated. Many stores were in the wrong locations. All required major (and costly) upgrading and expansion to respond to the new home decorating theme. Product lines were expanded to provide a complete offering ranging from floor coverings to fluorescent lights. At the time, critics observed that Sherwin-Williams lacked the experience in retail store management needed to carry out the strategy. Performance difficulties were compounded by the decision to pull the Sherwin-Williams brand out of paint and hardware stores so as to avoid direct competition with company stores. It was replaced by another company brand that was not supported by a strong national advertising effort. Because of this limitation, many dealers shifted to competing brands with established brand images.

■ *Corrective Action.* Following two years of declining earnings (the company lost $8 million in 1977), a new chairman and president, John G. Breen, was appointed. Under his leadership, the company experienced a strong turnaround. Obsolete plants and more than 100 of its 1,500 retail stores were closed. Half of the company's upper-level 100 managers were replaced, and several of the new executives had extensive experience in retailing. The new stores were smaller and were located near suburban shopping malls. The broad mix of decorating products was pruned. Large increases were made in advertising expenditures. To offer a strong brand to other retailers, the Dutch Boy trademark was acquired in 1980. Profits for 1979 were $18 million, and profits increased each year through 1985.

The Sherwin-Williams experience illustrates several important characteristics of successful marketing plans. First, a marketing plan involves far more than coming up with a good idea. A sound concept has to be translated into a cohesive and complete plan of action. Second, proper implementation is crucial. Third, few plans remain constant over time. Although the modifications made by Sherwin-Williams' management were more drastic than most, corrective action is the rule rather than the exception, a point that underscores the ongoing nature of marketing planning. Finally, the success of a marketing plan must be gauged by its results, not by how elaborate and innovative the plan is.

Contingency Planning

The rapidly changing marketing environment has caused many firms to include contingencies in their marketing plans. This issue should be considered in the development of marketing strategy. Contingencies may affect any or all of the planning steps and can cause firms to alter their marketing plans.

Contingency planning consists of considering assumptions that would be affected by changing conditions during the planning period, identifying the probable changes, and evaluating whether and how marketing strategy should be altered to respond to the new conditions. An interesting example of contingency planning occurred in June 1978, when changes were made in the rates savings and loan associations (S&Ls) were authorized to pay on six-month certificates. The objective was to prevent savers from moving their money out of S&Ls (disintermediation), because interest rates were expected to climb rapidly during the next year (which they did). Many S&Ls developed contingency strategies based on alternative assumptions concerning how high short-term interest rates would climb. S&Ls pay expenses and generate profits from the spread between the interest rate on savings and the interest rate on loans. Thus, the objective was to shift away from the aggressive marketing of six-month certificates if certificate rates approached home mortgage rates.

For many firms, contingency planning may be more significant in long-range than in short-range marketing planning. Even in a rapidly changing environment, the assumptions underlying the annual plan will often hold for the planning period; if conditions do change, the short-term plan can be modified by changing tactics. Plans should not be so rigid that adjustments cannot be made as market behavior, competition, and other influences shift over time. If contingencies develop over the short term, they should be included in the marketing plan.

Estimating Market Response and Resource Allocation

Two important activities cut across the entire marketing planning process: estimating market response and deciding how to allocate resources (people and money) to marketing activities.

Market Response

Market response is the reaction of a target market to a company's marketing effort, taking into account environmental influences, competitive efforts, and the influence of nonmarketing company influences.

Estimating **market response** to a marketing effort is the essence of deciding how to combine the marketing mix components. Market response occurs within a given target market due to a firm's marketing effort. Although market response can be measured in various ways (customer brand preference, market share, number of people exposed to a firm's marketing effort), sales are frequently used as a measure. When sales projections are combined with the costs of the marketing effort, profit contribution can be estimated. By examining alternative levels of marketing program expenditures, the most promising program can be selected.

As shown in Exhibit 9-6, there are various influences on market opportunities. Estimation of the individual effects of these factors is clearly difficult. And since several interrelated factors must be considered, including

EXHIBIT 9-6 Influences on Market Opportunities

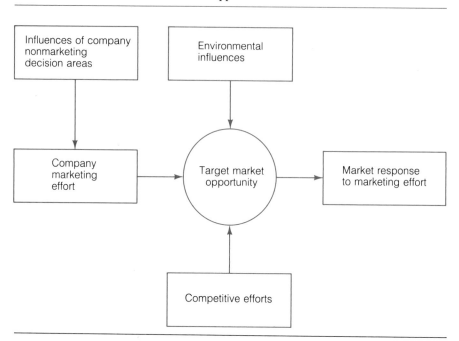

factors that cannot be controlled by the firm, estimating market response is also difficult. The marketing actions taken by a particular firm (an increase in the size of the sales force) may precipitate actions by competitors. Unfavorable changes in economic conditions may slow down consumer purchases. Analysis of market response is facilitated by studying the effect of varying a single controllable factor, assuming that the influences of all other factors (competition, environmental forces, and so forth) will remain at their present level. Then, the possible effects of the other factors can be incorporated into the analysis.

Varying One Factor.   Consider Exhibit 9-7, which shows the relationship of sales to a single marketing mix variable, advertising effort. All other marketing and nonmarketing factors influencing sales are held constant, while advertising is allowed to vary as indicated. At low levels of advertising effort, increases might be expected to yield only small rises in sales. In fact, initial advertising effort sometimes does not create any sales response until a threshold level has been reached. Large expenditures are necessary before a national television advertising campaign has any impact on the marketplace. After this initial buildup, advertising expenditures reach a level at which sales increase more rapidly than expenditures. Customers have become aware of the product and are responding favorably to the offer. Sales continue to

EXHIBIT 9-7 Illustrative Market Response Function

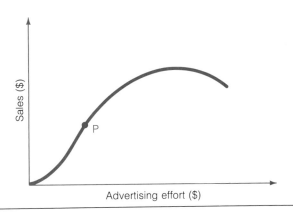

increase more rapidly than expenditures up to point P. Beyond point P, sales increases are slower in relation to additional advertising expenditures. The portion of the curve to the right of point P corresponds to the law of diminishing returns—when you increase the amount of any one input, holding the amounts of all others constant (as is done in Exhibit 9-7), the returns on that increasing input (advertising effort) will ultimately begin to diminish.[6] In a geographic area where a substantial portion of the available market potential has been obtained by a firm and its competitors, an increase in advertising may yield only modest increases in sales compared to the added expenses. Finally, a level of saturation may be reached beyond which more advertising effort would yield no increases in sales and might even result in decreases. Experience has shown that too much advertising can have a negative effect on sales.

Influence of Other Factors.   The influence of other factors on market response can be incorporated into the analysis just described, as shown in Exhibit 9-8. The estimated response for three sizes of sales force, including the present size of S_0, is shown in Exhibit 9-8A. This demonstrates the impact on market response when two marketing mix variables are used. Economies in marketing resources can frequently be achieved by using marketing mix elements in combination. As shown on curves S_1 and S_2, advertising and personal selling working together produce a greater response than does increasing advertising but holding the sales force at a constant level. This happens because additional advertising develops awareness and interest in the product, thus creating expanded personal selling opportunities. Of course, the costs of marketing resources as well as market response must be considered in determining the appropriate composition and magnitude of the marketing program.

EXHIBIT 9-8 Market Response Incorporating Factors in Addition to Advertising

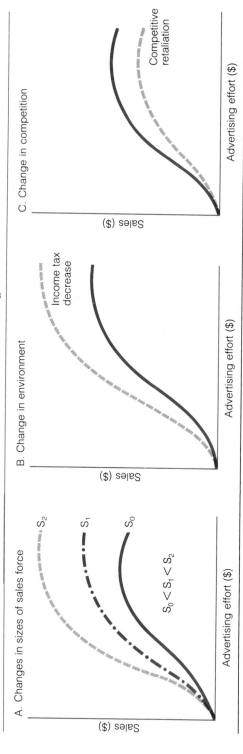

In Exhibit 9–8B, the influence of an environmental change is illustrated. A reduction in personal income tax is expected to increase sales response at all levels of advertising expenditures for the firm's target market. As shown in Exhibit 9–8C, aggressive retaliation by competitors to the firm's higher level of advertising expenditures is expected to have an adverse effect on the market response experienced by the firm.

Estimating Market Response.   There are three major approaches to estimating the sales response to marketing effort: judgmental, analytic, and testing.

Judgmental.   Judgmental approaches utilize management's experience and knowledge of market behavior as a basis for estimating response to alternative levels of marketing expenditures. For example, the marketing manager might estimate alternative levels of sales for a 10 percent increase and a 10 percent decrease in the marketing budget for the coming year. Such estimates are useful in determining whether to expand or contract marketing effort directed to a particular target market. If uncontrollable factors remain relatively constant over the short-to-intermediate term, judgmental methods may be a useful guide in developing decisions on the allocation of marketing resources. In the absence of historical data, such objective evaluations may be the only available means for estimating market response. Estimating sales of recordings for new performers falls into this category. CBS Records approaches the task as follows:

> An attempt may be made to compare the new artist or group with others whose track records are known, thereby yielding a forecast based partly on assumptions regarding analogous sales patterns. The reactions of audiences and reviewers to live performances of the artist are also assessed. Ultimately, however, much depends on a professional "feel," or a "sixth sense" of the company's planners for what the buying public will want.[7]

Analytic.   If historical data are available, analytic methods, such as multiple linear regression analysis, can be used to develop market response relationships. These methods involve identifying relationships between sales and possible determinants of sales, including uncontrollable factors (market potential). Such methods are often used to develop market response relationships for particular elements of the marketing mix. They are also used to prepare sales forecasts for specific target markets. CBS uses time series methods to forecast sales of recordings when a sales history is available.[8] These "catalog items" have steady sales year after year and thus lend themselves to historical analysis and projection, although this is adjusted by judgment to take into account new factors that are likely to influence market response.

EXHIBIT 9-9 Simulated Test Marketing

Consumers are intercepted in shopping centers (or sometimes at their homes), where they are interviewed for demographics and asked to rate various products on a point scale.

Next, they are shown commercials both for the test product and competitors' products and taken to a simulated store shelf environment where they are reinterviewed and given seed money or cents-off coupons to make a purchase. Those not purchasing the test product are given free samples.

After a use-up period, they are interviewed by telephone and asked to rate the test product against the competition on a series of attributes. They again are asked which product they would purchase. From their responses, anticipated market share is estimated.

Also known as premarket (sales) volume forecasts, volumetric projection techniques, and laboratory testing, among other terms, STM is used by a variety of consulting companies and corporate research departments to estimate the potential success or failure of new products or concepts.

Based on complicated mathematical models, the techniques predict sales volumes that would result from variations on a host of business circumstances, such as product name, packaging, levels of advertising and promotion, distribution, pricing, and quantity.

Source: Richard Edel, "Lab-to-Rollout Becoming More Traveled Path," *Advertising Age*, February 20, 1984, M-11.

Testing. Market testing of new consumer products can be used to determine the market response to a proposed marketing program. Testing "is a research technique in which the product under study is placed in one or more selected localities or areas, and its reception by consumer and trade is observed, recorded, and analyzed."[9] Testing can be used to evaluate market response to new products, advertising programs, package designs and sizes, pricing, and other mix elements.[10]

Consider an illustration involving the test marketing of disposable diapers by a large consumer products firm. During test marketing in Sacramento, the diaper was priced at 10 cents. Buyer response did not reach a level considered satisfactory enough to warrant national introduction of the product. Management was seriously considering dropping the product because of the poor test market results. It finally decided to try the product in another test market. Indianapolis was selected, and a price of six cents was used. The test was an immediate success, and a decision was made to introduce the product into the national market.

An interesting modification of test marketing is simulated test marketing (STM), described in Exhibit 9-9. This substitute for test marketing is a promising method for speeding up the introduction of a new product. Positive results from STM prompted Richardson-Vicks to introduce Climacel moisturizer in Australia and the Olay beauty bar in the United States in early 1984.[11]

Resource Allocation

An important activity in marketing planning is resource allocation. As an introduction to the subject, consider the illustration shown in Exhibit 9-10.

EXHIBIT 9-10A Comparison of Response in Two Markets

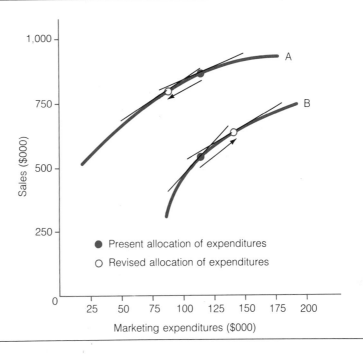

Assume that management has estimated (based on judgment, experience, and the analysis of historical information) the market response relationships shown for markets A and B and that you are asked (based only on the information in Exhibit 9-10A) whether you can improve the return on total marketing expenditures for markets A and B combined without increasing the total expenditures. It would be logical to reduce expenditures in A and to increase them in B. This shift would result in a gain in sales at no additional cost. The reallocation makes sense, given a long-run goal of profit maximization, because the sales increase per dollar of additional marketing expenditure in B is higher than the corresponding loss of sales in A. As shown in Exhibit 9-10B, decreasing marketing expenditures in market A by about $27,000 and increasing marketing expenditures in the main market, B, by the same amount results in a sales increase of $38,000.

The example in Exhibit 9-10 shows that shifts in the use of marketing resources should *not* be guided by average response (total sales divided by total expenditures). The average response in market A is $875,000 ÷ $113,000 = $7,700, whereas in market B it is $4,600. Using the average market response to guide the allocation decision might prompt us to shift more resources into A and away from B. Yet allocation into B, away from A, results in higher sales at no increase in costs.

EXHIBIT 9-10B Results of Reallocating Marketing Expenditures from Market A
to Market B ($000s)

Market	Marketing expenditures	Sales
Present allocation		
A	$113	$ 875
B	113	525
Total	$226	$1,400
Revised allocation		
A	$ 86	$ 800
B	140	638
Total	$226	$1,438

Marginal return rule is that the return from the last dollar spent on any one marketing mix component should equal the return from the last dollar spent on each of the other marketing mix components.

Exhibit 9-10 illustrates the **marginal return rule,** an important principle for use in deciding how to allocate marketing resources. In Exhibit 9-10A, returns are represented by sales. Before resources were shifted from market A to market B, the marginal return (slope of the sales response curve) was greater in B than in A. Increasing expenditures in B to a point at which the marginal returns are equal (the revised allocations), can increase revenues at no increase in marketing costs.

The marginal return rule is a key guideline for allocating resources to the various elements of the marketing mix. It is also useful in allocating resources within a particular mix area, such as advertising or personal selling. If a firm is serving more than one target market, the same marginal equality should apply for each target market.

Certain implications should be recognized in using the marginal return rule in making marketing decisions:

■ Marketing expenditures are made in chunks of dollars (increments) rather than a dollar at a time. Portions of a salesperson or an advertisement obviously cannot be considered. Thus, allocations among mix variables cannot be perfectly balanced in accordance with the marginal return rule.

■ Uncertainties in estimating revenue-cost relationships prevent the marketing manager from making precise allocation decisions. Yet the marginal return rule can be quite useful in indicating the direction of resource shifts.

■ The marginal return rule implies that the marketing manager can select the best use of resources for each marketing variable. Skill, experience, and creativity are essential in selecting alternative uses of marketing mix dollars. The rule itself does not identify the alternatives that should be evaluated.

Some Characteristics of Marketing Variables. In applying the marginal return rule, certain characteristics of marketing variables should be recognized. These include the time lag in market response, scale economies, substitution and combination effects, and the decay rate of marketing variables.[12]

Time Lag in Response.   The time lag in response to a marketing effort has an important bearing on allocation decisions. For example, increasing the sales force does not immediately produce an increase in sales. Salespeople must be trained, accounts must be assigned and developed, and competitive efforts must be countered. In industrial markets, a salesperson may have to be on the job for one or two years before contributing more than he or she costs. Similarly, all the effects of advertising may not be felt during the expenditure period. In making allocation decisions, the marketing manager must attempt to estimate the flow of revenues and costs that marketing actions will produce over time.

Scale Economies.   Certain economies (and diseconomies) of scale are inherent in the use of marketing resources. In particular types of retailing, such as fast-food retailing, local advertising costs are typically too high to be absorbed by a single outlet. Fast-food firms tend to locate in metropolitan areas where a network of stores can be provided with management assistance, advertising, and other marketing and operational support. In certain lines of agricultural products, growers often engage in cooperative marketing and distribution efforts to overcome diseconomies of scale. Scale economies may vary for different elements of the marketing mix. In selecting mix components, economies and diseconomies of scale relative to the marketing cost structure should be considered.

Substitution and Combination Effects.   The interrelationships among marketing variables are important in planning the marketing program. Different marketing mix elements can sometimes be used for the same purpose. Advertising and personal selling perform many similar functions. Some firms use direct mail rather than advertising and personal selling. The combined effects of two or more marketing mix elements working together should be assessed, since one mix element may be needed to complement another. Have you ever searched the shelves of a food store or a drugstore for a heavily advertised new product only to learn that the distribution system has not yet moved the product into your retail trade area?

Decay rate.   The effectiveness of marketing mix elements inevitably decays over time. Products are often modified after they have been in the market for a long time. New packaging designs are introduced on a regular basis for many consumer products. Similarly, business firms revise advertising programs to sustain the effectiveness of advertising expenditures. The marketing manager must make changes in the use of resources due to the loss of effectiveness over time.

Resource allocation in marketing draws on experience as well as on analytic tools. The principles and issues we have examined form a framework for guiding the marketing manager in deciding how to use products, distribution, pricing, advertising, and personal selling in building the marketing program.

Additional Considerations. Thus far, our discussion of decision analysis has utilized a time frame of one year. Frequently, the planning horizon is much longer, particularly in assessments of new product feasibility, new ventures, changes in distribution channel design, and other longer-term decisions. In such situations, the revenue and cost estimates used in decision analysis should be extended over the relevant time horizon. Marketing decisions of this type are similar to expenditures for plant, equipment, and other investments that influence business operations over a number of years. Capital budgeting techniques can be used to facilitate analysis of these decisions.

Various capital budgeting techniques are used, including the payback (the time required to pay back the investment) and discounted cash flow methods. The discounted cash flow approach is based on the time value of money, recognizing that a sales dollar received now is worth more than a sales dollar received at some future time. The difference in the time value of money is reflected in the interest that could be earned if the money were currently available. Since capital budgeting techniques are extensively covered in finance and managerial accounting textbooks, it is sufficient for our purposes to emphasize that they should be used when analyzing marketing resource decisions that may span a long time horizon.

Application

Allocating Resources

When a firm is serving two or more target markets, it is necessary to design a marketing program for each target. Since sales and corresponding profit opportunities are likely to vary from one target to another, the marketing manager must also determine what level of resources to use for each target market.

To illustrate the nature of decision analysis involving different marketing programs for separate target markets, consider a situation in which a manufacturer of small appliances is serving three target markets. The characteristics of each target and the type of marketing mix used are outlined below.

■ *Target A.* This target market consists of medium-income consumers who purchase through department and jewelry stores and other specialty outlets. The manufacturer's products are handled by distributors, and local cooperative advertising support is provided in major metropolitan markets. The products fall into a medium price range compared to those of the competition.

■ *Target B.* This upper-income prestige market comprises users of credit cards, airline travelers, and other consumers who can be reached through direct mail. The products are higher in quality and price than those marketed to target

A. Direct mail programs are conducted in cooperation with the credit card issuers and airlines.

■ *Target C.* This market is made up of business and institutional users of small appliances, such as hotels, motels, and government agencies. The products are comparable in quality to those marketed to target A. The marketing program is primarily personal selling in which direct selling efforts are focused on a relatively small number of customers that purchase large quantities of appliances.

The marketing manager has prepared the analysis of costs and profit contribution shown in Exhibit 9–A. At present, $500,000 in marketing expenditures is allocated to target A, $100,000 to target B, and $200,000 to target C, for a total level of marketing expenditures of $800,000 and a resulting total profit contribution of $1.52 million (net of marketing costs). Is it possible to improve the profit contribution with no increase in marketing expenditures? Based on the data in Exhibit 9–A, expenditures in target B could be eliminated entirely and the $100,000 used to increase marketing effort in target market C. This reallocation would result in a $90,000 improvement in total profit contribution—a $295,000 incremental profit gain in target C minus the $205,000 profit contribution that is eliminated due to moving out of target B. This, of course, assumes that there would be no adverse effects from discontinuing marketing efforts in target B. The improvement is possible because the incremental profit contribution that would result from shifting an additional $100,000 into target C is greater than the profit contribution that

EXHIBIT 9–A Marketing Costs and Profit Contribution in Three Targets ($000)

Level of Marketing Effort	Profit Contribution*			
	Target			
	A	*B*	*C*	*Total*
$100	$– 230	$ 205	– 45	$ – 70
200	– 45	385	430	770
300	215	370	725	1,310
400	525	215	810	1,550
500	885	65	795	1,745
600	1,095	– 185	605	1,515
700	935	– 370	315	1,150

* Net of marketing costs.
☐ Profit contribution for present allocation of marketing effort.

would result from adding that amount to target A or the profit contribution that would be lost by taking that amount away from target B.

Suppose that the marketing manager has been given the go-ahead to increase marketing expenditures by 25 percent in the coming year. By examining the incremental profit changes within and among the three markets, the marketing manager could determine that the most profitable allocation would be to spend $600,000 in target A, $100,000 in target B, and $300,000 in target C. This would yield an estimated $2,025,000 profit contribution. If no limit were placed on marketing expenditures, the $1 million budget could be increased by $200,000, moving expenditures in target B up to $200,000 and expenditures in target C up to $400,000. This would yield an estimated profit contribution of $2,290,000 ■

Summary

Marketing planning consists of the coordinated set of decisions that constitute a marketing strategy for one or more of a firm's target markets. The development of the marketing plan includes an interrelated sequence of analytic and decision-making activities. The planning process comprises these steps: conducting the situation assessment, selecting the target market(s) to be served by the firm, setting objectives, designing the marketing program positioning strategy, evaluating the organizational design and assigning responsibilities for implementation of the marketing plan, preparing sales forecasts and budgets, developing the operating strategies and tactics for the annual plan, and implementing and managing the annual plan.

Estimating the market response to the firm's marketing effort provides the basis for deciding how to use each marketing mix component. Environmental factors and competition also influence the market response. Estimates of the market response to marketing effort may draw on management judgment and experience, analytic tools, and test market results. Analysis of the market response to marketing effort provides management with a basis for deploying resources among marketing mix variables.

The marginal return rule is an important guideline to marketing resource allocation. It states that the return from the last dollar spent on any one marketing mix component should equal the return from the last dollar spent on any other marketing mix component. In applying the marginal return rule to marketing resource allocation, the characteristics of marketing variables should be recognized. These variables include time lag in response, scale economies, substitution and combination effects, and decay effects.

Working with controllable factors (the marketing mix) and taking into account various uncontrollable factors, a program must be designed and managed that will obtain the desired market response at cost levels sufficient to meet both short- and long-term profit contribution objectives. The task of building the marketing plan is not complete until decisions about each program component have been combined in an integrated marketing plan.

Exercises for Review and Discussion

1. The areas typically included in marketing plans are very similar, even though they have been developed for firms in different industries, size categories, and channel levels. Considering the wide differences in organizations, why are the planning areas so similar?

2. A situation analysis represents the first step in developing a marketing plan. Prepare an outline of the questions you would use to conduct a situation analysis for a regional supermarket chain.

3. As marketing manager, you have been asked by the chief executive of your firm to develop specific objectives for the marketing function. What information do you need before preparing these objectives?

4. While markets and products are the primary determinants of marketing strategy, they are both influenced by environmental forces. Discuss some effects of environmental forces in the 1980s that necessitated changes in the markets or products of various firms.

5. How would you explain to a corporate vice president of finance the difficulty of determining an optimal marketing program? What do you regard as the major issues in working toward more effective use of marketing resources?

6. With respect to sales response, how might management's assessment of the probable existence of a threshold level of marketing effort influence its decision to introduce a new product nationwide? Discuss this in terms not only of the new product's impact on the advertising budget but also of its impact on other marketing factors (channels of distribution, price, test marketing, sales force, etc.).

7. Use an example to demonstrate why the marginal return from the last dollar spent on one marketing variable should be equal to the marginal return from allocations to each of the other marketing variables. Develop your own figures or diagrams. What difficulties exist in applying this concept in marketing practice?

8. It is budgeting time at the Tofu Corporation.

The Tofu marketing budget was $1.2 million for the current year. This was allocated to the various marketing mix elements as indicated below:

Product	$300,000
Promotion	700,000
Channels	200,000

The president has suggested to the marketing vice president that since sales are projected to be roughly 10 percent higher next year, she should plan to increase product, promotion, and channels expenditures about 10 percent. (On this basis, next year's budget would be $1.32 million.) If you were asked to assess the above action, what questions would you want answered in developing a recommendation? Discuss.

9. The president of an electronic component manufacturing firm has asked the marketing manager to conduct a feasibility study regarding the introduction of a laserdisk player into the home entertainment market. Assuming that this will be the first firm to introduce the product, prepare a detailed outline of the areas that the study should assess.

Notes

1. This illustration is based on Lawrence Ingrassia, "Negative Images: Polaroid Faces Tough Sell with Its New Instant . . .", *The Wall Street Journal*, March 25, 1986, p. 31.

2. "Is Polaroid Playing to a Market That Just Isn't There?" *Business Week*, April 7, 1986, pp. 82–83.

3. Ingrassia, "Negative Images," p. 31.

4. Harry Allison, "Framework for Marketing Strategy," *California Management Review*, Fall 1961, pp. 75–95.

5. This account is based in part on Susan Wagner Leisner, "Cleaning Up: Sherwin-Williams Co. Is Recovering from Its Spill," *Barron's*, November 24, 1980, pp. 35–36.

6. William J. Baumol and Alan S. Blinder, *Economics: Principles and Policy* (New York: Harcourt Brace Jovanovich, 1979), p. 397.

7. David L. Hurwood, Elliott S. Grossman, and Earl L. Bailey, *Sales Forecasting* (New York: Conference Board, 1978), p. 176.

8. Ibid.

9. Jack A. Gold, as quoted in *Market Testing Consumer Products* (New York: National Industrial Conference Board, 1968), p. 11.

10. An excellent discussion of the purposes, strengths, weaknesses, and approaches of test marketing is provided in N. D. Cadbury, "When, Where, and How to Test Market," *Harvard Business Review*, May–June 1975, pp. 96–105.

11. Richard Edel, "Lab-to-Rollout Becoming More Traveled Test Path," *Advertising Age*, February 20, 1984, p. M-11.

12. Several guidelines that are helpful in making marketing programming decisions are discussed in R. P. Willett, "A Model for Marketing Programming," *Journal of Marketing* 27 (January 1963), pp. 42–44. The following discussion is based largely on this source.

CHAPTER 10

Strategic Forces Affecting Marketing Strategy

*T*he do-it-yourself segment comprises nearly 60 percent of the $75 billion home improvement market.[1] Sales in this market should exceed $100 billion by 1990. They are growing at two times the rate of retailing sales in general. The home improvement industry is fragmented. No single company has more than a 3 percent market share. Payless Cashways, Inc., one of the larger firms in the industry, is committed to market dominance and growth. The marketing strategy of its management is intended to establish a dominant position in the geographic markets served by the firm. In the three years through 1985, 76 new stores were opened, bringing the total to 169. Moving from this base, Payless Cashways will place future emphasis on developing new markets that can be served from the company's network of eight regional distribution centers. Acquisitions will be considered on a selective basis. Payless Cashways' management has assessed market, competitive, and environmental influences as being favorable to the firm's achievement of profitable growth. The firm's marketing strategy includes targeting serious do-it-yourselfers and tradespeople, who together comprise the dominant share of the home improvement market. The marketing program positioning strategy features the concept of one-stop shopping. Payless Cashways retail stores present a comprehensive mix of functional and fashionable goods in an appealing way. The company has made lumber the focal point of its product mix because company marketing research studies indicate that the consumer is most likely to purchase lumber first for a major home improvement project. Payless Cashways features lumber in its print and broadcast advertising.

An important basis for marketing strategy formulation is matching the strategy to the firm's strategic situation. This chapter examines the strategic forces that may affect marketing strategy. First, an overview of the major stages in marketing strategy development is presented. Next, illustrative strategic situations that occur as a consequence of these forces are identified and discussed. The marketing strategy alternatives appropriate to each situation are considered. Finally, an application illustration shows how a strategic situation analysis is conducted. The discussion complements the examination of marketing planning in Chapter 9.

Marketing Strategy Development

Various guidelines have been advocated to assist managers in formulating, implementing, and managing marketing strategy. These include:

- Matching marketing strategy to the market situation and the stage of the product life cycle.
- Analyzing competitive forces to identify a firm's unique advantages.
- Assessing the strategic implications of environmental forces.
- Incorporating the effects of corporate and business unit strategies into marketing strategy.

While each of these guidelines may be important for strategy development, concentration on a single factor can threaten the success of a marketing strategy. The discussion of Payless Cashways highlighted management's consideration of various influences on the firm's choice of a marketing strategy. Marketing strategy formulation should incorporate all of the relevant strategic factors.

The development of marketing strategy consists of these major activities:

- Monitoring the relevant strategic forces.
- Evaluating the strategic situation.
- Selecting a marketing strategy appropriate to the strategic situation.
- Implementing and managing the strategy.

Strategy development is a continuing process. Although major adjustments are not made frequently, periodic review of a firm's marketing strategy is appropriate, given the rapid rate of change in many product-markets caused by various strategic forces.

The management of Corning Glass Works was slow to recognize the firm's strategic situation. The firm produced the "little blue flower" casserole dishes, dinnerware, and other cookware. At first, management failed to assess the emerging threat of low-cost imports to Corning's line of Corelle dinnerware.[2] It also neglected microwave cookware, the most rapid growth segment in the housewares industry, even though Corning's products were suitable for the microwave oven. New competitors entered this market, capitalizing on a sales growth that escalated from nothing to $500 million a year. Corning's profits began to decline in 1982 and had not recovered by 1986. In 1985, Corning began to aggressively promote its products for microwave use and to invest in new product development. Although the company had an early dominant position in the market, it failed to adequately support

EXHIBIT 10-1 Factors Affecting Marketing Strategy

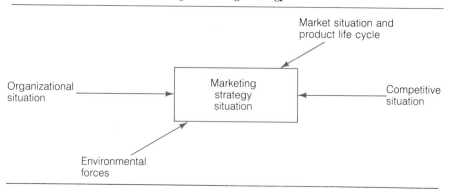

that position, allowing such competitors as Anchor Hocking, Nordic Ware, and overseas firms to gain positions.

Factors Affecting Strategic Situation

The four major types of factors that affect marketing strategy are shown in Exhibit 10-1.[3] These include the market situation and the product life cycle; the competitive situation; environmental influences on the firm and its markets; and the firm's strengths, weaknesses and other characteristics. Firms must continually monitor their marketing strategy to capitalize on new opportunities and to avoid the potential pitfalls that these factors may present. The dangers of complacency are illustrated by the experience of Corning Glass Works. An understanding of the strategic situation and its implications for marketing decision making is essential. Changes in the national and global marketing environment are increasing at a rapid rate, making strategy development significant to the success of organizations. Analysis of the strategic situation yields important guidelines for marketing decisions and provides a basis for effectively linking corporate and marketing strategy. Shifts in marketing strategy must be based on a thorough understanding of a firm's present situation and of trends affecting that situation.

Market Situation and Product Life Cycle

The market for manual typewriters in offices highlights the importance of understanding the market situation and the product life cycle (PLC). Nearly 500,000 manual typewriters were sold in 1966, compared to only 10,000 in 1984.[4] Electric and electronic typewriters and computers have virtually eliminated the demand for manual typewriters.

Products, like people, move through life cycles, and a firm's marketing strategy must be modified in response to changes in the product life cycle.[5] Studies of a variety of products from their introduction until they reach

EXHIBIT 10-2 Sales of Home Movie Equipment Falling: As Firms Abandon Market, Video Grows

Home movies appear to have gone the way of Ozzie and Harriet, bobby socks, and a new car every year.

The home movie buff who once would have bought an eight-millimeter camera and projector is now more likely to buy video equipment. Sales of video tape recorders and cameras are rising as steadily as sales of movie cameras are falling.

Movie cameras aren't even made anymore by the two U.S. companies synonymous with photography—Eastman Kodak Company and Polaroid Corporation. Japanese companies dominate the market now.

A Kodak spokesman says the company discontinued the cameras because "there were too many other attractive choices in photography," such as cartridge loading, instant, and 35-mm cameras. There was also "a fall-off in child bearing in those years," he says, considered significant because movie cameras are thought to be particularly attractive to parents of young children.

Video's rising fortunes aren't hard to understand. It has the same appeal as instant photography. The picture can be played back immediately through a videocassette recorder and shown on a TV set, whereas showing a home movie requires setting up a screen and projector that have to be put away later.

Videotape equipment prices have been dropping, encouraging people who might have decided on a less expensive movie camera system to wait until they can afford videotape. "People know video is coming and they're reluctant to invest in the old system, the system that's going to be replaced," says William Relyea, an analyst at Paine Webber Mitchell Hutchins.

The new system can also be acquired gradually. People who bought portable video recorders to tape television shows or show taped movies can, by adding a video camera, take movies. "I definitely bought a portable recorder with the idea of (eventually) using it with a video camera," says Mr. Relyea.

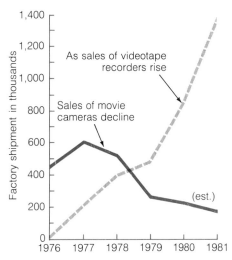

Sources: *Electronic Industries Association* (videotape recorders); *Wolfman Report* (8mm movie cameras).

Video, however, may not be the sole villain in the demise of home movies. Stanley Morten, an analyst at Wertheim & Co., says more important is the high cost per minute of home movies compared with other ways people can use their discretionary income and leisure time.

A resurgence in movie cameras seems unlikely. "It's sort of sad," says Andrew Schupack, a spokesman for Vivitar Corporation, a privately held photographic equipment manufacturer that stopped making movie cameras in 1974. "Movies used to be the only photographic record some people had, my parents included."

Source: Excerpted from Ann Hughey, "Sales of Home Movie Equipment Falling: As Firms Abandon Market, Video Grows," *The Wall Street Journal*, March 17, 1982, p. 33. Reprinted by permission of *The Wall Street Journal*, © Dow Jones & Company, Inc., 1982. All rights reserved.

maturity (and in some cases, death) suggest that sales and profits follow definite patterns during the product life cycle of *introduction, growth, maturity*, and *decline.*

An interesting picture of product life-cycle changes for home movie equipment is shown in Exhibit 10-2. New technology in the form of videocassette players/recorders, changes in consumer preferences, and the availability of less expensive photography options such as 35-mm color slides contributed to the demise of the home movie market. Note the huge decline of movie camera sales from over 600,000 units in 1977 to 180,000 units in 1981. Movie cameras had clearly moved into the decline stage of the PLC. These changes over the PLC for movie cameras substantially altered the strategic situations of firms in the industry. Adjustments in various aspects of marketing strategy were necessary, including the development of new products in order to survive.

Alternative PLC Patterns.   How valid is the product life-cycle concept? Certainly, not all products go through exactly the same life cycle. There are variations in the time it takes for products to go through particular stages of the cycle. For example, microwave ovens went through a very long introductory stage before moving into the growth stage. However, electronic calculators went almost immediately into a growth stage. On the other hand, the videodisc player had been expected to be the most important consumer electronics product of the 1980s, but it was being compared to the Edsel by late 1983.[6] The player was introduced by Magnavox in 1980 and by RCA in March 1981. Estimated industry sales for 1984 were only about one-half millon units, although RCA had expected to sell 500,000 units in 1981. In April 1984, RCA announced that it would stop producing the videodisc player.

In spite of such life-cycle differences, evidence supports the existence of definite patterns over the life of products. In a study of 140 categories of nondurable (health and personal care, food, and tobacco) consumer products, Polli and Cook used a hypothesized life-cycle model with introduction, growth, maturity, and decline stages. They assigned boundaries to the theoretical distribution of the stages based on percentage changes in sales. The introduction stage was defined as the period when annual sales were less than 5 percent of a peak level. Polli and Cook commented on the results of their life-cycle study:

> While the overall performance of the model leaves some questions as to its general applicability, it is clearly a good model of sales behavior in certain market situations—especially so in the case of different product forms competing for the same market segment within a general class of products.[7]

In a study of 258 ethical drug products introduced during the years 1955–59, Cox found that six different sales patterns (curves) were needed to describe the products in the sample.[8] These variations were probably caused in part by company actions to overcome declining sales.

The product life cycle is a key marketing planning tool beause the relative importance of various elements of the marketing mix will shift at different stages in the life cycle. Price is often more important during the maturity stage than during the introduction stage. Communicating the availability and features of a new product through advertising and personal selling is essential in achieving buyer awareness during the early stages of the life cycle. Later in the PLC, company promotion concentrates more and more on communicating advantages over similar brands in the marketplace. The life-cycle concept also emphasizes the need for a company to develop a stream of new and improved products so as to expand sales and profits over the long run. Above all, the life-cycle stages emphasize the limited time over which a company can enjoy sales growth and profitability with any given product.

New product planning is essential to ensure that replacements will be ready when existing products reach their inevitable end.

PLC Prediction. The exact pattern and timing of the life cycle for a product may be difficult to predict. Life-cycle patterns should be monitored, and projections should be revised on the basis of new information and experience. Environmental influences such as the rapid decline in world oil prices in 1986 may drastically change life-cycle patterns. Low-cost oil exerted favorable and unfavorable influences on several product life cycles.

The product life cycle is clearly dependent on the marketing effort of a firm or an industry, because sales response in the marketplace is partly the result of the marketing effort expended. When applying the PLC concept as a guide for planning, marketing management should attempt to estimate the effect of the marketing strategies pursued by the firm and its competitors on life-cycle patterns. It is essential to examine the market situation and PLC considerations in combination with the influence of other strategic forces that may be present (see Exhibit 10-1).

Competitive Situation

The U.S. market for heavy trucks offers an interesting illustration of a global competitive situation. Consider this description of the industry:

> "It's going to be a long, tough battle, and we're prepared to stand up and fight it," says Edson P. Williams, the vice president for truck operations at Ford Motor Company, one of the remaining domestic combatants. Can they win? "It's not a question of whether some U.S. manufacturers will have to leave the marketplace," says Robert Dickey, senior vice president of Paccar, Inc., another U.S. entry. "It's a question of when."
>
> The domestic companies have traveled a rough road. In the mid-1970s, a severe recession drove Chrysler Corporation and Diamond Reo, Inc. out of the business. In the 1981–82 recession, only Paccar among the U.S. heavy-truck makers was consistently profitable; Harvester, Ford, and General Motors Corporation don't break out truck-group earnings, but securities analysts believe that they sustained major losses during most of that period.
>
> And the latest recession left other domestic heavy-truck makers vulnerable to foreign shoppers seeking a foothold here. White Motor Corporation was in bankruptcy proceedings when AB Volvo of Sweden bought it in 1981. Freightliner Corporation was bathing in about $1 million of red ink a month when Daimler-Benz AG of West Germany acquired it the same year. And Mack Trucks, Inc. had losses totaling more than $60 million in the 21 months before Regie Nationale des Usines Renault, the auto and truck maker owned by the French government, bought a controlling stake from Signal Companies last summer.[9]

By 1983, European truck makers accounted for one third of U.S. truck sales, as shown in Exhibit 10-3. While Harvester was the market leader, Paccar was not far behind in market position. Emphasis throughout the industry was on quality improvement, cost reduction, and product development. American executives believed that government subsidy of European firms enabled them to gain market position by cutting prices.[10] This charge is

EXHIBIT 10-3 Truck Manufacturers' Market Shares

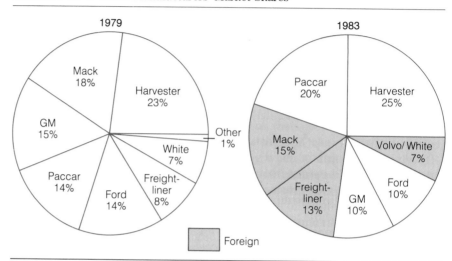

Because Volvo bought White Motor in 1981, truck unit sales are combined in 1983.

Source: "Collision Course: Heavy-Truck Makers Gear Up to Fight Europeans, Who Take Third of U.S. Market," *The Wall Street Journal*, May 26, 1984, p. 14. Reprinted by permission of *The Wall Street Journal*, © Dow Jones & Company, Inc. 1984. All rights reserved.

denied by executives in the European companies. The truck industry represents only one of a variety of competitive structures that exist in the United States and throughout the world.

Industry Structure.   Industry structures can be identified according to economic theory (monopoly, oligopoly, pure competition, etc.). This perspective can be expanded on the basis that an industry environment is influenced by the extent of concentration of firms, stage of maturity, and exposure to international competition.[11]

Emerging.   These industries are newly formed or reformed, created by such factors as new technology, changing needs of buyers, and identification of unmet needs by suppliers.

Fragmented.   In this type of industry, no company has a strong position with respect to market share or influence. Typically, the industry comprises a large number of relatively small firms. There are many fragmented industries in the United States, such as the home improvement industry.

Transitional.   These industries are shifting from rapid growth to maturity, as represented by the product life cycle. The personal computer industry is at or beyond the transitional stage.

Declining.   In this type of industry, real sales are declining. The movie camera industry is an example. A declining industry is not experiencing a temporary decline but actually fading away.

Global. Firms in these industries compete on a global basis. Examples include trucks, tires, and consumer electronics.

Types of Competitors. The firms in an industry can be classified according to their *size* and *market position* in the industry.[12]

Market Leader. This firm has the largest market share in the industry and is often the leader in strategic actions, such as introducing new products, pricing, and aggressive promotion.

Market Challenger. In some industries, one or more firms are attempting to gain market leadership through aggressive marketing efforts. The Avis strategy focused on Hertz is illustrative, as are the strategies of General Electric and Whirlpool in kitchen appliances. Kroger is a market challenger in grocery retailing.

Market Follower. Firms in this category are willing to follow the actions of the market leaders regarding new products, pricing, distribution, and other marketing actions. The better-performing firms in this category typically have one or more advantages over the market leaders—geographic concentration, lower wage rates, and so forth. For example, Magic Chef expanded its line of kitchen appliances by acquiring washers and dryers from Norge and refrigerators and freezers from Admiral, thereby increasing its product mix beyond its original line of ranges and ovens. Magic Chef, even after acquisition by Maytag, ranks behind the market leaders (GE, Whirlpool, and White Consolidated Industries), but its management has been successful in sharply reducing manufacturing costs by overhauling factories, consolidating plans, and retooling.[13]

Market Niche. Concentrating on one or more segments of the market is often an effective strategy for small firms. Examples of firms that employ this strategy include Ethan Allen in furniture, Nucor in steel joists, and Tootsie Roll in candy.

Environmental Influences

Environmental inflection point is an external change that shifts a sales or profit trend for a company or an industry away from its normal path.

Another factor affecting the strategic situation is the environment. Businesses throughout the world have experienced several periods of sudden change. A graphic example of an **environmental inflection point** for automobile sales is shown in Exhibit 10-4. Sales of large automobiles in the United States scored impressive gains in the years 1982-83, apparently due to the decline in gasoline prices and consumer expectations about future prices. The inflection point from the downward trend in sales of large cars occurred during 1981-82.

Because environmental inflection points are becoming increasingly important for corporate strategy, marketing—with its base of knowledge, experience, and information concerning the external environment—can contribute significantly to overall organizational strategy analysis and design. Shortages

EXHIBIT 10-4 Large-Car Sales and Gasoline Prices: Moving in Tandem

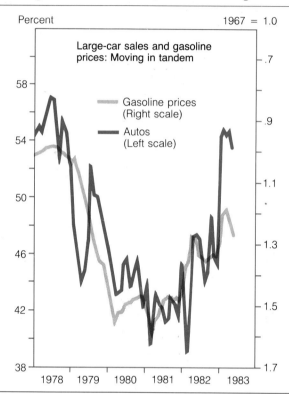

Note: Market share of standard- and intermediate-size autos. Gasoline price data, plotted on an inverted scale, show changes relative to the overall consumer price index.

Source: *Morgan Guaranty Survey,* July 1983, pp. 2–3.

and other environmental shocks only emphasize what astute business executives have recognized for many years—change is inherent in the marketplace. To be successful in the future, firms must identify strategic opportunities and constraints and guide marketing efforts by devoting increased attention to the global environment and to specific markets. The important tasks of environmental assessment and market opportunity analysis provide critical information and direction not only for marketing strategy design but also for overall corporate strategy development.

Organizational Situation

Thus far, only strategic forces external to the firm have been considered. However, the organization itself may influence the marketing strategy situation. Major organizational influences on the strategic situation include the stage of corporate development, the corporate culture, and company capabilities and market position.

Stage of Corporate Development. The various paths of an organization's development beyond the core business are examined in Chapter 2. A brief discussion of the contrast between a newly formed business and a mature business highlights the differences in firms based on their stages of development.

A company is started by one or a group of entrepreneurs. A common practice in some industries is for employees to leave a company and found a new one. The marketing of newly formed firms is entrepreneurial in character.[14] The founders rely on prior business and personal relationships to obtain sales. The products are often custom designed. After a few years, however, management may decide to expand the customer base using a more standardized product offering.

California Closets, a company that has recently carved out a market niche in the home-remodeling market by making closets more efficient, provides an interesting profile of business development.[15] Neil Balter started the firm as a part-time business while attending Pierce Community College in Los Angeles. In 1979, California Closets had sales of $50,000; by 1984, it was a $6 million business with franchises across the country.

> California Closets has started 24 franchises, from Jacksonville, Florida, to San Francisco, in less than two years. Operations outside California go by the name Creative Closets, Inc. Mr. Balter, who was born in New York City, feared the California name would give the company a flaky image elsewhere.
>
> Franchisees pay $45,000 for a package that includes vans, equipment, and inventory. The company gets 5 percent of their revenue. Franchisees agree to spend another 5 percent of their revenue on local advertising, or pay that amount to the parent company. The entire company spent about $600,000 last year on advertising, which Mr. Balter believes is crucial to its success. "We literally have to go out and educate the public," he says. "They've never heard about redecorating a closet before."[16]

When a company reaches maturity, it normally has expertise in its area of technology, in manufacturing or distribution, in accounting and finance, and in marketing. At the maturity stage of corporate development, a successful company should also have substantial financial resources. However, mature companies do not necessarily have strengths in all the business functions. Technology-driven firms may have weaknesses in marketing because these firms' management is often primarily concerned with technological achievements. Nonetheless, a mature firm may find competing very difficult if it does not have a coordinated marketing effort.

Market conditions may cause a reemphasis on marketing among mature firms. Hershey Foods Corporation lost the number one position in the candy market to Mars, Inc. in the 1970s. Until 1969, Hershey had spent no money on consumer advertising. Subsequently, it became an aggressive and highly successful marketer. New products, extensive advertising, and diversification into food-related businesses such as the Friendly chain of retail restaurants are major components of Hershey's marketing strategy. Friendly's 667 outlets had sales of $390 million and profits of $41 million in 1984:

Under Hershey, Friendly has become "much more marketing and new product oriented," says Carl DeBiase, president of *Restaurant Trends*, an industry newsletter. It has tripled its promotion spending, opened about 75 new units, and remodeled existing outlets. Along with new entrées, such as fried scallops and spaghetti, the chain has launched a bevy of new ice cream products, many using Hershey ingredients. Says Chairman Dearden: "Friendly seems to be a real growth vehicle on a real roll now."[17]

The Hershey example also shows that firms at the maturity stage of corporate development may diversify to avoid the risk of serving only one market, to utilize available cash, and to sustain or accelerate growth.

Corporate Culture.   The values, role models, rites and rituals, and cultural network of an organization are its corporate culture.[18] Every organization has a culture. That culture may be strong and cohesive, with everyone aware of the organization's mission and goals, or it may be weak. The corporate culture may have a major influence on the strategic situation of a firm. It is displayed in such ways as management's willingness to take risks, employee motivation, and employee commitment to company objectives.

Company Capabilities and Market Position.   An organization's situation is also affected by its position relative to competition. Recall the earlier discussion of types of firms in an industry. The situation of a market leader is quite different from that of a small firm. Contrast, for example, the situation of Payless Cashways with that of a small lumberyard in a local market. The lumberyard must determine how to compete with the market leader. This may involve selectively targeting buyers and offering special services such as credit. The strategic situation of the small firm is quite different from that of the market leader.

Illustrative Strategic Situations

Various marketing strategy situations occur due to the influence of the market situation and the product life cycle, the competitive situation, environmental forces, and the organizational situation. The nature, scope, and interaction of these factors can generate different strategy situations. Establishing a set of situational categories will facilitate the identification and analysis of strategic situations. Five situational categories can be determined on the basis of an industry's situation and a firm's competitive position:

- Market development.
- Market domination.
- Differential advantage.
- Market selectivity.
- No advantage.[19]

EXHIBIT 10-5 Illustrative Marketing Strategy Situations

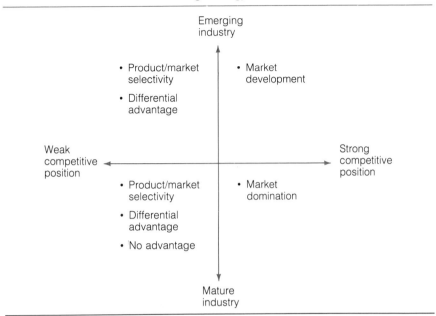

The categories are shown in Exhibit 10-5. Such strategic factors as market attractiveness, PLC, and environmental forces are not specifically included in these categories. These strategic factors must be analyzed and their effects evaluated to obtain a complete situational analysis. Two market development situations that are alike in other respects may vary substantially due to the effects of additional strategic forces.

Market Development

A market development situation may occur in a new, expanding, or fragmented industry. The firm in this situation has a strong competitive position. Payless Cashways, for example, holds a strong competitive position, although no single firm in its industry has more than a 3 percent market share. The company's strategy of developing a dominant position in existing geographic markets and selectively expanding into new areas could move Payless into a market domination situation. Competition is more likely to come from existing home center retailers than from new entrants. The competitors of Payless include Handy Dan, Home Depot, Lowes, and a variety of regional and local chains and independents. The target markets of these firms differ somewhat. The warehouse outlet concept in the building supplies industry has expanded rapidly, as illustrated by the fast growth of Home Depot. The income and other demographic characteristics of the target market served by Home Depot differ to some degree from those of the Payless Cashways target market.

The market characteristics of a market development situation are typically favorable. The nature and intensity of competition depend on the particular industry. In the building supplies industry, competition is very strong. This may prevent Payless Cashways from gaining a dominant position. In a less competitive environment, a leading firm can influence the nature and direction of market development. Segmentation opportunities depend on the characteristics of the market and the extent of differentiation in buyers' needs.

The environmental factors affecting the market development situation are typically very situation specific. The effects of environmental forces may therefore be favorable or unfavorable, depending on the circumstances.

Market Domination

The leading firm in an established industry and perhaps one or two challengers are in a market domination situation. The industry may be growing, mature, or declining, and it may be regional, national, or global in scope. The leading firm may have achieved its dominant position as a consequence of such strategic assets as a strong brand franchise, cost advantages, effective market segmentation, and patent protection.

A market domination situation typically occurs in a mature industry rather than an emerging or rapidly growing industry, even though a firm may be the market leader of such an industry. One of the larger firms in a fragmented industry may eventually achieve domination, as in the case of Payless Cashways. Until this occurs, a market development situation exists.

The consolidations of companies in the kitchen appliance industry that occurred in 1986 provide an interesting illustration of market domination. The trend toward industry dominance by a few firms offering a broad range of appliances began in the late 1970s. There are several advantages to producing and marketing a combination of kitchen ranges, washers, dryers, and refrigerators. The product lines share common control technologies and can be marketed through the same distribution channels. Builders and housing developers prefer to purchase all of their appliances from the same supplier.

In 1986, the acquisition of White Consolidated Industries (WCI) by AB Electrolux, the Swedish appliance giant, was announced.[20] This consolidation will make Electrolux the world leader in kichen appliances and the third-largest U.S. producer. WCI produces private brands for such retailers as Sears and Montgomery Ward as well as its own White-Westinghouse, Frigidaire, Gibson, and Kelvinator brands. Electrolux markets ranges and microwaves in the United States using the Tappan brand. General Electric and Whirlpool Corporation are the U.S. market leaders. At about the same time as Electrolux acquired WCI, Maytag announced the purchase of Magic Chef, which would substantially expand Maytag's product mix.

Differential Advantage

This situation may exist in various types of industries, although it is probably most common in mature industries. A firm in a differential advantage situation has some unique capability that enables it to operate at an advantage against competing firms. Differential advantage may exist because of geographic location, patent protection, product specialization, special skills, low costs, or other strengths. It is more likely to exist when buyers' needs are differentiated, although a low-cost producer in a commodity market has a differential advantage.

The personal computer industry provides an interesting example of differential advantage. By 1986, industry analysts assessed the personal computer as rapidly becoming a commodity with limited brand differentiation.[21] Price is typically the basis of competition in commodity markets. The transition to a commodity computer market gives Tandy Corporation a strong differential advantage (Exhibit 10-6). Since the cost of purchased components comprises most of the costs of manufacturing the personal computer, producers that buy computer components at low prices have an advantage. Industry experts believe that Tandy, which has extensive experience in electronic parts purchasing, is the lowest-cost U.S. producer of personal computers. This advantage in combination with an extensive distribution network gives Tandy a strong differential advantage over U.S. producers and the capability to compete with such importers as Leading Edge Products, Inc. and Epson America.

Market Selectivity

The market selectivity situation normally applies to smaller firms in markets where buyers have differentiated needs, offering firms an opportunity to concentrate on one or more market segments. For the market selectivity situation to occur, the product-type product-market must be segmentable. Avoiding head-on competition with market leaders is necessary because of the small firm's size, capabilities, resources, and market position. The market selectivity situation may occur in industries at various stages of development. Market segmentation strategies are appropriate for firms in market selectivity situations.

Failure to recognize that a firm is in a market selectivity situation may lead to serious consequences. Sperry Corporation's strategic situation appears to correspond to the market selectivity situation. Yet Sperry's management has apparently decided to compete as a full-line computer company with IBM.[22] Sperry is the world's fourth-largest mainframe computer producer but has only a 4 percent market share compared to IBM's 76 percent share. Concentrating in selected market segments would appear to be more logical than challenging IBM. The acquisition of Sperry by Burroughs Corporation in 1986 should strengthen both firms. Nevertheless, head-on competition against IBM appears inappropriate.

EXHIBIT 10-6

Tandy has a differential advantage in personal computers because they have become commodities. Tandy's advantages include low production costs and a strong distribution network.

Courtesy Tandy Corporation.

No Advantage

The no-advantage situation is not uncommon, particularly among the small firms in industries that are dominated by a few large firms and have other firms with special advantages or strong market segment positions. Overcoming the lack of advantage is the key strategic issue, since remaining in a no-advantage situation will typically prove unprofitable and may lead to failure of the enterprise. One option is to sell the business. Certain air carriers in the United States are in the no-advantage situation.

The implications of the five illustrative strategic situations should be recognized.[23] A strategic situation is not fixed. A firm's strategic situation will change over time due both to management's actions and to uncontrollable influences. A strategic situation such as differential advantage may break out into two or more specific situations, depending on the influence of market, competitive, and environmental factors.

Matching Situation to Strategy Options

By placing a particular strategic situation into one of the five situational categories, the strategic implications of the situation can be analyzed and feasible marketing strategy options considered. The objective is to demonstrate how one or more specific marketing strategy options are appropriate to a given strategic situation. Six strategy options encompass the range of possibilities:

- Multiple targeting.
- Selective targeting.
- Differential advantage.
- Acquisition/merger/joint venture.
- Diversification.
- Harvest/divest.[24]

It should be noted that other strategy classifications are available.[25] Comparison of other classification schemes with the six strategy options indicates a high degree of similarity in classification characteristics, although the names of the classifications vary. It is important to view the strategy options as illustrative rather than as representing a complete portfolio of marketing strategy options. Many specific strategies exist within each option, and a combination of two of the strategy options may be appropriate in specific situations.

Multiple Targeting Strategy

This strategy consists of selecting and developing a marketing program for each of several target markets. The company using a multiple targeting strategy would be marketing to a substantial portion of a product-type product-market by operating in various market segments. For this strategy to be effective, marketing segmentation must be feasible. The strategy can be used by a market leader to develop a relatively new market or to dominate a mature market. It may also be appropriate for use in a fragmented industry by a firm seeking to build a leadership position.

Market Development Situation.   In the early stages of the product life cycle, there may be an advantage to dividing the market into a few broad categories of users and potential users. The objective of this strategy is to rapidly expand the market by increasing the number of buyers. The strategy is appropriate when a sizable market potential exists compared to existing industry sales. In hotel room personal care amenities, Guest Supply has placed buyers into two groups: those seeking customized amenities and those seeking standard amenity packages.

Market Domination Situation.   An effective strategy for market domination is to target all or most of the segments in a mature market. By expanding into several segments, dominance can be gained or strengthened. Typically, mature markets contain buyers with differentiated needs, and thus segmentation is necessary and appropriate. Anheuser-Busch has been able to dominate and expand its share position in the U.S. beer market through multiple targeting using several brands. Other examples include IBM in computers and Hartmarx in men's apparel.

Selective Targeting Strategy

This strategy is appropriate in differential advantage and market selectivity situations. The strategy can be executed only if market segments exist. The strategy consists of targeting one or a few market segments.

Differential Advantage Situation.   The possession of special advantages may enable a firm to selectively target users that want the advantages provided by the firm. Those advantages may be the consequence of environmental influences or of the firm's efforts. Pier 1, the imported gift and home accessory retailer, has developed trading contacts with cottage industry sources throughout the world. Seeking out unique items at favorable prices has enabled this retail chain to offer buyers a differentiated array of products for the home. Pier 1's specialized merchandise differentiates it from many other retailers that are serving the same customers with other products.

Market Selectivity Situation.   Targeting one or a few market segments is a necessary strategy for small firms in mature industries that comprise large and small firms. Various bases of segmentation may be appropriate, depending on a firm's capabilities and on the nature and scope of competing firms. By concentrating efforts in one or a few segments, head-on competition can be avoided. European automobile producers such as BMW have competed successfully in U.S. markets against U.S. and Japanese producers by targeting higher-income, status-oriented buyers.

Differential Advantage Strategy

This strategy may be appropriate in any strategy situation, assuming that an organization has or can develop advantages over competition. Differential advantage may take various forms. The strategy is appropriate for firms of all sizes in an industry or a competing group.

Product differentiation is a frequently used strategy for gaining differential advantage. Minolta's Maxxum 35-mm single-lens reflex camera demonstrates the power of product differentiation. This completely automated camera enabled Minolta to improve its market position (Exhibit 10-7). *Product specialization* is another means of gaining differential advantage. This

EXHIBIT 10–7

The Minolta Maxxum automated autofocus camera was Minolta's differential advantage strategy for increasing its market position.

Courtesy Bozell, Jacobs, Kenyon & Eckhardt, Inc.

strategy has enabled Schlumberger to dominate the global market for wireline services in oil well drilling. *Low cost* is yet another method of gaining differential advantage. Low-cost airlines are illustrative of this strategy. Cost advantage may also be achieved by leading firms in industries where experience curve effects apply.

Marketing capabilities may offer a firm important strengths relative to its competition. Advantages may result from well-developed distribution channels, an established brand image, effective advertising, and a competent sales force. Firms that combine the marketing mix components into an effective integrated strategy that adds marketing value have a strong differential advantage over competing firms. In women's apparel specialty retailing, Limited, Inc. has developed a differential advantage with its marketing capabilities. Limited has built a strong retail image, effective distribution methods, and integrated promotion programs. The corporate culture encourages innovation and achievement and rewards high performance.

Finally, differential advantage may result from regulation, governmental control, or the possession of power. Utilities in the United States are illustrative of regulated monopolies. In diamond distribution, De Beers has demonstrated the power of an unregulated monopoly. This powerful global organization controls the distribution of most of the uncut diamonds produced in the world.

Acquisition/Merger/Joint Venture Strategy

Combining business capabilities through acquisition, merger, or joint venture may be an appropriate strategy for various strategic situations. This strategy frequently enables more rapid growth to take place than would be possible through internal development. Attractive value-cost ratios in such industries as food processing add to the attractiveness of acquisition. Limited, Inc. has used this strategy to expand into selected segments of the women's apparel market. The joint venture strategy is used to spread the risks of a market development situation over two or more venture partner firms.

In 1985, American Telephone and Telegraph Company (AT&T) was operating at a disadvantage in competing with International Business Machines Corporation (IBM) in the telecommunications market. IBM had acquired Rohm Corporation (office phone switch equipment) and had established a cooperative venture arrangement with MCI Communications (long-distance services). AT&T needed a strong computer capability to counter IBM's computer hardware and software strengths. AT&T's acquisition of a company such as Sperry Corporation could have been advantageous to both firms. Since the 1983 breakup of the Bell System, AT&T had been required to operate its equipment unit separately from its long-distance phone service unit. Customers (large corporations) wanted to buy from an integrated communications supplier rather than to coordinate the purchase of equipment, software, and services from different suppliers. These operating restrictions were relaxed in 1986.

Diversification Strategy

Moving away from the core business through diversification may be appropriate in certain strategic situations. This strategy option offers an attractive avenue for growth if the existing product-market area is growing slowly or declining, if competition is intense, or if improving market position in a firm's existing market is not feasible. Diversification provides the advantage of spreading risks over two or more business areas. Diversification may be achieved by moving into related product-market areas or by building the corporation into a conglomerate comprising unrelated product-market areas.[26]

Diversification has not had a good record of success in the United States. Examples of unsuccessful diversification efforts include Mobil's acquisition

EXHIBIT 10–8 Illustrative Matching of Situation to Marketing Strategy Options

	Feasible Marketing Strategies					
Strategic Situation	**Multiple Targeting**	**Selective Targeting**	**Differential Advantage**	**Acquisition/ Joint Venture**	**Diversification**	**Harvest/ Divest**
Market development	Guest Supply (hotel room personal care amenities)	N/A	California Closets (closet remodeling)	Used by leading firm for faster growth	N/A	N/A
Market domination	Seiko (time instruments)	N/A	Tupperware (kitchenware)	Consolidations in the kitchen appliance industry	IBM (acquisition of Rohm)	N/A
Differential advantage	N/A	Tandy Corporation (personal computers)	Minolta (35-mm cameras)	Strategy for expanding market coverage	N/A	N/A
Market selectivity	N/A	Volvo (automobiles)	Gold Star (Korean consumer electronics)	Consolidation of public accounting firms	Possible strategy if segment growth is limited	N/A
No advantage	N/A	N/A	N/A	Airline consolidations	N/A	Exxon (office equipment)

N/A = Not applicable.

of Montgomery Ward, Exxon's office equipment venture, Sperry Corporation's venture into farm equipment, and Amfac's hotel and recreational ventures. The strategic fit of a diversification is often an important factor in its success. Such a fit is not apparent between Sperry's computer business and farm equipment.

Harvest/Divest Strategy

A strategic situation that offers no advantage to a firm calls for a harvest/divest strategy if no opportunity exists for improving the situation. This strategy eliminates the business through sale or liquidation. Insider buyouts have been popular in recent years as a means of selling no-advantage businesses. Some of the insider buyouts have proven to be successful ventures for the new owners.

Strategy Analysis

A matching of strategic situations to illustrative marketing strategy options is shown in Exhibit 10–8. Several examples are given. It is important to recognize that the situations and the strategy illustrations apply to a particular point in time (1986). Moreover, several of the firms in the illustrations are involved in more than one strategic situation since their business areas encompass various products and markets. And a company may be using a combination strategy. Tandy, for example, is using both selective targeting and differential advantage strategies. Exhibit 10–8 highlights several illustrative links between the situational categories and feasible marketing strategy options. Nevertheless, penetrating analyses are essential in selecting a marketing strategy for a particular strategic situation.

Marketing strategy selection should result from:

■ A systematic assessment of the factors affecting a strategic situation.

■ Strategic situation determination.

■ Identification of marketing strategy options.

■ The selection of a strategy that corresponds favorably to management's selection criteria.

While the situations identified provide a starting point, comprehensive analysis of relevant strategic factors is essential to a complete situational analysis.

Application

Tupperware's Strategic Situation Analysis

Tupperware International, a subsidiary of Dart & Kraft, Inc., provides an interesting case study of strategic situation assessment and marketing strategy selection and implementation.

Analysis of Strategic Forces

Tupperware produces a variety of high-quality kitchen containers and related products. Its marketing approach is centered on direct selling using the party format. Tupperware accounts for 8 percent of Dart & Kraft's sales and for 14 percent of its earnings.[27] Tupperware's operating profits declined to $139 million in 1984 from a high of $229 million in 1981. Tupperware had sales of $777 million in 1984. Over half of its sales are obtained outside the United States.

Market Situation. In the late 1970s, Tupperware began encountering competition from firms using low-price strategies. Tupperware's products were at the mature stage of the product life cycle. The products were becoming commodities. One competitor, Eagle Affiliates, was selling its SuperSeal brand at prices 40 percent below those of Tupperware.[28] Rubbermaid was also an aggressive price competitor. The Tupperware party format was not attracting buyers as effectively as it had in the past. Lifestyles had changed due to the rapid increases in the numbers of working women. Many of the company's former partygoers were in their 50s and had no need for additional container items.

Competitive Situation. Tupperware was clearly the market leader, with an estimated 80 percent market share in 1985.[29] Nevertheless, aggressive competition was eroding Tupperware's strong market position. Low prices and acceptable product quality were favorably influencing buyers. The trend toward a commodity orientation of buyers was expected to continue. The entry of other competitors was possible.

Environmental Forces. The lifestyle changes of women, including more eating away from home, more limited discretionary time, a growth in the number of single families, and a declining interest in cooking, were having important effects on Tupperware's market. Changing demographics, including an expanding middle-age group, were also affecting that market.

Organizational Situation. Tupperware's profit contributions are important to Dart & Kraft. Tupperware's management had the financial resources needed to develop and launch an aggresive marketing strategy to help reverse its three-year decline in earnings. A new top-management team with a strong marketing orientation was appointed in early 1985. It was assigned the responsibility for responding to changing lifestyles with an effective marketing strategy.[30]

Tupperware is clearly in a *market domination* situation, although competitive threats and changes in the market situation have altered the effectiveness of its marketing strategy. The brand has a strong consumer franchise and a quality product. The need for examining marketing strategy alternatives was apparent in early 1985.

Strategy Options and Selection

Feasible marketing strategy options for Tupperware include multiple targeting, differential advantage, acquisition/joint venture, and diversification. In view of the characteristics of the strategic situation, a combination of multiple-targeting and differential advantage strategies appears appropriate. Acquisition is probably not feasible and might be prohibited by the federal government due to Tupperware's already dominant market position. Diversification would probably not be a logical strategy until the existing market situation has been improved.

The marketing strategy selected by Tupperware's management consisted of two major components: a major new product was developed and introduced; and substantial changes were made in the marketing strategy for the existing line of kitchenware.

Product Differentiation. Management invested $70 million to develop Ultra 21 Ovenware.[31] This proprietary plastic product can withstand conventional oven temperatures in excess of 500 degrees, is usable in microwave ovens, can be placed in the freezer or dishwasher, and is resistant to discoloration and stains. In test markets, Ultra 21 was a strong performer. The number of parties, average attendance, and party sales all increased. Those attending also purchased other Tupperware products. The Ultra 21 line was introduced in the United States in mid-1985 and in Europe and Japan in late 1985. The intensive marketing program for Ultra 21 included the largest advertising campaign in Tupperware's history. The profit margins are much higher on Ultra 21 than on the items in the regular Tupperware line.

Marketing Strategy Adjustments. The company's consumer research studies indicated several strengths of the Tupperware system, including informative product demonstration, superior products, swift distribution, personal service, and word-of-mouth product endorsement.[32] Tupperware's unique product features were considered important by buyers. The assessment of Tupperware's strategic situation also led to several changes in marketing strategy. The party format was made more flexible— one-hour, lunch-hour, and rush-hour gatherings were held. Custom kitchen parties are being tested. At these parties, a manager or dealer reorganizes available cabinet space using Tupperware containers to achieve expanded storage, efficiency, and convenience. The training of dealers was increased. Advertising expenditures were increased from $2 million in 1984 to $15 million in 1985.[33] All of these efforts are designed to help Tupperware attract new customers. Younger working women are a high-priority target market ■

—————————————————————— *Summary* ——————————————————————

The overall strategy selected for a company, a business unit, or a target market sets the stage for deciding the details of the marketing strategy to be used. The objective is to build a marketing plan for the strategy situation faced by marketing management. An analysis of the relevant strategic forces helps management apply the marketing planning process more effectively. After evaluating the strategic situation, management is better prepared to accomplish the steps in the marketing process.

The first step in marketing strategy development is to identify the strategic forces affecting the marketing strategy situation. Market targeting and positioning strategies must correspond to the strategic forces that exist in a given situation. Marketing strategy development consists of: a systematic assessment of the relevant strategic forces, identifying and evaluating the strategic situation, and selecting and implementing a marketing strategy that is appropriate to the strategic situation.

The factors that may affect a marketing strategy are the market situation and the product life cycle, the competitive situation, environmental forces, and the organizational situation. The importance of these factors will vary from one company situation to another, so it is important to consider each of the factors in a particular business setting.

Strategic analysis can be used to identify and evaluate the strategic factors that are important in a given marketing strategy situation. Five illustrative strategic situations illustrate the range of the situations created by the various strategic factors. These situations are designated as market development, market domination, differential advantage, market selectivity, and no advantage. By placing a particular strategic situation into one of these categories, the strategic implications of the situation can be analyzed and feasible marketing strategy options considered.

Six marketing strategy options encompass the range of possibilities: multiple targeting, selective targeting, differential advantage, acquisition/merger/joint venture, diversification, and harvest/divest. One or more of these strategy options are appropriate to a particular strategic situation.

Exercises for Review and Discussion

1. Assume the role of chief marketing executive of a major home movie equipment manufacturer in the mid-1970s. What recommendations should you make to top management in view of probable product life-cycle trends?

2. Will the nature and composition of the marketing mix be the same for all products at the same stage in the product-market life cycle? Discuss your answer.

3. The Consumers Products Corporation markets various products that fall into different product-market positions. The firm's major line consists of cosmetic products (shampoo, soap, body lotion). Management is considering the introduction of nongreasy french fries, a product entirely different from the existing product line. Discuss the strategic situation that the french fries product-market combination would occupy. What are the implications for the firm's existing strategic position and for the marketing program associated with that position?

4. Some bank authorities are convinced that small banks in the United States face a very tough battle for survival in the future due to deregulation, the high cost of money, and intense competition from such companies as Sears, K mart, and Merrill Lynch. Identify the strategic issues that sould be considered by the management of small banks.

5. Suppose you have been asked to advise a wealthy entrepreneur concerning possible entry into the fast-food industry beginning in 1987. What are your recommendations?

6. De Beers is the world's largest diamond distributor, holding a virtual monopoly on the distribution of 80 percent of all the diamonds produced. Discuss the feasibility of another company actively competing with De Beers. What changes in the industry might occur if De Beers were to lose its monopoly position?

7. Assume that you are developing a market-ing plan for a new product. What information do you need to prepare the plan?

8. Prepare a strategic analysis for Winnebago Industries (recreational vehicles), indicating the strategic situation as of the date of your analysis.

9. Discuss the environmental inflection point(s) that would probably occur for a firm dependent upon petroleum supplies assuming that a long-term (five years or more) cutoff should occur in Middle Eastern oil supplies.

10. Select a firm with which you are familiar, and identify the nature and significance of the strategic forces affecting the firm.

Notes

1. Payless Cashways, Inc., *1985 Annual Report*, pp. 6–15.

2. "Too Little, Too Late," *Forbes*, March 24, 1986, pp. 172–73.

3. The discussion in this chapter is based on David W. Cravens, "Examining Marketing Strategy from a Contingency Perspective," Working Paper Series no. 3, M. J. Neeley School of Business, Texas Christian University, May 24, 1985; and "Strategic Forces Affecting Marketing Strategy," *Business Horizons*, September–October 1986.

4. *The Wall Street Journal*, March 22, 1984, p. 1.

5. The product life-cycle concept is discussed in greater detail in Chester R. Wasson, "The Importance of the Product-Life Cycle to the Industrial Marketer," *Industrial Marketing Management* 5 (December 1976), pp. 299–308.

6. Laura Landro, "RCA Reaches Crossroads on Future of Its Troubled Videodisk Player," *The Wall Street Journal*, September 13, 1983, p. 35.

7. Rolando Polli and Victor Cook, "Validity of the Product Life Cycle," *Journal of Business* 44 (October 1969), p. 400.

8. William E. Cox, Jr., "Product Life Cycles as Marketing Models," *Journal of Business* 40 (October 1965), p. 382.

9. Jeffrey Zaslow, "Collision Course: Heavy Truck Makers Gear Up for Big Battle with Foreign Rivals," *The Wall Street Journal*, March 26, 1984, p. 1. Reprinted by permission of *The Wall Street Journal*, © Dow Jones & Company, Inc., 1984. All rights reserved.

10. Ibid., pp. 1, 14.

11. Michael E. Porter, *Competitive Strategy* (New York: Free Press, 1980), chap. 9.

12. Philip Kotler, *Marketing Management: Analysis Planning and Control*, 5th ed. (Englewood Cliffs, N. J.: Prentice-Hall, 1984).

13. Elizabeth Sanger, "White Goods Are Red-Hot," *Barron's*, April 9, 1984, pp. 11, 26.

14. Tyzoon T. Tyebjee, Albert V. Bruno, and Shelby H. McIntyre, "Growing Ventures Can Anticipate Marketing Stages," *Harvard Business Review*, January–February 1983, pp. 62, 64, 66.

15. Jennifer Bingham Hull, "California Closets Finds Niche in Remodeling Storage Space," *The Wall Street Journal*, March 19, 1984, p. 29. Reprinted by permission of *The Wall Street Journal*, © Dow Jones & Company, Inc., 1984. All rights reserved.

16. Ibid.

17. "Hershey: A Hefty Ad Budget Has Profits Flying High," *Business Week*, February 13, 1984, p. 88.

18. Terrence E. Deal and Allan A. Kennedy, *Corporate Cultures* (Reading, Mass.: Addison-Wesley Publishing, 1982), p. 4.

19. Cravens, "Strategic Forces Affecting Marketing Strategy."

20. Pat McGeehan, "WCI Buy Makes Electrolux World Leader," *Advertising Age*, March 17, 1986, p. 4.

21. Geoff Lewis, "Personal Computers: Just Another Commodity," *Business Week*, March 10, 1986, p. 118.

22. Ellen Benoit, "All Dressed Up," *Forbes*, March 24, 1986, pp. 106, 108.

23. Cravens, "Strategic Forces Affecting Marketing Strategy."

24. David W. Cravens, *Strategic Marketing*, 2nd ed. (Homewood, Ill.: Richard D. Irwin, 1987), chap. 7.

25. See for example, Porter, *Competitive Strategy*; Kotler, *Marketing Management*; and George S. Day, *Strategic Marketing Planning* (St. Paul, Minn.: West Publishing, 1984), chap. 5.

26. Cravens, "Strategic Forces Affecting Marketing Strategy."

27. Dart & Kraft, Inc., *1984 Annual Report*, p. 17.

28. "How Tupperware Hopes to Liven Up the Party," *Business Week*, February 25, 1985, 108–109.

29. Ibid., p. 108.

30. Ibid., p. 108.

31. Dart & Kraft, Inc., *1984 Annual Report*, p. 19.

32. Ibid., pp. 17, 19.

33. "How Tupperware Hopes to Liven Up the Party," p. 108.

CHAPTER 11

Segmentation, Targeting, and Positioning

Market segmentation is an important part of Marriott Corporation's marketing strategy in the $33 billion lodging market.[1] Traditionally, Marriott has targeted affluent guests at the high-quality and high-price end ($65–$100 a night) of the market. Within this price and quality range, management further segments by use situations, targeting to business travelers, consumers on vacation trips, special groups such as conventions, and contracted groups such as airline crews. In 1982, management decided to target a segment in the mid-price range. Marriott's new chain, Courtyard, is aimed at the $45–$65-a-night market. Many properties in this segment are old, and a successful entry by Marriott could result in a major expansion of its customer base. The product concept, based on extensive marketing research that determined lodgers' needs and preferences, is a two-story, 150-room suburban property. The rooms are close in quality to traditional Marriott hotel rooms. The lower room prices have been made possible by reducing public space and service. Marriott has committed over $2 billion to building Courtyard into a major chain. The objective is to build 300 Courtyard by Marriott hotels by the early 1990s, gaining market share from Holiday Inns and Ramada Inns. There are risks in that the venture requires different pricing and marketing strategies, different service levels, and a new customer segment. Profit margins are slimmer in the middle range compared to the high end (12 percent of sales as compared to 28 percent). Marriott is also looking into suites-only hotels, the time-share condominium market, and the retirement community business. It is committed to going after multiple market segments, and the stakes are high. The impact of the segmentation movement could drastically alter the composition of the lodging industry.

Deciding what people or organizations to target is the first step in developing a marketing strategy. This decision depends in part on the targeting options available to a company. These range from going after the mass market to targeting one or more segments, as illustrated by Marriott Corporation's target market strategy (Exhibit 11–1). Since many companies today are using some form of market segmentation to select target markets, most of

EXHIBIT 11–1

Aggressive competition by Hyatt Hotels and others at the high-price and -quality end of the lodging market encouraged Marriott's management to expand into new market segments, including its Courtyard by Marriott chain.

Courtesy J. Walter Thompson USA.

this chapter is concerned with analyzing, planning, and implementing a market segmentation strategy. The chapter begins with a discussion of mass and segmentation strategies and then examines the requirements for market segmentation. Next, the identification, description, and evaluation of the market opportunity in each segment of interest are discussed. The target market decision is then considered. Finally, marketing program positioning strategy is discussed and illustrated.

Mass versus Segmentation Strategy

Certain kinds of people are more likely than others to buy particular products. A baseball fan is more likely to buy tickets to a game than is a person who is not at all interested in the sport. No product or service has such universal appeal that everyone in a population is an equally good prospect for a sale. Company managers typically try to single out certain groups within a population as good prospects for their brands. This is sometimes done on the basis of experience with the kinds of people who have bought in the past. A successful restaurant owner in a medium-sized southern city frequently circulates from table to table. This gives the owner a very good idea of the characteristics of the people whom the restaurant has been attracting. Many decisions, including decisions on menu items, advertising media and messages, pricing, and table service, are based on the owner's descriptive profile of the people who typically eat at the restaurant.

Other firms use market opportunity analyses to identify and study prospects for their products. Anheuser-Busch has gone well beyond simply describing beer drinkers. With the help of marketing research, it has sorted beer drinkers into different market groups according to their preferences for such beer characteristics as price versus premium quality, lightness, and imported versus domestic origin. Different Anheuser-Busch beer brands and supporting promotion are aimed at each of these groups.[2] This strategy has enabled Anheuser-Busch to gain a dominant market position.

Both the restaurateur and the brewer have the same purpose in mind. Each wants to direct the marketing effort toward particular groups of people who are good sales prospects. Information about these groups helps managers to better match what the company offers to the requirements that potential buyers are trying to satisfy. And effective matching of offers with customer requirements should lead to greater sales and profits. This, in a nutshell, is the underlying logic for selecting a target market. The key to target market strategies, however, is to find targets where the company has a differential advantage over competitors.

Target Market Options

A company may have several target market options, as illustrated by Marriott's segmentation strategy. But regardless of the options taken, target markets are selected from either generic-class or product-type markets (see Chapter 4). The challenge facing managers is to decide which groups within a product-market provide the best opportunities for company brands. For example, some clothing manufacturers, including Lane Bryant, have targeted within the market for women's clothes (a generic-class product-market) a target market consisting of women who need special clothing sizes. The Limited, Inc., a successful women's apparel retail chain, acquired Lane Bryant in 1982 to enable it to appeal to the segment of the women's apparel market with special clothing requirements, a segment that its chain of retail stores was not covering.

Selecting target markets involves much more than using a market opportunity analysis (MOA) to describe potential customers. Targeting is a strategic decision that guides marketing objectives and marketing program decisions. Many considerations go into the choice of targets, including the

Mass market strategy
is the targeting of all
the potential buyers in
a product-market, using
the same marketing
mix to appeal to the
needs and wants of all
of them.

**Market segmentation
strategy**
is dividing all of the
potential customers
into groups that will re-
spond similarly to a
particular marketing
mix and selecting a
group, then aiming a
specific marketing mix
at that target market.

company's ability to satisfy the requirements of market groups, the coverage of markets by competitors, and the costs of reaching market groups. As a starting point, management must identify the alternative target market strategy options open to the company.

The available options depend primarily on how potential customers in the overall product-market are grouped together. A company may regard all of the potential customers within a product-market as sufficiently similar to warrant treating the entire product-market as a target. This is called a **mass market strategy,** but that name can be misleading. The size of the product-market is not the real issue. The distinguishing characteristic of the mass market strategy is that no attempt is made to concentrate on any differences among product-market customers.

Other target market options involve separating potential customers within product-markets into different groups, each of which is based on some demand-related characteristic. These options, called **market segmentation strategies,** recognize differences among potential customers that can be exploited by carefully tailoring marketing offers to the unique requirements of the groups selected as targets.

Mass Market Strategy

A mass market strategy consists of targeting the entire market. A profile is first developed to describe the typical or average customer within a product-market. Then, the marketing mix for a particular brand is aimed at this typical customer. If the description of the typical customer fits a large portion of the product-market, the brand strategy should match the market requirements reasonably well. Similarity among customers on the characteristics that are related to demand within the total market is a key to the success or failure of a mass market strategy.

Under the right conditions, a mass target market can be a very appropriate choice for a company. Of all the targeting options, it places the least emphasis on using an MOA to define and describe markets. Only one customer profile for a product market is needed to guide the company's marketing effort. Holiday Inns, for example, spent very little on marketing research during the first two decades of its existence. A mass strategy was very successfully aimed at the typical highway traveler (married couple, with kids, on vacation, traveling by car from one city or town to another).[3] Mass strategies are often more popular in new markets than in mature markets because in the former there are typically few competitors and because buyers have had inadequate experience with the product and have not developed differences in their needs and wants.

A mass strategy has a built-in cost efficiency that is very attractive to management. By designing and implementing the same marketing offer for everyone in a product-market, a company can take advantage of economies of scale. When a mass strategy fits the market situation, the combined lower costs of market analyses and greater scale economies can lead to attractive profits. Finally, the marketing management task is simpler for a mass strategy than for a strategy that targets multiple segments to gain an equivalent market coverage.

Segmentation

The life of marketing people would probably be less complicated, and less challenging, if mass target market strategies always worked well. But the fact is that they do not. When that is the case, a company must turn to segmentation. Product-markets are analyzed to identify different groups of potential customers called market segments or market niches. Each of these segments becomes a target market candidate. For many managers, however, the shift from a mass strategy to a segmentation strategy may be difficult. Instead of showing how customers are similar, market analyses must show how they differ. And ways must be found to match different marketing offers to the groups selected as market targets.

Segmentation groups together customers with similar needs and wants for the purpose of selecting a target market strategy. If the customers in one group respond to a particular marketing mix in the same way as do those in another group, then segments have *not* been formed. Segmentation is the process of matching marketing mix offers to the differences in the ways groups of customers will respond. As a part of the strategy, marketing mix guidelines are established for serving each segment.

It is important to recognize that segmentation consists of more than one option.

> Market segmentation is the recognition that groups or segments differ with respect to properties which suggest that different marketing mixes might be used to appeal to the different groups. These subsegments may then be aggregated if the reduction in cost exceeds the reduction in benefits (revenues). This aggregation is based on the fact that both subsegments respond most to the same marketing mix.[4]

Multiple-segmentation strategy
is the targeting of two or more market segments, using a different marketing mix for each segment.

If customers' needs and wants differ enough so that designing a specific marketing mix for each segment of interest to a company would obtain a more favorable market response than would be obtained from a mass market strategy, then **multiple-segmentation strategies** are used. An equally important incentive comes from competitors' use of a segmentation strategy to build differential advantages in targeted niches. Differences in the response of various segments are at the heart of the segmentation approach. Of course, the costs of marketing to each segment must also be considered.

Most product-markets contain buyers that differ in their needs and wants. Consider, for example, the still photography product-market. Clearly, camera and equipment needs vary between amateurs and professionals. Within these two user categories, variations include the use situation, such as the photographing of action sports versus the photographing of family and friends. Other differences concern user needs in regard to camera type, size, quality, features, and price. For example, Leica cameras appeal to advanced amateurs and some professionals:

> The Leica simply is different. "Our niche in the photo market is populated by people who want and need a little bit more; price isn't as important as in other areas," says Karl Keinz Hormel, head of the U.S. subsidiary of Ernst Leitz Wetzlar G.m.b.H., the West German firm that makes Leicas.
>
> Worldwide, the company, expects about 30,000 people to fork out that $1,600—or more—this year for a Leica single-lens reflex camera. Another 7,500 or so are expected to buy the slightly less expensive Leica rangefinder, which is focused through a viewfinder rather than through the lens.
>
> The Japanese camera makers deal in much larger production volumes and have gone after the mass market with lower-priced instruments. But Leitz, says Mr. Hormel, is "tied to the Leica; it's part of our tradition." There are other motives. Leitz's chief interest is scientific instruments such as microscopes and binoculars, and the research and development done for Leica, says Mr. Hormel, "helps to keep our expertise up."[5]

Since the 1980s, several changes have occurred in the 35-mm camera market. Growth has been explosive. The single-lens reflex camera has fueled sales, with the Japanese dominating the market. Leica continues to hold its small but loyal user group, primarily advanced amateurs.

There are both very large and very small segments. In contrast to the Leica, Kodak's 35-mm camera is aimed at people who want a relatively inexpensive camera that is simple to operate and will take good pictures. Kodak's mass target approach aims at the middle core or majority of the product-market. The portion of the market served by Kodak is very large, and Kodak's distribution through retail outlets is extensive.

Mass market strategies are becoming less common in the United States and other developed countries. Alvin Toffler and other observers of societal trends have identified fundamental changes that are "demassifying" societies in the United States and other developed nations.[6] These changes have important implications for target market strategies. One significant effect of demassification is increasing differences in preferences for goods and services. As a consequence, a proliferation of brands has been designed to appeal to people (and companies) in various segments (niches) of the market. Consider the many precooked foods that are aimed at singles, live-togethers, and two-career couples.

It is not just products that are segmented and targeted but also distribution and communication. Videocassette recorders can be purchased from department stores, catalog showrooms, upscale discounters, specialty stores, and mail-order catalogs. Toffler comments on this trend: "In all fields of merchandising and distribution, we are moving toward greater market segmentation. Computers and direct-mail marketing help target products to precisely identified minimarkets. Home shopping through computers will complete the customization of distribution."[7] Similarly, communicating with specifically defined target audiences is facilitated by such electronic media as cable TV and by targeted print media such as special-interest magazines—for runners, personal computer owners, amateur photographers, and so forth.

The size of markets in the United States and throughout the world allows the targeting of special market niches that are large enough to offer attractive opportunities to many firms. Improvements in technology allow smaller quantities of products to be produced at attractive costs. And improvements in distribution efficiency, achieved through technological advances in the storage and movement of goods, are making it easier to satisfy a growing variety of specialized demands.

Market Segmentation Strategy

It is essential to avoid identifying as segments groups of people or organizations within a product-market that are *not* market segments. The danger of doing this is that it can result in targeting groups that do not contain customers with similar preferences for a particular marketing program. Using demographics alone as a basis for segmentation can be misleading because other relevant variables are omitted.

> It is interesting that the X-rated moviegoer happens to fit nicely with the demographic profile of Salt Lake City. Omitted variables having to do with religious convictions and interests are all-important in this case. The problem is, of course, that demographics are rarely the cause of the behavior—they simply help to define some obvious constraints, at best. Demographics should be used for nothing more than reducing the set of feasible alternatives. For example, the X-rated movie exhibitor can select 20 alternative sites for his three new movie theaters from a possible set of 500 cities using demographic matching techniques. Next he should do an on-site survey or analysis to reduce the 20 choices to 3. The same should be done for media selection: screen out inappropriate media using demographics, and then use direct measurement of media exposure of the target population.[8]

Segmentation Requirements

Management must determine whether there are meaningful ways to group potential customers into segments. Identification of segments is operationally meaningful when:

- Customer differences in preferences for brand appeals do, in fact, exist.
- These differences can be identified and matched with customer groups.
- The segment preferences can be reached by the marketing program.

■ The segments have enough demand potential to justify their selection as target markets.

■ The segments are sufficiently stable to allow adequate lead time for the design and implementation of a marketing strategy.

Customer Differences. For market segments to exist, customer responses to a firm's marketing program (product, distribution, price, and promotion) must vary between market groupings. Suppose that a product-market has been divided into two segments, A and B, and that each segment contains 3 million people. Assuming that sales to segments A and B will occur as shown by the curves in Exhibit 11-2, then response differences clearly exist between the two segments. If the marketing program designed for segment A (horizontal axis) is directed toward segment B, then market response at any level of marketing program expenditure will be less for B than for A. The point is illustrated by promotion in the fast-food industry. Directing a Ronald McDonald advertising campaign toward adults is not likely to be very effective in attracting adult singles business.

Response elasticity is the ratio of the percentage change in market response to the percentage change in marketing program expenditure.

Successful market segmentation strategies depend on differences in the **response elasticities** of potential customers. Response elasticity refers to how favorably a customer will react to a marketing program. Response differences may exist for all or some of the components of the marketing mix. A demand curve showing how customers change their buying decisions in response to changes in price illustrates responsiveness to a single mix component. Similarly, customers will be more or less responsive to all the other components of a marketing mix, including product features, advertising messages, media, product availability, personal selling effort, and customer services.

Differences in response elasticities provide an opportunity to design marketing offers that are tailored to match segment preferences. Of course, a potential segment must be estimated to be responsive enough to a separate marketing program to more than pay for the added cost of serving that segment. Lack of differences in response elasticities suggests that a mass market strategy is more appropriate than a segmentation strategy. Customers do not appear to have very different response elasticities for such commodities as fruit, salt, and sugar.

Identifiable Differences. Probably the most difficult part of the segmentation process is finding the best way to group customers into segments. While information is needed on probable customer reactions to alternative marketing offer designs to develop a graph such as that shown in Exhibit 11-2, the analyst must be able to place people with similar reactions in the same segment. And the customer segments must be described so that management understands who is in each one.

Finding appropriate segmentation bases is often a trial-and-error process. A firm may have to conduct several research projects to find a workable way

EXHIBIT 11–2 Differences in Customer Response between Segments

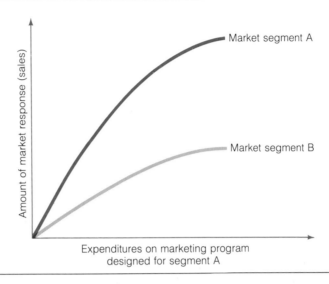

of forming segments, and may then have to use research periodically to monitor any changes. Such efforts can be expensive. A comprehensive segmentation analysis may cost more than $100,000 in a consumer product-market.

Reaching Segment Customers. Market segmentation is a competitive strategy, as illustrated by Marriott's targeting of the mid-price market served by Holiday Inns and Ramada Inns. Marketing appeals must be tailored to the defined target segments. Ideally, these appeals should have minimal "leakage" into other segments. Meeting this requirement is not always easy. Sometimes a firm may not have access to marketing program alternatives that will reach a segment's unique characteristics and preferences. Consider the difficulties of a department store in a small city that is trying to reach two or three market segments with different advertising appeals. Local media typically have broad coverage, reaching customers in various segments. Targeted forms of distribution such as direct mail, specialized print media, and telecommunications technology are overcoming historical problems in reaching specific customer groups.

A marketing mix designed for one segment may cannibalize (attract customers from) another segment. Cannibalization of the established TRAC II razor by the Atra brand, introduced in 1977, was a key issue faced by the Gillette Company in the late 1970s. Marketing management was trying to develop strategies that targeted different user groups, but overlap in the target segments was clearly a problem since both brands satisfied a very similar need.

Sufficient Demand Potential.   A segment must have enough demand potential to justify the costs of using a market segmentation strategy. The costs of research, of designing unique offers, and of managing the strategy are typically higher for segmentation strategies than for mass strategies. Segmentation entails a substantial initial investment that is justified only by appropriate increases in sales. RCA offers different lines of color televisions that vary in price and are aimed at target market customers who differ in price elasticity. By employing this segmentation strategy, RCA sacrifices economies of scale in product design, manufacturing, distribution, and selling that could be achieved by offering only one television model to everyone. Fortunately, modern production technologies such as modular components increasingly allow scale economies at lower volumes than were needed in the past, thus facilitating the serving of specific segments.

Sufficient Stability over Time.   Adequate lead time is needed to design and profit from a segmentation strategy. And what constitutes sufficient lead time will differ considerably among firms. In the toy industry, a company may profit if demand for a certain toy lasts only through the Christmas season. On the other hand, automobile manufacturers need several years of stability, due to the lead time required to design, produce, and distribute a new model. For a segmentation strategy to be viable, the targeted segments must remain stable over the necessary lead time.

Steps in Segmentation Strategy

Market segmentation is one of the most important strategic tools that a marketing manager has for matching marketing offers to customer preferences. The segmentation concept is so logical and straightforward that it is easy to overlook the difficulty and expense of implementing it. The more common problems mentioned above stress the skill and effort that must go into finding a workable approach. Segmentation is more likely to be successful if a step-by-step approach is used (Exhibit 11–3). Segmentation strategy does not just happen; it is the result of applying a systematic analytic and decision-making process.

   The step-by-step approach highlights the major parts of segmentation strategy. In step 1, the basis for forming segments must be selected and the segments evaluated, using the five requirements just discussed. In step 2, detailed buyer profile information is obtained for each segment of interest. In step 3, candidate segments are evaluated by means of financial and strategic criteria. In step 4, management must decide which segments to select as target markets.

EXHIBIT 11-3 Steps in Segmentation Strategy

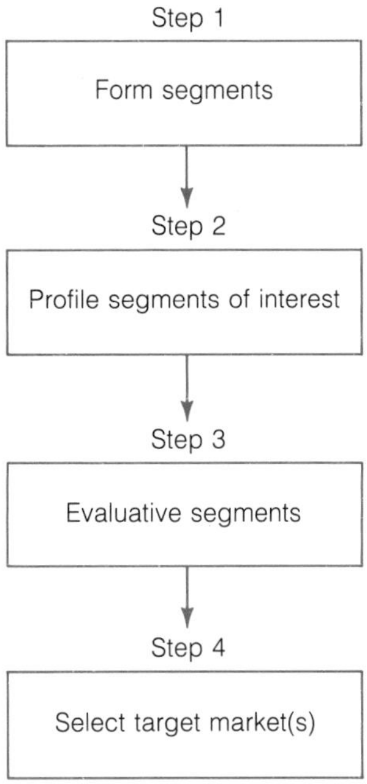

Step 1

> Form segments

Step 2

> Profile segments of interest

Step 3

> Evaluative segments

Step 4

> Select target market(s)

Forming Segments

There are two important considerations in identifying market segments. First, should segments be formed by aggregating individual customers (the buildup approach) or by separating a product-market into segments (the breakdown approach)? Second, what bases (income, benefits provided) should be used to form segments?

Buildup versus Breakdown. Exhibit 11–4 illustrates the essential difference between the buildup and breakdown approaches. Either approach may be appropriate in a given situation. A firm might group individual customers to form segments with similar needs, or a large product-market might be broken down on the basis of one or more customer characteristics.

Buildup Approach. When analyzing a market that contains millions of people, buildup may not be practical. It is particularly appropriate, however, in markets that contain a relatively small number of potential buyers, such as industrial markets. In fact, for some industrial products firms, each customer is a specific target market. Consider how an industrial motor manufacturer

EXHIBIT 11-4 Buildup versus Breakdown Segment Formation

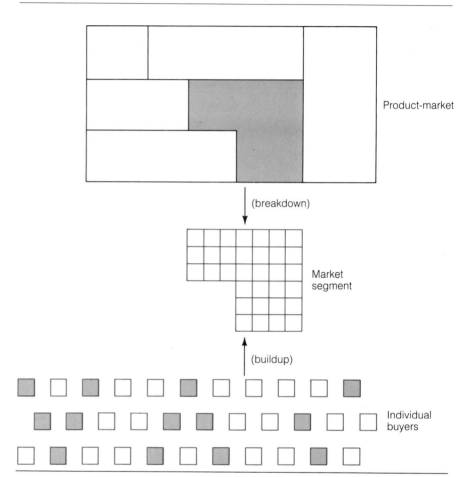

aggregated customers from 47 Standard Industrial Code (SIC) markets into four segments, A, B, C, and D (Exhibit 11-5). Note how common buying factors differ among the four segments.

The buildup approach is theoretically the logical approach to forming segments. Subsegments may be combined to satisfy constraints dictated by scarce resources or by management.[9] The people with needs and wants for a given product type are aggregated into groups with similar responses to a particular marketing offer.

In order to aggregate people into groups, the people who comprise a product-market must first be identified. Aggregation is useful in identifying habits and preferences in markets for generic products, such as foods. For example, a study of 1,000 households asked respondents their attitudes on

EXHIBIT 11–5 Buildup Approach to Forming Segments

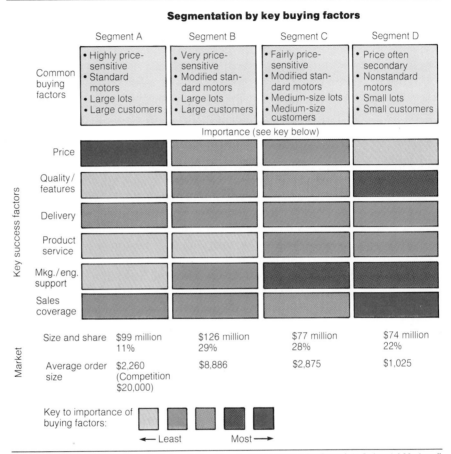

Source: Robert A. Garda, "Strategic Segmentation: How to Carve Niches for Growth in Industrial Markets," *Management Review*, August 1981, 21.

nutrition and food.[10] Participants kept a diary record of every snack or meal consumed during a two-week period. The results enabled the researchers to place the subjects in five major categories:

■ Meat and potato eaters

■ Families with kids—whose cupboards are stocked with soda pop and sweetened cereal

■ Dieters

■ Natural-food eaters

■ Sophisticates—moneyed urban types whose diets feature alcohol, Swiss cheese, and rye and pumpernickel.

But the groups did not stick to their stated preferences. The sophisticates were "above-average eaters of doughnuts and prepackaged cakes, including Sara Lee frozen cakes and Hostess Twinkies. They were also the most frequent eaters of cream cheese, probably because they were also the most avid eaters of bagels." Such research is very useful for the new product planning of food companies since it aggregates buyers into major groups and also identifies their true eating habits. Once the major groups have been identified, more comprehensive analysis can be conducted within each group to determine whether particular subgroups should be considered possible target markets.

Breakdown Approach. Breakdown is widely used in forming segments. Many marketing professionals consider segmentation to be a process of subdividing a product-market. Of course, to accomplish such a breakdown, the product-market must be well defined. The breakdown approach requires a basis for dividing the market. Banks are segmenting commercial and retail markets by analyzing their customer base and assigning officers to industry and consumer categories within the commercial and retail sectors.[11] Chemical Bank has a nonprofit organization segment. Commercial real estate developers, oil and gas energy producers, strip retailers, and medical services are other examples of segments for financial institutions.

    The buildup and breakdown approaches each have certain benefits and limitations. The buildup approach lends itself to situations in which there are many users (foods) or in which specific users can be easily identified, as in the case of several industrial markets. The breakdown approach requires identifying a basis for dividing the market (dividing the product-market based on amount of use).

Identifying Segmentation Bases. Finding some way to group customers in a product-market (either generic class or specific product type) into different segments is essentially a classification task. Marketing management needs to find the best basis for showing the segment in which a buyer belongs. Segmentation bases are characteristics on which potential buyers differ and reflect preferences for brand marketing offers. Ideally, a segmentation basis would be a direct measure of response elasticities to entire marketing offers. Such measures have not been developed, however, though progress is being made in this direction. In practice, segmentation bases are typically characteristics of potential buyers that are, at best, *proxy* measures of response elasticities.

    The wide range of bases that have been applied can be arranged in five levels, starting with general descriptors and ending with specific purchase behavior, as shown in Exhibit 11-6.[12] The levels begin with buyer characteristics, proceed to preferences and perceptions, and end with purchase behavior. While the levels correspond in a general way to a buyer's decision processes, interrelationships among the bases are not explicit. There is

EXHIBIT 11–6 Market Segmentation Bases

Basis Level	Examples	Basis Level	Examples
General customer/ prospect characteristics	Various demographic and socio-economic characteristics such as age, sex, income, occupation. Bases for industrial products include industry, company size, and growth rate.	*Brand perceptions*	Examples include attitudes toward brands, brand preferences, and perceived brand similarities.
Psychographics (lifestyle)	There is some variation in the factors that researchers place in this category. Psychographics is described as "seeing into consumers' world or life space."* Examples include activities, interests, attitudes, beliefs, and opinions.	*Purchase behavior*	Characteristics associated with the person and the buying/use situation, including the specific products purchased, brand loyalty, the use rate, deal proneness, the degree of planning for product purchases, and the choice of supplier.
Desired values	Examples include desired product attributes, the relative importance attached to attributes, and attitudes toward products. Bases applicable for industrial products include supplier assistance, service requirements, performance characteristics, and product benefits.		

* Peter R. Dickson, "Person-Situation: Segmentation's Missing Link," *Journal of Marketing*, Fall 1982, p. 59.

general agreement among marketing professionals that both the *person* and the *situation* offer potentially useful variables for segmentation.

The Person-Situation Framework. The framework shown in Exhibit 11–7 combines three basic segmentation bases: *person, situation,* and *person within situation*.[13] Linking personal traits and the use situation with benefits, preferences, utilities, and behavior, it provides a structure for integrating the different bases that have been used in market opportunity analysis and target market determination. One major implication of the person-situation framework is that more than a single characteristic should be considered in selecting a basis for segmentation. The framework calls for the identification of person-situation combinations that can be aggregated or disaggregated in terms of the predominant product benefits sought, product and attribute perceptions, and marketplace behavior.[14]

A demonstration of how the person-situation framework can be used in constructing a segmentation matrix is provided in Exhibit 11–8. The person-situation framework illustrates the potential of an integrated approach to identifying market segments. In some applications, use of one or more of the bases for forming segments may be adequate.

EXHIBIT 11-7

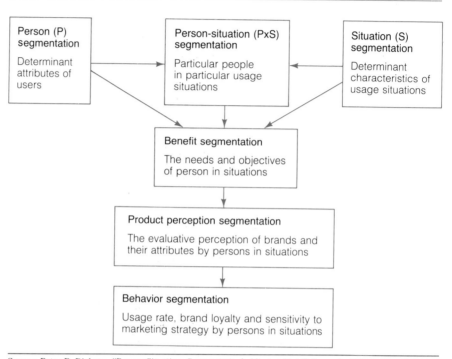

Source: Peter R. Dickson, "Person-Situation: Segmentation's Missing Link," *Journal of Marketing*, Fall 1982, p. 60.

Profile Segments

After segments have been formed, analysis turns to developing a sound understanding of what the typical customer in each segment is like (step 2 in Exhibit 11-3).

Developing Customer Profiles. A profile is built for each segment by searching for relationships among segmentation basis variables and descriptive characteristic variables. Strong correlations between the way in which customers score on segmentation basis variables and on a descriptive characteristic support the inclusion of that descriptive characteristic in the profile. Available statistical tools allow the simultaneous analysis of correlations between multiple descriptive characteristics and the segmentation basis.

Management is interested in both within-segment similarities and between-segment differences. However, there may be similarities in the profiles of different segments. Although a segmentation basis should clearly classify customers into segments, customers in different segments do not have to score differently on every profile variable. But if total profiles are too similar across segments, they will give management little additional insight into how

EXHIBIT 11–8 Speculative Person-Situation Segmentation Matrix for Suntan Lotion

Persons / Situations	Young children		Teenagers		Adult women		Adult men		Situation benefit features
	Fair skin	Dark skin	Fair skin	Dark skin	Fair skin	Dark skin	Fair skin	Dark skin	
beach/boat sunbathing	combined insect repellent				summer perfume				a. windburn protection b. formula and container can stand heat c. container floats and is distinctive (not easily lost)
home/ poolside sunbathing					combined moisturizer				a. large pump dispenser b. won't stain wood, concrete, or furnishings
sunlamp					combined moisturizer and massage oil				a. designed specifically for type of lamp b. artificial tanning ingredient
snow skiing					winter perfume				a. special protection from special light rays and weather b. antifreeze formula
Person Benefit/ features	special protection a. protection critical b. nonpoisonous		special protection a. fit in jean pocket b. used by opinion leaders		special protection female perfume		special protection male perfume		

Source: Peter R. Dickson, "Person-Situation: Segmentation's Missing Link," *Journal of Marketing* Fall 1982, p. 62.

to serve each segment with a specific marketing mix beyond that provided by the segmentation basis variables.

Evaluate Market Segments

Once segments have been formed and profiled, marketing managers evaluate the profit contribution expected from each segment (step 3 of Exhibit 11-3). Several kinds of information are needed, starting with the demand potential within each segment.

Forecasting Segment Potential. Estimating segment potential is essentially a forecasting task requiring one or more of the forecasting techniques presented in Chapter 8. However, segmentation analysis requires predicting demand for each component of a product-market rather than for the product-market as a whole. The profiles of the various segments are needed to guide the forecasts. The sum of the estimates for each segment should equal the estimate for the entire product-market, as shown:

$$MP = \sum_{i=1}^{n} sp_i$$

where:

MP = Market potential for the product-market

sp_i = Segment potential in the ith segment

n = Number of segments formed from the product-market

Analyzing Competitive Positions. Segment potential does not always translate into profits for a company. A segment's contribution to corporate sales and profits depends in part on the position of key competitors in the segment. An analysis of the competitors serving each segment is needed to help managers strategicallly evaluate the strengths and weaknesses of their positions (see Chapter 7). We know that company brand sales are dependent both on market potential and on the effectiveness of the firm's marketing offer relative to those of competitors:

Segment sales forecast = Segment market forecast × Segment share

To illustrate the danger of overlooking the positions of competitors, suppose that an analysis of two segments shows that segment A has expected sales of $20 million and that segment B has expected sales of only $10 million. On the surface, segment A may seem to present more market opportunity than segment B since it has twice the demand potential. However, suppose that two competitors are now serving segment A, that two more plan to enter the segment soon, and that market share of 11 to 15 percent is probably achievable for our firm. On the other hand, only one competitor is serving segment B and no other competitors are known to be contemplating entering this market, so that a much higher market share, say 40 percent, is attainable. Using the segment sales forecast equation, the sales opportunity in the smaller segment, B, turns out to be more attractive:

Segment A sales forecast = $20,000,000 × 15%
= 3,000,000

Segment B sales forecast = $10,000,000 × 40%
= 4,000,000

As has been indicated, firms looking for new opportunities in established markets should carefully assess the smaller segments because existing firms are likely to be successfully positioned in the larger segments. However, for untapped product markets, such as may exist for radically new products, the greatest opportunity will undoubtedly be in the larger segments, since competition will be minimal.

Both competitor analysis and customer profiles are needed to design segment marketing offers. With a marketing strategy for each candidate target segment, management can estimate the costs of serving segments. These costs provide a partial basis for comparing opportunities in different markets.

Analyzing Potential Goal/Objective Achievement. As a final step before selecting target markets, the potential for achieving corporate goals and objectives in market segments should be assessed. Organizational and marketing goals and objectives vary from corporation to corporation. Typically, there are both quantitative goals—profits, market share, return on investment—and qualitative goals concerning company image and reputation. Evaluating qualitative goals is more judgmental than evaluating quantitative goals. Here, managers have to gauge whether the marketing program needed to reach a segment will create or reinforce customer product and brand attitudes consistent with corporate image objectives.

Select Target Markets

After the candidate segments have been evaluated, management is ready to select the segments that will be target markets (step 4 in Exhibit 11-3). Alternative segmentation strategies are typically available. These can be classified according to the number of segments entered (full- versus limited-coverage segmentation) and the uniqueness of the marketing mix components used in catering to segment differences (see Exhibit 11-9).

Full-coverage market segmentation is the targeting by a firm of all or most of the market segments in a product-market, using a specific marketing mix for each segment.

Full-Coverage Market Segmentation. When a company decides to enter all or at least most segments, **full-coverage market segmentation** is used. This is a high-sales strategy, since greater penetration into each segment is combined with broad coverage of a total market. Extensive resources are required to implement the strategy because it affords limited opportunity for economies of scale. Full-coverage market segmentation is therefore most likely to be adopted by a large organization such as General Motors, IBM, or Anheuser-Busch.

A full-coverage market segmentation strategy can be implemented by designing unique marketing programs for every target segment (I). General Motors uses this approach. Its Chevrolet, Pontiac, Buick, Oldsmobile, and Cadillac divisions each appeal to different segments with different products, prices, promotion, and channels. On the other hand, a company will often try to achieve cost savings by designing only partly unique marketing offers for different segments (II). Holiday Inns uses the same facilities to appeal to business travelers, families on vacation, and local residents. However, adver-

EXHIBIT 11–9 Alternative Segmentation Strategies

| | Marketing Mix | |
	Totally Unique	Partly Unique
Full coverage	I	II
Limited coverage	III	IV

tising, promotion, price, and amenities are differentiated for these segments. The chain also allocates certain floors to executive guests at some of its properties, offering such amenities as snacks and drinks.

Limited-Coverage Market Segmentation.   When only one or a few segments are selected as market targets, **limited-coverage market segmentation** is used. This strategy requires fewer resources and is therefore effective for smaller companies trying to compete against the giants of an industry. American Motors has tried to remain viable in automotive markets by concentrating on small cars and on the recreational vehicle segment with its line of Jeeps. The company's market position is strong in the segment targeted by its Jeep line.

    A limited-coverage market segmentation strategy offers several advantages for the smaller firm. It does not require as great a resource commitment as the full-coverage strategy, yet is still a relatively high-sales approach. Tailoring a marketing offer to the unique needs of selected segments should lead to greater penetration and market share. When a few segments are selected, management may decide to design a totally unique offer for each segment (III), though cost economies are achieved by designing only partly unique offers (IV).

    A major risk of the limited-coverage strategy lies in dependence on one or a few segments for sales. A company using this strategy is highly susceptible to market segment changes—shifts in customer preferences or the entry of additional competitors. Over time, instability of sales and poor performance may result. Cummins Engine Company builds diesel engines for heavy-duty trucks. It dominates this segment of the truck market, holding a 50 percent market share. Sales in this market are highly cyclical—declining from 375,000 in 1979 to about 190,000 in 1982, then rising to 275,000 in 1984.[15] To help reduce the ups and downs of sales and profits in the heavy-truck market, Cummins is moving into the lower-horsepower segment of the market.

    Limited- and full-coverage market segmentation strategies represent the opposite ends of a strategy continuum. A small firm may begin with a limited-coverage strategy and then move into more and more segments as it grows. Or a firm having performance problems in multiple segments, as may happen when it is competing in a mature market, can move toward the limited-coverage strategy. Over the years, American Motors has been withdrawing

Limited-coverage market segmentation is the targeting of only one or a few of the market segments in a product-market, using a specific marketing mix for each segment.

from less profitable segments for larger cars and intensifying its efforts in the more profitable segments for smaller cars and recreational vehicles.

Methods for Forming Segments

Segmentation should involve a systematic analytic process. Research methods may be needed to help management identify segments. Several techniques can be used to select the bases for segmentation and to form segments. The many specific approaches for forming market segments usually fall into one of two categories: approaches using experience and available information and research approaches.[16] An examination of the two approaches will indicate how they are used in various applications.

Experience and Available Information

There are many situations in which management's knowledge of customer needs can be combined with analysis of *available* information to identify market segments. The industrial motor segmentation application in Exhibit 11-5 illustrates this approach. The four segments formed were determined by analyzing existing customer characteristics and average order size. An interesting description of the evolution of market segmentation in industrial product-markets is shown in Exhibit 11-10.

Utilizing experience and existing information to form segments is particularly applicable to industrial product-markets with a relatively small number of product users. In these markets, management often has a detailed knowledge of the customer base. Quaker Chemical, a producer of specialty chemicals used in manufacturing operations, considers each customer and prospect a target market. The main thrust of Quaker's marketing approach is its sales force. The firm's sales engineers work with a small number of customers, studying manufacturing processes to identify applications for Quaker Chemicals. Prospects are selected based on the sales potential for Quaker products.

Numerous sources of available information can be used by management to guide segment identification. Several services collect, analyze, and distribute to subscribers data on purchases of various products. Some services provide descriptive profiles of the people who purchase the products. Typically, a sample of households is questioned periodically concerning products and brands purchased, prices paid, the location of purchases, and other pertinent information. Frequently purchased products such as foods and drugs are particularly well suited to coverage by these information services.

Information Resources, Inc., a Chicago-based firm, illustrates how new information processing technology coupled with proven marketing research methods generates useful information for market segmentation. Its BehaviorScan system electronically tracks total grocery store sales and individual

EXHIBIT 11–10 How Market Segmentation Evolved

Stage 1 Segmentation by product

Stage 3 Product/market segments

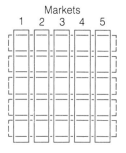

In the late 1950s and early 1960s industrial companies, following the lead of consumer goods manufacturers, installed product managers to make certain that each product received its fair share of support from the various functional groups influencing its success in the marketplace.

In the early 1970s, strategists began to concentrate on defining the product/market combinations in which their companies were involved and designing specific strategies for each segment. Some companies resorted to matrix organizations with both product and market managers.

Stage 2 Segmentation by market

State 4 Geographic product/market segments

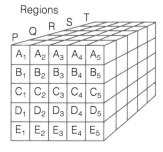

In the mid to late 1960s focus was on end-use markets. Market or industry managers were set up to plan for these end-use markets, each served by a particular group of products.

For the multinational corporation of today, the geographic dimension has been added. Many companies are now trying to develop niche strategies for each product/region they serve. In short, the art of market segmentation has been growing more and more sophisticated. But with the sophistication has come complexity, and many managers are now concerned that in contending with this complexity, their marketing analysts have lost sight of the real object of market segmentation: gaining competitive advantage.

Source: Adapted from Robert A. Garda, "Strategic Segmentation: How to Carve Niches for Growth in Industrial Markets," *Management Review*, August 1981, p. 18.

household purchase behavior through complete universal product code (UPC) scanner coverage. People in the 2,500 household samples in each of several metropolitan markets covered by the service carry special ID cards and are individually tracked via scanner in grocery stores and drugstores. An example of the type of information generated is given in Exhibit 11–11. Note how the information can be used to form market segments. The firm publishes *The Marketing Fact Book*, which provides consumer purchase data on all product categories, and provides access to the data base for follow-up, in-

EXHIBIT 11-11 Analysis of Age of Soap Purchasers

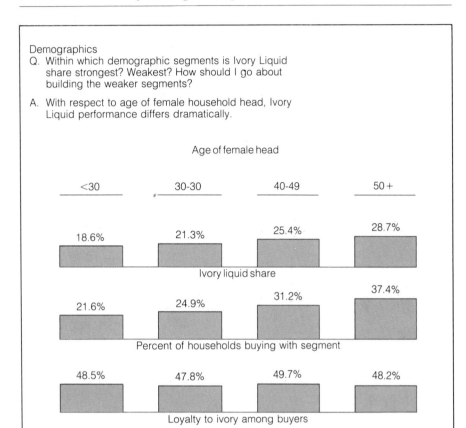

Demographics

Q. Within which demographic segments is Ivory Liquid share strongest? Weakest? How should I go about building the weaker segments?

A. With respect to age of female household head, Ivory Liquid performance differs dramatically.

Age of female head

<30	30-30	40-49	50+
18.6%	21.3%	25.4%	28.7%

Ivory liquid share

21.6%	24.9%	31.2%	37.4%

Percent of households buying with segment

48.5%	47.8%	49.7%	48.2%

Loyalty to ivory among buyers

The relatively weaker performance among younger households traces to fewer buyers. Among those who *did* buy, loyalty was similar in all segments.

To build share, promotions (perhaps high-value coupons) and/or advertising aimed at trial generation among younger female household heads should be considered.

This analysis can, of course, include a full range of additional demographic variables.

The above data are entirely fictional. Brand names are used only to add an element of reality. Any similarity to actual brand data is entirely coincidental.

Source: *The Marketing Fact Book*™ (Chicago: Information Resources, 1986), p. 10.

depth analyses. Although the service is expensive ($85,000 per year in 1986), its cost is a small fraction of the cost of collecting and analyzing the data.

Research Approaches

The research methods that can be used to identify market segments fall into two general categories—*predetermined patronage* and *perceptions and preferences*.[17] Methods in the first category involve some measure of patronage, such as product use rate, as the basis for forming segments. Thus, the segments are predetermined. Analysis distinguishes among customers that fall into the various patronage categories. Methods in the second category obtain measures of consumer perceptions and preferences to form segments. Predetermined patronage approaches are essentially customer self-selection, in that segment members are identified in advance based on some measure of patronage.[18] Perception and preference approaches (also referred to as "customer participation" approaches) build the customer into the segment formation process by asking a sample of customers questions and using the information obtained in this way to form segments.

Predetermined Patronage Segmentation. After predetermined patronage approaches create candidate segments, typically in terms of product use, statistical analysis is conducted to identify the characteristics of the people in each candidate segment (heavy, medium, and light users of a brand). The objective is to describe the customers in each candidate segment and to show that there are differences among customers across segments. Demographic variables have been used extensively in such analyses.

There is a supporting logic to predetermined patronage approaches in that the basis they use to form segments corresponds to customer responsiveness to a marketing mix. The problem with these approaches is that strong and distinct differences typically have not been found between customers in one candidate segment and those in another. Several reasons for the disappointing results have been offered. One explanation is that "past consumption generated in one particular environment had very little to say about potential actions necessary to capture future demand."[19] Thus, the stability of the segment may affect how useful predetermined patronage approaches may be in a given situation. It has also been noted that the predetermined segments are so large that substantial differences may exist among the customers within a candidate segment. Moreover, interrelationships in predetermined segments may be so complex that they cannot be identified. In addition, predetermined patronage approaches have made limited use of most of the segmentation bases listed in Exhibit 11-6, with the exception of general characteristics.

A study of heavy users and nonusers of shotgun ammunition illustrates how going beyond demographic variables to psychographics may improve the results of predetermined segment analysis (Exhibit 11-12). The demo-

EXHIBIT 11–12 Profiles of Heavy Users and Nonusers of Shotgun Ammunition

Demographic*

	Heavy Users (141)	Nonusers (395)
Age		
Under 25	9%	5%
25–34	33	15
35–44	27	22
45–54	18	22
55+	13	36
Occupation		
Professional	6	15
Managerial	23	23
Clerical/sales	9	17
Craftperson	50	35
Income		
Under $6,000	26	19
$6,000–10,000	39	36
$10,000–15,000	24	27
$15,000+	11	18
Population density		
Rural	34	12
2,500–50,000	11	11
50,000–500,000	16	15
500,000–2 million	21	27
2 million+	13	19
Geographic division		
New England–Mid-Atlantic	21	33
N.W. Central	22	30
South Atlantic	23	12
East South Central	10	3
West South Central	10	5
Mountain	6	3
Pacific	9	15

Psychographic†

	Heavy Users (141)	Nonusers (395)
I like hunting	88%	7%
I like fishing	68	26
I like to go camping	57	21
I love the out-of-doors	90	65
A cabin by a quiet lake is a great place to spend the summer	49	34
I like to work outdoors	67	40
I am good at fixing mechanical things	47	27
I often do a lot of repair work on my own car	36	12
I like war stories	50	32
I would do better than average in a fistfight	38	16
I would like to be a professional football player	28	18
I would like to be on the police force	22	8
There is too much violence on television	35	45
There should be a gun in every home	56	10
I like danger	19	8
I would like to own my own airplane	35	13
I like to play poker	50	26
I smoke too much	39	24
I love to eat	49	34
I spend money on myself that I should spend on the family	44	26
If given a chance, most men would cheat on their wives	33	14
I read the newspaper every day	51	72

*Percentage of each user group in the different age, occupation, income, population, and geographic classes.

†Percentage of each user group answering yes to each statement.

Source: W. D. Wells, "Psychographics: A Critical Review," *Journal of Marketing Research* 12 (May 1975), pp. 197–98.

graphic profiles show some differences between users and nonusers of shotgun ammunition, but the psychographic profiles provide a more revealing description of those differences. Nonetheless, both the demographic and psychographic profiles may be useful. The demographic profiles are helpful in targeting advertising and other marketing efforts, and the psychographic profiles can guide advertising messages and other promotional efforts.

Customer Perception and Preference Segmentation. Some of the more promising research approaches for forming segments use research data on customers to construct perceptual "maps" for products and brands. For example, product use situation and product attributes have been used to form maps based on customer perceptions. While the specific research methodology and techniques are beyond the scope of our discussion, the major steps of the customer perception and preference approaches can be summarized (brand may refer to a product or service or to an entire organization such as a restaurant, department store, or bank):

1. Selection of the product-market to be examined.
2. Determination of the brands in the product-market.
3. Collection of data on consumer perceptions regarding brands (and an ideal brand) obtained from a sample of people. The perceptions pertain to various product attributes (cost, features, trade-in value, etc.). The *ideal* brand would possess the proper amount of each attribute for each buyer.
4. Analysis of the data to form one, two, or more composite attribute dimensions, each independent of the others. For example, several attributes might be reflected in one composite attribute, such as cost.
5. Preparation of a two-dimensional map (X and Y grid) of attributes on which consumer perceptions of competing brands are positioned.
6. Plotting of consumers with similar ideal preferences to see whether subgroups will form.
7. Interpretation of the results in terms of target market and product-positioning strategies.[20]

A hypothetical example of a consumer perception map for videocassette recorders (VCRs) is shown in Exhibit 11–13. Brands A through D are positioned on the map as they are perceived by a sample of consumers, and the preferences of consumer segments I through V regarding expense and features are as indicated. Note that many research steps must be completed before this simple, yet revealing map can be constructed. For example, the two dimensions (features and expense) actually represent composites of several different attributes.

What are the market segment implications of the analysis if our brand is D? Clearly, we are in an attractive position in that our brand is relatively close to segments III, IV, and V, while brands B and C are close to segment III. Several

EXHIBIT 11-13 Consumer Perception Map for Videocassette Recorders

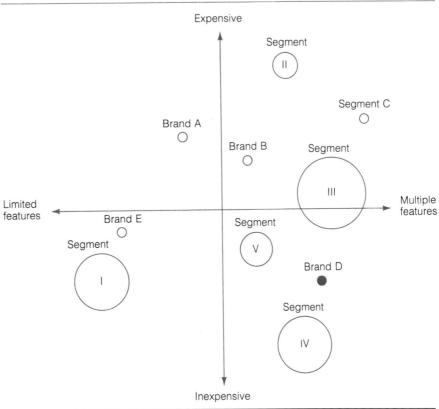

options exist for brand D. One is to attempt to alter consumers' perceptions of D as being somewhat inexpensive to perceptions of D as being somewhat expensive. It is probably more feasible to do this than to change quality perceptions. Brand C represents a competitive threat should its management decide to go after segment III rather than II. Interestingly, the people in segment IV appear to be unrealistic in their preferences. They want a VCR that is both high in quality and inexpensive. They may have to alter their price preferences, or they may decide not to purchase VCRs.

Positioning Strategy

Market segmentation strategy and marketing positioning strategy are like two sides of a coin. Segmentation strategy identifies the customers to be targeted. Positioning strategy is concerned with selecting a marketing mix appropriate to each target market segment. Thus, positioning of a firm's

EXHIBIT 11-14

Mercury Sable and Ford Taurus are Ford's all-new automobiles targeted toward higher-income, young-to-middle-age buyers that are attracted to European styling and high-performance cars like Audi, BMW, and Volvo.

Courtesy Young & Rubicam/Detroit.

product or brand is ultimately determined by the buyer in combination with the actions of competition. Positioning of a brand is how it is perceived by the buyer relative to the brands of the firm's key competitors (Exhibit 11-14). The objective of a positioning strategy is to have the brand favorably perceived by the people in the target market.[21] Two firms' have the same positioning strategy if their marketing offerings are perceived to be identical. Typically, there are differences in how buyers perceive marketing offerings. Consider the services of American and Delta airlines. Ask people who fly both airlines regularly, and you are likely to obtain somewhat different perceptions of the services offered by the two airlines. Often the product is the focal point of a positioning strategy since the other marketing mix components are working toward positioning the product in the eyes and mind of the buyer.

The marketing approach used by Kraft for its Breyers ice cream brand offers an interesting example of a positioning strategy:

In the late 1960s, Kraft was marketing an ice cream called Breyers in the New York, Philadelphia, and Baltimore-Washington areas. . . .

. . . Breyers ice cream does not contain any kind of artificial flavoring, nor does it contain any added coloring. And, more significantly, it does not contain any stabilizers or emulsifiers. . . .

. . . consumers' interest in natural foods was just beginning to emerge as a positioning consideration; and very few, if any, marketers were making much noise about it. An advertising campaign was developed that targeted the Breyers product as "The All-Natural Ice Cream." This positioning was deliberately designed to be more of an ingredient story than to have a health or ecological appeal. Copy reported on the quantity as well as the quality of the ingredients (e.g., Breyers takes more than a pound of peaches to make a half gallon of peach ice cream).

This new Breyers positioning caught on quickly, and in three years sales in its traditional marketing areas had doubled. It was then realized that this strategy could be an effective means of introducing the brand into new markets where the all-natural positioning had not yet been used to its fullest. This was a great idea, but how could we face up to the challenge . . . when we were already well represented in these markets by Sealtest, another premium quality brand? . . .

And what about the consumer? If we sell the consumer on the merits of Breyers as being the best quality product, what do we say about Sealtest? That it is almost as good? Might we really be only competing with ourselves for the same customer? . . .

In coming to grips with these and other somewat difficult strategic questions, a solution evolved that led to the creation of what was called "The Premium Ice Cream Program." Basically, this is a three-brand marketing strategy that recognizes several key consumer purchase and demand considerations.[22]

Kraft was faced with positioning three different brands: Breyers, Sealtest, and Light n' Lively (ice milk). Here is how each brand was positioned:

Breyers was aimed at people wanting a premium, all-natural product as described above.

Sealtest was positioned for people who were not attracted by the appeal of naturalness but wanted something special in an ice cream. Sealtest was promoted as "The Supermarket Ice Cream with that Ice Cream Parlor Taste."

Light n' Lively was targeted to people who cannot or do not want to pay the price for fine ice cream. Kraft developed a premium ice milk brand with texture and taste qualities similar to ice cream and priced it below the two premium brands but above other ice milks.[23]

There are several ways to develop a positioning strategy:

- By attribute—Crest is a cavity fighter.

- By price/quality—Sears is a "value" store.

- By competitor—Avis positions itself with Hertz.

- By application—Gatorade is for flu attacks.
- By product user—Miller is for the blue-collar, heavy beer drinker.
- By product class—Carnation Instant Breakfast is a breakfast food.[24]

These examples are not necessarily mutually exclusive. By definition, positioning is in reference to competition. Also, other positioning strategies are built on:

- Low cost relative to competitors' prices (The Price Club warehouse retailers).
- Distribution/service (IBM).
- Premium/prestige image (Breyers in ice cream and Mercedes-Benz in automobiles).

Developing a positioning strategy requires that management identify key competitors, determine how competitors are perceived and evaluated by buyers, determine the competitors' positions, analyze the customers, select the position, and monitor the position.[25] The choice of a target market segment answers several of the questions regarding positioning strategy.

Application

Segmentation Research and Positioning[26]

Differentiating automobile brands is a continuing challenge to automobile manufacturers. Those firms are increasingly using attributes other than body style to differentiate their cars. Consider the perceptual map developed by Chrysler Corporation (Exhibit 11-A). The map is based on consumer surveys asking owners of different makes to rank their autos on a scale of 1 to 10 for such attributes as "youthfulness," "luxury," and "practicality." The responses are analyzed using a computer model that reduces the set of attributes to a two-dimensional brand preference map like the one shown. Chrysler prepares brand preference maps about three times each year and uses them to analyze positioning of existing brands, to identify promising market segments, and to spot new trends in consumer preferences for automobiles.

The map in Exhibit 11-A measures the images of the major divisions of U.S. automakers and some imports. The individual models of a particular brand would probably occupy various positions on the map. For example, consumers undoubtedly perceive Chevrolet's Nova and Corvette models differently. The upper-right quadrant suggests a potential opportunity for U.S. manufacturers. The 1986 Mercury Sable and Ford Taurus automobiles appear to be targeting people who are seeking the attributes in this quadrant.

Information regarding consumer demand is incorporated into the map to show strong areas

EXHIBIT 11-A Chrysler's Automobile Brand Positioning Map

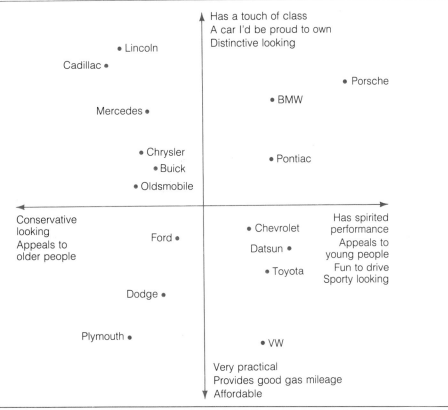

of demand. The map shows how people perceive various brands but does not indicate where their "ideal" brand would be positioned. Groupings of people with similar ideal points represent possible market segments. By comparing segment groupings and brand positions, market opportunities, intensity of competition, and gaps in market coverage can be identified.

The map has important strategic implications for Chrysler. Plymouth and Dodge need to be repositioned upward on the luxury scale. Management decided that Chrysler models need to present a more youthful image. Note also the similarity in the perceptions of General Motors Corporation's Oldsmobile and Buick divisions. This suggests that these divisions may be competing more against each other than against the brands of other carmakers. Gains in Buick's market share would probably be cannibalized from Oldsmobile customers.

Perception mapping is an important analytic tool for segmentation analysis and positioning. Perceptual maps combine consumer preference information and a product orientation. The maps are useful in planning strategy and in evaluating strategies that have been implemented ∎

Summary

This chapter establishes an important link between the market and the organization. The selection of one or more target markets by marketing management sets the stage for developing a positioning strategy for each target market. A target market is any group of potential customers toward whom a company decides to direct its marketing offer. A firm often has several target market options, each selected from a generic-class or product-type market. Targeting is a strategic decision that may result in going after the entire product-market (mass strategy) or targeting one or more market segments. Market segmentation is the process of matching marketing mix offers to the differences in the way one or more groups of customers will respond to offerings. Market segmentation is becoming the dominant strategy of many firms because of the wide differences in people's needs and wants, the ease of targeting segments, and the cost effectiveness of segmentation.

For market segments to exist, certain requirements must be satisfied. First, there must be differences in customer preferences for brand appeals (marketing mixes); customer response to a firm's marketing program (product, distribution, price, and promotion) must vary among market segments. Second, these differences must be identifiable and the people in each segment described. Third, the firm must be able to target segment preferences with an appropriate marketing mix for each target. Fourth, each target must offer enough market opportunity to justify the costs of a segmentation strategy. Finally, segment preferences should not change until the firm has had an opportunity to gain enough sales and profits to make the venture attractive to management.

The four steps involved in a segmentation strategy are: forming segments, profiling the segments of interest, financially and strategically evaluating the segments, and selecting one or more target markets. Step one requires that some way be found to group customers into segments. There are several categories of segmentation bases, including descriptive characteristics, psychographics (lifestyle), desired values, brand perceptions, and purchase behavior. Experience, available information, and research approaches may be used to form segments using one or more of these bases. Research approaches to forming segments involve either predetermined patronage segmentation or segmentation from customer research data.

In steps two and three, customer profiles are developed and each segment is evaluated as to potential, the competitive situation, the required marketing strategy, and the extent to which corporate objectives will be satisfied through the segment. Finally, in step four, management must decide which segments to target. The options range from serving all or most segments (full coverage) to targeting one or a few segments (limited coverage).

Marketing positioning is set into motion by the marketing mix that is developed and implemented to meet the needs and wants of a target segment. Actual positioning is determined by buyers' perceptions of the firm's brand relative to the brands of its key competitors. Thus, the essential issue is how the firm's marketing program (product, distribution, price, and promotion) is perceived by the people in the target segment relative to competing marketing programs.

Exercises for Review and Discussion

1. All Tennis was the first retail store devoted exclusively to selling tennis equipment and clothing in a medium-sized southern city. Sales were low for the first year, and then the store experienced nine years of rapid growth in sales and profitability. During this period, the popularity of tennis mushroomed. Then, the store's sales leveled off and its profits declined. The owner/manager was concerned. He knew that two new tennis stores had opened in the past two years. One was Basic Tennis, which seemed to appeal primarily on a low-price basis. The other was Tennis Love, which emphasized high-fashion clothing and well-known, prestigious brands. Yet the manager did not feel that two more competitors should have hurt business that much. The number of tennis players had grown substantially, and the manager felt that All Tennis appealed to "most everyone who played the game." What target market options should All Tennis consider? How would you evaluate those options? Discuss your answers.

2. Explain why Marriott Corporation is attempting to appeal to multiple segments while Days Inn (moderately priced accommodations) has a much more limited service offering.

3. As part of an MOA for a new snack food that your company is going to introduce (Bluebells, a corn chip with a unique shape), you have received the information in Exhibit A. Use this information to recommend target market and marketing mix strategy actions that you believe appropriate for this product.

4. A manufacturer of sailboats had been distributing its line of boats as a private brand sold under several distributors' names. Now the marketing staff is recommending that the line be

EXHIBIT A

	Heavy User	Light User	Nonuser
Average volume purchased	12-15 boxes per month	1-6 boxes per month	0 boxes per month
Demographics	Urban or rural residence Low-moderate income Blue-collar occupation Less than high school education Large family	Moderate income White-collar occupation High school graduate Suburban residence	High income Over 50 Suburban residence College-educated
AIOs	Socially active Prefers informal "get-togethers" with friends Nontraveler Concerned with high inflation Politically inactive	Socially inactive Very concerned with increasing food prices Sports enthusiast	Entertains by having formal dinner parties Socially active Churchgoer Politically active Concerned with community affairs
Behavioral characteristics	Heavy beer drinker Heavy TV watcher	Heavy TV watcher Heavy buyer of sporting equipment	Watches very little TV Wine drinker

sold directly to boating retail stores under the company's own brand name. After conducting a market opportunity analysis, the staff settled on a target market comprising families with a household head who is male and between 35 and 50 years of age, is in a professional occupation, earns more than $30,000 per year, lives in a suburban area near a city of 100,000 or more, and has children between 8 and 18. What kind of target market strategy is being recommended? Mass market? Market segmentation? Discuss your answer.

5. For which of the following products is a company most likely to choose a mass strategy? Automobiles; bus service; cameras; the first store in an area selling exclusively running/jogging clothes, shoes, and related equipment; salt; oranges; motorcycles. Discuss your answer.

6. A market segmentation study sponsored by a fast-food hamburger chain identified five market segments within the fast-food hamburger product-market. The chain was only the 25th-largest operation in its field, so management decided to go after only one market segment. The largest segment was selected because it had the greatest market potential. Do you feel that management made an appropriate target market selection? Discuss your response.

7. The brand manager for an all-purpose household liquid cleaner was reevaluating the target market strategy for this product. She had just taken over the position from a manager who had not developed a very well defined targeting approach. As far as the new manager could tell, a mass strategy came closest to describing her predecessor's marketing actions. Now she wondered whether such a strategy was best. What analyses of market conditions should the new brand manager use to help her evaluate whether to continue the mass strategy or to change to another? Discuss your reasons.

8. Under what conditions may segmentation not be feasible? Discuss your answer.

9. Why do companies alter their market target strategies over time? Discuss your answer.

10. The marketing vice president of a large savings institution in Texas indicates that the firm's primary target market for new customers consists of middle-income people seeking a new banking relationship because of relocation, divorce, marriage, or departure from the parents' home. Can you supply possible reasons for this targeting decision?

Notes

1. This illustration is based on Steven Swartz, "Basic Bedrooms: How Marriott Changes Hotel Design to Tap Midpriced Market," *The Wall Street Journal*, September 18, 1985, pp. 1, 16; and Richard Koenig, "Marriott Is Seen Announcing Tomorrow Its Move into Lower-Cost Hotel Market," *The Wall Street Journal*, June 6, 1983, p. 2.

2. "A-B Aims to Win by Segmenting Light Beer," *Marketing News*, December 29, 1975, pp. 1, 5, 6.

3. From a talk by Edward E. Phillipy, group president, sales, for Holiday Inns, Inc., University of Tennessee, Spring 1978.

4. Frederick W. Winter, "A Cost-Benefit Approach to Market Segmentation," *Journal of Marketing*, Fall 1979, pp. 103–11.

5. Ann Hughey, "Leica Cameras Sell Well at $1,600 Apiece, Filling the 'Rolls Royce' Niche in Market," *The Wall Street Journal*, June 22, 1982, p. 33. Reprinted by permission of *The Wall Street Journal*, © Dow Jones & Company, Inc., 1982. All rights reserved.

6. The following discussion is based in part on Alvin Toffler, "Reordering Industry as the Era of the Masses Passes," *The Wall Street Journal*, June 16, 1983, p. 24.

7. Ibid.

8. Frederick W. Winter, "Market Segmentation: A Tactical Approach," *Business Horizons*, January–February 1984, p. 58.

9. Frederick W. Winter and Howard Thomas, "An Extension of Market Segmentation: Strategic Segmentation," in *Strategic Marketing and Management*, ed. Howard Thomas and David Gardner (Chichester, England: John Wiley & Sons Ltd., 1985), p. 256.

10. Betsy Morris, "Study to Detect True Eating Habits Finds Junk-Food Fans in the Health-Food Ranks," *The Wall Street Journal*, February 3, 1984, p. 19.

11. "U.S. Bankers Are Flocking to Segmentation Strategies to Combat New Competition: Healy," *Marketing News*, October 15, 1982, p. 10.

12. William L. Wilkie and Joel B. Cohen, "A Behavioral Science Look at Market Segmentation Research," in *Moving Ahead with Attitude Research*, ed. Yoram Wind (Chicago: American Marketing Association, 1977), 138.

13. Peter R. Dickson, "Person-Situation: Segmentation's Missing Link," *Journal of Marketing*, Fall 1982, p. 60.

14. Ibid.

15. Alex Kotlowitz, "Truck Makers' Road Is a Rough One," *The Wall Street Journal*, November 20, 1985, p. 6.

16. David W. Cravens, *Strategic Marketing* (Homewoo, Ill.: Richard D. Irwin, 1982), pp. 173–74.

17. Ibid., pp. 178–81.

18. Ronald E. Frank, William F. Massy, and Yoram Wind, *Market Segmentation* (Englewood Cliffs, N.J.: Prentice-Hall, 1972), pp. 9–11.

19. Winter and Thomas, "Extension of Market Segmentation," pp. 253–66.

20. Cravens, *Strategic Marketing*, p. 180.

21. Ibid., p. 209.

22. This illustration was written by Samuel R. Gardner, vice president—marketing, Retail Food Group of Kraft, Inc., and is reproduced by permission from *Product-Line Strategies*, Earl L. Bailey, ed. (New York: Conference Board, 1982), pp. 40–42.

23. Ibid.

24. David A. Aaker and J. Gary Shansby, "Positioning Your Product," *Business Horizons*, May–June 1982, p. 62.

25. Ibid., p. 59.

26. John Koten, "Car Makers Use 'Image Map' as Tool to Position Products," *The Wall Street Journal*, March 22, 1984, p. 31.

CHAPTER 12

New Product Development

*T*he home computer market "will take off" as a result of IBM's entry, said William H. Millard, chairman of ComputerLand Corporation, the largest chain of computer stores in the country.

The hullabaloo of publicity surrounding the new product will attract many more newcomers who won't want to wait, dealers and competitors believe. "PC Jr. is the herald, the trumpet for the home market. . . . Many people may delay, but many others will think the computer revolution is really here and get with it," said an executive at ComputerLand, which has more than 600 stores.

These statements are from a *Wall Street Journal* article in late 1983 titled "IBM Unwraps Its Smallest Computer, PC Jr." By early 1984, negative signals were emanating from the marketplace. It began to appear that even IBM, typically cited as a magnificent marketer, had misjudged the likelihood of its success in the home market. Another *Wall Street Journal* article appeared, but this time it was, "IBM's Hotly Touted PC Jr. Receives Cooler-Than-Expected Reception":

All the hoopla preceding the announcement of International Business Machines Corporation's new home computer PC Jr. prompted Scott Prussing to wait. But once the hotly touted machine reached the stores, Mr. Prussing, a writer in Orange, California, wasn't impressed.

"I can't understand the keyboard," Mr. Prussing says. Worse, after adding the accessories he wanted, the expanded-memory PC Jr. "wasn't that much cheaper than the Macintosh," Apple Computer, Inc.'s new model.

Maybe expectations were impossibly high, but to this point the takeoff of IBM's little computer has been slow. Dealers, many of whom have received only about 25 PC Jr.'s so far, report that some are still sitting on the shelves. They wish IBM could rekindle the excitement that surrounded the introduction.

This cooler-than-expected reception for the PC Jr. could be an important break for IBM's smaller rivals. IBM's personal computer is by far the most successful product in the office desktop computer market, but dealers and software writers are beginning to hedge earlier projections that the industry giant would walk away with this year's $2.7 billion home computer market.

Dealers wonder whether the obvious market, executives who use the PC at the office and want to take work home, will be receptive. Dealers say IBM's timing was off in announcing the product months before delivery. "Interest was at fever pitch" after the introduction, says Patricia Vaughan, co-owner of the ComputerLand store in Ithaca, New York. "Once we had a demonstration model (in January), the only thing I can say is that the response was underwhelming," she says.

The PC Jr., however, has at least three invaluable assets: the letters I, B, and M. Many dealers, software marketers, and analysts believe the brand name and the compatibility with PC accessories and software guarantee a market.[1]

In 1985, IBM announced that it was dropping out of the home computer market, and the remaining inventory was being sold well into 1986. Even the best of marketers with ample resources can fail. There are no guarantees. But this chapter is devoted to showing how the probabilities of success can be enhanced and how advance planning can contribute to winning products.

The chapter is organized around commonly used steps for developing new products:

- New product strategy development.
- Idea generation.
- Screening and evaluating ideas.
- Business analysis.
- Product development.
- Market acceptance testing.
- Commercialization.

Each of these steps includes several essential activities. Suggestions for organizing new product development are provided. Finally, the importance of understanding the consumer new product adoption process is highlighted. This chapter summarizes what is currently known about new product development and will be of great interest to all who are the least bit fascinated by the flow of new products into the marketplace.

What Are New Products?

New products are those whose degree of change for customers is sufficient to require the design or redesign of marketing strategies.

New products provide new life for otherwise aging organizations and propel entrepreneurs to the top of new industries. The rate of new product introductions varies across industries, but new and better ways to serve needs and wants are ultimately introduced in all industries. If a product is introduced by a competitor, the organization must be defensive and "play catch-up." Introducing a product can mean moving into an industry leadership position. Thus, few decisions in an organization are as fundamental, pervasive, and long lasting as those concerning products. Still, the number of new products each year is striking. Just in the food industry, it is common to see over 2,000 new product introductions in a year.[2]

An important question concerning new products is, "New to whom?" If a product is new *to top management*, it clearly presents challenges and demands creative responses. If a product is new *to personnel in research and development* and in *production*, it requires change on their part as well. Yet from our marketing perspective, the question "New to whom?" must be answered, "*Customers!*"

A second consideration is how different and innovative a *new* product must be. Great new TV technology may be placed in a traditional television cabinet and involve few changes for consumers. Because marketing programs and strategies hinge on customer perceptions, attitudes, and behavior, a television incorporating that technology may not have to be treated as a new product. The marketing issue is whether or not *customers* have to change their view (and behavior) as to how to best fill a given need. New products require this change.

Generally speaking, the more newness and change a product presents to customers, the more risk-laden the product. Most customers tend to resist change. Products in which significant new benefits are not perceived will join the huge and ever-growing product failure junkyard. Newness is, of course, in the eye of the beholder.

While the Polaroid camera, the videocassette recorder, and digital watches were obviously new products, the truly new product is not common. Only 10 percent of all "new" products introduced over a recent five-year period were truly innovative and "new to the world."[3] Most product ideas represent a variation on an existing product, such as adding buffering ingredients to aspirin, changing automobile styling, attaching pull tabs to cans, or improving valves for aerosol packaging.

Booz•Allen & Hamilton, Inc., an international management and technology consulting firm with extensive experience in new product development, conducted a major study of 700 manufacturing companies. It identified six categories of new products in terms of their newness both to the *company* and to *customers* in the marketplace. As shown in Exhibit 12-1, these categories are:

■ *Additions to existing product lines:* products that supplement a company's established lines (26 percent of total).

■ *Improvements in/revisions to existing products:* products that provide improved performance or greater perceived value and replace existing products (26 percent of total).

■ *New product lines:* products that allow a company to enter an established market for the first time (20 percent of total).

■ *Cost reductions:* new products that provide similar performance at lower cost (11 percent of total).

EXHIBIT 12-1 New Product Introductions

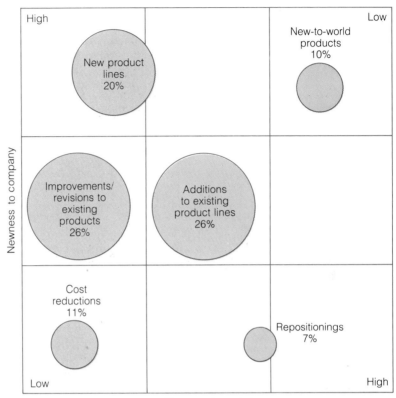

Size of circle denotes number of introductions relative to total.

Source: Adapted from *New Product Management for the 1980s* (New York: Booz•Allen & Hamilton, 1982), p. 9.

■ *New-to-the-world products:* products that create an entirely new market (10 percent of total introductions).

■ *Repositionings:* existing products that are targeted to new markets or market segments (7 percent of total).

Over 50 percent of the companies surveyed had introduced *no* new-to-the-world products over the previous five years, and 25 percent had introduced no new product lines. Yet the 30 percent total of new-to-the-world products and new product lines accounted for 60 percent of the new products considered most successful. The figures indicate a common tendency among management to adopt lower-risk, incremental product development strategies as opposed to higher-risk, higher-profit approaches.

Management must decide to what extent to treat a product as new because that decision guides such decisions as where to assign development of a product within the organization and how large a budget to allocate for its development. Responsibility for implementing an improvement is often assigned to managers of existing products. For truly new product innovations, however, managers specializing in new product planning may be needed. The cost of developing and carrying a truly new product through to market introduction is also much higher than the cost of improving an existing product. A product improvement may cost a company a few thousand dollars in consulting and research fees, whereas a major new product can cost more than a million dollars.

Importance of New Products

Replacing old products with new products is essential to the growth and vitality of organizations. The Booz•Allen survey found that U.S. companies expected the portion of their profits generated by new products to increase by 40 percent from 1981 to 1986. In Exhibit 12-2, the actual profit contribution of new products from 1976 to 1981 is compared to expectations for 1981 to 1986 for several industries. Although new products play an important role in all of the industries shown, their contribution was especially significant in information processing, consumer durables, and instruments and controls.

Even in more mature industries such as chemicals, new products can make all the difference. Hercules, Inc., a chemicals firm started in 1913, has always been in the shadow of Du Pont, its Delaware neighbor. In the 1970s, Hercules reported the first quarterly loss in its history. But the situation was reversed through a bold program of new product development. The company successfully reduced most of its dependence on commodity petrochemicals and developed new *specialty* petrochemicals to provide the specific properties that certain customer groups wanted—for a price. Over half of Hercules' assets are now committed to nonpetrochemical production, with such new ventures as graphite fiber parts for the space shuttle and Formula One racing cars. Today, the company is recognized as an industry leader due to its new product activities.[4]

Why New Products Fail

Despite the obvious importance of new products, they entail a certain amount of risk, as seen with IBM's PC Jr. Many forces are at work that alter consumers' needs and wants for products. Lifestyles change, populations age, and preferences rarely stay constant. Similarly, the needs of industrial buyers are affected by changing business opportunities, shortages of energy and

EXHIBIT 12–2 Contribution of New Products to Profit,* by Industry, as Percentage of Total Company Profits

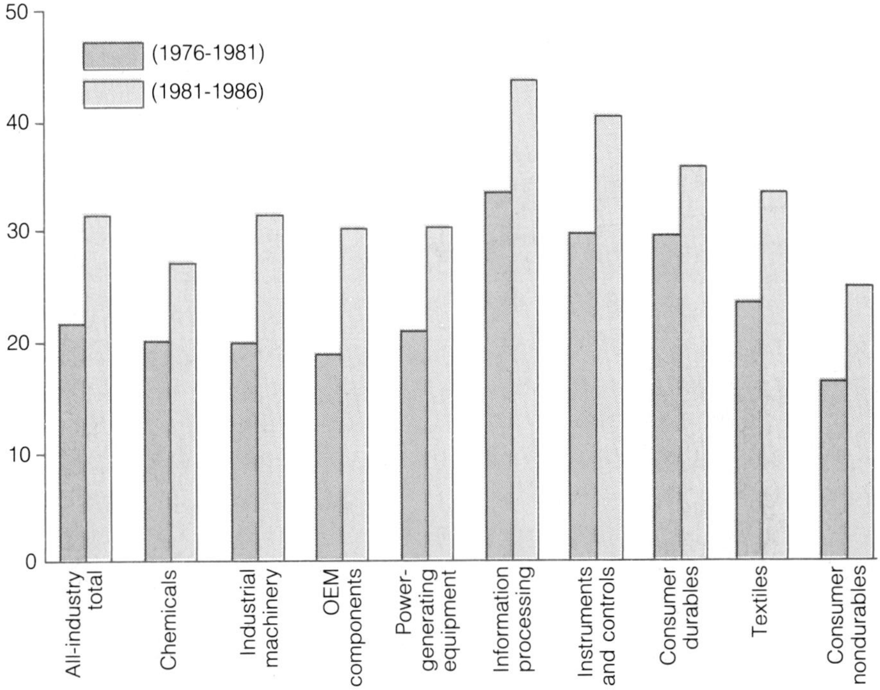

Source: Adapted from *New Product Management for the 1980s* (New York: Booz•Allen & Hamilton, 1982), p. 4.

materials, technological advances, actions of competitors, and industry trends—all of which can affect the success of a new product.

Shorter product life cycles, the cost of capital, government regulations, and increasing international competition further add to the risks and costs of new product development. Although new products are essential to a company's growth and survival, they are among the riskiest of all business actions. Estimates of the failure rate for new products range from 50 percent to 80 percent. The time between the generation of new product ideas and their introduction into the marketplace often spans several years. This means that changes in markets, competitive strategies, supply conditions, and economic trends can substantially alter a product's attractiveness by the time it reaches the market. The time needed to recoup invested resources can extend several more years into the future. The magnitude of the risk involved is indicated by the losses associated with product failures, which can be staggering (Exhibit 12–3).

A firm may also have difficulty in achieving new product successes because of an inappropriate organizational structure. The bureaucratic hier-

EXHIBIT 12–3 Cost of New Product Failures

Product	Estimated Loss ($millions)
RCA's Selectavision videodisk player*	$300.0
Ford's Edsel	350.0
Du Pont's Corfam (synthetic leather)	100.0
Scott Paper Company's Baby Scott (disposable diapers)	12.8
General Food's freeze-dried fruit cereals	5.0
Hunt's pizza and hickory-flavored catsups	11.2
American Home's Easy-Off household cleaner	0.8

* Laura Landro, "RCA Reaches Crossroads on Future of Its Troubled Videodisk Player," *The Wall Street Journal*, September 13, 1983, p. 37.

archy common to large companies can be highly efficient in controlling existing products, but that same structure can hamper new product planning. Consider the following:

> When dramatic new business possibilities do emerge internally, their most frequent immediate effect is to impinge on the status quo. Since the fundamental corporate thesis of most companies is squarely based on continuity, change appears as its antithesis. The more truly innovative a change seems to be, the greater the resistance to it that can be expected. . . . As a result, the history of innovation is a history of overlooked potential and demeaned ideas.
>
> Xerox saw the novel promise of Chester Carlson's copying machine; IBM and Eastman Kodak did not see it at all. RCA was able to envision the innovative opportunity of radio; the Victor Talking Machine Company could not. . . . Marshall Field understood the unique market development possibilities of installment buying; Endicott Johnson did not, calling it "the vilest system devised to create trouble." And so it has gone.[5]

Managerial problems also account for new product failures. These problems include inadequate budgeting to cover introduction costs, incomplete controls over performance, poor timing of introductions, and failure to establish a competitive market position. For instance, a new product may fail if no important differences over competitor products are evident. In a market segment containing only a few competitors, a me-too product can do quite well if the market is large enough. Eventually, however, an added brand will fail to make inroads against established brands unless the new brand offers a unique advantage to customers. Gino's, Inc., a regional chain of fast-food restaurants, tried to copy Wendy's and Burger King by introducing its Heroburger. The Heroburger's only distinction at the time was its rectangular shape. The new hamburger's lack of a differential advantage, plus problems with the process of making it, led to its failure.

Customers must comprehend a new product's advantages. Unless sound communication strategies support the introduction of a new product, failure usually follows. Head & Shoulders shampoo successfully communicated its point of difference as an effective "dandruff fighter." In contrast, Brown and Foreman's supporting strategy for a new "light whiskey" did not help consumers understand how to use the product. Consumers did not know whether the new product was intended to replace whiskey or to be used in place of gin or vodka. The result was a classic story of product failure.

Finally, product features must match appropriate markets. Different features of a product may appeal to different market groups. So finding the most effective combination of features *and target markets* is crucial to the success of new products. For example, Right Guard was first introduced as a men's deodorant, with its neutral scent as the primary selling feature. Later, the product was repositioned as a family deodorant by promoting both scent and the spray application, and sales increased by nearly $20 million a year.

New Product Development Process

The Booz•Allen & Hamilton survey of 700 U.S. companies (involved with 13,000 products) concluded that most companies use a formal new product planning process, usually beginning with the development of an overall new product strategy. In addition, companies that had already successfully launched new products were more likely to have had a formal new product planning process in place for a longer period of time and were also more likely to have a strategic plan.

It must be emphasized, however, that not *all* companies use a systematic, formal new product planning process. Indeed, Feldman and Page, based on in-depth interviews with product planning executives from nine major corporations (six industrial and three consumer goods producers), concluded that product planning was surrounded by three myths. The myths were that new product planners:

- Used a new product planning process that was orderly, logical, and sequential.

- Formulated new product plans that were strategically based.

- Utilized sophisticated management techniques in the new product planning process.[6]

Despite the small number of companies surveyed, the study raises important questions that demand further investigation. Feldman and Page concluded, however, that the three myths needed to become *reality* and that use of a strategic new product planning process was essential.

In this context, while most companies recognize the importance of studying new markets, some are more systematic than others. In a survey of 138 companies conducted by the Association of National Advertisers, 57 percent of the firms responding recommended that more time, money, and personnel

EXHIBIT 12–4 New Product Development Process

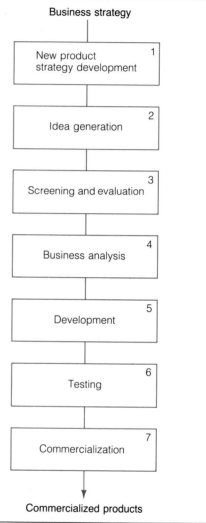

Source: Adapted from *New Product Management for the 1980s* (New York: Booz•Allen & Hamilton, 1982), p. 11.

be devoted to the search for promising product-markets. Yet when making a major "go/no go" decision on a new product, a substantial minority of 31 percent of the companies said that they relied more on intuition than on quantitative criteria, although 54 percent favored numbers over instincts.[7] The Booz•Allen & Hamilton new product development process is shown in Exhibit 12-4.

EXHIBIT 12-5 Strategic Approach to New Product Planning

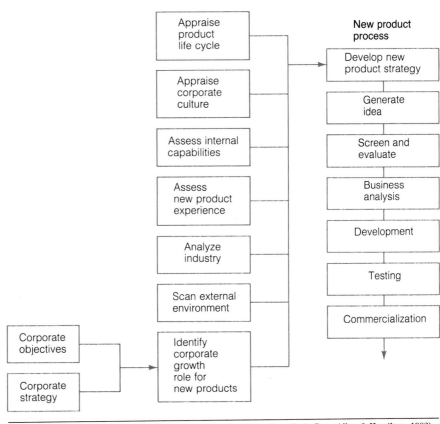

Source: Adapted from *New Product Management for the 1980s* (New York: Booz·Allen & Hamilton, 1982), p. 21.

Product Strategy Development

New product strategy provides corporate strategic guidelines for the new product development process through assessing internal experience and abilities and external opportunities.

Developing an explicit **new product strategy** is a new but widely used concept. In Booz·Allen's latest survey, 77 percent of the companies formally treated strategy as the first step in new product planning. The strategy links product development to corporate strategic direction (Exhibit 12-5). Based on corporate objectives and strategy, the corporate role for new products is determined, the external environment is scrutinized to identify emerging product threats and opportunities, industries are evaluated to determine the growth potential of existing markets, previous new product experiences in various markets are considered, internal capabilities are evaluated to identify relevant company strengths and weaknesses, the existing management style is weighed, and the position of existing products in the product life cycle is considered. A new product strategy (the outcome of Exhibit 12-5) provides a set of strategic roles that, in turn, help identify the markets for which new product ideas will be developed. It was found, in fact, that in the mid-1980s corporate CEOs were forging a closer link between marketing and strategic planning.[8] Also, the three steps through screening and evaluation were more closely linked. Developing a new product strategy, the first step, provides a focus for the second, idea generation step in that the ideas generated are intended to meet strategic objectives. The screening criteria used (in step 3) are also tied to strategic objectives. Between 1968 and 1981, the *proportion* of total resources expended on these first three steps in most companies more than doubled, from 10 percent to 21 percent. This dramatically reduced the number of new product ideas considered for each successful new product introduced—from an average of 58 in 1963-68 to 7 in 1976-81. Yet the percentage of total new product expenditures allocated to products that were ultimately successful increased from 30 percent in 1968 to 54 percent in 1981. Nonetheless, the success rates for commercialized new products across the two time periods (67 percent and 65 percent, respectively) did not improve.

Idea Generation

Idea generation involves using various idea sources and idea generation techniques to identify new ways to satisfy needs and monitor evolving technologies.

The development of Corning Ware cooking products began with an accident: an overheated experimental piece of glass did not break when a worker dropped it on the floor. From this incident, the idea for Corning Ware products was developed. Although such chance discoveries of new product ideas are sometimes made, **idea generation** is too important to rely on accidents.

Idea Sources.   Management must search for new product ideas so that it can *plan* introductions. Most new product ideas come from either identifying ways to satisfy customer needs and wants or understanding evolving new technologies (not only "things" but also concepts and the like). Exhibit 12-6 shows some of the better sources of these types of information. But new product ideas may also come from investors, patent attorneys, suppliers, consultants, and any number of other sources.

Creativity is essential, but so too is systematic organization. Customer complaint letters often contain ideas for improving products, but the ideas are lost unless the letters are read by people trained for this task. Salespeople should be trained to pass on information about customer reactions and competitor activities to the people in product planning. There is a general need to foster and manage the flow of ideas. Personnel must be given training and incentives to ensure that they submit their ideas. Researchers must be trained to search for ideas, and they need incentives to allocate a portion of their time and effort to this task. The organization structure should provide

EXHIBIT 12–6 Sources for New Product Ideas

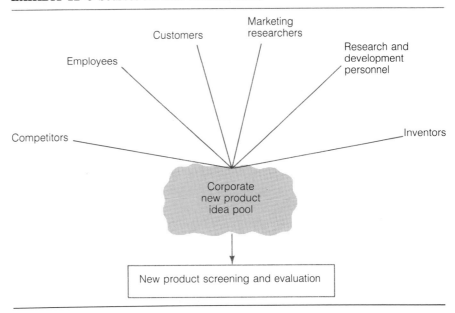

for a central "idea pool" into which ideas can be funneled, and personnel should be familiar with the procedures.

Research and Development versus Customers. Well-known products such as nylon, polyethylene, and the transistor were the result of R&D effort. The key role played by R&D in discovering new product ideas cannot be over-emphasized.[9] Yet the marketing concept cautions firms to first determine market needs and then to design marketing programs, including those for new products, to meet those needs. However, if this directive were taken too literally, R&D would only develop new products for known market needs. The caveat here is that consumers cannot always articulate their specific needs, particularly when there is no existing product to show that a need can be satisfied. Who could have visualized a need for home computers, videocassette recorders, or freeze-dried coffee before those products were developed? R&D sometimes determines what products are technologically possible; market opportunity analysis is used to determine whether a market need for those products exists. On the other hand, R&D is increasingly expected to develop products to meet needs that have first been uncovered by marketing research. This underscores the important role of customers as a source of ideas. More and more, customer feedback is being obtained by companies, both through research and through such mechanisms as telephone "cool" lines (Whirlpool, General Electric). Such feedback and studies of consumer satisfaction and dissatisfaction, which are also becoming increasingly common, are often a source of product ideas. A study of *industrial* products by Von Hippel found that *customers* were the first to create new need-fulfilling products in well over half of the cases examined.[10]

Signode Industries, Inc. creates independent venture teams, in which half the members have a technical background and half are drawn from marketing and sales.[11] The company, which was founded in 1916 and went private in recent years in a leveraged buyout, is a $750 million producer of steel and plastic strapping systems and industrial products. How do its teams work? After two weeks of listening to outside experts about trends and possible opportunities, a team spends about six months searching for unmet or unperceived market needs, its only preconceived direction being that the company's strategic strengths should be emphasized. The full-time task of the team members, performed away from the company itself, is to generate ideas. They are challenged to be creative and are forewarned against discouraging the flow of ideas by the reminder that it is easy to kill an idea, especially if it is someone else's. They search widely for information and ideas, with sensitivity to R&D but using a market-driven, customer-oriented approach. They narrow their list of ideas from a few hundred to two or three at a later stage, and eventually they carry a product to market.

Competitors.   Direct observation of competitors' products, customers' evaluations of their product features, and the grapevine of suppliers and others who serve competitors often contribute ideas. Ethical and legal issues can arise from clandestine activities, yet such activities sometimes occur. Disassembly and intensive analysis of competitors' products is common. Hiring away competitors' employees is another strategy, sometimes challenged in the courts.

Inventors.   Inventors and other "creators" represent a key source of technological innovation and product ideas from outside the company. Major companies are constantly approached with new product ideas that can be acquired or licensed for production or distribution. To make sure that ideas received in this way are appropriately screened, not just quickly rejected or lost, it is essential that those in the company most likely to be contacted by creators be identified and trained.

Employees.   All employees must understand how to make their ideas known and be encouraged to do so. One way to accomplish this is to offer employees rewards for ideas that are later deemed marketable. Employees often have an understanding and interest in company products that make them astute judges of ways to improve them.

Marketing Research.   Although marketing research is a method rather than a source, an exciting development is the use of marketing research techniques in the search for product ideas. *Direct observation* can be used when a firm is searching for ideas to solve a particular customer problem or need. If an appliance manufacturer wants to determine whether preparing a meal in the home can be made easier through new or modified products, a fully equipped kitchen can be set up and consumers brought in to cook a meal. The movements and activities of each cook can be observed for clues to new product ideas. If homemakers have trouble finding foods in the refrigerator, for example, ideas for modifying its interior may result.

Another approach is to use *brainstorming* sessions in which small groups of customers (and others) toss out new product ideas. Such sessions may last one or two hours and are largely unstructured and freewheeling. Leadership keeps the interchange moving and the discussion on the desired track. A brainstorming session may generate as many as 75 to 100 new ideas. Since the objective is to have the participants advance as many ideas as possible, no criticism or evaluation of the ideas presented is allowed. The ideas advanced are screened later.

Focus group interviewing is a technique similar to brainstorming. The sessions are freewheeling, but they often go beyond idea generation to include evaluation and discussion of related issues. Beckman Instruments Company, a manufacturer of precision instruments, used focus group interviewing to generate ideas and designs for a new line of process control equipment. At a per respondent cost of cocktails plus $40 for expenses, Beckman brought together 46 engineers (in small groups) from companies that used process control equipment. The participants began by filling out a questionnaire on the process control equipment field. The remainder of each session was spent in a tape-recorded focus group discussion of process control equipment. Beckman maintained anonymity to encourage openness among the engineers. Several important new product ideas resulted, including a different type of process printing device and a larger window for viewing measurement scales.[12]

Among the most promising research approaches to developing new product ideas are proactive modes, such as *consumer preference testing*, that use data from studies to build an understanding of customer decision processes. Five stages are involved:

1. Determine the product-market within which to conduct research.
2. Identify important product attributes.
3. Represent those attributes in a configuration perceived by customers.
4. Develop a model relating customer preferences to actual choice behavior.
5. Develop a method for searching the product configuration for new product ideas.[13]

The first stage identifies products that customers perceive as competitive for the same need. If headache remedies are being studied, customers are surveyed to find out which products from a predeveloped list they regard as

EXHIBIT 12-7 Attribute and Product Relationships

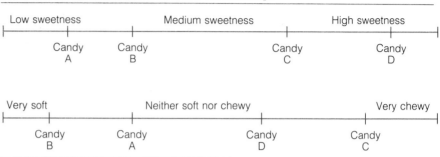

suitable for relieving headache pain. The results may indicate that such products as aspirin, cold remedies, and digestive ailment remedies (e.g., Alka Seltzer) are regarded as suitable for this purpose.

In the second stage, measurements are taken of the product attributes that customers use to compare and choose between product alternatives. These should be viable attributes, that is, attributes on which management can take action. The sweetness of a food product is such an attribute because consumer perceptions of a product's sweetness can be influenced by the amount of sugar or sugar substitute that is added to the product. However, the sportiness of an automobile may be less conducive to management action because it is more difficult to determine what design alternatives are viewed as sporty.

In the third stage, a sample of customers can be asked to describe how products compare to one another in terms of each characteristic. Exhibit 12-7 is an example of the positioning of four candy products along two attribute scales. The distances between products show how similar or different respondents perceive the products to be. For attributes that customers consider important when buying candy, the scales also show how products compare to one another on determinants of customer choice.

The fourth and most challenging stage is to develop a model that will predict customer product choice based on the viable product attributes.

Customers' stated preferences for existing products within the relevant product-market are first analyzed. The trick is to show how preference is related to the viable product attributes uncovered in the previous stage. One illustrative model is a preference-attribute relationship of the form shown below.[14]

$$P_{jk} = f \left[\sum_{i=1}^{n} (A_{ijk}) W_{ij} \right]$$

where:

P_{jk} = Preference of jth customer for product k

EXHIBIT 12–8 Location of Customer j's Ideal Point

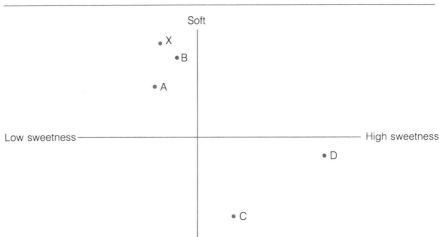

A_{ijk} = Level of attribute i perceived by customer j to be possessed by product k

W_{ij} = Salience of attribute i to customer j for choice in the product-market

n = Number of salient attributes for choice in the product-market

In addition to preferences for existing products, an ideal combination of attribute levels must be determined for each customer. This allows the search for new product ideas to consider customer wants as reflected by the ideal product. Exhibit 12-8 shows the relationship among four existing candy products in terms of two attributes, determined by plotting the scale locations for the products on the sweetness and softness attributes from Exhibit 12-7. Now suppose that customer j has ranked the four candy products from most preferred to least preferred: B > A > C > D. Using this preference assumption, point X represents an ideal product for customer j since that point is located closer to B than to A, closer to A than to C, and closer to C than to D. By simultaneously conducting the analysis for all customers in the sample, the model can be expanded to show the relationship between the four existing candy products and all respondents' ideal points.

The familiar distance function from geometry, the Pythagorean theorem, is used to predict preference for each of the real products or any other combination of attributes in this space. This approach quantifies the assumption that P_{jk} will be greater, indicating greater preference, for those attribute combinations that are closer to more preferred existing candy products and lower for those attribute combinations that are a greater distance away from such products.

EXHIBIT 12–9 New Product Idea Search

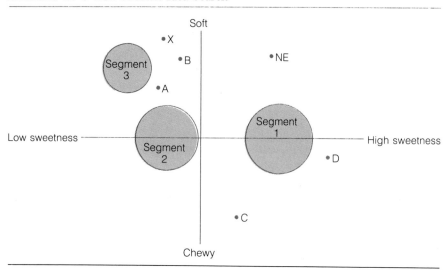

The search for new product ideas is diagrammed in Exhibit 12–9. This shows candy perceptions and preferences for a representative sample of customers. The circles represent customer segments (where their ideal products are sufficiently similar), and circle size indicates relative segment size. The points labeled A, B, C, and D are the four existing candy products. All the other points in the product space represent nonexistent but potential combinations of attributes. For example, point NE represents a unique combination of sweetness and softness that might be developed into a new candy product. Since an infinite number of such combinations are included in the product space, criteria for selecting ideas are needed. These typically include:

- The technical ability to produce a product with that combination of attributes.

- The closeness of new attribute combinations to large segments of customers' ideal points.

- The degree of differentiation (or distance) from existing competitive products.

- The complementary or substitute relationship of the new combination to existing products in the firm's mix.

New attribute combinations that pass this prescreening are added to the new product idea pool. NE would probably not be added due to its distance from clusters of ideal points.

This idea search process is more likely to generate product modification ideas than totally new products, which holds true for marketing research approaches in general. The reason is that customers use existing products as a frame of reference. The ability to foresee products totally unlike those that already exist is rare.

EXHIBIT 12-10

THE RAPHAEL
RESTAURANT
HAS ONLY 40 CHAIRS
FOR A GOOD REASON.

Every day we handpick only the choicest
meats, the best from the sea, and the ripest
produce. Then we prepare each meal one
at a time...when you request it.
Our dining room is intimate and our
service impeccable.
If we were any larger, we wouldn't be
able to maintain our high standards. So
there's a good reason why we have only
40 chairs...for your pleasure.
Reserve your chair today.

The Raphael
201 East Delaware Place
Adjacent to The Hancock Center
943-5000

Small size attribute emphasized to accent exclusiveness

Courtesy Barkley & Evergreen.

Mapping customer attribute preferences is used not only in identifying new products but also in developing product positioning strategies. Note the attributes that are emphasized in the advertisement in Exhibit 12-10. Here, a small restaurant size is effectively combined with high-quality food, atmosphere, and service to convey an exclusive image.

Finally, *environmental forecasting* methods are used to identify new product ideas. A changing environment often means changing markets, and these, in turn, lead to new product opportunities.

Screening New Product Ideas

New product screening
is the development and systematic use of criteria to evaluate the potential of new product ideas.

Ideas from the new product idea pool have to be screened to find those that are worthy of continued development and evaluation. **New product screening** is an evaluation that relies heavily on managerial judgment and experience (Exhibit 12-4). But a systematic approach to culling out ideas helps ensure that the judgments are good.

Criteria for Screening. New product screening should be designed to avoid making two types of errors:

EXHIBIT 12-11 New Product Screening Criteria

Corporate goal and objective criteria

Consistency with corporate mission
   Satisfying similar customer needs
   Similarity to existing products

Consistency with corporate image and reputation
   Type of product and quality
   Completeness of product offering
   Superiority over competitors' products
   Degree of newness

Consistency with desired financial performance
   Sales level (market size, existing and potential competition)
   Payback period
   Market share
   Return on investment

Market opportunity potential
   Ability to market to existing versus new customers
   Market potential size and growth
   International market potential
   Seasonal fluctuations
   Competitive threats

Corporate resource capabilities

Investment commitment

Market development required

Product life-cycle length

Technical skills required

Marketing program requirements
   Advertising (same media, etc.)
   Personal selling (use existing sales force?)
   Distribution channels (existing?/access?)
   Customer service (existing organization?)
   Probable price (image consistency, margins)

Patent protection (competitor entry?)

- Rejecting an idea that could become a very successful product.
- Accepting an idea that later fails.

The screening process should not require large expenditures. There are many ideas to screen, and resources must be conserved for development of those that pass the screening process. Because the cost goes up at each stage of the product planning process, it is desirable to drop as many product ideas at this stage as possible. The Booz•Allen & Hamilton study found that companies, in part because their idea generation had to fit within specified product strategies, were formally screening far fewer ideas than they had screened previously.

Central to the screening process is setting criteria that represent the standards that management believes must be surpassed by a new product opportunity. Two categories of screening criteria are commonly used, as shown in Exhibit 12-11. Management screens new product ideas against

EXHIBIT 12–12 Culling, Rating, and Scoring Criteria

	Yes	No
Illustrative culling criteria:		
1. Can the product be marketed through supermarkets?	_____	_____
2. Does any one competitor have a market share of over 50 percent?	_____	_____
3. Is this a high-technology product?	_____	_____
4. Can the product be marketed internationally?	_____	_____
Illustrative rating criteria:		
1. Is the product hard for competitors to duplicate?	_____	_____
2. Does the product offer a considerable market for after-sale parts and service?	_____	_____
3. Does the product fit the desired corporate image?	_____	_____

Illustrative scoring criteria:			
	Low	Medium	High
1. What is the annual market growth rate?	1	2	3
	Short	Medium	Long
2. What is the length of the life cycle?	1	2	3
	Not Likely	Quite Likely	Very Likely
3. How likely is it that competition will enter?	1	2	3

Source: Adapted from H. Ronald Hamilton, "Screening Business Development Opportunities," *Business Horizons* 17 (August 1974), pp. 20–21. Copyright 1974 by the Foundation for the School of Business at Indiana University. Reprinted by permission.

corporate goals and objectives to determine whether they correspond with the basic purpose and the expected performance of the firm. Management must also evaluate new product ideas in terms of whether the firm has the ability and the resources needed to take advantage of the opportunities they afford. These latter criteria reflect the key capabilities on which the firm builds its success. It has been noted that "firms are more successful with a new product for which they know the business."[15] IBM's PC Jr., entering a new type of market at the low end of the product line, apparently did not meet these criteria well enough.

Evaluation. Screening could be accomplished by considering all of the screening criteria simultaneously. But it is often more practical to proceed in evaluation stages in which these criteria are applied to a new product idea in sequence. Ideas are eliminated when criteria are not met at any stage in the process. The criteria sequence is an important concern for management. The order used may be based on the difficulty and expense of obtaining the information needed to apply the criteria, beginning with the low-expense stages. Or the order can be based on the importance of the criteria in predicting overall product success.

To implement a multistage approach, firms can screen an idea against culling criteria, then against rating criteria, and finally against scoring criteria (Exhibit 12–12).[16] Culling criteria are qualitative, dichotomous guidelines—either a product meets the criterion or it doesn't. Whether a new product can be sold through supermarkets might be a culling criterion for Procter & Gamble. Rating criteria can also be applied by using a dichotomous (yes/no) approach. However, management must establish definitional boundaries. Evaluating whether an idea fits the corporate image may require only a yes or no judgment as long as management has determined what is required to meet the image objective—a specific materials quality level, design configuration, or price. Scoring criteria are usually the most expensive to apply due to the more precise judgment required. If a product has not been screened out by this stage, it is likely to be worth the additional evaluation.

Decision rules are used to determine whether an idea will pass a particular screening stage. For culling and rating criteria, the rule may be simply the number of criteria that must be met (three out of five). When scoring criteria are used, each criterion has a predetermined range of values over which an idea is rated (Exhibit 12-12). Weights are often assigned to each criterion to indicate its relative importance. A score for the new product idea is calculated by multiplying the weights by the scores and then adding up the total. That total can then be compared with an established cutoff score for the given screening stage.

The available approaches for screening new product ideas are not without problems. One difficulty arises when screening is performed by a management team rather than an individual. Since team members will often disagree, a reconciliation method, such as the Delphi method, must be used. In addition, little guidance is provided for determining appropriate decision rules, criteria weights, or cutoff scores. These are usually subjectively derived for a specific organization. Finally, quantitative scoring approaches are not necessarily sensitive to changes in criteria weights or to score evaluations.[17] These approaches are more valuable for identifying extremely good or very poor new product opportunities than for finely differentiating ideas with similar potential.

Business Analysis

Business analysis is an in-depth study of the estimated economic feasibility of new product ideas.

New product ideas that successfully pass screening are further evaluated at the **business analysis** point in the new product planning process (step 4 in Exhibit 12-4). Assessing the profitability of a new product helps management decide whether to introduce the new product, continue the development and evaluation process, or drop the idea.

Break-Even Analysis. Break-even analysis determines the volume of sales that will provide just enough revenue to cover the costs of producing, distributing, and selling a new product. The sales volume is not a forecast of the actual sales that can be achieved: rather, it is the level necessary to recover costs. The equation used to determine the break-even point is:

$$S_{BE} = \frac{TFC}{P_u - VC_u}$$

where:

S_{BE} = Sales volume needed to break even

TFC = Total fixed costs incurred by the new product

P_u = New product price per unit

VC_u = Variable cost per unit incurred by the new product

The denominator, P_u minus VC_u, is the gross margin generated by each unit sold. Dividing this quantity into total fixed costs will determine how many units must be sold to cover all of the fixed costs.

Knowing the break-even point establishes the sales forecast accuracy needed. Here, rather than trying to pinpoint the actual sales of new product, a very difficult task, management instead has to judge whether sales will exceed the break-even volume. Management may want to go the extra step of estimating how much total sales (S_a) are expected to exceed the break-even volume to assess probability (P):

$$P = (S_a - S_{BE})(P_u - VC_u)$$

A determination of the break-even point may make it clear that the sales volume required is unrealistic or that it can be easily attained. The risks can then be weighed accordingly. Fixed costs are typically costs incurred prior to the generation of sales. The higher these front-end costs, the more that can be lost (the higher the downside risk). These costs must be weighed against the potential profit or upside gain.

Break-even analysis appears deceptively simple. In reality, a considerable amount of information and judgment is required. One complication is that break-even analysis must be conducted for a specified time period. One option is to view cost and price inputs as an *average* estimate over a stated number of periods (usually years). Break-even volume would then be the number of units that must be sold during each period, on average, to cover the fixed and variable costs incurred during that period. This approach is used only when price and costs are not expected to change dramatically during the periods included in the analysis. Another option is to use a *payback period* analysis. Here, total fixed costs and an average price and variable cost per unit are estimated over the entire time covered by the analysis. An estimate of expected sales per time period is also needed. These estimates show the expected timing or pattern of sales and costs over all time periods. The total time required for new product sales to be sufficient to recover all costs is calculated by:

$$S_{BE} = S_1 + S_2 \ldots + S_{n'}$$

where:

S_n = Sales expected in the nth time period

Break-even analysis also assumes particular production, distribution, and selling strategies, since these will determine the costs to be incurred. Break-even analysis may also be used to assess alternative strategies by comparing the resulting break-even volumes. The value of break-even analysis is clearly dependent on management's ability to estimate the costs of each strategy being considered. The complexities of cost analyses, such as classifying costs as fixed, variable, or semivariable, will influence the results from the break-even models.

Break-even analysis does not incorporate such key factors as the impact of the product on the company's other products. This is a serious omission when there are complementary or competitive relationships between a new product and existing products (e.g., new Coca Cola versus classic Coca Cola). However, a break-even model can be adapted to include that impact. Also, the uncertainty inherent in the estimates is normally not considered. Nonetheless, break-even analysis is a good starting point in evaluating the potential of a new product.

Discounted Cash Flow. A discounted cash flow analysis recognizes that both revenues and costs are likely to change over time. The time value of money is incorporated by discounting future revenues and costs by the opportunity cost of a company's capital.[18]

$$PV = \sum_{i=1}^{n} \frac{(R_i - C_i)}{(1 + k)^i}$$

where:

PV = Present value of the new product decision

R_i = Expected new product revenue in the ith period

C_i = Expected new product cost in the ith period

k = Company's opportunity cost of capital

n = Number of time periods over which the new product cost and revenue forecasts are made

Management must decide the number of time periods over which to evaluate a new product. Strategies must be designed for the time periods, costs must be estimated, and demand forecast. With these estimates and the company's opportunity cost of capital, the present value of the profits expected from the new product can be calculated. Then, the present value of the expected future profits can be compared with the required investment to determine whether or not to introduce the new product.

There is no explicit treatment in the equation of the uncertainty of revenue and cost estimates. This can be formally incorporated by requiring management to supply a subjective probability estimate, P_i, of the likelihood of obtaining the calculated present value. This is then used to weight the present value of the profit expected (EPV) from a new product before a comparison is made with the required investment. In equation form, the weighted discounted cash flow is:

$$EPV = P_i \left[\sum_{i=1}^{n} \frac{R_i - C_i}{(1 + k)^i} \right]$$

Another method for incorporating uncertainty requires management to supply a subjective probability estimate (S_{pi}) of achieving each time period's profit flow. This explicitly recognizes that uncertainty may change as estimates are made for time priods further and further into the future. The model would then be:

$$EPV = \sum_{i=1}^{n} S_{pi} \left[\frac{R_i - C_i}{(1 + k)^i} \right]$$

Bayesian Decision Model. Another framework for evaluating new product opportunities is the Bayesian decision model. A major advantage of the model is that it permits alternative new product strategies to be evaluated simultaneously. With this model, management provides payoff estimates for each of several decision combinations that might be employed. Uncertainty about future payoffs is incorporated into the evaluation through subjective probability estimates of the occurrence of various events that will affect payoff (e.g., competition entering with a similar new product). The advantages of the discounted cash flow model can also be retained by requiring that payoffs be estimated as discounted profits over a predetermined number of time periods.

An illustration of the Bayesian model is shown in Exhibit 12-13. Suppose that a firm is evaluating the opportunity presented by a radically new automated filling machine for pressurized containers. The new product is targeted toward contract packagers and large consumer goods firms. Distribution and promotional strategy have been developed, but still under consideration are the two best product designs and two pricing strategies. Management is uncertain about how quickly its major competitors will introduce a competitive machine, as well as about the level of sales that can be achieved in each of the first four years. The new product decision will hinge on the present value of the profits expected over this four-year period. Specification of these factors affecting the product decision allows the construction of the decision tree in Exhibit 12-13. For each branch of the tree, management must supply estimates of the likelihood of each competitive response and each sales forecast (optimistic, most likely, and pessimistic) in terms of subjective probability and the present value payoff. Sales, cost, and other information provide the basis for these estimates. Following through the calculations, the best set of decisions is to introduce product design 2 with a penetration pricing strategy, with an expected net income of $462,500.

Simulation Models. The Bayesian model yields a single expected value for each strategy alternative specified by management. This value may be viewed as the mean of a distribution of values that might be achieved with a particular strategy. In some cases, management may want to know the entire

EXHIBIT 12–13 Bayesian Decision Model Applied to a New Product

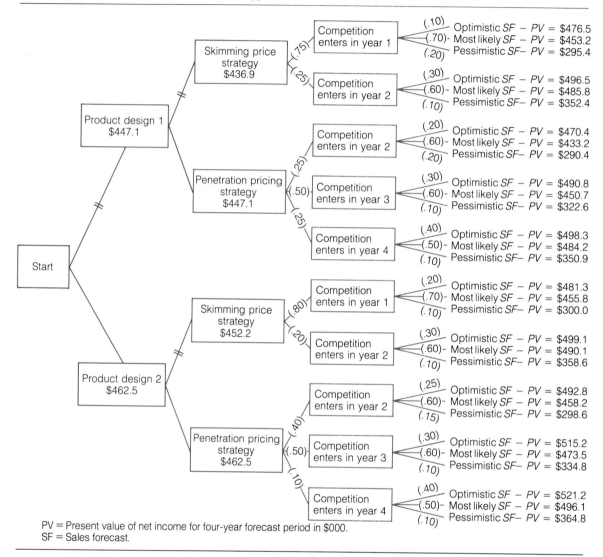

PV = Present value of net income for four-year forecast period in $000.
SF = Sales forecast.

distribution for each strategy alternative. The dispersions and ranges of the distributions may be helpful in selecting the best strategy for the firm. Exhibit 12-14 shows a new product strategy decision in which the highest expected value strategy might not be best for the firm. Strategy 2 has the higher expected rate of return (the mean of distribution 2 is greater than the mean of distribution 1), but the range of values might be much wider if this strategy were followed. On the other hand, strategy 1 has a much narrower range of possible rates of return, with higher probabilities of achieving a rate of return closer to the expected rate. A conservative management might select strategy

EXHIBIT 12–14 Estimated Probability Distributions of Rate of Return for Two Alternative New Product Strategies

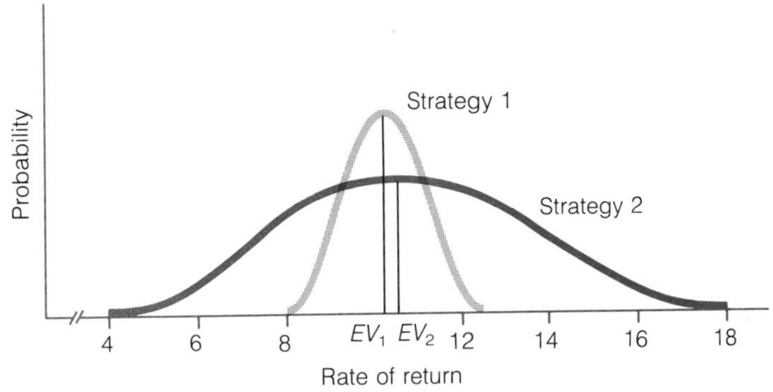

Source: Reprinted with permission from Philip Kotler, "Computer Simulation in the Analysis of New-Product Decisions," in *Application of the Sciences in Marketing Management*, ed. Frank M. Bass, Charles W. King, and Edgar A. Pessemier (New York: John Wiley & Sons, © 1968), p. 298.

1 even though the expected rate of return is lower than that of strategy 2. This decision minimizes the chances of obtaining returns much lower than the expected return. A risk-oriented management might find strategy 2 more attractive because of the higher expected return and also because of the higher probabilities of achieving greater rates of return.

Building such probability distributions into a new product decision analysis requires a simulation model. Looking back to Exhibit 12-13, suppose that management is asked for the mean, the .25 and the .75 quartile values of each sales forecast, and each competitive response branch. These estimates would be in lieu of the single payoff values and subjective probabilities of the Bayesian model. A simulation would then extend these estimates to the implied entire probability distributions for each branch, enabling a more complete evaluation of the strategy alternatives. Simulation models include more of the complexities of new product decisions than do other methods of analysis. A company is more likely to need simulations when a large number of decision alternatives must be considered or when the interrelationship between a new product and existing company products should be included.

One or more of the new product evaluation methods may be used and periodically applied as more and better information about new product performance becomes available. The real value of each method is that it provides an overall *framework for thinking* about the evaluation.

Product Development

The product ideas that pass the screening and business analysis stages are not usually "concrete" enough for extensive testing of customer acceptance. An idea must be developed into a functioning product (step 5 in Exhibit

Product development involves developing the product (or service) itself (with attention to attributes preferred by customers) and further development of manufacturing, packaging, and distribution cost estimates.

12-4). **Product development** is often a scientific and engineering task, leading to the design and building of *prototype* working models. Once a prototype exists, *functional testing* may take place. For technical products such as sound speakers or robots, this may be a complex and lengthy task. Government testing and approvals may also be required for such products as new cancer drugs or birth control devices. Alternative designs may vary the product's safety and its cost. Relatively simple products, as well as many services, may be developed and tested quickly and inexpensively. Others take years to develop and test. But in any case, marketing plays a valuable role. To determine which design is best, information on customer preferences is often needed in addition to comparative costs. Customer preferences can be obtained informally through personal contact, as when a product is developed for a few industrial customers. Or marketing research may sample customers' preferences when the target markets comprise many, widely dispersed customers.

Consumer *preference testing* (noted earlier) may also be used at this stage to help choose features to build into a particular product. Suppose that a firm has screened a new food product and is now trying to determine specific ingredients to create desired product characteristics and benefits. A key attribute is sweetness. Yet development personnel are unsure of the degree of sweetness to build into the product. Prospective consumers can be recruited and asked to taste samples that differ only in the level of sugar. Consumers choose the preferred version in a paired-comparison test, after tasting and comparing several pairs of products. Data from the choices made by all the consumers determine the distribution of preferences over the various levels of sweetness being tested (see Exhibit 12-15). Sweetness level A, which corresponds to a particular sugar content, is preferred by a majority of the consumers. Yet choosing this level could result in falling victim to the *majority fallacy*. If there are competitive products with a sweetness level at or near A, then the best strategy might be to build in a lower or higher level of sweetness. This would differentiate the product from its competitors and possibly capture a larger share of a smaller market.

Consumer preferences for softer, chewy cookies versus the traditional harder cookies led to substantial preference testing expenditures. The outcome of this research is described as the products enter the market:

> The cookie kings of Nabisco Brands, Inc. appeared to be crumbling under attack.
> Their turf was being invaded by Procter & Gamble Company, the soap people, and Frito-Lay, Inc., the potato chip maker owned by PepsiCo, Inc. For Nabisco's cookie bakers, used to unchallenged ownership of one third of the $2.2 billion retail cookie market, the situation looked serious.
> Frito-Lay introduced Grandma's, cookies "so fresh, they taste suspiciously close to homemade." About nine months later, Procter & Gamble's Duncan Hines chocolate chip cookies followed with the promise that their soon-to-be-patented process made them crispy outside and chewy inside, just as a homemade cookie should be.
> Unknown to the outside world, Nabisco had been busy baking its own version of the chewy, almost-like-homemade cookie. The 15-variety line, called Almost Home,

EXHIBIT 12–15 Customer Preference Distribution

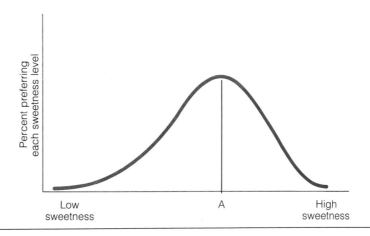

is Nabisco's biggest new cookie project in years. Billed as "the moistest, chewiest, most perfectly baked cookies the world has ever tasted . . . well, almost," the cookies appeared on grocery shelves in 10 percent of the United States.

"The whole situation is explosive right now because each of the companies is lining up for battle," says a cookie market researcher who asked not to be identified.

So tense are battle preparations that Nabisco, Frito-Lay, Procter & Gamble, and British-owned Keebler Company, in Elmhurst, Illinois, all refuse to divulge a single crumb of information about their cookie plans.[19]

Interaction between marketing and product development personnel is further illustrated by Gillette's experience with its roll-on antiperspirant, Dry Idea. From consumer research, management learned that many people thought roll-ons were wet when applied, forcing them to wait to get dressed. Chemists at Gillette's laboratory in Boston were told to develop a roll-on that would not go on wet. Several formulations were tried by consumers who judged the feel of each roll-on as it was applied as well as the roll-on's antiperspirant qualities. Then, one was selected.

The new product development stage also provides information on the estimated costs of manufacturing, packaging, and distributing the product. Because the development stage is yet another decision point in the new product decision process, the product idea may be dropped if building is not technically feasible; if the product can only be built with substantial, undesirable modifications; or if the costs of development or production are prohibitive. Minnesota Mining and Manufacturing Company (3M) once evaluated a new product concept involving the commercial farming of oysters in a controlled situation. Eventually, 3M rejected the idea because a small-scale test showed that it was not possible to cultivate enough oysters to make the project financially attractive.

Designing Supporting Strategies.   Once an idea has passed the screening stage, work on the design and testing of supporting strategies and tactics can begin, concurrently with product development. Planning supporting strategies at this stage can significantly reduce the total lead time between idea screening and product introduction. Returning to Gillette's Dry Idea roll-on, while chemists were working on a product formulation, engineers were creating a package applicator. An original design had to be scrapped because of leakage problems and because consumer tests showed that users could not feel the antiperspirant go on. Targeting women between 20 and 45, an advertising strategy was also designed and tested, and a brand name was selected from dozens that were proposed to consumers. Word-association tests were used to study proposed brand names. Drynamite, Feel Free, Omni, and Horizon were tried before Gillette settled on Dry Idea. With each of the rejected names, consumer tests showed that a potentially confusing or undesirable meaning came to respondents' minds. Drynamite sounded too much like a drain cleaner.[20]

In another application, a manufacturer of a new food-flavoring product tried out alternative package designs on small samples of consumers. Management learned that customers wanted to see the product before making a buying decision. A package with a clear plastic "window" was finally selected, so that customers could see the contents without actually opening the package.

Small-scale tests of supporting strategies should not be confused with marketing research intended to forecast sales. The results of small-scale tests are too limited in scope to provide much help in estimating demand, but they sound out consumer reaction to individual components of marketing programs.

Testing

New product decisions often require sales forecasts of 2, 5, or even 10 or more years, depending on the level of commitment required and the investment. And forecasting over long periods is by nature hazardous. Managers face the difficulty of foreseeing future events, including economic conditions, the effectiveness of supporting strategies, competitive actions, and customer preferences and decisions that will affect product performance.

Analysis of market opportunities during the idea generation stage or the screening stage helps managers settle on initial target markets and identify key demand determinants. This is essential, since all of the **testing** procedures below require drawing representative customer samples from target markets so that projections can be made from test results. The analysis of test data enables management to refine its selection of target markets by providing additional information on customer characteristics and preferences (Exhibit 12–4). Three different types of marketing research techniques are now examined; variations of each of these techniques exist.

Testing stage thoroughly evaluates potential market acceptance through the use of market research.

EXHIBIT 12-16 Concept Test Layout of Multiunit Housing Design and Spacing

Concept Testing. Concept testing helps managers estimate customer reaction to a proposed product early in the decision process. It may be used as early as the idea screening stage, before the product has been fully developed. Potential customers are asked to evaluate a product *concept* rather than the actual product. Respondents, usually a small sample, are shown a pictorial and verbal description of the product concept and are encouraged to visualize the attributes, performance characteristics, and actual use of the product. Then, the respondents are asked about their reactions to the product and about what their probable intentions to purchase the product would be if it were made available for sale.

Concept testing helped the management of a land development firm assess the feasibility of a planned unit development on a large tract. An advertising agency prepared layouts of the proposed development (Exhibit 12-16), which were presented to a sample of potential customers to illustrate the design of the units, the amount of space between them, and some of the planned recreational facilities. Previous market analyses had determined that these were important attributes to potential customers. A drawing of an aerial view of the development was shown to customers to provide a more complete perspective of the entire project. This drawing emphasized the amount of green space between units, easy access to units, and recreational alternatives. Together, the drawings helped the respondents imagine what the planned development would offer, highlighting features that were thought to be key determinants in their housing decision.

The sample was selected from the target market, and personal interviews were used to gather information. The respondents studied the layouts and asked questions. The interviewers had been trained to provide answers. After the interviewer was satisfied that a respondent understood the concept, questions were asked to obtain reactions to the proposed development. These questions covered the respondents':

- Current housing usage.
- Attitudes toward the key characteristics of the development.
- Preferences for alternative design options.
- Intentions to purchase, given certain prices.
- Characteristics.

The data were analyzed to determine the extent of interest and buying intentions.

A rough idea of demand can be calculated from the following equation:

$$\text{New product sales} = \text{N} \times \text{FR} \times \text{AP} \times \frac{\text{MS}}{\text{SS}}$$

where:

N = Number of people in the sample who said they intended to buy—estimated directly from an intention to buy question on the questionnaire

FR = Fulfillment rate, showing the percentage of intenders who are expected to actually follow through on their stated intentions—comes from management's experience with purchases of similar products from previous tests and from questionnaire responses about the probability of buying

AP = Average price of purchase—estimated from available price data

MS = Estimated size of target market—calculated on the basis of target market boundaries

SS = Sample size—the number of respondents in the concept test

The component of the forecasting equation that is most often overlooked and most difficult to estimate is the fulfillment rate. "Yea-sayers" usually bias the results, often dramatically. Sometimes it is impossible to make even a subjective estimate of the fulfillment rate. An alternative is to apply a conservative rule of thumb to the intentions data in deciding whether to move ahead with the new product. Companies sometimes set a very high number (between 80 and 90 percent) of respondents who must show a strong buying intention before deciding that a new product idea warrants further evaluation or introduction. IBM's PC Jr. may well have suffered from an overstated fulfillment rate.

Managers must be realistic about the sales forecasting capability of concept testing. It is not highly accurate or reliable. Experience suggests that concept testing is best used to predict sales for product modifications that do not require significant changes in consumers' use behavior (e.g., me-too brands such as the fluoride toothpastes that followed Crest into the marketplace). For innovative products that require changes in consumer use patterns (hot-air popcorn poppers, videocassette cameras), concept testing is much less reliable.[21] Remember that sample respondents are reacting to a product concept, not to the product itself. Their ability to anticipate future purchase and use is heavily dependent on how well they can visualize product characteristics and benefits and imagine how the product would be used. The more innovative and new the product, the less able people are to predict their future buying. Concept testing is more reliable for forecasting first-time or trial use than for forecasting repeat purchases over time. Customers' ability to envision the outcome of actual product use is limited.

Offsetting the problems with concept testing are several advantages. Concept testing does not require that the new product be developed, possibly avoiding expensive product development work. And concept testing may be used to help with a "go-no-go" decision that must be made before product development can be completed. In a concept test for a public bus service in Jacksonville, Florida the reaction of potential patrons was sufficiently cool to warrant discarding the product idea at that point, thus saving hundreds of thousands of dollars in final design work and equipment.

Concept testing is less complex than other marketing research alternatives and involves less costly procedures for collecting information—the land development concept test was conducted for less than $10,000. It entails no costs for producing prototypes. Moreover, due to management's greater tolerance for forecasting error at this early stage, a smaller sample size is required.

An important strength of concept testing is its diagnostic capability. Concept testing often uncovers major problems with a new product idea early in the planning process.

Product Use Tests. Product use tests measure market reaction to the actual characteristics and benefits of the physical product (or service). Because respondents examine and use the product before being questioned, their answers to intentions questions are based on much more than just an abstract idea of the product. Consider a package goods firm that evaluated the demand for a new spaghetti sauce. A representative sample of target market customers was drawn, and the respondents filled out a questionnaire concerning their current use of spaghetti sauces, including frequency of use,

EXHIBIT 12–17 Buying Intentions Responses

Intentions Categories	New Sauce	Popular Sauce
Definitely would buy	30%	30%
Probably would buy	45	40
May or may not buy	8	10
Probably would not buy	12	15
Definitely would not buy	5	5
Total respondents	100%	100%

brand preferences, and attribute preferences (hot, spicy, etc.). The respondents were then given a supply of unlabeled sauces (the new sauce and existing brands) to try for a period of time. Each person used one product a week.

After using the products, the respondents were asked to describe their reactions to the products and their intentions with regard to the purchase of each of them. The questions were similar to those asked in a concept test because the research objective was essentially the same. The distribution of the responses was more positive for the new sauce than for a popular existing brand, as shown in Exhibit 12–17. Management then compared the responses with a predetermined decision rule (70 percent of the respondents had to have a positive intention to buy), and the decision was made to proceed.

A product use test is usually more expensive than a concept test, but it does not depend as heavily on respondents' ability to predict usage from a mental picture of a product and its benefits. A product use test can cost from $20,000 to $1 million or more, depending on the sample size. However, while product use tests improve the reliability of data, they are better for predicting trial and first-repeat purchases than for predicting the full adoption of a product or frequency of purchase.

Test Marketing. Information from concept and product use tests does not directly measure what happens after a new product is offered for sale, nor does it give the market's reaction to an entire marketing strategy. Test marketing is intended to duplicate a real market situation for the new product, but on a smaller scale and at less cost. However, a market test can cost up to $1 million or more. Setting up a test market requires decisions on:

- The number and location of the test areas, usually cities.
- The marketing strategies to be tested.
- The data to be collected.

Test Cities. Results from test markets must be projected to the entire target market, so the candidate cities selected must possess population characteristics that closely match those of the target market. Population analyses often help in selecting representative test areas. The appropriate number of areas to test is determined by weighing cost factors against management's information needs and accuracy requirements.

Strategies to Be Tested.   Test marketing can be flexible in responding to different needs. In some situations, management uses test marketing as a kind of dress rehearsal for a single strategy that it already believes is best. More commonly, test marketing is used to evaluate the performance of two or more options. Procter & Gamble test-marketed a new dessert product in Dallas and Denver with substantially higher advertising expenditures in Denver than in Dallas. The test market demonstrated that the market was very sensitive to the amount of advertising, with higher sales in Denver.

Data Collected.   There are several test market data options, including product movements, sales, and use of customer panels. Product movement data measure the physical movement of products through such intermediaries as wholesalers and warehouses. Auditing the number of units flowing through intermediaries provides one kind of measure of the sales of the new product in test markets. Typically, this is the least costly way to estimate customer reaction, but it is also a crude measure since there is little indication of how many of the units are actually being purchased by customers versus how many are being inventoried by firms in the channel. Records can also be kept of the beginning and ending inventories and of the purchases of intermediaries, but this is more expensive. For products sold through certain types of retailers (e.g., supermarkets and discount drugstores), standardized audit information services from such firms as A. C. Nielsen Company and BehaviorScan, Inc. can be used to audit customer sales. Product scanning data have greatly facilitated this process in recent years.

Management may also want to analyze the composition of sales by breaking out different sales categories. These often include how many sales are made to customers who buy for the first time and how many are made to customers who buy the product again (repeat buying), how many customers have adopted the product, and how frequently customers buy. Management may also want to know why some potential customers did not buy the first time or why customers who did buy decided not to adopt the product. This kind of information can best be obtained by using a customer panel. Panel participants are not told the reason for the panel, because one objective is to measure how quickly they become sufficiently aware of a new product to make a purchase. They provide diary or questionnaire data on their product and brand purchases and are usually asked to give opinions about products and brands. Panel data are collected from the same respondents at different points in time so that their purchasing can be tracked.

Test Market Problems.   One of the most serious test market problems arises when a competitor discovers the existence of a test market and monitors the results. This is particularly dangerous if there are no barriers to duplicating the new product, such as patents or technological know-how. A competitor willing to assume the risk can quickly produce a me-too product and even enter target markets ahead of the innovating company. General Foods once test-marketed a snack product that was later introduced as the brand Toast'em Popups. But the Kellogg Company, without test marketing, was able to go into national distribution at about the same time with a very similar product, Pop-Tarts. General Foods' management believes that Kellogg was able to accomplish this feat because it monitored General Foods' test market results.

Competitors may also try to disrupt a test market, which can cause inaccuracies in test data. Competitors may buy large quantities of the new product, overspend or underspend on advertising, or significantly reduce prices. When Procter & Gamble test-marketed Crisco, a smaller competitor cut the price of its own product in the test market. P&G found out about the tactic and retaliated by cutting the price on Crisco, but this made the test market unreliable.

Finally, there is always the risk of unanticipated unique market conditions. Dow Chemical Company test-marketed a new lubricant for use in outboard motors in Florida, but in Florida motors were not stored for the winter. Under northern weather conditions, the lubricant congealed, allowing stored outboard motors to rust. Fortunately, Dow also test-marketed in Michigan, where the flaw was discovered.

Alternatives to Test Marketing. Modified test marketing techniques have been developed that are intended to overcome some of these problems. One is the *simulated store*.[22] The respondents are brought to a predesignated location at which they are exposed to test commercials along with programs and other commercials. They are then given money and asked to shop in a simulated store (a store set up to duplicate a retail store, with shelving, product assortments, point-of-purchase displays, aisles, and so forth). The respondents can use the money to buy products or can keep all or part of it. After shopping, they participate in a group interview, discussing the reasons for their purchase decisions. The respondents may also be contacted two or three weeks later to determine their usage of a new product, their satisfaction with it, and their intentions to buy it again. The advantage of this method is that it keeps the test secret while still obtaining information concerning actual customer purchase decisions. The simulated store technique differs from test marketing in that its data are primarily on trial purchases, and there is no opportunity to fully test the distribution, after-sale customer service, or personal selling components of the supporting strategy. This technique also lacks complete realism. Yet it can yield valuable information concerning whether or not to actually commercialize a product.[23]

Successfully predicting sales for a new product with much confidence requires that potential customers see and use the product and that they be given the opportunity to purchase the product over a period of time. There are thus four steps in the buying process: trial, the first repeat purchase, adoption and, finally, purchasing with some frequency. Concept tests primarily measure intentions regarding only trial use of the product. Market tests, at the other extreme, provide for customers going through all four steps, but market tests are very expensive and involve other risks. A method that falls in between the concept test and market tests is *sales wave research.* This is usually an in-home test, much like a product use test, but with several subsequent opportunities for the respondents to actually purchase the product. Frequency of purchase and customer attrition over a number of sales waves provide useful data for making sales forecasts. Sales wave research is also combined with the simulated store approach. Use of techniques that approach the reality of a market test, but do not incur the related costs and risks, appears to be on the increase.

Commercialization

Commercialization is the actual introduction of the product into the marketplace, with all of the related decisions and resource commitments.

A decision must finally be made on whether or not deciding on to introduce the new product into target markets (step 7 in Exhibit 12–4). In **commercialization** of a product, all evaluations are brought to bear as management assesses the degree to which the product and the supporting strategy can be expected to succeed. If the decision is to go ahead, resources are committed to implementing the new product strategy. Raw material and component contracts must be made with suppliers; channels of distribution must be selected; manufacturing facilities, equipment, and processes must be set into operation; salespeople may need to be hired and trained; and so forth. Typically, very large commitments of money and personnel are involved. Because of the tremendous resource commitment required by new product launchings, a crucial decision concerns the time frame over which the introduction will take place.

Crash Introduction. A crash introduction is the full-scale commercialization of a new product as quickly as possible. The resources needed to move into target markets are immediately committed. In this way, competitors are given little time to prepare their responses to the product. A crash program is most often selected when competitors can counter quickly and maximum lead time is needed to establish market position. A crash introduction tends to maximize other risks because substantial resources are committed quickly.

Rollout Introduction. For a rollout introduction, target markets are divided geographically and initially the new product is introduced in only one or a few areas. If the new product is successful in these areas, the process continues until all geographic target markets are being served. A rollout offers the advantage of giving management time to monitor and adjust the new product strategy before all resources are committed. This is not the same as continuing the test market stage, because an introduction decision has been made, much larger market areas are entered, and less elaborate monitoring of performance is conducted. When the resources needed for a crash program are not available, as is the case with smaller companies, the rollout procedure may be the only feasible alternative.

Timing. Highly innovative products are often introduced before potential customers are prepared to accept them. Introductions that occur before their time often fail. At the other extreme, delays or overly slow rollouts can help competitors gain a substantial advantage. There is often a window of opportunity that gradually closes due to changing preferences, competitive entries, and a changing environment. Most timing issues are specific to the product-market situation, so related analysis is essential.

Organizing for New Product Development

Nowhere is the need for cooperation among managers more pressing than in new product development. As in establishing a new business enterprise, all functions of the business must be integrated for a successful development effort. Several alternatives exist for organizing the new product development process.

■ *Product Manager.* Product managers are typically members of middle management who have marketing responsibility for an existing product or a group of related products. Their base of experience with a given type of product can be very valuable, as can their established relationships with people in other functions of the business. This alternative has serious drawbacks: (1) the product managers have to divide their time between "fighting fires" with existing products and developing new products; (2) *new* product development often requires a more entrepreneurial style than many managers possess; and (3) major new innovations are unlikely to be generated by managers, although product modifications are a natural outcome of their experience.

■ *New Product Manager.* New product managers are often part of the product manager organization, but have specific responsibility for new products. These managers use their product-type experience but specialize in the development of products. However, there are usually significant limitations to a new product manager's authority, and such managers tend to concentrate on product modifications for existing markets.

■ *New Product Committees.* Many companies have new product committees consisting of top-level executives from several key functional areas who periodically meet to discuss new product candidates. Such committees allow companies to take advantage of the specialized functional expertise of people with authority. But this approach does not usually involve new product specialists, and the demands on executives' time for ongoing *existing* product decisions are substantial. Periodic meetings may not provide adequate continuity.

■ *New Product Department.* A separate department can encompass new product decision specialists such as engineers, technical researchers, and functional managers. Usually placed at a high level, such departments have substantial authority and can offer a perspective that goes beyond existing product lines. But obtaining support from other units often comes down to individual persuasion, and resistance sometimes develops from executives who have not been involved in the early stages of a given new product idea.

■ *Venture Teams.* A venture team is a separate organizational entity that is established to develop and implement a new product strategy. The venture team is free from existing operations. This approach fosters the flexibility and entrepreneurship characteristic of smaller businesses. Venture teams comprise a mix of specialized expertise, can call on other corporate resources as needed, and often provide financial incentives to team members.

If new products are essential to corporate strategic planning, their development should not be left to chance. The use of departments and venture teams helps ensure that sufficient time and expertise are devoted to the new product decision area. Burying new product development in the corporate bureaucracy almost by definition retards substantial progress in this area. Further, it is important to have a "product champion" who, with some blind faith and a high sense of commitment, will work feverishly to ensure the success of a new product. Venture capitalists say that it is better to have a first-rate entrepreneur (who will make the venture work) with a second-rate idea than a second-rate entrepreneur with a first-rate idea. Ideally, new product development has both a first-rate entrepreneur and a first-rate idea.

Consumer Adoption Processes

Once a product has been introduced, a major challenge rests with the marketing function. The product must be adopted (purchased) and "diffused" throughout the markets—and the faster this happens, the better. Adoption is the decision of an individual to use the product. Diffusion is the collective spread of individual adoption decisions throughout a population or market.

As noted, there is usually a limited window of opportunity for new products. Venture capitalists often indicate that their projected sales for a product are more accurate than their *timing*. It often takes longer than expected to attain projected sales levels. And the rate of acceptance often differentiates a tremendously successful product from a disaster. So how can the *rate* of acceptance be increased?

EXHIBIT 12-18 Types of Adopters by Adoption Time Required

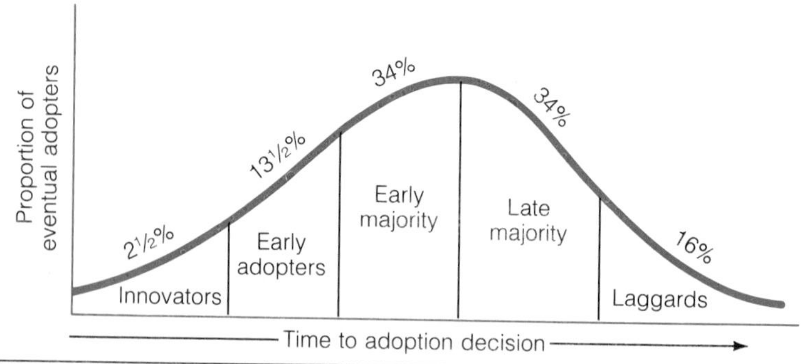

Source: Reprinted with permission of The Free Press, a division of Macmillan, Inc., from *Diffusion of Innovations* by Everett M. Rogers. Copyright © 1962 by The Free Press.

First, consumers go through a process of deciding to buy a product (Chapters 5 and 6). The usual steps in the adoption process, the buying decision process for new products, are:

Awareness ⟶ Interest ⟶ Evaluation ⟶ Trial ⟶ Adoption

(Knows it exists) — (Seeks information) — (Weighs whether or not to try it) — (Tries it once or twice) — (Purchases and repurchases)

Marketing in the introduction and early growth stages must be oriented toward facilitating the rapid movement of as many customers as possible through this process. The timing of various marketing tactics (informative advertising, coupons or incentives to try a product, and so forth) becomes critical.

Second, some customers adopt products more quickly than others, which has strategy implications. Individual customers may be labeled according to how quickly they adopt a product, ranging from "innovators" to "laggards," as shown in Exhibit 12-18. Marketing should, if possible, be initially directed to the innovators and early adopters, both to develop an early cash flow and to encourage a faster rate of diffusion into the majority of the market. Unfortunately, research has found little consistency of innovator and early adopter demographic or psychographic characteristics across different types of products. Marketers should, however, seek to find common characteristics for early purchasers in their particular product category and, if possible, target their marketing strategy accordingly. Some evidence exists for the general innovator profile (Exhibit 12-19), but again, those results should be viewed cautiously with respect to specific products.

Third, many diffusion studies have demonstrated that a product's characteristics as *perceived* by potential buyers are extremely important. Marketing activity can be partially directed toward helping minimize misperceptions

EXHIBIT 12–19 Comparative Profiles of the Consumer Innovator and the Later Adopter

Characteristic	Innovator	Noninnovator (or Later Adopter)
Product interest	More	Less
Opinion leadership	More	Less
Personality		
Dogmatism	Open-minded	Closed-minded
Social character	Inner-directed	Other-directed
Category width	Broad categorizer	Narrow categorizer
Venturesome	More	Less
Perceived risk	Less	More
Purchase and consumption traits		
Brand loyalty	Less	More
Deal proneness	More	Less
Usage	More	Less
Media habits		
Total magazine exposure	More	Less
Special-interest magazines	More	Less
Television	Less	More
Social characteristics		
Social integration	More	Less
Social striving (e.g., social, physical, and occupational mobility)	More	Less
Group memberships	More	Less
Demographic characteristics		
Age	Younger	Older
Income	More	Less
Education	More	Less
Occupational status	More	Less

Source: Leon G. Schiffman and Leslie Lazar Kanuk, *Consumer Behavior*, 2nd ed., © 1983, p. 526. Reprinted by permission of Prentice-Hall, Inc., Englewood Cliffs, N.J.

and enhancing strengths. Important perceived product characteristics and related marketing actions are shown in Exhibit 12–20. *Relative advantage* is the extent to which potential customers perceive a new product as superior to existing substitutes. *Compatibility* is the extent to which potential customers consider a new product to be consistent with their values, needs, and behavior. *Complexity* is the degree to which an innovation is difficult to understand or use. *Trialability* is the extent to which a new product or venture is capable of being tried on a limited basis by customers. Finally, communicability or *observability* is the ease with which a product's benefits can be seen by, imagined by, or described to potential consumers.

Although each of these product characteristics borders on being intuitively obvious, paying systematic and creative attention to them can be critical to the design of effective marketing strategies for new products. Apple Computer, Inc.'s MacIntosh personal computer was a good example of a product

EXHIBIT 12–20 Marketing Implications of Important Product/Venture Characteristics

Characteristic	Marketing Action	Characteristic	Marketing Action
Relative advantage	Clearly and credibly communicate the product's advantage. Obtain third-party/professional/objective endorsements. Price the product to compare favorably with others. Construct the product to "deliver" benefits quickly.	*Trialability*	Offer money-back guarantee (reduce the cost/risk of trial). Make small quantities available free or at low price. Provide incentives to encourage trial. Durable items: test drives for autos, etc.
Compatibility	Develop an understanding of customer lifestyles, behavior, etc. to minimize the required adaptation. Make the product fit in with related products. Make the product/brand fit customer's social situation.	*Observability*	Encourage visible use by customers. Make it easy for others to perceive the product/brand. Create incentives for customers to encourage friends to consider trial.
Complexity	Make the product readily understandable. Strive to make the product "user friendly." Make the product at a complexity level not exceeding that of substitutes.		

designed with the above characteristics in mind. Compared to IBM's PC, the relative price/quality advantage of the MacIntosh was assumed to be favorable and its compatibility and lack of complexity were major advantages. "Apple Pins MacIntosh Future on 'User Friendliness' of Lisa' was how *The Wall Street Journal* described the situation at introduction.[25] Given intense competition, however, it was uncertain how successful the MacIntosh would be.

=========================== *Application* ===========================

New Product Development At Campbell Soup

Campbell Soup Company introduced 334 new products over a five-year period, more than any other company in the food industry.[26] R. Gordon McGovern became president and CEO in 1980, and his goal was to turn the stodgy soup maker into a consumer-driven marketing company. Previously, emphasis had been placed on pro-

duction efficiency and products appeared to be designed on the basis of what the company could make easily, rather than what people wanted to buy. McGovern cut at bureaucracy and encouraged entrepreneurial attitudes by splitting Campbell into 50 autonomous business units. He also increased marketing expenditures by almost 150 percent between 1980 and 1985. Of the 10 major new brands introduced, 7 have been successful, each generating at least $25 million in annual sales. Prego spaghetti sauces and LeMenu frozen dinners became superstars, accounting for more than $450 million of Campbell's $4 billion in annual sales. However, earnings fell short of McGovern's goal of 15 percent annual growth. Now he is tightening the reins, with more emphasis on product quality, production efficiency, and cost control. He describes this new emphasis as a necessary phase of Campbell's evolution.

There is also more emphasis on the "fit" of new products into broader corporate and brand strategic directions and more rigorous screening and a slower pace of national introductions. The president of Campbell's huge U.S. division says that it can no longer afford to run "a new product boutique." An advertising executive who works with the company applauds the increased tendency of senior managers to first develop new product strategies. Campbell is screening and testing more ideas than ever before, but consistent with the Booz·Allen study cited earlier, fewer are going national. Ideas in the testing stage included refrigerated salads, soups in microwavable containers, Pepperidge Farm ice cream, and dry soups to compete with Thomas J. Lipton, Inc.

A good example of Campbell's more strategic focus and its greater emphasis on testing is provided by its Pepperidge Farm unit, a star performer until it introduced several product failures that had little to do with the brand's premium image. There was a growing impression that the unit had lost sight of its heritage and its strategic focus. Pepperidge Farm was founded in 1937 by Margaret Rudkin as an outgrowth of baking natural whole wheat bread for her asthmatic son. The natural, high-quality Pepperidge image continued along with rapid growth, and Campbell bought the company in 1961.

To put Pepperidge Farm back on track, 50 marketing managers attended a retreat in the fall of 1985. They listened to presentations on environmental and consumer trends as a backdrop for discussing the meaning of the Pepperidge Farm brand. This provided guidelines for new product idea search. As one manager said, "You started to see the company take shape. You started to see a [strategic] philosophy." Key product attributes were identified for positioning the brand, including premium quality, natural ingredients, building on the company's bakery image, and in general meeting a consumer need. From this discussion, new product criteria and priorities (weights) were developed. At the meeting, brainstorming was used to generate numerous ideas that were later screened against the criteria and priorities.

Monthly meetings of the once autonomous marketing managers were instituted, yet it was recognized that room should be left for innovation while keeping a strategic discipline across the business units. There are fewer crash introductions and more roll outs. Consistent with new product development trends, Campbell is carefully putting resources behind the products that have the greatest chance of success ▪

Summary

New products are those for which the degree of change faced by *customers* is sufficient to require the design or redesign of marketing strategies. Such products may be new to the world, new product lines, additions to existing product lines, improved or revised products, repositionings, or cost reductions.

New product development, an outgrowth of an overall business strategy, includes seven steps, the first of which is *new product strategy development.* This step links corporate objectives to a specific new product effort and provides overall direction for the new product planning process. Developing a new product strategy based on corporate objectives and strategy includes identifying the corporate growth role for new products; scanning the external environment; analyzing the industry; assessing the firm's new product experience, internal capabilities, and corporate culture; and appraising the product life cycle. The outcome is a set of strategic roles (Exhibit 12-5) that help identify the markets for which new products will be developed.

The second step, *idea generation,* involves identifying new ways to satisfy customer needs and wants and understanding evolving technologies. Sources of ideas include competitors, employees, customers, research and development, marketing research, and inventors. Idea generation techniques include direct observation, brainstorming, focus group interviewing, consumer preference testing, and environmental forecasting.

Screening and evaluating ideas, the third step, involves determining what the screening criteria (Exhibit 12-11) should be. These criteria can be sequenced in terms of the difficulty and expense of obtaining the information needed and/or in terms of their importance in predicting overall product success. A multistage approach can involve the use of culling, rating, and scoring criteria, although no generally agreed-upon process exists.

The fourth step in new product development, *business analysis,* involves using various methods to assess likely profitability. These include break-even analysis, discounted cash flow, the Bayesian decision model, and simulation models.

The fifth step, *product development,* is the scientific and engineering task of building a prototype and its functional testing. Consumer preference testing may also be used to guide the development of specific product attributes. At this stage, attention is given to the costs of manufacturing, packaging, and distributing the new product.

Market acceptance testing is the sixth step. Concept testing, product use testing, and market testing (and variations thereof) are used to evaluate likely market reaction. Market testing costs much more than concept testing, but the validity of the market information also increases with market testing (if the test market is not confounded by competitors).

The final step, *commercialization,* is the full introduction of the product, either on a "crash" basis or more slowly through a rollout. The timing of product introductions often spells success or failure.

The chapter concluded with a discussion of organizing for new product development. The more successful approaches involve well-supported, independent units. Finally, the consumer adoption process was presented with a view toward increasing the rate and level of new product acceptance.

Exercises for Review and Discussion

1. Sunergy, Inc., a solar heating company, has the R&D ability to construct an economically feasible solar reflector, making it possible for homeowners to convert to solar heating with substantial cost savings after the fifth year. As vice president of marketing, you are in charge of developing the new product. Outline how you would take this idea through the new product development process.

2. You are a vice president with Keserlis Product Development, Inc., a consulting firm. Subject the following new product proposals to your new product screening process, and identify possible problems: Del Monte marketing a sug-

ared fruit candy, Wang entering the traditional typewriter market, and the *New York Times* publishing a Hare Krishna newsmagazine.

3. The marketing vice president of a large chemical producer made a radical proposal regarding the role of R&D in generating new product ideas. Her proposal asked R&D to curtail most basic research that could not be tied to known market needs. Marketing research would be given the major responsibility for identifying new product ideas based on analyses of customers and markets. R&D would direct its efforts toward determining the technical feasibility of these new product ideas. This would bring the company's new product development function in line with the marketing concept. Do you agree with this proposal and its rationale? Why or why not?

4. A consulting firm, Environmental Research Associates, has built up a large cash balance from its business over the past 10 years. The board of directors has been concerned about the susceptibility of consulting and research contract work to swings in the economy. The recession of 1982 demonstrated what happens to consulting business sales in a downswing, and the company wanted to insulate itself from such periods. Two years ago, the company decided to move into the manufacture of temperature measurement instruments. The company was doing well, but it became apparent that companies in the instrument business

were working on new technologies for measuring temperatures. The president told the board, "We have to be prepared to innovate if we want to stay competitive in the temperature measurement business. We need to set up an ongoing program to find new product ideas." What recommendations would you make to the president of Environmental Research Associates if you were asked to advise him on developing ideas for new products?

5. A new product development team developed the revenue and cost estimates shown in Exhibit 12–A for a new snack food proposal. Use the break-even model and the discounted cash flow model to assess the decision alternatives (introduce versus not introduce this product). Then, compare and contrast the usefulness of these two models for helping management make new product decisions.

6. A consumer goods manufacturer, Parker, Inc., recently experienced a declining rate of success on new product decisions. You have been assigned to review the firm's new product decision process to evaluate whether weaknesses in the process could be a cause of the problem. After extensive interviews with key personnel, you conclude that the process is as follows: R&D is given the primary responsibility for initiating new product ideas, though ideas are occasionally suggested by company salespeople, based on contact with retailers. A management committee consisting of vice

EXHIBIT 12–A Proposed Snack Food Revenue/Cost Analysis

	Years after Introduction				
	1	**2**	**3**	**4**	**5**
Most likely sales volume (000 units)	275	290	500	875	1,450
Selling prices per unit	$ 1.49	$ 1.49	$ 1.30	$ 1.25	$ 1.25
Annual fixed costs ($000)	$38	$38	$50	$50	$77
Annual variable costs per unit					
Factory	$ 0.25	$ 0.25	$ 0.30	$ 0.30	$ 0.35
Distribution	$ 0.30	$ 0.03	$ 0.04	$ 0.04	$ 0.06
Selling	$ 0.40	$ 0.40	$ 0.25	$ 0.25	$ 0.20
R&D cost	$100,000				
Company cost of capital/(percent)	0.12	0.12	0.10	0.10	0.10

presidents from finance, manufacturing, advertising, and purchasing is formed to evaluate a proposed idea. If approved, the idea is passed back to R&D for prototype development. If this effort shows that the idea is technically sound, advertising is asked to develop an introduction strategy covering advertising, personal selling, and distribution. Cooperation is requested from personnel in all of these areas. A survey of retailer reaction to the new product is also conducted. At the conclusion of these activities, the management committee meets again to make a decision on whether to introduce the new product.

Evaluate the strengths and the weaknesses of this new product decision process. Make recommendations to improve the process.

7. One important activity in a new product decision is the technical task of turning a new product idea into a functioning product. Suppose that Vaughn Recreation Vehicle Company is developing a small four-wheel-drive vehicle for off-the-road driving. The innovative idea calls for the sale of different body kits with a basic chassis. The buyer can select the body design from a wide set of options. And for the do-it-yourselfer, the body can be purchased separately in kit form along with the chassis for a lower total price. How might marketing research be used to develop this innovative idea into a functioning product?

Notes

1. Excerpts from above two titles in *The Wall Street Journal,* November 2, 1983, pp. 2, 20, and *The Wall Street Journal,* February 21, 1984, p. 31. Reprinted by permission of *The Wall Street Journal,* © Dow Jones & Company, Inc., 1984, 1983. All rights reserved.

2. Estimated from "Manufacturers Undaunted by Failures in Quest for New Product Successes," *Marketing News,* November 22, 1985, p. 17. Published by the American Marketing Association.

3. *New Product Management for the 1980s* (New York: Booz•Allen & Hamilton, 1982), p. 8.

4. Ronald Alsop, "Big Gains at Hercules Reflect a Major Shift by Chemical Firms to 'Specialty' Products," *The Wall Street Journal,* September 19, 1983, p. 29. Reprinted by permission of *The Wall Street Journal,* © Dow Jones & Company, Inc., 1983. All rights reserved.

5. Mack Hanan, "Corporate Growth through Venture Management," *Harvard Business Review,* January-February 1969, p. 44.

6. Laurence P. Feldman and Albert L. Page, "Principles versus Practice in New Product Planning," *Journal of Product Innovation Management,* January 1984, p. 44.

7. "New Products: Still Kissing . . . Finding a Winner . . . Hassles," *The Wall Street Journal,* November 3, 1983, p. 27.

8. "Strategic Marketing Top Priority of Chief Execs," *Marketing News,* January 31, 1986, p. 17. Published by the American Marketing Association.

9. Robert G. Cooper, "Market-Push Strategy Inhibits Industrial, High-Tech Innovation," *Marketing News,* June 25, 1982, p. 1.

10. Eric Von Hippel, "Has Your Customer Already Developed Your Next Product?" *Sloan Management Review* 18 (Winter 1977), pp. 63–64.

11. Robert O. Null, "The Team Approach to Business Expansion," presentation to the Chicago Chapter of the Product Development and Management Association, February 26, 1986.

12. "Beckman Gets Customers to Design Its Products," *Business Week,* August 17, 1974, pp. 52, 54.

13. Proactive approaches to new product search processes are reviewed in Allan D. Shocker and V. Srinivasan, "Multiattribute Approaches for Product Concept Evaluation and Generation: A Critical Review," *Journal of Marketing Research* 16 (May 1979), pp. 159–80.

14. Allan D. Shocker and V. Srinivasan, "Consumer-Based Methodology for Identification of New Products," *Management Science* 20 (February 1974), p. 927.

15. Edward M. Tauber, "Less Daring Days Ahead for Marketers of New Products," *Marketing News*, August 11, 1978, p. 11.

16. H. Ronald Hamilton, "Screening Business Development Opportunities," *Business Horizons* 17 (August 1974), pp. 13-24. Also see Ted Karger, "A Rigorous Idea Screening Process Delivers New Products Which Gain Corporate Support," *Marketing News*, November 22, 1985, p. 20. Published by the American Marketing Association.

17. Marshall Freimer and Leonard S. Simon, "Screening New Product Ideas," in *Marketing and the New Science of Planning*, ed. Robert L. King (Chicago: American Marketing Association, 1968), pp. 103-4.

18. A firm's opportunity cost of capital is a percentage or rate measure of the average cost of obtaining resources through all sources. The rate reflects such out-of-pocket costs as the interest rate on bond indebtedness and also less tangible costs, such as the increased risk of business operation caused by greater debt.

19. Janet Guyon, "Nabisco's New Cookie Line Marks the Beginning of a Fierce Sales War," *The Wall Street Journal*, October 17, 1983, p. 8. Reprinted by permission of *The Wall Street Journal*, © Dow Jones & Company, Inc.

20. Niel Ulman, "Sweating It Out: Time, Risk, Ingenuity All Go into Launching New Personal Product," *The Wall Street Journal*, November 17, 1978, p. 41.

21. Edward M. Tauber, "Forecasting Sales Prior to Test Market," *Journal of Marketing* 41 (January 1977), p. 81.

22. Pieter P. deKadt, "New Techiques in Evaluating Test Markets," in *Combined Proceedings*, ed. Fred C. Allvine (Chicago: American Marketing Association, 1972), pp. 154-57. See also Alvin J. Silk and Glen L. Urban, "Pre-Test Market Evaluation of New Packaged Goods: A Model and Measurement Methodology," *Journal of Marketing Research* 15 (May 1978), pp. 171-91.

23. An excellent overview of other testing variations is in C. S. Chaterji, Ronald T. Lonsdale, and Stanley F. Stasch, "New Product Development: Theory and Practice," in *Review of Marketing, 1981*, ed. Ben M. Enis and Kenneth Roering (Chicago: American Marketing Association, 1981), pp. 147-50.

24. These five characteristics are cited by Everett M. Rogers and F. Floyd Shoemaker, *Communication of Innovations* (New York: Free Press, 1971), p. 102.

25. Dennis Kneale, "Apple Pins MacIntosh Future on 'User Friendliness' of Lisa," *The Wall Street Journal*, January 27, 1984, p. 25.

26. This application is based on Fancine Schwadel, "Burned by Mistakes, Campbell Soup Company Is in Throes of Change," *The Wall Street Journal*, August 14, 1985, pp. 1, 15. Used by permission of *The Wall Street Journal*, © Dow Jones & Company, Inc., 1985. All rights reserved.

PART

4

Marketing Planning

Analyzing the Situation

Marketing Strategy Development

Marketing Program Design

Implementing the Marketing Program

Marketing's Broadening Role

*A*t the heart of marketing strategy is the marketing program presented to customers in target markets. This offer determines what set of benefits will be provided to customers and how the company will position itself against competition. At management's disposal are the controllable components of this marketing offer. Part 4 examines the decisions required to effectively utilize these components.

In Chapter 13, "Product Decisions," the discussion centers on decisions made concerning the product component during the life of products after their introduction, including modification and drop decisions.

The other chapters in Part 4 deal with the components of the marketing offer that support the distribution and sale of company products. Chapter 14, "Channel of Distribution Decisions," and Chapter 15, "Physical Distribution Decisions," discuss the decisions required to manage the flow of products from the producer to end-user markets.

To meet company objectives, products must be priced. In Chapter 16, "Pricing Decisions," the role of price in the marketing offer is discussed and approaches to setting price are reviewed.

Three chapters examine the promotion component in the marketing offer. Chapter 17, "Promotion and Sales Promotion," discusses the nature of communication between a company and its audiences. Chapter 18, "Advertising Decisions," examines the importance of advertising by companies and presents an analytic approach to making advertising decisions. Chapter 19, "Sales Force Management Decisions," considers the personal selling function and the task of planning and managing sales force strategy.

Part 4 applies the crucial marketing activities of analyzing the situation and developing overall marketing strategy, the topics of Parts 2 and 3. Designing the marketing program initiates a strategy and tactics for achieving sales from markets, a company's major source of revenue. The components of the marketing offer are coordinated through planning marketing strategy. The success of this strategy is crucial to the viability of a company ∎

CHAPTER 13

Product Decisions

*T*he competitive battle between Coca-Cola and Pepsi was one of the most publicized marketing face-offs in recent decades. In the mid-1980s, Coca-Cola continued to outsell Pepsi but was gradually losing market share. A special concern for Coca-Cola management was that Pepsi consistently won out over Coke in blind taste tests. Coke's idea was to transfer all of the positive qualities associated with the existing product to a product with improved taste. So after extensive research and planning, Coke introduced the sweeter, reformulated New Coke in 1985.

Everyone knows the outcome of what many thought would be an easy product modification decision. Coke misjudged the willingness of consumers to go along with its concept. One report in *The Wall Street Journal* summed it up this way:[1]

> In one of the most stunning flip-flops in marketing annals, Coke publicly apologized for scrapping a 99 year old product that had perhaps become more American than apple pie. . . . in one stroke, Coke largely undid what 4½ years of elaborate planning and market research had dictated was the right move. The abrupt decision, without any detailed marketing and advertising plans, surprised industry analysts and Coke's competitors alike.

After the reformulated Coke experienced strong success in the first month, weekly surveys showed a major swing in consumer sentiment by the end of May. Management had expected howls from die-hard Coke fans, but it began to sense that the public at large was adopting a negative view. Extensive press reports fanned the resistance, and consumer surveys showed old Coke preferred two to one over new Coke by the end of June. Coke's bottlers were also up in arms, another crucial factor. Coca-Cola management found that consumers saw New Coke as a product that was putting an end to a significant piece of Americana.

Resting at home on July 4, Coke's president worldwide decided that the company had to bring back its old formula under the name Classic Coke. Other brand names were considered, including Coke 1986, Old Coke, and

Coke 1. On July 5, the president began ordering departments of the company to prepare for a relaunch, before a final decision was made. Some argued that Coca-Cola should wait and see and make such changes as removing the word *new* from the Coke can. But the decision to go ahead with Classic Coke was implemented with an entrepreneurial spirit. The design of the Coke Classic package was not begun until two days before the announcement, requiring the company to create a phony paper label for the can used in the first commercial.

Competitively matching a company's products to target market requirements is the heart of marketing strategy. The matching process is dynamic because market conditions constantly change. Products and industries move through life-cycle stages and each stage presents different challenges. So strategies are adapted to the competitive market situations that evolve.

This chapter discusses important strategy issues, many of which relate to the Coke experience. First, a definition of a product is presented that emphasizes how customers perceive products, since marketing management must base strategies on such perceptions. Then, several accepted ways of grouping consumer and industrial products are presented, because marketing strategies tend to be similar for each group. Services (as opposed to goods) are emphasized due to their growing importance in modern economies. Product policy decisions also receive attention. Guidelines should be set for determining the firm's product mix and product lines as well as specific products and their attributes. The last two sections of the chapter treat other product policy areas, including branding and packaging.

What Is a Product?

Product
is anything that is potentially valued by a target market for the benefits or satisfactions it provides, including objects, services, organizations, places, people, and ideas.

We have used the term *product* hundreds of times in the preceding chapters without a precise definition. This is because we all have an intuitive understanding of the term from our experience in the marketplace. But is the set of services provided by a travel agency a "product"? Does the United Fund sell contributors a "product"? Do political candidates with innovative ideas sell a "product"? How about a financial services firm? Is its consultation a "product"? Are graduating students who sell their talents to potential employers a "product"? As we define a **product,** the answer to all of these questions is yes. In each case, a customer is purchasing *benefits or satisfactions,* and from a marketing viewpoint this is the basic meaning of a product.

Customer Product Perception

Making product decisions is aided by grouping the various meanings of the term *product* into three levels (Exhibit 13-1). Level 1 comprises the basic *benefits or satisfactions* that a particular product delivers. The same product may provide different benefits to different people. To one person, a Cadillac

EXHIBIT 13-1 Customer Perception Hierarchy

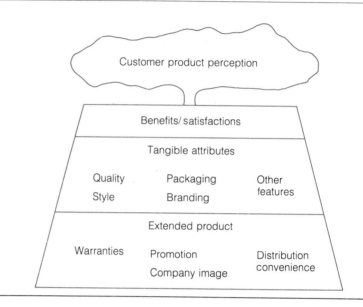

is a means for enhancing status; to another, it is a source of comfortable, quiet, and reliable transportation.

Marketers must also understand the linkages between objective, tangible *product attributes* (level 2) and subjective satisfactions. The Cadillac brand name, quality, and styling enhance the satisfactions that customers feel. Tangible attributes sometimes receive a disproportionate amount of attention in product decision making.

Finally, the *extended product* (level 3) comprises marketing elements that go beyond the specific product itself but are valued by customers. The extended product is the broader set of marketing elements within which the product exists. For a Cadillac, it includes such things as warranty service, status-oriented promotion, and delivery arrangements.

These three levels—the extended product, product attributes, and benefits/satisfactions—together create the customer's overall perception of a product. Management's task is to blend the three levels in a consistent, synergistic manner to meet the needs and wants of well-defined target markets. The levels imply that product perceptions in the marketplace are hierarchical; such perceptions are affected most by the customer benefits derived from products, second by the specific attributes of products, and last by the other marketing elements associated with products. There are exceptions, but in general management should adopt this customer-oriented perspective in attempting to create product images for target markets.

Product Classifications[2]

Marketing strategies must be tailored to fit different product-markets. The specific strategies for marketing cosmetics are different from those for marketing computer software. The fact that there are significant common marketing strategies for certain product groupings has allowed product classifications to be formed for consumer goods and for industrial goods.

Consumer Goods. One of the most accepted classification schemes for consumer goods is based on the problem-solving behavior of consumers. Grouping products according to how consumers go about buying them enables management to build customer-oriented strategies to fit customer needs. This classification scheme divides consumer products into these groups:

- Convenience goods.
- Shopping goods.
- Specialty goods.
- Unsought goods.

Convenience goods are products that the customer wants but is not willing to spend much time shopping for, such as candy bars, cigarettes, soap, and most grocery items.

Convenience goods are usually bought frequently, require little service or selling, are inexpensive, and may be bought by habit. Convenience goods may be subdivided into three types—staples, impulse goods, and emergency goods. Staples, which include food and drugs, are items that are used regularly in most households and are usually frequently and routinely purchased without much thought beyond the initial decision. Impulse goods are purchased on sight and without forethought; an ice cream cone bought to fulfill a sudden urge is an impulse good. Emergency goods, which might include tire chains, umbrellas, and ambulance services, are purchased when the need is urgent.

The most obvious strategic requirements for convenience goods are availability on short notice and availability in readily accessible locations. Convenience stores, which meet these requirements, were developed to specifically market convenience products. Homogeneous **shopping goods** are seen by consumers as very similar, so price becomes a major decision factor. Major appliances, despite feature differences, usually fit into this category. With heterogeneous shopping goods, consumers expect major differences other than price, so they carefully evaluate various features. Clothing, furniture, and other styled items are good examples of such goods. Here, price is less important as a strategy variable.

Shopping goods are products that are considered worth the time and effort needed to carefully evaluate them and to compare them with competing products—refrigerators and furniture are examples.

Specialty goods are products that consumers will make a special effort to buy, usually specific branded items of special importance to the consumers.

For **specialty goods,** the issue is not one of comparative shopping but rather the sheer willingness to search until the item is found. Polo and Izod shirts, for example, are often demanded by people who will not accept substitutes. Although such items need not be expensive, they often sell at a premium due to consumer insistence on the particular brand. Marketing strategies for specialty goods typically emphasize quality and branding (and sometimes advertising) rather than distribution convenience.

Unsought goods are products that consumers do not yet know they can buy or products that they usually do not want.

New **unsought goods** are products with which potential customers are not yet familiar. Many people are still not aware of real estate interval time sharing (two weeks' use of a mountain resort cabin can be purchased and traded against the use of other resort facilities) for annual vacations. The idea of selling real estate in such a shared arrangement is still very new. *Regularly unsought goods* are products that are often not aggressively sought, such as life insurance and gravestones. Unsought goods of either type require substantial, well-designed marketing strategies.

Industrial Goods.   Industrial goods classifications are even more valuable for marketing than consumer goods classifications because industrial buyers typically use a system of buying that is related to the classes of goods. Industrial goods classifications are based on how industrial buyers regard products and on how products are to be used. Expensive and. long-lived products are usually treated differently from inexpensive items. There are six categories of industrial products:

■ *Installations* are large, expensive capital items that do not become a part of the final product but are expended, depleted, or worn out during years of use. Installations include buildings (and land rights) and custom-made and standard major equipment.

■ *Accessory equipment* comprises tools and equipment that facilitate production or office activities—drills, lift trucks, typewriters, and so forth. Like installations, these are capital items that do not become part of the buyer's final product, but they are usually less expensive and shorter lived than installations.

■ *Raw materials* are basic commodities such as logs, iron ore, sand, and fresh fish that are processed only as much as needed for safe, convenient, economical transport and handling to reach the next processing stage or the place of end use. Raw materials are expense items that become part of a physical product. They include farm products (crops, livestock, etc.) and such natural products as minerals, maple syrup, and fish and game.

■ *Component parts and materials* are items that have undergone processing, usually to meet buyer specifications. They become part of a finished product and are treated as expense items. Component parts are ready, or nearly ready, to be assembled into a final product, whereas component materials require further processing. Examples of the former are automobile batteries, small motors, and castings; examples of the latter are wire, paper, and cement.

■ *Supplies* include maintenance, repair, and operating supplies (MRO items). These expense items are continually used up but do not become a part of the physical product. They include paint, nails, nuts and bolts, greases, and typing paper.

■ *Services* are usually supplied by specialists in support of the firm's operations. The services provided by engineering consultants and maintenance contractors are examples. Services are expense items.

The buying process, and therefore the appropriate marketing strategy, varies across these different types of industrial products. Buying process decisions often vary by whether one or more persons are involved in the decision; by the levels of involvement (e.g., president versus purchasing agent); by whether the purchase is a modified rebuy, a straight rebuy, and so on; by whether a lease option exists; and by the typical size of the market and the price elasticity of demand. These factors are important for marketing. The persons to whom marketing efforts should be targeted must be identified, and the decision process must be well enough understood to construct marketing strategies (Chapter 6). The same is true for yet another grouping: services.

Services

Those who say that the services economy is in our future are wrong. It's already here and has been for some time.

Today, 73 percent of the nonfarm work force is employed by services organizations. . . . And about two-thirds of the U.S. gross national product (GNP) comes from services.

About 47 cents of the consumer's dollar is spent on intangible services—everything from ball games to medical services and electricity to financial services. . . . Given the prominence of services in the economy and in consumers' lives, it's incumbent on us to pay more attention to how services are marketed.[3]

These words by Leonard L. Berry heralded an announcement that the American Marketing Association was establishing a new Services Marketing Division. Since the end of World War II, U.S. service industries have created 15 new jobs for every new manufacturing job.[4] The term *product* is used in this text to encompass services, but it is important to note that marketing services is somewhat different from marketing products because services are different themselves. They are intangible; they blend production and consumption; and they often involve unorthodox distribution channels.

Intangible

One of the most important differentiating characteristics of services is their intangible nature. A good is an object, a device, a thing; a service is a deed, a performance, an effort. When a good is purchased, something tangible is acquired—something that can be seen, touched, perhaps smelled, worn, or placed on a mantel. When a service is purchased, there is generally nothing tangible to show for it. Services are consumed but not possessed.[5]

EXHIBIT 13–2 Dominant Elements of Marketing Offers

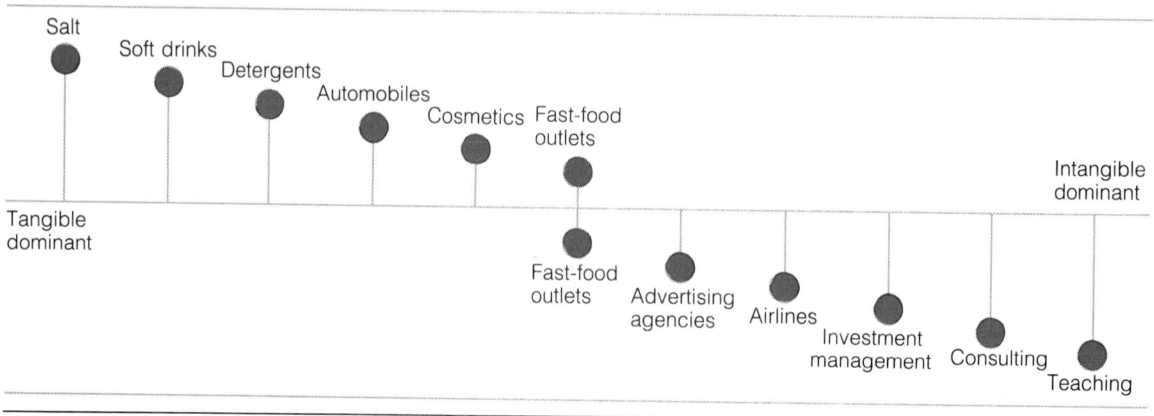

Salt

Soft drinks

Detergents

Automobiles

Cosmetics Fast-food
outlets

Intangible
dominant

Tangible
dominant

Fast-food
outlets

Advertising
agencies

Airlines

Investment
management Consulting

Teaching

Source: G. Lynn Shostack, "Breaking Free from Product Marketing," *Journal of Marketing* 41 (April 1977), p. 77.

Most offerings in the marketplace involve both tangible and intangible elements, so the distinction here is one of degree and emphasis. Exhibit 13-2 shows the relationship between tangibles and intangibles for a variety of consumer goods and services.[6] With services, the intangible elements are dominant. A fast-food outlet is a true blend of services and tangible products. Airlines could not deliver their transportation services without planes, but in contrast to buying an automobile, when these services are bought, the dominant product purchased is an intangible experience that is left behind at the airport.

The intangible nature of services has important managerial implications. First, defining the service attributes of importance to customers is a special challenge. Although this task is similar in concept to the task of identifying the key attributes of a tangible product (say a television set), the attributes of a service are more ephemeral and more difficult to define. An investment counseling firm sells advice. But what identifiable attributes exist as the foundation for a marketing program? Certainly the quality of the investment counselor's recommendations. But how about the counselor's appearance or the counselor's ability to communicate with an aura of self-confidence? Suffice it to say that these sometimes elusive attributes should be defined from the customer's perspective, even though this may be difficult. And once the important attributes have been identified, they must be "brought to life" in the minds of potential customers.

Doing this requires a reversal of what is done with goods marketing. With goods marketing, abstractions are often developed from objects. Coca-Cola "Brings Good Things to Life" and is featured in advertising portraying the good times that can accompany the drink. Services marketing starts instead with an abstract product, and the challenge is to show tangible evidence that

EXHIBIT 13-3

United Airlines makes services seem tangible to crystallize the perception of an intangible.

Courtesy Leo Burnett, U.S.A.

reflects favorably on the important service attributes (Exhibit 13-3). H&R Block shows a tax preparer sitting at a desk with an obviously happy client and cites the advantages of using its services. This marketing reversal is shown in Exhibit 13-4. Whereas marketing usually has the task of making inanimate objects more alive (e.g., cosmetics contributing to a beautiful physical appearance), with services the task is to make abstractions more concrete.

EXHIBIT 13–4 Relationship of Tangible and Intangible Elements: Goods versus Services

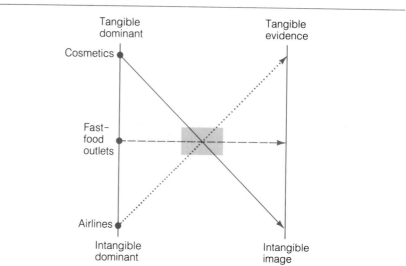

Source: G. Lynn Shostack, "Breaking Free from Product Marketing," *Journal of Marketing* 41 (April 1977), p. 79.

Production-Consumption Blending

A second difference between goods and services is that the sale of goods usually means that an object is transferred from inventory to a customer, whereas the sale of services involves interaction between the producer and the customer. The producer and the production of the service are both present at the point of receipt by the customer. This characteristic of services has several implications.

First, the direct producer-customer relationship provides an opportunity to be very customer oriented, even to the point of customizing the service to meet specific needs. The exact service may be designed at a meeting with the customer. It is therefore very important to hire producers who are in some degree marketers. Because one person carries out parts of both the production and marketing functions, both functions should be emphasized in employee training.

Second, the face-to-face (labor-intensive) nature of the services industry means that although on-the-spot customizing may offer advantages, delivery of a standardized product of consistent quality presents a special challenge. Quality standards and control must receive emphasis in employee training.

Third, the blending of production and consumption usually means that there is no inventory "cushion." Matching supply with demand becomes especially critical for management. Procter & Gamble maintains an inventory of Ivory Soap, in part to absorb variations in demand. But what if 200 people arrive for a "Starting a Business" seminar and the room capacity is 150? With face-to-face production and consumption, marketing targets demand to equal but not exceed supply. For this purpose, several demand-influencing strategies can be used—raising prices in periods of peak demand, increasing nonpeak demand to balance out capacity needs, and instituting reservation systems.[7]

Distribution Channels

With the explosion of information-based industries have come unorthodox, electronic "channels of distribution." Whether a standard telephone call or a computer modem is used, no physical transfer of goods occurs, yet a service is delivered. In most service businesses, the channel is very short or nonexistent (face-to-face transfer is the most common arrangement). A restaurant has the factory, retail outlet, and point of consumption rolled into one.[8]

Part of an information service may be distributed through the media. Investment information may be conveyed through newspapers or television in the hope that part of the audience will sign up for face-to-face counseling. Cable TV courses may be taken on a fee basis.

Developing a Product Policy

Corporations are careful to coordinate product decisions to avoid the risk of stretching company resources into product-markets-offering little competitive advantage. Companies can counter this risk by formulating an overall **product policy** that ties product decisions to the corporate product strategy (Chapter 12).

Product policy prioritizes product types and sets guidelines for grouping individual products to take advantage of using common marketing strategies.

The product policy covers several levels of product groupings, beginning with top management's decision to operate one or more business units. This establishes a strategic *business mix* that defines the product-market scope of the company. Each unit in the business mix has responsibility for products appealing to target markets that differ from those of other business units, and each unit is usually given responsibility to design, implement, and control its own marketing strategy. Within each strategic business unit, there are typically a product mix, product lines within the mix, specific products within each line, and specific attributes of each product, as Exhibit 13-5 shows. The myriad of decisions regarding products must be made with an understanding of how a given decision, such as adding a product, will fit within the existing product mix. One objective is to seek complementary or even synergistic product lines, products, and attributes as part of the product mix.

Major product policy decisions are illustrated in the strategy changes made by Magic Chef, a medium-sized manufacturer with ambitions to become more diversified:

EXHIBIT 13-5 Levels of Product Policy Decisions

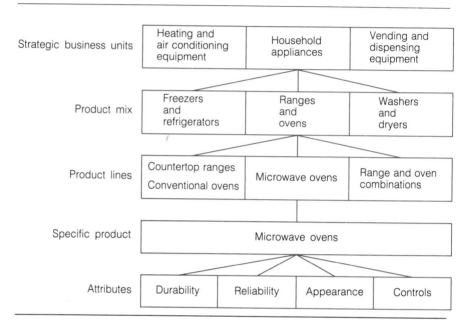

At the end of the 1970s, Magic Chef, fifth in size in the appliance industry, manufactured kitchen appliances, heating and air conditioning equipment, and soft-drink vending equipment. The kitchen appliance mix included ranges and microwave ovens built by the firm, and dishwashers, refrigerators, vents, garbage disposals, and trash compactors supplied by other manufacturers. In 1979, management announced the decision to expand Magic Chef's appliance product mix to include washers and dryers and refrigerators and freezers. The mix decision signaled management's strategy of becoming a multiline appliance manufacturer. The company announced agreements to purchase the Norge division (washers and dryers) of Fedders Corporation and the Admiral domestic appliance division (refrigerators and freezers) of Rockwell International.[9]

From 1974 to 1984, Magic Chef's home appliance sales grew 570 percent, to $862 million, breaking all previous profit records. The expanded product lines made Magic Chef an attractive acquisition for Maytag in 1986.

Product Mix

Product mix
is the entire collection of product lines and items offered by an organization.

Product mix decisions such as the one made by Magic Chef rest on the perspective that companies have of the product-market conditions they face. A key factor in Magic Chef's decision was the growing demand from home builders for a complete array of appliances from one source. Magic Chef's product policy was to offer a **product mix** that was sufficient to meet buyer needs.

Product mix decisions are usually the most important and fundamental of all marketing strategy decisions. Other marketing mix decision areas such as pricing and promotion build product mix decisions.

Among the important decisions regarding the product mix are decisions regarding width, depth, and internal consistency. *Width* refers to the number of types of products that are often organized into product lines. A major consumer products firm offers cake mixes, soups, salad dressings, and 17 other product types. The width of its product mix is 20 product types. Management may decide to offer one or more product lines to one or more target markets. Snap-on Tools Corporation offers one line of hand tools to one target market—mechanics. At the other extreme, Steel Company of Canada, Ltd. offers multiple lines (sheet steel, pipe, plate, bars, rods, and wire) to match several different target markets.

The *depth* of the product mix refers to the variations within each product type. For example, the consumer goods company mentioned above offers eight flavors of salad dressings and nine cake mixes.

The *internal consistency* of the product mix is the extent to which the types of products and their variations complement one another. A company that offers motor oil and potato chips would not try to associate the two in consumers' minds. The sale of one type of product does not help the sale of the other type. In contrast, a company that makes chip dip available in the grocery display space for potato chips not only complements its product but also creates a synergistic relationship, with more sales resulting for both types of items.

The overall product mix has a major effect on the image of the organization, and that image, as seen by customers, helps spell success or failure in the marketplace. The entire product mix is further enhanced by lines that consistently portray quality or reliability or a good buy for the money. Levi Strauss & Company introduced several new product lines (men's accessories, women's wear, and active sportswear) in recent years to capitalize on an overall company image of quality and value.

How wide and deep should a product mix be? The answer varies from market to market and with the related costs. If a company had to be concerned only with generating demand, it would offer an extensive array of types of products and variations of each to meet the wants and needs of all the customers in its target markets. But costs rise as each new line and item is offered, so the decision is based on estimates of additional revenue as compared to the additional costs.

Product Line

Magic Chef defined one **product line** (within its product mix) as ranges and ovens. Various range and oven combinations were offered, as well as microwave ovens. This product line could have been defined more broadly, with refrigerators, ranges, and dishwashers grouped together to meet the needs of homebuilders. Determination of the common relationship among products in a **product line** is based on managerial judgment. Yet the groupings become extremely important because similar marketing strategies typically are used for all the products in the same product line.

Among the types of decisions made regarding product lines are decisions regarding the length of the line, decisions regarding the positioning of products within the line, and decisions regarding whether to drop products.

Product Line Length.   Each product line should be effectively targeted toward defined markets, to minimize market overlap between products. If McDonald's Corporation introduced a variation on its Big Mac with, say, a spicy sauce, the new version would cut into the existing market for the Big Mac. This is *product cannibalization,* one product in a line eating away at the sale of another. Perhaps it was to avoid product cannibalization that McDonald's offered Chicken McNuggets rather than a product that would directly compete with the Big Mac. The intent was to capture new customers and not cannibalize existing products.

There are typically forces at work that tend to lengthen product lines over time. Entrepreneur John Koss, producer and marketer of Koss stereophones, refers to this as the "might as well" phenomenon.[10] On the surface, the addition of products may appear to be very natural. We "might as well" use our existing product expertise to serve a new market niche. Or we "might as well" use up idle production capacity. Or we "might as well" modify an existing product to meet the needs of another customer group. "Might as wells," without careful study, become disasters.

In some respects, it is worse when a product does not fail but just never succeeds. A product of this kind can sap management energies and profits without becoming a clear-cut product drop candidate. So product lines sometimes evolve into less-than-rational assortments, with poor performers limping along and products poorly positioned relative to each other.

Positioning.   When positioning products within a line, major cannibalization should be avoided and positioning should be made to optimize the number of products offered to target markets. Identifying gaps in the marketplace that justify product line additions is part of good marketing management, and gaps may be identified through attribute analysis of competitive products. Product lines may be characterized by their positioning on a price/quality continuum, and line-stretching decisions can be made in the hopes of capturing a lower or higher part of the market. IBM with its PC Jr. unsuccessfully stretched its PC line to the lower end of the market, the home user. American auto producers would like to stretch their lines to cover the upper end of the auto market, occupied by Mercedes and others, but face formidable challenges in doing so.

Product Drop Decisions. Eventually, all products reach the end of profitable lives. Even Ivory Soap will one day die. Whatever the reason for the demise, phasing out weak products calls for careful planning. Candidates for elimination from a firm's line are identified through management's regular monitoring of product performance. Once such candidates have been identified, there are typically considerable resources at stake when a drop decision is made:

- Du Pont's termination of the production of Corfam, a synthetic leather substitute for shoes, at a loss of about $100 million.

- General Motors' sale of its Frigidaire appliance business to White Consolidated Industries, Inc.

- RCA's exit from the videodisc market at a total loss of $780 million.

Decisions to drop a product are difficult. Sometimes powerful arguments for retaining products are given by the sales force, by manufacturing, and by other areas of the organization. Furthermore, the measurement of product performance is complex. A product's real contribution to operating results is difficult to determine because the product's sales and costs are interrelated with those of other products. Yet the elimination of a product can make important profit contributions and free scarce marketing resources for higher-priority needs.

As part of the marketing control process, product performance should be evaluated against standards on a regular basis. The results of such evaluation can lead to three possible actions—continue to market the product, modify the product to remedy the problem, or phase out the product (Exhibit 13–6). The option selected depends on what shows up during the evaluation.

Evaluation Criteria and Procedures. The criteria for evaluating product performance generally fall into these five groups:

- *Performance.* This could include analysis of sales and market share trends, profit contribution, financial requirements to support the product, cost and price trends.

- *Product Line/Mix.* This could mean examination of the market impact of a drop decision on sales of the firm's other products, customer needs for the product, and product/brand image contributed by the product.

- *Operations.* Analysis is needed to determine the impact on production operations and marketing activities, the demands on management time, servicing requirements, and the alternative uses of resources made available by a drop.

- *Channel Participants and Suppliers.* Assessment is made of the impact of a product drop on channel relationships, sales and profit impact of a drop on channel members, and the probable reaction of suppliers to a drop.

- *Competitive.* Advantages that a drop provides to competition are assessed.

EXHIBIT 13-6 Evaluation of Existing Products

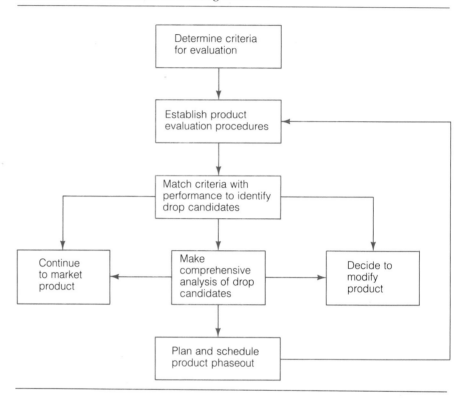

Some of these criteria can be quantified; for others, such as the impact of a proposed product drop on channel relationships, only a more subjective evaluation is possible. The selection of the criteria for a product drop should be based on assessment of the factors that relate to product performance in a particular firm. Since these factors may involve economic, market, and technical performance, a team of executives representing top management and the various functional areas of the firm should select and assign weights to the criteria.

Formal procedures should be established for regular monitoring of the firm's products. An evaluation team made up of representatives of key functional areas in the firm can review data on the performance of products and apply the criteria. How often this team meets depends on the rate of change in the product life cycle and in historical product performance. This varies from firm to firm. An annual review is usually a minimum time span; longer intervals may be appropriate, depending on the situation.

Matching Criteria with Performance.   The criteria set by management are used to measure the performance of existing products. When a company has

EXHIBIT 13-7 Product Rankings Generated Using the PRESS Model

Product	Total Contribution Margin ($)	Percent of Total (CM)	Cost of Facilities Used (FC)	Percent of Total (FC)	Selection Index*
810	$37,065.60	15.45%	60.15	4.78%	49.94
927	20,021.80	8.35	22.16	1.76	39.56
812	24,948.10	10.40	95.64	7.60	14.23
801	16,909.80	7.05	52.19	4.15	11.98
813	9,229.59	3.89	24.33	1.93	7.82
802	14,919.10	6.22	62.77	4.99	7.75
815	11.767.60	4.91	48.26	3.84	6.27
811	12,740.90	5.31	65.27	5.19	5.44
807	12,026.60	5.01	58.69	4.66	5.39
808	11,315.10	4.72	55.25	4.39	5.07
914	9,049.04	3.77	41.90	3.33	4.27
959	9,581.52	3.99	55.62	4.42	3.61
951	5,275.66	2.20	17.54	1.39	3.47
806	6,273.96	2.62	25.59	2.03	3.36
805	5,843.32	2.44	25.83	2.05	2.89
960	4,635.12	1.93	20.00	1.59	2.35
923	5,048.00	2.10	27.41	2.18	2.03
809	5,311.16	2.21	34.53	2.74	1.79
814	5,392.80	2.25	36.40	2.89	1.75
803	3,757.65	1.57	71.73	5.70	0.43
926	1,325.35	0.55	9.05	0.72	0.42
952	3,242.56	1.35	107.88	8.57	0.21
917	2,602.95	1.09	76.53	6.08	0.19
922	837.25	0.35	76.63	6.09	0.02
804	655.98	0.27	86.82	6.90	0.01
		100.00%		100.00%	

* The most profitable products have the largest selection indexes.

Source: Reprinted by permission from Paul W. Hamelmann and Edward M. Mazze, "Improving Product Abandonment Decisions," *Journal of Marketing* 36 (April 1972), pp. 20–26. Published by the American Marketing Association.

a large product mix, performance assessment should be done in steps, the first step being to quickly screen for possible drop candidates. It would be too costly and time-consuming to perform a comprehensive analysis for each product of a wholesale food or drug firm because of the thousands of products involved.

Computer models have been developed for screening when evaluative criteria and performance information can be quantified. The Product Review and Evaluation Subsystem (PRESS) model is one computerized approach to identifying product deletion candidates.[11] It utilizes standard cost accounting and marketing information to generate product rankings of the type shown in Exhibit 13-7. The products with low selection indexes (1.0 or less) are considered for elimination from the firm's line of products. The selection index (SIN) is calculated by using the following formula:

$$SIN_i = \frac{CM_i/\Sigma CM_i}{FC_i/\Sigma FC_i} \times (CM_i/\Sigma CM_i)$$

where:

SIN$_i$ = Selection index number for product i

CM$_i$ = Contribution margin for product i

FC$_i$ = Facilities costs for product i

ΣCM$_i$ = Summation of contribution margins of all products

ΣFC$_i$ = Summation of facilities costs of all products[12]

If products A and B have equal contribution margins, but A's facilities cost are double those of B, then A's SIN value will be one half that of B.

Depending on the particular evaluation criteria that are appropriate in a given firm, factors other than facilities costs could be used, such as shelf space or floor space in a retail firm. The PRESS model can also apply available subjective and historical data to examine price-volume relationships, sales trends, and product complementarity and substitutability.

Evaluation teams help ensure that the assessment process considers the impact of a proposed product drop on various areas of the firm (production, finance, marketing, personnel). Since it is impossible to quantify all of the evaluative criteria, the teams must subjectively assess the impact of the drop on customers, competitors, and suppliers.

Planning a Product Phaseout.   The phaseout of a product must be planned for and coordinated. Management may choose one of three possible strategies. First, selling the product to another firm may enhance the financial attractiveness of the product elimination decision. This strategy has been followed by many firms seeking to restructure their product mixes, as illustrated by Westinghouse's sale of its appliance business. Second, if selling a product is not feasible, management may decide to phase it out gradually, allowing time for inventory reduction, facilities conversion, assisting customers in finding new sources of supply, and other internal restructuring. Finally, it may be necessary in some instances to bite the bullet by rapidly eliminating the product and accepting the consequences. When Outboard Marine Corporation dropped its snowmobile line, the financial consequences were substantial.

Specific Product Attributes

Decisions concerning specific products and their attributes are the final level in product policy. Numerous attributes of an existing product may be changed to rekindle interest in it and to improve its image in the marketplace. Which attributes are important varies by the type of product. For stereo headphones, the key attributes include sound quality, durability, and wearing comfort. Dramatic improvement in headphone sound quality in recent years has forced producers to constantly strive to be at the cutting edge. Koss Corporation targeted its headphones primarily at the higher quality end of the product spectrum, although they span several price categories. It also added new attributes, among them a warning light that indicates when the sound level can be dangerous to one's ears.

Such improvements in product attributes typically occur because management is pursuing one or more of the following strategies:

■ *Programmed Change.* Regular changes in styling and features may be programmed annually or less often to stimulate sales. Automobiles and appliances illustrate the programmed approach to product modification.

■ *Product Life-Cycle Alteration.* Product improvements may be used as a strategy to maintain or improve sales and profits for products that have reached the maturity stage. This strategy is aimed at giving a lift to mature products and at delaying or avoiding the decline stage of the product life cycle.

■ *Leader in Technology.* Some companies invest heavily in research and development aimed at advances in technology and make regular improvements at all stages of the life cycle. Hewlett-Packard, the electronic instrument manufacturer, makes product development and the improvement of existing products major corporate objectives.

■ *Environmental Pressures.* Management may initiate product modifications in response to changing environmental conditions. Concern over energy conservation caused some firms to reduce the energy consumption of their products.

The planning process associated with making product improvements is similar to new product planning (Chapter 12), but there is usually less uncertainty about the product's performance in the marketplace. Nevertheless, product improvement decisions are often subjected to in-depth analysis, much like that for new products.

Branding Strategies and Decisions

Branding and packaging are increasing in strategic importance. We live in a world of brands that convey various meanings to consumer and industrial buyers. There are several terms associated with branding, and they are often used loosely:

■ *Brand.* A broad term encompassing most ways of identifying a product, such as its name, design, or symbol. A product's brand distinguishes it from the offerings of competitors.

■ *Brand Name.* The part of the brand that can be vocalized, such as "Ford" or "Nike."

■ *Brand mark.* The part of a brand identification that cannot be vocalized, such as a symbol, design, coloring, or lettering.

■ *Trademark.* The exclusive legal right to use a brand name or a brand mark. The golden arches of McDonald's and Puma brand footwear are trademarks registered with the U.S. Patent Office.

■ *Copyright.* The sole legal right to reproduce and sell a literary or artistic expression.

Common law may be used to protect brand names and brand marks, but it is legally advisable to register trademarks (good for 20 years and renewable) with the U.S. Patent and Trademark Office. Over 50,000 applications are received each year. Trademarks are typically used to register brand names and marks, although copyrights are sometimes used for such marks as artistic labeling.

Why Branding?

A few decades ago, very few products were branded, but today the branding of products is common. Why do firms make the investment? There are several important reasons:

■ Market identity. A brand helps position a company's product offering in terms of price level, quality, service, prestige, and other factors that are important to buyers in the firm's target markets. Consumers often use brand image as a proxy for quality and dependability, particularly if they find it difficult to evaluate the product because of its newness or complexity.

■ To legally protect a name or symbol for which huge promotional expenditures may have been made.

■ To create a basis for building customer brand loyalty for a successful brand, which can be an important competitive strategy. Repeat sales become more likely, and the position of other company products may also be enhanced.

■ Different brands may be used to serve different market niches. Similar products such as soft drinks with different brands can help provide a sufficient array of alternatives to increase sales in many markets.

■ Brand identity may itself increase margins and profits by enhancing the perception of quality.

■ Identity in the marketplace helps ensure that customers will demand the product from distributors, thus strengthening the producer's influence in the channel of distribution. A strong brand image helps "pull" manufacturers' products through the channel of distribution by establishing recognition and preferences among consumer or industrial end users. This can also establish powerful bargaining positions with suppliers and distributors.

It should not be assumed that a product *must* be branded. Although there are numerous advantages to branding, with some products a name identity can be de-emphasized and emphasis placed on other marketing mix elements instead. Offering a lower price is the most common strategy for unbranded or

EXHIBIT 13–8

Fannie May would like to remind you that February 14th is this Saturday.

Brand loyalty helped Fannie May expand operations from its historically concentrated market in the Midwest to new shops in Florida.

Courtesy Fannie May Candy Shops.

generic products. The grocery industry has offered lower-priced generic items for consumers who are willing to forgo the quality assurance and risk reduction that goes with branding.

Manufacturer's Brand versus Distributor's Brand

Strategy options differ according to who in the channel undertakes the effort to build brand name and image. Once the decision has been made to use a branding strategy, it must be determined whether this will be done at the producer or distributor level.

Producer branding involves building brand identity by applying a corporate brand to products. Several corporate giants have used this approach, particularly those that market to other firms, such as U.S. Steel, Exxon, and the Carrier Corporation. Seiko, the watch manufacturer, has done an impressive job in developing brand identity using its corporate name. A privately held boxed chocolates company, Fannie May Candy Shops Inc., both produces and retails chocolates that enjoy intense brand loyalty (Exhibit 13–8).

EXHIBIT 13-9 Apparel Branding and Changing Markets

When Bill Blass decided to sell a new line of pantyhose to off-price retailers, he did so at great peril.

Many people in the retailing and designing establishment consider clothes manufacturers who deal with the hated offpricers and other discounters downright evil. By doing so, Mr. Blass was risking his good name and the premium price that the name commands. Makers of brand-name and designer clothing have been caught in a cross fire between price-conscious consumers and full-price retailers, some of whom drop brand names that deal with discounters. The retail establishment has put further heat on designers by developing high-quality private-label goods that sometimes threaten to crowd designer names off the shelves.

Although national brand names account for a minority of U.S. apparel sales, they remain the backbone of retailing, the lures that draw customers to the store. Such merchandise is well advertised and often heavily promoted nationally. In contrast, private-label merchandise is sold by individual chains and stores. Few stores sell private labels alone, and some big mass merchandisers, such as Sears, Roebuck & Co. and J. C. Penney Company, have turned to national brands to polish their image or attract new customers.

Brand names have thrived since World War II, thanks to a surging economy and an affluent, free-spending baby-boom generation. But times made consumers thriftier and the success of off-price stores makes them difficult for clothes makers to ignore. But prestigious brand-name labels risk losing the "in" crowd by marketing to this lowbrow end of the market. They also risk incurring the wrath of the big retailers they depend on.

Source: Adapted from Steve Weiner, "Caught in a Cross Fire, Brand-Apparel Makers Design Their Defenses," *The Wall Street Journal,* January 24, 1984, pp. 1, 12. Reprinted by permission of *The Wall Street Journal,* © Dow Jones & Company, Inc. All rights reserved.

Private or distributor branding allows another channel member to put its brand on a product. Large retailers such as Sears establish contractual arrangements with suppliers to manufacture products that bear the retailer's name. The Kellwood Company produces apparel and related products primarily for Sears. The term *national brands* refers to nationally promoted products, whether at the distributor or producer level.

A firm may also pursue a combination of manufacturer and private branding. Whirlpool has its own brand but also sells appliances under the Sears name. At the retail level, K mart has created in-store comparisons by displaying nationally known manufacturer brands side by side with less expensive but similar private label K mart brands. Whereas manufacturer brands used to dominate the marketplace, powerful retailers that control shelf space and price-conscious consumers have helped build private brands into a substantial market position. This battle of the brands goes on, with distributors continuing to gain share. An example of producer-distributor conflict is presented in Exhibit 13-9.

Individual Brand versus Family Brand

Whether at the manufacturer or distributor level, another branding decision concerns the pros and cons of having "family" branding as opposed to having separate, individual brands for each product.

Family branding involves establishing brands for product groupings or particular product lines—Sears Kenmore appliances and Craftsman tools or Levi Strauss & Co.'s wide use of its brand across several clothing and accessory categories. Company names often become the family brand (Caterpillar tractors). Individual branding involves having separate brand names for each product. Procter & Gamble is well known for its many independent brands—Tide, Cheer, Oxydol, Gain, Bold, and Ivory Snow. A company may also use a combination of family branding and individual branding by having different product brands and affiliating them with an umbrella reference, such as the corporate name.

Individual product branding may be used to better position brands for particular target markets, or it may simply be a means of offering a variety of brands to buyers. Apparel manufacturers use brand names to appeal to different price/quality target markets. Hartmarx produces men's clothing under several different labels, including Hickey Freeman, Hart Schaffner & Marx, Society Brand, Ltd., Johnny Carson, Christian Dior, and Jack Nicklaus. Care must be taken not to offer too many brands that compete for the same markets. Otherwise, cannibalization of the sales of existing brands will occur, with an insufficient increase in total sales to justify a new brand introduction. In the mid-1980s, Procter & Gamble was watching to see how much damage its new Liquid Tide would do to its powdered Tide brand. The advantages of having several individual brands must also be weighed against the substantial development and promotional costs of maintaining them.

Family branding is more economical than individual branding, and with this type of branding, new products can to some extent live off the reputation of existing products. The collective image may also have a greater impact on customer awareness and recognition. Firms sometimes initiate *brand extension strategies*, using a strong existing brand name as a major advantage with new product introductions. Honda has introduced several new products in recent years, using its reputation for quality as an entry wedge. Gerber Products Company, best known for its baby food, has successfully extended its brand name to baby apparel furniture and day-care centers.[13] Observers in the mid-1980s attributed an increase in the use of brand extensions to a growing demand for quality assurance by consumers.[14] Extensions hitting the market included Ivory shampoo, Hershey chocolate milk (powder), and Mr. Coffee coffee. Also, major companies were, for the first time, spending millions to associate their corporate name with various brands (Nabisco Brands, Inc. with its Oreo cookies, Planters nuts, and Fleischmann's margarine; Beatrice Company with its Samsonite luggage, Martha White grits, and Stiffel lamps).

On the minus side, if a problem arises with one item, the negative effects can cause problems for the entire family brand. Serving target markets of different quality levels with the same brand is usually counterproductive. The battle for retailer shelf space may be more difficult to wage if there are not several independent brands, each with a loyal customer following. Finally, associating different types of products can confuse an existing image. In sum, the decision between family and individual brands (or a combination) is complex, with major trade-offs between costs and the potential market impact.

Packaging Strategy and Decisions

A final major product decision area concerns packaging. Most goods must be packaged. Furniture is protected by shipping cartons; pop-top cans provide drinks to purchasers; and the L'eggs container became a revolutionary success in the distribution of women's stockings. Whipped dessert topping is provided in aerosol cans, and gourmet dinners are available on trays ready for the microwave oven. The day of the country general store with its bulk containers of apples, pickles, and candy are long gone. There are several reasons for this:

■ *Store Efficiency.* It usually takes less labor to package items at the point of production rather than one by one as they are purchased at retail.

■ *Self-Service.* When stores went to self-service, packages had to help create a product identity and market the product.

■ *Convenience for Customers.* Affluent, time-conscious consumers have become more and more willing to pay for the convenience of packaged goods.

■ *Shelf-Space Battle.* As retail shelf space became scarce, retailers began to consider the package in deciding what to stock. The value of the package as a marketing tool and its ease of stacking are important.

■ *Strict Safety and Contamination Guidelines.* Government regulations have meant stricter distribution guidelines with required changes in packaging. The Tylenol-related deaths contributed to added voluntary design measures.

Packaging
is the process of designing the container(s) for a product.

There are three levels of physical **packaging**.[15] The first level is the *primary package*, the materials that envelop the product and hold it. This could be a Snickers candy bar wrapper or a Coca-Cola can. The *secondary package* is packaging that holds the primary package for transportation or display. A cardboard box that holds a medicine bottle (of Bayer aspirin) is a secondary package, as is a plastic bag that holds a pound of individually wrapped candies. The *tertiary packaging* is the bulk packaging—a cardboard box or pallet—that holds secondary packages for shipments. Sometimes the primary, secondary, and tertiary packages are combined, and usually at least two levels of packaging are used.

Packaging Strategy

Management must first decide what strategic and support roles its packaging should occupy. What functions should be performed, and in what degree, by the three types of packages?

Aid New Product Strategy. Some packaging is such an integral part of the product that it becomes a major part of new product strategies. Aerosol deodorants versus the *nonaerosol* spray packages are good examples. Kimberly-Clark's Kleenex tissues were successfully introduced in pop-up decorative boxes. Also consider the role of packaging in the motor oil industry:

"Say goodbye to America's favorite can of motor oil" trumpeted Quaker State Oil Refining Corporation in its advertising.

Quaker State wasn't urging drivers to abandon the company's best-selling motor oil. But its old green and white cans were about to become obsolete. Quaker State motor oil will be sold in plastic bottles.

Already the country's largest processor of motor oil, Quaker State was counting on its plastic bottles to attract new customers. The company's research shows that consumers not only prefer the plastic bottle, but may switch to Quaker State if their usual brand isn't available in plastic. The company hopes to increase its 21 percent share of the $2.2-billion-a-year industry by as much as 6 percentage points. Competitors of Quaker State took note. Pennzoil Company, the nation's second-largest motor-oil processor with 18 percent of the market, hired a design firm to create a new package.

Most people used to overlook the inconvenience because they bought oil at service stations, where the attendant took care of the spout and can. But today, 68 percent of all oil used by owners of cars and light trucks is purchased in quart containers at supermarkets, drug chains, auto parts stores, and discount department stores.[16]

Provide Access to Channels.   Packaging can open up new distribution channels, such as through vending machines. Characteristics of packaging—protection against pilferage, ease of shelf stacking, and convenient price marking—determine whether or not distributors will agree to handle the product. Shelf life is also often determined by the type of packaging.[17]

Support Pricing Strategy.   Package size decisions, such as offering 7- or 16-ounce drink cans, often relate to price positioning decisions. Premium quality and design packaging can contribute to being able to ask a premium price.

Serve as Part of Promotion.   The size, shape, design, and wording on a package can convey a particular image, not unlike advertising itself. Advance consumer testing of packaging is often conducted, in part to evaluate the image it portrays. Packages are often eye-catching, they create awareness, and they are informative. Key product attributes are often highlighted on packages to encourage trial purchases. Otto Roth & Co., distributor of Beaux Villages cheeses, found in research that most consumers did not understand the different types of premium cheeses, such as Brie, Gouda, and Muenster. It therefore developed special packaging with descriptive labels to help take away the mystery.[18]

Provide Protection and Containment.   Probably the most basic of packaging functions is protection. Virtually all products need protection, even bags of potting soil in garden centers. Another basic function of packaging is to hold products in specified quantities for transporting. Physical distribution considerations are vital to marketing success.

Provide Information to Customers. Packaging usually provides important information to customers regarding use, misuse, guarantees, and ingredients. This provides yet another opportunity to be of assistance to customers and thereby enhance the product.

Packaging Decisions

The basic packaging strategy, that of deciding how much weight to give each of the above roles, provides a foundation for tactical decisions. The packaging strategy must, of course, complement the overall product and marketing strategy and be carefully targeted to well-defined and well-understood target markets.

Packaging is often a very important element of the marketing mix, and its role in strategy should be explicitly defined. For the most part, the way packaging decisions are made parallels the new product development process. The following steps are usually required to develop a specific container design.[19]

Get Organized. Because so many organizational areas are involved in packaging decisions, they are best coordinated at a high level, rather than solely in the marketing department. As is true of other product decisions, packaging decisions often involve the highest-level executives in addition to marketing, physical distribution, manufacturing, research and development, legal, and purchasing personnel. Outside the firm, advertising agencies, distributors, and specialized engineers may be involved. It is therefore important for top management to give coordination a strong endorsement.

Conduct Packaging Research. Formal and informal marketing research is often needed to help position the product, brand, and package among competitive offerings. Advertising and image-related research may be carried out, as may package usage tests. Technical and engineering tests may be required. Colgate toothpaste's "pump" package had to be carefully tested.

Develop Graphics and Copy. Color, illustrations, and copy wording must be consistent with the overall image desired. Orville Redenbacher popcorn, for example, has a package with old-fashioned printing and homey coloring and is personalized with Redenbacher's picture.

Develop Physical Package. The container itself must meet the needs of customers and distributors. The physical design includes shape, size, materials, and color. Like graphics, the physical design must be functional, yet reflect the image desired. Package designs can sometimes be patented or trademarked.

Test the Design in the Market.   Marketing research using in-store tests or indirect psychological methods or obtaining distributor feedback is often appropriate before going to market with a packaging design. To obtain valid information, the tests must usually be subtle and indirect, rather than forthrightly asking customers which design is preferred. Packaging testing is sometimes part of an overall product concept test or test market.

Do an Environmental Check.   Environmental factors can constrain as well as dictate marketing decisions. Throughout the above steps, attention must be given to consumer and legal issues, including packaging safety, disposable packaging (e.g., biodegradable), the quantity of packaging, littering, and avoidance of misleading labeling and an unrealistic impression of the quantity purchased.

Application

A Product Decision[20]

Coca-Cola's decision to reintroduce Classic Coke clearly confirms that consumer perceptions of products are derived from a hierarchy of perceptions. Part of the extended product, the Coca-Cola company image and its position in the American culture, was underestimated. The tangible attributes of the product received considerable management attention, but the extended product perceptions held by consumers led to negative satisfaction from dropping the original Coke and substituting the new. Over-focus on product attributes and momentary consumer perceptions can be dangerous. Blind taste tests with 190,000 consumers had shown that the majority preferred the new recipe. (The tests also showed that only about half of the population has taste buds sensitive enough to distinguish between Coke and Pepsi.) But the extended product foundation for consumer product perceptions proved more powerful than analysis of specific attributes.

The New Coke experience also underscored the importance of product decisions to the entire corporation. Within a few days of announcing the return of Classic Coke, the company began an elaborate research effort to determine how the events had affected its overall reputation and its credibility with consumers. Although part of the marketing mix, product decisions involve the highest level of management.

The challenge to management was to effectively make key product line and branding decisions. In 1982, Diet Coke was introduced, the first brand extension to borrow the prized Coke trademark. Diet Coke quickly became the nation's number three soft drink. The advantages of branding were apparent. But the return of Classic Coke was different. There was concern that the return of the original version might irreparably discredit New Coke. The decision could also have been viewed as proof that management had doubts about both products.

The most optimistic view at the time was that the Coca-Cola brand perception would not be damaged and that even given the cannibalization effects of the Coke Classic on the New Coke, Coke would capture more retail shelf space and more customers with both products than it would have with just one of them. By the end of 1985, New Coke had a 15 percent market share and Classic Coke had 5.9 percent, for a total of 20.9 percent. In the previous year, the original Coke had had a 21.7 percent share, although that share was gradually declining. Because of the two Cokes, Pepsi became the nation's best-selling single soft drink in 1985, with a share of 18.6 percent. Sales for all of the Coca-Cola Company family and independent brands rose to 30.7 percent against Pepsi's 24.7 percent, giving Coca-Cola a greater lead than it had held previously. Each market share point was worth about $250 million in retail sales.[21]

The management of Coca-Cola had undoubtedly planned for years how to best announce what was actually a product modification. New Coke was a competitive repositioning of the product, with focus on the sweetness attribute. But it was presented to consumers as a new product, and most consumers perceived it in that light. One cannot help but wonder what the outcome would have been if the newness of New Coke had been downplayed or if New Coke had been introduced as just another brand extension with no immediate plan to phase out the original Coke. Yet given the company's marketing prowess, Coca-Cola may still become a net winner ■

Summary

A product is anything that is potentially valued by a target market for the benefits or satisfactions it provides. The term *product* includes objects, services, organizations, places, people, and ideas. Customers perceive products in terms of the satisfaction they provide, their tangible attributes, and their extended product dimensions.

A product policy should be developed that addresses what types of products to offer and how to group individual products to take advantage of marketing strategy commonalities in reaching targeted markets. Basic groupings of consumer goods are convenience, shopping, specialty, and unsought goods. There are also a number of industrial product groupings. Basic marketing strategy commonalities apply to each grouping.

The services sector of the U.S. economy is growing rapidly. Marketing services involves several unique aspects, among which are intangibility, product-consumption blending, and different forms of distribution channels.

There are several levels of product planning decisions—deciding the product mix, product lines, specific items within the lines, and the product attributes for each item. Product mix decisions determine the full collection of product lines and items offered by the organization and involve deciding the width, depth, and internal consistency of the mix. Product lines are groups of products that are related in some way—because they fulfill a given market need, employ similar distribution approaches, or belong to a common price category. Major product line decisions are determining line length, product positioning within the line, and whether to drop existing products. Product and attribute changes are often made to revitalize an aging product line. Product improvement decisions parallel the new product decision process described in the previous chapter, although they are usually less detailed and complex.

Brand identity and packaging are major product decisions, particularly for consumer product companies. Among the major branding decisions are determining the channel level at which to brand a product (manufacturer or distributor) and the extent to which to develop individual brands rather than a family brand.

Like branding, packaging has risen in importance in recent decades. Primary, secondary, and tertiary packages fulfill the functions of providing protection and containment, aiding new product strategy, obtaining channel access, complementing pricing strategies and promotion, and providing customer information. The packaging decision steps include getting organized, conducting packaging research, developing graphics and copy, developing the physical package, testing the package in the market, and doing an environmental check.

Product decisions provide the foundation and the rationale for designing entire marketing programs. Management's choice of products, the extent of its commitment to new product development, and the target markets for each product offering establish the basis for shaping marketing strategy. This chapter and the previous chapter have examined product planning. The product planning process follows a sequence of finding new product ideas, developing and introducing the products that are most promising, improving them over time, and eliminating them when they no longer fulfill needs.

Exercises for Review and Discussion

1. The "customer perception hierarchy" discussed in the chapter has significant managerial implications. Cite some specific implications of adopting a hierarchical view for marketing the following products: *(a)* automobile cassette tape decks, *(b)* high-quality gourmet frozen dinners, and *(c)* personal computer repair service.

2. The president of a medium-sized firm that manufactures bicycles was considering a proposal from Sears that it become the primary seller of the company's bicycle line. The agreement included allowing Sears to put its name on all of the bicycles it sold. The company used its own brand name, Hill Master Bikes, and sold through bicycle specialty stores. Its distribution was limited to 18 states in the Southeast and the Southwest. How should the president decide whether to accept Sears' proposal? Discuss the advantages of private branding through Sears versus continuing the Hill Master branding strategy.

3. Bondurant Brothers, a wholesaler of kitchen and bathroom construction supplies and appliances, has a product mix of over 2,000 items. Management has had difficulty in managing this large and diverse assortment. Suppliers are constantly proposing that the company carry new products. The president has asked for recommendations on how to monitor the current product assortment so as to identify products that might be dropped to make room for new products. What suggestions do you have for the president? Discuss your answer.

4. Higher-priced items are now appearing in convenience stores as "convenience goods." Identify some of these products from your own experience, and cite the product classification that they were formerly in. Discuss possible marketing implications due to these class changes.

5. A product such as a heavy-duty battery for consumer or industrial use can fall into both consumer and industrial goods categories. Identify and discuss several products that could fall into both of these categories, and based on material in this chapter, outline strategy differences that would probably exist between the two classifications.

6. Over the past few years, car leasing has increased in popularity for a number of reasons. Leasing provides both a vehicle and maintenance-free worries for the lessee. Based on your understanding of automobile leasing, would you classify this item as a product or a service? Why? Discuss your answer.

7. A major packaging change in recent years was Campbell Soup's elimination of metal cans in favor of plastic containers. Given the discussion of packaging functions in this chapter, discuss the benefits and advantages that probably resulted from this change.

8. Over the past decade, the U.S. economy has evolved to the point where most of the GNP comes from the service sector rather than from manufacturing. Discuss the changes in marketing that have accompanied this trend.

Notes

1. This example is based on John Koten and Scott Kilman, "How Coke's Decision to Offer Two Colas Undid 4½ Years of Planning," *The Wall Street Journal*, pp. 1, 13.

2. This section is based on E. Jerome McCarthy and William D. Perreault, Jr., *Basic Marketing*, 8th ed. (Homewood, Ill.: Richard D. Irwin, 1984), pp. 291–305.

3. Thomas E. Caruso, "New Services Marketing Division Will Help AMA Lead Growing Area," *Marketing News*, April 27, 1984, pp. 1, 13.

4. Joseph Neubauer, "Services: The New Management Challenge," Fourth Annual Conference, Strategic Management Society, The Wharton School, University of Pennsylvania, 1985.

5. Leonard L. Berry, "Services Marketing Is Different," *Business*, May–June 1980, p. 29.

6. G. Lynn Shostack, "Breaking Free from Product Marketing," *Journal of Marketing* 41 (April 1977), pp. 73–80.

7. W. Earl Sasser, "Match Supply and Demand in Service Industries," *Harvard Business Review*, November–December 1976, p. 138.

8. Christopher H. Lovelock, *Services Marketing* (Englewood Cliffs, N.J.: Prentice-Hall, 1983), p. 5.

9. Magic Chef, Inc., *Stockholders' Report*.

10. Presentation by John Koss, president and CEO of Koss Corporation, at the University of Illinois at Chicago, May 8, 1984.

11. See, for example, Paul W. Hammelmann and Edward M. Mazze, "Improving Product Abandonment Decisions," *Journal of Marketing* 36 (April 1972), pp. 20–26.

12. Ibid., p. 23.

13. John Gorman, "Gerber Isn't Kidding about Diversification," *Chicago Tribune*, December 9, 1985, Business Section, p. 5.

14. Ronald Alsop, "Firms Unveil More Products Associated with Brand Names," *The Wall Street Journal*, December 13, 1984, p. 27.

15. C. Merle Crawford, *New Products Management* (Homewood, Ill.: Richard D. Irwin, 1983), p. 595.

16. Abstracted from Susan Casey, "Quaker State's Move to Plastic Containers Shakes Up Lucrative Motor-Oil Business," *The Wall Street Journal*, May 2, 1984, p. 31. Reprinted by permission of *The Wall Street Journal*, © Dow Jones & Company, Inc., 1984. All rights reserved.

17. Robert D. Hisrich and Michael P. Peters, *Marketing Decisions for New and Mature Products* (Columbus, Ohio: Charles E. Merrill Publishing, 1984), p. 308.

18. "Packing Educates Supermarket Shoppers about the Subtleties of Specialty Cheeses," *Marketing News*, November 22, 1985, p. 22. Published by the American Marketing Association.

19. For more information on the subject, see Crawford, *New Products Management*, pp. 596–99.

20. Based on Koten and Kilman, "Coke's Decision," pp. 1, 13; and Ronald Alsop, "Coke's Flip-Flop Underscores Risks of Consumer Taste Tests," *The Wall Street Journal*, July 18, 1985, p. 23.

21. "Classic Example of Division Puts Pepsi's Cola out Front," *Chicago Tribune*, January 28, 1986, Business Section, p. 2.

CHAPTER 14

Channel of Distribution Decisions

Guest Supply is the leading supplier of personal care amenities to the hotel and lodging industry.[1] The company has established a distribution channel between producers of bathroom amenities (national brands of soap and shampoo) and hotels. Guest Supply created the distribution channel by contributing marketing value to the channel relationship. The company's marketing strategy of high-quality service and innovative supply of bathroom amenities meets the needs of hotels, motels, and resort areas. Guest Supply demonstrated to clients the value of offering lodging guests an attractive and functional group of in-room amenities that add a special touch to a traveler's lodging experience. Guest Supply's strategy begins with an initial consultation to determine what a hotel's requirements are, how it conducts business, and what types of amenities would be most suitable for its guests. After establishing the client's profile, Guest Supply designs an amenity program that corresponds to the hotel's image. The program recommendation is implemented after approval by the client. Guest Supply's customer service department monitors all phases of production to ensure on-time delivery and customer satisfaction.

Channel of distribution decisions are of vital importance to all types of firms—producers, wholesalers, and retailers. Each member of a channel is a link in a distribution network of organizations that extends from the producer to the end users of products or services. Although some firms perform all channel functions, typically several organizations are linked together in a distribution channel to carry out the various activities of storage, transportation, sales contact, service, sorting, and repacking. Organizations that perform these marketing functions between producers and end users are called *middlemen, intermediaries,* or *resellers.*

A look at the marketing system provides an understanding of the total distribution network and the various marketing organizations that link an economy's products and services with customers. Understanding the characteristics of channels of distribution aids in determining whether to sell directly to end users or to work through marketing intermediaries. If intermediaries are used, decisions must be made on the type of distribution channel to utilize, the design, and the selection of participants.

The Marketing System

Channel of distribution
is "an organized network [system] of agencies and institutions which, in combination, perform all the activities required to link producers with users and users with producers . . . to accomplish the marketing task".²

The marketing system is made up of a vast configuration of organizations and individuals, linked together by flows of information, products, negotiations, risks, money, and people. Specific firms are aligned to form a **channel of distribution** that connects producers of products with the people and organizations that consume the products. Each channel in the marketing system seeks to satisfy the needs and wants of targeted end users, and also to meet the objectives of the channel's participants (Exhibit 14-1).

Each organization in the distribution channel performs particular activities in connecting end users with desired goods and services. Consider the firms, the functions, the flows, and the relationships involved in transforming a steer on a Texas ranch into a roast on the dinner table of a family in Washington, D.C. The animal is sold by the rancher to a feedlot operator for fattening and then purchased by a meat packer for processing. The hindquarter of the carcass or bulk packaged portions are sold to a large retail food chain, transported from a regional warehouse of the food chain to a supermarket in Washington, D.C., and processed by the supermarket butcher into steaks, roasts, and ground beef that are finally placed in the meat display case.

Marketing Intermediaries

Most of the goods and services available in a modern economy are produced at relatively few locations to obtain the cost advantages of large-scale production. New York, California, Pennsylvania, and New Jersey account for 60 percent of the apparel plants in the United States; North Carolina, Virginia, and California ship more than half of all the wood furniture produced in the United States.³ Yet buyers of apparel and furniture are widely dispersed. This creates a need for a distribution function—a way of connecting suppliers with consumers. Three options exist:

- Each producer can go directly to consumers of its products or services.
- Each consumer can go to the producers.
- Intermediaries can help perform the activities necessary to link suppliers with consumers.

The marketing system contains examples of all three approaches. For many goods and services, due to the costs involved and the types of services desired by consumers, the direct producer-consumer exchange is simply not

EXHIBIT 14-1 The Marketing System

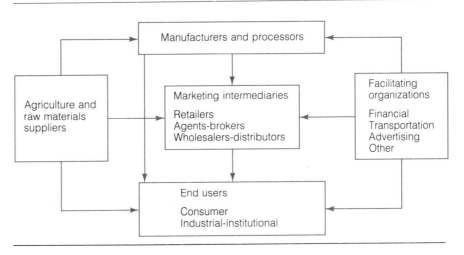

Marketing intermedi-
aries
are organizations that
perform the various
channel of distribution
functions necessary to
connect producers with
end users.

feasible. **Marketing intermediaries** form distribution channels to fill this gap between producers and end users.

Intermediaries drastically reduce the number of buyer-seller transactions. Suppose 10 customers each wanted to buy a Gant oxford button-down shirt, a pair of Calvin Klein jeans, an Aigner belt, and Bass loafers. Each person dealing directly with each manufacturer would have to conduct 4 transactions, for a total of 40. Now place a retailer between the 4 manufacturers and the 10 consumers, and the number of transactions is reduced from 40 to 14. This *transactional efficiency* is represented by the wide assortment of products carried by a Long's drugstore, a Neiman-Marcus department store, or a Kroger's supermarket. The size and complexity of the marketplace in advanced societies make the transactional function provided by intermediaries essential.

By taking advantage of the economies obtainable through large-scale purchases and specialization and by greatly reducing the number of transactions needed to bring end users and producers together, middlemen perform functions that are often not possible for manufacturers or end users.

Companies in the distribution channel perform various functions—procurement, storage, packaging, financing, transportation, and counseling. A substantial portion of the price paid by consumers for products and services is frequently accounted for by activities performed by these companies. For example, 69 cents of each dollar spent for food is used to pay for distribution and processing activities.[4] Contrary to popular opinion, most marketing intermediaries do not receive large profit margins for their services. In 1985, profit margins in pennies per dollar of sales were 4 cents for Wal-Mart Stores (discount retailer), 1 cent for the Kroger Company (food retailer) and 11 cents for McDonald's Corporation (fast-food chain).

Wetterau, Inc., the third-largest voluntary food wholesaler in the United States, is illustrative of many highly efficient marketing intermediaries that are able to operate profitably on very slim margins between revenues and costs.[5] Although Wetterau's revenues in fiscal 1985 were $3.1 billion, it has had a net profit of around a penny per dollar of sales for the past decade.

Over time, inefficient intermediaries are eliminated from the marketing system. The competitive marketplace generates new distribution alternatives when entrepreneurs see better ways to provide cost-effective services to buyers and when buyers are willing to consider different levels of customer service. Currently, one of the most rapidly expanding distribution concepts is nonstore marketing via such means as mail, telephone, vending machines, and door-to-door selling. Consumers made an estimated 15 percent of their purchases by mail in 1985.[6]

Classification of Intermediaries.   Marketing intermediaries can be classified by ownership of goods:

- *Retailers.* Businesses that buy and resell merchandise to consumer and organizational end users. Retailers may take title to goods or may handle them on a consignment basis without taking title and sell the goods on a commission basis.

- *Agents/Brokers.* Businesses that negotiate purchases or sales, or both, but do not take title to the goods in which they deal. They commonly receive a commission or fee and may or may not take physical possession of the goods they sell. Examples are brokers, selling agents, manufacturer's agents, and commission merchants.

- *Wholesalers/Distributors.* Businesses that buy and resell merchandise to retailers and other merchants or to industrial, institutional, and commercial users, but do not sell in significant amounts to end users. They normally take title to the goods they sell.

Retailers may also lease store space, as is the case with some camera departments in retail establishments. Unlike retailers and wholesalers/distributors (who take title to the goods they handle), agents/brokers, because they do not take title, do not assume market risk (the risk of price fluctuations).

Middlemen may also be classified by their level in the channel of distribution. Alternative vertical channels are shown in Exhibit 14–2. Closest to consumers and organizational end users are retailers. Manufacturers may employ salespersons for contacting wholesalers and distributors and sometimes own their sales offices and branches. If sales personnel cannot be economically justified by the sales volume and the profits from their ac-

EXHIBIT 14-2 Marketing Channels

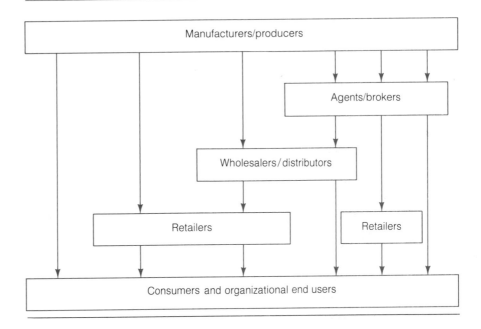

tivities (due perhaps to a limited product line), manufacturers may use agents or brokers on a commission basis.

There are important relationships between marketers at a given level of distribution. Marketers may join together for mutual advantage in voluntary groups and retailer cooperatives. Pooled buying groups include, for example, independent grocers who work cooperatively to lower the costs of goods purchased from wholesalers. Pooling of orders has allowed independent grocers to receive better prices from wholesalers and to compete with chain stores. Shopping centers also illustrate horizontal channel relationships, with the combination of stores creating a greater customer-attracting force than would the stores as separate and dispersed establishments.

Wholesaling versus Retailing.   The two principal distribution sectors are wholesalers and retailers. The retail sector includes such establishments as food stores, automotive dealers, general merchandise stores, restaurants, and specialty stores. On a dollar basis, food stores account for almost one fourth of total U.S. sales. Retail sales of food increased from $459 billion in 1972 to $1.1 trillion in 1982.[7] Employment in food retailing was 2.5 million in 1982, and there were 252,000 establishments. During the last decade, several new types of retailers have become a threat to existing establishments. The

EXHIBIT 14–3 Performance Profile of New Wave Retailers (1982)

	Strategic Profit Model Ratios					
Type of Retailer	**Net Profits as percent of Net Sales**	**Net Sales Times Total Assets**	**Net Profits as percent of Total Assets**	**Total Assets Times Net Worth**	**Net Profits as percent of Net Worth**	**Examples**
Hobby and craft centers	7.2%	2.2 ×	15.8%	1.8 ×	28.5%	Tandy-Crafts, Inc.
Home decorating specialty stores	7.0	1.8	12.6	2.1	26.5	Color Tile
Paint and home decorating "supermarkets"	7.4	1.8	12.6	1.8	24.0	Sherwin-Williams
Super hardware stores	5.8	2.7	15.7	1.6	25.1	Payless Cash-ways
Super drugstores	3.6	4.0	14.4	1.8	25.9	Long's
Combination stores	2.5	5.1	12.8	2.1	26.8	Skagg's Alpha Beta
Upscale discounters	3.2	4.1	13.1	2.0	26.2	Target

Source: Distribution Research Program, University of Oklahoma.

financial performance of this "new wave" of retailers is shown in Exhibit 14-3. The net profits on sales and net profits on net worth of these retailers are higher than those of many conventional retailers.

The wholesale sector comprises merchant wholesalers (who take title to goods sold); manufacturers' sales branches and offices; and commission merchants, agents, and brokers (who do not take title). In 1982, merchant wholesalers' sales were nearly $1.2 trillion, their employment was 5.3 million, and there were over 300,000 merchant wholesaling establishments.

Merchant wholesalers purchase, sort, assemble, grade, and store goods in large quantities, and sell this merchandise to retailers and to institutional, farm, governmental, professional, and industrial users. These wholesalers also extend credit and a variety of services both to customers and suppliers, many of whom are small businesses. For their customers, they provide delivery service and sales promotion suggestions. To their suppliers, they pass on marketing information about changes in consumer behavior and purchasing habits.[8]

In 1982, sales for all types of wholesalers were more than double retail sales. Even though the public probably perceives retail sales as higher because retail prices are higher, wholesale sales are higher because the wholesale market consists largely of large-scale purchasers: nearly 40 percent of such sales are made to industrial and other institutional users; 17 percent are made to other wholesalers; 4 percent are exports; and 1 percent are made to consumers and farmers.

Characteristics of Distribution Channels

A channel of distribution exists because its participants, through specialization of functions and transactional efficiencies, can perform the marketing function better with intermediaries than without them. Arrangements in a channel are continually modified to improve efficiency and to strengthen advantages over competing channels.

The producer often exercises control over the channel organization, and it is convenient to view the channel from the producer's perspective. Intermediaries tend to be used when:

- The number of sellers and buyers and the distance of product movement are relatively large
- The frequency of purchase is high
- The lot sizes needed by end users are small
- Markets are decentralized.[9]

Several channels of distribution are shown in Exhibit 14–4. Note the relatively large and complex channel of which the grocery wholesaler is a member as compared to the short, direct channel used by the computer systems manufacturer. Generally speaking, channel systems for industrial products are shorter and more direct than those for consumer products.

The channel is a competitive unit. The firms that make up a particular vertical channel of distribution compete as a coordinated unit with other channels. In designing marketing programs for target markets, management should consider the complete channel. Concern only with the adjacent links in the distribution channel provides an incomplete perspective of markets, competitive processes, and the tasks that the marketing program should be designed to perform.

Channel Flows

While the most obvious thing flowing through a channel is a physical product, there are other flows—transfer of ownership, communications (a new price list sent to distributors), financial transactions, and transfer of risk (insurance on warehouse inventory).[10] These flows connect the various channel participants and are essential to the performance of channel functions.

The *physical flow* of products occurs between suppliers, manufacturers, middlemen, and consumers. Movement is often accomplished by transportation firms. The direction of flow is from suppliers to end users, unless returns are involved. Some products are shipped to field warehouses and stored for a time before moving on through the distribution system. For a regional coffee processor, bulk coffee beans are received by truck and rail from suppliers, the coffee is processed, cases of canned and bagged coffee are transported to wholesalers and retail stores by company trucks, retailers stock their shelves, and consumers finally purchase coffee and carry it home for their own use.

EXHIBIT 14–4 Illustrations of Channel Systems

Company	Product Service	End-User Market Served	Participating Firms	Facilitating Firms
Burroughs Corporation (manufacturer)	Computer systems, business machines, and supplies	Business firms, government, and other institutions	Markets direct to end users using company sales force (no participating firms are involved)	Burroughs Finance Corporation, advertising agency, transportation firms
Ethan Allen, Inc. (manufacturer)	Furniture and furnishings for the home	Consumers	Retailers and other manufacturers furnishings	Advertising, transportation, financial institutions
Holiday Inns of America, Inc. (motel and hotel chain)	Motel and hotel facilities, motel equipment and services	Business and pleasure consumers of hotel services	Franchised motel operations (some owned by Holiday Inns), suppliers of services and equipment for motels (some corporate owned)	Insurance, finance, and construction firms (some corporate owned); advertising services
Coca-Cola Company (producer)	Carbonated beverages	Consumers	Independent and owned bottlers, brokers, food and beverage retailers	Advertising services, transportation firms
Fleming Companies, Inc. (wholesaler)	Foods (also distributes health and beauty aids)	Consumers and institutional end users (e.g., hospitals)	Suppliers of food products, brokers, retailers (independent voluntary groups, and corporate owned)	Banks, transportation firms, insurance firms

The *flow of ownership* concerns the transfer of title through the channel. In the coffee example, channel participants take ownership at the time of physical receipt of the product (the purchase or sale of coffee in commodity markets may alter the time of transfer of ownership). The movement of ownership is generally in the same direction as the physical flow of the product, though not all intermediaries participate in ownership flow. If the coffee processor uses food brokers to call on certain wholesalers, these brokers do not take title to or physical possession of the product. When goods are transported by public carrier, ownership rests with either the buyer or the seller, depending on the conditions of the sale.

Financial flow is payment for the goods and services that move through the channel. Payment generally moves in the direction opposite to physical and ownership flows and may involve such facilitating organizations as banks and other financial institutions. Financial flows also occur as producers and middlemen pay so-called facilitating firms for such services as advertising, marketing research, transportation, and storage. The terms of payment may be cash or credit.

The *flow of information* is communication in all directions within the channel. Information, the channel's "brain network," often determines its speed and efficiency in moving goods. Orders are placed by phone and mail; catalogs are sent to buyers; consumers see and hear advertising from various media; and salespeople inform buyers and persuade them to buy products and services. Communications also transmit complaints from users back through the channel. Marketing research is another form of information flow.

The *flow of risks* overlies all of the flows and affects virtually everyone involved in a channel. Product obsolescence, perishable goods, liability caused by faulty products, price fluctuations, and many other conditions create risks for buyers and sellers. As a result, those at different channel levels attempt to offset risk in a variety of ways. Farmers can hedge in grain commodity trading to reduce the risks of uncertain future price levels for their crops. Processors can also hedge via futures markets. At some levels, the product may be insured against loss or damage. Banks serving as facilitating organizations adjust by increasing interest rates for riskier customers.

Developing a Channel Strategy

The selection of an appropriate channel of distribution is a major determinant of an organization's success. Snap-on Tools Corporation developed the socket wrench nearly six decades ago. The wrench enabled the user to cut by two thirds the number of tools required for a wide range of sizes and uses. Dealers did not welcome this large reduction in sales opportunity. Frustrated by unsuccessful attempts to persuade distributors and retailers to stock the line, management decided to market it to professional mechanics, first using company salespeople and ultimately using independent retail dealers (over 3,000) with complete traveling "tool stores." The company built its own channel of distribution. With relatively high prices and production efficiencies, the company obtains attractive margins. Customer satisfaction is high due to quality products, a liberal replacement policy, quick response to changing needs, on-the-spot service, and credit arrangements. Sales and profits have grown rapidly, reaching $591 million in 1985.

Management's decision to serve the professional mechanic niche of the tool market and the development of a system of intermediary specialists were key factors contributing to Snap-on Tool's growth and profitability. Though the firm is small by comparison, it has been able to successfully compete with Sears and other giants, despite prices as much as 40 percent higher. It dominates the professional segment of the mechanic hand tool market.

Channel decisions represent much longer-term commitments than do other marketing decisions because of the time, costs, and intermediary relationships that are involved in building a new channel or in gaining access to an established one. And the channel, once selected, imposes certain constraints on other marketing mix elements. Kellwood Company, an apparel manufacturer producing private label brands for Sears, must comply with the retailer's product specifications and probably accepts lower prices than would be obtainable from an alternative channel. Private branding makes the manufacturer highly dependent on the retailer, if all or a substantial portion of the manufacturer's output is produced for the retailer. (About two thirds of Kellwood's output is produced for Sears.) Certain benefits compensate for the constraints—the retailer's strong brand image in the marketplace and the reduction in expenses for advertising and personal selling.

The length (number of intermediary levels) of the channel affects the methods used to promote the product or service. In a long distribution channel for a consumer product, a producer may direct advertising at consumers, thus stimulating interest in the product at the end-user level. This is a *pull* strategy—promotional efforts seek to pull the product through the channel levels (wholesaler and retailer). Alternatively, a *push* strategy seeks to promote the product with channel intermediaries, for example, by advertising in trade publications. Until 1975, Tylenol was advertised in medical and dental professional publications—not to end users. Thus, the promotional strategy used depends, in part, on the particular channel system selected by the firm.

J. P. Stevens, the textile giant, shifted toward a pull channel strategy in 1983 with its Lauren home furnishings line.[11] Central to the strategy is building merchandise lines for channels of distribution through department and specialty stores, thus countering the competitive impact of off-price stores on Stevens' channel members. Aggressive consumer advertising is part of the new marketing strategy. The merchandise lines offered by Stevens includes home furnishings manufactured by such noncompeting firms as Henredon (furniture) and Bardwil (table linens).

Choosing a Channel Strategy

Channel of distribution strategy consists of selecting the type of channel to be used, designing its specific configuration, selecting its participants, and managing it to achieve the organization's objectives.

Channel strategy is guided by the firm's target markets and marketing objectives. The channel chosen should enable the firm to reach its target markets. Given this key role, **channel of distribution strategy** must be carefully integrated with all components of the marketing program.

Channel objectives specify what the channel is expected to accomplish with regard to a firm's target markets and support of the firm's marketing program. These objectives should include *channel performance, extent of control, financial support* to be provided in channel development, and other operational considerations. Channel performance includes sales, market share, and profit contribution targets. A firm should also indicate what role it plans to play in the coordination and control of channel operations. Financial support concerns the amount of financial resources that the firm's management is willing to use in building the channel of distribution. For example, is the firm interested in and capable of owning such intermediaries as retail stores? Various operational objectives may be established, such as the extent of the support to be provided to intermediaries and product-servicing arrangements.

For a manufacturer, two decisions should occur early in the process of formulating a channel strategy:

■ Determining whether the firm will sell directly to end users or will utilize intermediaries.

■ Selecting the type of channel (conventional or vertically coordinated).

If the choice is direct distribution, the manufacturer performs all channel functions, making sales force or mail contact with consumer or industrial and institutional end users. This method has both advantages and limitations. Direct distribution simplifies the channel network, provides the manufacturer with control over marketing activities, facilitates buyer-seller communication, and eliminates the profit margins of middlemen. Direct distribution does not eliminate channel functions, however, and it often requires substantial resources. Direct distribution is more prevalent in industrial markets than in consumer markets. Marketing characteristics that indicate choice of a direct distribution approach are shown in Exhibit 14–5. Many of these characteristics apply to IBM in the sale and servicing of its large computer systems. Interestingly, IBM's management decided to use marketing intermediaries when it introduced its personal computer line. This was because the smaller computers, when sold one at a time, did not yield large enough margins to cover direct distribution costs.

Direct distribution becomes prohibitive for products that are frequently purchased in small amounts by a variety of users. Chemical processors such as Dow, Allied, and Pennwalt use independent industrial distributors to serve chemical users that purchase small amounts of chemicals. Although distributors buy from producers in carload lots, they, in turn, serve business and institutional customers that buy a variety of chemicals in small quantities for use in water treatment, metal cleaning and plating, food processing, and other applications.

If the conditions do not favor direct distribution, intermediaries are necessary. In some industries, either option may be viable. In cosmetics, Avon and Mary Kay have adopted a direct (door-to-door) approach, whereas Max Factor and Noxell work through intermediaries. If either direct distribution or the use of intermediaries is feasible, management should evaluate both approaches before making a choice.

Planning and implementing a channel strategy involves three interrelated decision-making areas:

■ *Type of Distribution Channel.* This includes decisions as to how the channel will contribute to corporate and marketing strategy, establishment of channel objectives, and selection of the type of channel utilized.

EXHIBIT 14-5 Factors Indicating Choice of Direct Distribution

Factor	Characteristics	Factor	Characteristics
Target markets	Relatively few customers Large purchase in terms of quantity or unit price Customers concentrated geographically Sufficient margin to support personal selling or mail contact efforts Purchase decision a major, long-term commitment by the buyer	*Product/service characteristics*	Manufacturer's personnel required in selling and service because of complexity of product (computer sales and service) Width of product line sufficient to support direct marketing approach (Avon Products, Fuller Brush) Product application assistance required (steam turbines) Product technology changing rapidly
Marketing program	Personal selling a major component of the marketing program Intermediary functions not needed (storage, local credit, inventory, packaging, etc.) or can be efficiently performed by the manufacturer	*Corporate capabilities*	Resources available to support a direct marketing approach (establishment of a sales force) Firm experienced in marketing similar products to comparable market targets (direct channels exist) Sufficient time available to develop direct distribution before potential competition becomes a threat (patent protection)

■ *Design of Channel Configuration.* Alternatives for the type of channel to be used must be identified and evaluated, and one or more channels must be selected. The specific organizations that the channel comprises must be identified, evaluated, and selected.

■ *Channel Management.* Once designed, the channel must be managed, its performance evaluated, and its configuration and participants revised to meet changing conditions.

The Type of Channel

There are two major types of distribution channels:

Vertical marketing system
(VMS) is a channel of distribution in which one member has the authority to manage all other organizations in the channel.

■ Conventional channels in which members have joined together by mutual agreement and are not coordinated or managed on any formal basis (members are loosely aligned and relatively autonomous).

■ **Vertical marketing systems** (VMS) in which the authority to coordinate is achieved through *ownership* of all members by a single firm, through *contractual arrangement* (franchising retail outlets by the producer) or through an *administered* relationship among channel members for a line or classification of merchandise (Hartmarx in men's suits).

EXHIBIT 14-6 Characteristics of Channel Types

Type of Channel	Characteristics	Examples
Vertical marketing systems*		
Ownership	Ownership may occur at manufacturer, wholesaler, or retailer levels	The Limited, Inc. (women's apparel)
	Firms may also utilize contractual systems (e.g., certain franchisers own a portion of retail outlets)	Sears, Roebuck & Co.
		Sherwin-Williams (paint)
		Tandy Corporation (electronics)
	Substantial financial resources and levels of investment required	
Contractual	Consist of wholesaler-sponsored voluntary chains, retailer cooperative organizations, and franchise systems	McDonald's Corporation
		Holiday Inns of America, Inc.
		Ethan Allen, Inc.
	Normally involve a written agreement in which responsibilities of channel participants are specified	Buick Division of General Motors Corporation
Administered	Coordination achieved through power and influence of dominant firm in channel	Hartmarx
		Kraftco Corporation (dairy products)
	Normally involve a line or classification of products	
Conventional channel systems	No dominant power in the channel	Channels used by independent supermarkets, shoe stores, and various other retail outlets
	Decision making centered in each firm	
	Channel entry and exit easier to accomplish than in vertically coordinated systems	Small-manufacturer use of agent-broker intermediary channels to reach industrial end users
	Lack integrated programmed approach to channel management	

* The VMS is discussed in greater detail in William R. Davidson, "Changes in Distributive Institutions," *Journal of Marketing* 34 (January 1970), pp. 7-10.

The VMS is so designated because the channel operates as a cohesive, integrated network of organizations and is managed by one of the channel members. In the conventional channel, the participants function on an independent basis, there is a lack of overall channel coordination, and the arrangement is usually less than optimal. Thus, it is not surprising that the VMS is rapidly emerging as the dominant type of channel system in the U.S. economy.[12] Characteristics of the major types of channels are shown in Exhibit 14-6.

Management must decide on the type of channel to be utilized. The VMS is the predominant form for consumer products, while direct distribution is often used by industrial firms. Many types of conventional channels of distribution also function within the marketing system. The selection of a channel strategy provides a basis for identifying suitable channel types for a given firm.

Designing the Channel Configuration

The major stages in channel design are shown in Exhibit 14-7. Specific channel alternatives that correspond to a given channel strategy must be identified and evaluated on a comprehensive basis. Using the appropriate

EXHIBIT 14–7 Channel Design Decisions and Decision Criteria

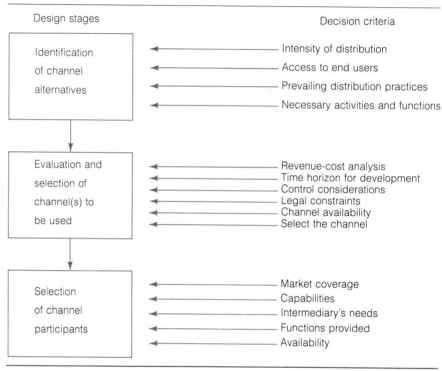

Design stages

Decision criteria

Identification
of channel
alternatives
— Intensity of distribution
— Access to end users
— Prevailing distribution practices
— Necessary activities and functions

Evaluation and
selection of
channel(s) to
be used
— Revenue-cost analysis
— Time horizon for development
— Control considerations
— Legal constraints
— Channel availability
— Select the channel

Selection
of channel
participants
— Market coverage
— Capabilities
— Intermediary's needs
— Functions provided
— Availability

criteria, one or more channels must be selected and specific channel participants must then be chosen.

Identification of Channel Alternatives. Although use of a particular type of channel eliminates some alternatives, within each type there is more than one channel configuration. A food manufacturer desiring to achieve broad distribution by using a conventional channel may consider the alternatives shown in Exhibit 14–8. While going directly to national chains would give broad coverage in the marketplace, even more extensive coverage could be obtained by using several of the channels shown. These criteria are useful in identifying channel alternatives.

Distribution intensity is the extent to which distribution for a particular brand at a specified channel level has reached saturation coverage in a specific geographic area.

Intensity of Distribution. The number of intermediaries relative to a saturation level that are marketing a manufacturer's brand in a trading area (state, county, or city) is designated as the **distribution intensity** being used for the brand. Complete saturation occurs when all middlemen that normally market a particular product type (such as soft drinks) carry a particular manufacturer's brand. Intensity alternatives include exclusive, selective, and intensive distribution through many intermediaries.

EXHIBIT 14-8 Channels of Distribution for Food Products

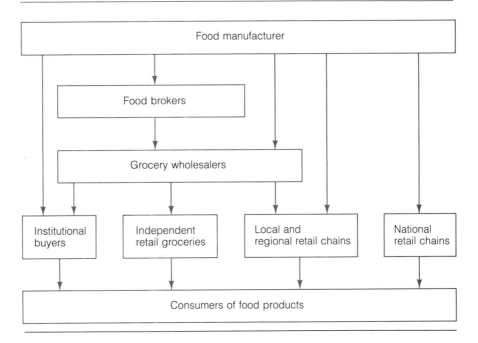

In an exclusive distribution arrangement, the wholesaler, distributor, or retailer does not market competing brands. Instead, the brand is carried by only one firm in a trading area. Ethan Allen Galleries retail the company's traditional American furniture line, and buyers must go to the one gallery in their trading area to purchase Ethan Allen furniture. With selective distribution, a product is available in more than a single outlet or chain, but not everywhere that such a product might be carried. Lines of medium- to high-priced men's and women's apparel are often found in a limited number of retail outlets operating in a trading area. In addition to type of product, a strong brand image that attracts sufficient customers, adequate margins to support the necessary services, and availability of qualified intermediaries are factors that suggest the choice of selective approaches. Over time, companies may change distribution intensity as the needs of target markets change or as marketing strategy is modified. Nikon used selective distribution initially but changed to more intensive distribution in the late 1970s to combat intense competition from other Japanese camera manufacturers. Intensive distribution involves a broad network (department stores, discounters, specialty stores, and other appropriate outlets). Kodak film is distributed through an intensive retail network.

A policy of exclusive or selective distribution may not be appropriate for certain types of products: "At retail, selective distribution is probably effective for most specialty lines and shopping lines, but it is not satisfactory for convenience goods which, by definition, must be available at many locations within easy reach of consumers."[13] Thus, such products as cigarettes, chewing gum, and candy are intensively distributed.

Although market and product characteristics influence the appropriate distribution approach, there is a reasonable degree of flexibility regarding the intensity of distribution. Ethan Allen moved away from department store distribution to the use of a relatively small number of retail dealers. The firm has successfully developed a selective distribution channel in an industry in which more intensive distribution approaches typically prevail.

Access to End Users.   By working back from an end-user target market, the intermediaries that might be used to reach the market can be identified. Consider what channels might provide access to consumer end users of a curling iron for use by women in the 16-to-35 age group (assuming a conventional type of channel and intensive distribution). Retail, department, and discount chains would certainly provide access to the target market. Similarly, drug chains and other wholesalers and distributors of small electrical appliances would be involved. Direct sales to large chains should be considered. Private branding for a firm such as J. C. Penney is another alternative. Attention should also be given to the geographic coverage and the approximate sales potential provided by each channel configuration.

Prevailing Distribution Practices.   Consideration of the channel practices used for similar products or services can be useful in identifying the types and functions of various intermediaries. Studying competitors' channel systems and market performance may yield useful insights. However, the channel alternatives considered should not be restricted to those currently used in a particular industry, because other options may also be feasible. Snap-on Tools and Ethan Allen have successful channel systems that are not typical in their industries.

Necessary Activities and Functions.   The manufacturer should also identify the functions (storage, transportation, customer contact) required to make the product available to end users in the marketplace. The functions that the firm can perform best should be separated from those appropriate for intermediaries. If a manufacturer of consumer products cannot make direct contact with prospective customers at the retail level, then resellers must be used. Providing inventories in various geographic locations suggests a need for wholesalers. Assessment of the channel flows (physical, ownership, financial, information, and risk) needed to serve target markets provides additional insight into necessary activities and functions in the distribution channel. Management should also identify the functions and capabilities of the different types of intermediaries that are feasible in a proposed channel. Factors to be considered include the services provided by

EXHIBIT 14–9

Seiko combines moon time with fine design to create an extraordinary clock. Track the phases of the moon while seconds sweep smoothly past. The gleaming silver-and-gold-tone makes it modern, marvelous. Seiko Quartz mantel, wall, table and travel clocks, priced from $29.50 to $795.00.*

SEIKO QUARTZ CLOCKS

Seiko uses a selective distribution strategy to reach various market segments with innovative top-of-the-line moon clocks like this one.

Courtesy AC&R Advertising Inc.

middlemen, the availability of middlemen, and the attitudes of middlemen toward the producer, sales opportunities, and costs.

A firm may select multiple channels. Certain motel and fast-food chains own some of their retail outlets and franchise others. The practice of distributing a manufacturer's brand through more than one distribution channel may create problems for the producer if the members of one channel object to having the product distributed in another channel (Exhibit 14–9). To determine whether alternatives of interest to a firm are feasible, each such alternative should be further investigated with regard to access to end users, prevailing distribution practices, and necessary activities and functions.

Evaluation and Selection of Channels. The evaluation of channel alternatives should include revenue-cost analysis, length of time required for channel development, control considerations, legal constraints, and channel availability.

EXHIBIT 14–10A Distribution Costs for Blenders

	Wholesaler Channel		Large Retailer Channel	
	Small Order	**Large Order**	**Small Order**	**Large Order**
East Territory				
Budgeted sales (units)	5,119	4,868	2,381	2,632
Cost per unit	$3.00	$2.40	$3.50	$2.80
Total channel costs	$15,357	$11,683	$ 8,334	$7,370
West Territory				
Budgeted sales (units)	2,881	3,132	4,619	4,368
Cost per unit	$4.00	$3.20	$2.90	2.20
Total channel costs	$11,524	$10,022	$13,395	$9,610

Revenue-Cost Analysis. A key factor in evaluating channel alternatives is the expected economic performance of each alternative. The estimated revenue and cost flows over the planning horizon should be determined. Intensive distribution through a variety of retail outlets may be more costly than other alternatives but should generate a larger sales volume than selective distribution. Evaluation is complicated by the interrelationships among the channel decision and other elements of the marketing mix, since the selection of a particular channel influences the costs of other marketing mix elements. The participation of other firms also makes revenue and cost analysis difficult.

Consider this situation. A food products manufacturer is evaluating whether to use food brokers to move the firm's products through the channel system or to develop a company sales force. The costs of a sales force are estimated to be in excess of the broker costs, but a sales force will give the manufacturer direct contact with wholesalers. Management and control of selling efforts are typically more effective with a company sales force. The use of brokers will substantially eliminate personal selling costs, but with brokers, the manufacturer may need heavier advertising and sales promotion expenditures at the consumer level to pull the product through the channel. The economic analysis of alternative channel systems must include all of the relevant cost trade-offs among mix elements, as well as estimates of probable sales for each alternative. The difference between revenues and costs can be used to compare the economic performance of each alternative.

An analysis of channel of distribution costs for one product by territory and channel is given in Exhibit 14–10A. By combining revenues with the channel costs and other costs, the contribution margin and segment income can be compared (Exhibit 14–10B).

Time for Development. It often requires several years before new channels reach the size and configuration desired by management. Thus, a channel may be more attractive if it can be developed quickly relative to another alternative. Consider the retailer life cycles shown in Exhibit 14–11. Some of

EXHIBIT 14–10B Analysis of Contribution Margin and Segment Income

	Small Order (4,619 units)		Large Order (4,368 units)		Total	
	Percent of Revenue		Percent of Revenue		Percent of Revenue	
Revenues		$175,522		$165,984		$341,506
Variable costs						
Marketing		$92,380		$87,360		$179,740
Selling	10.0%	17,552	10.0%	16,598	10.0%	34,150
Channel costs	7.6	13,395	5.8	9,610	6.7	23,005
Total		123,327		113,568		236,895
Contribution margin	29.7	52,195	31.6	52,416	30.6	104,611
Fixed costs						
Programmed advertising	1.8	3,084	1.8	2,916	1.8	6,000
Direct manu-facturing costs		30,793		29,120		59,913
Total		33,877		32,036		65,913
Segment income	10.4	$ 18,318	12.3	$ 20,380	11.3	$ 38,698

Source: Adapted from Patrick M. Dunne and Harry I. Wolk, "Marketing Cost Analysis: A Modularized Contribution Approach," *Journal of Marketing* July 1977, pp. 88, 91.

the newer retail chains have grown quite rapidly. During its first two decades, The Limited, Inc. grew from one women's specialty clothing store to a $1 billion corporate chain. Speed in channel development is important to gain (or protect) market position in many lines of business.

Control Considerations. Factors other than revenues and cost are also important in selecting channels of distribution. Given two channel alternatives with similar estimated economic performance, the choice may rest on the extent of management control that the firm can exercise in each of the channels. In addition to management control, bargaining processes, potential coalitions of participants, flexibility in responding to changing conditions, communications flows, and avoidance of possible conflict may be relevant in the channel choice process. Typically, the channel selected reflects several of these factors.[14] In this context, the long-term nature of the channel decision should be recognized by management. Major modifications in channels are constrained by costs, possible adverse influences on trade and customer relationships, and sales losses while making the shift to another channel (or intermediary).

The extent of control over channel participants is an important management issue, since the premise is that greater control will enable the firm to better achieve its objectives. A corporate-owned VMS gives the greatest degree of management control in terms of market coverage, price determination, inventory, customer service, promotion, and other aspects of marketing strategy and tactics. Since this type of channel is competing as a unit, all of its parts (organizations) are managed and coordinated as an integrated market-

EXHIBIT 14–11 Retailer Life Cycles—Timing and Years to Maturity

Department stores		100 years
Variety stores		60 years
Supermarkets		30 years
Discount department stores		20 years
Mass merchandisers		15 years
Fast-food outlets		15 years
Home improvement centers		15 years
Furniture warehouse showrooms		10 years
Catalog showrooms		10 years

1850   1870   1890   1910   1930   1950   1970   1990

Source: E. Jerome McCarthy and William D. Perreault, Jr., *Basic Marketing*, 8th ed. (Homewood, Ill.: Richard D. Irwin, 1984), p. 406.

ing system linking the producer to end users. Although management is facilitated by the ownership of all participants, administration remains a formidable challenge because conflicts can occur among organizational units as well as among firms, even when they are linked together for a common purpose.[15]

Legal Constraints.   Federal antitrust laws are of primary importance in channel selection decisions. Aspects of channel decisions that may be affected by such legislation include:[16]

▪ The extent of product or brand exclusiveness that can be granted to resellers.

▪ Geographic restrictions on intermediary coverage (and possible penalties).

▪ Other restrictions and requirements.

▪ The consistency of terms and arrangements between resellers.

▪ State and local laws and regulations.

   An example will illustrate the impact that antitrust laws can have on channel strategy. Malone and Hyde, a large grocery wholesaler pursuing a policy of expanding its channel network, arranged an acquisition of a smaller wholesaler that served an adjacent market area. The acquisition was viewed quite favorably by both firms, and it could have resulted in increased efficiencies for both because such functions as warehousing were combined. A request for approval of the merger was sent to the federal government. While awaiting a decision, the firms developed plans to facilitate the transition, since both managements and their legal advisers believed that approval would be forthcoming. The request was denied more than six months after it had been filed. The government held that the merger would place the large wholesaler in a dominant position in the markets it served, even though there was no market overlap in the previous coverage of the two firms.

Channel Availability. Management should determine whether there is a reasonable possibility of being able to enter a channel that is under consideration. The unwillingness of distributors and retailers to stock Snap-on Tools socket wrenches forced management to design a new channel system. At the final stage in channel selection, it may be appropriate to contact members of the channel alternatives to make a more comprehensive evaluation of availability. This step is sometimes included in the selection of channel participants.

Selecting the Channel. Using the various selection factors, one or more channel alternatives can be chosen. Economic considerations typically play a central role in channel choice. Testing alternative channel designs in different geographic areas may be useful in this context. Market testing generates actual results for review by management, and it may identify potential problems before full-scale adoption of a particular channel design. A manufacturer evaluating a factory sales force versus independent representatives could experiment with both distribution approaches.

A firm may utilize two or more channels of distribution to reach its target markets. It is important to consider the interrelationships between these channel systems. Will there be conflicts between intermediaries? How will end users respond if the channel systems charge different prices? The rapid growth of factory outlets in the clothing industry illustrates the conflicts that can develop with a firm's existing channels:

> Sales in factory outlets were an estimated $1 billion in 1976, and growing like crazy. They carry London Fog, Palm Beach, Hathaway, and other name brands, often with labels removed and irregular stamps. Prices range as low as 50 percent of retail. Manufacturers' store location and promotional strategies attempt to minimize adverse retailer reaction. Nevertheless, retailers located in factory outlet trade areas are very unhappy with manufacturers who operate or supply the discount systems.[17]

Nonetheless, consumers benefit from discount prices and manufacturers are apparently willing to chance adverse retailer reaction in return for the profits generated by an additional channel to end users. Off-price sales from factory outlets had increased to nearly $6 billion by 1982, and volume was expected to double in five years.[18]

In selecting a channel system, management should consider two major consequences of the decision. *First*, does the proposed channel offer the best available link to the firm's target markets? That is, is the system of intermediaries appropriate for implementing the company's marketing strategy? Once established, the channel will impose various constraints on the marketing program. Program elements that may be affected include distribution intensity, pricing policies, promotional requirements, inventory and stocking policies, and customer service. *Second*, is the alternative financially attractive? If the channel is developed properly, does it offer a high probability of meeting sales, market share, profit contribution, and other corporate and marketing objectives? Since it is often difficult to quantify all of the factors that may affect a channel decision, management must ultimately reach a decision based on judgment and experience coupled with various supporting analyses.

Choosing the Channel Participants.   The selection of intermediaries is essentially a matching process. The producer must identify specific middlemen who can perform the channel functions needed and must convince them that the relationship will be mutually beneficial. The selection decision should be examined from the point of view of both participants. Several factors that are important to producers are:

- Contacts and relationships of intermediary with customers in target markets.
- Capabilities, reputation, and past performance for sales and service.
- Match of functions provided with producer's needs.
- Potential contribution of producer's product or service to intermediary's needs (profit contribution, gaps in line, existing products, etc.).
- Probability of effective long-term working relationship.
- Financial status and management ability.

Factors that are important to intermediaries in establishing a relationship with a producer are:

- Producer's product or brand image.
- Support and assistance provided by producer.
- Compatibility of product with existing lines.
- Trade reputation of producer.
- Potential profit contribution of product to intermediary.
- Anticipated reaction of channel members to addition of producer to channel system.
- Estimated start-up costs in adding product.

Commitment and the ability to deliver sales results are essential qualities in intermediaries. Evaluation of intermediaries often consists of three types of comparisons: current sales versus past attainments, the performance of various sales outlets, and the intermediary's sales versus quotas and other measures of territory sales potential.

The experience of a manufacturer of custom-fabricated industrial heating equipment demonstrates the impact that proper selection of channel intermediaries can have on sales. The firm decided to use agents to reach its target markets. In establishing a channel for a new line of equipment, it retained a consultant who specialized in bringing together manufacturers and sales representatives. Thirty days after the firm had selected and approved a sales agent in the Northeast, the agent obtained an order totaling nearly a quarter of a million dollars. This rapid success was due to the customer relationships that the agent had already established, the agent's experience and capabilities, the effective support provided by the manufacturer, and the quality of the new line of equipment.

Building a new channel of distribution requires a careful study of channel participants' capabilities and needs. In a multilevel channel, the producer must look beyond the first level of contact. Although the firm may only be involved in selecting resellers at one level in the channel, careful appraisal of the entire network is important. Entering an existing channel system with a new product or service requires various changes in the channel network. These changes must be anticipated and properly implemented. The final choice of channel participants will normally involve compromise. Ideal candidates may simply not exist, or if available, they may be unwilling to handle the firm's product.

Management of Channel Relationships

The design of new channel systems is a decision that is made infrequently. However, an understanding of channel design and of the methods for evaluating and selecting channels and channel participants provides a necessary framework for channel management. As should be obvious, once the channel has been established, it must be managed. Yet failure to recognize the ongoing responsibilities of channel management is one of the most critical gaps in marketing practice today, particularly among firms that are not members of vertical marketing systems.

Consider this illustration. K mart, which has over 2,000 store locations in the United States, Canada, and Puerto Rico, is an extraordinary retailer whose management over the decades has been alert to the need for change:

> Unlike a number of other discounters—many of which have closed up shop— K mart has unblinkingly confronted changing times and sought to develop a strategy to deal with them and to exploit what it sees as its untapped potential.

Thus, it is busily transforming sections of its aging one-floor stores into spanking new kinds of merchandising space. Gone are the brown polyester slacks hanging limply from long pipe racks. Featured now are familiar, toney names like Calvin Klein, Sergio Valente, and Jordache, displayed on tiered and "waterfall" racks, seeking the same dollar, or more likely, many, many more dollars. K mart has opted for a different kind of expansion, sociological rather than geographic, in a drive to attract new customers, more affluent and sensitive to style, while holding onto its old faithful patrons.[19]

K mart's sales growth from $4.6 billion in 1973 to more than $22 billion in 1985 required that management direct regular attention to all aspects of channel operations.

Channel Management

The channel is much more difficult to manage than a single organization due to the differing (and sometimes conflicting) objectives of channel participants, the complexity of channel networks, the geographic dispersion of firms, and the lack of direct control. Nonetheless, operating policies and procedures must be developed for a channel. Territory responsibilities, financial support, pricing, promotion, training, and servicing are some of the many areas that must be worked out with channel intermediaries. When policies and procedures are not explicit, conflicts and problems will often occur. Written contracts are sometimes used to indicate the responsibilities of both parties—for franchise systems, automobile dealerships, manufacturer's representatives. In conventional channels, there may be no formal agreement between the parties involved.

Motivation of Intermediaries.

Motivation of channel members is essential to achieving the producer's channel objectives. Incentives and regular contact with channel members can be helpful in maintaining effectiveness. Automobile manufacturers offer rebates to dealers on automobiles sold during slow sales periods when increased selling effort is desired, or as a reward when sales quotas are exceeded. Many other manufacturers incorporate incentives into their channel tactics to place greater emphasis on certain channel activities. Meetings and conferences are often used to communicate information about new products, policy changes, and other matters. Meetings also provide feedback from channel members concerning problems, market conditions, and competitive activity.

Effective communications and information flows in both directions are necessary if the channel is to function properly. A producer that is part of a long channel system is quite distant from the end users of its product. Recognition of this problem, in combination with the pressures generated by consumer advocates, has prompted manufacturing firms in such industries as appliances, automobiles, and insurance to establish direct communications with consumers to handle complaints, requests for information, and other matters concerning products and services. Procter & Gamble, for example, places an 800 number on the package of every one of its brands to enable consumers to directly contact the company.

Channel Conflict. When two or more organizations in a channel of distribution cannot reach an agreement on some issue, policy, or operating practice, conflict may hamper the functioning of the channel. The most drastic outcome of a conflict is the exit of a channel member. Disputes may occur between channel members at the same channel level, such as two retailers. This situation is designated as *horizontal* conflict. An example would be a dispute over geographic boundaries in the case of exclusive distribution arrangements with a manufacturer. *Vertical* conflict is a dispute or disagreement between two organizations at different channel levels, such as a manufacturer and a distributor. The manufacturer may have sales objectives for the distributor that are much higher than the distributor's sales objectives. Continual pressures for sales growth by the manufacturer may lead to conflict.

The resolution of channel conflict is normally accomplished through negotiation. This may take such forms as making concessions, improving communications, and offering incentives. The relative power positions of the two organizations may influence the outcome; however, conflict resolution through power rather than equity may adversely affect ongoing operating relationships.

Evaluating and Revising Channels

One important channel management task is gauging how well the channel is performing. This continuing management function involves:

- Defining the channel system in terms of participants, interrelationships, functions, and flows.
- Setting objectives (sales, market share, costs, levels of end-user satisfaction).
- Based on objectives, establishing relevant criteria and measures of performance.
- Collecting and analyzing sales, cost, and marketing research information.
- Identifying performance gaps.
- Formulating and implementing needed corrective action.

The development of methods and tools for analysis and evaluation of channel results has been quite limited. This is understandable, considering the difficulty of describing the various economic, political, and social interactions involved in channels of distribution. Typically, channel analysis is concerned with sales and cost performance in combination with the results of various types of attitude, preference, and opinion surveys conducted among channel participants.

Distribution channels must be responsive to the changing needs and wants of customers and to the development of new channel systems by competitors, as the K mart example illustrates. And marketing management must continuously monitor channel effectiveness and improve distribution networks to match changing conditions and potential market opportunities. Channel change tends to be more prevalent for consumer markets than for industrial markets. This may be due to the greater attention that management gives channel decisions in the consumer sector. Also, the complexity of many consumer product channels provides greater opportunity for possible improvement. Changes can occur throughout a vertical distribution channel or at a particular level (e.g., wholesale or retail) in the system. Although shifts in distribution channels usually occur over a period of several years, assuming that channels will remain fixed indefinitely can be hazardous.

Application

How Komatsu Encourages Cooperation in Channels of Distribution[20]

The Japanese company Komatsu is one of the world's major suppliers of construction equipment. In addition to an extensive domestic sales network, Komatsu has approximately 180 distributors around the world engaged in marketing, servicing, and parts supply. This wide network gives customers in all locations access to the full support of a local distributor, including comprehensive services both before and after sale. Every effort is made to assist customers in controlling costs, minimizing equipment downtime, and making the most effective use of the equipment they purchase.

Komatsu distributors provide customers with all the information they need to select the equipment that best suits their requirements. Through the Optimum Fleet Recommendation (OFR) system, distributors and Komatsu's regional offices ask clients to provide a detailed project assessment, or company engineers are sent to survey

the site and examine climatic and geologic conditions. Data thus collected are analyzed by computer to offer clients alternative fleet selections, based on the performance and capacities of each machine, fleet owning and operating costs, and the type and number of machines required for maximum productivity and economy.

Once equipment has been purchased, additional computerized analysis is provided for assistance in planning utilization, maintenance, and repair. Distributors prepare service programs suited to conditions in their particular region, with emphasis on preventive maintenance and minimization of repair costs. Whenever called for, Komatsu engineers are dispatched to give instruction and assistance.

Komatsu operates 13 overseas and 7 domestic parts depots that work in close cooperation with distributors to help them maintain adequate parts inventories. Telex and computerized communications systems enable this parts distribution network to respond rapidly to emergency parts orders.

The Komatsu distribution network functions in a coordinated way to build long-term relationships of trust and reliability with purchasers and users of Komatsu's equipment. As customer needs and the types of products sold become more diverse, new services must be made available. The company is working to develop better diagnostic instruments for preventive maintenance, more efficient equipment for distributors to use in repair work, and comprehensive consulting services on the use of its products. In addition, constant attention is given to upgrading and updating the training of service personnel. The company operates the Komatsu Training Institute in Shizuoka Prefecture, where training sessions using highly sophisticated equipment are offered to distributors and users from around the world ∎

Summary

Channels of distribution exist because of the advantages they offer in specialization of functions and because of the transactional efficiencies they provide to manufacturers and end users. Through specialization, retail supermarkets are serviced far more efficiently by such middlemen as grocery wholesalers than they would be if each supermarket negotiated directly with various food processors. Thus, marketing channels have developed because they are needed to perform specialized marketing functions and because market information, contractual, communications, merchandising, storing, transporting, pricing, and transactional functions are performed more efficiently through the use of marketing channels than they would be if producers distributed directly to end users.

In selecting a channel of distribution strategy, a firm seeks the best means of reaching its target markets. Although some companies may find that going directly to consumers is more appropriate than using intermediaries, many are compelled to either form new channels or become members of existing channels. The decision to use a direct distribution approach is influenced by market characteristics, marketing program requirements, product/service characteristics, and company capabilities. In shaping a channel strategy, management must determine what intensity of distribution is required to meet corporate objectives and what type of channel system will be used. There are two types of channels: conventional and vertical marketing systems. Ownership, contractual arrangements, and administered relationships are examples of VMSs. A VMS is managed as a coordinated group of channel participants.

After selecting the type of channel that will be used and the desired intensity of distribution, management must identify the specific channels that it will consider. These alternatives are then evaluated, and one or more are selected. The channel is a delivery system that comprises not only the physical product but also the other parts of the marketing offer. Channels remain relatively fixed over long periods of time; indeed, they may outlast many products. Yet changes in distribution strategy and tactics are necessary responses to shifting environmental influences, customer needs and wants, and competitive pressures. Although firms do not frequently develop new channel systems or attempt to enter existing systems, a sound understanding of channel design is essential to managing an existing distribution system.

The selection of a channel is often influenced by management's estimate of the channel's ability to meet marketing objectives, its costs, its availability, and the time required for its development, as well as by control considerations and legal constraints. After the channel design has been selected, channel participants must be recruited and operating relationships developed. Finally, the channel is managed over time and modified, when necessary, to adjust it to changing conditions.

Exercises for Review and Discussion

1. Although the logic of transactional efficiency seems clear, some problems occur if we try to develop a marketing system whose primary purpose is minimizing the number of transactions. Discuss this statement.

2. What are some basic issues that need to be considered in debating the pros and cons of using marketing intermediaries?

3. In 1979, the Magnavox Company introduced a videodisc player that could be attached to any television set. In the past, Magnavox had very selective distribution practices. Assuming that there are no constraints on Magnavox's management, develop a rationale for what you consider to be the most appropriate distribution strategy for the videodisc.

4. Why is the decision about the type of channel system to be used often critical to corporate success?

5. The president of a firm that manufactures and markets a line of surgical staplers has asked you to evaluate the firm's channel strategy. The stapler is used by surgeons as an alternative to needle and thread. What questions would you ask to obtain the information you need to recommend a channel strategy?

6. In selecting the best channel strategy for reaching the potential end users of a new consumer product, what information do you need concerning the market opportunity?

7. What risks may be encountered if a "follow-the-leader" approach is used in selecting a company's channel of distribution?

8. Identify some of the difficulties in estimating revenues and costs for alternative channel systems. What suggestions can you offer for overcoming these difficulties?

9. A manufacturer is now using five channels for distribution: A, B, C, D, and E. Sales and cost data for the five channels are shown in Exhibit 14–A. Based on this information, what changes in the channels of distribution would you propose to improve profits? What additional information would enable you to make a more complete evaluation of the five channels?

EXHIBIT 14–A

Channel	Sales ($)	Variable Costs ($)	Profit Margins ($)	Percentage of Sales
A	$ 350,000	$ 350,000	—	13%
B	600,000	400,000	$200,000	22
C	200,000	300,000	– 100,000	7
D	700,000	600,000	100,000	25
E	900,000	400,000	500,000	33
Total	$2,750,000	$2,050,000	$700,000	100%
Less fixed expenses			300,000	
Net profit			$400,000	

10. National Music Corporation is a small manufacturer of musical instruments. Management is considering two alternative distribution methods: *(a)* having brokers sell the musical instruments to wholesalers and retailers and *(b)* making direct sales to wholesalers. What are the advantages and disadvantages of each method? On what criteria would you base your decision?

11. The channel of distribution decision may be part of the marketing mix, but at the same time it may be unlike such other parts of the marketing mix as advertising or personal selling, which are controllable by the management of a firm. Discuss this point.

12. Suppose the marketing manager of a firm has asked you to develop a plan for changing from the use of manufacturer's representatives to the use of a factory sales force. Outline an approach to this task. Identify the major components of your plan. (Make whatever assumptions are necessary.)

Notes

1. Guest Supply, Inc., *1984 Annual Report.*

2. Reavis Cox and Thomas F. Schutte, "A Look at Channel Management," in *Marketing Involvement in Society and the Economy,* ed. Philip R. McDonald (Chicago: American Marketing Association, 1969), p. 100.

3. *1981 U.S. Industrial Outlook for 200 Industries with Projections for 1985* (Washington, D.C.: U.S. Government Printing Office, 1981), pp. 408, 446–47.

4. "What Keeps Food Prices High—and Rising," *Citibank,* June 1980, p. 4.

5. Wetterau, Inc., *1985 Annual Report,* pp. 1–48.

6. Richard Greene, "A Boutique in Your Living Room," *Forbes,* May 7, 1984, p. 86.

7. *1983 U.S. Industrial Outlook* (Washington, D.C.: Department of Commerce, 1983), p. 48-1.

8. Ibid., p. 47-1.

9. Louis P. Bucklin, *Competition and Evolution in the Distributive Trades* (Englewood Cliffs, N.J.: Prentice-Hall, 1972), p. 40.

10. These flows are examined in greater detail in George Fisk, *Marketing Systems* (New York: Harper & Row, 1965), chaps. 9–13.

11. Pat Sloan, "J. P. Stevens Chief: Marketing Now in Fashion at Textile Giant," *Advertising Age,* July 4, 1983, pp. 4, 28.

12. An extensive discussion of channel systems is provided in Lewis W. Stern and Adel I. El-Ansary, *Marketing Channels,* 2nd ed. (Englewood Cliffs, N.J.: Prentice-Hall, 1982), chap. 7.

13. Edwin H. Lewis, *Marketing Channels: Structure and Strategy* (New York: McGraw-Hill, 1968), p. 86; see also pp. 85–88 for a discussion of general versus limited distribution.

14. Bert C. McCammon, Jr., and Robert W. Little, "Marketing Channels: Analytical Systems and Approaches," in *Science in Marketing,* ed. George Schwartz (New York: John Wiley & Sons, 1965), pp. 336–54.

15. The interactions and conflicts that occur in channel systems are examined in Larry J. Rosenberg and Louis W. Stern, "Toward the Analysis of Conflict in Distribution Channels: A Descriptive Model," *Journal of Marketing* 34 (October 1970), pp. 40–46; Frederick S. Sturdivant and Donald L. Granbois, "Channel Interaction: An Institutional-Behavioral View," *Quarterly Review of Economics and Business,* Summer 1968, pp. 61–68; and Louis B. Bucklin, "The Locus of Channel Control," in *Marketing and the New Science of Planning,* ed. Robert L. King (Chicago: American Marketing Association, 1968), pp. 142–47.

16. Stern and El-Ansary, *Marketing Channels,* chap. 8.

17. "Selling on the Side," *The Wall Street Journal,* December 24, 1976, pp. 1, 11.

18. Howard Rudnitsky and Jay Gissen, "Profits from Outlets," *Forbes,* June 7, 1982, p. 128.

19. Elizabeth Sanger, "Value at a Discount," *Barron's,* February 28, 1983, p. 24.

20. This illustration is from Komatsu Ltd., *1983 Annual Report,* pp. 8–9.

CHAPTER 15

Physical Distribution Decisions

*T*he operations of a large grocery wholesaler like Wetterau, Inc. clearly illustrate the essential role of physical distribution in marketing. Meeting the needs of the company's 1,700 retailers in 24 states requires the efficient acquisition, storage, and distribution of dry groceries, meat, produce, frozen foods, and dairy products.[1] Gaining efficiency in operations has been a major factor in Wetterau's impressive growth and profit performance. Achieving high performance in wholesaling requires coordinated management of purchasing, handling, storage, inventory, transportation, and communications with suppliers and customers. An on-line computer system in the company's food distribution centers links buying, receiving, and warehousing operations for greater control and efficiency. Another on-line system monitors the transportation fleet maintenance program. Wetterau's productivity improvement program includes warehouse automation, establishment of work standards, and operation of electronic trip recorders throughout the truck fleet. In fiscal 1985, Wetterau exceeded its objective of a 4 percent improvement in productivity.

When you consider that grocery wholesalers' net profits are about $1 per $100 of sales compared to transportation costs of $30 or more per $100 of sales, the importance of physical distribution is apparent.[2] Other physical distribution costs such as inventory carrying costs and warehousing costs further demonstrate that distribution costs comprise a substantial portion of a grocery wholesaler's sales dollar.

Physical distribution activities and decisions are important for many kinds of manufacturers, wholesalers, and retailers, affecting both customer satisfaction and bottom-line profit performance. Managing the physical distribution function is considered in this chapter. First, the scope of physical distribution is examined. The function is defined, its components are described; and its role in both the organization and the marketing channel is discussed. Each of the major activities comprised by the physical distribution system (PDS) is then analyzed and illustrated.

The Scope of Physical Distribution

The management of physical distribution provides an exciting opportunity for improving customer services and reducing costs. For many enterprises, the physical distribution function often determines how well channels perform to satisfy customers through product availability. Efficient distribution can increase profitability by increasing sales and reducing costs. The impact that **physical distribution management** can have on profits is increasingly recognized in companies where major benefits are obtained by managing an integrated system of activities for satisfying customers at efficient cost levels.

Physical distribution management is "the process of strategically managing the movement and storage of materials, parts, and finished inventory from suppliers, between enterprise facilities, and to customers."[3]

Major activities that are normally grouped together in an integrated approach to physical distribution management are transportation, inventory, warehousing, and order processing. Each activity with its many specific functions represents an important management task, and decisions about it must be coordinated with all other distribution decisions.

Levels of Physical Distribution System (PDS)

The difficulties of managing physical distribution as an integrated system are compounded by the various levels that exist in many systems (Exhibit 15–1). When first adopting a physical distribution management approach, a firm may find it beneficial to divide the system into key subsystems for analysis. The supplier/manufacturer and the manufacturer/middlemen/end-user portions of the total system represent two major subsystems. The latter portion corresponds to the channel system, which connects the firm with its end-user markets. The channel system frequently involves more complex design and management tasks because experienced manufacturers probably already have efficient distribution systems with their suppliers and within manufacturing operations.[4]

Physical Distribution's Role in the Organization

Physical distribution considerations are important in the design of new channels of distribution and in the modification of existing systems because channel arrangements become physical distribution operating parameters.[5] The channel configuration and participants and the operating arrangements between channel organizations form the base for planning the physical distribution system.

This system may vary by product. The role of physical distribution for Lockheed Corporation is far different from its role for Zenith, a television manufacturer. Commercial aircraft are produced to order, typically with long lead times. Once aircraft have been produced, their distribution is immediate and direct. On the other hand, consumers normally do not order TVs, and if one model is not available, consumers may switch to other brands.

EXHIBIT 15-1 PDS Levels

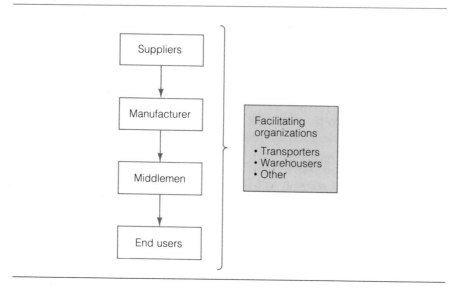

Management's concern and involvement with physical distribution depend to a great extent on its control and influence over the channels in which the firm participates. Members of conventional channels may be unable (or unwilling) to do more than provide for product flows from their firm to the next intermediary. The attention of a small grocery wholesaler is typically concentrated on purchasing, stocking, and distributing to the independent supermarkets it serves. In a vertically coordinated channel, however, the firm exercising control through ownership, contractual arrangement, or administrative clout often has the opportunity and the motivation to manage and coordinate distribution throughout the channel. Super Valu Stores, through ownership of some of its retailers and through influence on its suppliers, has a major impact on physical distribution management in its channels.

The more complex the channels (in number of intermediaries, participants involved, and facilitating firms), the greater are management's opportunities for improving physical distribution. Of course, there may be room for improvement in direct channels (producer to end user), through proper management. But because in direct channels cost and revenue information is normally available to the producer and communication is good, performance gaps are often more visible and less improvement is possible.

Signals that can alert management to possible problems with physical distribution include slow-moving inventory, abnormal stockouts, customer complaints, excessive interwarehouse shipments, and premium freight charges. Management should have available (or should develop) performance standards for spotting performance gaps in physical distribution. In many companies, distribution inventory turnovers of less than six times per year may indicate control problems.[6] Malone & Hyde, Inc., a profitable food wholesaler, has an annual inventory turnover of 15.

Components of the PDS

A look at the decisions that must be made for each PDS component indicates the nature and scope of designing an integrated distribution system.

Transportation

Transportation management is important to successful physical distribution decision making. PDSs involve such transportation-related decisions as:

- Measuring the cost and service aspects of transportation.
- Selecting transportation modes (rail, truck, ship, air, or pipeline) and specific carriers.
- Assessing the impact of regulatory changes (e.g., deregulation of carriers) on transportation operations.
- Deciding whether to use owned (or leased) equipment or to hire transportation services.
- Establishing criteria and methods for evaluating mode/carrier performance.[7]

Developing effective strategies for transportation requires a coordinated management effort.

Developing Cost-Effective Transportation. Identifying opportunities for improvements in distribution costs or customer service often involves gaining an understanding of the costs versus performance of a firm's transportation system. In 1983, Commodore International switched from air to sea shipment of its personal computer disk drives, which were made in the Far East.[8] The move represented a saving of $15 million annually, but the delay in delivery of the drives almost caused a revolt of dealers because they did not have the drives they needed to sell the computer consoles that were already in stock. Thus, savings achieved by changes in transportation modes have to be weighed against the effect that these changes will have on the service provided to customers.

Selecting Modes and Carriers. The choice of transportation modes often involves assessment of several operating characteristics, including cost, speed, availability, dependability, capability, and frequency (Exhibit 15-2). On the basis of cost per ton-mile, water shipment is the least expensive transportation mode, followed by pipeline, rail, truck, and air. After the

EXHIBIT 15–2 Relative Operating Characteristics of Five Basic
                Transportation Modes

Operating Characteristic	Transportation Mode Rating*				
	Rail	**Highway**	**Water**	**Pipeline**	**Air**
Speed	3	2	4	5	1
Availability	2	1	4	5	3
Dependability	3	2	4	1	5
Capability	2	3	1	5	4
Frequency	4	2	5	1	3

* 1 highest; 5 lowest.

Source: Donald J. Bowersox, *Logistical Management*, 2nd ed. (New York: Macmillan, 1978), p. 120.

transportation mode has been selected, the specific carrier must be chosen. Carrier choice involves evaluating the strengths and weaknesses of competing carriers. The carrier performance criteria that are important to a particular firm should be identified and used as the basis for selecting the transportation supplier. For such modes of transportation as railroad shipping, the available suppliers may be limited in certain geographic areas.

Regulatory Reform. Deregulation appears to be breaking down the barriers between transportation modes and to be bringing about a new breed of transportation companies that provide "multimodal" or "fully integrated" services. Consider this description of the new transportation environment:

> The shipper—the manufacturer or retailer, whose options were severely limited under strict regulation—is no longer the forgotten man. Now his options are limited only by economics, and he can take full advantage of containerization and other advances. It is becoming almost as simple for him to send an order overseas—a market he may have felt compelled to ignore before—as it used to be to send it to a neighboring city by truck.
>
> A truck trailer without its wheels is a container, and containerized freight can be whisked through a port to its overseas destination. In this increasingly high-tech world, more and more cargo is suitable for containerization. Add to all this a new generation of larger and fuel-efficient container ships now under construction, and the oceans soon could become superhighways carrying a vastly increased volume of world trade.
>
> In the United States, the use of combinations such as barge and rail or truck and rail, should enable transportation companies to time their deliveries more in line with shippers' needs. Thus, American manufacturers could emulate the Japanese "just-in-time" approach to inventory control. That, in turn, would reduce the costs of carrying large inventories, and the reduced costs could be reflected in prices.[9]

The Do or Buy Decision. A comparison of the cost of having the firm provide its own transportation services versus the cost of purchasing those services from outside suppliers is the starting point in making the do or buy decision. However, the decision involves assessment of several factors in

EXHIBIT 15-3

Leaseway Transportation helps customers reduce distribution costs by providing computer software systems for truck fleet management.

Courtesy Wyse Advertising.

addition to cost. Flexibility and control over transportation are much greater if a firm owns its truck fleet. With such a truck fleet, a firm can easily make routing changes and shift equipment in response to customer needs (Exhibit 15-3). Many firms own and operate trucks, and some firms own and operate ships, railroads, aircraft, and pipelines.

Transportation system audit
is a comprehensive evaluation of transportation objectives, operations, and performance.

Evaluating Mode/Carrier Performance. Among the criteria that are often used in measuring and controlling carrier performance are speed of service, size of order shipped, on-time delivery, transit time variability, and damage. In addition to day-to-day evaluation of transportation services, a periodic audit is needed in planning, implementing, and controlling a transportation system. A **transportation system audit** is useful in identifying performance standards, in measuring cost and service components, and in developing procedures for managing the transportation network. Characteristics related to the distribution of the product, customer service requirements, and geographic considerations should be identified and assessed. Next, transportation modal alternatives, including intermodal combinations (truck plus rail), should be examined. This is followed by consideration of the relationship of transportation to physical distribution. Finally, specific carriers are evaluated. The frequency of transportation system evaluation and the selection of criteria for such evaluation should be determined as a part of the system audit.

Inventory Management and Control

Inventory turnover refers to the number of times that the normal amount of inventory carried by a company is sold in a year.

A second component of the PDS involves inventory. Inventory decisions are concerned with balancing the costs of carrying inventory, ordering products from suppliers, and controlling other inventory costs to achieve a desired level of customer satisfaction. In the inventory for an appliance manufacturer, there are raw materials and parts inventories, stocks of partly manufactured products, finished goods inventory at the manufacturing level, and appliances stocked in the warehouses of distributors and retailers. Inventory accumulation is expensive, yet availability is essential to having satisfied customers. Thus, managing the trade-offs of inventory levels against other physical distribution activities is important. Decisions about **inventory turnover** should be influenced by the speed and cost of transportation, the location of facilities, the effectiveness of communication, and handling and storage requirements. However, reducing the costs of a particular distribution activity such as carrying inventory may increase the costs of other distribution activities or create unhappy customers.

Inventory management affects corporate profitability in two ways. First, maintaining higher levels of inventory leads to greater in-stock availability and more consistent service levels.[10] Second, inventory costs can be decreased by lowering carrying costs and by purchasing in economical lots. Thus, the higher the level of inventory, the more favorable will be the impact on demand and the higher inventory carrying costs will be. As a consequence, inventory decisions involve evaluation of various cost and benefit trade-offs. Several decision models can be used: economic order quantity (EOQ), fixed-order point, and fixed-order interval.

Economic order quantity

(EOQ) is the size of an order of an item to be placed in inventory that results in a minimum total cost, taking into account the ordering costs and the costs of carrying the item in inventory.

The EOQ Model.[11] When the inventory decision is being made under conditions of certainty (future demand is known) the **economic order quantity** model can be used. While clearly oversimplified, this approach is useful in showing how inventory trade-off decisions are made in balancing the costs of ordering inventory against the costs of carrying inventory. The typical relationships between these two sets of costs are shown in Exhibit 15-4. The EOQ is the order quantity that *minimizes* the total cost of inventory carrying and ordering.

EXHIBIT 15–4 Cost Trade-offs Required to Determine the EOQ

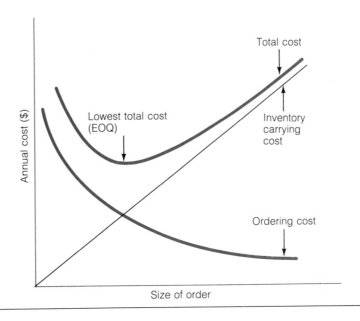

The calculation of EOQ is obtained from the following formula:

$$EOQ = \sqrt{\frac{2PD}{CV}}$$

where:

P = Ordering cost (dollars per order)
D = Annual demand (in units)
C = Annual inventory carrying cost *as a percentage* of product cost
V = Average cost of one unit of inventory

Suppose a retailer's ordering cost for a food processor is $500, annual demand is 10,000 units, annual inventory carrying cost is 10 percent, and the average cost of the processor is $50 per unit. What is the EOQ?

$$EOQ = \sqrt{\frac{2 \times \$500 \times 10{,}000}{10 \times \$50}}$$

$$= 141 \text{ units}$$

If the ordering cost were $1,000 instead of $500, would the EOQ increase or decrease? Repeating the EOQ calculation discloses that the new EOQ is larger than 141 units (200 units). Why? Because if all other aspects of the EOQ calculation do not change, then higher ordering costs would suggest larger orders.

Incorporating Uncertain Demand. Advanced inventory models incorporate more realistic assumptions than a continuous, constant, and known rate of demand and the other simplifying conditions of the EOQ. The uncertainties of demand and lead time can be included in the analysis using the fixed-order point (fixed-order quantity) model or the fixed-order interval model (Exhibit 15-5). The fixed-order point model follows the decision rule of ordering inventory when stock reaches a predetermined minimum required to satisfy demand during the order cycle. The reorder level is 150 units for the example shown in Exhibit 15-5A. The basis of the reorder point is that the remaining inventory (150 units) will satisfy demand during the order cycle (5 days). A calculated fixed-order quantity (500 units) is ordered every time the inventory level reaches 150 units.

The fixed-order interval model compares current inventory with forecast demand; replacement orders are made at regular, specified times. Orders are placed at 20-day intervals in the illustration shown in Exhibit 15-5B. Order amounts vary according to forecast demand.

The Warehousing Function

Manufacturing plants, warehouses, distribution centers, and retail outlets are PDS facilities. Given the large capital investment and operating costs required for the buildings and fixtures needed to perform the warehousing function, decisions on the size, number, and location of these facilities are critical aspects of PDS design. In an existing firm, much of the facility network may already be in place, constraining the opportunity to change the system. Nevertheless, consideration should be given to the potential impact on distribution system costs and service levels of warehouse additions and modifications, proposed new facilities, and so forth.

An illustration demonstrates the role of warehousing in physical distribution. W. W. Grainger manufactures and distributes its own motors, fans, blowers, and other products and parts, as well as those of other producers. Sales in 1983 were over $860 million, an increase of nearly three times over sales a decade earlier. One of Grainger's major strategic advantages is its distribution system—"having the right thing in the right place at the right time."[12] Grainger has 9,800 products and 24,000 parts that could present a distribution nightmare unless properly managed. Grainger's distribution is described as follows:

EXHIBIT 15-5 Models for Inventory Decisions under Uncertainty

A. Fixed-order point, fixed-order quantity model

Assumption: Order cycle is 5 days

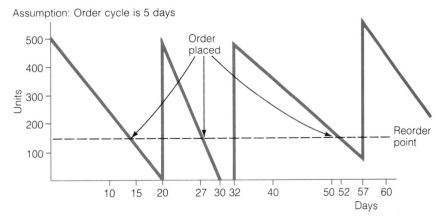

B. Fixed-order interval model

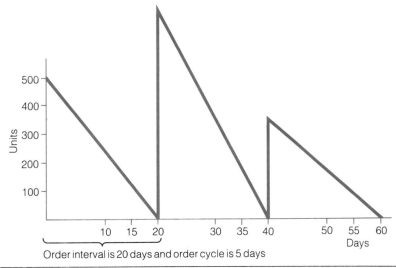

Source: Douglas M. Lambert and James R. Stock, *Strategic Distribution Management* (Homewood, Ill.: Richard D. Irwin, 1982), p. 287.

All merchandise is gathered through 1.6 million square feet of warehouses near its Skokie, Illinois, headquarters. (This hub will be duplicated with a 1.4-million-square-foot building to open in Kansas City this winter.) There it is arranged into assortments shipped at least weekly, in full truckloads, to the stores. With less volume, Grainger would have to settle for half-filled trucks or less-frequent deliveries. The weekly deliveries, in turn, enable branches to satisfy buyers without holding huge inventories of their own.[13]

An important aspect of warehousing is the handling and storage of inventories. These functions occur throughout the distribution channel and consume a sizable portion of total system costs. Efficient handling and storage can yield major cost reductions. The selection of improved methods of movement and packaging can yield huge savings when handling is extensive and repetitious. The following illustrates the impact that creative planning of handling and storage can have on physical distribution:

> Several enterprises have been able to design unit loads to move large assortments of products from the product line directly to the customer's shelf. Although such programs carry a proportional expense, if properly developed, they may more than pay for themselves through reduced handling, lower transportation costs, improved customer relations, and overall efficiency.[14]

Order Processing

The timely flow of correct information through the distribution network can reduce the costs of other PDS activities. Information connects the various organizations and distribution functions and serves as the nerve center of the distribution system. It provides data on order processing, transportation scheduling, delivery status, inventory turnover, and system performance. Planning for information flow, control, and feedback must be incorporated into the physical distribution design. The information processing technology available today is impressive; the challenge is to put together an effective and efficient communications network. Contrast, for example, the time and processing required for ordering by mail through one or more intermediaries versus ordering by an electronic terminal linked directly to the supplier's warehouse.

In vendor stocking, the supplier maintains an inventory for industrial customers, thus eliminating or reducing the customers' need to maintain inventory. Vendor stocking illustrates how order processing functions in coordination with such other physical distribution activities as inventory management and transportation. Vendor stocking programs can yield important benefits to suppliers and their customers. The Vallen Corporation distributes a wide variety of industrial safety and health products. For Dow Chemical's complex in Freeport, Texas, Vallen maintains enough inventory on 250 items to satisfy 95 percent of Dow's requisitions immediately, with deliveries every two hours.[15] If Dow needs 12 hard hats, it transmits the order via a computer terminal to Vallen's terminal in its branch office. This system eliminates Dow's need to keep a stockroom, shop by phone, or rush to locate out-of-stock items.

The PDS Planning Process

The design and management of physical distribution systems involve a number of business functions in addition to marketing, including raw materials management, inventory control, manufacturing, transportation, and warehouse and plant location. The major steps in designing the PDS are:

- Establish PDS objectives.
- Measure customer service.
- Examine cost trade-offs.
- Identify and select design alternatives.

Establish PDS Objectives

Customer service level
is a measure of how well the customer service function is being accomplished.

Customer service as it relates to the physical distribution function consists of providing products at the time and location corresponding to the customer's needs. The **customer service levels** that may be provided range from very good to very poor. A 100 percent level of satisfaction would indicate that all customers are completely satisfied with product availability.

The ideal solution to the problem of PDS design is to develop minimum cost systems for a range of acceptable levels of customer service and then to select the service level that makes the greatest contribution of sales less physical distribution costs. One major difficulty in this approach to PDS design is estimating the sales response to different levels of customer service.

Customers would be 100 percent satisfied if a wide range of products were available at the right place and time in sufficient quantities to meet the needs and wants of all who were willing and able to buy. Clearly, this condition rarely occurs, since the costs would be prohibitive. However, it is possible to achieve high levels of customer satisfaction with properly designed distribution systems. "Customer service is a complex collection of demand-related factors under the control of the firm, but whose importance in determining supplier patronage is ultimately evaluated by the customer receiving the service."[16] Five major factors affect customer service: *time, dependability, communication, availability,* and *convenience.*[17] The importance of these factors will vary by product and customer category. For example, delivery time may be a critical factor to customers when they find it necessary to order products. To establish service levels (90 percent, 95 percent), it is necessary to determine how important each factor is and what level of performance constitutes a particular level of service (95 percent customer satisfaction). Vallen Corporation's fulfillment of 95 percent of Dow Chemical's orders for 250 different items within two hours represents 95 percent customer service level satisfaction for time, dependability, communication, and convenience factors established between the buyer and the supplier.

There is a relationship among levels of customer service, sales, and the cost of the physical distribution system, as shown in Exhibit 15-6. A minimum-cost physical distribution system is the system with the lowest cost that can provide a specified level of customer service. As customer service approaches 100 percent, sales level off and distribution costs surge upward. The curves in Exhibit 15-6 probably resemble those that exist in a wide variety of firms.

EXHIBIT 15-6 Customer Service, Sales, and Distribution Cost Relationships

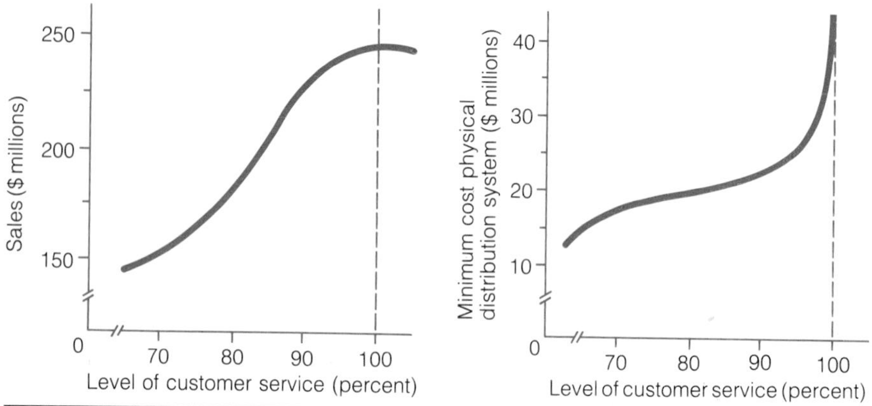

Measure Customer Service

Given the information in Exhibit 15-6, the physical distribution design task is clear. Within the range of customer service levels that management considers necessary to achieve the firm's marketing objectives (90 to 100 percent), the service level and system design that yield the highest contribution of sales minus physical distribution costs must be identified. The principal problem in doing this is the difficulty of measuring customer service and estimating sales response to service level. One way of resolving the problem is to regard customer service as a constraint on the system:

> A predetermined customer service level is selected as a minimum, and the system is designed to meet this level with a minimum cost. The level is arbitrarily selected and is often based on such factors as (1) the service levels established by competition, (2) the opinions of salesmen, and (3) tradition. There is no guarantee that a service level established in this manner will result in a system design that is the best balance between revenues and . . . costs.[18]

Several possible measures of customer service are shown in Exhibit 15-7. The choice of an appropriate measure or measures is situation specific and is based on the service factor(s) most closely linked to customer satisfaction. The *pretransaction* elements use measures that designate service capability before it is provided. A target delivery date indicates the planned time of delivery. The *transaction* elements gauge service performance for various components of buyer-seller transactions. The *posttransaction* elements measure customer service based on results or outcomes. An important factor in customer service is establishing communications between buyers and sellers. The direct computer contact between Vallen Corporation and Dow Chemical allows feedback from customers to assist the supplier's management in evaluating service and establishing service levels.

EXHIBIT 15–7 Possible Measures of Customer Service Performance

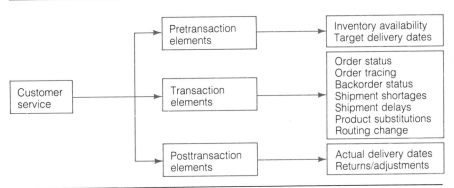

Source: Douglas M. Lambert and James R. Stock, *Strategic Distribution Management* (Homewood, Ill.: Richard D. Irwin, 1982), p. 75.

Examine Cost Trade-offs

The cost trade-offs for physical distribution components must be evaluated to determine how and to what extent each component will be utilized in the PDS. The interrelationships of various PDS components are shown in Exhibit 15–8. The arrows indicate the trade-offs between activities that must be evaluated in:[19]

- Estimating customer service levels.
- Developing purchasing policies.
- Selecting transportation policies.
- Making warehousing decisions.
- Setting inventory levels.

Analyzing the costs of alternative combinations of PDS components is essential to guiding the design of the system:

Trade-off analysis in PDS design is the evaluation of the costs of each system component with the objective of determining the combination of components that provides a minimum total cost system for a specified customer service level.

Storing all finished-goods inventory in a small number of distribution centers helps minimize warehousing costs but leads to an increase in freight expense. Similarly, savings resulting from large-order purchases may be entirely offset by greater inventory carrying costs. In a nutshell, reductions in one set of costs invariably increase the costs of other logistical components. Effective management and real cost savings can be accomplished only by viewing distribution as an integrated system and minimizing its total cost.[20]

Since certain elements of the distribution function are often more important than others in a given firm, **trade-off analysis** should be directed to those elements that comprise the major portion of distribution costs.

EXHIBIT 15-8 Cost Trade-offs in a Physical Distribution System

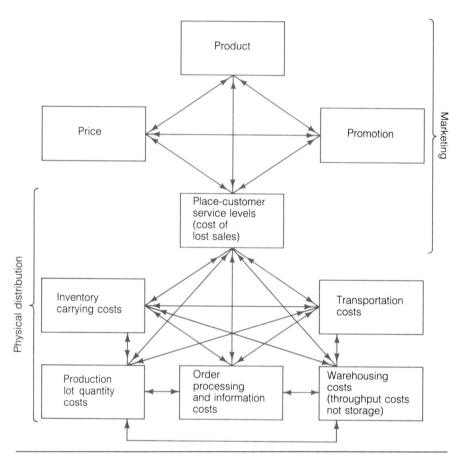

Source: Douglas M. Lambert. *The Development of an Inventory Costing Methodology: A Study of the Costs Associated with Holding Inventory* (Chicago: National Council of Physical Distribution Management, 1976), p. 7.

Identify and Select Design Alternatives

A key issue in designing the PDS is how to incorporate the customer service objective into the design process. Management judgment and experience will often dictate a range of customer satisfaction levels that are acceptable to the firm. In many cases, these levels may be expressed not as percentages, but rather in terms of lost orders, delays, stockouts, and other proxy measures. To illustrate alternative ways of handling the customer service objective, we consider three possible approaches to designing the PDS.

Estimate Sales Response to Customer Service. This approach requires information such as that shown in Exhibit 15-6. If it is possible to determine the relationship between sales and customer service, then a minimum-cost

EXHIBIT 15–9 Logistics System Design Costs as a Function of Various Customer Service Levels

Alterna-tive	System Design*	Annual Costs ($000)	Customer Service Level†	Alterna-tive	System Design*	Annual Costs ($000)	Customer Service Level†
1	Mail-order transmittal, water transporta-tion, low inventory levels	$5,000	80%	4	Mail-order transmittal, rail transportation, high inventory levels	$12,000	93%
2	Mail-order transmittal, rail transportation, low inventory levels	7,000	85	5	Mail-order transmittal, truck transportation, high inventory levels	15,000	95
3	Mail-order transmittal, truck transportation, low inventory levels	9,000	90	6	Telephone-order trans-mittal, truck transportation, high inventory levels	16,000	96

* Minimum-cost design to produce the stated customer service level.

† Percentage of customers receiving goods within one day.

Source: Ronald H. Ballou, *Business Logistics Management*, © 1973, p. 106. Reprinted by permission of Prentice-Hall, Inc., Englewood Cliffs, N.J.

PDS can be designed for the service level that yields the highest profit contribution. The difficult part of this approach is estimating the relationship of sales response to service level. What change in sales will occur if customer satisfaction is increased from 94 percent to 97 percent? Possible methods for estimating the relationship include management judgment and experience, analysis of historical sales and service data, customer research, and testing under controlled conditions.

Due to the difficulty of obtaining response information or the costs involved in estimating the response relationship, this approach may be unfeasible for many firms. The approach would be particularly difficult to apply in situations where customer patronage depends on several aspects of service. Developing a composite sales response function incorporating the effects of product substitutions, delivery delays, and inventory availability on sales response would be a demanding analytic task. However, the data available on customer service and buyer response should make the approach applicable to catalog mail-order distribution.

An example of estimating sales response to customer service is shown in Exhibit 15-9. The system designer must determine a minimum-cost design for each customer service level analyzed. In the six alternatives considered, the objective is to estimate the probable sales increases between customer service levels (e.g., the sales increase that would be obtained by moving from alternative 3 to alternative 4) and then to select the alternative that offers the greatest contribution over costs.

Minimize Total PDS Costs. With the second PDS design approach, management must estimate the total cost of customer service. This approach requires estimating costs of lost sales instead of sales response to customer

EXHIBIT 15-10 Revenue, Cost, and Profit Contribution Analysis for a PDS

Number of Warehouses Service level—93%, 24 hours	System Costs ($000)				
	3	6	10	15	20
Inventory costs—20%	$ 240	$ 300	$ 395	$ 540	$ 720
Probable obsolescence	130	160	210	320	450
Warehousing costs	155	203	270	350	430
Transportation to warehouses	415	370	395	435	500
Local delivery	310	220	165	134	90
Production or supply	80	40	35	40	50
Order processing costs	25	32	40	63	91
Total system cost	1,355	1,325	1,510	1,882	2,331
Forecast sales revenue	9,800	10,200	10,450	10,630	10,800
Forecast manufacturing profit contribution (20%)	3,920	4,080	4,180	4,250	4,320
Total system contribution	$2,560	$ 2,755	$ 2,670	$ 2,368	$ 1,989

Source: *Distribution Management Handbook* (Toronto: McGraw-Hill Ryerson, 1980), p. 314.

service. Management might specify a 95 percent service level that would mean 5 percent customer dissatisfaction. The cost of lost sales is estimated and included with other distribution costs.

$$\text{Minimize total PDS costs} = \text{Transportation costs} + \text{Inventory costs}$$
$$+ \text{Warehousing costs}$$
$$+ \text{Order processing costs}$$
$$+ \text{Cost of lost sales}$$

The objective is to minimize the total costs of physical distribution.

Reduce PDS Costs. The third approach to the design task involves analyzing the trade-offs between PDS components with the objective of improving physical distribution over the present level. This may mean increasing the customer service level at no additional cost or reducing total distribution costs with no loss of customer service. This approach is often the most feasible of the three, due to the inherent difficulty of the other approaches— the difficulty of estimating the relationships of sales response or cost to level of service. Although not an optimal solution, it represents a practical starting point for most firms.

Regardless of the approach used, management should attempt to assess the impact of improved physical distribution on sales. An example of sales, cost, and profit contribution for a physical distribution system is shown in Exhibit 15-10. The analysis considers alternative numbers of warehouses and other distribution activities for a service level of 93 percent on a 24-hour basis. Note how the costs of distribution elements and forecast revenue change in moving from 3 to 20 warehouses. The six-warehouse system offers the highest total system contribution of $2.755 million.

Managing Physical Distribution

After the PDS has been designed and implemented, it must be managed and controlled. Two key aspects of the ongoing management function require further explanation: assignment of responsibility for the PDS and development of a management information system for monitoring performance and spotting problems.

Organizational Options

Problems can occur when physical distribution activities are fragmented and uncoordinated. But deciding where to place responsibility for the physical distribution function may not be obvious. Like product management, distribution involves areas of the firm that have traditionally been separated. Approaches for organizing physical distribution include:

■ The use of a task force to monitor, coordinate, and, when necessary, modify distribution activities and interrelationships.

■ The assignment of management responsibility to an existing functional area in which several distribution activities are already being performed. Candidates include the executive responsible for channel management, manufacturing planning, or transportation.

■ The establishment of a separate organizational unit for distribution management and coordination. The unit should be headed by a professional physical distribution executive. It may range from a small staff organization that is primarily responsible for analysis, planning, and coordination to a line operation with responsibility for such distribution activities as warehousing, transportation, and order processing.

The integration of physical distribution activities may evolve over time, beginning with a task force approach and ultimately developing into a separate organizational unit. However, since the total integration of distribution-related activities cuts across an entire firm, it is unlikely that every activity can be placed under the auspices of one organizational operating unit. LaLonde suggests a three-stage approach to integrating physical distribution functions to reduce "organizational shock."[21] Traffic and warehousing would be combined first. Then, order processing and finished-goods inventory management would be added. The third stage—total integration—would incorporate production planning, packaging, and other physical distribution functions. Management's preferences and the costs versus benefits of total integration might make an intermediate level an acceptable organizational solution in a particular firm.

Controlling Distribution Costs

Physical distribution management has been given much attention by business executives during the past decade. Firms that have restructured their physical distribution systems in recent years include Hooker Chemical, Abbott

Laboratories, H. J. Heinz, Black & Decker, Bristol-Myers Products, and Johns-Manville Sales Corporation.[22] Many firms, however, continue to perform the distribution function in a highly fragmented fashion, and for some, the results may be acceptable. Still, it is advisable that management review and evaluate physical distribution operations to determine whether improvements are needed. Among the factors that may create a need for evaluation are rapid growth, new products, acquisitions, changes in channels of distribution, changes in the product mix, expansion from regional to national distribution, and such indications of inefficient distribution as customer complaints and slow inventory turnover.

The establishment of a PDS control system requires determination of performance standards, information collection, and comparison of actual with desired results. An illustration of one aspect of managing distribution costs indicates the importance of such a system:

> Most distribution costing systems are in their infancy and rely heavily on allocations to determine the performance of segments such as products, customers, territories, divisions, or functions. Company C provides an example of such allocations that led to erroneous decision making and loss of corporate dollars. The firm is a multidivision corporation that manufactured and sold high-margin pharmaceuticals as well as a number of lower-margin packaged-goods products. The company maintained a number of field warehouse locations managed by corporate staff. These climate-controlled facilities were designed for the pharmaceutical business and required security and housekeeping practices that far exceeded those necessary for normal packaged goods. To fully use the facilities, however, the company encouraged nonpharmaceutical divisions to store their products in these distribution centers.
>
> Although the costs of operating the warehouses were largely fixed, corporate policy was to allocate costs to user divisions on the basis of the square footage occupied. Due to the pharmaceutical warehousing requirements, this charge was relatively high. The corporate divisions were managed on a decentralized profit-center basis. [One] division's distribution executive realized that he could obtain similar services at lower cost to his division by using a public warehouse. For this reason, he withdrew his products from the corporate facilities and began to use public warehouses. Although the volume of product handled and stored in the corporate distribution center decreased significantly, relatively little savings were realized in terms of the distribution center's total costs. This was because of the high proportion of fixed costs. Consequently, the company allocated approximately the same cost over fewer users, which made it even more attractive to the other user divisions to change to public warehouses to obtain lower rates. The result was higher, not lower, total company warehousing costs. The corporate warehousing costs were primarily fixed and would not change significantly, whether the space [was] occupied or not. When the nonpharmaceutical divisions moved to public warehouses, the company continued to incur the same expenses for its own warehouses, as well as the additional public warehousing charges. In effect, the distribution costing system motivated divisional distribution managers to act in a manner that was not in the best interests of the company, and total costs escalated.[23]

Application

A Successful PDS[24]

Over a three-year period, sales for a large consumer goods manufacturer leveled off after a decade of rapid growth. Inventories rose 30 percent beyond previous levels, customers were unhappy, and service levels declined from the traditional 99 percent to less than 96 percent. The number of customer complaints was higher than it had ever been, and the morale of the sales force was impaired. The overall problem faced by the manufacturer was defined as, "How much inventory should we have to provide a competitive level of service, and how can we ensure that level of service?" A four-person task force was formed, consisting of managers from marketing, manufacturing, manufacturing systems, and production and inventory control, and assistance was obtained from outside consultants. The task force reported to a steering committee at the top-management level. The four managers were assigned to the task force on a full-time basis for the duration of the project, their regular positions being temporarily filled by subordinates.

Situation Analysis

Data collection and analysis took three months and generated several important findings. Among the major problems identified by the study team were inconsistent and inaccurate sales forecasts and inappropriate inventory levels. In total, the warehouse inventory was 50 percent higher than was required to provide a 99 percent customer service level, but it was far too low for a handful of products. Back orders had increased from an average of $10,000 to over $500,000. Inventory safety stock showed a variance of from one-half month of sales to six months of sales, rather than the intended quantity of two months of sales. There were also demand imbalances between the plant and the warehouses. This resulted in too much inventory in some locations and not enough in other locations. Inventory decisions were heavily based on freight cost, ignoring carrying and storage costs. Two different forecasts—one from manufacturing, the other from marketing—were being used in establishing inventory goals for each item. In the company's peak summer months, only 20 percent of sales were delivered on time; the principal component of lead times was waiting time rather than working time. Manufacturing capacity was severely overloaded during peak months. The identification of these problems provided a framework for redesigning the distribution system.

Actions and Results

The marketing and operations research team developed a sales forecasting system. Manufacturing and inventory control people designed a statistical safety stock system covering each product and each warehouse. A computer simulation was developed to help determine proper integration of distribution. A new manufacturing and planning system was designed to reduce lead time and to guide capacity planning on an overall basis so that inventory to handle peak demand requirements could be built up during slack periods. This last system design change resulted from raising the question of whether manufacturing could provide the product even if it had proper information. Had the project not been carried to this point, many of the other system changes would have been of little value in improving results.

Implementation of the improvements required one year. During that time, new computer systems were programmed and tested, users were trained, and the new and old systems underwent parallel testing. The results of the improvements were impressive. Inventories were reduced by $8 million (15 percent). Back orders declined from a $500,000 peak to the $10,000–20,000 range. Customer complaints were greatly reduced, and operating costs declined by over $300,000 per year, excluding savings in inventory and improved service ■

Summary

In many companies, physical distribution activities account for a major portion of the selling price of products. Increasing the effectiveness and efficiency of physical distribution offers an important opportunity and challenge for firms whose costs and demand are substantially affected by the physical movement of materials and products. Physical distribution activities include warehousing, inventory control, communications, transportation, and handling and storage. Physical distribution systems are important because of their influence on customer response and because of their high costs in many firms. The integration and management of distribution functions are important means of meeting customer satisfaction objectives at cost-effective levels.

Decisions as to each distribution system component, such as transportation, are a specific management task. Decisions in choosing the transportation mode and carrier must be made, taking into account the impact on costs and patronage of the other distribution system components (inventory, warehousing, etc.). The steps in physical distribution system planning consist of setting objectives, measuring the extent of customer service, examining cost trade-offs, identifying design alternatives, and selecting a design approach.

Three approaches to designing the PDS are considered. The first approach involves determining the service level and PDS cost that yields the highest profit contribution. This approach requires information on how sales respond to different levels of customer service. Using the information, a minimum-cost PDS can be designed for the service level that yields the highest profit contribution.

In the second approach, management selects the customer service level that it considers appropriate and then a minimum-cost PDS is developed. There is no attempt to examine the costs and sales response for alternative service levels. The third approach concentrates on improving customer service and/or reducing costs.

Finally, several options regarding the placing of responsibility for the PDS in the firm were considered, including the use of a committee or task force, assignment to an existing functional area, and establishment of a separate organizational unit. A three-stage approach to the integration of physical distribution functions is recommended. In the first stage, traffic and warehousing are confined. In the third stage, total integration is achieved.

Exercises for Review and Discussion

1. Identify and discuss the major factors that often influence the extent to which physical distribution systems offer a potential for favorable benefit/cost results.

2. Why is there likely to be a close correspondence between the type of channel (e.g., conventional, vertically coordinated) used by a firm and the firm's approach in managing the physical distribution function?

3. Measuring customer satisfaction at different levels of service is a critical input for the design of physical distribution systems. Suggest possible ways of measuring customer satisfaction for a company like Sears, J. C. Penney, or K mart.

4. What are some important issues that should be considered in deciding whether to establish a separate physical distribution organization or to manage the distribution function within marketing, manufacturing, or some other existing unit?

5. Explain why customer service objectives and physical distribution cost objectives conflict with each other.

6. How can a physical distribution system be

designed to overcome the conflicts between customer service objectives and physical distribution cost objectives?

7. What effect will an increase from 10 percent to 15 percent in annual inventory carrying cost have on the EOQ? What effect will a decrease in ordering cost to 70 percent of the previous level have on the EOQ?

8. As assistant to the president of an appliance manufacturer, you have been asked to develop a plan for analyzing the firm's physical distribution effectiveness and efficiency. Prepare an outline detailing how you intend to accomplish the assignment.

Notes

1. Wetterau, Inc., *1985 Annual Report*, p. 12.

2. Frank W. Campanella, "Wholesale Success: Retailing Also Helps Super Valu Keep Its Winning Streak Alive," *Barron's*, October 17, 1983, pp. 71–73.

3. Donald J. Bowersox, *Logistical Management*, 2nd ed. (New York: Macmillan, 1978), p. 3.

4. See, for example, David W. Cravens and Lowell M. Hoffman, "Analyzing the Supplier: Reversing the Marketing Process," *Management Review* 66 (July 1977), pp. 47-54.

5. Bowersox, *Logistical Management*, p. 42.

6. Steven B. Oresman and Charles D. Scudder, "A Remedy for Maldistribution," *Business Horizons*, June 1974, p. 72.

7. The discussion in this section is based on Douglas M. Lambert and James R. Stock, *Strategic Distribution Management* (Homewood, Ill.: Richard D. Irwin, 1982), chap. 5.

8. Dennis Kneale, "Commodore Hits Production Snags in Its Hot-Selling Home Computer," *The Wall Street Journal*, October 28, 1983, p. 31.

9. Bill Paul, "Moving It: Freight Transportation Is Being Transformed in Era of Deregulation," *The Wall Street Journal*, October 20, 1983, pp. 1, 22.

10. Lambert and Stock, *Strategic Distribution Management*, p. 282.

11. This discussion is based on Lambert and Stock, *Strategic Distribution Management*, pp. 282-86.

12. William Baldwin, "Dollars from Doodads," *Forbes*, October 11, 1982, p. 56.

13. Ibid., p. 56.

14. Bowersox, *Logistical Management*, p. 48.

15. Baldwin, "Dollars from Doodads," p. 52.

16. Ronald H. Ballou, *Business Logistics Management* (Englewood Cliffs, N.J.: Prentice-Hall, 1973), p. 96.

17. An extensive discussion of customer service is provided in John J. Coyle and Edward J. Bardi, *The Management of Business Logistics*, 2nd ed. (St. Paul, Minn.: West Publishing, 1980), chap. 11.

18. Ballou, *Business Logistics Management*, p. 104.

19. Douglas M. Lambert and Howard M. Armitage, "Managing Distribution Costs for Better Profit Performance," *Business*, September–October 1980, p. 46.

20. Ibid., p. 47.

21. Bernard J. LaLonde, "Strategies for Organizing Physical Distribution," *Transportation and Distribution Management* 14 (January-February 1974), p. 22.

22. Bowersox, *Logistical Management*, p. 442.

23. Lambert and Armitage, "Managing Distribution Costs," p. 49.

24. This illustration is based on Oresman and Scudder, "Remedy for Maldistribution," pp. 66, 68–69. Copyright 1974 by the Foundation for the School of Business at Indiana University. Used by permission.

CHAPTER 16

Pricing Decisions

*P*ricing decisions are usually critically important to both business and non-profit organizations. Local governments often seek added revenues by charging or increasing the charges for services that were once free or subsidized. Fares for public transportation have been subject to such increases. Yet transit management in Chicago decided in the mid-1980s that a general 10 percent fare *reduction* would be in everyone's best interest because such a reduction would bring about an increase in ridership. This change was successfully implemented. Chicago transit management also debated setting different prices for different markets:

> The interim chief of the Regional Transportation Authority is considering cutting non-rush hour fares on trains and buses by 10 to 25 percent as a way to increase ridership.
> It is a long overdue idea. The RTA and the Chicago Transit Authority out of necessity have traditionally considered fares as an accounting and political problem rather than a tool they can use to increase use of their systems. . . . reducing fares when there are empty seats ought to become a strategy of targeting transit fares to specific markets, just like [the] airlines.[1]

Pricing is also important to businesses facing competition from low-cost, international producers. One such business has been Cummins Engine Company, the leading maker of engines for heavy-duty trucks in North America. Having seen what happened to numerous U.S. companies because they underestimated Japanese competitors, the management of Cummins slashed prices as much as 30 percent on certain engines in the mid-1980s. Price wars over market share are nothing new; what was new in Cummins' pricing strategy was that the price cuts were made well before the Japanese products arrived in the United States. This was done because management estimated that Cummins' international competitors had a 25 to 30 percent cost advantage, so that any delay in reducing prices would be an invitation to disaster. The price cuts were followed by an ambitious effort to cut costs.[2]

Pricing
is the process of set-
ting objectives,
determining the avail-
able flexibility,
developing strategies,
setting prices, and
engaging in implemen-
tation and control.

Price decisions can enhance or impede the marketing strategy or program. Marketers seek to develop an integrated, internally consistent, and synergistic combination of marketing mix elements. Prices should fit into a firm's marketing strategy, increasing the appeal of the marketing program to the target market. **Pricing** begins with an understanding of the corporate mission, target markets, and marketing objectives. Then, pricing objectives (such as increasing market share) are developed. Next, management must estimate how much flexibility it has in establishing prices. Here, costs are studied to determine the lowest price level necessary to meet profit and other organizational objectives. Demand and competition determine the other end of the price spectrum—the highest possible prices, or "what the market will bear." Prices are set between these extremes by deciding on price strategies that are consistent with pricing objectives. Specific methods are then used to set prices. Finally, managerial skill is employed in pricing implementation and control, which includes effective monitoring to obtain feedback on the response of customers and competitors. These steps will now be discussed in some detail.

Role of Price in Marketing Strategy

Price is often used to enhance the image of a product, to increase sales through discount pricing, or, in combination with promotion, to build future sales. At times, however, price is an inactive element of the marketing mix, with firms using traditional markups over cost or following industry leaders. The use of price as a competitive tool may be avoided due to fear of retaliation and price wars. But whether pricing is an active or inactive element, it is an integral part of the overall marketing program. Determining the role that prices should play relative to other marketing mix variables establishes important boundaries and guidelines for pricing decisions.

Management faces two types of pricing decisions. New products must be priced, and the prices of existing products must be adjusted in the face of changing competitive, cost, and market conditions. Pricing strategies, particularly for new products, are a high-level responsibility shared by marketing and other executives. Pricing usually involves more executives from marketing and sales than from other corporate areas, but these executives share the responsibility for pricing with other high-level executives. Lower-level executives are usually given a narrow range of pricing discretion on specific items.

Price is used in different ways by different companies, depending on the role it plays in the overall marketing program. Service Merchandise, a catalog showroom discounter, uses low prices on name brands as its major basis for appealing to customers. In return for low prices, customers are willing to complete an order form and wait until their purchase is obtained from the warehouse. Through operating efficiencies, reduction in customer service, and high volume, catalog showrooms are able to compete with other retailers by using low prices. Ethan Allen assigned price a very different role. The company's high-priced traditional American furniture and fixtures provide buyers with high-quality products and allow attractive margins to independent retailers who serve as exclusive dealers. Both the manufacturer's and the dealers' margins make possible a variety of customer services and help support various promotional efforts.

The role assigned to price in the marketing program should be consistent with decisions about other marketing mix variables. Decisions to set a price on an item should consider the impact that the price might have on other items *in the product line.* Many firms carry substitute products (Procter & Gamble's Tide and All detergents) or complementary products (golf balls and gloves). In pricing one product, the impact on related products must be considered.

Pricing decisions are intertwined with *promotional* decisions. A price change may require changes in labeling, advertising copy, or advertising messages. The costs associated with such changes may be greater than the additional revenue generated by the price change. On the other hand, promotional expenditures, by increasing sales, may result in production and marketing economies of scale, thus reducing unit costs and allowing greater flexibility in setting prices. Recent reductions in the retail prices of children's toys were due to an increase in volume, resulting from promotion, that made narrower margins possible. Price levels must be appropriate to the promotional image that is projected.

Pricing decisions must also be made in light of *channel/distributor* interests. Palm Beach, Inc.'s pricing strategy for its Evan-Picone line of tailored apparel for women was developed, in part, as a way to strengthen relationships with retailers. Palm Beach management promised retailers designer-quality clothes at prices at least 30 percent lower than those of other distinguished labels, a price reduction made possible by the company's ability to mass-produce fine garments.

Specify Pricing Objectives

Pricing objectives are specific quantitative and qualitative operating targets that reflect the basic role of pricing in the marketing plan.

Many firms fail to establish specific objectives for their pricing programs. **Pricing objectives** should be clear, concise, and understood by all involved in making pricing decisions. Further, these objectives should be so stated as to enable those charged with pricing responsibility to compare performance with them.

A study of pricing in corporations highlighted the diversity of pricing objectives in some of the largest companies. Very few firms stated their pricing objectives in terms of maximizing profits. Rather, most tried to attain a satisfactory or target level of profits or return on investment. Examples of corporate pricing objectives were:

EXHIBIT 16-1 Pricing Objectives

Growth	*Cash flow*
Sales or profit growth.	Rapidly recover new product development costs.
Market share growth.	
	Enhancement of other strategy elements
Profit	Provide a promotional theme.
Maximize return on investment.	Make a product "visible," and create interest.
Maximize (or satisfice) short- and long-run profits.	Fill out the firm's product line.
	Contribute to the image of the product and the firm.
Competitive	Build traffic.
Discourage entrants, and speed exit of marginal firms.	Be regarded as "fair" by middlemen and customers.
Maintain price leadership.	
Discourage price-cutting and stabilize market prices.	
Rapidly establish market position.	

Source: Adapted from Alfred R. Oxenfeldt, "A Decision-Making Structure for Price Decisions," *Journal of Marketing* 37 (January 1973), pp. 48-53. Published by the American Marketing Association.

- "To meet the prices of competitors"—Goodyear.
- "To follow the price of the most important marketer in each area"—Gulf.
- "To maintain existing market share"—Kroger.

Even companies whose primary pricing objectives were stated in terms of profit margin or return on investment had collateral pricing objectives:

- "To promote new products"—Alcoa and General Electric.
- "To stabilize industry prices"—Exxon and Johns-Mansville.
- "To maintain a full line of food products and novelties"—General Foods.

Specific pricing objectives used by firms are shown in Exhibit 16-1. Organizations usually have a *set* of objectives—some primary, others collateral; some short run, others long run. Whatever their type, objectives should be specific, written, and operational.

Determine Extent of Pricing Flexibility

Determining the possible range of prices tells management how much flexibility it has in developing a pricing strategy. The extent of pricing flexibility is determined by costs, demand, competition, and legal and ethical constraints. Together, these elements establish upper and lower limits for prices.

Determine Costs

Since, over the long run, prices must exceed average unit costs, attention must be paid to costs. Analysis is essential to determine what cost level prices must exceed to yield a profit. Poorly managed firms sometimes naively

EXHIBIT 16-2 Costs and Prices: The Characteristic Pattern

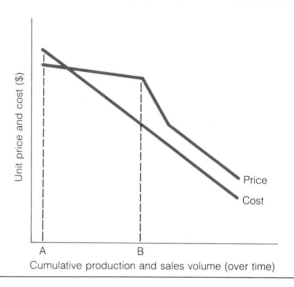

price "under costs," and it is sometimes said jokingly that such firms price under costs with the objective of making up the difference on volume! Pricing under costs is obviously not a long-term strategy. Misunderstanding overhead costs and unit costs at different production volumes as well as erratic inflation rates, sometimes leads to the problem of pricing under costs.

Manufacturers' costs vary not only with supply costs but also with cumulative production experience. One common relationship between costs and production experience, discovered long ago in the aircraft industry, is that with the increase in the cumulative number of units produced, production costs decline (the *learning curve* effect). This relationship between changes in production costs and changes in product prices is shown in Exhibit 16-2. When a new product is introduced, the price is sometimes set slightly below the initial total unit cost, at A. As cumulative production and sales volume grow over time, unit costs typically decline. If the price set does not reflect these declining costs, high profits may result, but typically only for the short run. High profits attract competition that, in turn, drives the price down to a more "reasonable" level above costs. Between A and B (say, year 1 and year 3), costs decline at a rate much greater than the decline in price. Thus, the benefits of experience and production economies are realized.

Various factors affect costs, so it is important that management understand the assumptions underlying cost estimates. Consideration must be given to probable production levels, manufacturing improvements that could result from experience, and the allocation of fixed costs. Understanding cost *behavior* is essential for estimating what product costs will really be. As a company gains experience in providing products and services, cost data are accumulated and management's understanding of costs is greatly improved. On the other hand, estimates of costs for new products may be imprecise. This is even true for automaking:

> An automaker starts by studying the market segment into which a new car will go [in] five or more years. . . . It checks the price of competing models, works out what features it wants, and allows for inflation. The result is a target price. . . . Then the company figures out whether it can design and build the car cheaply enough to leave a theoretical profit margin of at least 10 percent. Jockeying back and forth between desired price and the cost of production continues up to the moment the car is introduced.[3]

Evaluate Demand

Costs set the lower limits of price; demand and competition typically set the upper limits. The expression "what the market will bear" goes to the heart of evaluating demand. The traditional law of demand states that, other relevant factors remaining equal, price reductions will generate demand increases and price increases will cause demand reductions. This law determines the general character of the market demand curve, which depicts the quantity of a product demanded at each possible price. Most products have demand curves that slope downward and to the right when plotted on a vertical price axis and a horizontal quantity axis, as in Exhibit 16–3A. But some product price-quantity relationships are described by a positively sloped demand curve (as in Exhibit 16–3B). This can occur when price is perceived as reflecting product quality—assessing product quality is a difficult task for customers.[4] These graphs are, of course, estimates of customer responses to different price levels, which are difficult to estimate even with established products, much less new ones. Use of market opportunity analysis and demand estimation methods is essential.

Marketing strategists are concerned not only with the absolute level of demand at each price but also with the rate at which demand changes as price changes. If a 10 percent increase in price yields only a 5 percent decrease in unit sales and no change in average unit costs, the increase results in higher profits. Conversely, if a 10 percent price hike cuts sales by 20 percent, then total revenues will fall. If average unit costs are unaffected by the volume cutback, profits will decline. A measure of the responsiveness of demand to price changes is the **price elasticity of demand** coefficient (E_p). This coefficient is the ratio between the percentage change in the number of units demanded and the percentage change in a product's price.

Price elasticity of demand refers to the relationship between a change in sales (units demanded) and the percentage change in price.

$$E_p = \frac{\dfrac{\text{Absolute change in demand at new price}}{\text{Demand at old price}}}{\dfrac{\text{Absolute change in price}}{\text{Old price}}}$$

EXHIBIT 16–3 Downward-and Upward-Sloping Demand Curves

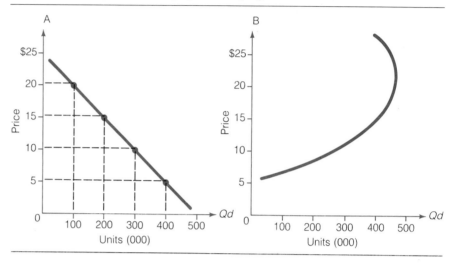

or

$$E_p = \frac{\text{Percentage change in quantity demanded}}{\text{Percentage change in price}}$$

Consider the product whose demand curve is shown in Exhibit 16–3A. A reduction in price from $20 to $15 (a 25 percent cut) increases demand from 100,000 to 200,000 units (a 100 percent jump). For this product, the price elasticity of demand for reductions from $20 to $15 is 4.0.

$$E_p = \frac{\dfrac{100{,}000}{100{,}000}}{\dfrac{\$5}{\$20}} = 4.0$$

When the elasticity coefficient is greater than 1.0, a product is *price elastic.* In this case, price changes yield greater- than-proportional changes in demand, so price hikes decrease *total* revenues and price cuts increase them (as determined by price times quantity demanded). When the coefficient is less than 1.0, a product is *price inelastic,* or not very responsive to price changes. Price hikes on price-inelastic products increase total revenues, and price cuts decrease them. When demand changes exactly in proportion to changes in price, a product is *unitary elastic* and the elasticity coefficient is 1.0.

Price elasticity of demand varies throughout the entire range of possible prices for most products. Raising the price of a marketing book 20 percent, from $30 to $36, may have an insignificant impact on sales. But if the price

EXHIBIT 16–4 Dayton Hudson Leaves Off-Price Retailing

Dayton Hudson Corporation announced [in 1984] that it was ending its experiment with off-price retailing and would sell its four test stores. The nation's fifth largest retailer said it was selling its "Plums . . . The Elegant Discounter" chain because the stores failed to meet performance goals. The Plums stores sold designer and brand-name men's and women's clothing at 20 percent to 50 percent discounts.

Unlike discount stores, which simply sell for less, off-price retailers buy from manufacturers for less because they pay cash, rarely return goods, and don't ask for advertising allowances.

A Dayton Hudson spokesman said the problem with the Plums approach was that its target market of upscale shoppers was so narrow that there was not a broad enough customer base nationally to promise the kind of growth they were looking for. They then attempted to broaden their market by lowering the price range of goods carried and sales picked up. But by lowering the price range, Plums placed itself in competition with other retailers.

Although leaving off-price retailing for now, Dayton Hudson insists the merchandising concept has a lot of potential.

Source: Adapted from Frank E. James, "Dayton Hudson Will End Test in Discounting," *The Wall Street Journal*, February 22, 1984, p. 12. Reprinted by permission of *The Wall Street Journal*, © Dow Jones & Company, Inc., 1984. All rights reserved.

were raised another 50 percent, to $54, demand could decline substantially. Thus, while average unit costs serve as price floors, price elasticity coefficients identify ceilings, or price levels perceived by many potential buyers as being too high. Estimating elasticity at alternative price levels is therefore essential.

Demand elasticity also varies by product type. Consider airfares and gasoline prices. Extensive airfare discounts have been offered by airlines. During one good year, the average price charged per passenger-mile dropped about 2 percent, but the airlines posted an 18 percent gain in traffic. Due to price elasticity, price competition benefited both the airlines and their customers. As for gasoline, most oil industry executives formerly believed that demand for it was not affected much by price changes (inelastic). An economist once estimated that a 50 percent price increase would reduce demand for gasoline by only 7.5 percent. This inelastic demand coefficient of 0.15 (0.075 ÷ 0.50) was later confirmed. But as gasoline prices moved to a higher price range, consumers began to scramble for smaller cars to reduce gasoline purchases. Price elasticity increased, even on gasoline, as the price of gasoline rose within a higher range. By the mid-1980s, however, consumers had become more acclimated to the *new* range of prices, and given reduced gas prices, they shifted back toward larger cars.[5] Elasticity can change over time and over price ranges, and it can be different for a price decrease than for a price increase. Elasticity, after all, is the result of customer behavior.

Finally, customer response to prices must be evaluated in light of the total size of the market. Reduced prices may increase demand, but not sufficiently in terms of the total quantity required to justify making a commitment to the target market. Dayton Hudson experimented with off-price apparel retailing, but decided that the responsiveness of upscale shoppers to lower prices was not sufficient given the limited size of the total market (Exhibit 16–4). That is, price elasticity was too low. Higher price elasticity or a larger target market could have made the venture successful.

Evaluate Competition

Implicit in the law of demand are the assumptions that buyers and sellers interact in a free market environment and that the prices at which goods are exchanged are determined by free market forces. But the extent to which free market forces determine prices depends on the competitive structure of industries. Thus, management must understand the industry structure within which it operates. Economic theory indicates that under conditions of pure competition the actions of buyers and sellers will result in prices that, in the long run, will cover all costs and allow a "fair" return on investment. Firms operating within a classic, purely competitive market do not set prices; market forces do. However, few markets in the United States represent this type of buyer-seller interaction. Most markets exhibit some degree of monopoly power, and this allows sellers to set prices somewhat by administrative fiat rather than having prices completely determined by supply and demand. Even agricultural industries allow some price-setting discretion by firms—and more concentrated industries allow for considerable price-making flexibility.

Johnson & Johnson used this flexibility in meeting Bristol-Myers' competition against its Tylenol. Bristol-Myers' entry into the $61 million market for nonaspirin headache remedies was a classic example of the difficulty of predicting competitive pricing behavior. Attracted by the high margins that Johnson & Johnson was getting on Tylenol tablets, Bristol-Myers decided to challenge J&J's virtual dominance of the acetaminophen market by introducing Datril. Bristol-Myers' management planned to introduce Datril, featuring it in television ads as a lower-cost equivalent to Tylenol. The pricing backfired as J&J's president telephoned Bristol-Myers' president to state that Tylenol's price to the trade was being reduced 30 percent and that ads claiming that there were significant differences in retail price between Datril and Tylenol would be misleading. At the end of a year, $20 million had been spent on Datril, but it had only a 1 percent share of the total analgesic market (then about $700 million), while Tylenol had moved from 10.6 percent to 11.5 percent. Some industry observers commented that Bristol-Myers' challenge was a classic marketing blunder.

Competitively oriented pricing sometimes leads to intense competition or even price wars, as evidenced in the retailing industry.

> These days, retailing seems to be one big price war. . . . Wherever one looks, retail advertising screams of super values, once-in-a-lifetime sales, inventory clearances, and huge savings. Retailing has become one giant sale. The most worrisome implication of retailing's "on sale" posture is the cumulative erosion of price credibility. . . . Retailers unwillingly are teaching consumers that they shouldn't buy something until it's placed on sale unless they absolutely, desperately need it.[6]

Such competitive practices, widely adopted, narrow the flexibility that managers have in setting their own prices. The competitive use of nonprice marketing mix elements is often more effective than the competitive use of price, because prices can be so easily countered by competitors.

Competition directly affects price elasticity because elasticity is higher if competitive substitutes are available to customers (cross elasticity). Thus, close attention to competitors' prices is essential in determining prices. In some industries price lists are sold by information services, and in other industries companies routinely "shop" competitors to monitor prices. Cummins Engine determined the cost advantage held by Japanese producers to estimate the potential price competition—then it cut prices by as much as 30 percent.

Legal and Ethical Constraints

Management must evaluate the effects on pricing flexibility of various legal and ethical considerations. The principal body of law governing price decisions is antitrust legislation, which provides the basis for tests of the legality of pricing decisions (Chapter 3). Pricing is one of the most narrowly and strictly monitored areas of marketing decision making. Overestimating the legal extent of flexibility in making pricing decisions can have serious consequences:

> In a unanimous ruling, the Supreme Court [in the mid-1980s] upheld a $10 million judgment against Monsanto Company. The high court said Monsanto acted illegally in 1968 when it severed ties with Spray-Rite Service Corporation, an Illinois distributor of Monsanto's agricultural herbicides.
>
> In the written opinion, the Court said there was "substantial direct evidence" that Monsanto and other distributors agreed to fix resale prices and to drive price-cutters out of business.
>
> Spray-Rite had sued Monsanto, contending that it was frozen out because it refused to join a Monsanto effort to maintain prices at a certain minimum level. A jury awarded Spray-Rite $3.5 million in damages, which were tripled by law, because the case involved an antitrust violation.[7]

Ethical considerations also influence price decisions. When do prices generate too much profit? Is a firm justified in setting prices equal to buyers' perceptions of values, even if such prices are far above actual costs? Questions of this kind are considered by management in light of the social and political environment, and with a sensitivity to the long-term moral effects of pricing decisions.

Develop Price Strategies

Price strategies are the guidelines and policies used to effectively guide pricing decisions to match target market conditions.

A firm follows **price strategies** when making price decisions. These strategies provide guidelines and policies for the development of specific plans for pricing a product or a line of products. Price strategies determine, among other things, the variability of prices, price levels, the use of price lining, price stability, pricing relative to the product life cycle, and the use of psychological pricing. Developing such strategies is the next step in the pricing process.

Price Variability/Discrimination

Will the selling price for each product be the same for all buyers? A variable pricing policy often enables a firm to achieve higher profits because it allows sellers to negotiate with potential buyers and set selling prices approximately equal to each buyer's perception of product values (and elasticity of demand). Automobile salespeople, for example, strive to assess each buyer's desire to own a new model and to make the sale at the highest price acceptable to the buyer. When purchasing a car, a dentist may consider her time valuable and not wish to haggle over a couple of hundred dollars, but a high school teacher with a family to support may make several shopping trips and bargain for days. Both buyers pay what they consider a fair price. But if a single price were set for both buyers, the seller might lose the teacher's purchase or sell the car at a price below what the dentist would willingly pay.

Because of limitations imposed on sellers by the Robinson-Patman Act, resellers or firms selling to industrial users typically avoid a completely variable pricing policy. In many companies, however, variable price policies allow the granting of trade (functional), quantity, cash, or geographic discounts to buyers. Other allowable price discrimination practices are:

- Charging different prices for goods offered for sale at different places (lower prices for warehouse sales).

- Charging significantly different prices for only marginally different products (higher prices for white sidewall tires).

- Charging different prices at different times (off-peak or non–rush hour pricing by the Chicago transit management).

If price discrimination is pursued, consideration must be given both to the legal limits (discussed in Chapter 24) and to the chances of negative market backlash because some customers are charged lower prices.

Price Level

Before specific prices are set, a general price level for the firm's products should be determined. To make this determination, management considers such factors as the current and desired image of the firm, product line objectives, competitive strengths and weaknesses, and the state of the economy. Sears' decision to alter its pricing strategy in the 1970s was influenced by these factors. Before World War II, Sears had appealed to price-conscious shoppers by charging less than its competitors. In the 1950s, Sears capitalized on rising American affluence and "traded up" to more expensive merchandise. Sears' profits grew steadily, but it lost more and more price-conscious shoppers to J. C. Penney, K mart, and Montgomery Ward. Sears' share of the total sales of retailing's Big Four (Sears, Penney, Kresge, and Montgomery Ward) fell, with K mart picking up a majority of the price-sensitive customers. When Sears' profits fell during the recession and inflation of the mid-1970s, it sought to shift back toward its basic low-price strategy. But Sears' management found it very difficult to change a firmly established image of somewhat

EXHIBIT 16–5

People Express is a firm that was founded on a general strategy of low prices.

Courtesy Plapler Russo & Associates.

higher prices and quality, and as of the mid-1980s it had not yet succeeded in implementing a lower-price image. People Express successfully created a low price image, but severe competition led to equally severe problems! (Exhibit 16–5).

Price Lining

Price lining
is setting several price levels within a product line to match with customers' preferences.

Price Lining is a strategy of offering a product at each price level demanded by customers and provided by competitors. The Chevrolet Division of General Motors offers automobiles at various price levels to appeal to various segments of the auto market. Models range from a stripped-down Chevette to a loaded Caprice Classic.

The ultimate in retailer price lining is *inverted pricing*. Whereas a traditional approach to setting prices is to build up a selling price by adding required markups to cost at each level of the marketing channel, inverted pricing begins with a target retail price, from which normal markups are deducted to identify a maximum production cost. Inverted pricing is used by manufacturers to fill gaps in the lines of goods that they offer at retail. The first step is to subtract distributor margins and costs from a retail price goal; this determines manufacturer prices. Based on these figures, products are designed to strategically fit into the line and yield the necessary manufacturer and reseller margins. For example, when prices of men's suits were polarized at the $175–225 and $65–85 levels, a clothing manufacturer identified a target market for conservative, yet stylish suits of average quality selling for approximately $130. Recognizing the required markups of 40 percent retail, 30 percent wholesale, and its own 25 percent, the manufacturer determined that it had to manufacture the suits for $57 or less ($130 − $37 − $21.50 − $14.50 = $57).

Price lining is often used to aid product positioning in the marketplace. The object is to serve various market segments but not to compete unduly with or cannibalize other products within the firm's product line.

Price Stability[8]

If resale price stability is adopted as an objective, any one of several strategies may be employed to accomplish that objective. Although resale price maintenance agreements with resellers (fair trade) are no longer legal, manufacturers are able to use other means to discourage price competition among resellers. Ethan Allen, Inc., for example, has done this by using selected dealers.

There are several options in maintaining price stability. First, firms may limit their resellers to those that provide a high level of service and traditionally adhere to manufacturers' suggested prices. Second, firms may sell almost all of their items to their distributors, but limit sales of special high-margin quality items to exclusive outlets. Third, firms may increase their influence on resale price decisions by shortening their distribution channel and marketing directly to retailers or consumers. Fourth, firms may achieve resale price stability through contractual agreements with independent distributors. Given sufficient brand competition, manufacturers may legally include price floors in contractual retailer franchise agreements and refuse to sell to violators. Fifth, firms may use consignment selling to maintain retail price stability. If a distributor acts as an agent for a manufacturer and the manufacturer retains title to the goods throughout the channel, the manufacturer is free to dictate all the terms of resale, including prices. Finally, firms may use promotional programs to encourage price stability. Manufacturers often share advertising expenses with retailers on the condition that the retailers advertise manufacturer-suggested prices. The policy of one photographic equipment manufacturer shows how cooperative advertising can be used to promote price stability:

■ When a dealer advertises the price of a product, that price must be at the dealer's actual selling price.

■ No advertisement is approved that advertises a price more than 15 percent lower than the suggested list price.

■ No advertisement is approved that makes a comparison between the dealer's advertised selling price and the suggested list price.

Manufacturers' national advertising, prepricing (ticketing), and price lists also tend to stabilize prices.

Life-Cycle Pricing

Some companies follow a policy of preplanning price changes as products move through the stages of the product life cycle. In general, average prices decline (in constant dollars) and the number of competing firms increases over the product life cycle. Companies assess their ability to effectively compete and develop a differential competitive advantage for each stage of the cycle. Semiconductor component manufacturers—Rockwell International, Texas Instruments, National Semiconductor Corporation—used a life-cycle pricing strategy that squeezed many firms out of the consumer calculator industry in the 1970s. About 70 percent of the manufacturing cost of calculators was accounted for by semiconductor components, so the main weapon of the semiconductor manufacturers was the learning curve. They anticipated manufacturing cost reductions associated with growth in production and sales and concurrently slashed prices to build volume. As a result, simple four-function calculators that had sold for up to $400 were selling for $25 in the 1970s and for well under $10 in the 1980s. Strategically staying ahead of competition on the life cycle was central to Texas Instruments' success. TI was less successful in the home computer market, however, and dropped out of that market in the mid-1980s.

Psychological Pricing

Psychological pricing is based on customer price perceptions so as to have special appeal in certain target markets.

The law of demand does not hold for some buyers of some goods. This accounts for **psychological pricing** strategies, which include odd-even pricing (e.g., $9.99), prestige pricing to benefit from snob appeal (the "If you ask the price, you can't afford it" psychology), and the setting of prices to imply quality. Psychological pricing strategies are dependent on consumer price consciousness, which means that management should determine whether consumers' perceptions of product quality are significantly influenced by the product price. If they are, this should be considered in setting prices.

For products difficult to evaluate, price sometimes serves as a surrogate indicator of quality. Taste studies show that beer drinkers have little success in differentiating beer quality and that they seem to partially base their quality perceptions on price. High prices also go with the "high-hat" shopping malls developed in recent years to serve affluent shoppers. High prices foster a snob appeal image, accented in such centers by valet parking, clerks from the country club set, and promotions built on highbrow themes, such as Beethoven's birthday parties. Determining the potential and the appropriateness of psychological pricing should be an early strategic decision by

EXHIBIT 16–6 Relative Importance of Price-Setting Methods as Seen by Executives

| | Type of Product | | |
Approaches to Setting Prices	Industrial	Consumer Durable	Consumer Nondurable
Competitive level	47%	45%	46%
Certain percentage above or below competitive level	7	8	11
Cost-plus	25	28	27
What the market will bear	13	16	14
According to government rules and regulations	8	3	2
Total	100%	100%	100%

Source: Jon G. Udell, *Successful Marketing Strategies in American Industries* (Madison, Wis.: Mimir, 1972), p. 152.

management, a decision directly related to the specific products involved and the target markets sought.

Establishing Prices

Setting pricing objectives, determining the extent of pricing flexibility, and selecting price strategies provide considerable direction to management for setting specific prices. But how are prices for specific products actually set? In a study of nearly 500 U.S. companies, each executive who responded allocated 100 points among five pricing approaches to indicate their importance. As shown in Exhibit 16-6, the results were very similar across industrial, consumer durable, and consumer nondurable manufacturing companies. All three groups regarded competition-oriented pricing as the most important approach. Cost-plus pricing ranked second. A sound approach to pricing must incorporate cost, competition, *and* demand factors. More than one price-setting method is typically used, and all three factors should be considered.

Cost-Oriented Approaches

Because costs establish the floor for a possible price range, two commonly used cost-oriented approaches show how cost is actually used to set prices.

Cost-Plus/Markup Pricing. Cost-plus pricing simply involves adding a percentage of the cost to set the price. Markup pricing is a variation of cost-plus pricing in that markups are calculated as a percentage of the selling price rather than as a percentage of the cost. But since only the cost and the

EXHIBIT 16-7 Markup Pricing by a Stereo Component Manufacturer

	Product		
	Receiver 101	**Speaker 201**	**Amplifier 301**
Unit variable costs	$120.00	$ 68.00	$ 90.00
Percentage allowance for overhead	12%	15%	10%
Overhead allowance	$ 14.40	$ 10.20	$ 9.00
Percentage markup on price (covers expenses plus profit)	40%	50%	30%
Selling price	$224.00	$156.40	$141.42

EXHIBIT 16-8 Markup Pricing for a Retail Department Store

	Product Category				
	Cameras	**Books**	**Dresses**	**Tobacco**	**Costume Jewelry**
Price to retailer	$135.00	$ 7.50	$44.25	$0.68	$4.30
Traditional markup	28%	34%	41%	20%	46%
Selling price	$187.50	$11.35	$74.99	$0.85	$7.99

desired percentage markup on selling price are known to the manager, a formula may be used to determine the price:

$$\text{Selling price} = \frac{\text{Average unit cost}}{1 - \text{Desired markup percentage}}$$

If an item costs $7 and the markup is 30 percent, then the price is set at $10 [$7 ÷ (1 − 0.3)].

Manufacturers usually add an allowance for fixed overhead costs to unit variable costs and then add a percentage markup (on price) to cover selling, administrative, and general expenses as well as a desired profit percentage. Prices for a receiver, speaker, and amplifier sold by a stereo component manufacturer are calculated by using markup pricing (Exhibit 16-7). A standard percentage is used to allocate overhead to each product. For the receiver, the average unit cost is $134.40 ($120.00 + $14.40). Using the 40 percent markup for receivers, the selling price is calculated as $224.00 ($134.40 ÷ 0.6).

Wholesalers and retailers typically mark up each class of products by a different fixed percentage over the prices they pay. Unlike manufacturers, trading organizations seldom attempt to allocate fixed and operating expenses to each product. Instead, percentage markups for each product category are most frequently determined by industry tradition, company strategy (e.g., price-level strategy), individual operating expenses (rent, insurance, pilferage, etc.), expected turnover, and a myriad of other factors. Using the markup price formula, prices for five different items sold in a retail department store are calculated in Exhibit 16-8.

Successful new ventures are sometimes founded on innovative, low-margin pricing, in the hope of high volume to provide a good return. In the 1930s supermarkets shook up the food distribution business using this approach, and in the 1980s the health care industry was experiencing similar changes. A health care think tank predicted that 10–12 "Supermeds" would control 50 percent of the hospital business by the mid–1990s. Traditional hospitals and HMOs (health maintenance organizations) are facing increased competition from major brand name health care providers, such as Humana, Inc.[9]

Break-Even and Target Return Pricing.   Another cost-oriented method, break-even pricing, determines the level of sales needed to cover all of the relevant fixed and variable costs. If fixed costs are $100,000, unit variable costs are $2, and the price per unit is $4, then the firm must sell 50,000 units to break even [$100,000 ÷ ($4 − $2)]. This relationship is graphically depicted in Exhibit 16–9A. Except for nonprofit organizations, break-even prices typically just set a pricing floor.

<hr>

Target return pricing is setting prices at a desired percentage return over and above the break-even point.

Target return pricing, popular among manufacturers, is based on break-even analysis. The total costs of producing and offering goods for sale are determined, and a target percentage return is then added to those costs at the standard output level. The sum of the total costs and the target return is the total revenue that must be generated. The selling price is determined by dividing the target total revenue level by the standard output level. Referring to Exhibit 16–9B, suppose that a firm has a standard output level of 80,000 units and that management wishes to achieve a 20 percent return on the total costs at that level of output ($260,000). Then, $52,000 (20 percent × $260,000) is added to $260,000 to obtain a target total revenue of $312,000 and the price must be set at $3.90 ($312,000 ÷ 80,000) to achieve that revenue. The obvious weakness of this and other cost-oriented pricing methods is that prices determined according to these methods are derived from costs without regard to market demand. The actual quantity sold at the determined price could easily be greater or less than the quantity required. Yet this method helps ensure that prices exceed all costs and therefore contribute to profit.

Inflation was a critically important cost factor at the end of the 1970s, and it could again be important. This means that crises could develop for firms whose prices are fixed by contract. Thus, it is essential to incorporate inflation factors into price-setting methods and to install systems that provide timely information on increasing costs.

Competition-Oriented Approaches

Many firms set prices largely in relation to the prices of competitors Exhibit 16–6. Although management in such a firm cannot totally disregard cost and demand factors, it gives primary attention to positioning its firm's prices relative to the prices of competing firms.

EXHIBIT 16–9 Using Break-Even Analysis to Determine Price

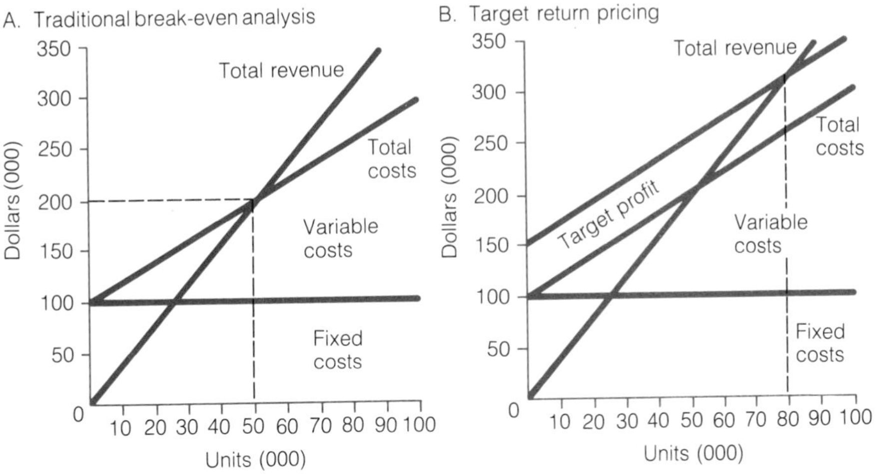

A. Traditional break-even analysis

B. Target return pricing

Going-Rate Pricing. One method is **going-rate pricing**—setting prices equal to or a certain percentage above or below competitors' prices. Whether or not this method is appropriate depends on the firm's pricing objectives; the structure of the industry (e.g., oligopoly); whether there is excess capacity; the relative production, selling, and administrative costs of competitors; and customers' perceptions of the firm's products compared to those of competitors. Furthermore, managers often use competitive pricing when:

Going-rate pricing is the method of setting prices in relation to the prices of competitors.

■ They believe that larger competitors are better able to select appropriate prices, so they "follow the leader."

■ Retaliatory price changes are likely beyond a given range, and price changes by competitors have a substantial effect on company sales.

■ Costs, demand, and other factors that affect sales and profits are stable enough to make it possible to rely on following general industry pricing trends.

Many retailers employ competition-oriented pricing methods in conjunction with the cost markup method. Retailers hire comparison shoppers who survey competitors' prices on selected items, and individual store managers are given the authority to adjust prices. This competition-oriented pricing program is used by a discount drug chain:

Headquarters distributes three lists—designated as AAA, A, and B—to its store managers every four weeks. For the items appearing on the lists, managers report prices and those of the closest (in proximity) competitors. For the AAA list, on which 20 to 24 most identifiable nonprescription drugs and cosmetic items appear (e.g., Crest toothpaste, family-size; Right Guard aerosol deodorant, large Bayer aspirin, 100s), the manager has *almost blanket* . . . authority to alter his store's prices to meet the competition's. . . . For A- and B-listed items, [the manager] must approach, but not necessarily meet, competitors' prices.[10]

Sealed Bid Models.   Many industries rely heavily on a competitive bidding approach to pricing. The higher the bid price submitted, the lower the odds of being selected; the lower the bid price submitted, the greater the negative impact on profits if the bid is accepted. For larger firms that can average their wins and losses, expected value computations are helpful in implementing the competitive bidding approach.

Firms engaged in competitive bidding may use mathematical models that have been developed for their specific situations.[11] Experience-based probabilistic bidding models can be developed to indicate the bid amount that is expected to yield the greatest profit. The general notation for a probabilistic model that will identify the most profitable bid is:

$$E(X) = P(X)Z(X)$$

where:

X = Amount of the bid

$E(X)$ = Expected profit of a bid of X

$P(X)$ = Probability of a bid of X being accepted

$Z(X)$ = Profit if a bid of X is accepted

The amount of profit made if a bid of X is accepted [$Z(X)$] equals the difference between the bid price (X) and the expected costs associated with the project for which the bid is submitted. These data are obtained from financial and accounting analyses of the project. The probability of a bid of a certain amount above project costs being accepted can often be determined by an analysis of historical patterns. A firm might discover that a bid of 30 percent above its direct costs on certain types of products has been below competitor A's bid 95 percent of the time, below B's bid 85 percent of the time, and below C's bid 90 percent of the time. Since these events are independent of one another, the probability of underbidding all three major competitors with a bid of 130 percent of direct costs is 72.7 percent (.95 × .85 × .90). A bid price of 130 percent of direct costs yields a contribution margin of 23 percent. Therefore, the expected contribution margin for bids 30 percent above direct costs is 16.7 percent (.727 × .23). Expected contribution margins for other bid prices as a percentage of direct costs are shown in Exhibit 16-10. Bids of 130 percent of direct costs are expected to yield the highest value to the bidder.

Few applications of models for pricing decisions have been made beyond the limited use of competitive bidding models and Bayesian or decision tree analysis. Unfortunately, many of the models that have been developed are

EXHIBIT 16–10 Expected Contribution Margin when Bidding against Three Competitors

Bid as a Percentage of Estimated Direct Cost	Z(X): Contribution Margin (percent)	Probability of Underbidding			P(X): Overall Probability of Having Lowest Bid	E(X): Expected Contribution Margin (percent)
		Firm A	Firm B	Firm C		
110	9	1.00	.98	1.00	.980	0.9
120	17	.98	.90	.95	.838	13.8
130	23	.95	.85	.90	.727	16.7
140	29	.80	.50	.55	.220	4.8
150	33	.40	.25	.30	.030	0.9
160	38	.20	.05	.10	.001	0.0
170	41	.05	.00	.00	.000	0.0

Source: Wayne J. Morse, "Probabilistic Bidding Models: A Synthesis," *Business Horizons* 16 (April 1975), pp. 67–74. Copyright 1975 by the Foundation for the School of Business at Indiana University. Reprinted by permission.

simplistic and their usefulness is therefore limited. An opportunity exists for developing more useful models.

Demand-Oriented Approaches

Firms that set prices based on costs or competition alone must assume that a close relationship exists between traditional markups or competitors' prices and market demand considerations. Yet demand schedules can be usefully incorporated into price determinations through several methods.

Demand-Modified Break-Even Analysis. Estimates of market demand used in conjunction with traditional break-even analysis can approximate profit-maximizing decisions. **Demand-modified break-even pricing** re-

_____

Demand-modified break-even pricing is setting prices to achieve the highest profit (over the break-even point) in consideration of the amount demanded at alternative prices.

_____

quires estimates of market demand at each feasible price; break-even points and expected levels of total sales revenue can then be calculated. In the example presented in Exhibit 16–11, the fixed costs are $200,000, the unit variable costs are $2.50, and demand forecasts are given for prices of $5, $10, $15, and $20. Of the four prices considered, the $15 price yields the highest profit ($362,500).

The primary challenge in demand-oriented pricing is obtaining accurate estimates of the price/quantity relationships shown in Exhibit 16–11. For established products, firms may employ time series analyses of historical prices (in constant dollars) and sales volume levels to derive a price/quantity demand schedule. In using historical data to plan future prices, however, it is assumed that the factors that affected sales in the past will affect future sales in much the same way, and this assumption often does not hold true.

A second approach is to conduct direct customer interviews, asking respondents within a target market a series of questions to measure their likely response at different price levels. This approach is complicated by customers who find it difficult to judge how they would actually respond.

EXHIBIT 16–11 Break-Even Analysis with a Market Demand Schedule

Unit Price ($)	Market Demand (units)	Total Revenue ($)		Total Costs ($)	Break-Even Points (units)		Expected Profits ($)
5	65,000	(d')	325,000	362,500	(d)	80,000	(37,500)
10	55,000	(c')	550,000	337,500	(c)	26,667	212,500
15	45,000	(b')	675,000	312,500	(b)	16,000	362,500
20	30,000	(a')	600,000	275,000	(a)	11,429	325,000

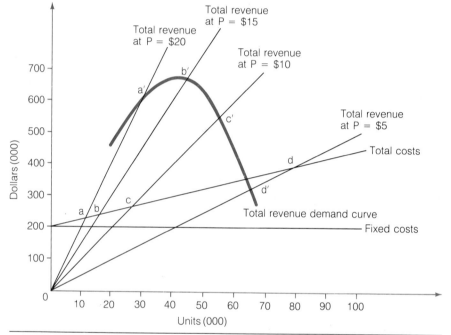

A third approach is to use controlled store experiments. This method may be used with new as well as existing products, and it promises greater validity than time series anlaysis. In store experiments, buyers make actual purchase decisions within a short time period, and the influence of external variables can be controlled. The Quaker Oats Company once selected two products that were not contributing adequately to profitability and considered raising the price of each product by four cents. To determine the likely impact of the higher prices on sales and, more important, on the profits of the line, the company conducted an in-store experiment.

Within 120 grocery stores, a research design was used to test four combinations (treatments):

- Raise price of item A by four cents; no change in price of item B.
- No change in price of item A; raise price of item B by four cents.
- Raise price of item A by four cents; raise price of item B by four cents.
- No change in price of item A; no change in price of item B.

Three monthly audits were conducted in the 120 stores to determine the effect of each treatment on sales. Analysis of the sales results produced the following conclusions:

- Increasing the price of A alone would reduce total product line profits.
- Increasing the price of B alone would not significantly change total line profits.
- Changes in the price of both A and B would not have any impact on line profits.[12]

If properly planned and executed, controlled experiments can be valuable in setting prices. Coca-Cola U.S.A. has used trailer simulations to estimate the impact of price changes on sales. The company creates major product displays in a motorized van that simulates part of a retail outlet. Shoppers are then selected and invited to shop in this simulated supermarket. Although somewhat artificial, this approach offers research efficiency because it permits many price changes (e.g., on eight-packs of 16-ounce Coke) to be easily tested.

Perceived Value Pricing. The task of determining prices for industrial products is basically the same as the task of determining prices for consumer products. Yet the price of an industrial product is probably determined somewhat more by the exact potential benefit that the product offers the buyers. This is especially true when an industrial product faces little direct competition. In one instance, a small manufacturer developed a new electronic temperature measurement instrument, and management was unsure about how to price it. The variable costs were about $1,200. Management usually set a selling price of about four times the variable costs to cover other costs and contribute to profits, but the fixed costs were to be proportionately lower for the new product. Management estimated that a price of $3,600 for the new product would cover costs and meet the profit objectives. But then several potential users were asked to rate the new product and key competitive products on product attributes. Management learned that less accurate competitive instruments were available at $3,200. After assessing the product's potential benefit to users and the willingness of users to purchase the product at different price levels, management set the price at $4,500. Demand factors ultimately dictated the appropriate price.

Perceived value
pricing
is setting prices to either match or go below customers' perceptions of the value of products.

Perceived value pricing is also applicable to consumer products, for which it is often based on a psychological pricing strategy. Izod shirts are priced in part on consumers' perception of their value. This pricing method is, of course, based on an understanding of price elasticity, but it underscores the behavioral foundation underlying price elasticity. The willingness of customers to pay a higher price depends on their perception of the fairness of the price—of the quality they get for the price they pay.

Perceptions sometimes stray from reality, and conducting market research on perceptions as they affect demand elasticity can be very useful. Ford Motor Company developed a high-quality sports sedan, but industry observers speculated that the price might exceed the car's *perceived* value. As reported in the business press:

> Marketing any new car is no cinch, but Ford Motor Company's Lincoln-Mercury division faces some special obstacles with the new Merkur. That's right—Merkur with a K. The new model, the Merkur XR4Ti, is made in West Germany by Ford's West German subsidiary. It is a turbocharged, fuel-injected, two-door hatchback sports sedan designed to compete with such European cars as the Saab 900 Turbo and the BMW 325e and priced accordingly at $16,000 to $18,000.
>
> In other words, the Merkur XR4Ti is the kind of car that buyers don't normally go looking for at Lincoln-Mercury dealers, and that's just the first problem. It is also a kind of car that Lincoln-Mercury dealers have little experience selling; they're more used to hawking heated side mirrors than hot engines. Even the car's name is a headache. Lincoln-Mercury picked it to stress the car's German origins, but the correct pronunciation doesn't trip naturally off American lips (it's MARE-COOR). Moreover, Lincoln-Mercury tried once before, from 1970 to 1978, to sell a German-made car, the Capri, and ended up disappointing some early enthusiasts by moving production to the United States.
>
> Lincoln-Mercury is forging ahead, because opportunity beckons. Lincoln-Mercury's general manager, Robert L. Rewey, thinks sales of Merkur models alone could total 100,000 units a year within three to five years.
>
> But how do you convince the guy who's looking for a BMW that he really wants a Mercury? That's where the real marketing challenge comes in.[13]

Implementation and Control

Once prices have been established, plans to implement and control pricing decisions must be executed. Company salespeople, channel resellers, and ultimate consumers or users are most immediately affected by price decisions. The responses of customers to price decisions are often anticipated through marketing research. But the reactions of salespeople and distributors should also be sought, because these two groups are usually responsible for implementing price decisions.

Successful implementation of price decisions and price changes is dependent on coordination with salespeople and resellers as well as marketing, accounting, manufacturing, and purchasing personnel. Final price decisions affect and are affected by the decisions of each of these groups, so their inputs to the decision process should be solicited. Because salespeople and distributors are the voice of the company in explaining prices to buyers, they should understand the rationale for price decisions. Since prices often reflect corporate goals, policies, and philosophies, steps should be taken to minimize differences between the messages that corporate executives want to convey and the messages received by resellers and consumers. Corporate messages should rarely be unexpected or perceived as unjustified by salespeople or distributors.

To control price decisions, the firm must monitor:

EXHIBIT 16–12 Price Decision Warning System

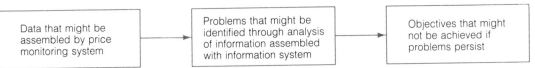

Data that might be assembled by price monitoring system	Problems that might be identified through analysis of information assembled with information system	Objectives that might not be achieved if problems persist

1. Sales—in units and in dollars:
   a. Previous year comparisons.
   b. Different markets/channels comparisons.
2. Rivals' prices.
3. Inquiries from potential customers about the line.
4. Company's sales at "off list" price:
   a. Measured as percent of total sales.
   b. Revenue as percent of sales at full price.
5. Types of customers getting the most and largest price reductions.
6. Market shares—in individual markets.
7. Marketing costs; production costs; production costs at nearly full output.
8. Price complaints:
   a. From customers.
   b. From sales staff.
9. Inventories of finished goods at different levels.
10. Customer's attitudes toward firm, prices, etc.
11. Number of lost customers (brand switching).
12. Inquiries—and subsequent purchases.
13. Marketing costs.
14. Entry and exit of competitors from industry.
15. Consumer and reseller responses to competitors' price reductions.

1. A decline in sales.
2. Prices are too high—relative to those charged by rivals, relative to the benefits of the product. (Prices might be too high in a few regional markets and very appropriate elsewhere.)
3. Price is too low, (again perhaps in certain markets and not in others).
4. The company is regarded as exploitative of customers and not to be trusted.
5. The firm places excessive financial burdens on its resellers.
6. The price differentials among items in the line are objectionable or unintelligible.
7. Price changes are too frequent—or do not take account of major changes in market circumstances.
8. The firm's price reflects negatively on itself and on its products.
9. The price is unstabilizing the market which had finally become stabilized after great difficulty.
10. The firm is offering its customers too many price choices and is confusing its customers and resellers.
11. The firm's prices seem higher to customers than they really are.
12. The firm's price policy attracts undesirable kinds of customers who have no loyalty to any seller.
13. The firm's pricing behavior makes customers unduly price sensitive and unappreciative of quality differences.
14. The company has fostered a decline in market discipline among sellers in the industry.

1. Maximum long-run profits.
2. Maximum short-run profits.
3. Growth.
4. Stabilize market.
5. Desensitize customers to price.
6. Maintain price leadership arrangement.
7. Discourage entrants.
8. Speed exit of marginal firms.
9. Avoid government investigation and control.
10. Maintain loyalty of resellers.
11. Avoid demands for "more" from suppliers—labor, in particular.
12. Enhance image of firm and its offerings.
13. Be regarded as "fair" by customers (ultimate).
14. Create interest and excitement about the item.
15. Be considered trustworthy and reliable by rivals.
16. Help in the sale of weak items in the line.
17. Discourage others from cutting prices.
18. Make a product "visible."
19. "Spoil market" to obtain high price for sale of business.
20. Build traffic.

Source: Adapted from Alfred R. Oxenfeldt, "A Decision-Making Structure for Price Decisions," *Journal of Marketing* 37 (January 1973), pp. 48-53.

- Their impact on corporate and distributor performance.
- The reactions of competitive firms.
- Customer satisfaction.

The firm's information system should provide assistance to those who make pricing objectives and strategies. A price decision warning system is highlighted in Exhibit 16–12. Such a system would, for example, provide advance warning of negative reactions by resellers toward not allowing end-of-season price discounting. And with such a warning, remedial actions could be taken in good time.

New Product Pricing

Determining the prices for new products is basically similar to determining the prices for any other products. Pricing objectives for new products consider the role that these products (and their prices) will play in the organization's overall marketing strategy. Typically, the pricing objectives for new products have more latitude than those for existing products.

Pricing flexibility is also greater for new products. For products in the growth, maturity, or decline stages of the product life cycle, there is usually growing competition and a smaller number of acceptable prices. The prices of such products often have to be reduced. New products with little competition usually offer the option of a skimming or penetration strategy.

A **skimming pricing strategy** sets introductory prices at high levels relative to costs so as to "skim the cream" off the market. In the absence of immediate competition and price-inelastic customers, firms often consider it safe to set initial new product prices high relative to costs and to lower the prices gradually as market conditions dictate. Skimming profits allows sellers to recover their investment rapidly, though the high margins tend to attract competition. Makers of personal computers charged high prices at the outset, but there has been competitive price warfare in recent years.

A **penetration pricing strategy** sets new product prices low relative to costs. This strategy is usually employed to rapidly acquire a large share of a potential market. Relatively low margins discourage the entry of competitors and often allow the entering firm to establish itself with a large market share. However, if a market is large enough, even low prices may attract competitors. The appropriateness of a penetration strategy depends on the firm's ability to retain its desired market share once competition develops.

If the odds are against retaining an initial foothold, it may be better to skim and profit more heavily for a short time. Du Pont was the first company to make cyclohexane, a product used in oil refining. Knowing that oil refiners with an inherent cost advantage would soon develop competitive products, Du Pont set the initial price for cyclohexane at a high level (skimming strategy) and discontinued production when the number of competing producers increased as anticipated.

Setting specific new product prices within the strategies selected, given limited competition, normally involves first establishing a price floor through break-even analysis. Unit costs may be high at first, so a long-run viewpoint may be essential in deriving cost estimates. Cost and demand uncertainties are high, so building in alternative cost assumptions and using *sensitivity analysis* to determine important cost thresholds can be very important. Sensitivity analysis answers such questions as, "What *if* production costs are 10 percent higher than anticipated? What happens to the break-even point, and what are the odds of achieving the required higher sales level?"

The uncertainty that accompanies new products cannot be totally eliminated. Monitoring new product prices is therefore particularly critical. Although well-developed strategies should not be abandoned lightly,

Skimming pricing strategy involves setting a high initial price to first profit from price-inelastic customers, and then successively lowering prices, often under increasingly competitive conditions, to the levels that more price-sensitive customers are willing to pay.

Penetration pricing strategy involves setting a low initial price to establish market share, preempt competitors, and/or capitalize on production economies.

management must be prepared to make ongoing adjustments to better match prices with distributor and customer requirements.

Changing Prices and Responding to Competitors

Nonprice competition is often stressed in marketing strategies, in part because price changes are easy for competitors to counter. It is far more difficult to directly counter a strong brand image with unique product features than with a price change. Marketing strategies comprise an array of marketing mix variables, of which the price variable is sometimes considered best left alone.

Whether or not price is an active strategy variable is partly determined by the economic structure of the industry. The deregulation of several industries in the past decade has meant a new market structure and a new pricing environment for them. (Exhibit 16-13).

Price Contingency Planning

When competitors make price changes, there is often little time for careful research on competitors or on likely customer responses, so contingency planning can be very important. If key competitors can have a substantial pricing impact on the market, doing some "what if" planning is usually in order. Unless management gathers information on competitors from various sources, it may misinterpret a competitor's pricing move. Knowing why the competitor made the move is critical in determining the most appropriate response. Is the move intended to temporarily alleviate certain conditions, or is it part of a conscious strategy for obtaining a greater long-run market share?

Other key questions are:

■ *How will customers interpret and respond to the price change?* Price elasticity in a particular market is central to answering this question. Just as management can misperceive a pricing move by competitors, so can customers. And this can be to a firm's advantage or disadvantage. To minimize negative customer reaction, General Motors has gone to two or more modest price hikes a year rather than one major hike at the beginning of the model year. Also, the announced price hikes do not include the cost of quality improvements or new features. The perception is what counts.

■ *How will other competitors respond to the price change?* One must attempt to judge how other firms serving the same markets will interpret and respond. An extreme response is "following the leader." Appropriate responses include no change, a limited change, or a move to match or exceed the change made by the competitor. Further, the price response may be combined with nonprice changes, such as a dramatic increase in the advertising of product quality or the addition of a new product feature or service benefit.

EXHIBIT 16–13

Deregulation of the telephone industry has brought about demand- and competition-oriented pricing.

Reprinted courtesy AT&T and Young & Rubicam/New York.

■ *How will customers and competitors in the industry respond to our response?* One needs to judge not only where one's own price will be after the change but also what subsequent moves our move will allow competitors.

■ *Will a price increase benefit the entire industry?* If demand is high and customers are not highly price sensitive (low industry elasticity), a general hike in prices may be beneficial to all producers.

Competitive Pricing Models

Bayesian and other theoretical pricing models aid management in judging the desirability of alternative competitive responses, including those involving price. Decision tree analyses normally begin with identifying two or more possible price decisions along with a key competitor's possible reactions.

The reactions might be: no response, a cut in price, or a cut in price combined with an increase in service. Then, a subjective probability of occurrence and an estimate of the financial impact are assigned to each combination of a price decision and a likely competitive response. Finally, the expected value for each price decision and each price response alternative is calculated, and the best alternative is determined. Other cost-oriented, price-volume and heuristic simulations can also be used as aids to making price change decisions.

— *Application* —

A Competitive Pricing Oriented Marketing Strategy

United Airlines, a firm in a previously regulated industry, had historically de-emphasized prices as a strategy variable since monopoly power over prices was periodically approved by the regulatory agencies. With deregulation, pricing suddenly became a critically important management task. A previously oligopolistic industry with mostly undifferentiated services changed dramatically, with new, smaller airlines providing lower-cost services. United Airlines was forced to shift to a responsive, competitive pricing orientation.

By the mid-1980s, the number of scheduled airlines had risen to 100, up from 36 before deregulation, and there was all-out price warfare between the low-cost airlines and the majors. The four largest airlines, which had carried 53 percent of industry traffic in 1978, were down to 45 percent in 1985. To combat market share erosion, the 12 major airlines carried more than 85 percent of their traffic on discounted fares in 1985, up from 50 percent in 1979. In the early years of deregulation, these carriers usually only matched, or even ignored, the low fares offered by the low-cost airlines. But by the mid-1980s their "gloves were off," with the majors seizing the initiative on fare cuts and fighting all competitive moves of even the smallest and newest airlines. People Express and others posted major losses and looked to adding services, using more innovative marketing and seeking less competitive routes to increase profits.[14]

Here is how United Airlines' Director of Pricing outlined the firm's approach to the changed competitive environment.[15]

On pricing objectives, flexibility, and strategy:

Our [pricing] strategy is to maintain a price structure that appeals to as wide a range of the traveling public as possible—while providing an acceptable financial return to United. In concert with this, we support the market management team by maintaining competitive prices with a competitive product.

With every pricing decision we make, our goal is to protect or increase United's on-board revenue.

We think discount fares should be used to generate new traffic.

[Pricing stability is] something we all would like to see happen tomorrow, but I believe it's an unrealistic wish. As long as there are new low-cost carriers entering the marketplace, and as some established carriers continue to suffer from overcapacity, erosion of market share, or financial difficulties, we'll face a volatile pricing environment [with little flexibility].

On establishing prices:

[United does not] match every low fare filed by a competitor. We price on a market-by-market basis, and prior to making a pricing decision we contrast United's posture in the market with that of our competitors. Factors considered include schedules and service, load factors, price structure and levels, traffic mix, market size, seasonality, cost structures, and distribution. In other words, we look at our market position versus the competition when we price our product.

The only way to [offer discount fares] without significantly compromising revenue from higher-yield passengers is to apply restrictions to these fares, such as advance purchase and minimum/maximum stay requirements. Unrestricted discount fares merely divert traffic from the full fare.

[Concerning price changes,] in one recent week, the airline industry initiated almost 60,000 fare changes in our markets. United alone made 40,000 of those changes—or 8,000 a day. Since the company serves more than 5,000 markets, the volume of pricing activity is extremely high.

On implementation and control:

Timing is extremely important when reacting to competitive moves. If a competitor has initiated a constructive upward pricing action, we must quickly give a favorable response to prevent him from prematurely withdrawing the increase. If a downward pricing action has been started which we feel offsets United's product advantages, it's imperative that we respond quickly to thwart traffic or revenue erosion.

Sometimes restrained response is chosen to avoid a fare war—which we know from past experience can destroy our bottom line.

In our major markets, United can change a fare within two hours and sometimes even faster. Computers are becoming much more important in the analysis and decision-making process. This is our most important tool for alerting travel agents about rate changes. Our regional pricing coordinators are another valuable link for communicating with our sales force.

United updates and maintains more than 2 million industry fares. We receive about 70,000 local and joint-fare pricing changes for 195 airlines every day and update them within 24 to 72 hours; we also update about 100 industry price rules daily.

Why is price competition a major factor in the airline industry? Actually, for the same reasons that it is important in other industries:

■ Underutilized capacity or inventory.

■ Threatened market share.

■ Changing cost/financial conditions (e.g., crisis cash flow squeeze).

■ Aggressive pricing strategy by one or more competitors.

These factors contribute to an unstable, volatile pricing situation and make United's pricing objectives, strategies, and implementation an exceptionally active and important part of its overall marketing strategy ■

Summary

In both profit and nonprofit organizations, prices may be an active or inactive element within an overall marketing strategy. The first step in the pricing process is to set prices with attention to their effects on the overall product line, the promotional program, and distributor relationships. Then, specific objectives for the pricing program are established. They should be clear, concise, and understood by all involved, whether they are oriented toward achieving profit, discouraging competition, or striving for growth, cash flow, or the enhancement of other strategy elements.

The second step is to determine the extent of pricing flexibility. Unit costs provide the floor for prices, so it is important to determine those costs, taking into account possible learning curve effects, inflation rates, and other factors that affect costs. Demand must be evaluated, with attention given to estimating the shape of demand curves for different price/quantity combinations. Estimating the price elasticity of demand is also necessary. Elasticity varies over the range of possible prices, over time, and by product type. The likely effect of price changes on the size of the market must be considered. Competition also helps determine the amount of pricing flexibility. The range is from pure competition (no flexibility) to pure monopoly (high flexibility). The chance of sparking a price war is a deterrent to aggressive competitive pricing. Legal and ethical constraints often help set the bounds of pricing flexibility.

The third step is to set pricing strategies. Should there be high *price variability* for different customers, using price discrimination to the firm's advantage? Trade, quantity, cash and geographic discounts are often offered, as are different prices for goods sold at different places or different times. Prices sometimes vary greatly for only slightly different products. In matters concerning price variability, the legal limits and possible customer backlash need to be considered. The *general price level* should also be decided upon, with consideration given to the desired image of the firm. *Price lining* may be used, a strategy of offering a product at each level of competitive products in a particular category. A strategy of encouraging distributor *price stability* or discouraging reseller price competition may also be pursued. A *life-cycle pricing* strategy involves anticipating pricing pressures at different stages of the product life cycle and responding with pricing changes that are to the firm's best advantage. *Psychological pricing* strategies include odd-even pricing, prestige pricing, and setting prices to connote quality.

The fourth step is to set prices for each product or service. Cost-oriented approaches include cost-plus (and markup) pricing and break-even (and target return) pricing. Competition-oriented approaches include going-rate pricing and sealed bid models. Demand-oriented approaches include demand-modified break-even and perceived value pricing.

The fifth and final step in the pricing process is to implement the prices set and to monitor the response of customers, distributors, and competitors to those prices. Price adjustments are made, if necessary, to better achieve the pricing objectives stated at the beginning of the process.

Setting prices for new products often presents the option of a skimming versus a penetration strategy. Changing prices hinges on understanding the industry structure and on management's decisions as to how active a strategy variable pricing should be. Contingency planning with regard to the pricing moves of key competitors can help prevent disastrous price wars. Management must understand why price changes are made and judge the likely responses of customers and competitors to their perception of changes in the marketplace. Competitive pricing models are sometimes helpful in this process.

Exercises for Review and Discussion

1. A new refrigerator has been developed that needs no energy source—it is a self-sufficient unit. Evaluate the pros and cons of skimming and penetration pricing strategies, and come up with a recommended strategy. (Assume no competition *at this time.*)

2. This chapter uses the example of Mercury's Merkur to explain perceived value pricing. What are other examples of products, both consumer and industrial, in which perceived value would strongly influence final pricing?

3. Douglas Company in Mount Upton, New York, is a new producer of component sound systems (e.g., speakers, receivers, tape decks), and management is debating how to price its products. The target market consists of young middle-income couples who are not interested in understanding the technical aspects of the products and who have difficulty in evaluating the quality of the components. Could price play a special role in this marketing mix? Are there potential opportunities as well as risks in setting the price level? What would you do?

4. Identify and discuss major factors to consider in pricing a new snack food product. The product will be distributed through a conventional channel of distribution from the manufacturer to food brokers, to retailers, to consumers.

5. Under what circumstances would penetration pricing for a new product be most appropriate? Skimming? Could you implement one and then the other?

6. A new brand of bar soap has been developed that has no drying effects on the skin, has a refreshing and pleasant smell, looks attractive, and yet is a more effective cleaning agent. It can be produced at no greater cost than the two brands that the company already markets. Start at the beginning of the pricing process discussed in this chapter; make any essential as-

sumptions; and "walk through" the process, identifying the necessary tasks and the primary questions at each stage to ultimately arrive at an appropriate price.

7. What role does price occupy in the marketing mix (program) for Bayer aspirin? For a privately labeled or drugstore brand of aspirin?

8. A critical element in determining the commercial potential of a new consumer product is obtaining information on the probable response of potential buyers to different price levels. Discuss several types of marketing research studies that might be developed to obtain this type of information (refer to earlier chapters).

Notes

1. "Marketing Mass Transit," Editorial, *Chicago Tribune*, April 5, 1984, sec. 1, p. 18.

2. Matt O'Connor, "Cummins Cut Headed Off the Japanese," *Chicago Tribune*, March 3, 1986, Business Section, p. 1.

3. "Why Detroit Can't Cut Prices," *Business Week*, March 1, 1982, p. 110.

4. See Zarrel V. Lambert, "Product Perception: An Important Variable in Price Strategy," *Journal of Marketing* 34 (October 1970), pp. 68–76; and Kent Monroe, "Buyers Subjective Perceptions of Price," *Journal of Marketing Research* 10 (February 1973), pp. 70–80.

5. Charles W. Stevens, "Car Buyers Start Returning to V-8 Engine as Gas Prices Drop, Big Autos Sell Better," *The Wall Street Journal*, May 25, 1983, p. 25.

6. Leonard L. Berry, "Multidimensional Strategies Can Combat Price Wars," *Marketing News*, January 31, 1986, p. 10. Published by the American Marketing Association.

7. Stephen Wermiel, "High Court Upholds $10 Million Judgment against Monsanto in Resale Price-Fixing," *The Wall Street Journal*, March 21, 1984, p. 8. Reprinted by permission of *The Wall Street Journal*, © Dow Jones & Company, Inc., 1984.

8. Much of this section is based on Louis W. Stern, "Approaches to Achieving Retail Price Stability," *Business Horizons* 5 (Fall 1964), pp. 75–86.

9. Kevin T. Higgins, "Supermeds Apply Brand Identity to Health Care Alphabet Soup," *Marketing News*, January 17, 1986, p. 11. Published by the American Marketing Association.

10. Leonard J. Parsons and W. Bailey Price, "Adaptive Pricing by a Retailer," *Journal of Marketing Research* 9 (May 1972), p. 128.

11. See Wayne J. Morse, "Probabilistic Bidding Models: A Synthesis," *Business Horizons* 16 (April 1975), pp. 67–74.

12. For a detailed description of the study, see William D. Barclay, "Factorial Design in a Pricing Experiment," *Journal of Marketing Research* 6 (November 1969), pp. 427–29. Published by the American Marketing Association.

13. Adapted from Melinda Grenier Guiles, "New Functional Luxury Car from Ford Faces Big Hurdles," *The Wall Street Journal*, June 7, 1984, p. 25. Reprinted by permission of *The Wall Street Journal*, © Dow Jones & Company, Inc., 1984. All rights reserved.

14. Francis C. Brown III, "Major Airlines, Tired of New Lines' Inroads, Cut Fares, Woo Public," *The Wall Street Journal*, February 28, 1986, pp. 1, 17.

15. Based on "Walsh: The Price is Right when Profit Is in the Picture," *Friendly Times* (published by United Airlines), May 1984, pp. 10–11 and "Major Airlines," pp. 1, 17.

CHAPTER 17

Promotion and Sales Promotion

*T*he Swedish automaker Saab-Vabis faced a difficult situation in the United States. Management had been unable to handle rapid growth and had let customer service levels slip. To revive performance, Saab introduced the 900 Turbo series, a completely redesigned line of cars with three models. Management was confident that the line was a winner. Yet sales of the 900 Turbo were initially low because very narrow market segments had been targeted. There was almost no awareness of the 900 Turbo outside this small market niche. To widen its appeal, Saab turned to promotion. Three objectives consistent with Saab's overall marketing strategy were set for promotion of the 900 Turbo:

- Change the positioning of Saab to that of a luxurious and high-performance car.
- Establish the competition, not as inexpensive compacts, but as high-performance, high-quality automobile brands such as BMW and Volvo.
- Inform potential customers of the price range of the three 900 Turbo models.

Saab's promotion was very effective even though its promotion budget was relatively small. The company's marketing research documented tremendous increases in awareness by the mid-1980s: 50 percent of U.S. car buyers in general and 75 percent of U.S. car buyers in the new target markets recognized the Saab name. Just as impressive was the 75 percent of current owners who said that they planned to buy another Saab.[1]

A well-designed product that meets customers' needs is important for effective marketing but not sufficient for market success, as Saab found out. Customers must also know that the product is available and must understand its benefits and its advantages over the competition. Marketing is charged with the responsibility of *informing* and *reminding* prospective customers of the company's offer and of *advocating* a position in the minds of this audience. Informing, reminding, and advocating are the purposes of the promotion component of the marketing mix.

This chapter provides an overview of a company's promotion decisions. First, the variety of audiences for promotion are reviewed, and the promotion tools are introduced. Then, promotion is viewed as a communication process between the company and its target audiences. This process provides a very useful framework for understanding the decisions that marketing managers must make to manage promotion tools. Next, the key strengths and weaknesses of each major promotion tool are reviewed to emphasize the importance of blending the different tools into a promotion mix. Finally, the decisions required to plan and implement sales promotion, an important tool in the promotion mix of many companies, are discussed.

The Promotion Mix

Promotion is not restricted to communicating with the company's customers. Companies may direct promotion to a wide variety of audiences. Many large companies try to establish a particular reputation, a *corporate image*, with the general public. The oil companies especially have spent huge amounts for this purpose. Their promotion tries to sway public opinion by demonstrating concern for preserving the environment while meeting the country's energy needs (Exhibit 17–1).

Other audiences for promotion include investors and stockholders, government officials, suppliers, distribution company managers, and company employees. All of these audiences comprise people who can influence how well a company achieves its mission and objectives. Promotion must often aim at a mix of these important audiences, though different objectives are set for each audience.

As you might expect, planning, implementing, and controlling promotion is the same regardless of the audience.

Promotion is considerably more than just advertising. In fact, a marketing manager can draw on four major tools: *advertising, sales promotion, publicity,* and *personal selling.* Together, these tools make up the **promotion mix.**

Promotion mix is the particular combination of promotion tools used by a company to communicate with its audiences.

■ *Advertising.* Communicating with an audience through nonpersonal, paid media; the audience clearly perceives the source of messages as the organization that paid the media.

■ *Sales Promotion.* Communicating with an audience through a variety of nonpersonal, nonmedia vehicles such as free samples, gifts, and coupons; the audience clearly perceives the source of messages as the organization paying for their delivery.

■ *Publicity.* Communicating with an audience by personal or nonpersonal media that are not explicitly paid for delivering the messages; the audience is

EXHIBIT 17-1

SUN, OIL AND THE FISHERMAN'S SON. People get a lot of fish from the Santa Barbara Channel. And this is where Sun Company gets a lot of oil—more than three million barrels a year! Around here oil is our business. But Sun people like Stan Blossom can tell you it's not our only concern.

"I work for Sun, but I also fish in these waters. And I want my son's generation to fish here too. That's why precautions like our containment unit are so important. In case of a spill, it would quickly surround the oil and help prevent damage.

"This is just one of the ways we're helping to make sure there'll be many more years of fishing around here."

At Sun, we think putting energy back into the environment is as important as getting it out.

**WHERE THERE'S SUN
THERE'S ENERGY.**

Sun Oil Company aims advertising at the general public to help build a corporate image of caring for the environment.

Courtesy N W Ayer Inc.

likely to perceive the media rather than the organization as the source of messages.

■ *Personal Selling.* Communicating directly with an audience through paid personnel of the organization or its agents; the audience perceives the communicator's organization as the source of messages.

Each major promotion tool includes a wide variety of activities, some of which are listed in Exhibit 17-2. Many companies use all four of these tools to achieve promotion objectives but place different weights on each of the tools. Industrial companies typically spend more for personal selling than for advertising or publicity. In contrast, consumer products companies are likely to place very heavy weight on advertising and sales promotion to reach the vast numbers of customers in their target markets.

The promotion tools open many options to organizations. Some companies and many nonprofit organizations elect to use only some of the tools. Forgo-

EXHIBIT 17–2 Selected Promotion Mix Tools

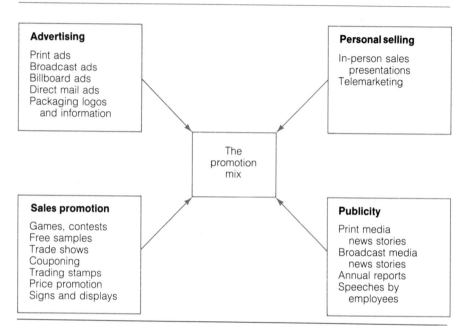

ing one tool may help hold down costs but puts an added burden on the other tools to achieve promotion objectives. Haagen-Dazs, the premium ice cream manufacturer, has performed very well without using advertising.

Only in smaller organizations is responsibility for the promotion mix given to one manager or even one department. In most cases, a few managers are insufficient to coordinate the many different activities involved in promotion. In larger firms, personal selling is managed under a field sales department and advertising is assigned separately, to either an advertising department or product managers. Sales promotion may also have its own department, if the budget allocation is large. However, many sales promotion activities may be part of the responsibility of field sales or advertising. Salespersons are often encouraged to create sales promotion activities for their territories. At the same time, the advertising department may handle artwork for promotions, such as that for in-store signs and displays.

Publicity may be included in advertising, or it may be a part of a public relations department, particularly in a larger organization. Public relations is charged with communicating the corporate image and the company's points of view on issues important to its welfare. News stories and other publicity-type activities are used for this purpose. The expertise of public relations in conducting such activities equips it to handle product publicity more expediently than other departments. However, marketing managers sometimes have difficulty convincing public relations to give adequate attention to products as well as to the corporate image and issue advocacy.

Company/Audience Communication

Promotion can be viewed as the flow of information between a company and its audiences. Because this flow is very important to a firm's marketing effort, marketing managers must understand what happens during the flow process.

A **communications model** describes the essential components of a communication occurring when information from a source is received by audiences (Exhibit 17–3).[2] Information is contained in a message created to inform, remind, or advocate a point of view. A channel is needed to deliver it to an intended audience. If the message and the delivery are effective, the audience will react in a way favorable both to itself and to the source (e.g., by buying the advertised product). The communications model provides a very useful framework for understanding promotion.

In the model, an organization is a key source of information flowing to target audiences. However, the model also shows two other directions of information flow. First, information can move from an audience back to the organization. G. D. Searle & Co., the originator of NutraSweet brand sweetener, has been very successful in harnessing this kind of information flow. In response to the many letters from consumers asking for the names of products in which the sweetener was used, Searle developed a logo to identify products containing NutraSweet.[3]

Information can also flow between individual audience members. This is word-of-mouth communication. Because customers rely heavily on the opinions of other people—particularly family members, neighbors, friends, and colleagues—when making buying decisions, word of mouth is crucial to the success of many companies' marketing programs. Service organizations such as hospitals, restaurants, and brokerage houses are particularly dependent on favorable word of mouth to attract new customers. The benefits received from services can be quite intangible and difficult for buyers to evaluate. Opinions of important others help to overcome this problem.

Communications model is a representation of the flow of information in a message from its source to audiences and of the audience's reaction to the message.

Managing the Communications Flow

Promotion mix decisions are needed to manage the flow of communications between the company and its target audiences, with each step in the flow requiring a different type of decision.

Source. Messages originate with a source—either a person or an organization. How the audience perceives the source can have an impact on the effectiveness of the message in achieving its intended purpose. Generally,

EXHIBIT 17–3 A Model of the Flow of Communications between an Organization and Its Audiences

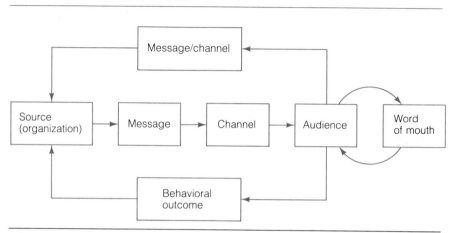

two characteristics of the source are important: credibility and attractiveness.

Source credibility refers to the source's trustworthiness and expertise with respect to the content of the message, as perceived by the audience.

Audience members typically evaluate the **credibility of the source.** This judgment determines how much they will use the information in the message as opposed to information from other sources. In buying a new stereo, a consumer may view advertising as less trustworthy than a close friend, believing that the advertiser, unlike the friend, has something to gain from influencing the buyer. On the other hand, a salesperson who is a stereo buff may appear to have more expertise than the friend, and therefore to possess more credibility. While advertising is generally not high in credibility, some other tools in the promotion mix can be.

Source attractiveness refers to the physical attractiveness of a source as perceived by the audience, or the degree to which the audience sees the source as being similar to itself in age, interests, values, or other characteristics.

Source attractiveness may also be judged by an audience, either physically or in terms of the perceived similarity of the source to itself. More attractive sources are likely to be more effective. Retail stores often try to build source attractiveness by using salespersons who are similar to the store's shoppers. It is no accident that Its for Levi, a jeans store chain, employs college-age salesclerks to sell to a clientele similar in age. Management believes that shoppers will be more likely to accept advice on fit and style from these clerks than from older personnel.

To some extent, a company can control how credible the audience perceives its communications to be. Carefully training sales personnel so that they fully understand the products they are selling is one way to influence customers' perception of credibility. Nowhere is this more evident than in the selling of emergency care drugs to doctors and hospital staff. American Critical Care, a fast-growing division of American Hospital Supply Corporation, extensively trains its sales personnel so that they can provide information that will influence doctors' choice of drugs and other critical care products. In many cases, doctors rely on salespeople for assistance in the purchase and proper application of these products.

Credibility may also be fostered by using promotion to build a strong corporate image or a reputation that audiences trust. Such trust is easily transferred to the company's products. Gerber Products has used promotion based on the theme "Babies are our business" to build a solid reputation for expertise. IBM, Procter & Gamble, AT&T, and many other organizations have achieved like results through promotion. Of course, high product quality and strong distribution and service have backed up the promotion.

What kinds of promotion are best at building image? An executive for Chevron Corporation commented:

> Ads which emphasize marketing attributes such as service and product quality may do more to foster positive overall attitudes about the advertiser than image ads. In addition, they sell the product.[4]

This statement suggests that credibility is developed from the entire promotion effort. Institutional advertising that informs audiences of the corporation and what it stands for is important. But advertising, sales promotion, personal selling, and publicity for individual products also play a crucial part in the image-building effort.

Message content, the information provided by promotion, can include facts, opinions, and persuasive arguments.

Message format or layout is the way that a message is presented, the arrangement of text and visual displays in such a way as to capture an audience's attention and convey the message.

Messages. Two of the most creative aspects of promotion involve determining what to say to audiences and how to say it. **Message content** is the facts, opinions, and persuasive arguments that are intended to inform, remind, or persuade an audience. **Message format or layout** is the means that are used to present and enhance the message communicated to an audience. Content and format come together in the eye-catching and informative advertisement in Exhibit 17–4.

Designing effective messages would be easy if the only messages aimed at an audience were those of one company. However, an overwhelming number of messages compete for the attention of audiences. A message that is not highly interesting or relevant can be lost in the sea of communications. Further, a message must be understood to be effective. Miscomprehension, the inability of audience members to correctly recall or recognize message information, is a problem that promotion managers face constantly. One study has shed some light on the magnitude of the problem for television advertising in the United States:

■ Most members of test audiences miscomprehended some aspects of the advertisements they saw.

■ Every advertisement tested was miscomprehended by some audience members.

■ On the average, about 30 percent of the information in advertisements was miscomprehended.[5]

EXHIBIT 17-4

Jaguar uses message content and format to create an attention-getting and informative advertisement.

Courtesy Jaguar Cars Inc. and Bozell, Jacobs, Kenyon & Eckhardt, Inc.

These findings emphasize the importance of careful design of message content and format. Skilled promotion managers must understand their audiences and be willing to test a promotion for indications of potential miscomprehension.

Message Channel.   Even the best-designed promotion will not be effective unless it reaches the target audience. Delivering promotion is accomplished by **promotion media,** which comprise many different vehicles. The mass media—newspapers, television, magazines, billboards, and radio—are one kind of promotion media. Other kinds are salespersons, point-of-purchase signs and displays, and direct mail. No single vehicle is likely to reach an entire target audience, much less a mix of audiences. Thus, a combination of vehicles is typically needed to ensure desired coverage.

Promotion media are the various vehicles that companies can use to carry their promotional messages to audiences.

Audience. As discussed earlier, promotion should be targeted toward a particular group of people. Not only must this target audience be defined, but the makeup and special characteristics of the people in the audience must also be studied. How promotion managers see these people influences most of the other decisions required to manage the communications flow. We have already noted how message and media channel decisions hinge on the characteristics of the people in the audience. Consequently, selecting the target audience is the central promotion decision on which the others are based.

An important characteristic of all audiences is the ability of their members to interact not only with sources of communication but also with one another. When making purchases, people may seek information both from the promotion of organizations and from such personal sources as family and friends. Promotion managers are much more able to manage the flow of promotion communications than word-of-mouth flow. However, these managers must be alert to opportunities for fostering favorable word-of-mouth communications. One way is to ensure that customers are satisfied, while another is to get highly visible and influential people to use the company's products.

Behavioral Outcomes. Promotion communications attempt to influence the overt, observable behavior or the intangible beliefs or feelings of people in target audiences. The overt behavior sought is behavior beneficial for the source, such as visiting a dealer showroom, redeeming a coupon, buying a particular brand, or telling a friend about a favorable experience with the product.

A more intangible influence of promotion is the impressions of the company or its products that it creates in the minds of the audience. Such impressions—including buying criteria, beliefs, attitudes, and intentions—influence buying decisions. American Express, MasterCard, Visa, and other charge card companies spend millions of dollars each year on consumer promotion for this purpose. They are all trying to create the impression that there are important differences in the services the cards offer and the prestige they confer. Each brand is battling to get cardholders to prefer its card over those of competitors. For people who carry more than one card, such preferences have a great impact on which card is pulled out for purchases.[6]

Promotion Decisions

Each step in the communications flow model is a point at which management can decide how to guide the promotion process. Exhibit 17–5 provides a framework for organizing these decisions into a logical sequence. The direction for all promotion decisions comes from the overall marketing plan. Target audiences for promotion typically coincide with all or some portion of

EXHIBIT 17-5 Promotion Decisions

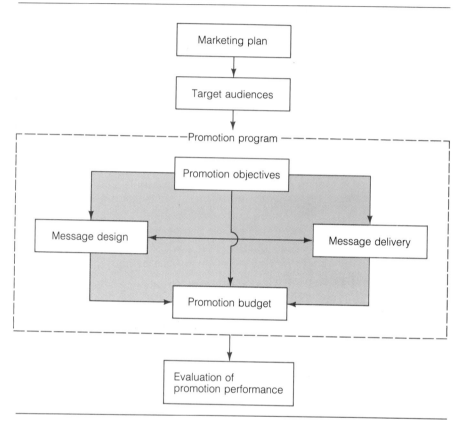

the marketing plan's target markets. Furthermore, the entire promotion program—objectives, creative content of messages and format, selection of delivery vehicles, and the budget—should follow directly from marketing objectives and help achieve them. In this way, the marketing plan ensures that promotion is coordinated with marketing strategy. This point is emphatically made by the president of an advertising agency:

> Once the marketing plan has been devised—by the agency or client—it can be used to develop a total marketing communications program. This includes a budget for each element including public relations, direct mail, trade shows, internal promotion, and an ad media plan with a creative platform to reach marketing objectives (and taking into account any predetermined market problems).[7]

The promotion program comprises highly interrelated decision areas. No particular sequence applies to all firms. In some firms, top management imposes a budget limit on promotion activities. When this happens, objectives, message content and layout, and message delivery decisions are made so that the cost of promotion falls within that limit. In other firms, the opposite approach is used. The promotion program is designed to support the marketing plan in the desired way, and the cost of the promotion program is set by the budget required to implement the marketing plan. Top management reviews the promotion budget for approval. If it considers the promotion budget too high given resource limitations, then management must scale back the program.

Promotion objectives should be set before message content, layout, and delivery decisions are made. Message content, layout, and delivery are highly interrelated. Content and layout decisions must take into consideration the strengths and weaknesses of the various media vehicles, and delivery decisions must consider the requirements for carrying particular kinds of messages.

Determining the Promotion Mix

Firms rarely rely on only one of the four tools of promotion—advertising, sales promotion, publicity, and personal selling. Each tool has particular strengths and weaknesses. The challenge for management is to combine these tools in a way that will take advantage of their strengths and avoid their weaknesses.

Managers typically use five criteria to determine the role of each promotion tool:

- Cost of reaching an audience member.
- Ability to reach target audiences with little leakage to persons not included in them.
- Ability to deliver a complicated message.
- Ability to engage in interchanges with the target audiences.
- Credibility.

Exhibit 17-6 summarizes how well the four tools compare on these criteria.

Advertising is particularly difficult to evaluate because it includes so many different types of delivery vehicles. Direct mail advertising can be good at targeting a particular audience if a select mailing list is found. On the other hand, TV network, newspaper, and billboard advertising typically reaches many more people than are in target audiences. Thus, advertising varies from poor to good on two of the five criteria.

Looking across the four promotion tools, it is evident why promotion managers must use a mix. There are very clear trade-offs to be made between the tools. A comparison of advertising and personal selling illustrates such trade-offs. Advertising reaches far larger audiences than personal selling for a given total cost. But personal selling is better able to target a particular audience and can develop an interchange with customers, responding to their questions and refuting their objections. Further, complicated messages, such

EXHIBIT 17-6 How Promotion Tools Compare on Selected Criteria

| Criteria | TOOL | | | |
	Advertising	Sales Promotion	Publicity	Personal Selling
Cost per audience member	Low	Low	Very low	Very high
Confined to target markets	Poor to good	Good	Moderate	Very good
Deliver a complicated message	Poor to good	Poor	Poor to good	Very good
Interchange with audiences	None	None	Low to moderate	Very good
Credibility	Low	Low	High	Moderate to high

as explaining how a technical product works or how a product may be applied in an unusual way, are much better presented in person than by advertising. Finally, because salespeople can build rapport with customers over time, personal selling has the potential to build much greater credibility with audiences.

Determining the proper organizational structure to manage the promotion mix can be difficult because of the importance of coordinating promotion decisions. Only in a small organization would the same managers make decisions on all aspects of promotion. A small county hospital in rural Tennessee, for example, has a director of promotion who is responsible for all communications. The top administrators approve all promotion plans. The hospital relies almost exclusively on publicity and very limited forms of sales promotion, primarily a hospital brochure that is handed out to all patients and occasionally mailed to county residents. This hospital is the only one in the county, so many citizens are familiar with its services. Thus, the minimal promotion effort required can be managed by a few people.

As an organization gets larger, more managers become involved in planning, implementation, and control of the different promotion tools. In a moderately sized regional chain of jeans stores selling in cities across the Southeast, management coordinates advertising and sales promotion in the central office. Personal selling is handled by the store managers. The size of the company and the location of markets far from the central office require decentralization of some promotion tools and specialization by promotion tool. The president of the chain coordinates promotion by approving all plans.

Even in organizations with separate departments planning and managing each of the promotion tools, promotion activities must be coordinated through a middle- to- high-level executive such as a product manager or a marketing vice president.

Sales Promotion Decisions

Emphasis on sales promotion varies considerably among organizations. Some firms do very little sales promotion, while others spend more on sales promotion than on advertising. Sales promotion budgets in the United States have been increasing rapidly in recent years. One marketing executive estimates that there has been a 10 percent annual increase since 1970.[8] Some aspects of sales promotion have been increasing even faster than that. In 1983, spending on point-of-purchase signs and displays reached almost $7 billion, an increase of more than 18 percent over the amount spent in 1982.[9]

The expanded role of sales promotion is expected to continue through the 1990s. Slow sales growth in many consumer goods markets and more intense competition mean that more and more firms must try to wrest sales away from competitors. Sales promotion can play an important role in this kind of environment. Joseph Sullivan, former president and chief executive officer for Swift & Co., makes this case persuasively:

> Slow growth, volatile markets, and intense competition between consumer goods producers will mark the U.S. business climate for the next 15 years, and that will place new emphasis on sales promotion. In a stagnant or slow-growth market, the need to take business away from the competition in order to survive and grow is mandatory. It's increasingly apparent that sales promotion is finally being perceived at the top levels of progressive companies as a critical business tool.[10]

Another factor in the increasing use of sales promotion is the explosion of costs for network TV advertising and personal selling. As the cost advantages of sales promotion grow greater, recognition of its value should increase among top-level managers. Such recognition is essential in expanding the role of sales promotion as a communications tool.[11]

Not only consumer products companies but also many industrial firms are spending more on sales promotion activities. The same benefits of sales promotion are available in industrial communication situations as in consumer communication situations, as the sellers of business software for personal computers (programs for word processing, spread sheet analysis, and data management) have learned. Sales of these products reached $1.8 billion in 1984 and are expected to grow to nearly $4 billion by 1988.[12] But the industry is very crowded, comprising several thousand software firms. Sales promotion and advertising are being used extensively, particularly by the larger firms, to develop brand awareness and preference among business buyers. Coupons and trial samples of programs are appearing in the market. Techniques have been developed to capitalize on brand names—Lotus Development Corporation gave away tickets to the local orchestra concert with the purchase of its Symphony program.[13]

The Marketing Plan Guides Decisions

Sales promotion decisions follow the promotion management framework presented in Exhibit 17-5. All promotion decisions should be guided by the marketing plan, and sales promotion is no exception. The marketing plan determines target markets, and these markets become targets for sales promotion. SureWay Air Traffic Corporation developed a clever target market strategy for competing against the U.S. Postal Service and such firms as Federal Express and Purolator for courier sales in the New York City area. Through marketing research on an industry by industry basis, companies not committed to the large couriers were identified. These companies were targeted as markets by SureWay and at the same time became targets for several of its sales promotion activities.[14]

A key component of the marketing plan is the statement of marketing objectives. Management must determine which of these objectives can be achieved with sales promotion tools. For SureWay, a crucial marketing objective was to get uncommitted segments of business customers to notice it and try its service. Sales promotion helped introduce SureWay to customers in such segments. Coupons worth 50 percent off the regular price of document delivery service were sent to law firms to get them to try SureWay. Trade shows were used by the company to gain awareness in several uncommitted segments.[15]

Target Audiences for Sales Promotion

The target markets specified by a marketing plan are but one of three types of target audiences for sales promotion. As Exhibit 17-7 suggests, sales promotion can be aimed at target markets, but also at channel of distribution companies (called "the trade") and at the company's own sales force. Usually, the trade or the sales force is a target when management wants to encourage its cooperation in a company's total marketing effort. Offering a free vacation to the persons with the highest sales volumes is a sales promotion activity of this type.

Sales promotion may be used simply to help gain the attention of the trade (or the sales force). If that is done, later communication will have a higher likelihood of being persuasive. American Telecom Inc., a supplier of telecommunications equipment, used sales promotion to help implement a strategic marketing decision to set up a network of independent distributors. At the outset, the company was not well known in the industry, so it was difficult to get the time needed to present the proposal to prospective distributors. A free gift promotion overcame this problem. The gift was a chocolate telephone sent in advance of a salesperson's call. This sales promotion tactic was

EXHIBIT 17–7 Target Audiences for Sales Promotion

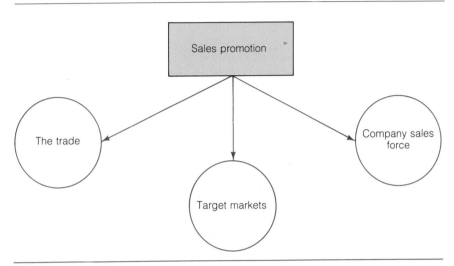

very successful in getting prospective distributors to listen to the sales presentation.[16]

Sales promotion aimed at the trade or the sales force acts as an incentive to increase the selling effort directed at target markets. Grocery manufacturers use price promotions (price discounts to stores) to encourage retailers to lower prices to consumers, arrange special displays of products, and give products a featured position in advertising. Similarly, many manufacturers periodically offer gifts (appliances, vacations) to motivate sales personnel to push particular brands or models.

If there are several target audiences, a company may use a number of sales promotion activities at the same time. A real estate developer selling houses, condominiums, or lots for a development project uses sales promotion tactics that are aimed directly at consumers as well as sales promotion activities directed at real estate brokers who might steer consumers to the project. The developer's promotion includes:

■ Special events to draw consumers' attention to the development; these events include family barbecues and picnics.

■ Price promotions on slow-moving property.

■ Attractive signs at the development site.

■ Prizes and other incentives for high-selling real estate brokers.

■ Participation in trade shows in other cities to acquaint out-of-town real estate brokers with the project.[17]

Once target audiences have been selected, sales promotion managers must study the nature and makeup of those audiences. A market opportunity analysis can help in this effort by providing descriptions of target markets and of distribution companies and their managers. In some cases, special studies may be needed to supplement data already on hand.

Understanding audiences helps sales promotion managers select activities that will achieve communication objectives or weed out ineffective activities. Many banks use such special promotions as free gifts and interest-bearing checking accounts to attract consumers. Yet a study showed that interest-bearing checking accounts are considerably more effective than free gifts. In fact, about 25 percent of the people surveyed said that free gifts were irrelevant to their decision or were not really free since the customer would ultimately have to pay for them in some way.[18] The results have caused some banks to reconsider using free gift sales promotion.

Objectives for Sales Promotion

Sales promotion is usually intended to promote overt actions in target audiences, and well-formulated promotion objectives state exactly what these actions are for each target audience. The objectives differ somewhat for different audiences. A company may want customers to:

- Try its product.
- Switch brands.
- Stock up on its product.
- Visit a dealer's showroom.
- Make an inquiry about the company's product.

Sales promotion may also be used to encourage salespeople to make more calls on selected target markets or to emphasize certain brands or models in a sales presentation. At the same time, sales promotion may motivate distributors to give more shelf or floor space to the company's product, to lower price, or to cooperate in advertising. Consider what Polaroid expects from a recent sales promotion activity:

> On the lush grounds of the Century Plaza Hotel in Los Angeles, a giant walk-through Polaroid camera is being constructed. Next week, hundreds of camera dealers, Wall Street analysts and journalists will tour it. They will be given new Polaroid Spectra cameras and all the film they want, and then will scurry around the palm trees and blue reflecting pools taking shots of "Fame" dancers, Nina Blanchard models and colorful props. When it's all over, Polaroid Corporation hopes, the guests will marvel at the terrific photos Spectra takes—and head home to spread the word.[19]

The time horizon for achieving sales promotion objectives is usually short, ranging from a few weeks to a few months. Managers know that the economic benefit of a sales promotion activity can easily be eroded by competitors.[20] If one fast-food restaurant chain starts a contest that attracts customers from the other chains, competitors can quickly counter with contests of their own. The contests are concluded in a few months because they no longer cause switching. Other sales promotion activities are then initiated to achieve new action-oriented objectives.

Message Design and Delivery

Sales promotion is a catchall category that encompasses a wider variety of activities than do the other promotion tools. One way to organize these many activities is by the way they reach audiences:

- *In-store sales promotions* are activities aimed at communicating with customers while they are shopping in a store; they include in-store signs, displays, and brochures.
- *Audience-direct sales promotions* are activities aimed at reaching audiences directly, through the mail, through advertising media, or through delivery by sales personnel; they include samples, gifts, contests, and cents-off coupons.
- *Trade shows* are events in which a number of companies display their wares in exhibits at a central location and invite dealers or customers to visit the exhibits.

In-Store Promotions. Sales promotions are intended to evoke immediate action from audiences, and the best time to do that is when customers are shopping in the store. Drawing attention to the company's brands at the place where purchase is made (point of purchase) provides a last opportunity to sway customers before they purchase. Thus, manufacturers selling through retail stores use point-of-purchase displays of the product (Exhibit 17-8), signs, such audiovisual aids as a televised film of the product being used (e.g., a cooking demonstration), cents-off specials, brochures, and a variety of other means to influence shoppers while they are in a store.

Growth in sales promotion activities presents a dilemma for manufacturers that are trying to get their promotions into stores in the distribution system. Stores with large merchandise offerings—supermarkets, discounters, department stores—are overwhelmed with requests to run special promotions. Each of these promotions takes up precious floor or shelf space that might otherwise be devoted to displaying more products. As a result, the store manager must select only some of these promotions to prevent the store from being overrun with them.

One way to encourage a store manager to run the manufacturer's sales promotion is to offer inducements. Trade promotion is used for this purpose. A manufacturer might give a price discount or a merchandise allowance (extra units of the product) to encourage the store manager to run a promotion. Of course, trade promotion inducements do not always work. Many store managers have opinions, based on experience, concerning which types of products are most likely to show increased sales from in-store promotions.

EXHIBIT 17–8

An in-store display attracts customers' attention to the company's brand.

Courtesy L'Eggs Products, Inc. and Dancer Fitzgerald Sample Worldwide.

These managers will only select those promotions that they believe will contribute significantly to store sales. One study provides corroborating evidence showing that in-store displays are more effective for some products than others. The study found that displays work better for slow-growth products than for fast-growth products.[21]

Manufacturers' sales personnel often play a part in obtaining in-store promotions, since part of their responsibility is to convince store managers of the sales or profit contribution benefits of the sales promotion activity. Advertising aimed at the trade may also help by reinforcing these efforts.

Audience-Direct Sales Promotions. Trade promotions are one way of delivering sales promotions directly to the audience. Other ways include coupons sent through the mail or placed in (or on) packages; free samples of

EXHIBIT 17-9

Magazine media deliver a sales promotion coupon directly to customers.

Courtesy National Oats Co.

a product delivered to homes or businesses; games, sweepstakes, and contests that do not involve store participation; and gifts sent to customers. Many of these methods can be used equally well with any of the three major audience groups targeted by sales promotion—trade, customers, or salespeople.

To deliver sales promotion to audiences, management must select the most advantageous vehicles, which may differ by the type of audience reached. Direct mail is used extensively for sales promotions intended to reach customers in their homes or businesses. Couponing, free samples, gifts, games, contests, and sweepstakes are promotion activities that rely on mail. Another delivery technique is the use of advertising media. Newspaper advertising can include coupons redeemable for price discounts or free gifts with purchase of the advertised product. Magazines and direct mail advertising are also used in this way (Exhibit 17-9).

Finally, company personnel can carry sales promotion to audiences. Middle- and upper-level managers can make their support of the promotion very visible by directly meeting with the target audience. In publishing, for instance, at sales meetings upper-level managers may announce special incentives on books in the publisher's product mix. They explain the nature and purpose of the promotion to encourage sale personnel to direct greater selling effort to the highlighted books.

Choosing the best vehicle, or the best combination of vehicles, is based on weighing costs versus expediency and audience coverage benefits. The costs of direct mail for a free sample campaign include the expense of purchasing or developing a mailing list containing the names and addresses of audience members and the expense of postage and packaging. The counterbalancing benefits depend on the quality of the mailing list in singling out target audience members and the speed with which samples reach the target audience. Other vehicles—hiring local workers to deliver the samples door-to-door or attaching the samples to another product bought by target audience members—must be weighed, using the same criteria.

Trade Shows.   Trade shows offer an opportunity for a company to display its products to a select audience. Exhibits or booths are staffed by company personnel such as salespeople or executives. Buyers attending a trade show circulate among the exhibits and can examine products and talk to the seller's representatives. Orders are often taken on the spot. In addition, contacts made at the show can be followed up by sales personnel.

Through trade shows, companies can reach distributors and dealers or end users. Manufacturers of tennis clothing and equipment sponsor an annual trade show in Atlanta at which they introduce new lines to retail store buyers. These buyers base most of their purchasing decisions for the upcoming year on the communication interchange at the show. In contrast, many industrial goods companies participate in trade shows to reach their end users. Computer manufacturers such as IBM, Digital Equipment Corporation, and Apple use trade shows for this purpose. These manufacturers can demonstrate their products' capabilities to the many business users attracted to their booths by the attention-getting power of the whole show.

To obtain the desired level of attendance, trade show sponsors must make audiences aware of the show and persuade them to attend. Mailed announcements, advertisements, and personal contacts are needed to bring the audience to a show. These supporting promotions capitalize on the fact that buyers often see trade shows as sources of new product information.

Sales Promotion Budget

Marketing managers must plan for the cost of sales promotion activities. In developing a sales promotion budget, marketing managers delineate the expense categories required to implement planned activities and specify the amounts that they expect to be spent. They also establish an overall limit on expenditures.

The limit on a sales promotion budget can be determined in one of two ways: the top-down or bottom-up approach. In a top-down procedure, top management informs sales promotion managers of the total budget expenditure authorized. This budget amount becomes a constraint on the planning of specific activities. The top-down approach has a serious drawback. Without a plan to evaluate, top management may be tempted to resort to arbitrary rules of thumb to come up with a budget limit. A financial control executive may set the promotion limit as a certain percentage of forecast sales, with the percentage figure being one that has been used in the past. While such an approach is expedient, its logic is not sound, because the budget is set before managers plan a sales promotion campaign and assess what return—orders, sales, profit contribution—the campaign can make to the company.

The other approach is to set the budget from the bottom up. Target audiences are selected and sales promotion objectives set; then, activities are planned to achieve these objectives. The costs of these activities are estimated to determine the budget, and the total of these costs becomes the recommended budget limit. At this point, higher-level management can review the plan and the budget for approval or revision. The advantage of the bottom-up approach is that the potential contribution of sales promotions to the company's performance can be considered during the budget approval process.

In companies without a formal sales promotion department, the budgeting process is more complicated. Sales promotion activities may be planned by more than one department, say, advertising and field sales. In this case, sales promotion expenses show up in more than one departmental budget. The costs of point-of-purchase display materials and artwork may be part of the advertising budget, while expenditures for trade show participation may be underwritten by field sales. Attaining coordination in such a situation is a challenge. Product managers or a higher level marketing manager may have to perform this task.

Evaluation of Performance

Pretesting
is a marketing research study used to evaluate audience reaction to a promotion activity before a decision has been made to implement the activity on a full scale.

Evaluation of performance may come at two points in the process of managing sales promotion activities. **Pretesting** is done before a commitment has been made to a full-scale implementation of an activity, while **posttesting** occurs during or after a full-scale run. Surprisingly, many companies do not evaluate their sales promotion activities as extensively as they evaluate advertising and personal selling. Over 72 percent of the companies participating in one study did not pretest consumer promotions. Among the reasons given were insufficient time and money for pretesting.[22] Nonetheless, evaluation is as important for sales promotion as for any other component of the promotion mix.

Posttesting
is a marketing research study used to evaluate audience reaction to a promotion activity during its implementation or after it has been implemented on a full scale.

Whether pretesting or posttesting, performance evaluation is guided by the objectives set for sales promotion. Most of these objectives are couched in terms of eliciting certain actions among audience members, and the evaluation data are measures of these actions. A very simple measure is a count of the frequency with which an action occurred. An automobile trade show may be evaluated by counting the number of orders for new automobiles taken during the show; the evaluation of a couponing campaign is based on the number of coupons redeemed.

When desired actions are not so easily counted, other measures of performance are needed. One procedure is to record sales of the products before, during, and after a sales promotion campaign. Suppose this procedure is used to determine the sales effect of a supermarket's cents-off promotion on a product such as cereal or toothpaste. If the price promotion is the major new marketing activity during the period, sales changes after the promotion will give managers an adequate view of the promotion's success. On the other hand, if other influences on sales are at work (competitors' countermoves with promotion tactics or a successful push by sales personnel to get more shelf space in stores), a before/after measure of sales is not good enough. Then, marketing research techniques must be used to control for non–sales promotion influences on sales. A supermarket chain may vary the amount of sales promotion in comparable geographic areas in a market test, and then compare the sales across the areas to see the effect of the promotion. In addition, the costs of sales promotion in each area can be used to estimate profit contribution.

Summary

Effectively managing a company's promotion mix is a challenging task for marketing managers. The great variety of promotion tools complicates the planning and control of communications with audiences. Further, coordination becomes increasingly difficult as a company gets larger and the various promotion tools are assigned to different departments. Product managers, promotion committees comprised of managers from each promotion department, and other organizational units have been used with some success to deal with the communications responsibility.

Promotion involves a flow of communications. Understanding the nature of the communications flow from a company to its audiences, as well as the flow among audience members by word of mouth, is essential for effective promotion decision making. Each promotion decision—selecting target audiences, building source credibility, designing messages, selecting delivery channels—combines with the others to determine the nature of the communications flow and how well it works for both the company and its audiences.

Only in the smallest companies are promotion decisions made by one or a few managers. As companies allocate promotion responsibility to more managers and departments, promotion decision making becomes more specialized. Managing each tool, such as sales promotion, requires making a sequence of decisions that include selecting target audiences, setting objectives, determining the activities needed to achieve those objectives, setting a budget, and evaluating the performance of promotion.

Exercises for Review and Discussion

1. For many years, Hershey Chocolate Company used no advertising in its promotion mix. Only recently has the company begun to advertise. Why would the company choose to use no advertising for so long and then decide to include advertising as part of its promotion? Discuss possible reasons.

2. D'Lites, a new fast-food chain specializing in low-calorie, but highly tasty foods, is a new entry in the industry. It must contend with strong and well-established competitors such as McDonalds, Burger King, and Wendy's. How can promotion help with the introduction of D'Lites? More specifically, does the communications flow model suggest kinds of communications that management should use to build sales and market share against these competitors? Discuss your answer.

3. Many companies allocate a substantial part of their sales training programs to providing trainees with information on company products. What is the purpose of this part of the programs? How does extensive product knowledge add to a salesperson's effectiveness with customers?

4. Wendy's popular "Where's the beef?" advertising campaign relied heavily on humor, using a little old lady to ask rival hamburger restaurants where the beef was on their hamburgers. Why do you think this campaign performed as well as it did? What were the desired actions of the target audiences? Why was the humor in the advertisements needed?

5. The management of a firm manufacturing specialized instruments that contain microprocessor components learned that customers often believed that these instruments were too delicate for the intended uses. The customers are engineers and purchasing agents in manufacturing firms. Management knows that the microprocessor-based instruments are, in fact, very rugged. How can promotion be used to communicate this product characteristic to buyers? Which promotion tool or tools would be best for this message and target audience? Discuss your answer.

6. Sales promotion expenditures are growing even faster than expenditures for advertising. Does this mean that sales promotion is a substitute for advertising? Can the two promotion tools achieve exactly the same kinds of objectives? Discuss your answer.

7. Suppose salespeople for Procter & Gamble are having trouble getting supermarkets to purchase enough units of Crest toothpaste. How can sales promotion be used to help them increase supermarket orders of Crest? Discuss your answer.

8. Ace Appliance Company, a distributor of kitchen appliances, ran an off-price promotion for its microwave ovens. The promotion allowed retailers a 15 percent discount on all microwave ovens ordered in the next 30 days. How can Ace's management find out how effective the sales promotion is? Discuss your answer.

Notes

1. Information for this illustration is in Bernie Whalen, " 'Tiny' Saab Drives Up Profits with Market-Niche Strategy, Repositioning," *Marketing News*, March 16, 1984, sec. 1, pp. 14–15.

2. For a related discussion of the communication process, see David A. Aaker and John G. Myers, *Advertising Management* (Englewood Cliffs, N.J.: Prentice-Hall, 1982), pp. 233–36.

3. Kevin Higgins, "Searle Plots a Dual Marketing Strategy for NutraSweet Brand," *Marketing News*, August 3, 1984, p. 1.

4. "Brand Ads Can Do More to Boost Corporate Image than Image Ads Do in Most Cases," *Marketing News*, August 17, 1984, p. 1.

5. For further discussion of this study, see Jacob Jacoby and Wayne D. Hoyer, "Viewer Miscomprehension of Televised Communication: Selected Findings," *Journal of Marketing* 46 (Fall 1982), pp. 12–26.

6. "A New Marketing Blitz in the War of the Plastic Cards," *Business Week*, July 23, 1984, pp. 126, 128.

7. Kenneth E. Bowles, "Develop Marketing Plan, with or without Agency, before Trying to Devise Ad Budget," *Marketing News*, March 18, 1983, p. 17.

8. Jeffrey K. McElnea, "Save Time, Money with Five-Phase Promotion Pretesting Model," *Marketing News*, May 25, 1984, sec. 2, p. 2.

9. "Marketing Briefs: Point-of-Purchase Spending Surpassed $6.8 Billion," *Marketing News*, June 8, 1984, p. 8.

10. "Bigger Role Is Seen for Sales Promotion in 1980s and 1990s," *Marketing News*, June 8, 1984, p. 5.

11. Ibid.

12. Maggie McComas, "The Hard Sell Comes to Software," *Fortune*, September 17, 1984, pp. 59–60.

13. Ibid.

14. Kevin Higgins, "Courier Firm Employs a Brand Approach to Establish a Niche," *Marketing News*, April 27, 1984, pp. 1, 13.

15. Ibid., p. 13.

16. "Sweet Sell Garners 100% Response for Phone Equipment Manufacturer," *Marketing News*, April 1, 1983, p. 3.

17. Shirley Green, "When Competition Heats Up, Real Estate Marketing Is Vital," *Marketing News*, August 3, 1984, p. 13.

18. Robert W. Johnson, "Better Targeting Is Needed from Financial Institutions when They Shape Promotions," *Marketing News*, May 27, 1983, p. 9.

19. Lawrence Ingrassia, "Negative Images: Polaroid Faces Tough Sell with Its New Instant . . . ," *The Wall Street Journal*, March 25, 1986, p. 33.

20. Robert C. Blattberg, Gary D. Epen, and Joshua Lieberman, "A Theoretical and Empirical Evaluation of Price Deals for Consumer Nondurables," *Journal of Marketing* 45 (Winter 1981), p. 117.

21. Michel Chevalier, "Increase in Sales due to In-Store Display," *Journal of Marketing Research* 12 (November 1975), pp. 426–31.

22. McElnea, "Save Time, Money," p. 2.

CHAPTER 18

Advertising Decisions

*C*hevrolet, a division of General Motors Corporation, recently made a bold new marketing strategy move that has important implications for its advertising. Management decided to target women as a key market segment. In the past, men have been Chevrolet's primary target market and consequently the dominant audience for its advertising, as indicated by the company's extensive spending on sports-related media. Now, however, women have been designated a high-priority audience for Chevrolet advertising. Funds formerly spent on television sports are being slashed to make room for advertising media that Chevrolet has heretofore used very little—women's magazines, direct mail, and direct-response print ads. In addition, the creative design of many ads is being tailored to appeal to women. The reasons for the strategic move are explained by Chevrolet's general marketing manager:

> Women today are making higher salaries and they have more responsible positions than ever before. Today they account for about a third of all new-car and truck sales and by 1990 they'll be buying more than half. Even today, counting their influence on purchase decisions, they're responsible for a majority of sales.[1]

Chevrolet's advertising agency has formed a group headed by a woman to design ads for the female audience. At the same time, Chevrolet has an all-women executive marketing committee to guide the planning of marketing and advertising strategy directed toward this target. The impact of the new strategy is evident in the many Chevrolet advertisements that portray women in lifestyle situations. The company has high hopes for the new strategy because it was relatively successful in selling to women even before the strategy was adopted.[2]

Organizations in the United States allocate billions of dollars for advertising, and each year the amount allocated for this purpose reaches a new high. This spending is a vote of confidence in advertising as a marketing tool. It is also a mandate to make effective use of the advertising resources. Thus, management must develop sound approaches to planning and implementing advertising and to controlling advertising resources. While the specific procedures employed vary from company to company, there are systematic steps that can be taken to manage these resources:

- Determine a mission for advertising.
- Determine an advertising budget.
- Design an advertising campaign.
- Develop a creative strategy and a media plan.
- Measure how effective advertising has been.

Advertising's Mission

Three key decisions determine advertising's mission. First, the role of advertising in the company's promotion strategy must be established. Then, target audiences are selected. Finally, specific objectives are set whose achievement enables advertising to fulfill its role.

Advertising Plays a Role

Advertising's role is determined by how much emphasis or weight is given to advertising relative to other marketing mix components. Companies vary considerably in deciding how extensive this role should be. Exhibit 18-1 lists expenditures of the top 10 advertisers in the United States. It is no accident that all 10 are large consumer products companies. Although a company must be large to afford such huge amounts, the types of audiences being targeted also determine the weight given to advertising. Consumer markets contain many more customers and are more geographically dispersed than industrial markets. Consequently, consumer products companies typically assign a larger role to advertising than do industrial products companies.

Before assigning advertising's role, management must compare the capabilities of the alternative promotion tools. Each of these tools has certain strengths and offsetting weaknesses, as can be seen by contrasting advertising and personal selling. Advertising is less effective than personal selling in persuading customers to buy. A salesperson can tailor an appeal to individual customers, respond directly to questions, and refute objections as they are raised. On the other hand, salespeople are severely limited in the number of customers they can reach. Advertising, because it reaches so many, is far less expensive than personal selling for each target audience contact made.

Assigning the appropriate role to advertising is complicated by the fact that the roles of all the promotion tools should be coordinated. This function may be performed by a chief marketing executive or by a committee that is established to weigh the merits of alternative allocations across the promotion tools. If such a committee is formed, executives from sales, marketing staff, advertising, the advertising agency, and corporate staff meet periodically to discuss problems and opportunities for the promotion mix.

EXHIBIT 18–1 Top 10 Advertisers in the United States, 1983–1984 ($ millions)

Company	Advertising Expenditure			
	1984	Rank	1983	Rank
Procter & Gamble Company	$872.0	1	$773.6	1
General Motors Corporation	763.8	2	595.1	4
Sears, Roebuck & Co.	746.9	3	732.5	2
Beatrice Companies	680.0	4	602.8	3
R. J. Reynolds Industries	678.2	5	593.4	5
Philip Morris, Inc.	570.4	6	527.5	6
American Telephone and Telegraph Company	563.2	7	463.1	8
Ford Motor Company	559.4	8	479.1	7
K mart Corporation	554.4	9	400.0	9
McDonald's Corporation	480.0	10	311.4	16

Sources: *Advertising Age*, September 26, 1985, p. 1; and *Advertising Age*, September 14, 1984, p. 1.

Target Audiences

A central part of the advertising mission is communicating with specific audiences. A well-developed marketing strategy guides decisions concerning who the target audiences for the advertising program should be. New Jersey Bell has effectively coordinated advertising's mission with overall marketing strategy for its customized call-waiting service (a special signal is activated whenever someone is calling the number of a phone in use; these incoming calls can then be acknowledged). One target market is families with teenagers, since teenagers are active phone users. Advertising has been designed specifically for this target market by communicating such service benefits as reaching a family in an emergency.[3]

Trade advertising is advertising aimed at informing, reminding, and persuading managers of wholesale or retail firms in a company's channel of distribution.

Another important audience for advertising is the trade (resellers in a company's channel of distribution). This audience is reached through **trade advertising** intended to enlist wholesaler or retailer cooperation in selling the company's products. Retail stores, for instance, may be encouraged to stock the advertiser's product, to participate in a cents-off price promotion, or to buy larger quantities of the product.

How managers split budgets between trade and end-user advertising depends on the type of marketing strategy used. A push strategy emphasizing placing products into the distribution channel requires relatively more trade advertising. In contrast, a pull strategy to build a strong preference for a company's brands among end users must have a higher proportion of consumer advertising. Of course, many marketing strategies fall somewhere in between push and pull and have more balanced allocations.

Some of the other audiences for advertising—stockholders, investors, the general public, government officials, employees—have little to do with target markets. A railroad ran advertisements showing the deplorable condition of track and equipment so as to win support for subsidies among government legislators. Michigan Seamless Tube Company changed its name to Quanex Corporation to launch a new corporate image and used advertising directed toward investors to strengthen the price of the company's stock.[4]

Advertising Objectives

To be effective, advertising aimed at supporting the marketing strategy for a company's products (services) must ultimately influence buyer purchase decisions (sales). However, the relationship between advertising and sales is difficult to sort out. Advertising combines with a host of other influences to determine buyers' purchase decisions. The problem is to figure out what contribution advertising made to those decisions.

This dilemma causes marketing managers to disagree about the objectives for advertising. Some managers believe that advertising should achieve communication objectives, while others argue for setting sales objectives.

Communication objectives
for advertising state how audiences should think and feel about the product or company as a way of influencing later buying decisions.

Communication Objectives. Proponents of **communication objectives** believe that advertising should contribute to the entire company sales effort but should not be expected to achieve any given level of sales. They argue that it is not fair to expect advertising to do the whole job of meeting a company's sales objectives. Instead, advertising objectives should state expected performance in terms of what audiences should think and feel—developing awareness of product benefits, generating positive attitudes and emotions toward the product, or creating a strong intention to buy should the need arise. Proceeding along these lines, the International Apple Institute used advertising and publicity to increase consumer awareness of the varieties and uses of apples available in the United States. By telling consumers about the choices, advertising and publicity were aimed at building sales of apples. Marketing research data subsequently showed that sales did, in fact, increase.[5]

Advertising's primary purpose is to convey to audiences information about a company and its products. On the basis of this information, customers form beliefs, likes and dislikes, predispositions, and intentions that later influence purchase decisions. In this way, advertising contributes to the total selling effort of a marketing strategy but does not carry the entire burden of generating sales. Advertising objectives guiding a Marathon Oil Company campaign illustrate communication objectives:

- To increase awareness of the Marathon brand and instill confidence in it.

- To introduce the Marathon guarantee and convince motorists that it is a legitimate offer, completely backed by the company.

- To increase the number of persons who regard Marathon as a major oil company.

- To increase the number of persons who regard Marathon's gasoline and oil products as being of the highest quality.[6]

Communication objectives should be derived from studying people in target audiences. The fundamentals of buyer behavior offer guidelines on what to study. A marketing research and consulting firm, Elrick and Lavidge, Inc., developed a model based on communication objectives (Exhibit 18-2). The model portrays buyers as relying on information—whether from per-

EXHIBIT 18-2 A Communications Model for Advertising

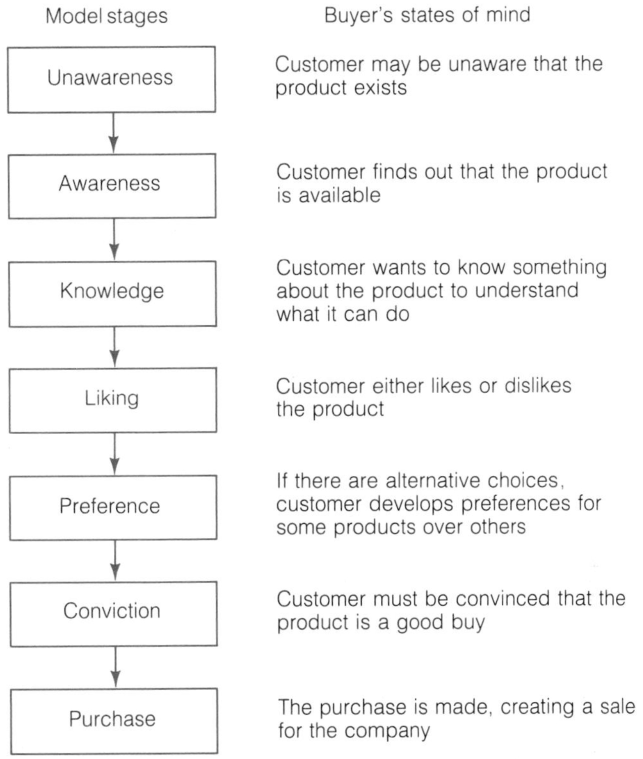

Model stages	Buyer's states of mind
Unawareness	Customer may be unaware that the product exists
Awareness	Customer finds out that the product is available
Knowledge	Customer wants to know something about the product to understand what it can do
Liking	Customer either likes or dislikes the product
Preference	If there are alternative choices, customer develops preferences for some products over others
Conviction	Customer must be convinced that the product is a good buy
Purchase	The purchase is made, creating a sale for the company

Source: Robert J. Lavidge and Gary A. Steiner, "A Model for Predicting Measurements of Advertising Effectiveness," *Journal of Marketing* 25 (October 1961), pp. 59-62. Published by the American Marketing Association.

sonal experience, product packages, friends and family, salespeople, or advertising—to help them make purchase choices. While the model is more applicable to high-involvement purchases than to other kinds of purchases, it can serve as a framework for setting advertising objectives.

Marketing research helps to implement a communications model by measuring how many people from target markets are in each stage—how many are unaware of the product, how many are aware of it without knowing what it has to offer, and so forth. This enables managers to evaluate the worth of influencing customers to move from one stage to the next, closer to purchase. Such worth is based on the increased probability of purchase when a customer goes to the next stage. Probabilities of this kind can be estimated by monitoring how many people starting in a given stage actually end up buying. Suppose data indicate that 10 percent of those who become aware of the product proceed to purchase it. A manager can apply this fact to calculate the worth (number of people aware × .10 × the profit contribution of each unit sold) of using advertising to achieve an awareness objective.

**Sales-related
objectives**
state the level of sales
or sales-related per-
formance that
advertising is expected
to achieve.

Sales Objectives.   Proponents of **sales-related objectives** hold that advertising should achieve such performance as growth in sales, market share,
or even profits. Wesson Oil set an objective of this kind when threatened by a
powerful competitor. Management found that it was losing market share to
Procter & Gamble's Crisco Oil. Advertising was expected to stop the slide. An
advertising objective was established to increase Wesson's market share at
P&G's expense.[7]

Advocates of sales-related objectives argue that such objectives tie advertising directly to the same kinds of performance objectives that are expected
from the overall marketing strategy. Further, they point out that the relationship between achieving communication objectives and generating sales
is not clear. In fact, the controversy would not exist if effective communication always led to higher sales, market share, and profits. However, being
aware of a product and knowing certain benefits may not be enough to
influence consumers to purchase, particularly if these benefits are not important to them.

There is probably a middle ground. Sales objectives provide little guidance
to those who must design advertising campaigns, and sales as a measure of
advertising effectiveness do not explain why an advertising campaign was (or
was not) successful. Communication objectives are more useful than sales
objectives for determining what to say to audiences. Furthermore, measures
to determine how well communication objectives have been achieved are
widely available. For these reasons, communication objectives should play at
least a part in determining the mission of advertising. At the same time,
managers should be concerned about the extent to which achieving communication objectives contributes to sales-related measures of performance.

Advertising Budgeting

An advertising budget is a financial document that shows the total dollar
resources allocated to advertising and should also list the way those dollars
are to be spent. Expenditure categories typically concern production of the
advertisements and the media to deliver them to audiences. One of the most
difficult decisions is determining the limit on the size of the advertising
budget—the allocation decision.

Allocating Resources to Advertising

Management should, of course, allocate company resources to advertising on
the basis of its potential contribution to corporate and marketing objectives.
Determining this contribution is not easy. Marginal analysis, an idealized
approach to determining an advertising budget allocation, serves as a standard for evaluating the alternative approaches actually used by businesses.

Marginal analysis assumes that management wants to maximize profits. To
simplify, it is also assumed here that the company has sufficient resources to

EXHIBIT 18-3 Marginal Analysis Identifying the Profit-Maximizing
Advertising Budget ($000)

(1) Advertising Expenditures	(2) Marginal Ad Costs	(3)* Net Revenue	(4) Marginal Revenue	(5) Total Profit	(6) Marginal Profit
$ 30		$20		$ - 10	
35	$5	24	$ + 4	- 11	$ - 1
40	5	30	+ 6	- 10	+ 1
45	5	40	+ 10	- 5	+ 5
50	5	55	+ 15	+ 5	+ 10
55	5	77	+ 22	+ 22	+ 17
60	5	88	+ 11	+ 28	+ 6
65	5	95	+ 7	+ 30	+ 2
70	5	98	+ 3	+ 28	- 2
75	5	99	+ 1	+ 24	- 4
80	5	99	0	+ 19	- 5
85	5	97	- 2	+ 12	- 7
90	5	95	- 2	+ 5	- 7
95	5	90	- 5	- 5	- 10
100	5	83	- 7	- 12	- 7

* Sales less all advertising costs.

meet the profit-maximizing objective and that increases (or decreases) in advertising spending must be made in $5,000 increments. Exhibit 18-3 illustrates the kinds of data needed to analyze the profit contribution of advertising.

The data show that spending less than $50,000 on advertising does not allow the company to generate enough sales to cover all costs. Thus, this amount sets a floor or minimum allocation for advertising. The ceiling, or upper limit, is $90,000, with any further spending on advertising causing a loss. The task is to find the profit-maximizing expenditure somewhere between these upper and lower limits.

To find the optimal advertising expenditure, management must compare marginal revenue (column 4) with marginal cost (column 2). The difference between them is advertising's contribution to total profits (column 6). Advertising continues to add to profits until a budget level of $65,000 is reached. At that level, profits are maximized at $30,000. Beyond that level, profits start to decline.

The most inhibiting problem with marginal analysis is obtaining appropriate data. Consider the marginal revenue estimate. To determine changes in revenue with different advertising budgets, management must know exactly how advertising influences customers' purchase decisions. We have already seen that obtaining such information is difficult since there are so many other influences on sales. Costs are easier to estimate, although there are complications here, too, including short-run cost changes, unanticipated costs, and joint advertising costs across products. Consequently, marginal analysis is seldom if ever used in practice, but can serve as a standard for budget-setting procedures to emulate.

Advertising Budget Rules of Thumb

Some companies rely on budgeting procedures that are essentially rules of thumb, such as the following:

- Percent of sales.
- Competitive parity.
- All resources available for advertising.[8]

Percent of Sales.   Percent of sales allocations set aside a predetermined percentage of sales for advertising. The sales may be the last period's sales or forecast sales. A jeans store uses this approach when it allocates 8 percent of forecast sales to advertising. If sales are expected to reach $150,000 for an operating period, then the store's advertising budget is set at $12,000. The percent of sales procedure is very versatile. It can be applied to a company's total advertising or to advertising for various units—stores in a chain, individual products in a product mix, or particular target markets. It is a simple procedure to understand, and it ensures that managers consider the company's ability to pay for advertising out of revenues.

How well does the percent of sales procedure compare to the marginal analysis ideal? Not very well! Too often the percentage is historically determined—this year's percentage is the same as the percentage that was used last year and the year before. However, the opportunity for using advertising productively changes over time as the market and competition change. A further problem occurs when forecast sales are used in the calculation. Notice that sales are forecast before advertising expenditures are determined. This is illogical because advertising's purpose is to help stimulate sales for the company, and so future sales are dependent on the amount and quality of advertising.

Competitive Parity.   Managers usually keep an eye on the marketing activity of competitors. Sometimes data can be obtained that show how much competitors are spending on advertising. Burger King's managers know that McDonald's spends about $200 million on advertising annually.[10] While Burger King is not big enough to match that budget, this information probably influences how much money it allocates to advertising. Common competitive parity rules of thumb are:

- Spend on advertising so that the ratio of the advertising budget to that of a competitor is the same as relative market shares of the two firms.

- Spend on advertising an amount equal to the average advertising expenditure for the industry.

- Spend on advertising a set percentage of a key competitor's advertising expenditure.

The parity approach ensures that managers consider competitive advertising strategies when setting a budget. If advertising is an important influence on sales and market share, management will try to keep up with the competition. To set a budget based only on competitive spending, however, is a risky approach. One problem is obtaining accurate information on what key competitors are doing. Published sources may not give a complete estimate of a competitor's spending (sometimes only media budgets are reported, rather than total advertising budgets).

When competitive data or industry averages data are available, advertising managers usually want to compare their own spending on advertising with that of the competition. In the 1970s, studies of marketing by industrial companies—the Advisor Projects—were conducted to learn about marketing and advertising allocations. The results provided insight into average spending on advertising in terms of percent of sales (0.7 percent in 1975) and percent of total marketing budgets (10 percent in 1975).[11] These data offered industry standards that some companies have used to guide their advertising allocations.

A serious problem with competitive parity budgeting approaches is the implied assumption that all competitors have the same advertising opportunities. This is seldom true. A company introducing a new product to compete with another company's established brand has a mission for advertising very different from that of its competitor. Even for established brands of competing companies, opportunities are not likely to be identical. Consider AT&T's battle with MCI for long-distance telephone service. AT&T's quality reputation is well established among long-distance callers, while MCI's reputation is still developing. MCI must use advertising to continue to expand its appeal among buyers, while AT&T can set other objectives for advertising, such as maintaining favorable impressions of the company and its services (Exhibit 18–4).

All Resources Available.   Finally a company may allocate all available resources to advertising. The amount of the available resources may be analytically determined by estimating sales, deducting all nonadvertising costs, and deducting a planned amount of profit. Sometimes a financial control executive gives a "guesstimate" of the amount available. Either way, advertising is treated as a residual activity. All other functions are funded before advertising receives its allocation.

This approach has advantages. It requires that managers budget for advertising after considering the firm's profit objectives. Further, managers must set a priority on advertising relative to other functions that contribute to profits. Offsetting these advantages is a serious potential pitfall. Managers can too easily use this rule of thumb without specifically considering opportunities for using advertising to achieve marketing objectives. This may lead to spending too little or too much on advertising. Moreover, the advertising

EXHIBIT 18-4

MCI uses advertising to expand its appeal among long-distance callers.

Courtesy MCI Telecommunications Corp.

budget is set after sales have been estimated even though the amount spent on advertising ought to be a factor in the sales forecasting procedure.

In practice, only very poorly trained managers base advertising budgets solely on one of these rules of thumb. Managers are more likely to use the rules of thumb as guidelines for evaluating alternative budgets. A top financial executive, for instance, may check a proposed advertising budget by calculating a percentage of sales to see how the budget compares with what has been spent in previous years. A budget out of line with past figures will receive close scrutiny. However, even used in this way can be a problem. One expert describes the danger in applying advertising budgeting rules of thumb:

There is a temptation in some companies to let arbitrary guidelines loom a bit too large in the equation, with perhaps not quite enough attention paid to the analysis and research which provide the factual underpinning for a rationally defensible budget.[9]

Building the Budget by Objective and Task

Rather than relying on arbitrary rules of thumb, managers can use an analytic approach to setting an advertising budget. They can construct an advertising budget through analyses of the objectives and tasks of advertising. Briefly, management begins by examining the contribution of advertising to the company's overall marketing strategy. Objectives are set based on that contribution. Then advertising managers design a campaign to accomplish these objectives. The cost of this campaign becomes the advertising budget.

To gain a better perspective on how this approach works, consider the marketing strategy of Humana, Inc., the Louisville-based hospital chain. Humana has already become known for its artificial heart program. Management of the chain has been aggressively trying to establish widespread brand name recognition for its hospitals and its health care–related services. Currently, it is building reputation and sales for Humana Care Plus (HCP), a preferred-provider organization (PPO). PPOs offer reduced-cost medical services to subscribers through a network of physicians and facilities. Humana wanted to build awareness of HCP, to educate potential subscribers to the benefits of its services, and to expand the number of subscribers. Advertising was assigned a major role in the strategy. In 1984, an advertising campaign was designed with these strategic objectives in mind, and an estimated $12 million was allocated to the advertising budget as necessary to accomplish the communication and sales objectives. The campaign was quite successful, as indicated by a more than 10-fold increase in the number of subscribers in a six-month period.[12]

As the Humana situation illustrates, an objective and task approach to budgeting follows the ideal framework of marginal analysis more closely than do the budgeting rules of thumb. The objective/task approach requires managers to evaluate the potential contribution of advertising to company marketing objectives. The resulting advertising budget matches the resource allocation with specific advertising goals. At the same time, the approach requires a more thorough analysis of market opportunity than do the rules of thumb, and so it can be expensive to implement.

Models for Advertising Budgeting

Quantitative models can be used in making advertising budgeting decisions. These models guide the collection of information for analysis and allow quick evaluation of the information collected so as to produce a budget for approval. Management retains the ability to accept or modify the budget allocation as it sees fit.

A model called ADMOD[13] illustrates the value of budgeting decision models. ADMOD offers a way of quantifying the value of a given budget using the objective function:

$$V = \Sigma \, N_s/n_s \sum_{i\in s} W_s \sum_{Z_i = 0}^{\infty} A_{ci}(Z_i)f_{ci}(Z_i) - \sum_j k_j X_{cj}$$

where:

V = Value of an insertion schedule

c = Index referring to the copy alternative c

i = Index referring to the ith individual in sample population

j = Index referring to the jth vehicle (media)

s = Index referring to market segment s

N_s = Size of market segment s

n_s = Size of sample from market segment s

W_s = Value to firm of consumer action (e.g., a trial purchase) by member of market segment s

Z_i = Number of exposures received by individual i, given the insertion schedule

$A_{ci}(Z_i)$ = Probability that the desired consumer action will occur, given that Z_i exposures occurred

$f_{ci}(Z_i)$ = Probability that individual i will receive exactly Z_i exposures, given the insertion schedule

k_j = Cost of insertion in vehicle j

X_{cj} = Insertion of copy alternative c into vehicle j ($X_{cj} = 0,1$)

The model has several interesting characteristics. First, the objective function ensures that the budget is set based on the value of advertising *insertion schedules*. The model examines different schedules to find the one that maximizes V, advertising's objective of achieving a desired action from consumers (e.g., a store visit, a trial purchase). The budget size is $\sum_j k_j X_{cj}$ in the objective function.

Second, the model requires an explicit evaluation of the contribution of alternative copy designs (messages and layouts in ads) and media combinations to the firm. The term $\Sigma \, W_s \sum_{Z_i = 0}^{\infty} A_{ci}(Z_i)f_{ci}(Z_i)$ accomplishes this purpose. The remaining term, $\Sigma \, N_s/n_s$, converts the value of advertising for the sample data to the segment populations as a whole. Implementing the model is similar to the objective and task approach of designing a campaign to achieve objectives before determining a budget.

Advertising managers must use marketing research data to estimate the parameters in the model. Each parameter serves as a guide to specifying the data needed. Thus, the model is a useful framework for analyzing budgeting decision considerations.

Creating an Advertising Campaign

Advertising campaign is a combination of messages communicated in a particular way to audiences to achieve advertising objectives.

The most creative part of advertising is planning an **advertising campaign.** The campaign determines what to say to target audiences and how to say it so that people will listen to and understand the messages and remember them when buying decisions are made. Exhibit 18-5 shows the steps that creative specialists follow to design a campaign.

Marketing Position Statement

A marketing plan should provide a position statement explaining how a company's product (or service) is to be differentiated from those of key competitors. This statement is derived from an analysis of market opportunities. The most important assessments are those of customers' market requirements and competitors' strengths and weaknesses. The advertiser's own strengths and weaknesses must also be considered.

Burger King effectively used such analyses when developing its successful "Battle of the Burgers" campaign, which ran from 1982 through most of 1985. Management was frustrated by the fact that McDonald's dominated the markets for fast-food hamburger restaurants. However, marketing research revealed that Burger King had several product benefit advantages perceived as important by consumers, including larger hamburgers and a cooking process based on broiling rather than frying. To counter the dominance of McDonald's, management decided to position Burger King as "the quality fast-food hamburger restaurant." Advertising took its direction from this position statement.[14]

Advertising's Selling Proposals

Selling proposal is a statement describing the important facts, images, and persuasive arguments to be communicated to target audiences.

A position statement helps advertising managers plan a **selling proposal.** This describes the specific selling points—product benefits, emotions enhanced by the product, service benefits—to be made in advertising copy (the text of the ad). Burger King's creative strategy was guided by a selling proposal that led to using comparative advertising. Copy for television and print advertisements compared its hamburgers with those of McDonald's on the cooking process, the size of meat patties, and related benefits. The Battle of the Burgers campaign was very successful, though by the end of 1985 it

EXHIBIT 18–5 Advertising Creative Strategy Decisions

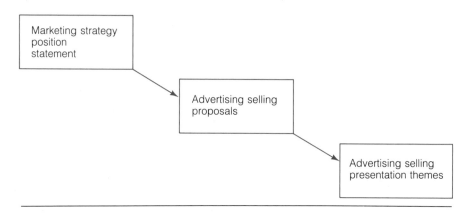

had lost its effectiveness. Realizing that the selling proposal had to change, Burger King created a new marketing and advertising strategy to concentrate on food quality and other benefits.

Advertising Presentations

Selling points provide essential direction for creative specialists. These specialists create the advertising copy and layout to translate selling points into an advertising presentation. Copy and layout are coordinated and integrated into a proposed advertisement. Typically, several alternative presentations are designed. Market research tests can then be conducted to see which alternative is best at communicating selling points to the audience. Armed with the test data, management selects the presentation for a campaign. Exhibit 18-6 illustrates the application of this process by several companies, as indicated by recent advertising themes.

Managing Creative Specialists. Successful advertising requires fresh and interesting ways to communicate selling points to target audiences. The competition for the attention of target audiences is intense. The forte of creative specialists is their ability to use insight and imagination in the design of presentations. However, these specialists should be managed to ensure that advertising presentations are consistent with marketing strategy.[15]

Marketing is responsible for ensuring that creative specialists understand the requirements of an advertising campaign. Information from the marketing plan and supporting market opportunity analysis are essential to acquaint

EXHIBIT 18–6 Advertising Presentations Reflecting Positioning of Company Brand

Position Statement	Selling Proposal	Selling Presentation
Wendy's is positioned as a fast-food chain offering high-quality food.	Wendy's uses fresher ingredients than its competitors and does not pre-cook its food.	"Choose fresh, choose Wendy's."
Dodge is positioned as the best-built and most durable brand of small trucks.	Dodge makes a durable small truck that can take rough use.	"Dodge is Ram-tough!"
Subaru is positioned as a better-designed car in the low-price end of the competition.	Subaru offers a simply designed and dependable car with a low price.	"Subaru is inexpensive and built to stay that way."

creative specialists with the product, its competition, the position strategy and selling proposal, the advertising objectives, and the characteristics of the target audience. A profile of the target audience is particularly important. Creative specialists have to visualize the flesh and blood persons in the audience. Information on the demographic characteristics of the audience can be helpful, but even more helpful are descriptions of lifestyle, values, product use situations, attitudes, product-related beliefs, preferred product benefits, and other data that together paint a picture of real people.

Only after reviewing such information can creative specialists begin to concentrate on the way that the messages will be communicated. At this point, they must be given the freedom to use their talents. William Bernbach of Doyle Dane Bernbach, Inc., a well-known advertising agency, described the task of the creative specialists very well when he said:

> Truth is essential in advertising. . . . You're not going to make it without it. But I must tell you that, while it may make you feel virtuous, it isn't its own reward. As far as your advertising budget is concerned, the truth isn't the truth until people believe you; and they can't believe you if they don't know what you're saying, and they won't listen to you if you're not interesting. And you won't be interesting unless you say things freshly, originally, imaginatively.[16]

Pretesting Ad Presentation Alternatives.   Marketing research plays another important role in the creative process by testing alternative presentations. Data gathered from the tests help managers evaluate how audiences are likely to react. Many kinds of tests are available, and no one kind is always more appropriate than the others. Tests must be matched with the type of presentation being developed. An ad intended to create a mood or emotion that consumers associate with the product, as might be the case for cosmetics, should probably not be tested in the same way as an ad communicating tangible product characteristics. Creative specialists must work with research personnel to decide what kinds of tests are needed.[17]

Media Strategy and Tactics

Media mix
is the combination of vehicles (e.g., magazines, newspapers, TV, radio, direct mail, billboards) that will carry advertisements to target audiences.

Media schedule
is the combination of specific times (e.g., by day, week, month) when advertisements are inserted into media vehicles and delivered to target audiences.

Media plan
is the designated media mix and media schedule that will be used to deliver advertisements to target audiences.

Developing media strategy is complicated by the fact that many different vehicles are available, each having its advantages and disadvantages. Typically, no one vehicle reaches an entire target audience. Consequently, media planners must evaluate the many alternatives so as to construct a **media mix** that will meet objectives. Further, the timing of advertisements—a **media schedule**—must be determined so that they are properly sequenced when the advertising campaign is run. Together, the media mix and media schedule decisions form a **media plan.** The media plan lists the media to be used, the times or issues in which each advertisement is to be carried by each vehicle, and the cost of the media mix. It serves as a blueprint for implementing the delivery of an advertising campaign.

A high percentage of an advertising budget is allocated to the cost of the various media. Thus, many companies assign the task of developing a media plan to specialists. These specialists may be personnel working for the advertiser, or may be in the advertising agency used by the advertiser. They know or can quickly determine rates for advertisements placed in vehicles. Further, they are experienced in working with the media to buy space for advertisements. However, even these experts can be overwhelmed by the sheer number of different vehicles to consider, particularly for a large and diversified advertising campaign. As we shall see, many advertising agencies have brought the power of the computer, in the form of computerized media models, to bear on this task as an aid to media planners.

Media Mix Decisions

There are a relatively few major media types. Exhibit 18–7 describes important advantages and disadvantages of various media types. Each type comprises a large number of alternatives. There are hundreds of magazines and trade journals, each reaching a somewhat different audience. There are also a wide variety of newspapers, television and radio programs, and billboard locations. In addition, each vehicle has multiple issues or time slots—newspapers are usually printed daily or weekly; magazines are published weekly, monthly, or quarterly; and television programs are run daily or weekly, or may even be onetime specials. Choosing the best combination of these vehicles and deciding how many and what size advertisements to place in each of them requires a systematic selection process.

Advertisers deal with this complexity by setting criteria for comparison to ensure that the vehicles selected meet advertising objectives and budget constraints. Three particularly important criteria are:

- Overlap of vehicle audience with target audiences.
- Media communication capabilities.
- Cost.

EXHIBIT 18–7 Advantages and Disadvantages of Major Advertising Media

Media	Advantages	Disadvantages	Media	Advantages	Disadvantages
Television	Reaches large audiences Has visual and audio capabilities Provides great flexibility in getting attention Short lead time needed to place ad	Not easy to reach specific target markets Total cost is high relative to other media Requires production specialists Short exposure time	*Radio*	Audio capability Low cost relative to costs of the other media Short lead time needed to place ad Can reach demographic and geographic segments Reaches large audiences Reaches audiences in cars	No visual capability Short exposure time Provides little flexibility in gaining attention
Magazines and journals	Issues reach is high for demographic and geographic segments High-quality production Ad lasts as long as magazine or journal is kept Issues are often read by more than one person Credibility of magazine or journal can benefit ad	Must place ad well in advance of publication Provide limited flexibility in gaining attention Provide incomplete control over location of ad in issue	*Newspapers*	Reach large audiences Can reach segments by locale Short lead time needed to place ad Credibility of newspaper can benefit ad	May be relatively expensive Provide little flexibility for use of creativity Limited reproduction quality (e.g., little or no use of color) Short life carries over to ad
Outdoor advertising	Relatively inexpensive Many repeat exposures	Only very limited message possible Cannot reach well-defined target markets Very short exposure time	*Direct mail*	Provides great flexibility in reaching target market segments No clutter from competing ads Easy to personalize copy and layout	Easily thrown away as "junk mail" Obtaining appropriate mailing lists can be expensive

Vehicle Audience Overlap.   The value of a particular media mix depends on how well it reaches a company's target audiences. Consequently, the characteristics of the vehicle's audience are examined to determine how well they match those of the target audiences. Most media supply advertisers with detailed information on the kinds of people reading, listening to, or watching their vehicles. Breweries such as Miller Brewing Company, for instance, rely extensively on sports-oriented television and radio programs and magazines because men dominate the audiences of these vehicles and men are more likely than women to decide which brand of beer to purchase.

Before evaluating how well alternative vehicles reach target audiences, an advertiser sets **audience delivery objectives.** These objectives typically concern several aspects of audience delivery, including:[18]

Audience delivery objectives
specify the target audience for advertising and the extent to which that audience is to be exposed to advertisements during the scheduled period.

■ The desired target audience segments to reach.

■ The percentage of a target audience that receives at least one exposure to the advertisement (i.e., reach).

■ The average number of times that the typical target audience member is exposed to the advertisement (i.e., average frequency of exposure).

■ The total number of exposures among the audience, not counting duplications (i.e., gross impressions).

Like creative specialists, media planners need information describing target audiences. They must also know the characteristics of different media audiences. In addition to the research of media on their own audiences, information on vehicle audiences is collected and sold by research companies. The characteristics used to describe vehicle audiences are very similar to those typically used to describe target markets—demographics, lifestyle, and product use data.

Media Communication Capabilities. Each of the major types of advertising media has special capabilities and limitations for delivering advertising presentations. Media planners seek media with the capabilities needed to effectively communicate selling points. One study highlighted the importance of these capabilities when it found that listeners' feeling for the background music in an advertisement can become associated with the product.[19] Yet radio and television are the only media that allow advertisers to take advantage of music's ability to influence.

Media planners rely heavily on judgment to match media communication capabilities with copy and layout requirements. Through extensive experience, media planners become very familiar with the unique advantages and disadvantages of each media type and of many vehicles. Thus, they are in a good position to weigh the capabilities of the various media vehicles against their cost.

Vehicle Costs. Advertising budgets place a limit on the amount of resources that can be used to buy media space or time. This means that media vehicle costs must be carefully assessed to develop a media mix. However, comparing vehicles solely on the basis of cost is not very practical. Cost must be related to some measure of value. A widely used value-to-cost criterion is **cost per thousand.** *Time* magazine charges $81,590 to run a full-page advertisement and has an audience of 4,600,000 persons.[20] Its cost per thousand, $17.74, can be compared to that of other vehicles with similar audiences to see which vehicle is the most economical.

Cost per thousand
measures the cost of reaching each thousand persons in a vehicles audience with a single advertising insertion.

Applying the cost-per-thousand criterion may appear deceptively easy. Its usefulness depends on the way the vehicle's audience is measured. In many cases, the figure given is based on the total audience of a vehicle. This may seriously overstate the vehicle's value because many of those in the vehicle's audience may not be in the firm's target audience. Only the portion of a vehicle's audience that overlaps with an advertiser's target audience is important, but this is harder to measure.

Measuring the actual audience for a given issue or time period is even more difficult. The problem is that not everyone in a total vehicle audience will be exposed to the advertisement for any particular insertion. In evaluating television programs for which to buy advertising time, the current cost of the advertising time should be compared with the predicted audiences (using program ratings) at the time the advertisements are run. Models are available to help with these predictions, which consider such factors as program content, audience demographics, audience loyalty to program, viewing preferences, and historical program ratings.[21]

Cost per thousand should also be used cautiously for decisions on the number of insertions per vehicle because multiple insertions typically do not all have the same value. The fifth time an audience member sees an advertisement may not be as effective as the first, second, or third time. Further, audience composition and exposure to the advertisement can change for each insertion. Using a single cost-per-thousand criterion for each insertion does not take such changes into account. Finally, cost per thousand does not take into consideration the communication characteristics of media.

All of these limitations of cost per thousand emphasize that it is only one of several criteria that should be considered when selecting a media mix. Advertisers must devise an evaluation process that incorporates all of the criteria for determining a media mix.

Media Selection Models

Quantitative models are often employed to assist in media selection decisions. With appropriate data, these models can be used to compare and evaluate large numbers of vehicle alternatives very quickly and efficiently. Advertising managers can review a model's recommended media mix and make adjustments where judgment and experience dictate. The available models generally fall into one of two categories: optimizing approaches and nonoptimizing approaches.

Interactive Optimizing Models. The building of media models has been spearheaded by advertising agencies. At some agencies, interactive models involving an iterative search routine are used to find an optimal media mix. The routine is a computer algorithm for searching through a list of candidate vehicles to select individual insertions, one vehicle and insertion at a time, until some constraint (generally a budget limit) has been reached. After each

EXHIBIT 18–8 Interactive Optimizing Media Selection Model

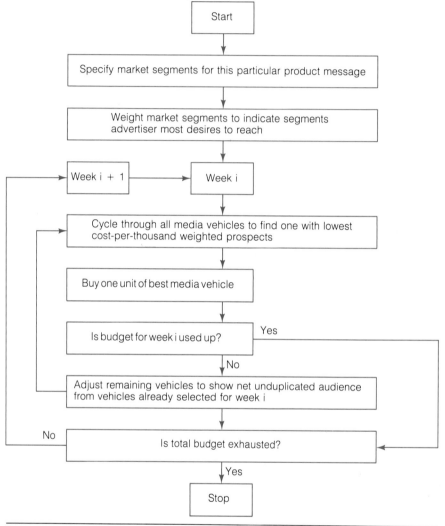

Source: Reprinted with permission from Dennis H. Gensch, "Computer Models in Advertising Media Selection," *Journal of Marketing Research* 5 (November 1968), p. 416. Published by the American Marketing Association.

vehicle insertion has been selected based on its contribution (e.g., cost per thousand, target audience reach, gross exposures), the contribution from all other vehicle insertions not yet selected is recomputed. Each iteration allows the model to consider audience duplication between vehicles. Exhibit 18–8 illustrates a flow diagram of one interactive media selection model.

Nonoptimizing Models. Simulation models have also been used in media selection decisions. This type of model simulates the process by which vehicles reach and influence target audience members. Marketing research collects data on the viewing habits of individuals and on the vehicles' probable impact on customer purchasing behavior. Advertising managers can enter alternative media mixes into the model to evaluate each of them.

Unlike optimization models, simulation models do not yield an optimal solution to the media mix decision because they cannot evaluate all possible alternatives simultaneously. On the other hand, simulation models are typically more descriptive than optimization models of the way in which media work in the real world. Optimization models must make simplifying assumptions in applying mathematics to find a single best media mix. Simulation models can relax these assumptions by incorporating more realistic constraints and conditions that characterize actual communication between companies and target audiences.

Research Needs for Media Modeling. The most important contribution of both types of media models is the analytic framework they provide. They help advertising managers evaluate key factors in media selection. Use of the models does not eliminate the need for judgment, rather judgment is improved through application of the models. In addition, the factors built into a model guide a company's use of marketing research in collecting relevant data.

The potential for computerized media models will improve over time as marketing professionals learn how to gather better data. According to one authority, eight kinds of data are needed by most media selection models:[22]

1. A list of candidate vehicles.

2. The size and composition of target audiences.

3. A list of the size and color units of candidate vehicles.

4. The cost of each unit in each vehicle.

5. Special restrictions on vehicle use.

6. Weights indicating the relative importance of persons in target audiences (heavy users).

7. Weights measuring the relative impact of each unit in each vehicle (exposures).

8. Weights measuring the cumulative impact of multiple insertions (awareness, attitude change, probability of purchase).

Clearly, the weights (items 6 through 8) remain the most difficult to measure, and further research is needed to improve measurement techniques.

EXHIBIT 18-9 Media Schedule Alternatives

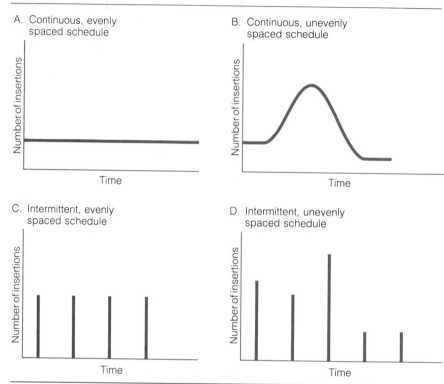

A. Continuous, evenly spaced schedule

B. Continuous, unevenly spaced schedule

C. Intermittent, evenly spaced schedule

D. Intermittent, unevenly spaced schedule

Media Scheduling Decisions

Frequency
is the number of insertions placed in a vehicle during a specific time period such as a budget year.

Continuity
is the timing of insertions spaced throughout a period such as a budget year.

In addition to selecting vehicles, advertising managers decide on the **frequency** and **continuity** of advertising insertions. These decisions determine the number and spacing or insertions in media and together result in a media schedule. Exhibit 18-9 illustrates a few of the kinds of media schedules that are used. However, there are many additional variations.

A number of factors enter into an advertiser's choice among schedule alternatives. One is the normal seasonal buying period for the product. This explains the uneven media schedule of U.S. automobile manufacturers. Traditionally, new models are brought out in the late summer or early fall. To generate awareness and interest among prospective new car buyers, the media schedule of automakers is heaviest immediately before and during that period. Advertising frequency tapers off at other times of the year. In contrast, frequently purchased products such as cereal and catsup benefit from a more evenly spaced schedule. The absence of seasonal buying for these products calls for a more constant level of advertising exposure.

Another factor is the nature of the target market. Repetition of an advertisement affects audience learning and remembering. Managers must decide how many ad exposures are necessary to achieve a desired level of learning of an advertisement's selling points. Insertions above this level would be a waste of resources, but too few insertions mean that the advertisements will not achieve objectives.

Audiences differ in their ability to learn advertising messages. For some audiences, an advertiser may have to use intermittent bursts of exposures to achieve a desired learning level. With a fixed media budget, the greater number of insertions in each burst must be offset by fewer insertions between the bursts. Learning will decline during the periods of low or no advertising, so new bursts are needed to bring it back up.

Finally, the competition's use of advertising should be considered. If a key competitor is large and can afford to spend many more dollars on advertising, a continuous, evenly spaced media schedule may get drowned out by all the noise from the competitor. The huge advertising expenditure of McDonald's has this effect on the advertising of the smaller fast-food chains. Although the smaller company cannot spend as much in total as McDonald's, it can spend at competitive levels for short periods of time by using an intermittent schedule. The objective is to be heard during the bursts of advertising.

Evaluating Advertising's Effectiveness

To get the most out of advertising resources, management must evaluate the ability of advertisements to achieve a campaign's objectives. Marketing research is needed to study the effect that advertisements are having on target audiences. This research is part of the overall control activity shown in Exhibit 18-10.

Control usually means collecting data during or after the full-scale running of an advertising campaign—posttesting. To evaluate alternative ads, managers may also want pretest data before a campaign is run. Marketing research expenditures are typically allocated to both kinds of studies.

Alternative tests of advertising effectiveness have been developed because different types of objectives are set for advertising—communication objectives and sales objectives. Correspondingly, there are communication and sales pre- and posttests.

Communication Tests

To measure the effectiveness of advertising in achieving communication objectives, measurements of customer awareness, attitude change, or degree of persuasiveness can be used. These can be pre- or posttests, or both.

Measuring Awareness. Awareness objectives state what percentage of a target audience should be aware of the advertisements and selling points. Consistent with this objective, effectiveness tests have been developed that

EXHIBIT 18–10 Advertising Control Activities

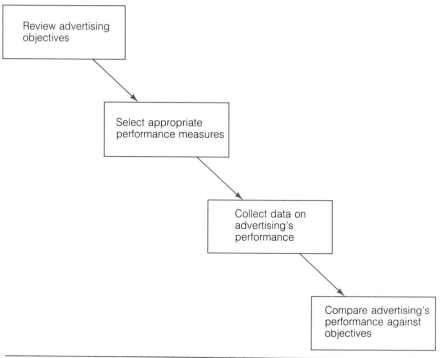

measure the awareness of audience members. Common awareness measurement techniques are *recognition tests, recall tests,* and *physiological tests.*

Recognition Tests. These tests measure the percentage of a sample who say they remember seeing an advertisement in a particular vehicle (e.g., a magazine or television ad). The degree of attention given to the advertisement can then be examined among those who remember it. Typically, simple indexes are calculated to facilitate comparisons. To illustrate, if 220 respondents out of a total sample of 500 say that they saw an advertisement, the advertisements recognition index is:

$$220/500 \times 100 = 44$$

Starch Readership Service is a commercial marketing research firm offering recognition tests for clients. Starch conducts personal interviews with an equal number of men and women from various geographic areas who have read the particular issues of magazines covered by the service. An interviewer pages through a magazine asking whether the respondent saw each test advertisement. If a respondent recognizes an ad, the respondent is asked

EXHIBIT 18–11 Starch Readership Scores for Alternative Fleischmann's Magazine Advertisement Copy

Tested Ad Copy	Noted Score	Associated Score	Read Most Score
Cardiologist endorsement copy	34%	25%	8%
Appetite appeal copy	53	38	14

Source: "Which Ad Attracted More Readers," *Advertising Age*, June 2, 1975, p. 40.

what he or she remembers about it. After analyzing the data, Starch sends a report to the client that contains statistics for a test advertisement measuring:

■ The percentage of respondents who said they saw the advertisement (noted score).

■ The percentage who said they saw or read specific parts of the advertisement, including the name of the product or advertiser (associated score).

■ The percentage who said they read more than half of the advertisement's copy (read most score).

The readership scores in Exhibit 18–11 were obtained from a test of the relative effectiveness of two advertisements for Fleischmann's margarine. The advertisements had different selling points and copy presentations. One advertisement explained that cardiologists at a convention requested Fleischmann's margarine as the table spread for meals because the brand was low in saturated fat and cholesterol. The copy for the second advertisement, which showed Fleischmann's margarine among a variety of other foods on a table, was intended to appeal to the appetites of audiences. The test results showed that the appetite appeal was more effective than the health concern appeal on all three recognition scores.

Recall Tests. These tests require respondents to prove that they saw and read an advertisement. Those who say they saw an advertisement are asked to recall its copy and layout. Recall can be *unaided* (no help is given by the interviewer) or *aided* (the interviewer gives such cues as a product name or a key word or phrase from the copy). Aided recall is intended to correct for the possibility that a respondent has seen an advertisement but under the pressure of the interviewing situation cannot remember what the advertisement said.

Gallup and Robinson, Inc. offers an aided recall testing service for magazine and television advertisements. Respondents are asked to pick from a list those products they remember seeing in advertisements. For each product recalled, they are asked a series of questions concerning content and product attitudes. Advertisers receive indexes of audience recognition, proved recall, remembering of ideas communicated, and attitudes toward the product.

Norms or averages for these indexes are also provided based on tests of many other advertisements for the same product category. An advertiser uses the norms to evaluate recall of its own advertisements.

Physiological Tests.   Some advertisers worry about the validity and reliability of recognition and recall data. Several problems can occur. People who have been exposed to an ad may not remember what they have seen at the time they are interviewed. Some people may not want to tell the interviewer what they saw in an advertisement. Or people may reconstruct what they have seen so that it is consistent with the way they see the world. One solution to these problems is to use nonverbal awareness measures.[23]

Physiological tests of advertising effectiveness are used routinely, primarily for pretests. These tests measure bodily reactions (eye movements, pupil dilation, brain waves, electrical resistance of the skin) in response to advertisements. Since people have much less control over such reactions than they have over what they say, some advertisers believe that physiological data are a more reliable indicator of an advertisement's impact than verbal responses.

Eye-tracking studies are commonly used to measure how consumers react to print advertisements. Respondents scan through a vehicle or a single advertisement. Tracking equipment accurately records eye movement. Data indicate an advertisement's ability to attract a person's attention (stopping power), who read the advertisement being tested, and which parts of the advertisement were seen/read and in what order.

Some very interesting and relevant conclusions have been drawn from experience with eye-tracking studies:[24]

▪ Recall scores do not always indicate how involved a person is with an advertisement.

▪ Eye tracking can explain why an advertisement is effective (or not effective) by showing what people see in an advertisement, what they ignore, and what they miss.

▪ Creative copy/layout design can work even if established "rules" (e.g., a headline should be at the top of an advertisement) are not followed.

▪ Consumers in America would rather look at pictures than read copy—they are visually oriented.

Evaluating Awareness Tests.   Reliance on awareness measures assumes that gaining exposure and attention leads to higher probability of future purchase. Many marketing managers challenge this assumption on intuitive grounds: people may remember an advertisement that was unpleasant or obnoxious but not change their intention to purchase the advertised product. In fact, studies show that awareness and the persuasive power of advertisements are not highly correlated.[25] In contrast, proponents of the assumption argue that if an advertisement is not seen by a target audience, it cannot influence buying. A compromise position is that awareness measures are necessary to see whether target audiences are being reached but that by themselves these measures do not sufficiently indicate how effective an advertisement is.

Measuring Attitude Change. In assessing advertising effectiveness, management can go beyond awareness tests to measure the persuasiveness of its advertisements. Persuasiveness is the ability of an advertisement to create or change attitudes toward the company and its services. Recall from Exhibit 18-2 that attitudes are a step closer to influencing purchase than is awareness. Awareness and attitude change are not necessarily directly related; a test of a 1981 AT&T advertisement showed very high attitude-change scores but awareness scores that were slightly below average.[26]

Measuring attitude-change effectiveness is more complicated than testing for awareness. Except in new product situations, research must contend with the fact that people already have attitudes toward a company's products before advertisements are run. Thus, marketing research must measure the change in attitudes from before to after the running of the advertisements. An effectiveness score is the difference between a measure of attitude obtained before an advertisement has been run and a corresponding measure taken after it has been run.

Eric Marder Associates, Inc. has offered a service that illustrates one approach—an experimental design.[27] In a typical study, two test groups and one control group of 800 respondents each were formed from a magazine's readership in New York, Chicago, and Philadelphia. A different test advertisement was inserted in the magazine issues sent to the two test groups but omitted from the issues sent to the control group. Several days after the three groups received the magazine, telephone interviews were conducted to measure awareness of the advertisements and attitudes toward the product. The interviews were identical for all of the respondents, and no mention was made of the advertisements being tested. Differences between the groups on the attitude effectiveness measures were attributed to the influence of the test advertisements.

Multiple exposures to the same advertisement or to different individual advertisements can also be tested for attitude-change effectiveness. Ogilvy & Mather, Inc., a large advertising agency, developed a multiple-exposure testing system for its clients. A sample is drawn of 200 respondents who represent a target audience, subscribe to a cable TV system, and agree to watch selected movie previews at specified times. The test advertisement and two control advertisements are broadcast during four 15-minute movie previews. The previews are run four times during a four-day period. Attitude data are obtained from telephone interviews conducted before, during, and after the multiple exposures. With this experimental design, data on attitude change for the test and control advertisements before and after exposure are used to evaluate advertising effectiveness.[28]

Change in Predisposition.   Predisposition refers to customers' preference for a product over others or to their intentions to buy that product. Measuring advertising's ability to influence predispositions requires essentially the same procedures as those required for measurement of attitude change. Effectiveness is determined by changes in predispositions traced to advertising.

Sales Effectiveness

Companies that set sales objectives for advertising should measure the impact of advertising expenditures on sales. In general, sales effectiveness measures are difficult to obtain because there are so many possible influences on a company's sales. Advertising managers cannot merely look at the current period's sales compared to the last period's sales to determine the impact of current-period advertising, because the observed change in sales could have been caused by changes in competition, consumer needs, price, distribution, state of the economy, and even past advertising. Nonetheless, two approaches to the measurement of sales effectiveness are used in practice: analysis of historical sales-advertising relationships and experimental studies.

Historical Sales-Advertising Relationships.   Most companies have data on sales for their brands and on advertising expenditures over several historical periods—quarters, six-month periods, years. Advertising effectiveness is analyzed by searching for the relationship between changes in advertising and corresponding changes in sales.[29] The contribution of advertising to variations in sales is estimated, using correlational techniques, for the time periods covered by the data. Advertisers know that current-period sales may be caused by current advertising plus a carryover effect from previous-period advertising. Thus, the statistical models used in historical studies may be quite complicated because of the attempt to separate the carryover effect from that of current advertising.

Experimental Studies.   To gain a better understanding of the cause-and-effect influence of advertising on sales, experimental studies can be used. Such studies can be used to pretest presentation alternatives, media schedules, or budgets and to posttest the effectiveness of advertising campaigns.

One widely used experimental approach is a test market study. Du Pont used test marketing when it developed advertising intended to reverse a declining sales trend for Teflon-coated cookware. Management used a test market study to determine the level of advertising expenditures needed to meet the sales objective.

In this study, a complicated crossover experimental design tested the sales effect of five different levels of advertising in 13 test cities (Exhibit 18–12). Control cities were also designated in which no advertisements were run. A

EXHIBIT 18–12 Experimental Design for Testing Sales Effectiveness of Advertising for Teflon-Coated Cookware

Period 2 Product Advertising	Period 1 Product Advertising		
	10 Daytime Ads per Week	**5 Daytime Ads per Week**	**No Ads**
7 daytime ads per week	Detroit Springfield	Dayton	Wichita
3 daytime ads per week	Columbus	St. Louis Bangor Youngstown	Rochester
No ads	Omaha	Pittsburgh	Philadelphia Grand Rapids

Source: James C. Becknell, Jr., and Robert W. McIsaac, "Test Marketing Cookware Coated with 'Teflon,'" *Journal of Marketing Research* 3 (September 1963), p. 3.

telephone survey of female heads of households was conducted in each city during the winter and again in the spring to measure purchases of all cookware and of Teflon-coated cookware. The data showed, among many findings, that Du Pont had to advertise at the higher levels to achieve significant increases in sales.[30]

An experimental approach for products sold through supermarkets is to use scanners to collect data on consumer purchases. Before shoppers enter the store, they are intercepted and asked about their recent viewing of advertisements. Two groups are formed—a viewer group reporting exposure to a test advertisement and a nonviewer group that had not seen the advertisement. After shopping in the store, group members present a card to the checkout clerk for a discount on the total bill. Scanners record the products purchased, the number of items of each product, and the amount of money spent. Comparisons of purchases in the viewer and nonviewer (control) groups are made to evaluate the effectiveness of advertising. In one scanner study for a soft drink, the data showed that the viewer group averaged almost twice as many unit purchases as the nonviewer group.[31]

Communication Effectiveness versus Sales Effectiveness Measures

Which approach—communication effectiveness or sales effectiveness—should a company use to measure the effectiveness of advertising? There is no single or easy answer to this question. Two key dimensions of the decision must be considered. The first is the relevance of advertising objectives to company performance objectives. The type of advertising objective chosen determines the effectiveness measure needed. Ideally, advertising managers would like to evaluate advertising's contribution to the overall performance of the organization in terms of return on investment and profitability. As measures of advertising effectiveness become further removed from these objectives, they become more open to the criticism that they lack relevance.

EXHIBIT 18–13 Dimensions of Advertising Effectiveness Measures

Advertising effectiveness measure	Decision relevance	Ease of measurement
Sales	High	Difficult
Change in predisposition		
Change in attitude		
Awareness	Low	Easy

Source: Adapted from David B. Montgomery and Glen L. Urban, *Management Science in Marketing* (Englewood Cliffs, N.J.: Prentice-Hall, 1968), p. 96.

In this sense, sales are more relevant than awareness because sales are so much more clearly related to corporate performance objectives.

The other key dimension is the difficulty and cost of obtaining the data needed to evaluate effectiveness. Generally, communication measures are easier to obtain than sales measures. Within the communication measures, awareness is easier to measure than attitude or predisposition change. Both the relevance and the ease of measurement of effectiveness measures are ranked in Exhibit 18-13.

Advertising managers face a dilemma. The more relevant the advertising effectiveness measures, the more difficult and costly they are to obtain. This means that management must make a trade-off between the two dimensions. If marketing research resources are limited, then advertising managers may have to settle for the less expensive, and less relevant, measures. The larger firms with more access to research and greater training in its use are more likely to employ the more relevant and expensive measures.

Summary

This chapter presented a framework of the advertising decision process to aid in understanding advertising management's responsibilities. The process begins with the advertising mission, which requires that management determine the role of advertising, select target audiences, and set specific objectives for advertising. Next, management must allocate to advertising enough resources for advertising to achieve its mission. The advertising budget decision has this purpose.

Within budget limits, advertising managers plan the development of an advertising campaign. This includes creating advertising presen-

tations and planning a media strategy for carrying advertisements to target audiences. The creative decision begins with the position statement in a marketing plan. From this statement, key selling points are combined into a selling proposal. Then, formats for presenting these selling points are created and tested. Media planning involves selecting a combination of vehicles to reach target audiences and a schedule of insertions in these vehicles over a period of time.

Finally, advertising managers must evaluate the effectiveness of advertising's performance. A variety of measurement approaches are available. Which should be used depends on the type of advertising objectives chosen. These approaches differ in relevance and cost. The more relevant approaches are also the approaches that are more expensive and more difficult to implement. Consequently, advertising managers must inevitably make trade-offs when choosing a measurement approach.

Exercises For Review And Discussion

1. National Control Systems' advertising manager wants a greater allocation of corporate promotion resources to advertising. The company manufactures quality-control monitoring systems. Most of its current promotion is devoted to personal selling. The manager believes that advertising is capable of reaching buyers more economically than salespersons can. The average cost per sales call is $72, while the advertising cost per audience member is $8.40. The advertising manager argues that advertising can substitute for a portion of salespersons' calls on customers and save the company money. Do you agree with the advertising manager? Why or why not?

2. "Advertising must compete for resources against other corporate functions by demonstrating its ability to contribute to performance. Because the most important operating objectives of the corporation are to achieve specified sales volume and profit, the most appropriate objectives for advertising are also sales and profitability." Do you agree with this point of view? Discuss your reasons.

3. Ride the Wind, Inc., a manufacturer of sailboats, budgets annual advertising expenditures in January of each year. To determine the budget limit on these expenditures, management first forecasts company sales. Then, all nonadvertising expenses are estimated, including those for manufacturing, distribution, overhead, and the sales force. The total of these expenses is subtracted from the sales forecast. From this amount is subtracted enough profit to yield a 17 percent return on investment. The remainder is allocated to advertising. How good is this advertising budgeting procedure? Discuss your answer.

4. Critics of advertising assail creative advertising copy for not presenting an unbiased description of product characteristics and weaknesses. Instead, advertising regularly uses such techniques as humor, gimmicks, imagery, and boasting. Why do advertisers use these techniques? Should advertising copy present an unbiased view of the company's product? Discuss your answer.

5. "The creative design of advertising messages and layouts requires a special kind of creativity and unstructured thinking of which only a few people are capable. Managers should not try to encumber creative personnel with a lot of market information. Just demonstrate the product and its advantages to these people, and then turn them loose to come up with creative ways to tell audiences about a company's product." Do you agree with this point of view? Discuss your reasons.

6. A brand manager for a line of tennis rackets manufactured by a large sports equipment company received the advertising effectiveness information in Exhibit 18–A.

EXHIBIT 18–A

	Number of Respondents	Number of Respondents Who Recalled the Ad	Number of Respondents Who Recalled the Brand Name in the Ad
Advertisement 1	405	221	115
Advertisement 2	395	218	153
Advertisement 3	415	209	165

For this information to be an appropriate measure of advertising effectiveness, what kind of advertising objective must have been set? Which advertisement is most effective, and why?

7. Suppose the brand manager in Exercise 6 decided to supplement the recall data with sales data. The level of sales of the tennis racket brand was measured for the year immediately preceding the one in which the advertising was run and for the year during which the advertising was run. The difference between these two sales amounts is the measure of advertising effectiveness. Since this difference showed a sales increase of five times the cost of the advertising, the brand manager believed that the campaign had been very effective. Do you agree with the brand manager? Why or why not?

8. The marketing manager of a brewery just received data for the initial four waves of a longitudinal study of the effectiveness of advertising for her beer brand. The figures in Exhibit 18-B show the average attitude scores of the respondents toward selected attributes of the brand.

EXHIBIT 18-B

Brand Attribute	Average Attitude Score of Respondents*			
	Wave 1	Wave 2	Wave 3	Wave 4
Lightness of taste†	2.43	2.67	3.34	4.28
Bitterness of taste	3.78	3.72	3.23	3.01
Premium quality†	2.12	2.26	2.34	2.29
Competitive price	4.05	4.09	3.98	4.02
Thirst quenching†	3.42	3.38	3.96	4.29
Fillingness†	1.94	1.87	2.01	2.50
Golden color	4.06	4.22	4.18	4.28

* 1 = very negative and 5 = very positive attitude.
† Brand attributes featured in the advertising.

The advertising campaign began after the wave 1 data were collected and is still running. Using these data, evaluate the effectiveness of the advertising campaign. Then evaluate the usefulness of this information for setting future advertising objectives.

Notes

1. Verne Gay and Paul L. Edwards, "Chevy Woos Women," *Advertising Age*, September 9, 1985, p. 1.

2. Information for this illustration came from Gay and Edwards, "Chevy Woos Women," pp. 1, 30.

3. "Phone Company Finds Direct Mail Is Most Efficient Seller of Service," *Marketing News*, July, 22, 1983, p. 18.

4. Ellen Graham, "The Image-Makers: To Get New Identities, Companies Often Hire Specialists in the Field," *The Wall Street Journal*, March 1, 1978, pp. 1, 22.

5. Kevin Higgins, "Marketing Becoming Essential for Commodity Producer Groups," *Marketing News*, April 29, 1983, p. 1.

6. Steuart Henderson Britt, "Are So-Called Successful Advertising Campaigns Really successful?" in *Marketing Management and Administrative Action*, ed. Steuart Henderson Britt and Harper W. Boyd (New York: McGraw-Hill, 1973), p. 556.

7. Ibid., p. 554.

8. For more discussion of these procedures, see *Some Guidelines for Advertising Budgeting* (New York: Conference Board, 1972), pp. 5-13.

9. Ibid., p. 6.

10. "Comparative Ads Paying Off for Burger King," *Marketing News*, April 27, 1984, p. 18.

11. Gary L. Lilien, "Advisor 2: Modeling the Marketing Mix Decision for Industrial Products," *Management Science* 25 (February 1979), pp. 191-204.

12. Kevin T. Higgins, "Supermeds Apply Brand Identity to Health-Care Alphabet Soup," *Marketing News*, January 17, 1986, pp. 11, 19.

13. David A. Aaker, "ADMOD: An Advertising Decision Model," *Journal of Marketing Research* 12 (February 1975), p. 42.

14. "Comparative Ads Paying Off for Burger King"; and Mary J. Pilzer and Amy Dunkin, "Burger King Takes the Bite out of Its Ads," *Business Week*, October 28, 1985, pp. 38, 40.

15. Bruce G. Vanden Bergh and Keith Adler, "Take This 10-Lesson Course on Managing Creatives Creatively," *Marketing News*, March 18, 1983, sec. 1, p. 22.

16. "Bill Bernbach Defines the Four Disciplines of Creativity," *Advertising Age*, July 5, 1971, p. 22.

17. "Ad Agency Creatives Attack Copy Research because They Don't Understand Testing Goals," *Marketing News*, August 7, 1981, p. 11.

18. William O. Bearden, Robert S. Headen, Jay E. Klompmaker, and Jesse E. Teel, "Attentive Audience Delivery of TV Advertising Schedules," *Journal of Marketing Research* 18 (May 1981), p. 187.

19. Gerald J. Gorn, "The Effects of Music in Advertising on Choice Behavior: A Classical Conditioning Approach," *Journal of Marketing* 46 (Winter 1982), pp. 94–101.

20. These data were obtained from *Consumer Magazine and Agri-Media Rates and Data*, May 27, 1984, pp. 439–42.

21. For more discussion, see Dennis Gensch and Paul Shaman, "Models of Competitive Television Ratings," *Journal of Marketing Research* 17 (August 1980), pp. 307–15.

22. Russell I. Haley, "Do We Really Know What We Are Doing?" in *1971 Combined Proceedings*, ed. Fred C. Allvine (Chicago: American Marketing Association, 1972), p. 217.

23. Elliot Young, "Use Eye Tracking Technology to Create Clutter-Breaking Ads," *Marketing News*, November 27, 1981, sec. 1, p. 19.

24. Ibid.

25. " 'State-of-the-Art' Recall/Persuasion Pretest Measures AT&T's Advertising Effectiveness," *Marketing News*, September 18, 1981, sec. 1, p. 16.

26. Ibid.

27. David A. Aaker and John G. Myers, *Advertising Management* (Englewood Cliffs, N.J.: Prentice-Hall, 1982), pp. 399–400.

28. "Ogilvy & Mather Finds M.E.T.S. Expensive but Appropriate, Useful," *Marketing News*, May 23, 1975, p. 8.

29. Robert P. Leone, "Modeling Sales-Advertising Relationships: An Integrated Time Series–Econometric Approach," *Journal of Marketing Research* 20 (August 1983), pp. 291–95.

30. For more detail on this example, see James C. Becknell, Jr., and Robert W. McIsaac, "Test Marketing Cookware Coated with 'Teflon,' " *Journal of Advertising Research* 3 (September 1963), pp. 2–8.

31. John L. Carefoot, "Scanner-Based Copy-Testing Methodology Links Purchase Behavior to Ad Exposure," *Marketing News*, September 17, 1982, sec. 1, pp. 11, 16.

CHAPTER 19

Sales Force Management Decisions

Personal selling is important in Cray Research, Inc.'s marketing strategy. Cray is the leading manufacturer of supercomputers, designed for such complex applications as weather forecasting and oil exploration. The huge special-purpose computers sell for prices ranging from a few million dollars up to $20 million. Cray's 1986 sales are estimated to be $500 million. Selling these large computers depends heavily on the salesperson, who may spend several years in sales development efforts. For Zellars C. West, a district manager, the efforts in selling a $9.5 million supercomputer covered five years.[1]

1981

April — Salesman West first visits General Electric's R&D center in Schenectady.

June — GE's computer programs are tested on Cray computers.

September — Twenty GE scientists and managers hear informal Cray presentation.

1982

April — Cray analyzes GE divisions to see which needs its machine most.

1983

September — West makes two-hour presentation for the most likely prospect, GE's Evendale (Ohio) aircraft engine manufacturing facility.

1984

October — West briefs 50 Evendale employees on Cray applications.

1985

January — GE approaches West with inquiries into specific Cray model.

August — West arranges two-day seminar on Cray's potential uses.

September — GE signs letter of intent to buy a $9.5 million Cray X-MP/28.

1986

February — Anticipated signing of purchase agreement.

This calendar shows the various stages in the selling process and the interactions among West, other Cray personnel, and various customer participants in the computer selection decision.

Personal selling accounts for a substantial share of the marketing budget in many firms. Annual expenditures for personal selling in the United States currently exceed advertising expenditures by as much as 50 percent. Often the personal selling function accounts for the major share of the personnel assigned to the marketing department.

Management is involved in decisions regarding the scope of personal selling and in key decisions affecting sales force development, sales force staffing and training, supervising and motivating salespeople, and evaluation and control of the sales force.

Personal Selling in Perspective

Salespeople comprise about 1 out of every 14 persons employed in the United States—as many as 8 million persons in the mid 1980s.[2] Sales jobs vary according to whether consumer or industrial products are sold and whether selling is done in the field or in the firm's store or office. A comparison of average annual compensation in 1985 for various sales positions is shown in Exhibit 19-1.[3] Positions that include opportunities for earning incentive pay based on sales results enable top sales performers to earn considerably more than the average pay levels.

The Scope of Selling

The selling function varies from firm to firm. The person selling health and beauty aids for a wholesaler is concerned with delivering such products as aspirin, toothpaste, and razor blades and arranging them on the shelves of supermarkets and other retail outlets. Here, very little actual selling effort is involved. In contrast, the primary function in life insurance is closing the sale, and it is a very creative selling task because of the intangible nature of the product.

The sales job consists of three main activities: generating sales, providing market information, and providing customer service.[4] Selling includes locating prospective customers, planning calls, making sales presentations, interacting with customers (e.g., overcoming objections), and closing sales. Obtaining business is central to most selling. In addition, salespeople collect information on competitive products, price, customer reactions to product use, stock levels, and service and delivery problems. Customer service can encompass a variety of responsibilities, including delivery, marketing assistance (e.g., promotional and display advice), credit evaluation, product application assistance, and repair of products. The importance of these job components varies with different sales positions. The automobile salesperson's major responsibility is generating sales, whereas "detail men" in the pharmaceutical field spend much of their time providing physicians with information, samples, and assistance to encourage them to prescribe certain drugs. The characteristics of the product being sold, customer needs and preferences, and the financial resources available influence the nature and role of personal selling in a particular company.

EXHIBIT 19–1 Salespeople's Annual Compensation

Salesperson Level	Consumer Products, 1985	Industrial Products, 1985	Salesperson Level	Consumer Products, 1985	Industrial Products, 1985
Sales trainee			*Senior salespeople*		
Straight salary	$18,700	$21,600	Straight salary	$35,700	$37,400
Salary plus incentive			Salary plus incentive		
Salary	18,000	20,300	Salary	30,700	32,300
Incentive	3,300	4,500	Incentive	8,500	10,300
Total	21,300	24,800	Total	39,200	42,600
Experienced salespeople			*Sales supervisor*		
Straight salary	26,300	28,200	Straight salary	37,000	47,600
Salary plus incentive			Salary plus incentive		
Salary	23,000	26,400	Salary	39,300	39,500
Incentive	6,200	6,780	Incentive	8,600	10,300
Total	29,200	34,100	Total	47,900	49,800

Source: Executive Compensation Service, Inc., a subsidiary of the Wyatt Company, published in "Compensation," *Sales & Marketing Management Magazine*, February 17, 1986, p. 56.

Salespeople are being viewed increasingly as managers of their assigned market areas.[5] They are involved in the coordination and management of various territory activities such as analyzing markets, developing selling strategies, engaging in local advertising, and providing support to the home office.

Classifying Sales Positions

Given the variety of activities involved in selling, one way of classifying sales positions is by the technical knowledge and creative skills required to perform the job successfully. Technical knowledge involves the product and its application. Engineers often sell complex industrial equipment because for such equipment, product and application know-how are central to the selling function. Creative skills are required when the need for a product or service has not been clearly established from the customer's point of view. Sales positions range from relatively simple, routine sales functions to very complex sales tasks that demand the highest level of technical knowledge and selling ability, as the Cray example illustrates.

Personal Selling and the Marketing Mix

Advertising and personal selling represent alternative ways of informing and persuading buyers. Each has certain communication advantages over the other. Often both are used in a firm's marketing program. Salespeople can interact with customers and prospects, answering questions, overcoming objections, and supplying needed information. With personal selling, messages can be developed to match the unique circumstances of each situation, and these messages can be modified to respond to customer needs identified during the sales call. Salespeople can demonstrate products to prospects. Industrial sales representatives often study the customer's operations to recommend equipment or products for particular applications.

With new products, prospective buyers are not easily identified, so searching and screening may be necessary to develop the market. Salespeople can obtain feedback from the marketplace. They can also instruct customers on the use and care of products.

The size and characteristics of each target market help determine how personal selling will be used in a firm's marketing mix. When the number of customers is very large, as in mass markets, and the size (in dollars) of the purchase is relatively small, personal selling costs become prohibitive. A sales call is expensive, although its cost is influenced by the salesperson's qualifications, the degree of customer concentration, the size of the territory, waiting time, and the time spent with the customer. The average cost of an industrial sales call exceeds $200. In contrast, a minute of national television advertising during prime viewing time costs less than $10 per thousand viewing homes. Although customer exposures to mass and personal communications are not equivalent, comparisons suggest how the characteristics of the market influence the extent to which personal selling is used in a firm's marketing program.

The sales force forms a major part of the marketing mix when customer needs can best be met through personal selling efforts and when there are sufficient margins between the purchase price and the costs to cover sales force expenses. Personal selling is often used in industrial markets since the number of customers and prospects is relatively small (compared to consumer markets) and the dollar amounts of purchases are sufficient to support salespeople. The same characteristics may exist in some consumer markets, for example in encyclopedia sales. In other situations, the marketing of consumer products may combine personal selling to channel intermediaries with heavy use of advertising at the consumer level.

Marketing management's task is to select the best combination of marketing mix elements to obtain the desired responses from target markets. The role of personal selling should be determined in conjunction with that of the other marketing mix components. Several characteristics of marketing programs that may indicate a relatively important role for personal selling are shown in Exhibit 19-2. Management has some flexibility in assigning a role to personal selling as part of a firm's total marketing effort—one company may sell its products by mail, while another may use sales agents. Advertising and other forms of sales promotion may be used to accomplish certain tasks that salespeople can perform (creating product awareness and transmitting product information). Yet the salesperson has several unique communications

EXHIBIT 19-2 Conditions Suggesting Personal Selling as a Major Element of the Marketing Mix

Mix Area	Characteristics	Mix Area	Characteristics
Product or service	Complex products requiring customer application assistance (computers, pollution control systems, steam turbines)	*Price*	Final price negotiated between buyer and seller (appliances, automobiles, real estate)
	Major purchase decisions, such as food items purchased by supermarket chains		Selling price or quantity purchased enable an adequate margin to support selling expenses (traditional department store compared to discount house)
	Features and performance of the product requiring personal demonstration and trial by the customer (private aircraft)	*Advertising*	Advertising media do not provide effective link with market targets
Channels	Channel system relatively short and direct to end users		Information needed by buyer cannot be provided entirely through advertising and sales promotion (life insurance)
	Product and service training and assistance needed by channel intermediaries		Number and dispersion of customers will not enable acceptable advertising economies
	Personal selling needed in "pushing" product through channel		
	Channel intermediaries available to perform personal selling function for supplier with limited resources and experience (brokers or manufacturer's agents)		

capabilities. An experienced and capable sales force with strong customer relationships is more difficult for new competitors to duplicate than is, for example, a price or advertising strategy.

Sales Force Management Decisions

The major decision areas involved in managing the sales force are shown in Exhibit 19-3. Management must first decide what functions the sales force will perform. This defines the role and objectives of personal selling and guides deployment—the size of the sales organization, and the location of salespeople in the marketplace. Once these deployment decisions have been made, management of the sales force involves recruitment and selection of the sales team, product and sales training, and motivation and supervision. Finally, marketing management is concerned with the evaluation and control of sales operations on a continuing basis so that performance gaps will be identified and corrective action taken.

Sales Force Role and Objectives

Objectives are essential in controlling selling effort according to marketing management's priorities for customer coverage, sales development, product emphasis, and other sales force activities. Objectives are needed to plan the sales program and to evaluate the sales organization's results. Sales force

EXHIBIT 19–3 Sales Force Management Decisions

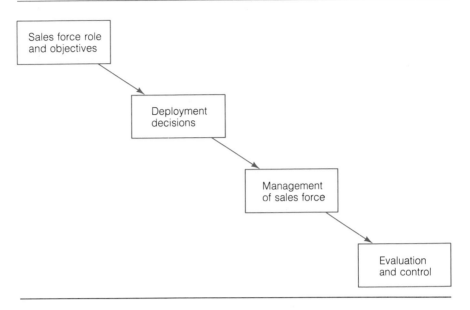

objectives should be determined concurrently with decisions on other elements of the marketing mix to indicate what contribution the sales organization is expected to make to the marketing program. Close coordination between the chief marketing executive and the manager of the sales force is essential. New product introduction is illustrative of the need for coordination. It is important that specific objectives and tasks in the new product introduction regarding the role of salespeople be determined and communicated to salespeople. Without such emphasis, the new product may not receive the sales effort necessary to gain market position.

The sales management objectives should include more than sales targets. Major areas in which sales management objectives are set include:

- Market performance.
- Contribution to profits.
- Customer relations and service.
- Development of sales personnel.
- Marketing program support.

These objectives provide the basis for more detailed objectives for individual salespeople (sales quotas, customer service, time with accounts, information collection, and product training). The first step in planning, therefore, is setting objectives against which the performance of the sales organization and specific salespeople can be monitored. This involves translating corpo-

EXHIBIT 19-4 Action Electronics, Inc. Sales and Expense Budget Analysis. January 1-March 31, 1986 ($000)

	Region					
	Eastern			Western		
Sales	**Budgeted**	**Actual**	**Variance**	**Budgeted**	**Actual**	**Variance**
Product Line						
A	$2,800	$3,125	$379	$2,500	$2,425	$ (75)
B	300	418	118	800	917	117
C	1,250	1,186	(64)	1,500	1,346	(154)
Total	$4,350	$4,729	$379	$4,800	$4,688	$(112)
Expenses						
Sales salaries	$ 324	$ 318	$ 6	$ 402	$ 397	$ 5
Travel	106	111	(5)	120	126	(6)
Entertainment	23	22	1	35	40	(5)
Advertising	75	80	(5)	82	85	(3)
Office rentals	6	7	(1)	10	10	0
Warehousing	8	8	0	9	8	1
Utilities	1	2	(1)	2	2	0
Miscellaneous	2	3	(1)	4	5	(1)
Total	$ 545	$ 551	$ (6)	$ 664	$ 673	$ (9)

rate and marketing goals into overall performance targets for the sales force and for each salesperson.

The sales and expense budget is an important part of objective setting. Budgeting is based on the sales forecast. When the sales forecast is combined with an estimate of the expenses necessary to meet it, we have a budget. The sales force budget is useful in several ways:

> A *budget* is simply a tool, a financial plan, which an administrator uses to plan for profits by anticipating the revenues and expenditure of funds. By adopting various budgetary procedures, management hopes to guide the operations of the organization to a predetermined end—a given level of profit on a certain volume of operations. Without a budget, management could never be certain whether operations were going successfully. Executives would not know if the goals of the firm were being met until the final accounting had been made for the fiscal period. Then it would be too late to revise the plan or provide remedies.[6]

An example of a sales and expense budget analysis for a quarter is shown in Exhibit 19-4. Note how the analysis highlights the points at which sales and expenses are above and below forecasts.

Deployment Decisions

In one survey, increasing the productivity of personal selling expenditures was cited as a major marketing management responsibility in the 1980s.[7]

EXHIBIT 19-5

The productivity of selling effort is being increased in many firms through the use of telemarketing in combination with face-to-face sales calls.

Courtesy Bozell, Jacobs, Kenyon & Eckhardt, Inc.

Deployment is the determination of the organization and size of the sales force, assignment of the salesperson's work responsibility, and allocation of the salesperson's effort among the assigned customers and prospects.

Incorrect **deployment** of a sales force has a major influence on productivity. Deployment decisions include the organization of the sales force, the size of the sales force, the territorial design, and the allocation of selling effort. If deployment is out of balance, even competent and hardworking salespeople will be unable to achieve their full potential (Exhibit 19-5).

Organizing the Sales Force. When the sales organization is so large that it cannot be effectively supervised by one person, organizational units must be created. One of the more popular bases for organizing a sales force is geographic area. With this organization, depending on the size of the sales force, different levels can be established for successively smaller geographic areas, and at each level multiple units can be formed. A sales department can be organized into two or more regions, each region comprising several districts and each district comprising several branches; a group of salespeople make up a branch. The salesperson's territory is a designated geographic area.

In some firms, salespeople may be organized according to some basis of specialization such as type of *customer* and type of *product.* Organizations sometimes combine geographic coverage and specialization by product.

Sales Force Size. In determining the size of the sales force, management must consider how market opportunities, environmental factors, competition, and company marketing effort will influence market response. Management also needs a proper unit for analysis of sales force size. Often this management control unit is related to the market. It may be individual customers or groups of customers, such as geographic trade areas. A control unit is normally some portion or all of the salesperson's **work unit.**

Work unit
is the assigned job
responsibility of the
salesperson, consisting
of a geographic area
(territory) or a group
of customers and
prospects.

Regular examination of sales force deployment effectiveness is essential to determine whether expansion or reduction is needed. The size of a company's sales force may not be optimal because of changes in opportunity, competition, costs, and other factors. The complexity of analyzing these influencing factors may make it impossible to determine an optimal sales force size. Nonetheless, by analyzing the various influences on market response, management can identify the direction of needed change. As people are added (or eliminated), management can analyze changes in sales organization performance, using profit contribution and other measures. Among the approaches used in making decisions regarding sales force size are break-even and workload analyses.

Break-Even Analysis. The sales results of individual salespeople can be compared to average break-even levels for the entire sales force to determine the extent to which each salesperson is contributing to profits. As an example of how this is done, an analysis of sales and customer call effort for two salespeople at a manufacturer's branch office in Albany, New York, is shown in Exhibit 19-6. The product is a line of industrial controls. Smith was hired three years ago to join Jones in the Albany office because the regional manager was convinced that the addition of a second salesperson was warranted by the market potential of the area served by the Albany branch.

When an analysis like the one conducted for the Albany branch is completed for all sales territories, the information obtained will provide guidelines for making needed size and deployment adjustments. Management judgment should be used in conjunction with historical information, since such an analysis cannot take into account all of the factors that may affect the situation.

Requests for additional sales personnel are often initiated by field managers at branch, district, or regional levels. Unless the chief sales executive (CSE) has guidelines available for evaluating possible sales force additions, there is a danger that a persuasive field manager will obtain an authorization to hire when a greater need exists elsewhere in the organization. The CSE

EXHIBIT 19–6 Analysis of Sales and Customer Call Effort

Salesperson	Customer Category*	Number of Customers	Calls		Sales†	
			Number	Percent	$000	Percent
Jones	A	19	503	74	244	95
	B	12	177	26	13	5
		31	680	100	257	100
Smith	A	5	202	23	111	71
	B	41	678	77	45	29
		46	880	100	156	100

Jones is operating above a break-even sales volume, while Smith is not. Since the results shown are typical of those obtained for the past three years, it is unlikely that Smith will reach break-even if changes are made. Unless customers with potential business are not being called on or substantial sales increases are pending from existing accounts, the assignment of two people to the Albany branch is questionable. The equivalent of one person's time (26 percent of Jones's time and 77 percent of Smith's) has been used for sales development (B category customers). Allocating one half of total selling effort to business development is excessive, particularly in view of the poor results obtained over the past three years. Smith has worked hard and is no doubt frustrated by his results. It is unlikely that he will tell his manager that he cannot obtain much additional business from his B accounts. Yet this seems to be the case. The indicated action is to assign all of Smith's A accounts to Jones and to operate the office with one person. This will require substantial reductions in call effort to most of the B accounts. Use of telemarketing coverage could be considered. Smith should be transferred, or if an opportunity within the firm is unavailable, it may be necessary to help him locate a position with another firm.

* A accounts are considered profitable; B accounts offer potential but are not currently profitable.

† Break-even sales per person = $200,000.

should be concerned about whether salespeople should be added and where additions will have the greatest impact on sales force performance. Consequently, unless changes in the sales force are infrequent, additions to (or eliminations from) the sales force should be based on periodic analysis of the entire organization.

Workload Analysis. When the size of the sales force needed for a new venture or other planned increase is being estimated, workload analysis is a useful guide.[8] The major steps in the workload approach are as follows:

1. Select an effort measure to distinguish variations in salespeople's time requirements to service a firm's customers and prospects. Accounts are classified to achieve equal workload (required effort to service accounts and prospects) within classification categories (large, medium, and small accounts). Possible effort measures include sales or potential sales, sales profitability, and other customer-servicing requirements.

2. Determine the number of accounts in each classification, and select the proper level of selling effort (e.g., call frequency) for each classification based on analysis of past call patterns, sales results, experience, and recommendations from salespeople.

3. Calculate the total amount of selling effort required for the customers and prospects of a firm. This is the estimated total workload.

EXHIBIT 19–7 Illustration of the Workload Approach to Determining Sales Force Size

Customer Category	Number of Customers	Desired Call Frequency (per year)	Total Calls Needed
A	300	52	15,600
B	700	30	21,000
C	1,000	12	12,000
D	2,000	6	12,000
	4,000		60,600

Calls per year that can be made by an average salesperson: 900.
Number of salespersons needed: $60,600 \div 900 = 67$.

4. Estimate the number of calls an average salesperson can make during the planning period (e.g., one year), taking into account the geographic distribution and concentration of accounts, the average time per call, the waiting time, and other relevant factors.

5. Calculate the sales force size by dividing the total number of calls required (3 above) by the number of calls an average salesperson can make (4 above).

An illustration of the workload approach is given in Exhibit 19-7. Various factors can be incorporated into the analysis to account for other workload influences, such as the allocation of time to different products. Product workload can be included using a combination customer and product classification scheme. The calls required for each account classification category (large, medium, small) and product type (motors and controls) are determined. In this example, six classifications would be needed.

Allocation of Selling Effort.   Management and salespeople are faced with several types of allocation decisions:

▪ How much sales effort should be devoted to each customer? How should time be divided among customers and prospects? Should the available effort be increased for some customers and decreased for others?

▪ What is the proper allocation of selling effort to such geographic units as trading areas, zip codes, and cities? When a large number of customers are involved, analysis by customer may not be possible.

▪ How should effort be allocated to various products in the line? Because many firms have several products, the allocation of selling effort to products is a type of allocation decision that goes beyond customer or geographic allocation.

▪ What basis should be used to assign salespeople to territories, customers, products, or other work assignment variables? Deciding how salespeople should be assigned selling responsibility is important to achieving sales results and to obtaining a fair distribution of opportunities among salespeople.

The crux of allocation is selecting the amount of selling effort in each management control unit (customers, trading areas). Allocation is optimal when shifts of selling effort between control units will produce no improvement in sales response.

The design of work units for sales personnel largely determines a salesperson's opportunity for achievement, so initial territorial assignments, the splitting or combining of territories, and other work unit changes are important sales management activities. Work unit design should pinpoint responsibility for market coverage and avoid duplication of selling effort.

The choice of a salesperson's work unit is based on two major considerations: the time required to serve customers and prospects (based on their importance to the firm) and the specific time demands that particular customers and prospects place on salespeople. In some instances, the buying potential of an account and the time needed to perform the sales function may make it necessary to assign a full-time salesperson to a single customer. Two accounts that purchase the same amount from the salesperson may require different amounts of effort. The various needs (e.g., how products are used) of particular types of customers may require specialization of the sales force. If complex products are involved, more than one person, each with a different product line, may call on the same customer.

Two basic approaches are used to allocate selling effort. The first is based on experience and judgment using such simple guidelines as market potential, workload, and return on time invested. For example, the previously discussed workload approach can be used to allocate the selling effort of the salesperson. The second basic approach involves the development of computer decision models. Some models can be used for both size and allocation decisions.

Investigating Reallocation Potential.[9]   The first step in allocation is to determine whether changes are needed. A useful screening technique to determine the potential for improving sales force size and deployment is the Sales Resources Opportunity Grid. This grid, which is similar to the strategic business unit (SBU) and product portfolio grids, can be used to evaluate current deployment. A 34-person sales force for a regional processor of low-priced consumer grocery products distributed through wholesalers and chain warehouses calls on nearly 4,000 retail outlets. This personal selling effort is augmented by advertising and sales promotion. The firm's market position varies widely throughout its market area. The screening grid shown in Exhibit 19-8 is used to position a sample of 204 accounts served by the firm according to account opportunity and sales organization strength dimensions, obtained from a questionnaire filled out by salespeople. Once the accounts have been properly positioned on the grid, average sales and

EXHIBIT 19-8 Sales Resources Opportunity Grid

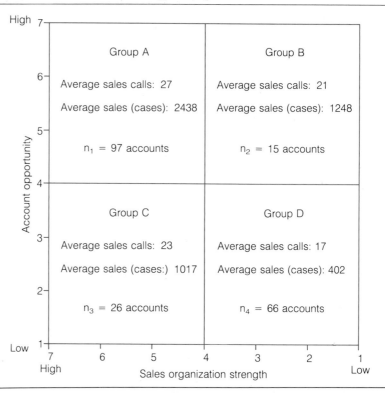

average number of sales calls are calculated for each quadrant. Note the wide variation in average sales between groups A, B, C, and D. In contrast, average sales calls vary over a much narrower range. If current allocations are correct, average sales calls in groups A and D should differ by greater amounts.

Suppose that the relatively high call level in group D and the relatively low call level in group A, compared to position on the grid, indicate an opportunity for improving deployment. The analysis alerts management to this opportunity. An appropriate measure of benefits from redeployment can be obtained using the information shown in Exhibit 19-8. Suppose calls in group D are reduced to a level equivalent to the average call-to-sales ratio across all groups (22/1,452). This would reduce the average level in group D from 17 to 6 calls (22/1452 × 402 = 6). Assuming that there is the same proportion of group D accounts in the population as in the sample, then the population contains 1,294 accounts (66/204 × 4,000). Suppose the average cost per call is $50. A reduction to 6 calls per account in group D represents a saving of $711,700 (11 calls × 1,294 accounts × $50). The available sales effort could be directed toward more promising sales opportunities (group A), or the size of the sales force could be reduced. The important point is that the estimated benefits from redeployment are much greater than the costs of obtaining the data needed for this analysis. For the size of the sales organization in the application, $60,000 to $80,000 should be adequate for development of the model. Even smaller, out-of-pocket, expenditures would be required if company personnel assisted in data collection and other development tasks.

Building a Deployment Model. The size and allocation of the sales force are both aspects of the deployment decision, and should be combined to achieve optimal deployment. The basic approach to deployment decision modeling is to first develop a sales response function (relationship between sales and selling effort) that corresponds to the control unit (e.g., customer) being analyzed. Then, a computer analysis is used to examine alternative allocations to each control unit. The allocations that yield maximum total sales for the available selling effort represent the best (optimal) allocation. Two basic types of decision models are available for this purpose: multideterminant *empirical models* and *judgment-based models.*

The empirical approach looks at sales response from control units (e.g., assigned accounts) for the previous period and tries to determine which variables or predictors are related to sales response. The typical procedure is to determine the important variables, measure their value for each control unit during the previous period, and then use a statistical procedure to develop a function that explains variation in control unit response for the previous period. Typical variables used as predictors in the sales response function are market potential, intensity of competition, and company business strength. The estimated parameters for the sales response function are then used as a basis for evaluating expected control unit response at alternative levels of effort for a future period.

The judgment-based approach develops the response function for the future period directly from estimates by salespeople or management of sales response to various amounts of selling effort. A major distinction between this approach and the empirical approach is that the judgmental model considers a single factor (selling effort) in estimating sales response, whereas the empirical model is based on a multivariate relationship. Typically, the salesperson estimates likely sales response from a control unit, taking into consideration several possible levels of effort. A curve-fitting procedure is used to convert these point estimates into a continuous response function. The judgment-based approach provides a separate response function for each control unit, which can be used to evaluate the potential effect of alternative levels of effort.

Data from the regional grocery products processor were used to develop a multideterminant sales response function deployment model. A summary is provided in Exhibit 19-9 for the accounts shown in Exhibit 19-8. Interestingly, the reallocations indicated by the empirical model (model sales calls) are consistent with the above assessment of reallocation potential. The

EXHIBIT 19–9 Sales Force Reallocation Using a Grid-Type Decision Model

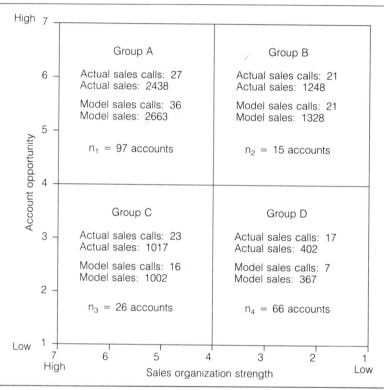

total actual sales for groups A to D are 5,105. Reallocating available effort as indicated in Exhibit 19-9 yields sales estimated at 5,360. The savings from even small changes in allocation indicates the great potential offered for improving sales force productivity.

A complete evaluation of the results of redeployment should be accomplished over one or two periods after implementation. The firm used in the illustration was pleased with the improvements in sales productivity obtained by implementing the model recommendations in a small number of high-impact areas.

Management of the Sales Force

Management of the sales force involves three activities: staffing, training, and supervising and motivating. These aspects are considered in the three following sections. A Conference Board study of more than 500 companies revealed that "by the end of the fifth year of employment, typically half of a given year's new sales recruits have terminated employment."[10] Although certain factors influencing turnover (economic conditions, family problems) cannot be adjusted or modified by sales management, other highly significant influences cited in the study, such as compensation, job content, and career patterns, can be controlled or influenced by sound management practices.

The costs of recruiting and training a salesperson range from a few thousand dollars to as much as $100,000. Consider an engineer hired as a sales trainee at an annual salary of $26,000, trained in product applications for one year, and then assigned to a field territory. An additional year may be required for this salesperson to reach a break-even sales level. Recruiting costs, salary, expenses, and supervision could easily require a company investment of $100,000 before the engineer becomes fully productive. If the engineer proves unsatisfactory or decides to leave the firm after two years, much of that investment is lost. This highlights the importance of developing a good sales recruiting program and of effectively supervising and motivating salespeople after they have been hired.

Sales Force Staffing. One of sales management's more demanding responsibilities is planning to meet future staffing needs resulting from turnover and growth. Sales force staffing activities include:

- Defining the selling job in a given organization.
- Developing selection procedures.
- Recruiting candidates.
- Selecting suitable people.

To conduct these activities, management must have a clear definition of the required skills, knowledge, and experience appropriate for particular selling positions. Job specifications guide selection procedures, the location of suitable applicants, and the choice of the people who best meet job requirements.

Defining the Selling Job. The personal selling function may include several activities of differing importance and with differing time demands—soliciting and servicing orders, "prospecting" (developing new customers), engaging in "missionary work" (helping channel of distribution intermediaries), accumulating information, assuming management responsibilities (e.g., supervision of service personnel), and engaging in nonsales work.[11] Sales management's first tasks are to identify the components of the sales job and to determine the relative importance of each. A written description is useful.

Suppose that manufacturer has decided to market a new electronic temperature measurement instrument that will require a sales force of about five people. Management has prepared an analysis of the selling job (Exhibit 19-10). The venture represents both a new product and a new market for the firm, so locating prospects and obtaining sales are big factors in the success of the effort, with a major portion of the salesperson's time allocated to these activities. For a new product, application assistance is important, so the firm

EXHIBIT 19–10 Sales Position Analysis

Major Activities	Estimated Time (percent)	Importance*
Locating prospects	20%	10
Obtaining sales	45	10
Providing customer application assistance	15	7
Dealing with instrument service problems	10	4
Engaging in nonselling activities	10	3

* 10 = highest.

plans to provide salespeople with home office technical assistance and to furnish each customer with a complete applications manual, including troubleshooting guidelines. Thus, there are applications and service demands on the sales force. The nonselling activities are limited to following up on orders, maintaining product knowledge, conducting correspondence, and reporting. Management can use this analysis to prepare a more detailed job description and to identify the characteristics desired in prospective salespeople.

Developing Selection Procedures.   When asked what kinds of people to look for to fill sales positions, a sales vice president replied, "We want producers, people who are results oriented." When asked how to spot potential producers, the vice president indicated that they should be:

■ Effective and interested in working with customers to help them solve problems.

■ Willing to work hard, dependable, highly motivated, thorough, and efficient in the use of time.

■ Interested and able to learn about the product and its applications.

Although the characteristics of a good salesperson have been debated for decades, those cited above are often mentioned by professionals in recruitment and selection. The difficulty, of course, is determining which people have the desired characteristics. Large firms with historical data on the characteristics and performance of salespersons are often able to identify more specific criteria for use in screening candidates for sales jobs. Management must determine which characteristics match the selling job in a given firm. Several sources of information can be used to identify factors that will be helpful as indicators of good sales performance. Study of the job description, analysis of the personal histories of salespeople, and failure analysis are possible sources of information for developing sales selection criteria.[12] In designing a selection procedure, management must comply with the equal employment opportunity requirement that the employer prove that any factor used in the selection process is related to performance. Selection guides should be explicit, yet avoid the arbitrary use of criteria to screen candidates.

Most studies of salespersons' performance have failed to identify factors that are always good predictors of performance. Predicting sales performance is an elusive task, and in the absence of research findings, a great deal of reliance is typically placed on management judgment and experience.

A major problem is pinpointing relevant influences on sales performance, since a number of influences are involved, some of which are interrelated, and the impact of each is often impossible to estimate. Possible determinants fall into the following categories:

■ *Aptitude.* Includes *physical* factors, such as appearance; mental abilities, such as education and past experience; and personality characteristics (empathy, ego strength, sociability, etc.).

■ *Skill Level.* Learned proficiency at performing the requirements of the job. Includes salesmanship and the interpersonal and technical skills needed in the selling environment.

■ *Motivation.* The amount of effort that the salesperson chooses to expend on each of the activities associated with the job.

■ *Role Perceptions.* The salesperson's perceptions of the activities or behaviors necessary to meet the expectations, demands, and pressures communicated by management, customers, and family.

■ *External and Constraining Factors.* These kinds of factors may directly facilitate or constrain performance or interact with other performance determinants. Among such factors are the intensity of competition, the quality of management, and the market potential.[13]

Aptitude and skill-level factors are often used in selecting salespeople. Here, the difficulty is that factors in the other three areas may also affect eventual performance. Although some of the determinants of sales performance can be controlled or influenced by training, supervision, and motivational tools, others are uncontrollable. Considering the variety of the possible influences on sales performance and the meagerness of the available research findings, it is not surprising that sales force management places heavy reliance on experience and judgment.

One method often used to identify possible selection factors is comparing the people in an organization whose performance is ranked *high* with the people whose performance is ranked *low*. When aptitude factors such as experience, education, age, and technical skills distinguish good from poor salespeople, these factors are often used to screen job applicants.

Statistical procedures are available that permit the simultaneous evaluation of these factors. But screening criteria should be used with caution since many other variables must be taken into consideration when selecting people. These criteria are primarily useful in screening job applicants, so that persons who qualify on the basis of initial screening can be subjected to a more comprehensive analysis.

EXHIBIT 19-11

We're looking for computer salespeople who are as aggressive as we are.

If you know anything about Burroughs, you know we don't give up easily. In fact, we don't give up until we accomplish what we set out to do.

That's the same quality that enabled us to put together some of the most cost-efficient, most productive computer systems (not to mention one of the best service organizations) in the world.

And it's exactly this quality of not accepting anything less than total success that we look for in a computer salesperson.

If you're that kind of salesperson, and you've had four or more years' experience selling computer mainframe systems in manufacturing, distribution, health care, government, finance or education —or if you're a six-year veteran of those fields—call now for an immediate interview at **1-800-221-3333**, extension Burroughs, 24 hours a day, seven days a week. Or send a resume to President, U.S. Marketing, Room 2A53, One Burroughs Place, Detroit, Mich. 48232.

Why shouldn't you work for a computer company that's every bit as aggressive as you?

 Burroughs

© 1986 Burroughs Corp.

Attracting and retaining successful salespeople is an important part of managing a sales force.

Courtesy Penchina Selkowitz, Inc.

Recruiting Candidates and Selecting Salespeople. The procedures for selecting salespeople vary from formal systems to very informal approaches. Formal selection procedures are more likely to exist in firms with a specific personnel function (Exhibit 19-11). The responsibility for recruiting and selecting salespeople may range from highly centralized systems to situations in which the primary responsibility is assigned to field (district, branch) managers. Since there are advantages to having personnel specialists, sales management, and field managers participate in the selection process, a selection procedure that includes all of them is recommended. Because the new salesperson will be assigned to a field unit, its manager should have a voice in the selection decision. A logical approach is to develop procedures centrally (with input from the field) for use by all field units.

Given the job to be accomplished and the selection criteria chosen, several tools are helpful in designing a selection procedure. These include application forms; references and credit reports; personal interviews; evaluation forms; physical examinations; and intelligence, aptitude, and psychological tests.[14] Applications are useful in screening people and in helping interviewers to identify particular areas in a candidate's background and experience that should be discussed. Checks of the references listed on the application are frequently included in the selection procedure. The interview is probably the most important selection tool. Salespeople are rarely hired without an interview; the exceptions include positions in which straight commission are paid, such as selling magazine subscriptions and greeting cards. To supplement the interview, rating or evaluation sheets are sometimes used to obtain interviewers' reactions to sales candidates. The use of tests in selecting salespersons varies considerably, and this is one of the more controversial aspects of the selection process because the validity of test results for predicting performance has been questioned. Nonetheless, some firms use tests to screen applicants. When tests are used, they should be selected, administered, and interpreted by professionally qualified personnel.

With the exception of very small sales organizations, locating suitable candidates for sales positions is a continuing activity due to turnover, promotions, retirement, and growth. Firms that employ college graduates in sales conduct regular recruiting visits to college campuses to identify interested and qualified candidates. Other means for locating salespeople are advertising in newspapers and magazines, employee referrals and transfers, and employment agencies.

The objective of the selection decision is to match the qualifications of the available candidates against the criteria for the position. In many cases, however, not all of the job offers extended will be accepted, so it will be necessary to offer jobs to more people than are needed. Decisions on selection may then be made by the sales manager, field managers, personnel, or in some cases on a joint basis, depending on company practices.

Training. Expenditures for sales training are substantial. According to the Dartnell Institute of Financial Research, the average cost to train a sales representative in 1981 was $12,600.[15] Training for industrial salespeople often lasts for a few months to as much as a year or more. Although management in many companies is convinced of the need for training, there is "an almost complete vacuum of published knowledge concerning the effects of these training programs on salespersons' skills, behavior, and performance."[16] Firms simply provide training in the belief that it is essential.

Most firms give new salespeople an orientation on company procedures, products, and other aspects of day-to-day sales operations. Many of these efforts are informal and occur on the job. The first issue facing sales management is whether or not to provide a formal training program. Executives in small and medium-sized companies often comment that they hire experienced salespeople rather than invest in training inexperienced people. Consequently, firms with impressive training programs, such as IBM and General Electric, have for years been a source of prospects for other firms seeking experienced salespeople. Organizations with sale forces in excess of 50 people typically engage in some form of training that is aimed primarily at imparting product knowledge and a knowledge of company operations. In addition, salespeople must be informed about the company mission, policies, and operating procedures. Training programs should have a major impact on a salesperson's skills and possible secondary influence on his or her role perceptions. The skills affected relate to *salesmanship, interpersonal relations,* and *technical capabilities.*

The Training Task. If the decision is made to train, management must decide what it wants training to accomplish and who will participate. Objectives should be established in terms of the skills that training is intended to influence and, where possible, the skill levels that are to be attained through training. Since many aspects of skills are difficult to measure, it may be necessary to express these objectives in qualitative terms. A key basis for setting objectives is identification of those areas in which training can contribute to improving sales force results. In most firms, product training and, to a lesser extent, training in salesmanship tend to dominate sales training efforts. Training on a new product can help existing salespeople initiate their sales efforts on the product more quickly and effectively.

Training program participants are often people who are new to the organization, since management considers their needs to be more critical than the needs of established employees. However, people who have been with the firm for some time may also require training as a part of their career development activities. Both new and longtime salespeople may require various types of training, depending on training objectives and particular needs. Since training is expensive, the program participants should be carefully selected. A new salesperson with previous selling experience in the same industry may require substantially less training than one without selling experience.

Designing the Training Program. Training should cover four main areas:

- Selling concepts and techniques.
- Time and territory management.
- Product knowledge.
- Company policies, procedures, and practices.

The job description provides a good guide to the training needs of new salespeople, who are typically trained when they enter the organization, either on the job or at a central location (e.g., the home office). The training of existing sales representatives may best be handled by gathering them in various locations in the field, particularly if the organization is widely dispersed. If the sales force is small, on-the-job training may be the only feasible alternative.

The number and location of the people to be trained and the type of training required are major determinants of when and where training should be conducted. Training can be accomplished by staff personnel (e.g., sales trainers), management, experienced salespeople, or outside specialists. The selection of trainers should be based on their knowledge of the training areas and on their ability to teach—a top salesperson may be a very poor teacher.

Various training methods are employed in industry, including lectures, demonstrations, observation, role playing, seminars, workshops, and self-study. The methods selected should be those that best accomplish training needs at favorable cost-benefit levels. Information technology such as personal computers, video tapes, and telecommunications provide useful training aids.

Management should continually monitor the results and the costs of the firm's sales training programs. Although evaluation of training is admittedly difficult, benchmarks for measuring benefits should be an integral part of the training program. The criteria for assessing program effectiveness include reduced training time, lower turnover, reduced selling costs, and improved sales performance. Tests of such things as product knowledge can be used to monitor the effectiveness of certain types of training.[17] The salespeople themselves should also be asked to provide evaluations of training programs.

Supervising Salespeople. Supervising and motivating the sales force are among the most challenging and perplexing management jobs in any enterprise. Management's understanding of what causes a salesperson to expend more (or less) effort on his or her job activities falls far short of the desired state of knowledge:

> The practice of sales management has resembled the practice of medicine by tribal witch doctors. Sales managers have often had to rely on large doses of folklore, tradition, intuition, and personal experience in deciding how to motivate and direct the performance of their sales forces. While many firms spend thousands to discover why their customers behave the way they do, too few expend much money or effort on studies of the motivation and behavior of their own salespeople.[18]

Our knowledge of the motivation and behavior of sales personnel is improving, but much work remains to be done.

Sales Management in Perspective. The selling job places special demands on management. Depending on the degree of direction and control of salespeople considered appropriate in a particular firm, the geographic dispersion of the salespeople, the information needed both by and from salespeople (e.g., competitive intelligence), the assistance provided to salespeople, and the quality of the sales force, various management and supervisory levels must be established. The following functions are typically included in sales management:

- *Creating the Work Environment.* Sales management is the salesperson's main link to the company, sometimes the only link, so the environment created by sales management is a major influence on the performance of salespeople.

- *Establishing Standards of Performance.* The salesperson looks to sales management to develop an understanding of the job, including performance goals. The sales manager must make company expectations clear to the salesperson and must evaluate the salesperson's performance against standards.

- *Developing Sales Personnel.* The training and development of salespeople are continuing responsibilities of sales management. The sales manager is in the best position to monitor training and development needs and to see that high-priority needs are met.

- *Maintaining Communication Links.* Information flows in the sales organization are important to management, salespeople, and customers. Information on prices, products, policies and procedures, customer needs, competitive activity, and other matters continually flows upward and downward in the sales organization. The sales manager plays a major role in facilitating communication.

- *Interpreting and Enforcing Policy and Procedures.* Salespeople must comply with various company policies and procedures. The expenses of salespersons are often a major selling cost, and these expenses must be utilized in the most effective manner. Similarly, policies on pricing, credit approval, and the collection of bad debts must be coordinated with the salesperson, and when necessary, their interpretation and enforcement must be accomplished by the sales manager.[19]

Motivating Salespeople.   Motivation, though clearly an important determinant of performance, must be considered along with the various influences on the sales force. Although management cannot affect some of the factors that bear on sales performance (e.g., aptitude), it has motivational tools that can influence how much effort the salesperson chooses to expend on each of the activities associated with the job. Walker, Churchill, and Ford see a salesperson's motivation with regard to a given task as a function of:

- The salesperson's perceptions of the linkages between effort and job performance. If I expend effort on something (e.g., selling a new product), what are the chances that this will lead to an improvement on some performance dimension (e.g., sales)?

- The salesperson's perceptions of the linkages between job performance and the various rewards that he or she will receive. For most selling positions, these linkages range from neutral to positive.

■ The salesperson's perceptions of the desirability of the resulting rewards. Inclinations toward rewards generally range from neutral to positive.[20]

Simply stated, this view of the salesperson's motivation can be described as follows. If I expend effort to do some part of my job: Will this move me to a higher level of performance? Will that performance generate a particular reward? How desirable is that reward? This description of motivation should be adopted by sales management with caution. Its simple, yet powerful, logic should not be allowed to overshadow other potentially important determinants of a salesperson's performance—aptitude, skill level, role perceptions, and situational factors.

The view of salespeople's motivation sugggested by Walker, Churchill, and Ford raises two questions of importance to sales management: What rewards will best generate the desired responses from the sales force? What are the best means of helping salespeople understand the effort/performance/reward linkage? Not surprisingly, financial rewards are widely used to motivate salespeople. Other rewards used for this purpose include promotion and various forms of recognition.

Compensating Salespeople. Arrangements for compensating salespeople range from a straight salary to a straight commission. Sales compensation plans often include some type of incentive or commission based on performance. The results of an American Management Association survey of sales compensation plans used by companies are:[21]

Straight salary	22%
Draw against commission	6
Salary plus commission	28
Salary plus individual bonus	30
Salary plus group bonus	2
Salary plus commission plus bonus	12

Nearly 80 percent of the firms in the survey compensated their salespeople by an arrangement other than a straight salary. Nearly three fourths (72 percent) of the firms utilized a salary plus incentive arrangement. Other studies report similar results. The sales compensation plan will often influence how salespeople direct their efforts, and it will determine how much management control can be exercised. Salespeople operating on a straight commission tend to be quite independent in channeling their efforts.

A good compensation plan should satisfy four broad objectives:[22]

■ It should correlate efforts, results, and rewards.

■ It should act as an unseen supervisor, assisting in controlling and directing salespeople's activities.

■ It should encourage salespeople to treat customers properly.

■ It should be attractive to both prospective and existing salespeople.

EXHIBIT 19–12 Incentive Pay Factors

Factor	Number of Plans Including Factor		Factor	Number of Plans Including Factor	
	Measured Objectively	**Measured Subjectively***		**Measured Objectively**	**Measured Subjectively***
Increased overall volume	96	2	Promotional activity	11	16
Balanced volume categories	47	4	Credit handling	8	13
Expense control	29	9	Length of service	4	7
New accounts	28	11	Season or timing of the sale	4	9
Territory growth	21	15	Report handling	3	22
Profit contribution of a sale	18	1	Product knowledge	2	23
Type or class of account	12	8	Personal selling effectiveness	2	28

* Subjective measures were mentioned by 38 of the 100 plans.

Source: *Incentive Plans for Salesmen,* Studies in Personnel Policy no. 217 (New York: National Industrial Conference Board, 1970), p. 42.

To achieve these objectives, the plan should provide for steady income and incentive income, should be sufficiently flexible to operate properly across differences in territories, economic conditions, and other variations, and should be understandable, fair, and economical to administer.

Selecting and designing the sales compensation plan best suited for a particular company begin with analyzing the selling job and determining what objectives the plan should achieve. Incentive planning should be coordinated with salesperson objectives and performance evaluation.

When incentive compensation plans are used, management must select the factors on which to base incentive pay. Although sales volume is often used as the single criterion for incentive compensation, other factors may be important in a particular firm, as illustrated by the survey of 100 companies shown in Exhibit 19–12. A company may use a weighted combination of two or more factors. It is important to avoid making the incentive arrangement too complex, because salespeople must be able to easily relate their results to the corresponding rewards.

Evaluation and Control

A primary sales management responsibility is the evaluation and control both of the sales organization at all levels and of individual salespeople. These tasks consume a substantial portion of management time.

Selling Operations.   Sales management is responsible for monitoring personal selling operations to determine whether objectives are being achieved and whether corrective action should be taken. The director of sales of Industrial Equipment, Inc. has prepared an analysis of sales effort and results

EXHIBIT 19-13 Comparison of Sales Effort and Results by Product Group for Industrial Equipment, Inc.

Product Group	Annual Sales ($000)	Gross Profit* ($000)	Estimated Annual Growth† (percent)	Company Market Share (percent)	Sales Effort (percent of total calls)
A	$ 871	$ 217	5%	43%	17%
B‡	2,273	1,135	12	16	24
C	767	115	−2	28	19
D	583	71	1	39	11
E‡	1,793	538	8	26	13
F‡	1,216	324	7	18	16
Total	$7,503	$2,400	—	—	100%

* After deduction of cost of products.

† For the next five years.

‡ The products in these groups are relatively new.

by product group, as shown in Exhibit 19-13. Sales last year were $7,503,000 for the six major product groups. The director of sales is concerned about the allocation of sales effort to various products. Sales effort (based on the number of sales calls) has generally been allocated according to product sales volume, with limited attention given to the gross profit contribution of and probable growth in the various product-markets. Nearly half of the sales effort has been focused on the three older product groups (A, C, and D). Yet 83 percent of the $2.4 million profit contribution was accounted for by the three newer product groups. These are clear indications that better allocation of sales effort can be made by shifting sales time away from the older products with low profit contribution and low growth potential toward product groups B, E, and F. The current market shares for these product groups also indicate that further increases may be possible, although competitive strengths must be assessed in each product-market to confirm that possibility.

Given the analysis in Exhibit 19-13, sales management is faced with the task of shifting selling effort to achieve higher profit contributions and growth opportunities. Very likely, the firm added products over time without developing specific plans for reallocating selling effort. Since Industrial Equipment, Inc. paid salespeople a straight salary, they had no incentive to make major shifts in selling effort. In evaluating this situation, management should first analyze the existing and potential customer requirements for the various product groups to estimate how much additional selling effort is needed for the new products. Since the sales and profit contributions for groups B, E, and F have been relatively high, additional sales effort may not be needed. In that case, management should investigate the size of the sales force to assess whether reductions are needed. If substantial shifts in effort appear appropriate, a plan for accomplishing them should be developed, including proper communication with salespeople, possible product training, and possible incentive program based on profit contributions.

Individual Performance. The individual salesperson is the basic unit of management control. A major issue in developing an evaluation and control system for a sales force is how to determine proper performance standards (and information on performance) with which to compare salespeople and assess the overall productivity of the sales force. Although the standards used to evaluate salespeople vary across organizations, in most organizations such standards are linked to sales, profit contribution, product mix, expenses, or activity (e.g., number of new customers). In some organizations, multiple standards are used. When performance standards are communicated to the sales force, they become a basis for individual planning. Compensation plans are often linked to performance standards. The salesperson's portion of the selling job is often designated by a quota, which serves as a performance standard. Quotas are used to monitor performance, provide salespeople with goals, and determine incentives. They are often based on such factors as market potential and historical sales. In determining quotas, management normally considers the capabilities of salespeople. In some firms, salespeople are involved in the quota process.

If quotas are determined subjectively by management, a major problem is taking into account all of the factors that should be considered. A promising approach to the development of performance standards, including quotas, is to investigate the relationship in a given organization between performance targets (criteria) and possible predictors (determinants) of performance.[23] Statistical analysis may make it possible to develop a relationship between a performance factor such as sales volume and possible predictors (the market potential, the salesperson's experience, the workload) for all work units. In that case, standards can be generated from the statistical relationship for each salesperson. The result is a performance benchmark that has been adjusted for factors beyond the salesperson's control.

An example of this approach, using multiple regression analysis for 25 salesperson work units (geographic territories) of an appliance manufacturer, is shown in Exhibit 19-14A. The performance criterion was sales volume (in dollars). A substantial portion of the variation in sales across territories was accounted for by the eight predictor variables, thus indicating a reasonably strong relationship. All eight variables except "salesperson's performance rating" are beyond the control of the salesperson. Note that most of the variation in sales was accounted for by only a few of the variables.

Subsequent analysis was performed, using only length of employment and average market share (weighted average for the prior four years) as predictors; the predicted values of sales for each territory were used as performance benchmarks (standards).

The rankings of the 25 territories for sales, benchmark achievement (predicted/actual sales), management ratings of salespersons, and quota achievement are shown in Exhibit 19-14B. There is no apparent relationship between management ratings of salespersons (column 4) and quota achievement

EXHIBIT 19–14A Summary of Stepwise Multiple Regression Analysis Using Data Transformed to Logarithmic Values

Step Number	Variable Entered*	Multiple R^2	Step Number	Variable Entered*	Multiple R^2
1	Length of employment	.730	5	Average workload per account	.878
2	Average market share	.809	6	Number of accounts	.879
3	Salesperson's performance rating	.871	7	Average market share change	.879
4	Advertising expenditures	.876	8	Industry sales	.879

* The predictor measures included in the regression relationship at a given step consist of the measure shown for that step plus the measures shown for all previous steps.

Source: Reprinted by permission from David W. Cravens and Robert B. Woodruff, "An Approach for Determining Criteria of Sales Performance," *Journal of Applied Psychology* 57 (1973), p. 244. Copyright 1973 by the American Psychological Association.

EXHIBIT 19–14B Rankings Based on Sales Volume, Benchmark Achievement, Quota Achievement, and Performance Ratings

(1) Territory Number	(2) Sales Volume	(3) Benchmark Achievement	(4) Management Rating	(5) Quota Achievement	(1) Territory Number	(2) Sales Volume	(3) Benchmark Achievement	(4) Management Rating	(5) Quota Achievement
1	15	2	4	1	14	21	11	10	6
2	6	9	2	16	15	4	1	1	14
3	18	7	20	15	16	11	21	14	21
4	8	23	17	22	17	9	14	15	20
5	2	5	5	17	18	13	3	11	11
6	24	17	7	2	19	14	13	13	10
7	3	16	6	24	20	10	18	19	25
8	12	25	24	18	21	23	22	25	5
9	1	4	3	13	22	16	19	16	12
10	5	10	21	19	23	25	24	23	3
11	19	20	18	9	24	7	6	22	23
12	22	15	9	4	25	17	12	12	7
13	20	8	8	8					

Source: Reprinted by permission from David W. Cravens and Robert B. Woodruff, "An Approach for Determining Criteria of Sales Performance," *Journal of Applied Psychology* 57 (1973), p. 245. Copyright 1973 by the American Psychological Association.

(column 5). But there is a statistically significant relationship between benchmark achievement (column 3) and management ratings of salespersons (column 4).[24]

If it is assumed that sales management can establish reasonable ratings of salespeople, then these results suggest that analytically determined performance standards are more relevant than subjectively determined quotas (which often are based largely on market potential). Because it is difficult for management to systematically consider the relevant determinants of performance without some method for processing the information (such as the analytic approach described above), it is not surprising that the rankings of management ratings (column 4) vary somewhat from the rankings of benchmark achievement (column 3). As the exhibit shows, benchmark achievement and management ratings are not similar for all territories (see, for example, territories 3, 7, 10, and 24). The use of an analytic performance standard that adjusts for factors beyond the salesperson's control can help management improve salesperson evaluation processes.

After reviewing the performance standards in Exhibit 19–14B, the firm's management indicated that the standards appeared to be appropriate gauges of salesperson performance. An executive of the firm commented that the results of the analysis supported management's dissatisfaction with the existing quota system and reinforced its judgment about the performance of various salespeople.

Other performance criteria can be used in conjunction with the same type of approach. Standards can be developed for profit contribution and for various product groups. Personal selling objectives should be linked to the performance criteria, and the analytic tools should be used to assist management rather than to replace judgment and experience.

Summary

The sales force is a major element of the marketing mix in many firms, and in these firms the salesperson is the most visible part of marketing strategy. Personal selling and advertising make up a substantial portion of the marketing manager's budget. The role and scope of the personal selling function are constantly changing. During the past decade, equal employment opportunity requirements have altered recruitment and selection procedures. Deregulation has changed the role of selling in many companies. Inflation and deflation have also affected the selling function, as have slower growth in many industries and global business competition. With costs increasing rapidly, much greater emphasis will be placed on sales force productivity and the cost effectiveness of personal selling activities will receive greater attention from management. All of these trends promise to make sales management more challenging and exciting in the decade ahead.

Among the important decision areas comprised by sales management are: selecting the role of the sales force in the firm; deciding how many salespeople are needed and how they should be allocated; selecting, training, and motivating them; and evaluating and controlling their performance. The efficient management of personal selling resources is more difficult than the efficient management of capital and physical resources, but this is not a valid reason for neglecting the task.

The role and size of the sales force and the allocation of salespeople to work units have been examined. Decisions on these matters are typically not changed frequently. Although major changes in the size of the sales force often occur over time, they do not typically occur on an annual basis. Yet substantial changes are sometimes necessary because of shifts in opportunities, changes in workload (perhaps because of new products), and competitive influences. More frequent reallocations are necessary because of changing customer needs and competitive pressures. Several of the more important factors influencing size and allocation decisions have been discussed.

Sales management decisions consist of an integrated system of actions that are aimed at achieving the objectives assigned to the selling organization. Once sales force size and allocation decisions have been made, much of the sales manager's time is devoted to managing people. Sales planning is needed to develop strategies for carrying out the marketing objectives assigned to the sales organization. Finding and selecting good salespeople is a continuing activity in most firms due to turnover, retirements, and growth. The training of new and existing employees must be planned and carried out. Training has a major impact on the sales-

person's skill level. Supervising and motivating salespeople is unlike any other management job in a company. Management's understanding of the motivation and behavior of salespeople is growing, but is limited at present. Incentives play a great role in motivating sales personnel.

Exercises for Review and Discussion

1. What factors primarily determine the personal selling job in a particular company? Which of these factors are under the control of management?

2. Why do companies such as Avon and Revlon assign very different roles to personal selling?

3. A metal products manufacturer is selling to customers in five different industries. The number of customers in each industry category is as follows: A = 500; B = 1,000; C = 2,000; D = 5,000; and E = 7,000. The desired call frequency per customer per month in each of the categories is: A, 5; B, 6; C, 1; D, 2; and E, 3. An average salesperson can make three calls per day for categories A and B and seven calls per day for categories C, D, and E. Based on the above information, what should be the approximate size of the sales force? How should the company allocate its salespeople to the five customer categories? What additional information would be useful in making a more complete assessment of sales force size?

4. A salesman has been assigned to sell a product in trading area X, trading area Y, and trading area Z. There are different types of customers, and some require a greater call frequency than others. The number of accounts and the number of calls per month for each trading area are as follows:

Trading Area X—20 accounts where two calls per month are necessary; 10 accounts where

one call per month is necessary; 10 accounts where one call every two months is necessary.

Trading Area Y—5 accounts where two calls per month are necessary; 15 accounts where one call per month is necessary; 5 accounts where one call every two months is necessary.

Trading Area Z—10 accounts where two calls per month are necessary; 5 accounts where one call per month is necessary; 10 accounts where one call every two months is necessary.

Based on this information, if our salesman averages a frequency of five calls per day, would he be able to handle the three trading areas? Would he have some extra time left to work in another territory, or would an extra salesperson be needed?

5. A food products wholesaler is currently selling in six districts. Based on a market potential analysis, a percentage of total sales has been allocated to each district. Two salespersons are assigned to each district. The sales figures are shown in Exhibit 19–A.

EXHIBIT 19–A

District	Market Potential (percent of total)	Sales Goals	Actual Sales
A	15%	$ 450,000	$ 825,000
B	20	600,000	225,000
C	17	510,000	330,000
D	13	390,000	370,000
E	25	750,000	740,000
F	10	300,000	520,000
Total	100%	$3,000,000	$3,010,000

What observations can you make concerning the performance of the salespersons in the six districts? Should there be a readjustment of the sales force in some districts? What additional information would be helpful in making an assessment of the six districts?

6. Compare the measurement of advertising effectiveness with the measurement of sales force effectiveness (in terms of both individual salespersons and the entire sales force).

7. Assume that you have been asked by the vice president of sales of a pharmaceutical firm to develop a sales force evaluation program. Outline an approach to this assignment, including in your presentation the information that will be needed and how you propose to obtain it.

8. Some firms prefer to hire and train inexperienced salespeople (e.g., recent business

school graduates), whereas other firms prefer to lure experienced people away from competitors. What are the relevant factors in deciding which of these approaches to utilize?

9. The shape of geographic sales territories is subject to several factors, including account location, account concentration, travel patterns, and method of travel. Illustrate different configurations arising from possible variations in the above factors that would favor different sales territory shapes.

10. Some industry observers argue that the importance of the personal selling function will decline in the 1980s due to such influences as gasoline costs and electronic communications. Identify and discuss the issues that need to be considered in assessing the validity of this contention.

Notes

1. "Where Three Sales a Year Make You a Superstar," *Business Week*, February 17, 1986, pp. 76–77.

2. Projected from *U.S. Statistical Abstract*, 1973 (Washington, D.C.: U.S. Government Printing Office, 1973), pp. 233–34.

3. "Compensation," *Sales & Marketing Management*, February 17, 1986, p. 56.

4. Kenneth R. David and Frederick E. Webster, Jr., *Sales Force Management* (New York: Ronald Press, 1968), p. 44.

5. For a detailed examination of the salesperson's role as a manager, see Gerald J. Carney, *Managing a Sales Territory* (New York: American Management Association, 1971).

6. William J. Stanton and Richard H. Buskirk, *Management of the Sales Force*, 6th ed. (Homewood, Ill.: Richard D. Irwin, 1983), p. 424.

7. Frederick E. Webster, Jr., "Top Management's Concerns about Marketing Issues for the 1980s," *Journal of Marketing*, Summer 1981, pp. 9–16.

8. Walter J. Talley Jr., "How to Design Sales Territories," *Journal of Marketing* 25 (January 1961), pp. 7–13. The following discussion is based on this source.

9. The discussion in this section is based in part on David W. Cravens and Raymond W. LaForge, "Salesforce Deployment Analysis," *Industrial Marketing Management* 12 (1983), pp. 179–92.

10. *Salesmen's Turnover in Early Employment* (New York: Conference Board, 1972), p. 1. This report contains a detailed analysis of turnover in a broad cross section of industries.

11. Robert E. Sibson, *Wages and Salaries: A Handbook for Line Managers*, rev. ed. (New York: American Management Association, 1967), pp. 161–62.

12. Stanton and Buskirk, *Management of the Sales Force;* chap. 4 contains a detailed discussion of job definition and the determination of the characteristics of the people who can perform the job.

13. An excellent comprehensive discussion of these factors is provided in Orville C. Walker, Jr., Gilbert A. Churchill, Jr., and Neil M. Ford, "Where Do We Go from Here? Selected Conceptual and Empirical Issues Concerning the Motivation and Performance of the Industrial Sales Force," presented at the American Institute for Decision Sciences Sales Management Workshop, St. Louis, Missouri, October 30, 1978.

14. See Stanton and Buskirk, *Management of the Sales Force*, chap. 6, for an extensive discussion of these selection tools.

15. "Average Sales Rep Pay Hits $30,444; Up 12.8% over '79," *Marketing News*, February 5, 1982, p. 1.

16. Walker, Churchill, and Ford, "Where Do We Go from Here?," p. 13.

17. See Stanton and Buskirk, *Management of the Sales Force*, chaps. 8 and 9, for discussion of the major considerations in the development of training programs for salespeople.

18. Walker, Churchill, and Ford, "Where Do We Go from Here?," p. 1.

19. The various supervisory functions are examined in greater detail in Davis and Webster, *Sales Force Management*, pp. 564–70.

20. Walker, Churchill, and Ford, "Where Do We Go from Here?," pp. 16–17.

21. "Compensation," *Sales & Marketing Management*, February 21, 1983, p. 70.

22. Stanton and Buskirk, *Management of the Sales Force*, pp. 260–61.

23. For an expanded discussion of this approach, see David W. Cravens and Robert B. Woodruff, "An Approach for Determining Criteria of Sales Performance," *Journal of Applied Psychology* 57 (1973), pp. 242–47.

24. The Spearman rank-correlation coefficient (R_s) for the benchmark relationship was at the .001 level. The quota relationship was not statistically significant.

PART 5

*T*he implementation of a marketing strategy ultimately determines its success. The people in marketing and throughout the organization are essential to moving marketing programs into action. Once marketing strategies are implemented, their performance must be evaluated and adjusted to bring actual and desired results as close together as possible. Marketing research and information systems are essential tools of the marketing manager and staff in planning and implementing marketing strategies. The marketing organization, the analysis of marketing performance, and marketing information are examined in Chapters 20, 21, and 22.

Organizational effectiveness is important in strategy implementation. Organizational design is a key factor in the effectiveness of the people in the organization. All organizational levels are involved to some extent in marketing strategy development and implementation, including the marketing department, the corporation and business unit, and organizations outside the firm, such as distributors and advertising agencies.

Marketing control is concerned with analyzing the performance of marketing decisions, uncovering performance problems and opportunities, and implementing actions to achieve favorable results. The control process is the basis for tracking marketing performance. It consists of developing performance standards, evaluating variations from standards, and implementing corrective action when necessary.

Marketing research and information systems help the marketing manager and staff in analysis, planning, and control. Information is needed for a wide range of decision-making activities. Identifying information needs, obtaining the needed information, and analyzing and interpreting that information are essential in facilitating marketing decision making■

CHAPTER 20

The Marketing Organization

General Motors Corporation, the world's largest carmaker, announced in the mid-1980s that it was reorganizing its massive structure. In what was heralded as the largest corporate restructuring in U.S. history, it reassembled the pieces to improve its competitive standing and its flexibility in responding to changing conditions. Several layers of organizational structure were eliminated, and two operating groups were formed, each with complete responsibility for design, manufacturing, and assembly functions. These functions had previously been spread across GM's five automobile divisions, each of which also had to coordinate with the Fisher Body Division on design and the General Motors Assembly Division on production. One of the two new groups produces small cars (and vehicles developed through joint ventures with other companies), and the other group concentrates on larger cars and specialty vehicles. The five automobile divisions (Cadillac, Oldsmobile, Buick, Pontiac, and Chevrolet) and their distribution systems were retained, however, in part to provide contact with the marketplace so as to determine what types of vehicles should be developed and produced.

The reorganization was intended to create a greater decentralization of decision making and more participatory management, making GM more quick-footed in responding to market and other changes. Another objective was to reduce duplication of effort. Attention was also given to improving employee attitudes and the corporate culture. This was a corporate reorganization rather than just a marketing reorganization, but it better equipped GM to respond to the marketplace. The organizational principles that the change entailed were the same as those applicable to marketing management in that a marketing organization, like any other, should facilitate responsiveness, flexibility, an appropriate level of decentralization, and minimal overlap and waste. In short, whether the company is General Motors or any other, its organization should facilitate the achievement of corporate and marketing objectives.

In this chapter, the term *organization* is defined and desirable organizational characteristics are discussed. Organizational issues are addressed at three levels: the marketing organizational unit itself (the marketing department), the corporation as a whole (the attempt of General Motors to encourage a market orientation throughout the firm), and the relationships of the corporation with outside companies such as advertising agencies and distributors. To be effective, marketing must operate at all three levels.

What Is an Organization?

Organizations are comprised of structure, processes, culture, and people.

Over time, an **organization** can fall out of sync with what is needed to achieve the corporate mission. As the macroenvironment (social, technological, etc.) and the task environment (competition, markets, etc.) change, as happened in the automobile industry, the mission and objectives of a company must change. As the mission and objectives change, the activities and personnel required to accomplish them change. And as activities and personnel change, it is good to consider the grouping of various personnel into a different organizational structure. An organization is ideally an open behavioral system, receiving and processing information and then adapting strategies. A well-designed organization facilitates the adapting process. For new companies, the challenge is to design a viable, first-time set of arrangements. For established companies, the challenge is to keep the organization responsive.

Structure is the formal arrangements of people's roles and relationships so as to achieve corporate and marketing objectives.

The **structure** of an organization is often depicted in an organization chart, but organizational structure also encompasses flows of authority, communication, and work. If a marketing objective is to become the industry leader in market share, then the organization, strategies, and related activities should be oriented toward attaining that objective. In creating a new organization, the next step is identifying what types of individual talent and what positions are required to implement the strategies and what means are required for effective deployment of that talent—deciding who reports to whom, whether there are to be groups or teams or a department, and whether people should be placed in different geographic locations. This hypothetical approach of assuming a clean slate and a new start can be valuable. It answers the question "What would be the ideal organizational structure to carry out the current mission and objectives of our marketing unit?" Once that question has been answered, the existing structure can be compared to the ideal structure, the differences between the two can be identified, and structural adjustments can be considered.

Organizational culture is the collection of beliefs, expectations, and values shared by employees.

The *processes* of an organization are its dynamics—communication flows, both formal and informal, and work flows. The relationships between positions and organizational units are largely determined by day-to-day flows and exchanges. Over extended periods, an **organizational culture** evolves from these relationships. That culture is deeply embedded and is passed on from existing to new employees. It guides which behavior and decision-making

EXHIBIT 20–1 Resistance within the AT&T Culture

William F. Buehler was 43 years old, named a vice president at American Telephone & Telegraph Company, given a work force of 3,000 and put in charge of marketing phone systems to small businesses all over the United States. What's more, his bosses at AT&T gave him considerable freedom to break with the Bell way of doing things.

And that's exactly what he did. In place of Bell's rigmarole of endless memos, interminable meetings, and strict chain of command, the boyish-looking Buehler discarded planning manuals, threw out employee tests, put salespeople on the highest commission-based compensation plan in AT&T history, and fired those who couldn't meet his tough quotas.

It worked. Salespeople say they caught "Buehler fever," and sales figures soared off the charts. His boss and the chairman of AT&T Information Systems conceded that the Buehler unit that sold the smaller business systems outperformed the rival unit selling larger ones.

But 12 months later, Buehler wasn't bathing in accolades. He was being removed from his job and put in an obscure planning position, though he remains a vice president.

* * * * *

As a result, the new corporate culture that he created was weakened, if not snuffed out, and many of his subordinates were apprehensive, even though they often found him difficult to work for. "We're all upset and worried that we'll lose our new culture," says James R. Lewis, an AT&T account executive in Southfield, Michigan.

Source: Adapted from Monica Langley, "AT&T Manager Finds His Effort to Galvanize Sales Meets Resistance," *The Wall Street Journal*, December 16, 1983, pp. 1, 8. Reprinted by permission of *The Wall Street Journal*, © Dow Jones & Company, Inc., 1983. All rights reserved.

styles are deemed acceptable and unacceptable. Issues central to an organization's culture include:

- Whether major career risks are associated with risk-laden decisions.
- The extent to which employees protect their turf and control information flow.
- The freedom of individual employees to make significant decisions without multilevel approvals.
- The extent to which disagreement or even confrontation is allowed or encouraged.

One of the best marketing examples of a person who challenges the existing corporate culture is the new product "champion." Due to a deep belief in a product's potential, this person typically takes above-average risks within the organization to champion the product. Champions put their necks on the line to guide products over various corporate hurdles toward the marketplace. Because of the importance of new products and their high failure rates, some organizations make special arrangements to foster new product development—creating separate new venture teams—on the ground that a different culture is needed for that purpose.

It is a slow and difficult process to change an organization's culture, and new executives and strategies often fall victim to employee resistance (Exhibit 20-1). A new vice president at AT&T was first given freedom to innovate and put the entrepreneurial spirit into action. But in the battle between corporate traditionalism and innovation, the victory went to the old line at AT&T. The new vice president had implemented too much change too quickly, and his maverick style did not synchronize with the style of the existing executive group.

In addition to structure, processes, and culture, an organization is comprised of *people*. Human resource management is a critical task for marketing as well as for all other business functions. Within the organizational structure and processes are individual positions, job descriptions, and employees. Having able, well-trained, experienced people in such areas as sales, brand management, and marketing research is critical to success.

The finest marketing strategy will be successful only if employees possess the needed expertise and understand how their detailed responsibilities fit into the overall strategy. General Electric Company committed to a new organizational mission and recognized the central role that individuals play. In a report to its shareholders, it stated:

> Whether it's bringing new technologies and services to the marketplace or revitalizing our strong core businesses, we want GE to be a place where the bias is towards action—a high-spirited, world-class enterprise that uses the resources of a large company but moves with the agility of the youngest and smallest. A goal of GE is to become the most competitive enterprise in the world. The goal is an immense challenge. But it is not an unreasonable one because General Electric has been fortunate enough to assemble a talented—and in many ways unique—team of men and women. GE's "corporate culture" is dominated by the skill, perseverance, vision, and ambition of its employees.
>
> Becoming the world's most competitive enterprise will require extraordinary effort in all aspects of management and individual performance. . . .
>
> * * * * *
>
> But General Electric is a very large enterprise. For GE to achieve world leadership, many people—at all levels—will have to be personally committed to excellence, to innovation, to individual entrepreneurship. Such dedication and drive will not be achieved through wishful thinking.
>
> At the heart of the company's success are broad-based systems of rewards for achievement that give personal meaning to the company's overall quest for excellence. Success depends entirely on the personal involvement of General Electric men and women throughout the company. Being a part of the world's most competitive enterprise must be a rewarding experience for all concerned; that is the chief focus of GE's managerial philosophy.[1]

A persuasive case can be made that marketing employees, perhaps more than any others, must be entrepreneurial and action oriented. Most marketing employees are boundary agents, at the interface between the organization and its environment. Marketing people cope daily with new information and with the uncertainties that come from marketplace and competitive forces. So matching individual talent with positions that have these types of responsibilities is no small order.

Designing the Marketing Organization

One basic rule in marketing organizational design is to build the organization around the basic marketing plan rather than forcing the plan into a predetermined organizational arrangement.[2] Organizations should not be assumed to be static or immovable. A good marketing organizational design should possess these characteristics:

- The organization should correspond to the marketing plan. If, for example, the plan is structured around markets or products, then the organizational structure should reflect that emphasis.

- Activities should be coordinated. Coordination of activities is essential to the successful implementation of plans, both within the marketing function and in conjunction with other company and business unit functions. But the more highly specialized marketing functions become, the more likely it is that coordination and communications problems will arise.

- An appropriate balance between coordination needs and specialization should be sought. Marketing activities should be specialized. Specialization of these activities tends to create greater efficiency in performing them. Specialization can provide technical depth—product specialization in a field sales force, for example, enables salespeople to provide specialized expertise to customers.

- Responsibility for results should correspond with a manager's authority and influence. While it is often difficult to fully achieve this objective, the objective is a leading consideration in designing the marketing organization.

- The organization should be adaptable to changing conditions to facilitate responses to competitive and customer moves. A real danger in a highly structured and complex organization is the loss of flexibility. Marketing's close links to the external environment require ongoing adjustments in the organization.

- The organization should foster integration rather than fragmentation of customer-influencing activities—publicity, for example, should portray the same images as personal selling.

- The organization should be cost effective and not involve undue duplication of effort or excess staff. The advantages of specialization by functions, products, and markets should be evaluated against the costs and against the resulting difficulties in coordinating marketing strategy and tactics.

- The organization should represent customer interests within the company.[3] The philosophical basis for this objective is derived from the marketing concept. By representing customer interests within the company, marketing helps ensure the long-term survival of the firm. A good marketing organization explicitly includes this element through job descriptions and positions.

The challenge in this list of desirable characteristics is to seek a balance among elements that inherently conflict with one another. Organizational design involves assigning priorities and balancing conflicting consequences. There is rarely one right or best organizational design; rather, some organizational design fits the particular situation better than others.

Organizational issues can be divided into three levels and the remainder of this chapter is organized accordingly.

- *Within Marketing.* This level involves organizational issues that fall within the marketing organizational unit.

- *Within Corporate.* This level involves organizational issues that determine what role marketing will play within the larger organization. The specific functions allocated to marketing vary from firm to firm. In implementing a well-integrated and consistent marketing strategy, customer-influencing functions that do not fall within marketing pose special coordination challenges. Thus, there is a need to foster cooperation and minimize conflict throughout the corporation.

- *Intercorporate.* Organizational units such as advertising agencies, transportation companies, and distributors are outside the corporate walls but influence the success of marketing strategies.

Organizational Decisions within Marketing

Managers are continually searching for better ways to structure the marketing organization. For a company serving one target market with a single product, marketing activities are often assembled into an organization comprising several functions, such as advertising, the sales force, distribution, marketing information, and customer services. Far more challenging is choosing a design for an organization serving several customer groups with a wide range of products. Management must decide how much specialization is needed for the different products and target markets and how marketing functions will be aligned when two or more product and/or market organizational units are formed. In addition to these functional, product, and market-based organizational units, certain components specialize in defined geographic market areas as well.

The necessary marketing functions, the mix of products or services, the characteristics of firm's customers, and geographic coverage are the four primary approaches that can be used in the design of a marketing organization. Depending on the scope and complexity of these influences, one organizational approach may be superior to another. Yet no one design is suited to all companies, and some degree of flexibility exists in choosing an organizational design. Today, most marketing organizations are a combination of functional, product, customer (market), and geographic specialization.

Functionally-Based Organization

Regardless of which approach is used, the marketing organization must accommodate the various functions assigned to the marketing manager. The functional approach is often used by large manufacturers of consumer prod-

EXHIBIT 20–2 Functionally Based Organization

ucts for which mass marketing strategies are appropriate. A single uncomplicated product or line of products (e.g., cigarettes or beer) is usually sold, and various marketing activities are specialized so as to serve a single market with a particular product. Exhibit 20–2 shows a typical functional organizational structure for marketing. It may be seen that the marketing organization has specialized units in advertising, customer service, personal sales, marketing research, new products and planning and administration. The **functional organization** encourages development of managerial and technical skills in each specialized function with an offsetting negative effect on day-to-day integration of the marketing program. Integration becomes a major task for the chief marketing executive.

Functional organizations are divided into specialized marketing functions such as advertising, selling, and marketing research.

Product-Based Organization

Product-based organizations are divided into units that specialize in marketing certain products or types of products.

The **product-based organization** or brand management approach pioneered by Procter & Gamble nearly half a century ago is illustrative of this organizational design. Marketing managers are assigned to various product groups with responsibility for coordinating marketing activities for their products (Exhibit 20–3). One of its strengths is that the product manager develops in-depth knowledge of the product itself, as well as of the unique aspects of marketing the product (or product group). Its main limitation is that too much emphasis can be placed on products, actually short circuiting implementation of a customer orientation. It also tends to increase the number of management levels.

A perplexing issue is how much emphasis to place on products versus markets in the organizational design, since both are important. Often neither products nor markets alone are a logical basis for grouping marketing functions. The strategic business unit (SBU) concept offers considerable promise as a basis for organizational design, because a single product-market or a group of related product-markets provide a basis for forming one or more organizational units. (SBUs, however, are within-corporate rather than within-marketing units.)

EXHIBIT 20-3 Product-Based Organization

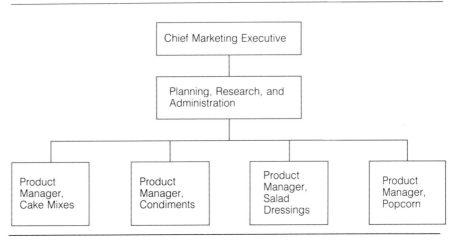

Using a narrow product focus can create problems—as Atari, Inc. discovered. Atari was purchased in the mid-1980s by the former president of Commodore International, Ltd. His objective was to make Atari profitable again. Atari's peak sales had been $2 billion, but then the video game market fell apart and competition in computers continued to grow. Several problems were involved, and analysts cited the company's basic structure as one of them. The video games and computer divisions had been run separately, and this product-oriented structure was viewed by many as costly and overlapping. More important, Atari handled the two product groups as if they had two different markets. "That was a big mistake," said the former vice president of sales. "They had the best computer on the market for three years, voted as the hobbyist's choice. They should have tried to combine the two and sell their low-end computer as a video game."[4] Although it is easy to have 20-20 hindsight, it is striking that using a product (rather than a customer) organizational structure was blamed for Atari's bad fortune. A product grouping offers advantages, but firms such as Atari learned that this approach can lead to inadequate emphasis on the needs of particular customer groups. Also consider the experience of the H. J. Heinz Company:

> One of the biggest complaints against the product/brand manager is his preoccupation with the internal functions of his own company. . . . he must constantly work at getting his share of advertising, market research, sales promotion, and other services. "He just does not get involved with the ultimate user of the product and with other external marketing functions," says Richard L. Johnson, general manager of the Foodservice Marketing Department of H. J. Heinz Company. Heinz, which switched to product management . . . , tried to correct that with a management structure that combined product management and market management.[5]

EXHIBIT 20-4 Customer-Based Organization

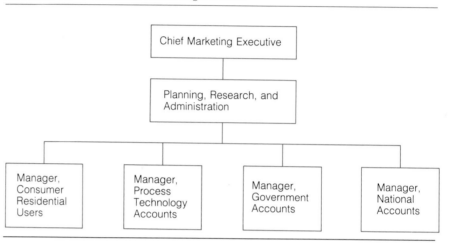

Customer-Based Organization

_____

**Customer-based
organizations**
are divided into groups
that specialize in serv-
ing the needs of certain
types of customers.

When a firm serves more than one product-market, the logic of building the
marketing organization around customer or market groups is difficult to
dispute. The usefulness of this approach is supported by Heinz and a growing
number of firms. A **customer-based organization** concentrates on a similar
group of users, with a comprehensive marketing effort managed by each
organizational unit serving a particular market (Exhibit 20-4). The organizational design focuses on customer needs, and marketing resources are integrated to serve customer groups. However, this type of organization can lead
to inefficient duplication of functions in each unit unless the scale of operations is sufficiently large. It can also contribute to the creation of more
management levels.

Consider the National Cash Register Company, which markets office
equipment ranging from cash registers to computers. NCR made a radical
shift in its organizational design, changing from a product-oriented approach
to a customer-oriented approach. In a massive marketing reorganization that
reached into every corner of NCR's far-flung and increasingly complex empire, the $6.6 billion business machines company began selling by "vocation"
or industry rather than by product line. Following the lead of more and more
industrial and consumer goods giants—ranging from IBM to General
Foods—NCR reassigned its 3,000-person domestic sales force from products
to specific customer markets—retailing, financial (banks and savings and
loan associations), commercial/industrial, and medical/education/govern-
ment.[6] NCR is representative of a growing number of firms that are looking to
the marketing concept as a basis for designing a new marketing organization
or reshaping an existing structure. These firms are recognizing the impor-

EXHIBIT 20–5

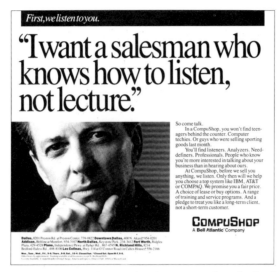

First, we listen to you.

"I want a salesman who knows how to listen, not lecture."

So come talk.
In a CompuShop, you won't find teen-agers behind the counter. Computer techies. Or guys who were selling sporting goods last month.
You'll find listeners. Analyzers. Need-definers. Professionals. People who know you're more interested in talking about your business than in hearing about ours.
At CompuShop, before we sell you anything, we listen. Only then will we help you choose a top system like IBM, AT&T or COMPAQ. We promise you a fair price. A choice of lease or buy options. A range of training and service programs. And a pledge to treat you like a long-term client, not a short-term customer.

COMPUSHOP
A Bell Atlantic Company

Dallas, 8201 Preston Rd. at Preston Center, 739-0822 **Downtown Dallas,** 400 N. Akard?-954-0201 **Addison,** Beltline at Montfort, 934-3107 **North Dallas,** Keystone Park, 234-3412 **Fort Worth,** Ridglea Plaza, 429-4528 **Plano,** Independence Pkwy. at Parker Rd., 867-4595 **N. Richland Hills,** 8214 Bedford-Euless Rd., 498-8106 **Las Colinas,** Hwy. 114 at O'Connor Road (in Cullen House)? 556-2166

Mon., Tues., Wed., Fri., 9-6; Thurs., 9-8; Sat., 10-4. Closed Sun. *Closed Sat. Open M-F, 9-6.

CompuShop is a customer-based organization targeted to the business computer user, with well-trained, specialized employees to analyze customer needs.

Courtesy Tracy-Locke Advertising, Inc.

tance of customers' needs and wants as a basic guide to their business orientation. A customer orientation is also shown by the ad in Exhibit 20–5.

Geographically-Based Organization

Geographically-based organization
is divided into groups to efficiently and effectively serve different geographic areas.

In the **geographically-based organization,** certain marketing personnel specialize in specified geographic areas and are often physically located in those areas. For organizations that serve large areas, it is common to have some specialization by geographic markets. The sheer size of a market area may require breaking it down into smaller units to reduce logistic costs. A geographically based organization may be consistent with a customer-based approach in that somewhat different customer preferences exist in different regions of the United States and across different international markets. One limitation of the geographically based organization, however, is that it reduces the flow of communication between personnel in different geographic areas. The most common marketing application of a geographically based organization is the allocation of personal selling representatives. As shown in Exhibit 20–6, companies normally have separate managers or divisions to serve various countries, and within the United States there are often regional, zone, and district managers. The regionalized listing of CompuShop locations at the bottom of Exhibit 20–5 reflects a partially geographic organization.

EXHIBIT 20-6 Geographic Approach to Marketing Organization

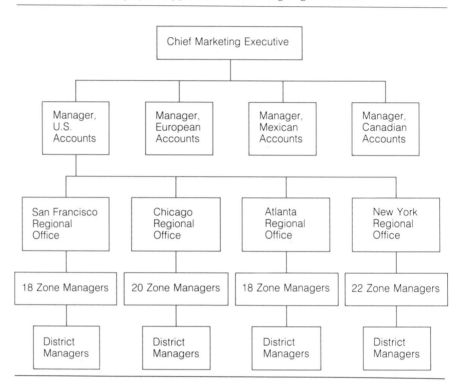

Combination of Bases

Large organizations usually select a combination of functional, product, customer, and geographic approaches, as shown in Exhibit 20-7. Various functional positions are shown as well as product, customer-based (e.g., government and institutional), and geographic units (regional sales managers and Caribbean sales). This structure evolved to fit various needs for specialization as well as the people and organizational culture involved.

An overview of the characteristics, strengths, limitations, and suggested applications of the four organizational approaches is provided in Exhibit 20-8. General Motors decided to have functional specialists in two new operating divisions with a product basis (small versus large cars), but to retain its five divisions with their franchise systems that matched somewhat different customer groups in a wide variety of geographic areas. Although the general form of the marketing organization can be selected from one of the four approaches, some specific decisions must be made to complete the design. In organizations not structured according to functions, such activities as advertising, personal selling, and marketing research must be assigned in some way. In making these assignments, three methods may be used:

EXHIBIT 20-7 Marketing Organization: Combined Approach

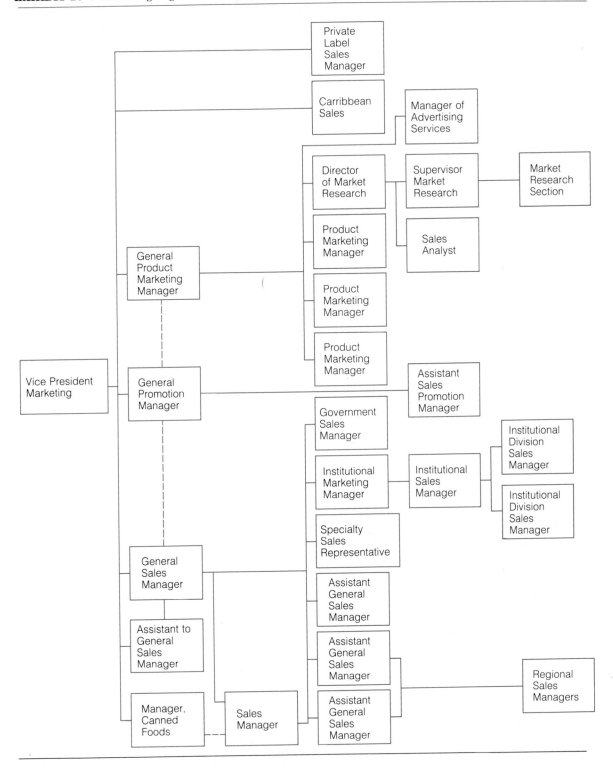

EXHIBIT 20–8 Comparison of Approaches to Marketing Organization

Characteristics	Strengths	Limitations	Applications
Functional approach			
Grouping of marketing activities into areas of specialization, such as advertising, sales, and marketing research	Encourages development of managerial and technical skills in each specialized marketing function	Places integrating responsibility on chief marketing executives, since specialization by activity tends to inhibit integration	Large firms utilizing several marketing functions and specialized personnel Firms concentrating on one primary product market; firms with a single, simple product line
Product approach			
Specialization by product line or product group; sometimes used by multidivision firms in which each division is responsible for a group of products	Permits direction of management attention to the requirements of different products; facilitates coordination of product decisions with other areas of the firm	May place too much emphasis on products, thus working against the philosophy of the marketing concept Tends to increase the number of organizational levels	Where several products are marketed and technical/application differences exist among product groups Where products require special knowledge/skills of personnel marketing them
Customer approach			
Emphasis on managing for customer groups rather than functions	Organizational design focused on customer needs; marketing resources integrated to serve customer groups with similar characteristics	May lead to duplication of functions and inefficiencies unless scale of operations is sufficiently large Requires more management levels (e.g., manager for each market area) and coordination	Where substantial differences exist between target markets, such as industrial and consumer markets Where market opportunities are large enough to justify separate marketing approaches
Geographic approach			
Specialization by geographic area	Provides for logistic efficiency as well as a customer orientation where regional market differences exist.	Reduces communication among personnel in different geographic areas.	Most often used for the organization and allocation of the sales force
Combinations			
Combining of functional, market, product, and geographic approaches to obtain multiple advantages and to overcome the limitations of a single approach	Enables combination of functional, market, and product characteristics in organizational design; Encourages integration and specialization of marketing efforts; more flexible than the other approaches	May make allocation of responsibility for various marketing activities more difficult May result in duplication and inefficiences if organizational units are not large enough to provide economies	Firms with several product groups and/or target markets serving various geographic areas

■ Providing functional capabilities across all product, market, or major geographic units—instead of assigning an advertising group to each product management area, one advertising department can serve each of the product managers.

- Locating all marketing functions within each product or market group. In this way, all marketing functions can perform within a particular product, customer, or even geographic group.

- Using an approach in which some functions are performed for all groups and some are handled separately by each group—marketing research and advertising might serve all groups, whereas product-market planning, the sales force, pricing, and distribution could be specialized within each group.

Organizational Patterns

Another important structural characteristic is how the organizational units are arranged—in a hierarchy, in teams, or in a matrix type of organization.

In large organizations, functional, product, customer, and geographic specializations are usually mixed in various ways and include hierarchical, team, and matrix elements.

Hierarchical. The traditional organization comprises several layers, with every employee reporting to one boss. Several of the previous exhibits illustrated a hierarchical approach, with a marketing executive at the top and subordinates fanning out below, creating a pyramid-shaped organization. Usually, the greater the number of layers, the more centralized the authority structure. Recently, organizations have tended to decentralize, with fewer levels and a more horizontal structure.

In a hierarchical structure, the flows of authority and the chain of command are clearly specified. The advantage of the hierarchical structure is its clarity to all involved because each domain is delineated. The disadvantages come from looking at the reverse side of the same coin. Due to its clearly defined turf, the hierarchical structure makes for narrowly focused objectives that, over time, can become suboptimal relative to overall marketing objectives. Each organizational unit largely rules its own kingdom, and this can impair cooperation and coordination.

Organizational Teams. Various types of teams, committees, and task forces are established to accomplish important goals. Such groups are usually established outside the existing hierarchy to pool various specialized talents essential to goal attainment. A team allows the required talent to be assembled, usually without permanently altering the rest of the structure. Work on the team may be a full-time or part-time responsibility. New product teams provide an example. Various talents inside and outside marketing are needed to carry the new product planning process forward. New ventures may be coordinated by a division, but rely largely on teams where a new product idea involves, say, television and solid-state technologies and requires the expertise of research and development, manufacturing, marketing, engineering and finance (Exhibit 20-9).

EXHIBIT 20-9 New Product Venture Teams in the Organization

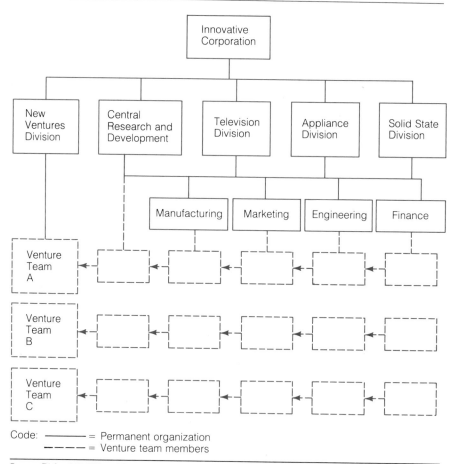

Code: ——————— = Permanent organization
        ------- = Venture team members

Source: Richard M. Hill and James D. Hlavacek, "The Venture Team: A New Concept in Marketing Organization," *Journal of Marketing* 36 (July 1972), p. 47. Published by the American Marketing Association.

One problem with the team approach is that it sometimes detracts from the permanent organization by "stealing" people from their usual responsibilities. Another problem is that it is often unclear who will evaluate the performance of each team member. Budget issues sometimes arise: Should the venture team be given its own budget, or should existing units be expected to contribute the time of their employees? Sometimes employees themselves resist getting caught in the middle. These issues, like all other organizational design issues, must be resolved in terms of the specific organizational culture and other situational factors.

Matrix organizations
create units with spe-
cialists in more than
one organizational
basis (e.g., functional,
product, customer),
with personnel typ-
ically reporting to two
superiors.

Matrix Organization.   Organizational teams are usually a form of **matrix organization,** an approach that originated with the NASA space program. Today, many companies have adopted the matrix approach on a permanent basis. The term *matrix* comes from the concept of a structure with two axes. Frequently, one axis is a set of functional responsibilities and the other is an array of products or markets. Each cell at the intersection of the two axes (e.g., the advertising function and the stereo receiver market) receives dual attention. The employee or manager represented by that cell reports equally to superiors in advertising and to superiors in the stereo receiver market. This differs from the combined approach shown in Exhibit 20-7, where each position shown has one superior in a hierarchy. Therefore, a combined approach does not have to be arranged in a matrix form, although matrix organizations do represent a combined approach.

The objectives of a matrix organization are to reduce the narrow focus that exists in a hierarchical organization and to increase flexibility and communication. But there are problems associated with matrix organizations. A study of such organizations found:

- *Tendencies toward Anarchy.* Having two bosses is often worse, not better, than having one.

- *Power Struggles.* The matrix permits a balancing of interests in fast-moving or especially complex situations where conflicting interests abound. However, the process of achieving this balance creates opportunities for power grabbing.

- *Severe "Groupitis."* Committee-like behavior evolves in cases where the matrix is misunderstood.

- *Collapse during Economic Crunch.* The matrix is an expensive and often a slow, democratic form of management, so tough times can cause its abandonment.

- *Excessive Overhead.* If the matrix mode is successful, productivity recaptures the investment, but the up-front investment is heavy.[7]

Matrix organizations offer substantial advantages as well as disadvantages, and as with other organizational structures, the degree to which this structure is implemented depends on a variety of situational factors.

Implementation and Marketing Organization

Developing marketing strategy is well recognized as an important task, but the actual implementation of marketing strategy is often overlooked.[8] Yet the finest strategy that is poorly implemented will probably fail. Poor implementation can also cloud poor results and leave it unclear whether or not the strategy itself failed. For this reason, when the results are poor, it is usually

**Marketing implemen-
tation**
is the execution of
marketing practices,
consistent with market-
ing programs and
strategies.

best to first consider making **marketing implementation** adjustments. Marketing implementation brings us to the lowest level of marketing, actual day-to-day execution of marketing tactics and practices. Successful implementation requires attention to organizational processes, culture, and people.

When it comes to implementation, managers probably have the most trouble with sales force management, distributor management, and pricing moves. When these functions go awry, it is often because of poor organization. Headquarters often assumes that the function in question will be executed by "someone" and ignores it until a crisis develops. But a poorly specified and detailed functional organization may be little better, or even worse, than none at all. Job descriptions provide the flesh for the bones of an organizational structure, so that each person knows what to do when. And the job descriptions must be current and well understood so that the lowest-level marketers in the organization can contribute to achieving the firm's marketing objectives.

A second implementation pitfall is spreading resources and talent democratically across marketing functions, rather than selecting one or two functions for special concentration and competence. The result may be global mediocrity, with pricing, advertising, promotion, and distribution all satisfactory but with no one outstanding function. Frito-Lay is an example of a company that has refined two functions, selling and distribution, to such heights that they serve as the company's marketing foundation.

At the marketing program level, the marketing functions are combined to penetrate a target market. Implementation pitfalls arise here as well. A computer vendor, for example, decided to set up a national accounts program to better serve its key customers. But deciding how to organize its personal selling unit was a major problem. Was it best to create a headquarters-based national accounts sales force that would overlap with the established sales offices around the United States? Or was it best to work through the existing sales managers, and attempt through persuasion to better serve major national customers? The answer had to come from a situation analysis and good judgment. Even though there was no standard answer, it was clear that faulty implementation could spell disaster.

At lower organizational levels, implementation pitfalls can occur with marketing systems, such as reporting and control. The wrong reporting systems can encourage standard patterns and industry practices that may be suboptimal relative to successfully implementing strategy. Reports from the sales force can be used as a way to punish sales representatives, which in turn can lead to representatives providing misleading market information and dangerous sales intelligence. Many companies still have no system for reporting profitability by target market, by product, or by customer account. "Accounting won't give it to us that way" is the classic problem. The design of such systems can be costly, so their added value for decision making and implementation must be carefully weighed. The wrong system, a misused system, or no system at all presents implementation pitfalls.

Perhaps the most basic implementation pitfall that affects execution and practices is the absence of a shared, common understanding of the firm's marketing purpose or theme. Marketing and nonmarketing managers who convey conflicting signals to the troops inevitably generate conflicts. The marketing theme could be "premium product quality with high-quality service to match" or "high quality for the price paid." The implications of these two themes could be quite different at the implementation level. Asking the key management people to write in one sentence the marketing theme of the firm can be revealing. And maintaining a common agreement on this theme is important. The marketing culture—the often unspoken, lunchroom, social web of management—also "speaks" to employees about the identity and role of marketing in the firm. It subtly but powerfully channels managers' behavior into comfortable ruts, and it may or may not be consistent with the marketing theme.

Another intangible factor between structure and performance is the quality of marketing leadership. Good leadership helps build a sense of marketing direction and a culture conducive to that direction.

Companies seem to be effective at marketing implementation when they have:

- A clarity of marketing theme.

- A culture with engrained customer concern.

- An employee willingness to stray from existing systems when this is best.

- An allocation of ample support to only a few programs and marketing functions.

- A readiness to overcome structure, if necessary, to achieve the mission.

Successful marketing management, after all, depends on people, as part of the organization, to implement the strategic plans.

Marketing within the Corporate Organization

The achievement of marketing objectives is influenced by units in the corporation organization other than marketing. In a company that produced huge custom-designed, glass-lined storage tanks used by chemical and other companies, a single sale from a field representative could total $250,000. Credit checks were run on potential customers before orders were accepted. This led to occasions when salespeople were utterly frustrated because the credit department would not approve an order. The marketing objectives were in conflict with what the financial administrators viewed as prudent credit risks. Some orders were lost, but sometimes negotiating led to a compromise—a higher payment in advance from the customer or a smaller order.

Dynamic processes surround the apparent order of organizational structures. Empire building and turf battles sometimes grow out of conflicts

EXHIBIT 20–10 Within-Corporate Conflicts

Marketing Orientation versus	Organizational Unit Orientation:	Marketing Orientation versus	Organizational Unit Orientation:
	Research and Development:		**Accounting and Finance:**
Conduct marketing research to determine customer needs.	Develop innovative, state-of-the-art technologies.	View marketing as a revenue-generating investment.	View marketing as a cost and seek to measure a short-run return on marketing expenditures.
Identify market opportunities, whether technological product oriented or not.	Develop new technologies, and then obtain customer reaction.	Initiate new activities with an entrepreneurial style.	Control costs relative to an approved budget.
Identify customer-satisfying products that can be produced at a reasonable cost.	Pursue next level of technological advancement for its own sake.		**Production:**
		Make what the company can most easily market.	Make what the company can most readily produce.
	Engineering:	Production levels should match demand.	Production levels should produce economical lots, etc.
Build an effective mousetrap for a good price.	Build the perfect mousetrap.		
Sell product benefits.	Sell product features.	Incur cost on quality control, etc. to enhance marketability.	Keep costs within budget.
	Credit:		
Use credit as a marketing mix variable to increase sales and make credit easily available.	Minimize risk of losses and approve customers who are most creditworthy, and seek early payments or high finance charges.		**Distribution:**
		Distribution methods convenient and fast for customers.	Cost and low-damage orientation.
Extend credit quickly.	Do a thorough credit search, checking references, etc.	Packaging as a marketing mix variable.	Packaging to protect products.

between organizational units. Personalities enter the process and complicate matters further. Beyond individual differences, organizational subunits may have objectives that *by design* tend to counteract each other.

Consider the conflicts listed in Exhibit 20–10, which sometimes arise between marketing and other organizational units. For technically oriented companies, the relationship between marketing and R&D is very important, yet the different orientations of the two groups have long led to communication and goal-oriented conflicts. Developing mechanisms as simple as monthly meetings between market specialists and technical personnel is highly desirable.

Engineering, like R&D, tends to be product oriented rather than market oriented, and production is committed to an efficient production process. A production orientation can conflict with marketers who often want small production runs of certain styles and colors to meet customer demand.

Credit tends to be viewed by marketers as a variable that can be adjusted or even negotiated. However, credit administrators often take a more conservative stance than marketers.

Accounting and finance personnel tend to view marketing expenditures as controllable *costs*, whereas marketers view them as an *investment*. This conflict has important dimensions. First, marketing costs often generate little immediate return but instead are designed to build sales over a period of several months or even years. Second, measuring an exact return on marketing costs is an extremely difficult task—in some degree, an impossible task. Yet when a marketing expenditure (e.g., direct mail advertising) clearly generates more revenue than the costs incurred, marketers will want to increase that expenditure. This, however, usually means exceeding budgeted expenditures and would therefore be viewed by some as a cost-control problem. Marketers then become frustrated because budgets are not increased to provide for more revenue generation.

Distribution methods and packaging are considered marketing mix variables by marketing personnel but are often under the control of another corporate unit. So differences can arise over the appropriate designs for packaging and over distributor arrangements.

There are numerous challenges within organizations that impede the implementation of marketing programs. These challenges have the desirable effect of requiring that various factors be weighed in making decisions. But they can also have the undesirable effect of unduly hampering the revenue-generating specialists (marketers) in the organization.

To cope with intraorganizational forces that impede marketing, awareness of subunit objectives that tend to conflict with marketing is needed so as to identify tensions early and to develop strategies for dealing with them. Mutual respect and constructive cooperation between corporate units can enhance the performance of all of them. Implementing the marketing concept requires that the entire organization, not just marketing, adopt a market-oriented perspective.

Intercorporate Linkages

The intercorporate level of organizational issues concerns organizations beyond the corporate boundaries on which marketing is dependent for success. As Exhibit 20-11 shows, many of these are organizations that the corporation compensates for services performed. It is usually possible to hire personnel to perform these services within the company itself, but companies often find it advantageous to use outside firms. Achieving the company's marketing objectives requires that the activities of independent firms be synchronized with activities in the company. Synchronization is legally accomplished through contractual agreements, compensation arrangements, or special incentives. These structural arrangements provide a basis for determining the relative power and control of the organizations.

Management should view outside organizations as essential in implementing marketing programs and, to the extent possible, should coordinate, com-

EXHIBIT 20-11 Intercorporate Linkages

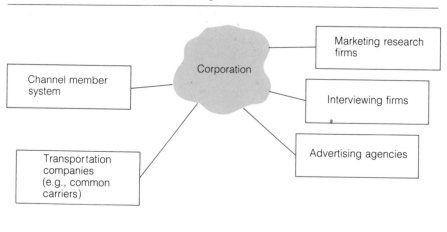

municate, and provide guidance to help ensure that the desired results are achieved. It is sometimes tempting to simply assume that these organizations will independently accomplish the necessary tasks. But doing their job well usually requires that they thoroughly understand marketing objectives and have an in-depth, qualitative sense of how their activities fit into the overall marketing program.

Consider the ties with an advertising agency. To perform well, the agency must understand the corporate mission and the image that the company wishes to convey to its public. The agency should be given adequate incentives to do the best job possible. Traditionally, much of a full-service advertising agency's revenue has come from media commissions (often 15 percent). The media (e.g., television stations) bill the advertising agency at the regular rates less the commission. Agency clients are then billed for the regular rates. As an alternative, an advertising agency may charge an agreed-upon fee and rebate all commissions to the client. This approach helps ensure that the agency will use the most cost-effective media and tends to foster professionalism.

An example of the importance of outside agencies concerns channels of distribution. Companies sometimes use contractual franchise agreements to build an independent distribution network while retaining some influence over channel members. A restructuring of Coca-Cola's bottling network in the mid-1980s was regarded as a critical contribution to Coca-Cola's success. All of Coca-Cola's franchises are granted in perpetuity, so how was this done?

Coca-Cola owns only about 10 percent of its U.S. bottling operations. The remainder were 300 independents ranging from units of big companies to mom and pop operations. Each buys Coke syrup or concentrate from the company, makes the soft drink, puts it in bottles or cans, and sells it. Officially, the company has almost no control over these operators.

But Coke can still affect the bottlers in many ways, such as by offering or withdrawing marketing funds. Using its powers of persuasion and plenty of cash, Coke managed to oversee changes in the ownership of about 120 of its 400 franchise territories. . . .

It sought to oust the feeble, the incompetent and the uninterested and replace them with bottlers who believed in "intelligent risk taking and no-holds-barred marketing." Coke executives insist that no one was forced out. At worst, some bottlers were told, "We would like you to get out of the business." In many franchise changes, Coke urged a sluggish franchisee to sell, lined up an aggressive replacement, helped arrange financing, and subsequently increased marketing budgets.

If no one was pushed out, many jumped when Coke and its hand-picked buyers demonstrated with cash just how much the company wanted to see them leave. But not all unsatisfactory bottlers were urged to get out. Some changed their ways after a chat with Coke's new management, Coke says.[9]

This case dramatically shows both the dependence of companies on external organizations and the need to ensure that those organizations fulfill their responsibilities. Whether distributors, advertising agencies, marketing research companies, transportation companies, or other organizations beyond the corporate boundaries are involved, maintaining a management-type role and viewpoint in dealing with them is essential to marketing success.

Application

Customer-Based Reorganization

In the mid-1980s, Xerox was still losing money on its computers. The firm decided to merge its separate product-based sales forces into a team to sell customers both copiers and computers. "It's one thing to have the technology and another thing to be able to sell it," said Donald J. Massaro, chairman of Metaphor Computer Systems and former president of Xerox's high-tech unit, the office products division. "Xerox's problems all were in sales and support."

In the past, Xerox had been reluctant to market high-tech products through its copier sales force, which was preoccupied with fierce competition from Japanese brands. Instead, it relied on three much smaller sales groups—one each for printers, computer workstations, and personal computers. Together, these groups amounted to a fourth of Xerox's entire sales staff.

So Xerox merged the three high-tech sales groups into its main copier division. But "Team Xerox" meant more than rewriting the organization chart; it entailed an entirely new sales approach, and possibly an end to the corporate turf battles that had long hampered the company's computer marketing.

Traditionally, Xerox's copier and computer systems salespeople had been rivals rather than partners, working out of separate offices—sometimes even separate buildings—under separate management. Worse still, corporate customers interested in more than just copiers had to deal with different sales representatives for each product. There were no incentives for cooperation on the same accounts. Referrals between sales divisions were rare.[10]

It was believed that a new customer-based organization would help make Xerox profitable in lines other than its copiers. Marketing resources were integrated for copiers and computers to serve customers more efficiently. Usually, a team approach helped ensure that both technical and customer-oriented expertise would be available. Finally, the teams were organized geographically to serve regions and districts ■

--------------------------------- *Summary* ---------------------------------

To achieve their mission, companies strive to establish an effective organizational *structure* in which appropriate *processes* and an appropriate *culture* are combined with talented *people.* Striving to achieve marketing objectives requires strategies and activities; performing these activities requires personnel in positions; and these personnel are grouped into organized units that make up the organizational structure. Structure formally arranges people's roles and relationships so as to achieve corporate and marketing objectives. Processes are the dynamic interchanges between people and units that, over time, evolve into a culture—a collection of shared beliefs, expectations, and values. Ultimately, it is the talents of individuals within the culture and the structure that make the organization perform.

The marketing organization should be built around the fundamental marketing plan. Other desirable features of the marketing organization are an appropriate level of specialization, responsibilities that correspond to a position's (or unit's) authority and influence, openness and flexibility, integration rather than fragmentation, minimal duplication of effort, and formal representation of customers' interests.

There are three levels of marketing organizational issues: within marketing, within corporate, and intercorporate. *Within marketing,* an organization may be built around a function, product, customer, or geographic specialization,

and it may be arranged in a hierarchical, team, or matrix configuration. Each of these bases has its advantages and disadvantages, and the organization should be molded to fit the situation. Many companies have moved toward a customer- or market-based organization in recent years, but there is no one "right" organizational design. Large organizations, whether profit or nonprofit, typically blend several of these bases.

Within the corporation, hurdles for marketers may arise from the turf consciousness or overly narrow viewpoints of other organizational units or from a misunderstanding of their role relative to marketing. This intraorganizational environment can influence marketing decisions. Some of the conflicts between marketing and other units arise from an organizational design that is intended to provide checks and balances over marketing decisions. Understanding the potential for conflicts of this kind and planning to cope with them are essential to successful implementation of marketing strategies.

The *intercorporate* level of marketing organizational issues concerns relationships with independent organizations outside the corporation. These organizations include advertising agencies, distributors, marketing research firms, and transportation companies. Although complete control of these organizations is not possible, it is essential to develop a managerial posture in dealing with them.

One should view an organization as an open behavioral system: dynamic and evolving. An organization should never be allowed to become inflexible and brittle. When an organization controls people and marketing plans, rather than the reverse, it has outlived its usefulness.

Exercises for Review and Discussion

1. This chapter discussed four types of marketing structures used today, also noting that combinations of these structures are commonly found. With this in mind, outline a marketing structure that might be appropriate for the following organizations:

a. A company similar to Anheuser-Busch that markets both beer and snack foods. Take into account that the beer market has become segmented into light beers, dark beers, premium beers, lager beers, etc.

b. An international accounting firm specializing in tax accounting. Here, "international" refers either to branch offices in various countries or to firms serving international corporations.

c. A microchip manufacturer holding the fifth-largest market share in the world.

2. For each of the three examples used above, suggest an organizational structure to best fit its type of business environment (technical environment necessitating R&D, large consumer promotions, etc.).

3. Many companies find that to compete in a certain market, they have to expand regionally *or* internationally. Explain how an organization might restructure its marketing approach when expanding in one of these two ways. Use Exhibit 20-6 as a guide.

4. You have been hired as senior vice president of Systems, Inc. The company manufactures, designs, and sells individual communications packages used by large corporations. For this reason, it must be highly market oriented. Outline a structure that might enable it to achieve this orientation. Assume that Systems, Inc. has R&D, production, accounting, finance, marketing, and sales departments.

5. List several types of intercorporate linkages that a company such as IBM has to "manage." Discuss each type briefly.

6. You have been asked to recommend a marketing organizational design for an industrial chemical distributor ($50 million in sales). What are several questions that you must answer in order to choose an appropriate design?

7. What type of marketing organizational structure is most common today? Why do you suppose this is so?

Notes

1. General Electric Company, *1982 Annual Report,* inside cover and pp. 17, 19.

2. This section is partially based on David W. Cravens, *Strategic Marketing* (Homewood, Ill.: Richard D. Irwin, 1982), p. 390.

3. Robert W. Haas and Thomas R. Wotruba, *Marketing Management: Concepts, Practice, and Cases,* (Plano, Tex.: Business Publications, 1983), p. 33.

4. Christine Winter, "New Atari Owner Not Playing Games," *Chicago Tribune*, July 8, 1984, Business Section, p. 8.

5. "The Brand Manager: No Longer King," *Business Week*, June 9, 1973, pp. 60–61.

6. "NCR's Radical Shift in Marketing Tactics," *Business Week*, December 8, 1973, p. 102, © 1973 by McGraw-Hill, Inc., New York, N.Y. 10020.

7. Reprinted by permission of the *Harvard Business Review*. Excerpt from "Problems of Matrix Organizations" by Paul R. Lawrence and Stanley M. Davis (May–June 1978). Copyright © 1978 by the President and Fellows of Harvard College; all rights reserved.

8. This section is based on Thomas V. Bonoma, "Making Your Marketing Strategy Work," *Harvard Business Review*, March–April 1984, pp. 69-76.

9. Excerpts from Thomas E. Ricks, "Coca-Cola Celebrates New Success after Restructuring Its Bottlers," *The Wall Street Journal*, June 28, 1984, p. 27. Reprinted by permission of *The Wall Street Journal*, © Dow Jones & Company, Inc., 1984. All rights reserved.

10. Adapted from Dennis Kneale, "Xerox Takes New Marketing Tack to Improve Poor Computer Sales," *The Wall Street Journal*, May 9, 1984, p. 31. Reprinted by permission of *The Wall Street Journal*, © Dow Jones & Company, Inc., 1984. All rights reserved.

CHAPTER 21

Analyzing Marketing Performance

*I*n the United States, coffee has lost considerable ground to soft drinks. A 1985 survey by the International Coffee Organization showed that coffee was no longer Americans' favorite beverage. Further, per capital consumption of coffee had dropped to an all-time low, due partly to health concerns over caffeine and to aggressive marketing by soft-drink companies.[1]

According to one expert, coffee makers were slow to recognize and correct the sagging performance of their industry. The coffee industry has not been known for innovation in products or marketing. At long last, however, coffee makers seem to recognize the seriousness of the situation and are fighting back. New products are being introduced, including flavored coffees, decaffeinated blends, and gourmet coffees. More creative promotion is being used to draw attention to improvements. One campaign is aimed at helping restaurants brew better coffee, while another is focused on college students. As one industry expert put it: "We have to stop thinking of ourselves as just coffee processors and marketers and position ourselves in the 'total beverage' category. If we do our product development right, coffee can compete with other beverages in price and product offerings."[2]

Experience demonstrates vividly that marketing plans do not always work exactly as expected. Sometimes performance will exceed management's expectations, suggesting opportunities for even greater returns. However, as the situation facing the coffee industry illustrates, marketing strategy may not yield the performance anticipated, indicating the existence of problems. How to deal with strategies or tactics that go awry is the task of **marketing control.**

All managers, from the chief executive on down, have responsibility for control. While the control procedure itself varies little from manager to manager, the job position dictates the types of performance controlled, the information used, and the nature of the analyses conducted. Illustrations of control at various levels in retail operations, service organizations, and manufacturers' product and sales departments are discussed in the chapter. How-

Marketing control is concerned with analyzing the performance of marketing decisions, uncovering performance problems or opportunities, and taking actions to resolve the problems or to take advantage of the opportunities.

ever, the essential control activities apply to all marketing positions in all types of organizations.

The Marketing Control Process

Problems or opportunities may become apparent on their own, but when this happens, valuable lead time that could have been spent in implementing solutions is often lost. Even more serious, a performance problem or opportunity may never be uncovered if it is camouflaged by better performance in other areas. A restaurant manager may not realize that desserts are losing money if they are lumped together with complete meals, or even worse, with meals and drinks on which profit is high. Experienced marketing managers establish a formal control procedure to identify problems and opportunities as quickly as possible.

Controlling Activity Centers

Control is equally important to both large and small organizations. A larger organization, however, must cope with the sheer size of operations. In such an organization, one or even a few managers probably cannot plan and control an entire function's activity. Responsibility is therefore delegated to managers of **marketing activity centers.** These centers establish control over designated components of the company's total sales effort. The manager of a marketing activity center may also be responsible for such objectives as market share, profit contribution, or even return on investment. Activity centers can be organized around products or brands, geographic areas, market segments, individual customers, distribution channels, and salespersons.

Marketing activity center is a component of a marketing program assigned to a manager responsible for achieving sales objectives for that component.

The need for marketing activity centers is especially apparent in the management of a large sales force. The sales department for just one division of American Hospital Supply Corporation has hundreds of salespeople spread across the United States. These salespeople sell to the thousands of doctors, hospitals, and other health care facilities that buy the company's products. One way to control this sales force is to organize by geographic area activity centers so that control is parceled out to sales managers, each responsible for a limited portion of the total selling function. The nation is broken down into a few large regions, each of which has a regional sales manager who reports to the national sales manager. Each region is split into several districts, each headed by a district sales manager who reports to the regional manager. Finally, each district is organized into individual sales territories that are assigned to salespeople. The performance of these salespeople is under the control of the district managers.

EXHIBIT 21-1 Control by Managers at Different Organizational Levels

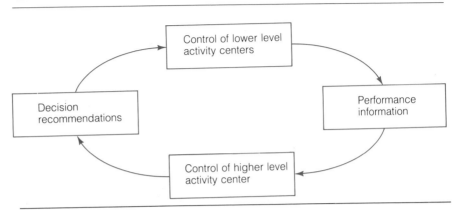

Marketing activity centers are carefully created so that each manager can concentrate on controlling a well-defined portion of company sales. The coordination of marketing activity centers is the responsibility of the manager at the next level in the organizational hierarchy. For this reason, control starts at the bottom and moves up the ladder, with the marketing manager at each higher level overseeing a more aggregate activity center. Information on performance at the lower levels is accumulated for use by a manager at a higher level. In turn, higher-level managers provide control inputs for the management of lower-level activity centers by making recommendations and setting limits. Exhibit 21-1 illustrates these relationships.

The Control Process

Control is a matter of establishing a logical process for monitoring, evaluating, and improving performance in each activity center. This process is highly analytic. Data are regularly collected to monitor a center's performance. Management compare these data with a performance standard to spot unusual performance. Typically, unusual performance signals a problem, but it may also reveal an opportunity. An automobile dealer recognized an opportunity to sell many more conversion vans when customer requests suddenly outstripped current inventory levels.

When a problem or an opportunity has been uncovered, the next step is to learn why it occurred. To correct problems or capitalize on newfound opportunities, managers must determine the reasons for unusual performance. If sales of a new kitchen appliance are low because of higher than normal stockouts, management must try to improve the company's distribution. On the other hand, if sales are low because consumers do not like some of the appliance's features, a different action must be taken.

Monitoring Marketing Performance

To identify problems promptly, an early warning system is needed. Managers must be alerted to a problem far in advance of serious consequences, with sufficient time to make and carry out decisions that will bring performance back into line. An early warning system is also needed to identify and deal with opportunities. Adequate lead time is provided if actual performance is regularly monitored. This means that the monitoring system must be planned in advance. An early warning system begins to take shape when managers specify exactly what kinds of performance to monitor, set standards showing what these kinds of performance should be, and collect data that measure the performance in question.

Specifying Performance and Setting Standards

As part of planning strategy, marketing managers set specific objectives that clearly define the types of performance expected. The most common types of marketing performance objectives are:

- Sales-oriented performance.
- Contribution to profits (or contribution margin).
- Budgeted costs.
- Market support performance.

Sales-Oriented Performance. Sales-oriented performance objectives specify performance in terms of sales volume and market share. Sales volume may be stated in different ways—total sales in units or dollars or total sales less such adjustments as defective products returned to the supplier. Market share may also be stated in different ways. It may be a percentage of an industry's total sales, a percentage of the sales obtained by a group of selected competitors (e.g., the largest competitors in the industry), or a percentage of the total sales in a defined market.[3] The administrators of a county hospital calculated their market share at 70 percent. This was the percentage of patients from the county (a market area) who used the hospital rather than competitive hospitals outside the county within a one-year operating period.

Sales volume and market share are undoubtedly the most common types of marketing performance objectives. The focus of marketing on buyers and markets makes it natural to assign such objectives to marketing managers. Recently however, more firms have been adding other types of objectives to the responsibility of marketing managers.[4]

Contribution to Profits. In the 1980s, responsibility for **profit contribution** has been assigned increasingly to managers of marketing activity centers. Environmental pressures such as economic fluctuations, high interest

---

Profit contribution is the portion of revenue that exceeds the costs directly attributable to a marketing activity center's operations and makes a contribution to the company's unallocatable overhead and profits.

rates, and escalating costs have caused top management to be concerned with coordinating marketing and financial performance. Responsibility for profit contribution requires marketing managers to consider both the costs and the sales directly attributable to a marketing activity center.

Profit contribution objectives are typically added to the marketing manager's responsibility for sales and market share objectives. This addition of a new performance to be controlled can change the way decisions are made, because each standard can lead to very different conclusions about problems—a marketing activity center may be doing well on one kind of performance but not on another. The chef of a New York restaurant reported to management that the breakfast hour was quite strong but that the lunch hour was weak. The chef, however, based this conclusion only on the number of customers served. Management analyzed profit contribution from these two periods and came to the opposite conclusion. While there was less customer traffic during the lunch hour, lunch customers were buying higher-margin menu items than breakfast customers. Considering both customer volume and profit margin per meal, profit contribution was greater for the lunch hour.[5]

A small but growing number of companies have been moving beyond profit contribution to set marketing objectives in terms of financial performance that is even more closely tied to owner equity. These objectives, which are usually applied to higher levels of management, take into consideration discounted cash flows and return on the assets used by a function or department. Such firms as Sears, Borden, and Combustion Engineering actually tie managers' compensation to the achievement of these types of performance.[6] Financial performance objectives consider sales, the costs attributed to marketing activity center, and the assets used by the center, as the following relationship demonstrates:[7]

$$
\begin{aligned}
\text{Return on assets} &= \text{Operating income/Assets} \\
&= \text{Operating income/Sales} \times \text{Sales/Assets} \\
&= \text{Margin} \times \text{Turnover}
\end{aligned}
$$

Notice that in this case management's attention has been shifted to control of both margin and turnover.

Budgeted Costs.   Implementing a marketing plan requires the expending of resources. Budgets are developed to anticipate the amounts needed. At the same time, expected costs for each item in the budget also establish standards for cost performance. Consequently, controlling costs is as important to controlling profit contribution and return on assets as is controlling sales performance. Procter & Gamble's product managers applied this idea as they looked for ways to improve the performance of Pringle's potato chips. Package and distribution changes were made to cut costs for the product in order to help boost profit contribution for a given sales volume. At the same time, product and advertising changes were made to boost sales.

Market support objectives
are those that state what target audiences should be aware of, believe, or feel about the company and its products or services.

Market Support. Finally, marketing managers may be expected to achieve **market support objectives.** Managers of the promotion functions, in particular, are charged with creating impressions of a product or company in the minds of people in target audiences. The advertising communication objectives—awareness, attitude change, purchase intentions, and customer satisfaction—are kinds of market support objectives. Achieving these communication objectives supports a company's sales effort because influencing awareness, attitude change, purchase intentions, and customer satisfaction can bring target audiences closer to purchase.

Data for Monitoring Performance

A second aspect of performance monitoring involves the data used for this purpose. Performance standards dictate the kinds of data that are needed to measure the actual performance of a marketing activity center.

A professional marketing manager must be able to work with different kinds of performance data since diversity of data can be used to measure marketing performance. In general, the objectives that marketing plans set for an activity center will dictate the types of data needed. These objectives must be carefully worded to specify performance that can be controlled. A company must not only be able to measure the performance being controlled but also to do so at a reasonable cost. Two of the most important sources for performance data are a firm's accounting system, and marketing research.

Accounting-Derived Performance Data. Although marketing managers are not accountants, they must understand how to use a company's accounting system. In fact, being able to communicate with accountants may be absolutely necessary to ensure that proper data are provided. Accountants are responsible for reporting on the financial condition of the firm to several external groups, including stockholders, the Securities and Exchange Commission, and the Internal Revenue Service. They are also responsible for providing internal data to managers, but collecting and recording performance data usually requires a different system. Consequently, accountants and marketing managers must be able to work together to determine what kinds of data are needed to monitor performance for control purposes.

Modular accounting system
gathers and stores data for individual activity centers designated by management; sales and costs are assigned to these centers so that reports on the performance of each center can be developed.

A **modular accounting system** is the heart of an effective internal source for sales, cost, and profit contribution performance data.[8] This system stores performance data by activity center so that sales and costs directly attributable to each center can be accumulated. Management can then monitor actual performance for each and every center. The need for such a system is evident in the management of a full-service hospital. The different health care treatment services—critical care, surgery, obstetrics, emergency room, drug dispensation, psychiatry, pathology—call for an organization of activity centers by type of treatment. A modular accounting system helps managers control these centers because it accumulates and stores revenue and cost data by treatment-defined activity centers. Management must designate the activity

EXHIBIT 21–2 Pinpointing Performance Problems of Activity Centers with a Modular Accounting System

Account	Total Hospital ($000)	(A) Psychiatry ($000)	(B) Pathology ($000)	(C) Obstetrics ($000)
Patient receipts	$4,260	$61	$400	$850
Direct expenses:				
Staff salaries	1,270	38	185	420
Supplies	458	12	23	78
Equipment depreciation	587	12	135	200
Profit contribution	1,945	(1)	57	152
General expenses:				
Building depreciation	425			
Administration	278			
Publicity	15			
Utilities	128			
Janitorial services	45			
Market reseach	18			
Food service	428			
Laundry service	98			
Net profit	510			

centers so that accountants can tackle the task of determining which performance data to assign to them. Costs that cannot be directly attributed to a center—general administration, utilities, building depreciation, publicity, and accounting—are recorded separately as unallocated overhead.

Exhibit 21-2 illustrates a hospital's abbreviated income statement, with selected activity centers reporting contribution to overhead and profits. By using a modularized accounting system, administrators can monitor the performance of the activity centers. A single display of data for the entire hospital can hide the high or low performance of particular activity centers. Sorting out performance data by activity center provides a clear picture of where problems and opportunities lie. Note that psychiatry (column A) is performing very poorly compared to the other centers.

A modular accounting system requires deciding which data to assign to each activity center and which data to keep in a general overhead pool. As a general rule, sales and costs that can be traced to each activity center are allocated direclty to the corresponding centers. Cost data not traceable to centers are treated as overhead and kept separate.[9] Similarly, nontraceable revenue remains unallocated. These allocation decisions influence the amount of contribution shown by a center. In the general expenses category, a case might be made for allocating building depreciation, utilities, food service, and laundry service expenses to the different activity centers. If each activity center occupied a definite space in the hospital, with no overlapping use of common spaces, the argument might be sound. Otherwise, the approach taken in Exhibit 21-2 would be more appropriate. The amount of profit contribution for the centers would be greatly affected by the choice made. Accounting can play an important role here by offering recommendations.

Marketing Research Data.   Management may not want to wait for sales or profit contribution data to work its way into and through the accounting system, or data on certain kinds of marketing performance, such as measures describing customers' states of mind—awareness, attitude change, and brand preference—may simply not be available in the accounting system or other internal records. In such situations, marketing research offers an alternative way of generating performance data.

An interesting illustration of the need for marketing research for control concerns customer satisfaction. As a senior consultant for Ernst & Whinney pointed out:

> "Research indicates 96 percent of dissatisfied customers never complain to the company. Instead, 60 to 90 percent of them simply switch stores or brands. Insofar as it costs five times as much to attract a new customer as it does to retain an existing one, it makes sense for a store to try to ensure customer satisfaction."[10]

Only by keeping track of customer satisfaction through marketing research can managers see whether customer dissatisfaction is reaching problem levels. Ernst & Whinney offers an information service based on satisfaction data. It conducts periodic consumer satisfaction studies for Canadian tire dealers, providing them with data on consumer reactions to product quality and availability, customer relations, refund policy, and location. The data alert managers to aspects of the marketing offer that are creating customer dissatisfaction so that corrective action can be taken before the problem becomes too severe.[11]

Comparing Performance to Standards

When monitoring performance data for activity centers, managers must know what to look for. Problems (or opportunities) only become apparent when performance data are compared to some standard. Thus, managers search for performance that is out of line with respect to standards.

Control Requires Standards for Performance

Objectives set targets for actual performance, and targets become standards for control because they state what managers expected performance to be. These standards can be stated in several different ways. In the three statements below, the different forms of the sales objectives provide alternative standards:

■ "Sales are projected to be $3.5 million by the end of the operating year"

■ "Sales are expected to grow by 15 percent over last year's sales"

■ "Sales are expected to grow to a level that will yield a market share of 22 percent"

In the first objective, an absolute number is the standard against which actual performance is measured. This amount may or may not be related to past sales. Absolute number targets can be set for profit contribution, return on assets, or any market support objective. The second objective clearly ties the standard to past performance. This kind of objective is common because managers are oriented toward growth. The third objective sets competitive performance as a standard. No target level of company sales is specified because the sales performance needed to meet the market share objective depends on the sales achieved by competitors.

The standard set for performance influences how comparisons are made. Managers use either or both of two types of comparisons to spot problems:

■ Static comparisons are more likely to be used when an absolute number target has been set.

■ Time-oriented comparisons are more likely to be used when the standard involves growth or when greater understanding of the nature of a problem is sought.

Finding Problems with Static Comparisons

Static control comparisons search for deviations of actual performance from standards set for a designated time period.

A well-stated marketing objective gives the exact time period within which the target performance is to be met. This may be a month, a quarter, a year, or any other period deemed appropriate by management. **Static control comparisons** are made for the designated time period only. Managers examine performance to see whether the standards have been met within that period. The comparison is simple because managers only need to look for deviations between standards and measures of actual performance.

Suppose that product managers for a pharmaceutical company wanted to evaluate performance of its two brands of chewable vitamins.[12] The primary users of chewable vitamins are children, though sales are made to parents. An annual sales objective has been set for each brand. At the end of the year, actual sales are tabulated and reported to management. Exhibit 21–3 shows a static comparison that enables management to look for a performance problem.

Product managers for the chewable vitamin brands can see from the "Difference" column that the Hercules brand more than met its sales objective, while the Batman brand fell far short of its sales objective. Without the expected sales standard, management could not say whether a performance problem existed. The differences between standard and actual performance highlight whether a problem exists.

EXHIBIT 21–3 Static Comparison of Sales Performance for a One-Year Period

Chewable Vitamin Brand	Year Sales ($000)	Expected Sales ($000)	Difference ($000)
Hercules brand	$12,546	$11,765	$ + 781
Batman brand	5,323	5,745	− 422

When the number of activity centers is large, the organization of a report to highlight differences among activity centers helps management quickly find those centers that require further analysis. A regional sales manager who has to evaluate 10 or more districts, each with 5 to 10 sales territories, should be able to find the problem districts and territories by quickly scanning the report. The report's format should make the "exceptional" territories stand out, so that managers will have no trouble spotting them.

Finding Problems with Time-Oriented Comparisons

Time-oriented control comparisons search for deviations of performance from standards set by actual performance achieved in other, usually past, time periods.

Tracking studies measure performance for each of several, usually sequential time periods, so that it can be monitored, or "tracked," from one period to the next.

Management can use **time oriented control comparisons** to learn more about problems by examining performance over several time periods. **Tracking studies** are one approach to finding out what has been happening to performance in the past. Suppose the pharmaceutical company's product manager wanted to see what parts of the year have been best and worst for sales of the Batman brand. Exhibit 21-4 shows results from tracking sales data throughout the year. Expected sales are based on applying seasonal adjustments to yearly sales.

The data suggest that the Batman brand started slowly during the first four months of the year. The next four months showed an improvement, however, coming closer to expected sales, even though performance was still not up to standard. In the last four months of the year, sales actually exceeded the standards set. This pattern suggests that the sales problem was being corrected during the year. Obviously, the situation is of less concern to management than it would have been if the negative sales deviations were increasing during the year.

Tracking studies are very versatile. They can be used with data from an accounting system or from marketing research. Marketing research allows much more flexibility in the categories set up for tracking. Product managers at Miles Laboratories take advantage of this flexibility by employing marketing research to track usage of its chewable vitamins by children in age groups ranging from age 2 to age 12. This enables managers to spot changes in usage patterns among user groups that may indicate potential problems.

Tracking studies can be applied to controlling costs as well as to any of the other performance objectives. They can also be used to track performance for any kind of activity center of interest to management. Miles Laboratories has found that control is enhanced by having product managers track sales of its chewable vitamin brands through major distribution outlets such as food

EXHIBIT 21-4 Tracking Brand Sales over a Year ($ millions)

	Period					
Sales Category	January–February	March–April	May–June	July–August	September–October	November–December
Actual sales	$0.85	$0.86	$0.79	$0.77	$1.03	$0.97
Expected sales	1.05	1.07	.86	.82	1.00	0.94
Difference	(0.20)	(0.21)	(0.07)	(0.05)	0.03	0.03

EXHIBIT 21-5 Market Shares for Brands of Soft Drinks Tracked over Two Periods

Brand	Market Share in Period 1	Market Share in Period 2
Coke	.307	.304
7Up	.172	.177
Tab	.025	.028
Like	.046	.062
Pepsi	.266	.242
Sprite	.070	.092
Diet Pepsi	.043	.038
Fresca	.075	.062

Source: Adapted with permission from Frank M. Bass, "The Theory of Stochastic Preference," *Journal of Marketing Research* 11 (February 1974), p. 17.

stores, drugstores, and mass merchandisers. The reason is that distribution is a key component of the company's marketing mix.

In some product categories, management may want to improve its understanding of the dynamics of brand switching by customers. If there is considerable switching, the problems may not be obvious from simply tracking total sales, market share, or profit contribution. To illustrate this point, consider the data in Exhibit 21-5. What can you conclude about performance of the soft drink brands?

At first glance, the market looks very stable, with few changes in market share for any of the brands. A brand manager noting this pattern might be lulled into thinking that most of the brands have very loyal customers who are very difficult to switch to another brand. As long as market share is not being steadily lost, the manager may become complacent. Further study, however, may indicate a very different picture.

Brand-switching study

measures consumers' actual brand purchases within a product category over several time periods, so that the amount of brand switching can be analyzed.

A **brand-switching study** can be very revealing in this situation. In this type of study, marketing research is used to collect data on the brands purchased by consumers from period to period. A common technique is to ask a sample of consumers to keep a diary of the brands bought each time they make a purchase. Analysis describes the amount and direction of brand switching in the market to gain new insights into performance problems.

Exhibit 21-6 illustrates the way in which data from a brand-switching study can be reported to managers. The data for an industry with three brands—A, B, and C—show the percentages of customers who switched from one brand

EXHIBIT 21–6 Brand-Switching Table

Brand Purchased in Time Period $t+1$

		A	B	C
Purchased in Time Period t	A	Repeat percent	Switching percent	Switching percent
	B	Switching percent	Repeat percent	Switching percent
	C	Switching percent	Switching percent	Repeat percent

to another over two purchase periods (from time t to time t + 1). Reading across the row for brand A, the two horizontal cells show the proportion of consumers who switched from brand A to each of the other two brands between time periods t and t + 1. The brand manager for brand A would like these percentages to be low. Reading down the column for brand A, the two vertical cells show the proportion of consumers who bought a competitor's brand in time t but switched to brand A in time t + 1. These percentages should be high if brand A is performing well. Finally, the diagonal percentages show the proportion of customers who bought the same brand in both periods. A brand manager would want this percentage to be as high as possible for the company's brand.

Exhibit 21-7 presents data from a consumer study showing repeat and switching percentages for eight soft-drink brands. These percentages were derived from the data used to calculate the market shares for the brands in Exhibit 21-5. The percentages add to 100 percent across the rows, meaning that the base numbers are the consumers who bought each soft-drink brand in time t. The switching percentages highlight the fact that the market is much more dynamic than the tracking of market shares suggests.

An experienced marketing manager can gain valuable insights into performance problems from switching data. The brand manager for Pepsi can determine several things about Pepsi's performance. First, whether Pepsi has a performance problem depends on the standards set for marketing strategy. If one of Pepsi's objectives was to become the market leader (have the highest market share), Exhibit 21-5 shows that this objective was not achieved during the periods covered by the study.

Faced with this market share performance problem, the manager next examines the switching data and can conclude:

■ Pepsi is not as good as Coke at retaining its customers from one period to the next (51.5 percent versus 61.2 percent, respectively).

■ Pepsi is losing its customers primarily to Coke (17.7 percent), 7Up (13.2 percent), and Sprite (7.5 percent).

EXHIBIT 21–7 Brand Switching for Eight Soft-Drink Brands

| | Brand Purchased in Time *t* + 1 | | | | | | | |
	Coke	7UP	Tab	Like	Pepsi	Sprite	Diet Pepsi	Fresca
Coke	61.2	10.7	0.9	3.3	13.4	5.5	1.4	3.6
7UP	18.6	44.8	0.6	6.3	14.0	9.9	1.2	4.6
Tab	8.0	12.0	16.0	36.0	8.0	4.0	8.0	8.0
Like	8.7	15.2	8.7	15.2	23.9	4.4	13.0	10.9
Pepsi	17.7	13.2	0.8	3.0	51.5	7.5	2.5	3.8
Sprite	11.4	18.6	2.9	7.1	15.6	32.9	2.9	8.6
Diet Pepsi	9.3	4.7	18.6	9.3	11.6	9.3	25.6	11.6
Fresca	22.7	9.2	5.3	10.7	14.7	10.7	6.7	20.0

(Left axis label: Brand Purchased in Time t*)*

Source: Adapted with permission from Frank M. Bass, "The Theory of Stochastic Preference," *Journal of Marketing Research* 11 (February 1974), p. 17.

■ Pepsi is losing more customers to noncolas (7Up and Sprite) than to Coke, a similar cola.

■ Pepsi is gaining surprisingly similar percentages of the other brands' switching customers.

These observations provide important insights into the nature of Pepsi's performance problems. The data suggest that the market share leadership problem can be broken down into two parts:

■ Pepsi is good at retaining its customers compared to most brands, but not as good as the market leader.

■ Pepsi is being hurt on two competitive fronts—Coke is successful in getting Pepsi customers to switch to its cola, and the popular noncolas are also getting Pepsi customers to switch to them.

Searching for Causes of Problems

The performance control data discussed so far are only useful for discovering performance problems. These data do not explain why the problems occur. Yet, control decisions to be effective should be aimed at correcting causes.

Management's search for the causes of performance problems is dependent on a sound understanding of the major influences on marketing per-

EXHIBIT 21–8 Contribution Margin for Three Channel of Distribution Activity
Centers ($000)

Account	Total	Food Stores	Drugstores	Mass Merchandiser
Gross sales	$5,323	$2,395	$2,236	$692
Allowances	852	335	313	204
Cash discounts	80	36	31	13
Net sales	4,391	2,024	1,892	475
Commission expenses	11	5	4	2
Freight	64	29	27	8
Net revenue	4,316	1,990	1,861	465
Cost of sales	1,597	718	671	208
Gross profit	2,719	1,272	1,190	257
Marketing expense	213	86	80	47
Field sales expense	266	95	89	82
Distribution expense	53	22	21	10
Sales promotion expense	1,490	670	626	194
Contribution margin	697	399	374	(76)

formance. Such problems occur because something unexpected happened to one or more of the influences on performance. Managers typically look for two important kinds of influences: the company's marketing effort in an activity center and external influences (competitive strategies, shifts in the economy, market preference changes, etc.).

Examining Marketing Effort in Activity Centers

Often the search for the causes of a performance problem can benefit from evaluating performance in each activity center in greater depth. Sometimes clues are provided by further pinpointing the source of the problem.[13] Let's return to the pharmaceutical company situation. If the Batman brand sales performance problem were compounded by a lower-than-expected profit contribution, management might want to see whether the problem was equally severe in the three major distribution channels: food stores, drugstores, and mass merchandisers. Exhibit 21–8 presents data that can be used for this purpose. Here, profit contributions are broken down by distribution channel activity centers. (This can be done only if a modularized accounting system is used.)[14]

The contribution margin data show that the mass merchandiser channel is making a negative contribution, whereas the other two channels are performing well. Apparently, the performance problem is centered in distribution through mass merchandiser outlets. Comparison of marketing, field sales, and sales promotion costs shows that a disproportionate amount of effort is going into the mass merchandiser channel.

EXHIBIT 21-9 Performance in the Mass Merchandiser Channel for Chewable Vitamins ($000)

Account	Mass Merchandise Chains			
	K mart	**Target**	**Ardan**	**Sears**
Gross sales	$263.0	$207.6	$173.0	$48.4
Allowances	77.5	61.2	44.9	20.4
Cash discounts	4.9	3.9	2.9	1.3
Net sales	180.6	142.5	125.2	26.7
Commission expense	0.8	0.6	0.4	0.2
Freight expense	3.0	2.4	2.0	0.6
Net revenue	176.8	139.5	122.8	25.9
Cost of sales	79.0	62.4	52.0	14.6
Gross profit	97.8	77.1	70.8	11.3
Marketing expense	17.9	14.1	11.8	3.3
Field sales expense	29.5	23.0	18.0	11.5
Distribution expense	3.8	3.0	2.5	0.7
Sales promotion expense	66.0	54.3	42.7	31.0
Contribution margin	(19.4)	(17.3)	(4.2)	(35.2)

The next logical step might be to analyze contribution margin from the major mass merchandiser chains in order to find out whether the problems are uniform across this channel or are confined to certain mass merchandisers. Exhibit 21-9 illustrates this kind of analysis for four chains. The profit contributions for all four chains are negative, but Sears' negative contribution is much greater than that of the other three chains.

Product managers will now want to see what is happening in the channel. Discussions with field salespeople, managers of mass merchandiser stores, and buyers in central offices of mass merchandisers can reveal possible reasons for the discrepancy. It may be that private-label chewable vitamins are more successful with the mass merchandisers. Or the mass merchandisers may be cutting back on the shelf space devoted to chewable vitamins, making the sales task more competitive.

Searching for External Causes

Management must be alert to possible changes in the external environment that may be causing performance problems. Monitoring competitors' marketing strategies, population changes, customer preferences, economic growth patterns, government regulation, and technological developments keeps management up to date on important environmental influences. Analysis is necessary to discover how environmental shifts are associated with performance problems. Seeing its sales drop over several years a school desk manufacturer used analysis of the environment to discover causes of the problem. Analysis of census data showed declines in the growth of the school-age population coinciding with the sales drops in the manufacturer's market area.

Interviews with school administrators revealed that they were aware of the population trend and were cutting back orders for new desks accordingly.

Another intriguing illustration of the environment's impact on performance problems concerns the situation faced by U.S. hospitals in the 1980s. Since the government began to support elderly hospital patients through Medicare programs, hospitals did not aggressively economize on costs. Payments to hospitals were based on length of stay and extent of treatment. Health care costs under this system exploded as Medicare payments became a very large component of hospitals' total income.

To slow down cost increases, the federal government changed the way in which payments to hospitals were made. Limits were placed on payments for the treatment of specific illnesses, regardless of the cost incurred by a hospital. This cut the flow of income from Medicare patients. In response to these changes, many hospitals have been increasing cost-control efforts with modular accounting systems that track costs directly to patient care. Hospitals have also been reeducating doctors on the way treatments for Medicare patients should be prescribed.[15] Increased control allows hospitals to survive in the new environment.

Sometimes marketing research is necessary to discover the cause of a performance problem, particularly when management suspects that the reasons lie in customers' response to market conditions. Marketing research was helpful to the advertising manager of a major department store in a southeastern city when he discovered that sales of fashion clothing to a market segment were lower than expected. Since the store had a reputation for being a fashion leader in the city, the advertising manager was not sure why these sales were so low. A study was conducted to find out how consumers perceived the store on key criteria used in store selection (merchandise variety, merchandise quality, salesperson friendliness, salesperson helpfulness, convenience of location, etc.). The results showed that customers in the segment of interest believed that the store was not very accessible and that its salespeople were not very helpful in suggesting appropriate styles. This understanding of the causes of the problem enabled the advertising manager to take corrective action.

The Marketing Audit

A company may find that performance problems recur regularly. In fact, trying to deal with such problems bog down managers to the point where they neglect other important responsibilities. This could happen to an entire marketing function of an organization, or it could happen in one department, such as field sales or product management. Determining what causes performance problems to recur may require a **marketing audit.**

Marketing audit is an in-depth assessment of the marketing function (or department).

A marketing audit is essentially an evaluation of where the company's marketing function is at the present time.[16] Such an audit can include analysis of:

- The commitment of top management to the marketing function.
- The external environment faced by marketing.
- The marketing planning approach.
- The organization of the marketing function.
- The contribution of marketing to the company.

This analysis should generate concrete recommendations concerning both the approach to carrying out marketing's responsibilities and strategies for the future. To succeed, a marketing audit must be carefully planned in advance. Major phases of the audit include assigning responsibility for performing the audit, developing a comprehensive program for the audit, investigating and analyzing the findings, and recommending needed changes, including a plan for implementation.

Assigning Responsibility. One of the more difficult tasks is deciding who should conduct the marketing audit. In a small firm, one person may be enough. In larger firms, a team or task force is needed. Several considerations are important in selecting people to perform the audit. The participants must be objective and have knowledge of the areas being studied. They should be experienced in marketing and either have or be able to develop a thorough understanding of the firm's business environment. Management must be willing to accept the auditors' recommendations, so the auditors must have the experience, judgment, and track record necessary to command support for these recommendations. Finally, enough time must be set aside to conduct the audit. Marketing staff must be available and willing to meet with the audit team and to assemble the information it requests.

The audit team may consist of company executives and staff, outside consultants, or a combination of the two. Lack of objectivity is often cited as a limitation of company personnel, whereas a drawback of consultants is that they may not be familiar with the particular business environment. A combination of company people and outside consultants is often the best approach in larger firms, if the necessary time and resources are available. In smaller firms, an experienced consultant can be effective working alone or with a small team of outside experts, provided that management can supply information and analysis when needed.

Designing the Audit Program. The auditing team should prepare a detailed outline showing what is to be studied, the responsibilities of the team members, a time schedule, a list of the information to be assembled, and the procedures to be used. An audit requires considerable information, including financial statements, product descriptions, corporate and marketing plans, market opportunity analyses, attitudes and opinions of managers, and analyses of activity center performance. Exhibit 21-10 is a checklist for planning the coverage of a marketing audit. Much of the information needed is available in company records, but some will have to come from extensive interviews with company personnel.

EXHIBIT 21–10 Checklist for Coverage of a Marketing Audit

I.   Mission
   A. Does the mission statement offer a clear guide to the product-markets of interest to the firm?
   B. Have objectives been established for the corporation as a whole and for marketing?
   C. Is information available for the review of corporate progress toward objectives, and are the reviews conducted on a regular (quarterly, monthly, etc.) basis?
   D. Has corporate strategy been successful in meeting objectives?
   E. Are opportunities or problems pending that may require altering marketing strategy?
II. Marketing strategy
   A. Situation analysis
      1. Is marketing's role and responsibility in corporate strategy clearly specified?
      2. Are responsibility and authority for marketing strategy assigned to one executive?
      3. How well is the firm's marketing strategy working? Do problems exist?
      4. Are changes likely to occur in the marketing environment that may affect the firm's marketing strategy?
   B. Marketing plan and organization
      1. Were annual and longer-range marketing plans developed, and are they being used?
      2. Are the responsibilities of the various units in the marketing organization clearly specified?
      3. What are the strengths and limitations of the key members of the marketing organization? What is being done to develop people?
      4. Is the organizational structure for marketing appropriate for implementing marketing plans?
   C. Market targets
      1. Has each market target been clearly defined and its importance to the firm established?
      2. Have demand, industry, and competition in each market target been analyzed, and have key trends, opportunities, and threats been identified?
      3. Has the proper market target strategy (mass, grouping, or segmentation) been adopted?
      4. Should repositioning in or exit from any product-market be considered?
   D. Objectives
      1. Have objectives been established for each market target and are these consistent with corporate objectives and the available resources? Are the objectives realistic?
      2. Are sales, cost, and other information available for monitoring the progress of planned performance against actual results?
      3. Are regular appraisals made of marketing performance?
      4. Where do gaps exist between planned and actual results? What are the probable causes of the performance gaps?
   E. Marketing program
      1. Does the firm have an integrated marketing program made up of product, channel, price, advertising, and sales force strategies? Is the role selected for each mix element consistent with the overall program objectives, and does it properly complement the roles of other mix elements?
      2. Are adequate resources available to carry out the marketing program? Are resources committed to target markets according to the importance of each?
      3. Are allocations to the various marketing mix areas too low, too high, or about right in terms of what each is expected to accomplish?
      4. Is the effectiveness of the marketing program appraised on a regular basis?

Analysis of Findings. Analyzing the information collected by a marketing audit is a painstaking task. Not only is there a large volume of information to digest, but the analysis must delve into rather diverse issues. Generally, auditors use the information collected to address four major questions:

- Does marketing have the commitment of top management to accomplish its purpose?

- Is marketing properly organized to achieve coordination between departments, and are the departments staffed by personnel with the skills necessary to carry out its purpose?

EXHIBIT 21–10 *(concluded)*

III. Marketing program activities
  A. Product
    1. Is the product mix geared to the needs that the firm wants to meet in each product-market?
    2. Does the firm have a sound approach to product planning, and is marketing involved in product decisions?
    3. Are additions to, modifications of, or deletions from the product mix needed to make the firm more competitive in the marketplace?
    4. Is the performance of each product evaluated on a regular basis?
  B. Channels of distribution
    1. Has the firm selected the type and intensity of distribution appropriate for each of its product-markets?
    2. How well does each channel reach its market target?
    3. Are channel intermediaries carrying out their assigned functions properly?
    4. Is the physical distribution function being managed as an integrated set of activities?
    5. Are desired customer service levels being reached, and are the costs of doing this acceptable?
  C. Pricing
    1. How responsive is each market target to price variations?
    2. What role and objectives does price have in the marketing mix?
    3. How do the firm's pricing strategy and tactics compare to those of competition?
    4. Is a systematic approach used to establish prices?
    5. Are there indications that changes may be needed in pricing strategy or tactics?
  D. Advertising and sales promotion
    1. Have a role and objectives been established for advertising and sales promotion in the marketing mix?
    2. Is the budget adequate to carry out the objectives assigned to advertising and sales promotion?
    3. Do the media used represent the most cost-effective means of communicating with market targets?
    4. Do advertising copy and content effectively communicate the intended messages?
    5. How well does the advertising program measure up in meeting its objectives?
  E. Sales force
    1. Are the role and objectives of personal selling in the marketing mix clearly specified and understood by the sales organization?
    2. Do the qualifications of salespeople correspond to their assigned role?
    3. Is the sales force of the proper size to carry out its function, and is it efficiently deployed?
    4. Are sales force results in line with management's expectations?
    5. Is each salesperson assigned performance targets, and are incentives offered to reward performance?
    6. Are compensation levels and ranges competitive?
IV. Implementation and control
  A. Have the causes of all performance gaps been identified?
  B. Is implementation of planned actions taking place as intended? Is implementation being hampered by other functional areas of the firm (e.g., manufacturing, finance)?
  C. Does the marketing plan require modification due to changing conditions, experience, or other factors?
  D. Has the audit revealed areas requiring additional study before action is taken?

■ Are proper procedures being used for marketing planning, plan implementation, and control?

■ Do marketing plans properly recognize the existing environmental constraints and opportunities?

Answering these questions takes time. Depending on the size and complexity of the firm's operations, the size of the audit team, and the time required to obtain and analyze information, an audit may take from a few weeks to several months. Because the answers to these questions are so important to the future direction taken by the company's marketing function, top management must be willing to commit the time and resources needed to do the job thoroughly.

Implementing Recommendations.   The marketing audit can contribute major improvements in marketing operations, provide guidelines for strategy modifications, uncover new opportunities, and highlight product-markets that have been neglected. To obtain these benefits, a plan must be developed for implementing the recommendations of the marketing audit. Far too often, however, management gives inadequate attention to implementation.

The chief executive officer of a small manufacturer of electrical components initiated a marketing audit because sales had leveled off and profits had declined. He believed that new markets were needed to turn performance around. The audit uncovered problems in trying to serve too many product-markets, unusually high manufacturing costs, and lack of internal coordination of marketing, engineering, and manufacturing. Recommendations were developed from the audit findings and placed in immediate, short-term, and long-term action categories. Follow-up a year later indicated that a few of the immediate actions recommended had been carried out but that no action had been taken on the other recommendations of the audit and no plans had been developed to act on them.

The chief executive officer was in full agreement with the audit recommendations. Due to demands on his time, however, he was unable to develop and implement an action plan. The audit fell far short of its potential impact on the firm's performance because several key recommendations were not implemented. For best results, an audit plan should assign responsibility, schedule actions, and provide follow-up guidelines.

Action to Correct Problems

Proper control includes the actions needed to correct problems. Management must see that performance is brought back in line with standards. Of course, the actions taken depend on the causes uncovered in the previous step in the process.

Sometimes doing anything about the causes of performance problems is beyond management's ability. In this situation, management may have to reset standards at a more realistic level. The impact of government changes in Medicare reimbursement procedures is an illustration. Administrators in many hospitals must readjust revenue objectives downward so that these objectives will be more in line with what can now be expected from Medicare payments. Changing objectives is one way to increase the likelihood that performance will match standards.

However, management seldom simply adjusts objectives in response to environmental changes. Instead, lowered performance standards in one activity center are usually coupled with marketing strategy decisions that raise performance standards in other centers. This kind of action was taken by Saga Corporation, the leading operator of college dining halls, when it found that the number of people of college age in the U.S. population was declining. More realistic sales growth objectives were necessary. At the same time, management steered the company into markets with more attractive growth opportunities by acquiring several restaurant chains, including Black Angus, Spoons, and Grandys.[17]

In cases where the causes of problems can be corrected, improving marketing performance becomes the focus. A county hospital, for instance, found that a key cause of poor market share performance was the belief of county citizens that the hospital was insufficiently skillful in dealing with difficult illnesses that required specialist treatment (e.g., cancer, heart disease). Patients with such illnesses were going to doctors and hospitals in a nearby city. The hospital developed a marketing strategy aimed at correcting this attitudinal problem. Several coordinated actions were taken to build the hospital's reputation for quality care:

■ Publicity was used to highlight the educational background and experience of doctors affiliated with the hospital.

■ Publicity was used to show the hospital's technical capabilities for dealing with illnesses requiring specialist treatment.

■ New equipment and staff were acquired to build specialist capability in an area of treatment not emphasized by competing hospitals.

■ Hospital administrators and staff were encouraged to give talks to community groups discussing the progress that the medical profession in general and the hospital in particular were making in the treatment of diseases that were difficult to cure.

Corrective marketing actions are being increasingly directed toward controlling costs as well as toward improving sales. As more concern is placed on marketing's profit contribution and its return on assets, marketing managers must look for ways to improve cost efficiency. Typically, cost-related actions are tied to revenue-generating actions. Cost control may result in more efficient ways of performing activities. But effective use of assets also requires looking for the best allocation of resources to support revenue-producing activities.

Consider the complexity of managing a large university. Faced with decreases in the high school–age portion of the U.S. population, universities are developing strategies to compete for students. Budgets have been pared to slow cost increases, and university administrators are allocating available monies into educational programs and recruiting activities that offer the greatest opportunities for revenue. Even the largest universities are looking for their market niches and then allocating funds where the payoff is highest.[18]

Summary

Analyzing marketing performance is part of a continuing process of developing plans for marketing activity centers, implementing those plans, controlling performance, and adjusting plans when performance gets out of line. A marketing control system must be planned and must be integrated into marketing operations. At the heart of effective control is the collection and use of information. Management must identify the types of information needed. Information can help in two ways. First, information is needed to monitor the performance of activity centers. Clearly stated objectives provide performance standards. Actual performance is then compared with the standards. Second, information is needed to identify the causes of performance problems. Sometimes analysis of existing information is sufficient for this purpose. But in some situations, marketing research must be conducted to identify such causes.

Regular control of activity center performance accounts for the bulk of the control process. However, management should conduct periodic marketing audits to assess the entire marketing operation. The results may indicate that the operation is working well, or they may lead to recommendations for reshaping marketing organization, staffing, or strategy.

Control relies heavily on management's judgment and experience. Effective managers are often able to sense when performance is out of line even before the results of formal monitoring are available. Because lead time for taking corrective action is needed to prevent problems from getting out of control, managers must be skillful at following up on any indications that problems are arising. Again, the key is to find causes so that proper action can be taken to deal with those problems.

Exercises for Review and Discussion

1. Owners of the Rock-A-Bye day-care center wanted to set up a process to help them control the center's performance. Recently, a consultant helped them design a marketing planning process that they are now following annually. In what ways should the control process be coordinated with the planning process? In what ways is the control process different from the planning process.

2. In a conversation with the regional sales manager, a salesperson was told that "good managers expect problems with performance to arise and are prepared to see them." Do you agree with the sales manager's statement? Discuss your reasons.

3. John Harvins started a marketing research firm. Within five years, the business had grown to over $2 million in revenue. Its customers typically fell into three categories: (1) those that purchased a standard kind of research that the company performed on a regular basis, (2) those that wanted consulting help with marketing planning, and (3) those that wanted special marketing research tailored to their needs. Harvins operated the business from a central office in Nashville, Tennessee, though customers were increasingly coming from other cities. Recently, Harvins concluded that he was no longer able to control the performance of the business and needed to parcel out responsibility to other managers. How can the activity center concept help him organize for more effective performance control? Discuss your answer.

4. Control requires comparing performance with standards. What kinds of standards do marketing managers use when monitoring perform-

ance and looking for problems? Discuss your answer.

5. Suppose that a company is currently manufacturing three products: product A, product B, and product C. The company is considering dropping product A from the product line. The information In Exhibit 21-A has been gathered for management.

EXHIBIT 21-A

	Product A	Product B	Product C	Total
Sales	$100,000	$80,000	$10,000	$190,000
Variable costs	80,000	56,000	6,000	142,000
Fixed costs:				
Direct	15,000	10,000	1,500	26,500
Allocated indirect	6,000	10,000	2,000	18,000

The direct fixed costs for a product can be eliminated by dropping that product. The allocated indirect fixed costs will continue regardless of whether the product is dropped. Based only on the information in Exhibit 21-A, what products (if any) should be dropped? What

factors other than sales and costs should be considered when deciding whether to drop a product from the line?

6. Using the information given in Exercise 5, suppose that product A and B are two substitute products and that if the company drops product A, the sales of product B will increase by 10 percent. Should product A be dropped?

7. Suppose that the idle facilities made available by dropping product A could be used to produce product D. The following are estimates of the sales and costs of product D:

Sales	$50,000
Variable costs	35,000
Direct fixed costs	7,000

Should the company drop product A and add product D? Discuss your answer.

8. Suppose that you have been appointed marketing vice president for a bank with assets approaching $1 billion. The bank services a metropolitan area through several branch offices. No one has held this position before, and top management does not understand the marketing management function. Develop a plan showing how you will handle your new responsibilities.

Notes

1. Information for the coffee illustration came from Trish Hall, "While Coffee Makers Fight Loss of Younger Drinkers," *The Wall Street Journal*, March 19, 1986, sec. 2, p. 33.

2. Ibid.

3. Bernard Catry and Michel Chevalier, "Market Share Strategy and the Product Life Cycle," *Journal of Marketing* 38 (October 1974), pp. 29-30.

4. Frederick E. Webster, Jr., James A. Largay III, and Clyde P. Stickney, "The Impact of Inflation Accounting on Marketing Decisions," *Journal of Marketing* 44 (Fall 1980), pp. 13-14.

5. Peter Nulty, "How Personal Computers Change Manager's Lives," *Fortune*, September 3, 1984, p. 40.

6. "Rewarding Executives for Taking the Long View," *Business Week*, April 2, 1984, p. 99.

7. Webster, Largay, and Stickney, "The Impact of Inflation," p. 14.

8. For a very good discussion of accounting data for control applications, see Patrick M. Dunne and Harry I. Wolk, "Marketing Cost Analysis: A Modularized Contribution Approach," *Journal of Marketing* 41 (July 1977), pp. 83-94.

9. For more discussion of the allocation issue, see Jimmy D. Barnes and Douglas V. Leister, "Profitability Accounting: Implications for Marketing Management," in *1979 AMA Proceedings*, ed. Neil Beckwith, Michael Houston, Robert Mittelstaedt, Kent B.

Monroe, and Scott Ward (Chicago: American Marketing Association, 1979), pp. 562–66; and Dunne and Wolk, "Marketing Cost Analysis."

10. Dale R. Harley, "Customer Satisfaction Tracking Improves Sales, Productivity, Morale of Retail Chains," *Marketing News*, June 22, 1984, p. 15.

11. Ibid.

12. The chewable vitamins examples throughout the chapter benefited greatly from an unpublished Miles Laboratories 1984 business plan and a supporting fact book. The exhibits using chewable vitamin data have been disguised for proprietary reasons. However, the illustrations are representative of the company's actual practice.

13. Barnes and Leister, "Profitability Accounting."

14. The data in Exhibit 21–8 (and Exhibit 21–9) generally follow a financial report format used by Miles Laboratories' product managers.

15. This illustration is based on information in "The Medicare Squeeze Pushes Hospitals into the Information Age," *Business Week*, June 18, 1984, pp. 87, 90.

16. Hal W. Goetsch, "Conduct a Comprehensive Marketing Audit to Improve Marketing Planning," *Marketing News*, March 18, 1983, sec. 2, p. 14.

17. Kenneth Labich, "The Dean of College Cuisine Smartens Up," *Fortune*, August 6, 1984, p. 28.

18. "How Academia Is Taking a Lesson from Business," *Business Week*, August 27, 1984, pp. 58–60.

CHAPTER 22

Marketing Research and Information Systems

*P*illsbury used marketing research in the planning and market introduction of Totino's Crisp Crust Frozen Pizza.[1] The planning for this new product was guided by information obtained from interviews with small groups of consumers in several cities to find out what people did not like about frozen pizza. The response from these interviews and other marketing research studies clearly indicated that the taste of the crust was a serious problem. Improving the crust could give Pillsbury an important advantage over competing brands. After several months of development, a new method of frying the crust was perfected. Consumer taste tests of the new crust were very favorable. Pillsbury's management decided to introduce the product. The advertising campaign emphasized that the crust did not taste like cardboard. Totino's new Crisp Crust Frozen Pizza moved the brand from an 18 percent market share to an impressive 30 percent share.

Because of the high costs of launching a product in the marketplace, more and more firms are turning to marketing research to help screen out unpromising product ideas and to guide the development and marketing of products that show signs of being successful.

Marketing research can contribute to all phases of marketing management planning, implementation, and control. Information from marketing research is used to identify market opportunities, design advertising campaigns, evaluate distributors, improve products, and for a host of other applications. Firms may conduct their own marketing research or contract with research suppliers to collect and analyze information needed in various activities.

This chapter discusses and illustrates alternative strategies for obtaining information. Techniques for estimating the costs and benefits of needed information are presented. The major steps in designing a marketing research study are examined, and the issues that are important in evaluating and selecting a research supplier are considered. Finally, several key aspects of building a marketing information and decision support system are identified.

Strategies for Obtaining Information

A marketing manager can draw from many sources of information that vary as to their availability, cost, and usefulness and as to the time needed to obtain the information they provide. Several strategies can be used to obtain information, as shown in Exhibit 22-1. Often a combination of two or more strategies is used.

Deciding What Information Is Needed

Specifying the information needed in the starting point in marketing research. The first step in such specification is to clearly define the situation in which the information will be used. A marketing manager concerned because the sales of her firm's major product line (portable power tools for home and professional use) have declined steadily for the past six months identified the following possible causes:

■ Environmental changes—economic conditions, technological advances, and governmental requirements that might cause a decline in buyer preferences for the product.

■ Alterations in the marketing strategies of competitors—the introduction of an improved product, price reduction, and increased advertising.

■ Weaknesses in the firm's marketing strategy—target markets, objectives, product, price, advertising, sales force, and distribution.

Obtaining information in all of these areas would be prohibitive in terms of time and cost. Consequently, the marketing manager must identify the most probable causes of the sales decline and the information needed to investigate them. Trade source information and market and competitive intelligence from the sales force have helped eliminate the first two possible causes, leaving as the probable cause of the sales drop a weakness in her firm's marketing strategy.

She is now in a position to identify the aspects of her marketing strategy that may be responsible for the problem. A review of customer sales (available through computer analysis on a monthly and year-to-date basis) over the past six months compared to the same period in the previous year reveals that the company's sales to dealers who sell to professional users of power tools have fallen off, thus suggesting a shift in preferences or an overall decline in purchases by this target market. But trade association reports indicate no overall reduction in power tool purchases by professionals. She recalls that several complaints have been received from the field concerning delays in service (by either the factory or the dealer, depending on the service that is required) and that there have been some unusually long delays in shipping tools to dealers.

EXHIBIT 22–1 Strategies for Obtaining Information

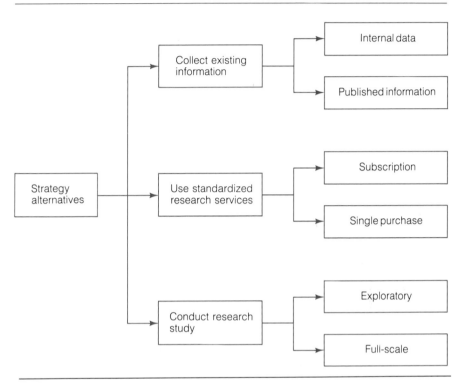

The marketing manager is reasonably certain that the quality and performance of her products compare very favorably with those of her competition based on regular factory tests of competitive tools. She is confident that her pricing structure is competitive and that her advertising program is sound. Thus, the most likely cause of the problem in the professional market for power tools is inadequate servicing and distribution of the firm's products. These factors could be of major significance to professionals, causing them to purchase competitive products.

After consultation with the marketing staff, the marketing manager has identified these information needs:

- Attitudes and preferences of professionals toward the firm's products.
- Brand preferences of professionals who use the tools.
- Factors most important to purchasers of power tools.
- Types and frequency of service problems.
- Needed improvements in service operations.
- Service practices of competitors.

EXHIBIT 22–2 Internal Information on Analysis of Passbook Savings Accounts for XYZ Bank

Passbook Balance	Percent of Total Accounts	Total Amount ($000)	Percent of Deposits
Below $100	40%	$ 200	1%
$100 to $999	31	2,450	9
$1,000 to $9,999	26	13,900	51
$10,000 to $19,999	2	5,450	20
$20,000 and above	1	5,450	20
Total	100%	$27,450	100%

- Possible product improvements that would reduce service problems.
- Reasons for increased delivery time.
- Particular products involved in slow delivery.
- Distributors' opinions concerning service and delivery.

The relative importance of these needs must be established to guide cost-benefit analysis and planning.

Collect Existing Information

Managers frequently use internal information such as sales and cost studies, financial reports, product profitability analyses, and other data furnished by the firm's information system.

As an example of internal information, an analysis of passbook savings accounts for XYZ Bank is shown in Exhibit 22-2. It highlights an important finding that should be examined in greater depth by management. Nearly half (40 percent) of all depositors account for less than 1 percent of all deposits. Serving this large group of customers is clearly unprofitable for the bank unless they have other accounts that are profitable for the bank. Further management study of this possible problem is needed to fully evaluate the situation.

Using existing information is often a useful starting point in meeting a particular information need. It is important to take advantage of this relatively inexpensive source. In fact, in some instances existing information may satisfy all of management's information needs.

Several external sources can be useful in particular instances. Information from these sources can be obtained in a short time, and it is often inexpensive (Exhibit 22-3). Such information is called *secondary data* because it is not prepared for one primary user. Examples include U.S. census data; publications of federal, state, and local government agencies; and industry and trade association reports. Information of this kind can be compiled to aid a decision maker.

Many secondary data reports are based on field studies conducted to serve a variety of users. Because of the multipurpose nature of secondary data,

EXHIBIT 22-3

The Beef Industry Council is using published nutrition research information to communicate Meat Nutri-Facts and to encourage consumers to fit beef into a balanced diet.

Courtesy Beef Industry Council.

such information may not correspond to a company's needs. The manager must evaluate published data as to purpose, scope, and usefulness for a particular problem. Thus, caution is necessary in using published information, since it may not deal directly with the manager's problem. It may also be inaccurate, incomplete, and out of date. Nevertheless, used carefully, secondary data represent an important information resource for many firms.

Use Standardized Research Services

Management may find one or more standardized information services useful in meeting information needs.

Information may be collected and prepared by commercial research organizations for sale to several users. Some services supply information on a subscription basis; others supply it as the need arises. The costs for these services range from less than $1,000 to $50,000 or more. Since the expenses of information collection and analysis are spread over many users, this information is typically less expensive than it would be if a company did the research itself. Examples of standardized services for industry information are:

- Dun & Bradstreet "Market Identifiers"
- Economic Information Systems Annual Purchase Data
- Predicasts Industry Studies
- Frost and Sullivan Industry Studies

The following services supply distribution information:

- Nielsen Retail Index
- Audits and Surveys National Total-Market Index
- Selling Areas-Marketing, Inc.

The following services supply consumer information:

- National Purchase Diary Panel
- Nielsen Television Index
- Starch Advertisement Readership Service
- Simmons Media/Marketing Service
- National Family Opinion

A brief look at one popular standardized information service in the food and drug industry will illustrate the nature of the information provided. The A. C. Nielsen Company is the largest marketing research firm in the world, operating in 25 countries. One of its major services is the Nielsen Retail Index System. This service consists of regular audits of a sample of food stores, drugstores, and mass merchandisers. Field representatives annually conduct over 76,000 audits in over 11,350 retail outlets. The audit consists of inventories and purchases, as well as observations made by Nielsen's representatives. Using this extensive base of information, various standard and custom reports are generated. An illustration of the information provided by the Nielsen Retail Index System is shown in Exhibit 22–4.

Conduct Research Study

When information cannot be obtained from internal records, external publications, or standardized sources, the marketing manager may decide to

EXHIBIT 22-4 Nielsen Food and Drug Retail Index System

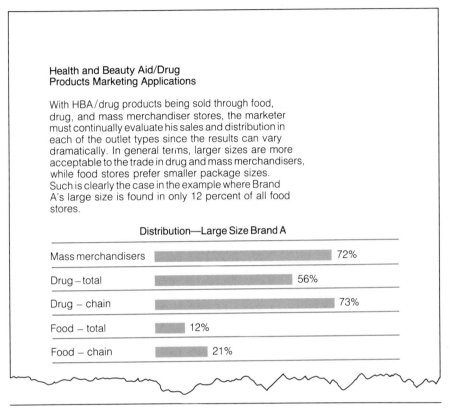

Health and Beauty Aid/Drug
Products Marketing Applications

With HBA/drug products being sold through food,
drug, and mass merchandiser stores, the marketer
must continually evaluate his sales and distribution in
each of the outlet types since the results can vary
dramatically. In general terms, larger sizes are more
acceptable to the trade in drug and mass merchandisers,
while food stores prefer smaller package sizes.
Such is clearly the case in the example where Brand
A's large size is found in only 12 percent of all food
stores.

Distribution—Large Size Brand A

Mass merchandisers	72%
Drug – total	56%
Drug – chain	73%
Food – total	12%
Food – chain	21%

Source: A.C. Nielsen Company.

Marketing research
is a step-by-step
process of planning for,
acquiring, analyzing,
and interpreting infor-
mation relevant to a
marketing decision-
making situation.

conduct a **marketing research** study. This is normally the most costly
method of securing information, but it can generate information that is
geared specifically to the needs of the decision maker. The costs range from a
few thousand dollars to many, many thousands, depending on the scope of
the study, the method of data collection used, and the information required.

A marketing research study may be either exploratory or full-scale; in some
instances, both types of studies are used.

In one exploratory study, a member of an appliance manufacturer's marketing staff collected and analyzed published information on the microwave
oven market and obtained information from discussions with knowledgeable
individuals. This investigation, conducted over a two-week period, generated
guidelines and recommendations for a more extensive, formal study of the
market. Such exploratory studies are important; they may provide adequate
information on a decision situation, or they may greatly facilitate the design
of formal research studies.

In a full-scale research study, established marketing research procedures should be used. The study may be carried out by a firm's marketing research staff or purchased from a marketing research firm. Some firms must rely on outside suppliers of research services. Even firms with the internal capability to conduct marketing research may choose to contract for certain phases of a project (such as interviewing). In weighing the make or buy decision, such factors as internal know-how and experience, costs, and the required completion time should be considered.

An illustration will demonstrate the nature and scope of a research study. The marketing vice president of a large savings and loan association developed a new type of savings account that he believed would attract a substantial amount of new savings with limited cannibalization of existing accounts. He needed support for this assumption, since marketing and operating the savings plan would involve a large expenditure. A marketing research firm was retained to plan and conduct a research study to obtain the information that the vice president needed to decide whether to recommend that the association offer the plan. Completion of the study required 45 days. A three-page questionnaire was administered by telephone to a randomly selected sample of 700 people (400 customers and 300 others). Each phone interview required 15 to 20 minutes. The 40-page final report included the background and objectives of the study, the methodology, and a summary and discussion of the findings. Interestingly, the vice president used the results of the field research to support a recommendation to top management that the new savings account *not* be offered.

Evaluating Costs and Benefits of Alternative Information Strategies

How much should be spent on additional information and what its probable contribution will be should be estimated early in the information strategy selection process. Information costs money and should contribute benefits. Yet it does not generate sales or profits. Rather, the potential contribution of information is to reduce uncertainty, enabling the marketing manager to make a better decision.

Although new information cannot guarantee improved results, any decision situation should include an assessment of its potential benefits. In some cases, information will not be worth the cost of obtaining it—additional information will not change the alternative most favored. In other cases, the benefits of information can be estimated from past experience in working with similar decision situations. Firms that have conducted advertising recall tests for several years have a useful base of experience concerning the costs and benefits of these tests. Firms with well-developed marketing information functions have accumulated a wide range of information on both costs and benefits.

Coping with Uncertain Benefits

Where a clear need for additional information is coupled with uncertainty on the probable benefits, two or more stages can be scheduled. The first stage consists of a preliminary investigation to better define the problem. An expenditure is chosen that falls within budgetary constraints and is acceptable to the decision maker. Then, depending on the information obtained in the first stage, more precise estimates of costs and benefits for subsequent stages can be made.

In some situations, the benefits may be apparent and the costs low compared to the significance of the decision. Companies know the appropriate costs of conducting a test market for a new product and have experience in evaluating the important factors in deciding whether to do so. In such situations, the information decision can be based on prior experience.

Decision Models

An increasing number of managers in firms such as Pillsbury, Du Pont, and General Foods use decision models to help them estimate the potential benefits of information in a decision situation. A decision model such as the payoff matrix or the decision tree can be used if the decision maker can specify:

- The alternatives in the decision situation.
- The possible outcomes for each alternative.
- The likelihood (or probability) of occurrence of each outcome.
- The payoffs (expected decision results) for each outcome.

In one use of decision models, value is estimated for the gap between present information and the complete elimination of uncertainty. In this approach, based on Bayesian decision theory, the decision maker's estimates of the probability of outcomes of future events are essential to the analysis. The approach consists of these stages:

1. Analyzing the decision situation using existing knowledge.

2. Extending the analysis by assuming that the decision maker knows what will occur in the future (a type of "what if" analysis) to estimate the maximum impact that new information will have on the decision situation.

3. Examining alternative methods of obtaining additional information to determine which method offers the most favorable cost-benefit contribution.[2]

This approach to information analysis begins with the decision maker's estimates of the probability of occurrence of future events that will affect the attractiveness of decision alternatives. For a decision on three alternative prices for a new product, the marketing manager estimates the probability of high, medium, and low future sales. The most favorable price alternative is determined by using a payoff table with net profits estimated for each sales outcome and then calculating the expected value of each alternative. In stage 2, the expected value of perfect information is calculated by selecting the most favorable payoff of all alternatives for each future sales outcome. This analysis provides an estimate of how much the payoff will be increased if the decision maker knows what sales outcome will occur before choosing an alternative. The payoff improvement is an estimate of the maximum value that additional information will contribute. Alternative information strategies (stage 3) can be evaluated in terms of their costs and their contribution to improving the accuracy of the decision maker's initial probability estimates of future sales. A study of consumer reaction to the proposed price alternatives is one way to obtain the additional information needed.[3]

Designing the Research Study

When existing information or standardized information services do not satisfy management's information needs, a decision may be made to conduct a research study. The major steps in planning and conducting a marketing research study are:

- Problem formulation
- Research design
- Data collection methods/forms
- Sampling design
- Data collection
- Analysis and results

Problem Formulation

The problem formulation stage consists of two major activities: clearly defining the problem situation for which the research study is being conducted and indicating the information needs that are to be satisfied by the research study.

One of the more valuable roles marketing research can perform is helping to define the problem to be solved. Only when the problem is carefully and precisely defined can research be designed to provide pertinent information. Part of the process of problem definition includes specifying the objectives of the specific research project or projects that might be undertaken. Each project should have one or more objectives, and the next step in the process should not be taken until these can be explicitly stated.[4]

Research Design

There are two primary alternatives in designing the research study. One is to collect data at a particular point in time. This is called a *cross-sectional study*. The survey of beer drinkers is an example of a cross-sectional study (Exhibit 22-5). The second alternative is to collect data from the same respondents (or different matched respondents) at two or more points in time. This is called a *longitudinal or panel* study. The marketing research firm Information Resources, Inc. has a panel of 2,500 households in each of several markets. The panel supplies longitudinal data for the firm's custom research studies and standardized information services for food and drug products.

There are three types of marketing research studies: exploratory, descriptive, and causal. Exploratory studies are used to help define research problems, typically using existing information. Descriptive studies are more extensive in scope. In such studies, information is collected from a representative sample of respondents and the information collected is analyzed by means of tables and statistical techniques, such as regression analysis. An example of a descriptive study is a demographic profile of heavy and light users of a brand. Descriptive studies do not measure cause and effect. If management is interested in determining the effect (amount of purchases, attitude change, etc.) of advertising on a target audience, the research design must incorporate features that will allow the researcher to measure the cause and effect of such marketing variables as advertising and price.

Information Resources, Inc.'s BehaviorScan studies provide cause-and-effect information for selected marketing research situations (Exhibit 22-6).[5] In each of several metropolitan markets, 2,500 households carry special ID cards and are individually tracked by checkout scanners in grocery stores and drugstores. The purchases of these households are electronically recorded. Marketing plans can be tested at both the consumer and store level. The effects of test commercials can be measured using computer-selected household test groups and controlled advertising exposure via cable television. Such marketing variables as shelf configuration, price, and promotions (displays, coupons, and newspaper ads) can also be evaluated. Data are collected for all brands to measure competitive activity. BehaviorScan studies cost up to 50 percent less than conventional test marketing.

Outside of a laboratory setting, measuring cause and effect is expensive and difficult. Consequently, marketing research studies are typically exploratory or descriptive.

Data Collection Methods

Information can be collected in two ways: by asking *questions* of respondents and by *observing* people or things (e.g., store inventory levels).

While questions are the primary means of obtaining information, there are

EXHIBIT 22-5 Results of Research Study on Beer Marketing

In December,[*Advertising Age*] asked R.H. Bruskin Associates, New Brunswick, N.J., to survey beer drinkers across the country about their favorite brand of beer. In addition, consumers were queried about their main reasons for preferring one brand over another, as well as their knowledge of advertising slogans.

Using the weekly OmniTel service of Bruskin Associates, a nationally representative sample of 1,000 adults was contacted, allowing for equal representation of men and women. Fifty-nine percent of men 18 years of age or older said they drank beer, either at home or away from home within the past month. The incidence of beer consumption among women was about half the level reported for men. An equal proportion (44 percent) of men and women drank wine (44 percent).

**Selected alcoholic beverages
drank in the past month**

	Total Sample	Men	Women
Beer	43%	59%	29%
Wine	44	44	44
Vodka	17	19	16
Scotch	9	14	5

To achieve a reliable estimate of beer usage among the general population, several alcoholic beverages were included in the preliminary questioning.

Other findings showed that the younger the adult, the more likely he or she was to drink beer (61 percent among 18- to 24-year-olds versus about 25 percent among adults 50 years of age or older).

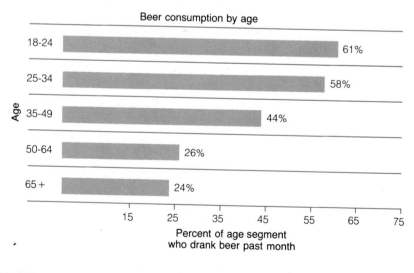

Beer consumption by age

EXHIBIT 22–5 *(concluded)*

According to Barbara Adago, vice president, client services at Bruskin Associates, men and women differed in their beer preferences, particularly with regard to low-calorie and imported beers. For example, 27 percent of female beer drinkers preferred low-calorie beer, compared with 8 percent of male drinkers. On the other hand, twice as many men preferred imported beer (8 percent of male beer drinkers versus 4 percent for females).

Types preferred

	Male	Female
Domestic (regular)	68%	59%
Low calorie (domestic/imported)	8	27
Imported	8	4
No particular brand	7	5
Undetermined type	9	5

What is America's favorite beer? Seventeen percent of all the adult beer drinkers chose Budweiser. Next in line were Miller High Life (10 percent), Miller Lite (9 percent), Michelob (8 percent), and Coors (7 percent).

Top five favorites

	Adults over 18
Budweiser	17%
Miller High Life	10
Miller Lite	9
Michelob	8
Coors	7

The primary reason people preferred their favorite brand of beer was taste (76 percent). Other reasons cited included low in calories (6 percent), price (5 percent), and conveniently available (5 percent).

Six slogans used in advertising of various brands of beer were tested within the study. The slogans and corresponding identification scores follow:

Slogan	Percentage of beer drinkers correctly identifying slogan
"Welcome to _____ Time" (Miller)	77%
"King of Beers" (Budweiser)	66
"When You're Out of _____ You're Out of Beer" (Schlitz)	36
"Come To Think of It, I'll Have A _____" (Heineken)	18
"Let It Be _____" (Lowenbrau)	14
"Bring Out Your Best" (Bud Light)	8

Questions regarding this study may be addressed to Barbara Adago, vp, R.H. Bruskin Associates, New Brunswick, N.J.

Source: "Peoples' Choice," *Advertising Age,* January 16, 1984, p. M-10.

EXHIBIT 22–6

IRI's BehaviorScan marketing research service tracks new product test sales and evaluates marketing mix effectiveness using consumer panels, electronic grocery and drug scanner tracking, and cable television.

Courtesy Information Resources, Inc.

several situations in which observation is an appropriate means. The license plates of cars parked at a shopping mall or motel can be analyzed to determine the geographic location of customers (provided that plate numbers indicate geographic location). However, many kinds of information, such as opinions and preferences, can be obtained only through questioning.

Responses to questions can be obtained from personal interviews, from telephone interviews, or by mail. Each of these methods has certain advantages and limitations, as shown in Exhibit 22-7. Regardless of the method used, the responses obtained are normally recorded on a questionnaire. Questionnaires vary in type and format according to whether the questions are structured or open-ended and according to whether the respondent knows *why* the question is being asked (i.e., disguised or not disguised). One page from a questionnaire used by a speciality retailer to survey its custom-

EXHIBIT 22-7 Advantages and Limitations of Questioning Methods

	Advantages	Limitations		Advantages	Limitations
Personal interviews	Most versatile and flexible Long questionnaires handled more easily Presence of interviewer allows more flexibility in procedure More enjoyable for respondents Fewer refusals	High cost Possibility of interviewer bias Possibility of cheating by interviewer due to lack of supervision Project time often lengthy	*Mail surveys*	Higher-quality information Better for collecting information on possibly embarrassing subjects Relatively cheaper to conduct No interviewer bias	Questionnaire cannot be changed Complex Can be completed by person other than intended respondent Follow-up expensive Response often slow in coming
Telephone interviews	Fewer interviewers needed Relatively inexpensive Rapid method of data collection Can reach large number of households More control over interviewers	More noncommittal answers Some households overrepresented Lengthy and detailed questions often not feasible			

Source: Harper W. Boyd, Jr., Ralph Westfall, and Stanley F. Stasch, *Marketing Research: Text and Cases*, 5th ed. (Homewood, Ill.: Richard D. Irwin, 1981), Chap. 4.

ers is shown in Exhibit 22-8. It was administered when shoppers visited the store.

Sampling Design

An important concern in designing a research study is *who* should be included. In many instances, the entire population of interest cannot be assessed. Consequently, the sampling of a population offers a powerful alternative. Sampling is much less costly than taking a complete census, and it is faster. The essential idea underlying sampling is that a very small portion of a population can be used to estimate values (e.g., brand preference) for the entire population of interest.

In the survey on consumers preferences for beer, a nationally representative sample of 1,000 was used. The key to successful sampling is to obtain a *representative* sample of the population—that is, a minipicture of the true characteristics of the population. Probability or nonprobability sampling may be used. With probability sampling, the researcher uses statistically sound methods to select the sample. With nonprobability sampling, statistical methods are not used to select the sample. The major limitation of a nonprobability sample is that a statistical level of confidence cannot be assigned

EXHIBIT 22-8 Example from Retail Store Survey Questionnaire

Office Use		
	31.	What is your age?
(38)		__1__ Under 25 __4__ 45 to 54
		__2__ 25 to 34 __5__ 55 to 64
		__3__ 35 to 44 __6__ 65 or over
	32a.	Do you have children?
(39)		__1__ No (Skip to Ques. 33)
		__2__ Yes (If yes, answer Ques. 32b & c)
	32.b	How many children are living at home?
(40)		__1__ None __3__ Two or three
		__2__ One __4__ Four or more
	32c.	Children's ages (circle ages of all children):
(42–44)		__1__ Preschool
		__2__ Elementary school
		__3__ Junior high school
		__4__ High school
		__5__ Older than high school
	33.	What was the last grade of school you completed?
(45)		__1__ Some high school or less
		__2__ High school graduate
		__3__ Business or technical school; some college
		__4__ College graduate
		__5__ Graduate or professional degree
	34.	Are you:
(46)		__1__ Single
		__2__ Married
		__3__ Separated, widowed, divorced
	35.	What is *your* occupation? (Circle *one*)
(47–48)		__01__ Professional __07__ Teacher/professor
		__02__ Manager/small business/large __08__ Homemaker
		business owner/executive __09__ Government or
		__03__ Outside sales/sales rep/agent military
		__04__ Worker or craftsman __10__ Farmer/rancher
		__05__ Skilled worker or craftsman/ __11__ Retired govt/military
		mechanic/service worker/ __12__ Retired other
		operative __13__ Student
		__06__ Secretarial/clerical/office worker
	36.	Total family income:
(49)		__1__ Under $15,000 __4__ $35,000–$49,999
		__2__ $15,000–$24,999 __5__ $50,000 or over
		__3__ $25,000–$34,999

to the responses obtained. A 95 percent level of confidence means that the estimate will include the true value of what is being estimated 95 percent of the time. The confidence level (95 percent) applies to the estimating process being used rather than to the estimate obtained from a specific sample.

Data Collection

This stage in a study moves the research process from planning to implementation. Communication between the researcher and the sample begins at the data collection stage. Even if everything has been done correctly up to this stage, incomplete data collection procedures and careless execution can ruin a study. Research results can include various errors because of data collection problems. Respondents may not understand a question even though they answer it. Respondents' answers may be incorrectly recorded. To minimize such problems, proper training and coordination of interviewer activities are essential. Firms with their own marketing research departments often contract with interviewing services in local markets because these services provide trained personnel.

Analysis and Results

The final step in a research study consists of analyzing the data and interpreting the results. The results are usually reported in tables, graphs, charts, and other easily understood forms for consolidating data to effectively communicate with the users of the research. As an example, the responses to one question asked in a survey of a sample of consumers are shown in Exhibit 22-9.

Analysis methods serve three general purposes. The first purpose is to summarize the information obtained from respondents—Exhibit 22-9 is illustrative of this type of analysis. The second purpose is to compare the differences between groups. A comparison of the lifestyle characteristics of frequent users and nonusers of a particular soft-drink brand is an example. The third purpose is to examine the relationships between two or more variables. An example is a correlation between family size and annual consumption of a particular brand of cereal.

Such advanced statistical techniques as multiple regression analysis and cluster methods may be useful in analyzing survey data. Applying these techniques requires statistical skills, so that only selective use is made of them. Interpretation of statistical results is more difficult than interpretation of data in tabular form. Properly applied and interpreted, however, statistical techniques can provide management with powerful tools for evaluating research results. These techniques can identify complex interrelationships among several variables, which is not possible with classification tables.

EXHIBIT 22-9 Analysis of Responses to a Survey Question

Question: Compared to other, competing stores where I regularly shop, XYZ Retail is better, about the same, or not as good when I consider:

	Percent of Respondents		
Factor	Better	Same	Not as Good
Prices	58%	40%	2%
Cleanliness	57	42	1
Appearance	71	29	—
Attractive display	64	31	5
Helpful clerks	24	68	8
Knowledgeable clerks	27	68	5
Value	49	48	3
Quality	41	56	3
Unique	85	12	3
Speedy service	45	49	6
Ease of finding	39	54	7

Evaluating Research Suppliers

Often marketing research firms perform at least some portion of research studies. The scope of activity of the 10 largest marketing research firms worldwide is indicated by the data in Exhibit 22-10. Numerous small marketing research firms also provide a wide range of research design, information collection, and analysis services.

Supplier Services

Commercial marketing research suppliers provide *customized* and/or *standardized* (syndicated) research services. These customized services accomplish all or some of the steps necessary in a research study. Some firms offer complete capabilities; others specialize in data collection, analysis, or other parts of the research process.

Standardized services involve either monitoring or data collection. The services provide ongoing standardized research efforts over time.

The services are offered by commercial marketing research firms in their attempts to provide specialized, routine information needed by a particular industry. Normally syndicated marketing research services take one of two forms. The service might provide uniform, ready-to-use, standard marketing data to various subscribing or client organizations at periodic intervals; this form of syndicated service is termed a *monitoring service*. Or the service might exist only as a *data collection service* wherein data are simultaneously collected for a number of subscribing organizations by means of a common data collection vehicle.

In either form, a syndicated research service differs from a customized research service in that it is simultaneously paid for by several different, sometimes competing, organizations. Specifically, organizations subscribing to a syndicated service

EXHIBIT 22–10 Ten Largest Research Groups Worldwide

Organization	Home Country	Approximate Research Revenues, 1982 ($ millions)	Number of Countries Served
1. A. C. Nielsen Company	United States	$433.1	25
2. IMS International	United States	124.8	34
3. SAMI	United States	85.0	1
4. Arbitron Ratings Company	United States	80.3	1
5. AGB Research PLC	United Kingdom	73.6	20
6. Burke Marketing Service	United States	52.1	2
7. Research International	United Kingdom	48.2	29
8. Infratest Forschung GmbH	West Germany	32.2	5
9. Market Facts, Inc.*	United States	25.4	1
10. GFK Numberg Gesellschaft F Konsum	West Germany	23.9	6
Total		$978.6	

* Does not include Market Facts of Canada, with volume of about $2.3 million, of which the parent owns about 50 percent.

Source: Reprinted with permission from the July 18, 1983, issue of *Advertising Age.* Copyright @ 1983 by Crain Communication, Inc.

share its expense. Sharing, in turn, reduces the cost incurred by each individual participating organization. Moreover, data from syndicated research services are often of very high quality since the commercial research supplier possesses considerable expertise in, and experience with, the syndicated service. Finally, research data may be obtained rather quickly from a syndicated service since the research procedures and mechanisms are constantly in use and available.[6]

Companies may need both customized and standardized services.

Evaluation Guidelines

If an outside research firm will be involved, the nature and scope of the project requiring its services must be defined. A useful tool for this purpose is a project proposal form that includes essential information on the project's purpose, objectives, and method of accomplishment. The form is useful not only in evaluating whether to undertake the project but in communicating with outside research suppliers.[7]

Before a decision is made to use a research service, evaluation is necessary. The central considerations in evaluating a research service are *competence* and *experience* in handling the client's particular research problem. Management is also interested in obtaining the study at a reasonable cost. A research firm with specific experience in the area of the proposed research may be able to provide the study at a lower cost than another firm. A large regional department store chain headquartered in the Dallas/Fort Worth Metroplex was expanding store locations to take advantage of the rapid

EXHIBIT 22–11 Managing the Marketing Research Buyer-Supplier (Seller) Relationship

Philosophical suggestions	*Operational suggestions*
Have a clear understanding of the problem before contacting a marketing research seller. Know what information you need and what you will do with it.	Personally check past . . . clients to evaluate the seller's prior experience with your problem, industry familiarity, and overall past performance in achieving research objectives.
Open lines of frank and honest communication with the research seller early in the research process, and maintain them throughout project implementation. Provide whatever information you have that bears on the problem at hand.	Familiarize yourself with the marketing research procedures and techniques that are to be used, including their applicability to your problem, the seller's expertise with them, and who in the agency will actually be responsible for performing them—in writing. Maintain a healthy interest in research activities (expect periodic reports, conduct independent data checks), but forgo unnecessary interference.
Written communication during all phases of the research process is imperative.	
Enter into the buyer-seller relationship with the understanding that marketing research sellers are professionals with expertise and experience.	Match the cost of marketing research services with the problem under investigation. The absolute cost of research must be evaluated with regard to the opportunity cost of not obtaining problem-relevant data.

Source: Robert A. Peterson and Roger A. Kerin, "The Effective Use of Marketing Research Consultants," *Industrial Marketing Management,* February 1980, pp. 69-73. Copyright 1980 by Elsevier-North Holland, Inc.

growth in its market area. Store location was a critical component of the chain's marketing strategy. A small local marketing research firm was chosen to assist management in making store location decisions because of its knowledge and experience of real estate and population trends in the market area.

Some useful guidelines for effectively managing marketing research buyer-supplier (seller) relationships are shown in Exhibit 22-11. Note that more than selection is involved. The client must manage the relationship while the project is under way. Close coordination and communication between supplier and client are important until the project has been completed and the user is familiar with the results. Both parties should share responsibility for making the relationship successful.

Building a Marketing Information System

Marketing information systems are integrated combinations of information, information processing and analysis equipment, software, and information specialists that serve the various analysis, planning, and control needs of marketing decision makers.

The computer age has ushered in a new era in marketing research. Available computer technology has made possible more sophisticated data analysis and new research applications.

Marketing information systems (MISs) that utilize computer capabilities permit analysis of marketing data for both long-term and day-to-day decisions—more sophisticated applications are called decision support systems. An MIS is a firm's effort to acquire and process information that meets regularly occurring marketing decision needs.

The major aspects of information planning for an MIS are shown in Exhibit 22-12. Normally, needed information falls into two categories:

EXHIBIT 22–12 Information Planning for an MIS

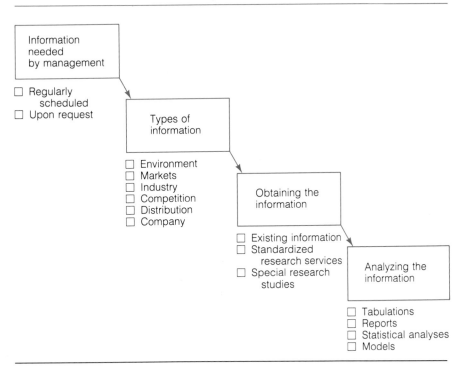

1. Regularly scheduled information supplied on a continuing basis to marketing management by internal and external sources—sales and cost analyses, market share measurements, and customer analyses.

2. Information that is obtained when it is required for a particular problem or situation—new product concept tests, brand preference studies, and studies of advertising effectiveness.

Management may need several types of information, and the importance of these categories of information will vary from one firm to another. There are three main sources of information for marketing planning and evaluation:

■ The *internal information system* is the backbone of any MIS. This information may consist primarily of sales and cost reports. Alternatively, an increasing number of firms are developing highly sophisticated marketing information systems for use in strategic and tactical planning and control activities.

■ A wide variety of *standardized information services* can be purchased by subscription or on a onetime basis from information services. The costs of these services are often a small fraction of what they would be if the reports were prepared for a single firm. Nielsen's TV ratings are an example.

■ From time to time, marketing decision makers require *special research studies* that may include one or a combination of the types of information shown in Exhibit 22-12. A study of distributor opinions concerning the services provided by a manufacturer is an illustration.[8]

Often data are simply tabulated or tabulations are included as a part of a formal report. The low cost of processing information using a computer is leading to greater use of statistical analyses and models by marketing executives.

Uses of an MIS

An internal system is the main center of information activities in most firms.[9] Using a variety of company information, often supplemented by external information, various reports are generated for management use in planning and control activities. The nature and scope of the internal information system may vary from basic analyses of operating data to elaborate computerized information storage and processing systems. The Quaker Oats Company has a sales and marketing information data base that contains about 500,000 time series and 20 million members. This data base is described in Exhibit 22-13. The system has a wide range of capabilities for report generation, statistical analyses, retrieval of information, and special studies. Among the kinds of information that can be supplied to management are shipment data, data on market shares and trends, advertising performance measures, and socioeconomic analyses (e.g., consumption per capita, brand development indexes, and maps).

Considering the costs of systems such as Quaker's MIS, are the benefits worth the expense? The record over the past decade has been mixed. However, the general trend is clearly toward wider adoption of MISs throughout the business community. An impressive control system for strategic and tactical planning is used by B. Dalton Bookseller, a retail chain owned by the Dayton-Hudson Corporation. Competitors acknowledge the MIS as a major Dalton advantage. It is a book-tracing system that codes each book order and monitors it on a computer. Users of the system are provided with such capabilities as "weekly sales reports, by title and topic, for every outlet, city, or region, and use of the data to restock fast sellers, drop slow movers, and choose new books to buy."[10]

The product mix and the nature of business operations have a strong bearing on the type of internal marketing information system that is appropriate in a particular firm. High-volume sales transactions, such as those for books, groceries, drugs, and other low-price consumer products, require computerized tracking and analysis capabilities. In contrast, a producer of low-volume, high-cost products such as ships or steam turbines may have far less need for systems like Quaker's and Dalton's.

EXHIBIT 22–13 Data Base for Quaker Oats Company

Data Source	Data Availability
Quaker data	
Dollar and quantity shipments Dollar and quantity promotion shipments Standard costs	These data are available by item and brand, by Quaker and SAMI (Selling Area Marketing Index) markets, and by month for three-year period.
Selling Areas-Marketing, Inc. data	
Dollar and pound withdrawals	These data are available by brand and category, by SAMI markets, and by SAMI period for three years.
Advertising data	
Ad expenditures from Advertising Information Services	These data are available by brand and category, by SAMI market, and by month for three-year periods.
Socioeconomic data	
Various sources such as the U.S. Census	These data are available by population, consumer price, household income, and food store sales.

Source: George A. Clowes, "Data Management Should Be No. 1 Priority in Developing On-Line MIS," *Marketing News*, December 12, 1980, p. 10.

Components of an MIS

Although the composition of MISs vary, certain basic components are present. A decision maker must activate the MIS in some manner, such as requesting needed information. The result is an "output" that feeds back to the decision maker. The system comprises three interrelated components: a data base (accumulated information); various capabilities for processing information; and system functions (file creation, report generation, etc.).

Data Base. The simplest form of data base is the conventional file system maintained by a business organization (customer files, order files, product information, etc.). The data base for an MIS is also information that has been collected to serve various purposes. But developing a data base for use in a computerized system is far more complex than maintaining a file system because of the precise requirements that must be met. A significant body of technical knowledge and experience is available on computerized data base design and utilization. A typical computerized marketing data base might include information on internal operations (salesmen's call report, costs, etc.), customer information, channel information, competitive intelligence, and environmental information.

Information Processing Capabilities. The information processing capabilities of the MIS involve both hardware and software (programs for storing and analyzing information). These capabilities generally fall into four categories: data retrieval, classification and comparison, statistical analysis, and modeling and simulation. Thus, the MIS user has available a wide range of capabilities extending from tabular comparisons to the more powerful decision analysis tools, such as multivariate techniques and computer modeling.

System Functions. Several types of activities can be performed by the MIS:

- Creating and Maintaining the data base.
- Processing information.
- Generating regular reports and responses to special requests.
- Responding to on-line inquiries from remote computer consoles.

Outputs of the MIS may include scheduled reports and analyses on product line sales performance, district sales, customer sales by size of account, and so forth. Since it would be difficult (and expensive) to design a series of reports and analyses to meet all the needs of marketing decision makers, the MIS should be capable of providing information on an ad hoc basis—historical market share analysis for a particular sales territory, a detailed analysis of particular customers, and so on.

Decision Support Systems

The marketing decision support system (MDSS) is a sophisticated form of the MIS. It is a technology that integrates data, software, and hardware to provide the marketing executive with information needed for decision making. The MDSS differs from a basic MIS in that it concentrates on:

- Analysis rather than retrieval.
- Provision of relevant data.
- Use of models to investigate relationships between marketing variables.
- Interactive computer analysis.[11]

The capabilities of a properly designed and implemented MDSS are impressive. The decision maker has immediate access to the system and can rapidly examine decision situations using the system's data, models, and display features. A successful system MDSS developed by a large packaged-goods firm has a data base that includes product sales, marketing expenditure data, and research information (panel and store audit results). Various analytic routines and models have been incorporated into the system.

> The bread and butter business of the MDSS consists of responding to a remarkable variety of small requests from brand managers and higher levels of marketing management. Rarely does raw data retrieval provide the answer. Almost always, data are manipulated and presented in a special way because of some issue at hand. Service is so good and turnaround on short requests is so fast that, at one point, it became necessary to reduce requests and maintain quality control on jobs performed. An important block of time goes into data base maintenance and updating.[12]

Perhaps the most significant feature of the MDSS is its ability to supply rapid "what if" analysis of several variables linked to the decision alternatives being considered by management. By means of the MDSS, analyses of sales response to advertising, price elasticity, and other strategic and tactical issues can be quickly incorporated into the consideration of these alternatives.

Summary

This chapter examines marketing research and information systems. The various information strategies that the marketing manager may use in planning and control are considered. The uses of internal and published information, standardized research services, and marketing research studies are discussed and illustrated. Information planning starts with a clear definition of a problem and with specification of the information that is needed to help solve it. Once information needs have been determined, management must weigh the costs and benefits of obtaining the needed information and select a strategy for obtaining it. Existing information may be utilized, standardized information services purchased, or a research study conducted.

When management's information strategy requires a formal research study, an interrelated sequence of steps should be followed in designing and conducting the study. These steps include problem formulation, research design, data collection methods and forms, sampling design, data collection procedures, and analysis and interpretation of the results. Errors in the execution of any of these steps will affect the validity of the overall results.

Many companies use outside research suppliers to meet at least part of their information needs. These services may be customized to the client's unique needs or syndicated to meet the needs of several users. The research proposal is a useful tool for defining the nature and scope of a proposed research project. It is helpful in evaluating whether to undertake the project and in communicating with outside suppliers. Guidelines for evaluating and working with research firms are discussed—competence and experience in handling the client's particular problem are of primary importance.

Finally, several aspects of building a marketing information system are considered. The basic task of planning for marketing information is outlined and illustrated. The major components of an MIS are the data base, various capabilities for processing information, and such system functions as generating reports and analyzing relationships between variables.

Exercises for Review and Discussion

1. Assume that a large bank is trying to identify potential locations for new branch bank sites. How might management determine what amount should be spent to obtain additional information that would be helpful in making location decisions?

2. If you were assigned the responsibility for describing the size, characteristics, and partici-

pants (e.g., suppliers and distributors) of the microwave oven market, how would you proceed?

3. A brewer has been considering the introduction of a beer-based beverage that does not taste like beer, though it would have roughly the same alcoholic content. Presumably, the product would appeal to people who do not like the

taste of standard beers but are not turned on by soda pop either. The company does not know exactly which taste it should use for its new beverage. What information needs should management consider? Suggest an approach for establishing priorities among these information needs. Indicate the probable impact that this information could have on the decision of whether to introduce the new beverage.

4. Under what conditions might a firm with a very competent marketing research department decide to purchase the services of a marketing research firm in obtaining additional information?

5. A cigarette manufacturer is considering changing the design of one of its cigarette packages. Use the information planning process to indicate probable information needs in this decision situation, and then outline an information strategy for obtaining the needed information. Make whatever assumptions are necessary in developing your analysis of the situation and

your associated recommendations concerning an information strategy.

6. How would the task of determining the information needs of a manager interested in assessing the performance of the sales force differ from that of determining the information needs of a manager concerned over a long-run decline in the firm's sales?

7. Discuss the probable impact of cable television on marketing research methods during the next decade as this medium penetrates U.S. households.

8. Compare and contrast the use of standardized information services and special research studies for tracking the performance of a new packaged food product.

9. What should the role of industry trade associations be in the development and distribution of standardized information services? What problems could develop in using trade groups as information sources?

●

Notes

1. Lawrence Ingrassia, "Matter of Taste: There Is No Way to Tell if a New Food Product Will Please the Public," *The Wall Street Journal*, February 26, 1980, pp. 1, 36. Reprinted by permission of *The Wall Street Journal*, © Dow Jones & Company, Inc., 1980. All Rights Reserved.

2. See Ralph L. Day, "Optimizing Marketing Research through Cost-Benefit Analysis," *Business Horizons* 9 (Fall 1966), pp. 45-54, for an excellent discussion of these phases. See also Gilbert A. Churchill, Jr., *Marketing Research*, 3d ed. (Hinsdale, Ill.: Dryden Press, 1983), Chap. 2.

3. A Parasuraman, *Marketing Research*, (Reading, Mass.: Addison-Wesley Publishing, 1986), pp. 104–17.

4. Churchill, *Marketing Research*, p. 21.

5. Information Resources, Inc., *BehaviorScan: Test Marketing Redefined*, 1986, pp. 1–3.

6. Robert A. Peterson, *Marketing Research* (Plano, Tex.: Business Publications, 1982), pp.130–31.

7. Thomas C. Benedict, Jr., "Flow Diagram Shows How to Evaluate Research Proposals," *Marketing News*, May 14, 1982, p. 11.

8. David W. Cravens, *Strategic Marketing* (Homewood, Ill.: Richard D. Irwin, 1982), pp. 420–21.

9. The discussion in this section is drawn from Cravens, *Strategic Marketing*, pp. 431–32.

10. "Waldenbooks: Countering B. Dalton by Aping Its Computer Operations," *Business Week*, October 8, 1979, p. 116.

11. John D. C. Little and Michael N. Cassettari, *Decision Support Systems for Marketing Managers* (New York: American Management Association, 1984), p. 9.

12. Ibid., pp. 28-29.

PART

6

*M*arketing exists only because it plays an important role in serving human needs worldwide. The two topics addressed in this concluding section help broaden one's view of the marketing task.

In Chapter 23, special aspects of marketing—international marketing and nonprofit marketing—are given attention due to their growing importance. The pursuit of international markets, long accepted in such countries as Japan and the Netherlands, is becoming a way of life for U.S. business managers. Although the marketing tasks of domestic and international marketing are basically the same, the macroenvironment in other nations often dictates the adoption of different marketing strategies. Analyzing the environment, selecting international markets, deciding on strategic entry strategies, and designing the marketing program are discussed. Then, the uniquenesses of nonprofit marketing are highlighted.

In Chapter 24, the social and legal environments of marketing are considered. Marketing and the quality of life provide the umbrella for more specific issues such as the profit motive, consumerism, the inner-city marketplace, and the physical environment. Then, marketing ethics are discussed, prior to a review of legal issues that are important to marketing management. Ethical and legal factors provide the boundaries that limit management behavior.

Marketing activity occurs in a broader environment and is partially shaped by that environment. The success of marketing, whether in an organization or as part of an economic system, is dependent on an adaptive orientation that uses the principles and concepts covered in the 24 chapters of this book ■

CHAPTER 23

Marketing in a Changing World

*I*t was an ill-timed blooper in Japan for a company known as one of America's most aggressive and sophisticated marketers. In the mid-1980s, United Airlines promoted its new flights with an advertisement that pictured a map of Japan—a map that left out Hokkaido, the nation's large northernmost island. Widely publicized in Japan, the incident was an embarrassing one for the noncommunist world's largest airline as it tried to gain a foothold in the lucrative, fast-growing transpacific market. "Hokkaido was ticked," acknowledged Colin Murray, United's Pacific region vice president in Tokyo.

The Orient, with its tradition-bound culture and its unique ways of doing business, proved perplexing for United in more ways than one. Despite United's formidable reputation in the U.S. marketing arena, it found the Far East a hard nut to crack. The unfamiliarity of the airline with Japan was a major handicap. Japanese tour operators and travel agents maintain strong loyalties to long-term business relationships and were hesitant to switch to a new player in the market, even for a price break. Agent support was crucial, because it accounted for about 90 percent of ticket sales in Japan, compared to about 60 percent in the United States.

At the time, United's Murray said, "We were the corn-fed kids from the Midwest coming over here. We knew the Orient is different, but not how much different it is. Here, it isn't enough to come in with a competitive price and fine product." For example, language can be important to Japanese travelers in choosing an airline. "The first thing they ask is, if I put them on United, will there be someone who will understand them," said a travel agent.

United attributed much of its growth in Japan to a "Visit USA" fare promotion that coincided with a peak travel period. And United was doling out generous commissions to travel agents overseas as an additional incentive for business, competitors said. United boosted its commissions to as high as 40 percent, while the standard rates ranged from 10 to 20 percent. Japanese Air Lines cried foul, contending that the fares were discriminatory and violated the U.S.-Japan air traffic treaty. "There are very serious legal questions over those fares," said one CAB source. "If they are continued, air traffic negotiations between the countries involved could be jeopardized."[1]

As United Airlines learned, domestic marketing strategies can be misapplied in an international environment.

It is critically important for firms to be globally oriented in their thinking and perspective, and even though the marketing mix is basically the same in international and domestic markets, important differences in institutional arrangements and business customs usually demand that adjustments be made in international markets. Moreover, in international markets as in domestic markets, marketers must continually adapt to changes in the macroenvironment, in industry conditions, markets, and competitive forces while keeping a keen eye on changing customer needs. Companies and countries will rise to the challenge or be left behind.

In this chapter, we first discuss marketing as it is applied in international markets. Then, marketing applications in the nonprofit sector are considered.

International Marketing

International marketing is not just for large companies. Three out of every five U.S. exporters have fewer than 100 employers. Consider the following success stories:

Alex Brunner, a native of Australia, started a small manufacturing/wholesaling business in Livonia, Michigan, in the mid-1970s. After two years, he entered the foreign trade market by exhibiting his products at the European Microfilm Kongress in Vienna, Austria. From a simple two-day exhibit, he obtained a $40,000 purchase contract. His principal product, microfilm controllers, had a good reception, and an order for 16 units was received from the Commerzbank in the Federal Republic of Germany. In the 1980s, his company, Visual Systems Corporation, moved to larger quarters in Southfield, Michigan, and was looking optimistically at other foreign markets. International markets appeared to be the answer to future growth for Visual Systems Corporation.

Another company, Dynatech Laboratories, Inc., was established in the 1950s as Cooke Engineering Company. Dynatech decided to pursue exporting in the late 1960s, when its sales of laboratory instruments were also growing in the United States. It was observed that there should be markets of at least equal size overseas. By the 1980s, the Virginia Company had total annual sales of $27 million, with $19 million in exports. Although the main purpose of Dynatech's expansion into foreign trade was to seek business growth, other important reasons were to obtain marketing and scientific feedback, to look for products that the firm might sell in the United States, and to get into the foreign market before foreign competition copied its products. The number of Dynatech employees grew from 70 persons before exporting to 340 by the 1980s.[2]

United States marketing executives no longer view their realm as domestic markets versus international markets; instead, they consider the United

States as just one of their markets.[3] This dramatic change in perspective toward the world marketplace will help place the United States in a much more competitive position. Overseas markets are becoming an increasingly important factor. Exports occupy a huge and expanding role in the U.S. economy, totaling about $200 billion in the mid-1980s. At that time, more than 4.6 million people had export-related jobs, about 1 million more than in 1973 and twice the total of the early 1960s. In the 1980s, 1 U.S. manufacturing job in 6 involved an export product, whereas in the mid-1960s the comparable ratio was 1 in 14. In the 1980s, more than 3,500 U.S. companies had more than $200 billion invested in 24,666 foreign affiliates; in the 1950s, 2,800 U.S. companies had about $25 billion invested abroad.[4] Imports, on the other hand, rose to about $270 billion in the mid-1980s, creating a whopping $124 billion trade deficit and costing the United States about 1.5 million jobs. Imports also create some U.S. employment, but only imports that carve out new markets are likely to create new jobs.[5]

Why are U.S. companies going abroad? First, growth in many domestic markets has leveled off, due in part to increased foreign competition. More foreign firms are coming to the United States, attracted by its huge markets, political stability, and their fear of U.S. protectionism. At the same time, many foreign markets are growing. Second, these companies are finding new market opportunities abroad. Finally, there is also ample evidence that exporting strategies are generally more profitable than domestic operations. Moreover, in view of balance-of-payments deficits, the U.S. government has been promoting increased exporting by domestic firms.

International marketing differs from domestic marketing mainly in that it involves different macro and task environments. The marketing management functions are the same for both, as are the basic marketing mix variables. So the definition of international marketing is the same as that for general marketing, except that marketing activity is directed to customers in more than one nation. Despite this basic similarity, the macro and task environments are often drastically different and a superficial understanding of international markets often leads to failure.

Opinions vary on how to conduct an international marketing effort, dividing over the issue of uniformity across markets versus adaptation to local markets. Standardizing a marketing mix worldwide is less costly than adapting to local markets, with savings in product development, production, advertising, and distribution.[6] Theodore Levitt and others argued that **global marketing** should be used more, given the savings and the resulting uniform image. This stirred intense debate, leading to a survey of large **multinational corporations** by Grey Advertising (a large agency with 88 offices worldwide). Grey called the global marketing drive "a dangerous siren song for naive marketers" but revealed that half of the companies surveyed favored a uniform ad campaign.[7] Nonetheless, different customer wants and needs and different stages of product acceptance across nations often necessitate different strategies and tactics. Increasing regulation of advertising is also complicating global marketing efforts. As examples:

International marketing
is designing and implementing marketing strategies to attain marketing objectives in the markets of other nations.

Global marketing
is using a standardized marketing strategy in worldwide markets to achieve marketing objectives.

Multinational corporations
directly invest in several countries and conduct their marketing without regard to an assumed home country.

■ References to iron and vitamins in a 30-second Kellogg cereal commercial produced for British TV would have to be deleted in the Netherlands.

■ A child wearing a Kellogg's T-shirt would be edited out in France, where children are forbidden to endorse products on TV.

■ In Germany, the wording "Kellogg makes their cornflakes the best they've ever been" would be axed because of rules prohibiting such claims.[8]

Deciding whether or not to use global marketing hinges on legal issues as well as on cost savings and effectiveness in different environments.

The special nature of international marketing is further illustrated by its extensive use of practices that are virtually unknown to those who engage solely in domestic marketing. Barter, counterpurchase, and compensation arrangements are three techniques that are worth exploring by the executive who is stymied by some of the difficulties of international trade.[9] Guesses as to the magnitude of such arrangements worldwide range as high as $200 billion a year.

Barter simply consists of swapping goods or services. It is the most primitive sort of international trading. For example, two parties may sign a contract in which one agrees to deliver, say, 100,000 pounds of ingot aluminum in return for 2,370 barrels of Saudi light crude oil. Since the market value of the two products is about the same, this is a fair arrangement for each party.

There are several advantages to bartering:

■ It usually moves a large quantity of product in a single transaction, because government bureaucrats and international traders seldom look for barter partners when small quantities are involved.

■ It creates no balance-of-payments problems. The amount of goods being taken by a cash-short country is matched by the amount of goods being shipped, so the net effect on the national income statement is zero. This is appealing to government bureaus in countries that are short of foreign exchange, where matching imports and exports is vital.

■ Each of the parties presumably gets something that it needs, though one party may be a somewhat more eager barter partner than the other.

Counterpurchase agreements are much like barter, but somewhat more flexible. Two parties enter into an arrangement to purchase products from each other that are roughly equivalent in value. This type of agreement overcomes some of the restrictive features of barter. A major advantage is that the reciprocal purchases can usually be made over an extended period. A German company may trade typewriters with a value of 160,000 marks to Rumania and agree to take back Rumanian products worth the same amount during the next three years. Another advantage is that the partner may be given a list of products from which to select.

Under a *compensation arrangement*, a company helps another company or a country to build a facility in exchange for the end products once the facility is operational. When Pullman-Kellogg won a contract to build a $340 million fertilizer plant in Nigeria, the agreement called for the U.S. company to sell part of the plant's output. Thus, like it or not, Pullman-Kellogg will someday be called upon to find an outlet for Nigeria's petroleum-based fertilizer.

Barter, counterpurchase, and compensation arrangements point up certain differences between domestic and international marketing, but the similarities between domestic and international marketing are sufficient to permit the use of the same framework for international marketing as that used for domestic marketing:

- Analyze the macro and task environments.
- Determine which markets to enter.
- Select entry strategies.
- Design the marketing program.

Analyze the Macro and Task Environments

The international marketing task largely involves adapting the controllable variables of the marketing mix to the environments in the various markets (Exhibit 23–1). The exhibit comes to life when the struggle by United Airlines to enter the Japanese market is considered. Even after having fought a 15-year battle to win landing rights in Japan, the airline continued to be buffeted by domestic environmental forces as well as by Japanese political, cultural, competitive, economic, distribution, and other environmental forces.

The U.S. environment most immediately affects the international marketing task, so it is necessary for international marketers to cope with at least two levels of environmental uncertainties (domestic and foreign) instead of one. Domestic political forces are sometimes combined with economics in fascinating ways. Trade barriers, for example, may be erected if a nation is engaging in political or military actions not supported by the domestic government. Protectionism rears its head when domestic industries are threatened. Second, domestic competition is often a factor in selecting which markets to enter. Large companies usually compete not only in the United States but also abroad. Finally, domestic economic vitality, which depends in part on having a healthy international balance of payments, is fundamental to the health of any marketer.

The outer circles in Exhibit 23–1 illustrate the different environments that often exist in various national markets.

Cultural Forces. Culture is learned behavior that is passed on from generation to generation and is manifest in social structures, habits, faiths, customs, rituals, and religions. Each of these affects lifestyles, which in turn shape consumption in the marketplace. Thus, what the people of a particular country buy, when they buy, where they buy, and how they buy are in large part culturally determined.[10]

EXHIBIT 23–1 The International Marketing Task

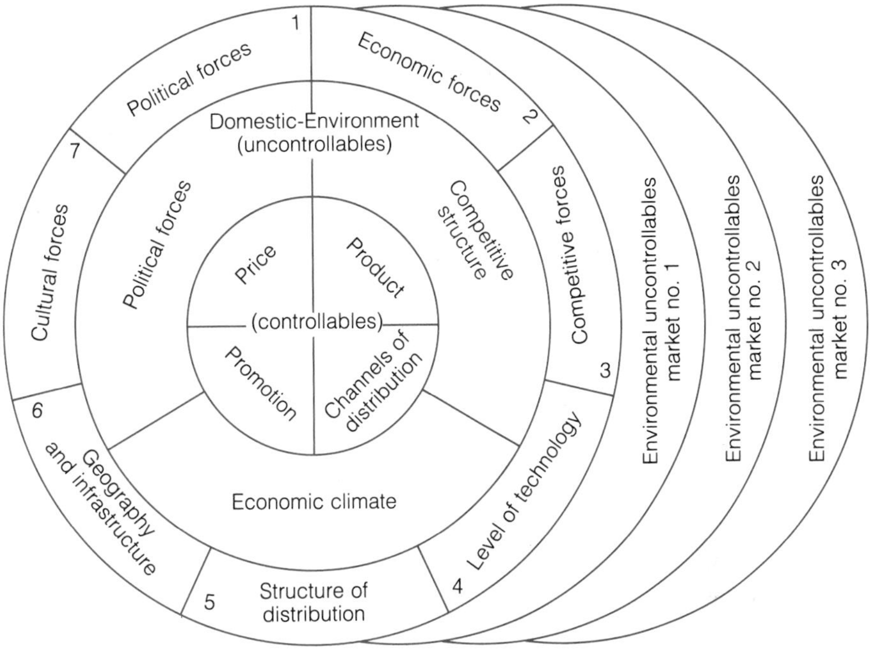

Political forces
Economic forces
1
2
Domestic-Environment
(uncontrollables)
7
Cultural forces
Political forces
Competitive structure
Competitive forces
Price
Product
(controllables)
Promotion
Channels of distribution
6
Geography and infrastructure
Economic climate
Level of technology
Environmental uncontrollables market no. 1
Environmental uncontrollables market no. 2
Environmental uncontrollables market no. 3
5
Structure of distribution
4

Foreign-Environment
(uncontrollables)

Source: Philip R. Cateora, *International Marketing* (Homewood, Il.: Richard D. Irwin, 1983), p. 7.

Cultural elements include the material culture, social organization, languages, religions, values, and attitudes.[11] Each of these elements varies from nation to nation, with related challenges to marketers. Social organization is the role played in a society by different groups and individuals, such as families, social classes, and ethnic groups. Marketing requires knowledge of who plays what role in influencing and ultimately making purchase decisions. Knowledge of the roles of men, women, and children (and large extended families) in purchase decisions is essential. Because communication is central to marketing, language differences are critically important in the international environment. Having bilingual local managers is usually essential, just to cope with language differences. Social classes, or strata within cultures, almost always exist and often have important market segmentation implications. Religion, values, and attitudes also play a critical role. Some products are taboo, and patterns of consumption are often tied to basic values and religious principles. Attitudes toward material possessions and consumption vary greatly.

Adjusting to a different culture is perhaps the greatest challenge confronting international marketers.[12] Marketing managers must be aware of their

Marketing relativism
is the interpretation of
marketing information
and activities and mar-
ket feedback in terms
of one's own experi-
ence and culture.

personal frame of reference, which modifies reactions to various situations. Many marketing programs fail because of unconscious responses from frames of reference that fit the manager's own culture. Marketers must bear in mind **marketing relativism.** When marketing decisions are made, the business problem should first be defined in terms of the marketer's culture, then it should be defined in the context of the foreign environment (without value judgments), and finally the net influence of the marketer's frame of reference should be carefully examined and the problem redefined as needed.

International marketers often differentiate between nations and sovereign states. By definition, the former are culturally based, with a common history, culture, and language. The latter are political units. There can be different nations within states, and nations can cut across states. Markets are often more closely related to nations than to states, because consumer tastes and preferences are more homogeneous in nations than in states.

Political Forces.   Governments, particularly those of less developed countries, often intervene in international business affairs. Some political factors that marketers should consider are:

- The political stability of the host nation.

- Whether the product involved pertains to the national defense and the defense capability of the host nation.

- Whether certain brands, products, or companies are readily identified with the United States and may therefore be especially vulnerable in times of stress.

- The importance of the product to the host nation.

- The possible threat to competitive suppliers in the host nation.

- Employment-generation advantages in the host nation.

These types of factors tend to determine the political vulnerability of a U.S. company's exporting activity.[13]

The legal environment is also central to the decision of whether to engage in international marketing. Consider the following:

- In Sweden, comparative ads must be significantly complete, citing all major differences between the products, including shortcomings.[14]

- Norway's Marketing Act has been interpreted to require full information in mail-order and credit sales advertising.[15]

- France has a law against door-to-door selling, and in Muslim countries salespeople are not allowed to see the woman of the house.[16]

- Mexico, France, and other countries have imposed controls over prices in recent years.

In addition to the legal regulation of marketing mix decisions, the "hassle level" should be considered. The responsiveness of the host government in such areas as legal processing and customs clearance can affect the desirability of marketing in a given nation.

Economic and Competitive Environment. Marketing decisions are, of course, directly intertwined with assessments of economic conditions. The potential size of various markets is determined by first looking at population and income statistics. Less developed countries may offer a market opportunity for certain types of products despite low income levels. Consequently, studying economic conditions in several alternative countries is an important early step.

Measures of economic progress may need to be used to understand markets. GNP should be considered, but more important may be the number of work-time minutes required to purchase basic products. Other important measures are the number of automobiles, TVs, and telephones per 1,000 population and per capita energy consumption. Care must be taken to use the most appropriate measures for a given country. Because many countries have bimodal income distributions, per capita figures must be viewed cautiously. Also, people in less developed countries usually live off the land to some extent, so their economic well-being may be far greater than income statistics indicate. Finally, because exchange rates are based on what is actually imported and exported (e.g., heavy machinery), the standard conversion may distort the market statistics for other products, such as food.

The economic environment also contributes to an observed pattern concerning U.S. exporting.[17] Exporting itself often goes through a product life cycle as the foreign country progresses through four stages of economic development:[18]

- The United States has an export monopoly for a new product.
- Foreign production begins.
- Foreign production becomes competitive with that of the United States in export markets.
- The United States actually imports the no-longer-new product.

United States producers are often the first to exploit market opportunities for high-income and laborsaving new products because such opportunities often appear first in the United States. These new products are first produced in the United States because proximity to customers and suppliers is important for design and marketing flexibility. In this first stage, U.S. producers have a monopoly in export markets and build sales with no concern for local competition. In the second stage, producers in other industrial countries start to manufacture the product, whose design and production is now standardized. So the growth of U.S. exports declines as competition enters. In the third stage, foreign producers displace U.S exports in the remaining export markets. Finally, foreign producers achieve sufficient competitive strength, often due to economies of scale and lower labor costs, to export to the United States itself. In short, the export effects of product innovation are undermined by lower costs abroad and technological diffusion. Management strategies in U.S. companies should therefore be constructed to capitalize on this natural evolution by extending the early stages if possible and by taking advantage of cooperative strategies such as joint ventures in the later stages.

Economic infrastructure is the set of basic systems that facilitate modern economic activity.

Other Environmental Factors. **Economic infrastructure** is important to marketing in that roads, other transportation and communication facilities, and the like are central to distribution and promotion. Rural areas in some countries are ignored in marketing efforts, due in part to lack of an infrastructure to support economic activity.

Geographic differences (climate, topography, natural resources, etc.) can also be very important, as can the distribution systems and the level of technology within the host country. Once the environment has been analyzed, a decision must be made as to which markets to enter.

Determine Which Markets to Enter

Becoming an international marketer not only means facing risks not seen in the domestic market; it also means pursuing significant opportunities. About 95 percent of the world's population and 75 percent of its income is located outside the United States. The decisions to enter international markets, enter specific countries, and pursue target markets within each country involve the same type of analysis, in stages progressing from general screening to detailed market analysis. The decision to "go international" is ultimately based on analysis of specific markets in specific countries.

The process of planning for international marketing is shown in Exhibit 23-2. Cateora recommends two phases for determining which markets to enter.[19] Phase 1 involves preliminary analysis and strategic screening by matching company and country needs, and phase 2 determines how much adaptation is required in the marketing mix to effectively enter the market. In phase 1, a company's strengths and weaknesses, product, philosophies, and objectives must be matched with the constraining factors and potential in the foreign country. In this phase, countries are screened to eliminate those that do not offer sufficient potential. The reasons that company is entering a foreign market and the returns expected need to be made explicit. Then, screening criteria must be established in light of the objectives—minimum acceptable market potential, minimum profit and return on investment, acceptable competitive conditions, acceptable transportation costs, and so on. Other criteria pertain to the environment—political stability and limited trade barriers, for example. Once the criteria have been set, a full analysis of the environment is conducted. At the conclusion of phase 1, the marketer should have enough basic information to:

■ Evaluate the potential of a proposed country market.

■ Identify problems that would eliminate a country from further consideration.

EXHIBIT 23-2 International Marketing Planning

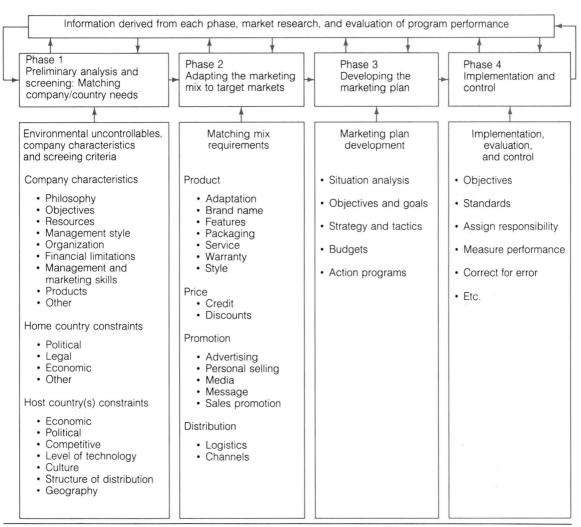

Source: Philip R. Cateora, *International Marketing* (Homewood, Ill.: Richard D. Irwin, 1983), p. 369.

■ Determine which elements of the marketing mix, in general, must be adapted to meet local market needs.

Phase 2 involves the more specific task of tentatively selecting country target markets and identifying problems and opportunities in each of these markets. In this phase, marketing mix components are examined in greater detail. The mix must be adapted to the cultural requirements of the foreign market and then costed out to see whether it is still feasible to enter the market. Sometimes essential changes, such as product modifications, cost more than can be absorbed through the added volume.

Finally, a full-scale target market analysis is conducted, based on both secondary and primary data. Sales are forecast and potential risks carefully evaluated. Then, based on projected costs, profits, and related risks and uncertainties, a "go" versus "no-go" decision is made. This is done for each product-market in each nation.

One strategic decision is whether to initially concentrate on one target market in one country or, at the other extreme, many target markets in many countries. Several factors must be considered in making this concentration versus diversification decision.[20]

Select Entry Strategies

If the decision is made to enter a country, the third step is selecting an appropriate entry strategy.[21] This is part of phase 3 (Exhibit 23-2). Varying levels of commitment and resources are involved, depending on the entry method selected. A company may use different entry methods for different markets or "get on the learning curve" using one method and later switch to another method. The costs, as well as the risks involved, vary by strategy. The strategies used include exporting, joint ventures, and the creation of subsidiaries, and each offers advantages and disadvantages as an entry strategy.

Exporting
is producing products in the home country and then distributing them to one or more other countries.

Exporting. **Exporting** may be direct or indirect, with involvement, costs, and risks increasing as one goes from indirect to direct exporting.

Indirect Exporting. With indirect exporting, a domestic firm deals with another firm in the home country that, in turn, acts as a sales intermediary and typically takes responsibility for moving products overseas. This approach gives smaller firms with little export expertise a way of penetrating foreign markets without becoming directly involved in exporting complexities. There are several kinds of intermediary firms, each with its own advantages.

■ *Commission Agents.* Commission or buying agents are "finders" for foreign firms that want to purchase products. They seek the desired items at the lowest possible price and are paid a commission by their foreign clients.

■ *Country-Controlled Buying Agents.* These are foreign governmental or quasi-governmental agencies that are empowered to locate and purchase desired goods.

■ *Export Management Companies (EMCs).* These act as the export department for several manufacturers of noncompetitive products. They solicit and transact business in the name of the manufacturers. In return for this service, they receive a commission, a salary, or a retainer plus commission. Many EMCs will also carry the financing for export sales, ensuring immediate payment for the manufacturers' products.

- *Export Trading Companies (ETCs).* These are firms that purchase goods for resale in foreign markets. They are generally well-established organizations that handle a variety of products, and they have efficient networks throughout their home markets. They may represent and favor suppliers in their own countries, however.

- *Export Merchants.* These purchase products directly from the manufacturer, packing and marketing the products according to their own specifications. Then, they sell overseas through their contacts, in their own names, and assume all risks for accounts.

- *Export Agents.* These operate as the manufacturer's representative, but the risk of loss remains with the manufacturer.

Direct Exporting. In direct exporting, the domestic firm takes responsibility for selling its own products abroad. It deals with foreign firms and is usually responsible for shipping its own products overseas. Often direct-exporting arrangements are initiated by the foreign firms involved. However, direct exporting may be initiated by domestic firms as a strategy that requires more commitment and risk than indirect exporting but also yields a chance of higher returns. A domestic firm may engage in direct exporting through one or more of the following:

- *Foreign Sales Representatives or Agents.* Like a manufacturer's agent in the United States, a foreign sales representative usually works on a commission basis, assumes no risk or responsibility, is under contract for a set period of time, and may have an exclusive or nonexclusive arrangement with the exporter.

- *Foreign Distributors.* A foreign distributor is a merchant who takes title to merchandise from a U.S. company and resells it at a profit.

- *Foreign Retailers.* Consumer products may be distributed by retailers in the foreign country who are contacted by sales representatives (or via direct mail).

- *State-Controlled Trading Companies.* In some countries, business must be conducted through a few government-sanctioned trading entities.

- *Corporate Marketing Division.* Rather than rely on agents and distributors, a company may establish its own sales force in another country to help ensure a well-planned and aggressive marketing effort. This requires a substantial resource commitment.

Joint Ventures. The second major strategy for tapping international markets is some form of joint venture.[22] There are several possible arrangements:

- *Licensing.* The firm's patents, designs, and the like are made available to a foreign producer and marketer for an established fee or royalty. The firm may also provide technical aid and know-how and allow the use of its trademark by the licensee. This method provides for rapid and low-cost entry, but it may also create a future competitor if the deal sours when the arrangement expires. Franchising (e.g., Coca-Cola bottlers), a licensing variation, is a growing form of international marketing.

■ *Management Contracting.* Typically, this arrangement provides participation and management control in a foreign venture without a capital investment. The return to management is usually a share of the profits plus fees, and sometimes stock options. Management contracting is often used in countries where firms must by law be owned by nationals.

■ *Contract Manufacturing.* The firm contracts for the production of products by foreign firms but carries out the marketing function in the foreign market. With this approach, less control is relinquished than with licensing, yet the approach eases entry into foreign markets.

■ *Joint Ownership.* This arrangement offers the advantage of having local principals who understand the country's markets, competitors, and government. It also reduces the investment that would otherwise be required. The disadvantages of this arrangement usually center on the differing goals and different management philosophies of the partners, which sometimes lead to management conflicts.

Wholly Owned Subsidiary.   The third strategy is to invest directly in a subsidiary operation. This multinational strategy requires the largest commitment and entails the greatest risks, but it can also yield the best return. This strategy is usually selected only after previous experience with another entry strategy. (Because the subsidiary is located and operates within another country, some question whether this is truly "international" marketing.)

A wholly owned subsidiary arrangement usually offers several advantages, including:

■ Flexibility in controlling marketing and production operations.

■ Patent and trademark protection in the host country.

■ Investment or tax incentives often provided by the host government (because, for example, jobs are created).

■ The added marketing know-how that comes from full commitment and immersion in the local environment.

The disadvantages of this arrangement center on risks involving political and monetary system considerations and on the risks of going it alone rather than having experienced, full-fledged local partners.

Designing the Marketing Program

The basic question at this stage is, "To what extent should existing product, promotion, pricing, and distribution variables in the marketing mix be changed to fit a given country's environment?" There are advantages to global standardization of the marketing mix across countries:

- Lower production costs.
- Less time spent by management.
- Easier control from the home office.

But some adaptation is almost always required to better meet market requirements (phases 3 and 4 in Exhibit 23–2).

Product Decisions. United States products often do not match the environment or markets in a foreign environment as well as in the domestic environment. In some countries, religious or cultural factors make certain products taboo: a developing nation offers a better market for plows than for computers; and a tropical country with low per capita incomes is not the best market for an exporter of shoes. Local customs often exist regarding product sizes, colors, speeds, and other attributes that require product redesign:

- In West Germany, refrigerators are much smaller than in the United States.
- Purple is a death color in Brazil, and in France a gift of yellow flowers suggests infidelity.
- Electrical standards vary from country to country.
- The metric system often requires product redesign.

Eastman Kodak Company launched its Ektaprint copier-duplicators in the Western European market in 1981, and by the mid-1980s it was third in the market.[23] But to achieve this, the product line had to be substantially revamped. Variable reduction capabilities were added (due to different paper sizes); the language on the keys was changed, the logic and electrical systems were alternated; and new safety doors were added (to meet safety codes). Thus, Eastman Kodak used a *product adaptation strategy.*[24] If no changes are made, the strategy is a simple *product extension* (Exhibit 23–3). A third strategy is *product invention*, that is, creating a new product, often one that is less costly, specifically to fit a market in another country. A $10 plastic, hand-powered washing machine was invented for the Mexican market, and its early sales were promising.

Packaging adaptations are often required. Coca-Cola and Pepsi-Cola standardize their packages globally, but many companies alter packages to fit local customs concerning, sizes, colors, and printing quality.[25] External packaging for shipping must also be designed to protect against the added perils of ocean travel, moisture, and pilferage.

Pricing. Costs, demand, and competition must be weighed in each market to determine appropriate prices. Conditions may be drastically different in various foreign markets than they are at home, and this may dictate changes in pricing strategies. A computer peripheral product that faces severe competition in U.S. markets may be a new product in foreign markets. So a high skimming price might be appropriate there, or a lower penetration price

EXHIBIT 23-3

For Jack Daniels, the marketing program includes a product extension.

Courtesy Jack Daniels Distillery.

might be used to build market share. Demand elasticities may also be very different in foreign markets, particularly if incomes are significantly lower in the foreign country than in the United States or if the product is perceived differently abroad than it is domestically. But the greatest pricing differences are often cost related. Tariffs, taxes, transportation and communication costs, fuel costs, and distributor margins can add significantly to expenses. Prices are also greatly affected by whether an exporting, joint venture, or wholly owned subsidiary is used, because these are likely to have very different cost structures.

Local environmental conditions such as inflation and fluctuations in the domestic country's monetary exchange rates for the foreign currency also affect pricing decisions. In addition, the foreign country may impose controls on price changes. Thus, as is true for all marketing mix components, the advantages of a largely standardized pricing system must be weighed against the more complex, but possibly more profitable, use of differential pricing across countries.

Promotion. The same global promotion may sometimes be used in different countries. In the Ektaprint introduction, Kodak chose to go with a single ad agency, the same ad graphics, and except for language, the same theme, "First name in photography, last word in copying." However, promotions must usually be adapted or even changed in foreign countries. Several barriers can impede using the same advertising:[26]

- Language differences
- Government controls
- Media availability
- Agency availability
- Economic differences
- Tastes and attitudes

Language itself may pose certain problems. Ford Motor Company named its low-cost "Third World" truck Fiera, which in Spanish-speaking countries means "ugly old woman." Rising nationalism in many countries (France, Mexico, the Philippines) has necessitated the recasting of advertising in the native language. In some countries, low literacy rates preclude the use of print advertising. The advertising task is further complicated in countries where more than one language is used (e.g., Switzerland).

In many foreign countries, there are *government controls* on advertising. For example, if broadcast media are publicly owned, ads may not be allowed on radio or television. Governments often regulate the advertising of socially sensitive products, and in some countries advertising expenditures are taxed. In Italy, television commercials can be broadcast only 10 times in a year, with at least 10 days between broadcasts. Such restrictions often mean that the relative use of different advertising media must differ from country to country.

The *availability of media* may also be a problem. The number of available radio and TV stations, print media, billboards, and the like varies significantly across countries. In some countries, use of direct mail is impossible due to poor mail service.

The number and quality of advertising agencies vary greatly. *Agency availability* often determines the feasibility of formulating an effective campaign in a foreign country.

Probably the most important communication barriers other than language are the different levels of *economic development* and the culturally based *tastes and attitudes* in various countries. Religious values may mean that a message appropriate in Europe is inappropriate in Saudi Arabia. And the needs and interests of people in Zaire are very different from those of people in Switzerland, due to different standards of living.

Personal selling is an important part of the international promotional mix, particularly for industrial products. Sales management methods are basically the same in foreign countries as in the United States, although recruiting, training, and managing local sales talent can present special challenges. Sales salaries may be lower, but higher expenses (e.g., transportation costs) may offset any salary advantage. Also, expensive benefits are sometimes specified by law. Cultures vary in their acceptance of personal selling, so adjustments in messages and levels of aggressiveness are sometimes required.

Distribution.   The channel decisions that must be made for international markets are similar to those that must be made for domestic markets. But distribution institutions and the way they function are often very different from country to country, and environmental conditions are also different. Distribution is more complex in international than in domestic marketing because there are usually more stages in the channel. Rather than a producer selling to an intermediary that sells to the end user, as often happens in domestic markets, a process such as that shown in Exhibit 23-4 may be involved.

United States companies engaging in international marketing should assume a perspective of coordinating and managing the flow of goods through the entire distribution channel, not just the first stage or two. Why? It is particularly tempting, given the length of the channel, to insufficiently study end-user markets. However, in international marketing as in domestic marketing, channel decisions must be made as part of a distribution strategy to effectively serve end-user needs and preferences. The institutional distribution options are basically the same as the domestic options—through agents, merchant wholesalers, or a firm's own sales and distribution system—but their precise form varies greatly. The degree of channel control, the level of channel efficiency, and the size of distributor margins are key factors in establishing both domestic and international distribution systems.

In most countries, middlemen are predominantly very large or very small, while in the United States there are many medium-sized firms.[27] The length of the channel may vary. Channels in Korea are notoriously long and complex. Generally speaking, however, the more advanced the stage of economic development, the shorter the channels.

One of the first things companies discover about international channels of distribution is that, in most countries, it is nearly impossible to gain adequate

EXHIBIT 23–4 Channels of Distribution for International Marketing

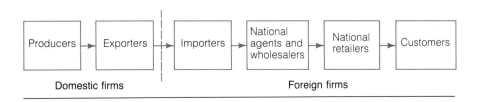

market coverage through a single channel. Appropriate channels may not even exist. So companies may have to depart from their customary channel patterns. Procter & Gamble, known as a mass merchandiser in the United States and Europe, sells soap and other products door-to-door in the Philippines, Iran, and other developing countries. Finally, channels may also be blocked by competitor connections, cartels, or accepted marketing practices. General Tire Company was forced out of Europe because a tire cartel would not tolerate its presence. The cartel used duress to render General Tire's channels of distribution ineffective.

International marketers must, of course, also develop feedback and control systems and strive to make marketing program adjustments as conditions dictate.

Nonprofit Marketing

A few years ago, there was relatively little sophisticated marketing in nonprofit organizations. Some nonprofit organizations even viewed marketing with great suspicion. But as the world changed, marketing has been applied more and more in nonprofit organizations. (Nonprofit organizations may be public or private. But we use the terms *nonprofit marketing* and *nonbusiness marketing* interchangeably.)

Marketing activity is clearly visible in United Fund campaigns, Reverend Billy Graham's crusades, numerous volunteer programs, and efforts to eliminate drug abuse. Millions of dollars go to recruiting the volunteer army, the promotion of state and local tourism (Exhibit 23-5), and political campaigns. Nonbusiness organizations comprise over one fifth of the U.S. economy. Nonprofit groups increasingly employ professional marketers and compete with business to obtain marketing expertise.

The Uniquenesses of Nonbusiness Marketing

It is a mistake to regard nonbusiness marketing as totally different from business marketing. The basic marketing concepts and techniques are applicable to both, yet imagination is required to creatively apply to non-

EXHIBIT 23–5

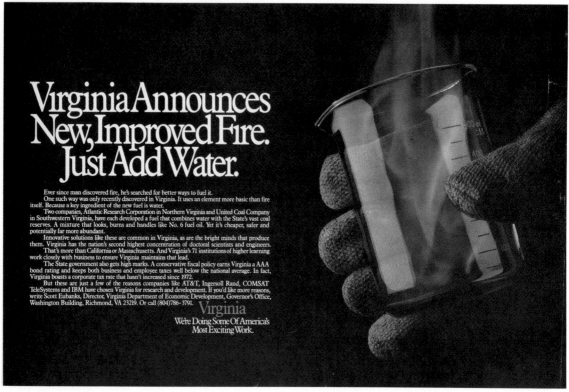

Nonprofit organizations such as state governments manage extensive marketing programs.

Courtesy Siddall, Maters, & Coughter, Inc.

business areas the same managerial tools that are applied to business areas. Indeed, nonprofit marketing does appear to differ somewhat from business marketing, although this view is debated.

Nonbusiness marketing more often strives to achieve something *other than stimulating demand* (Exhibit 23–6). Mass transit companies try to reduce demand at certain times of the day and to increase it at other times. Antismoking groups try to reduce the demand for cigarettes. Multiple objectives (as opposed to profit) complicate marketing in nonprofit organizations.

Nonprofit organizations more often *depend on a number of groups* or "publics," whereas business, even today, is considered primarily responsible to three groups (stockholders, employees, and customers). A state university must respond to students, faculty, legislators, alumni, contributors, and many other groups. Due to the high dependence of nonbusiness organizations on a number of groups, *environmental analysis may be more important* for nonbusiness organizations. And the marketing activity of nonbusiness organi-

EXHIBIT 23-6 Basic Marketing Tasks

Demand State	Marketing Task	Formal Name
Negative demand*	Disabuse demand	Conversional marketing
No demand	Create demand	Stimulational marketing
Latent demand†	Develop demand	Developmental marketing
Faltering demand	Revitalize demand	Remarketing
Irregular demand‡	Synchronize demand	Synchromarketing
Full demand	Maintain demand	Maintenance marketing
Overfull demand	Reduce demand	Demarketing
Unwholesome demand§	Destroy demand	Countermarketing

* A major part of the market dislikes the product (e.g., vasectomies, ex-convicts seeking employment).

† Consumer desire for something currently unavailable (e.g., comfortable cars that travel 85 miles per gallon of gasoline).

‡ Peak loads on mass transit, irregular use of recreational facilities.

§ Guns, drugs, cigarettes.

Source: Philip Kotler "The Major Tasks of Marketing Management," *Journal of Marketing* 37 (October 1973), pp. 42–49. Published by the American Marketing Association.

zations may be equally directed at several of their publics. Universities, for example, should analyze the needs of each of their publics.

Nonbusiness activity is *more often socially sensitive* and controversial and therefore more subject to environmental constraints, such as legislation and public scrutiny. Abortion clinics, for example, face severe local pressure in many communities.

The *products* of nonprofit organizations are often services and *more often intangible,* especially the marketing of "ideas." Consider, for example, antismoking and antialcoholism campaigns.

Nonbusiness organizations use *advertising (versus marketing)* more often than do business organizations. By definition, marketing requires an analysis of market needs and the coordination of product development and all other marketing variables to match those needs. Nonprofit groups sometimes adopt promotion but not marketing.[28]

The channel of *distribution* components of nonprofit organizations often *overlap with promotional media* in that idea "distribution," for example, uses communications media as channels of distribution. There is a growing body of literature on nonprofit marketing that students may wish to pursue.[29]

Social and Nonbusiness Marketing

Social marketing is the design, implementation, and control of programs seeking to increase the acceptability of a social idea, cause, or practice in a target group.[30]

Some nonprofit organizations have goals and activities that are similar to those of business organizations. But many nonprofit organizations pursue strictly social objectives. **Social marketing** is a subset of nonprofit marketing. A wide variety of such social marketing organizations exist, including:

- Educational and research organizations (universities, community colleges, think tanks, etc.).
- Cultural organizations (symphonies, art associations, museums, etc.).

- Health care organizations (hospitals, health maintenance organizations, etc.).
- Professional and trade associations (unions, lobbying organizations, membership groups, industry groups, etc.).
- Religious organizations (churches, religious foundations, evangelical groups, etc.).
- Political organizations (political parties, campaign organizations, etc.).
- Social cause organizations (antinuclear groups, consumer groups, environmental groups, etc.).
- Government organizations (post offices, police and fire departments, parks, etc.).
- Philanthropic institutions (foundations, social welfare organizations, etc.).

The categories listed are not mutually exclusive.

Some nonprofit organizations provide services to the general public, some to their members, and some to carefully defined target groups. As the list indicates, most provide intangible services and information to their constituencies. Some, such as government organizations and hospitals, receive considerable taxpayer support, while others depend on donations, membership fees, or volunteers for their existence. With the latter, marketing is not only essential for attaining the organizational mission but also for obtaining donations and members.

To clarify these points, it is useful to consider some examples of nonprofit marketing, beginning with colleges and universities. Public universities have several constituencies, including state legislatures and taxpayers, but the survival of private colleges depends on donations and student enrollment. To help ensure sufficient enrollment to create a financially sound and successful private college, a marketing audit of the college should be conducted. The following questions form the basis for such an audit.

- Mission/Goals. Is there a well-developed, market-oriented statement of mission and goals that personnel understand and accept?
- Marketing Concept. Is the entire organization, from the chancellor to the professors, united in providing a quality educational experience to the marketplace in a cost-effective manner?
- Marketing Organization. Do position descriptions adequately reflect the marketing role that must be assumed by people in all types of positions, from the librarian to the custodians? Does the structure include specialists with authority to develop true marketing programs as opposed to fragmented efforts?
- Marketing Environment. Is the broader environment understood? Are the full implications of demographic changes (which point to declining numbers of college-age students) understood? Does government support to private

EXHIBIT 23-7 Marketing Communications in Nonbusiness Situations

| | | | **Factors Affecting Success of Communication** | | | | |
Case	Target Group Interest/ Involvement	Benefits/ Reinforcers	Costs	Cost/ Benefit	Preexisting Demand	Segmentation	Conclusion
Military enlistment	Little past experience	Personal intangibles	Several years of one's life	Very good for some segments	Fairly high	Very specific and limited	Marketing communications can impact
55-mph speed limit	Little interest Low	Few personal benefits Weak societal benefits	Time Ego/macho	Poor	Virtually none	All drivers	Low likelihood of marketing communication impact
Antilitter campaign	Little interest Low	Few personal benefits Moderate societal benefits	Inconvenience	Poor	Low	All members of community	Short-run impact possible Long-run impact difficult
Voting	High to low. Depends on political race	Good citizenship feeling	Time inconvenient Infrequent/ low	Favorable	Moderate	All citizens ≥18 years of age	Short-run impact likely Long-run impact not necessary

Source: Adapted from Michael L. Rothschild, "Marketing Communications in Nonbusiness Situations or Why It's So Hard to Sell Brotherhood like Soap," *Journal of Marketing 43* (Spring 1979), p. 17. Published by the American Marketing Association.

EXHIBIT 23-8 Challenges in Implementing Nonprofit and Social Marketing

Market analysis problems

Fewer secondary data are available on consumers than are available in business marketing. Fewer research and syndicated services are available than are available in business marketing.

Primary data collection is often difficult due to sensitivity (e.g., concerning smoking, sex, or charity).

It is often difficult to convince funding sponsors of the justification for marketing research expenditures (e.g., sponsors often want to see tangible output quickly).

Market segmentation problems

There is pressure against segmentation, particularly against the de-emphasis of certain groups (e.g., egalitarian view of higher education versus targeting selected students).

Organizations often select as target markets the groups that are most negatively predisposed to the "product" (e.g., nonsmoking ads to heavy smokers).

Product strategy problems

There is often difficulty in formulating complex, behaviorally related products (e.g., drug therapy maintenance).

Positioning strategies may be hindered because of the different perceptions held by different publics (e.g., describing a social organization as a service organization rather than a research organization will appeal to some publics but not others).

Pricing strategy problems

The challenge is to reduce the monetary, psychic, energy, and time costs incurred by consumers when engaging in the desired behavior (e.g., convenience and guaranteed privacy with a family planning clinic).

Channels strategy problems

There is often difficulty in utilizing and controlling desired intermediaries, sometimes due to being unable to offer these intermediaries a monetary incentive (e.g., encouraging physicians to teach patients about the benefits of nonsmoking). The intermediaries are often volunteers.

Communications strategy problems

Paid advertising may not be used due to the sensitive nature of the message or concern over charges of wasting money. Public service announcements often fail to reach the targeted audience.

The complexity of, for example, changing salt consumption patterns requires large amounts of information. Multiple messages are often required, which makes public service announcements even less effective.

There is difficulty in conducting meaningful pretests of messages due to the lack of established standards and, in some cases, due to message sensitivity.

Organizational problems

Marketing in nonprofit organizations is often poorly understood, weakly appreciated, and inappropriately assigned. Marketing is often equated to promotion. The environment within the organization may doom the effectiveness of the marketing effort.

Source: Selected items abstracted from Paul N. Bloom and William D. Novelli, "Problems and Challenges in Social Marketing," *Journal of Marketing* 45 (Spring 1981), pp. 79-88.

colleges or to students seem likely? Can new technology increase cost effectiveness in delivering educational services?

■ Markets/Competitors. Do those in charge of generating student demand understand the demographic and behavioral characteristics of current and potential students and their families? Have conscious target market decisions been made? Are perceptions of the college and its programs understood, particularly perceptions that affect its market positioning relative to that of competitors? Are differential advantages perceived by potential students?

■ Marketing Mix. How are the college's services defined at different levels? Do some programs need to be dropped and new programs added? Is tuition at an appropriate level given not only costs but also demand and competition? Are the courses "delivered" at locations and times convenient to different target markets? Could an executive MBA program, for example, be designed and priced differently from other MBA programs? Does promotion convey the desired images and messages? Is there any attempt to track effectiveness over time? Are "salespeople" in the admissions function fired if they do not perform satisfactorily?

This audit listing illustrates the application of marketing concepts to a nonprofit organization and the substantial adjustment that marketing may require in the perspectives of personnel in nonprofit organizations. Other examples of nonprofit marketing are shown in Exhibit 23-7.

Marketing will inevitably be applied more and more by nonprofit organizations. Consequently, business students with formal marketing training will be employed increasingly by nonprofit groups. Some of the special hurdles and challenges facing nonprofit marketers (particularly social marketers) are reviewed in Exhibit 23-8.

As more and more nonbusiness groups engage in sophisticated marketing practices, it may become necessary for government to monitor conflicts and practices.[31] Clearly, it is not socially desirable for a nonbusiness group to do marketing well if the price of the group's success is the demise of a more deserving competitor.

Summary

The future will be exciting and challenging for marketers. International marketing is being accepted increasingly as a way of life. The task of defining a firm's environment, markets, and competition is no longer limited by national boundaries. The four steps in international marketing are to analyze the macro and task environments, to determine which markets to enter, to select entry strategies, and to design the marketing program.

The most important differences between domestic and international marketing relate to the environment of different nations. The social/cultural environment (language, social organization and religion, values, attitudes) is difficult to fully understand unless we are sensitive to marketing relativism (i.e., that our assumptions tend to be unconsciously based on our own culture). The political and legal environment is often different in other countries than in our own, whether because of political instability, international politics, or the maze of laws and regulations that differ from country to country. It is also essential to analyze the level of economic progress and the existing infrastructure as well as the technology, distribution structures, competition, and geography.

Determining which markets to enter involves two steps: preliminary strategic analysis and screening through matching company and country needs and more detailed study of how much adaptation is required in the marketing mix and the cost and revenue implications of such adaptation.

Selecting one or more entry strategies means choosing among exporting (indirect or direct), joint ventures (e.g., licensing, management contracting, contract manufacturing, and joint ownership), and the acquisition or creation of a wholly owned subsidiary.

Finally, the marketing program must be designed to take into account all the unique aspects of the international setting. While a simple product-extension strategy may be selected, product adaptation or even product invention may be preferable. The pricing, promotion, and channel decisions made in international marketing are similar to those made in domestic marketing, but substantial adaptation to international differences may be necessary.

Special adaptation is also required to effectively engage in nonprofit marketing. The differences between profit marketing and nonprofit marketing become apparent as one considers specific examples of nonprofit marketing, such as marketing higher education, military recruitment, the 55-mph speed limit, antilittering campaigns, or participation in voting. The marketing process is basically the same in nonprofit and profit marketing, but nonprofit marketing has several unique aspects.

Exercises for Review and Discussion

1. This chapter identified three unique methods for engaging in international trade (barter, counterpurchase, and compensation arrangements). Can you think of some disadvantages associated with each method?

2. First identify the types of environmental factors that should be considered before entering an international market. Then select a foreign country and identify for each factor the special environment and its possible implications for marketing.

3. After doing Exercise 2, select one or more specific products and design an appropriate marketing mix (for each product to be introduced in the country chosen). Make whatever assumptions are necessary.

4. As vice president of marketing for a medium-sized manufacturer of cordless phones, you have decided to market your products overseas and must develop an entry strategy. Outline some alternatives; discuss the pros and cons of each option; and tell why a particular strategy should be chosen.

5. Select a nonprofit organization with which you are familiar (or have access to), and demonstrate the applicability of the marketing planning process as discussed in Chapter 1 to that organization. Briefly discuss and interrelate environmental analysis, market opportunity analysis, and marketing strategy development. Cite major information needs for each of these tasks as well as the means for controlling the marketing program.

6. Using a specific nonprofit organization, select a specific chapter in this textbook and evaluate the transferability of each of the major concepts taken up in the chapter to its operations.

Notes

1. Adapted from Carol Jouzaitis and Sheila Tefft, "Japan's Skies Become Friendlier for United," *Chicago Tribune*, July 13, 1984, Business Section, pp. 1, 3. Reprinted by courtesy of the *Chicago Tribune.*

2. Grant C. Moon, *Success Stories: Small Business Exporters* (Washington, D.C.; Small Business Administration, 1980), pp. 3–4, 9; also see Tom Peters, "Boom Years Taught Executives They Didn't Have to Compete," *Chicago Tribune*, March 3, 1986, Business Section, p. 20.

3. The next two paragraphs of this section are partially based on Philip R. Cateora, *International Marketing* (Homewood, Ill.: Richard D. Irwin, 1983), pp. 3–5; also see Bernard J. O'Keefe, "Shooting Ourselves in the Foot," *Marketing News*, March 28, 1986, pp. 20–21. Published by the American Marketing Association.

4. "Companies Profit from Investments They Made Years Ago in Plants Overseas," *The Wall Street Journal*, March 11, 1981, p. 48.

5. "Imports, Often Blamed for Killing U.S. Jobs, Create New Ones, Too," *The Wall Street Journal*, February 29, 1984, pp. 1, 16.

6. Steuart H. Britt and Norman F. Guess, eds., *Marketing Manager's Handbook* (Chicago; Dartnell, 1983), p. 1157.

7. Ronald Alsop, "Efficacy of Global Ad Projects Questioned in Firm's Survey," *The Wall Street Journal*, September 13, 1984, p. 29.

8. Ronald Alsop, "Countries' Different Ad Rules Are Problem for Global Firms," *The Wall Street Journal*, September 27, 1984, p. 25.

9. The following overview is abstracted from Robert E. Weigand, "International Business via Barter, Counter-Purchases, and Compensation Agreements," in *Marketing Manager's Handbook*, ed. Steuart H. Britt and Norman F. Guess (Chicago; Dartnell, 1983), pp. 1226–29.

10. Paragraph based on Subhash C. Jain and Lewis R. Tucker, Jr., eds., *International Marketing: Managerial Perspectives* (Boston: CBI Publishing, 1979), p. 5.

11. Vern Terpstra, *International Dimensions of Marketing* (Boston: Kent Publishing, 1982), pp. 34–37; also see Vern Terpstra, *The Cultural Environment of International Business* (Cincinnati: South-Western Publishing, 1978).

12. This discussion is based on Cateora, *International Marketing*, pp. 9–13.

13. See also F. T. Haner, "Rating Investment Risks Abroad," *Business Horizons*, April 1979, pp. 18–23; and "A Rising Tide of Protectionism," *Newsweek*, May 30, 1983, pp. 75–78.

14. J. J. Boddewyn, "Advertising Regulation in the 1980s: The Underlying Global Forces," *Journal of Marketing* 46 (Winter 1982), p. 28.

15. Ibid.

16. Terpstra, *International Dimensions of Marketing*, p. 40.

17. This paragraph is adapted from Franklin R. Root, *International Trade and Investment* (Cincinnati: South-Western Publishing, 1978), pp. 102–3.

18. Raymond Vernon, "International Investment and International Trade in the Product Cycle," *Quarterly Journal of Economics*, May 1966, pp. 190–207; and

Louis T. Wells, Jr., "A Product Life Cycle for International Trade?" *Journal of Marketing* 32 (July 1968), pp. 1–6.

19. Discussion of exhibit from Cateora, *International Marketing*, pp. 368–73.

20. See Igal Ayal and Jehiel Zif, "Market Expansion Strategies in Multinational Marketing," *Journal of Marketing* 43 (Spring 1979), pp. 84–94.

21. These strategies are from *A Basic Guide to Exporting* (Washington, D.C.: Department of Commerce, 1981), pp. 15–19, 78–79.

22. For an excellent and more detailed discussion of ~perative arrangements, see Robert E. Weigand, ..rketing through Foreign Subsidiaries and Joint Venture Arrangements," in *Handbook of Modern Marketing*, ed. Victor P. Buell (New York: McGraw-Hill, forthcoming), chap. 194.

23. Joseph A. Lawton, "Kodak Penetrates the European Copier Market with Customized Marketing Strategy and Product Changes," *Marketing News*, August 3, 1984, p. 1.

24. These strategies are from Warren J. Keegan, "Multinational Product Planning: Strategic Alternatives," in *Readings in Internu.ional Marketing* (Chicago: American Marketing Association, 1969), pp. 58–62.

25. "Ten Commandments Guide Multinational Packaging," *Marketing News*, December 23, 1983, p. 3.

26. Adapted with permission from Vern Terpstra, *International Dimensions of Marketing* (Boston: Kent Publishing, 1982), p. 158.

27. This and the next paragraph are from Cateora, *International Marketing*, pp. 617–21.

28. Kevin T. Higgins, "Hospital Marketers Lack Technical, Analytical Skills," *Marketing News*, April 11, 1986, p. 1.

29. See, for example, Philip Kotler, *Marketing for Nonprofit Organizations* (Englewood Cliffs, N.J.: Prentice-Hall, 1982).

30. Philip Kotler, *Marketing Management: Analysis, Planning, and Control* (Englewood Cliffs, N.J.: Prentice-Hall, 1980), p. 687.

31. G. Laczniak, R. Lusch, and P. Murphy, "Social Marketing: Its Ethical Dimensions," *Journal of Marketing* 43 (Spring 1979), p. 34.

CHAPTER 24

Contemporary Marketing Issues

A company is considering the introduction of a new plastic container to the market. The firm regards itself as socially responsible; therefore, it undertakes an extensive impact assessment program. One of its environmentally minded employees suggests that people might light the containers and then cook their meals over the fire. Although the idea sounds bizarre, research and development doesn't want to take any chances, so for over a month hamburgers cooked over a fire made from the plastic bottles are fed to rats. The rats are carefully monitored for negative side effects, and tests indicate that they suffer no ill effects.

An extensive series of tests involving energy usage, disposal problems, and recycling opportunities are performed. The public is invited to carefully scheduled hearings across the country to encourage consumer input. Finally, the new product is marketed, landing a major soft-drink company as a customer.

Does it seem that the company has fulfilled its social responsibilities? In the mid-1970s, Monsanto went through this very process in developing Cycle-Safe bottles and spent more than $47 million to market the product. But the FDA later banned the bottle because when the bottle was stored at 120 degrees for an extended period of time, molecules strayed from the bottle into the contents. Rats, fed with doses equivalent to consuming thousands of quarts of soft drink over a human lifetime, developed an above-normal number of tumors.

Monsanto managers believed they were providing a product that did something for society—a plastic bottle that could be recycled. But social responsibility is unavoidably a matter of degree and interpretation.[1]

Marketing has an outstanding record of adapting to change. To adapt or not to adapt in a competitive environment is ultimately a decision for or against survival. Indeed, the only thing certain *is* change. Adaptation occurs in response to changing customers and changing competitive conditions, and these often result from broader macroenvironmental changes in society.[2]

In recent decades, considerable attention has been given to higher-level consumer needs, including clean air, better treatment in the marketplace, and a higher quality of life in general. Attention is given in this chapter to several related issues, including the role of profit, consumerism, the natural environment, and marketing ethics. Laws and regulations are often the outgrowth of social concerns over the functioning of the market system and its effects on the participants. Attention is given in this chapter to legal guidelines for pricing, channel, product, and promotion decisions.

Social Issues

The raison d'être of a social system is to serve the needs of the people. Society's needs are the basis for societal goals, and a fundamental goal of a society is usually to contribute to the happiness of its people or, a related goal, to the quality of their lives. These goals are also the social justification for marketing. A public examination of business demonstrates that marketing cannot be isolated from the many groups, organizations, and larger systems from which it derives its justification and its sustenance. It must serve social needs and contribute to a higher quality of life.

Social issues are a collective concern in a population based on a perceived gap between societal standards and the effects of marketing performance.

Immediate complications arise in striving for a higher quality of life because, given limited resources, it is impossible to satisfy all the desires of all people. The quality-of-life goal also requires a clear understanding of what generates happiness for different people. The means to achieving happiness obviously vary greatly for different people. These associated problems do not preclude using quality of life as a normative guideline for marketing decisions at the societal level, though the realities of social, governmental, and market processes should be taken into account. **Social issues** arise with regard to marketing when a concern arises over marketing practices, such as advertising to children.

Quality of Life

Quality of life refers to the perceived well-being of people, in groups and individually, and to the well-being of the environment in which these people live.[4]

There are as many definitions of **quality of life** as there are people. But if the quality-of-life concept is to be useful to marketers and public officials, some definition is essential. It is generally agreed that for most people in the United States, quality of life goes beyond purely economic issues. Most of the research on this matter has used such objective social indicators as economic wealth and unemployment and such noneconomic factors as crime rates and pollution to measure quality of life. These indicators are not adequate "if we believe, as most psychologists do, that the quality of life lies in the experience of life. Then these objective indicators are surrogate indicators. They describe the conditions of life that might be assumed to influence life experience, but they do not assess that experience directly."[3] More direct measures of the quality of life require attention to people's beliefs, feelings, states of happiness, and other cognitive, affective, and be-havioral measures that directly tap the subjective experience of life.

How does marketing affect the perceived well-being of people and the environment in which these people live? Gaps sometimes exist between customer's expectations (their standard) and their perception of actual mar-keting performance.

Consumer Issues and the Quality of Life

Whether the social issue is consumerism or pollution, its basic nature is captured in Exhibit 24–1. When consumer standards (partly based on expec-tations) are higher than perceived performance, consumer dissatisfaction may follow, ultimately leading to attempts to close the gap. It follows that, for consumers, the quality of life is negatively affected by a sense of dissatisfac-tion over such issues; this helps explain demands for a cleaner environment, a more equitable marketplace, and a higher quality of life in general. Implicit in the exhibit is the notion that consumer perceptions of marketing perform-ance may be inaccurate and that consumer standards (and expectations) may be unrealistic.

Consumer Education.

It is in the best interest of marketers to understand the level of consumer standards and the nature of consumer perceptions, as well as what is required to foster realism and accuracy among consumers. To reduce the chances that social issues will arise, management must deal with inadequate marketing performance, with unrealistic consumer standards, or with a combination of the two. In dealing with these matters, marketers should note that there is often a consumer information gap. As the number and complexity of products have grown over the years, the average buyer has not had the time, interest, or capacity to obtain the information needed to make optimal product decisions.[5] As the quantity of available information has increased, so has the time required to sort, digest, and evaluate it. Consequently, many companies have begun to specifically address the infor-mational needs of consumers and to develop programs for disseminating information to consumers. Kraft estimates that over a three-year period it distributed about 1.4 million informational booklets on food and nutrition terms, packaging, and labeling. To publicize the booklets, the company mailed a four-page newsletter to 8,000 educators and consumer profes-sionals, sent out news releases to papers around the country, and distributed 130 public service spots to more than 1,000 radio stations.[6]

Addressing Social Responsibility.

Marketing managers within different firms will see some social issues as more relevant than others. The relevance of a given social issue is determined by the company's products, promotional efforts, and pricing and distribution policies but also by its philosophy of social responsibility. A company may:

EXHIBIT 24-1 Marketing and Social Issues

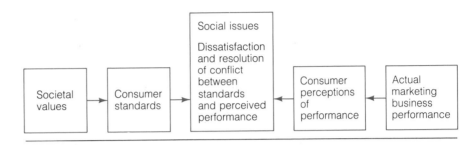

- Focus entirely on profits (and profitable firms typically serve society well).
- Explicitly incorporate social responsibility into its day-to-day marketing decisions to minimize negative effects on society and enhance positive effects.
- Go even further and engage in social projects that are unrelated to the corporate mission and even detrimental to profits (which could net out to be socially undesirable).

Management must decide which of these three levels of social responsibility to adopt and which social issues are relevant to its business.

> Control Data Corporation is a 25-year-old computer and financial services company that has had sales in excess of $4 billion. But it is also a company that, largely because of the whims of William C. Norris, its founder and chairman, dabbled in numerous ventures such as developing urban renewal plans, providing health care on Indian reservations, and computer education. Control Data says these projects are positioning the company for prosperity for years to come and showing corporate America how to solve social problems.
>
> Mr. Norris sees nothing less than a new role for private enterprise: Corporations, not government, increasingly will take the lead in finding new ways to solve unemployment, rehabilitate criminals, redevelop inner cities, and improve schools. But a former vice president of Control Data says, "The best thing they can do to be socially responsible is to make better products to increase demand so they can hire more people."[7]

Inner-City Marketplace.   One area of social concern and a notable example of marketplace failure is inner cities. Inner-city marketing problems have included price discrimination against the poor, exorbitant credit charges, and unethical merchant practices. Residents became increasingly dissatisfied with inner-city retail services; expectations rose; and the resulting gap between services and expectations contributed to frustration and even violence in the 1960s and early 1970s. During this period, attention was given to problems involving business practices, the market structure, and the behavior of consumers.[8] These factors, in combination, determine the performance of the retail system in inner cities still today.

Studies identified a higher incidence of fraudulent *business practices* in the inner city, including price discrimination, exorbitant credit charges, high-pressure salesmanship, and trickery. Prices for food and durables tend to be somewhat higher in inner-city areas, although operating costs such as insurance, pilferage, and labor turnover costs are also often higher. Just as important, mom-and-pop operations prohibit scale economies that large retail chains take for granted. Clearly, however, there is no economic justification for some shady retailer practices, and a higher proportion of merchants in the inner city take unfair advantage of consumers.

The inner-city retail *market structure* is atomistic, composed of tiny retail businesses that are often inefficient and poorly managed.[9] Mass merchandising and discount stores are underrepresented or nonexistent because there are serious barriers to entry, including high costs. Large retailers have pressed Congress for tax incentives and investment guarantees to make inner-city investments more attractive, but with little success.

The most basic problem of the inner-city marketplace is not retailer practices or the retail structure but *consumer behavior.* Compared to middle-income consumers, lower-income consumers tend to spend less time looking for information before making purchase decisions, are less mobile in their shopping, rely more on personal contacts and friendly merchants, and in general engage in purchasing behavior less characteristic of the "economic man" model. Less comparative shopping leads to less competition among retailers, and overly tolerant shoppers prolong the existence of marginal shops. Unethical merchants are attracted by these naive consumers, and the atomistic retail structure is to some extent required by consumers who search less. However, it is difficult to alter entrenched consumer behavior patterns, except over the long run. Thus, the social problems of the inner-city marketplace remain a challenge to the social conscience of marketers and public policymakers.

The Market System and Profit

An issue fundamental to the U.S. marketing system is the role of the profit motive.

Centralized versus Market Economies. In centralized economies, government planners rather than consumers make decisions concerning needs, the priority of need satisfaction (e.g., capital versus consumer goods), and the allocation of resources and production output. Despite the role of central planners, however, marketing functions are still performed—marketing is not eliminated. However, marketing activities may be performed in somewhat different ways and by different types of institutions. In a centralized economy, there may be less emphasis on advertising, so consumers must search for information on their own. Consumers may wait in lines outside stores to perform part of the usual advertising function—finding out what is available. But the same basic marketing functions, such as pricing and physical distribution, are performed in varying degrees in both centralized and market economies.

Market economies place much of the allocation responsibility on individuals. The degree of decentralization becomes apparent when one considers the millions of decisions that individual consumers make every day in the United States. These decisions collectively spell success or failure for products, companies, and even industries. The "votes" cast every day by customers ultimately determine how resources are allocated to satisfy various needs.

Reliance on markets and the market mechanism resolves the allocation of scarce resources to producers through the levels of consumer demand. The decisions of customers, via the market mechanism, lead to production decisions, which, in turn, result in the utilization of resources.

The Role of Profit. A key characteristic of the free market system is reliance on the profit motive as an incentive for people to contribute capital and human resources to the production process. The returns to investors and laborers (profits, wages, etc.) for the use of their resources provide the dollars (votes) that consumers expend in the marketplace. Individuals are allowed to accumulate capital and resources and to provide these for the production process in return for compensation.

In a now-classic letter to his grandson, Fred I. Kent, a former member of the Federal Reserve Board, used the following example to explain the nature of profit (and specialization):

> Our primitive community, dwelling at the foot of a mountain, must have water. There is no water except at a spring near the top of the mountain: therefore, every day all the 100 persons climb to the top of the mountain. It takes them one hour to go up and back. They do this day in and day out, until at last one of them notices that the water from the spring runs down inside the mountain in the same direction that he goes when he comes down. He conceives the idea of digging a trough in the mountainside all the way down to the place where he has his habitation. He goes to work to build a trough. The other 99 people are not even curious about what he is doing.
>
> Then one day this 100th man turns a small part of the water from the spring into his trough and it runs down the mountain into a basin he has fashioned at the bottom. Whereupon he says to the 99 others, who each spend an hour a day catching their water, that if they will each give him daily production of 10 minutes of their time, he will give them water from his basin. He will then receive 990 minutes of the time of the other men each day; this arrangement will make it unnecessary for him to work 16 hours a day to provide for his necessities. He is making a tremendous profit—but his enterprise has given each of the 99 other people 50 additional minutes each day.

The enterpriser, now having 16 hours a day at his disposal and being naturally curious, spends part of his time watching the water run down the mountain. He sees that it pushes along stones and pieces of wood. So he develops a water wheel; then he notices that it has power and, finally, after many hours of contemplation and work, he makes the water wheel run a mill to grind his corn.

This 100th man then realizes that he has sufficient power to grind corn for the other 99. He says to them, "I will allow you to grind your corn in my mill if you will give me 1/10th of the time you save." They agree, and so the enterpriser now makes an additional profit.[10]

This example illustrates the advantages of specialization and entrepreneurship, and it also suggests the rudiments of marketing, in that exchange becomes necessary as specialization is initiated. The entrepreneur trades his creative time for a proportion of the output resulting from the efforts of others. The value of profit as a motivator is provided by an extension of the example:

But suppose that, when the 100th man had completed his trough down the mountain and said to the other 99, "If you will give me what it takes you 10 minutes to produce, I will let you get your water from my basin," they had turned on him and said, "We are 99 and you are only 1. We will take what water we want. You cannot prevent us and we will give you nothing." What would have happened then? The incentive of the most curious mind to build upon his enterprising thought would have been taken away. He would have seen that he could gain nothing by solving problems if he still had to use every waking hour to provide his living. There could have been no advancement in the community. Life would have continued to be drudgery to everyone, with opportunity to do no more than work all day long just for a bare living.[11]

Centralized economies tend to remove much of the return on investment provided by market economies, in return for promises that the greater and longer-run good will be served. There are tremendous merits to using the profit motive, yet in every society the social good must be balanced against individual incentives. There is some inherent conflict between the two. Consumer suspicions about corporate profit motives tend to contribute to mistrust, despite the powerful rationale for having a profit-oriented system.

Consumerism

Consumerism
is an environmental force intended to aid and protect the consumer through the exertion of legal, moral, and economic pressure on business.[12]

Consumerism has been defined as simply "let the seller beware." Consumers, politicians, and various groups sometimes engage in actions intended to stir public opinion and generate public pressure—thus making consumerism a social force protecting the consumer (e.g., ensuring product safety) and aiding the consumer (e.g., providing better product information). Consumerism also generates pressure for regulation and legislation, appeals to the executive conscience, and exerts economic pressure through boycotts and negative publicity.

Consumerism exists in part because rising expectations outpaced business performance. Increasing incomes, higher educational levels, and changing values all helped create more demanding consumers. Add the impact of mass communications on consumer awareness, catalysts such as Ralph Nader, inflation, and a certain cynicism regarding institutions (including marketing), and one begins to understand why consumerism arose. The causes underlying consumerism go far beyond some failures of marketing and business, though these are partly to blame.

Is consumerism dying in the 1980s? There were major consumer movements in the early 1900s and 1930s that gradually disappeared. And the anticontrol mood in recent years has turned the tide of regulation that exploded during the 1970s. Yet the numerous laws and institutions that were then created to deal with consumer problems are still operational. Some longtime students of consumerism observed:

> One estimate made in 1980 identified some 4,000 consumer issues that had not been resolved by the federal government. . . . It is our opinion . . . that consumerism is neither declining sharply nor awaiting dramatic new growth but is rather in a mature, active stage that should continue through the 1980s and beyond. However, the thrust and character of the movement are bound to change, partly in response to evolving issues and partly in response to the mature phase of the product life cycle.[13]

The late 1970s and the first half of the 1980s were characterized as a back to basics period for Americans. Consumerism was affected, but it did not go away.

Organizational changes in response to consumerism are seen in the fact that over 200 companies have created high-level positions to deal with consumer problems. To be successful, the occupants of these positions must have the full support of top management, and many, in fact, report directly to the president. As the director of corporate social responsibility at Standard Oil of Indiana stated: "Social policies will remain placebos for the tortured executive conscience until they are implemented with the same iron-fisted management tools that are routinely employed in other areas of activity to measure performance, secure accountability, and distribute penalties and rewards."[14]

The Natural Environment

Another significant area of social concern is the environment. Marketing is ultimately dependent on the use of scarce resources to fulfill human needs. Actions that upset the ecological balance by either harming or unnecessarily using scarce resources can be the object of social and governmental action.[15] Consumer-oriented firms provide goods and services that meet needs—but sometimes without fully considering the social costs.

Marketing managers help determine which products are produced, and this indirectly affects:

- The natural resources and materials used.
- The amount of energy required in the production process.
- The residuals (e.g., wastewater) that result from production.
- The consumption of resources and energy that is required to use products (cars, air conditioners).
- The generation of pollutants (e.g., exhaust fumes) in using products.
- The amount of packaging material that may have to be discarded. (Packaging comprises less than 14 percent of collectible solid waste, but consumers often estimate its share of that waste at 40 to 80 percent).

Ecology groups and government offices pressure marketers to consider the social costs of production. However, many consumers are unwilling to pay higher prices for products that conserve resources or pollute less. Marketers can alter consumer's product preferences by limiting choices (either dropping existing products or not offering new products), but then questions of consumer freedom arise. Proponents of a free market system argue that consumers should be made aware of the social costs associated with the production and use of products and then should decide whether or not to purchase them.

Although marketing can have negative environmental effects, marketing techniques can also be used to help solve environmental problems. Marketing methods contribute to the development of products that improve the environment (Exhibit 24-2) and help business and social organizations inform and educate consumers on the environmental effects of their buying decisions. In an age of scarce resources, management may even engage in demarketing, encouraging less consumption—as with electricity and gasoline if energy shortages occur. Marketing can also be used to ensure efficient recycling, because recycling is, after all, a reverse channel of distribution. Consumers become the de facto producers, with middlemen channeling products for reuse (e.g., returnable bottles) or for reprocessing into different products or raw materials.[16]

> Turning trash into a valuable commodity (resource recovery) was one of the goals of the environmental movement in the 1970s, but the efforts failed. Yet *burning* trash to generate electricity or steam has demonstrated its commercial viability, particularly in the Northeast where landfill sites are scarce and energy is expensive. At a plant in Saugus, Massachusetts, garbage trucks from Boston and 16 nearby communities bring in 1,500 tons of trash a day and dump it into a 100 by 200 foot pit. Forced air and a 1,500-degree flame heats water in pipes surrounding the furnace and creates steam that is piped to the GE jet-engine plant a half mile away.[17]

The process has become a viable new service that generates revenue from the sale of power, the sale of recovered scrap metals, and the fees charged trash haulers.

EXHIBIT 24–2

Want to see the old mill stream turn out clean new energy?

Borg-Warner mini-hydroelectric turbines turn the energy in small rivers and streams into pollution-free electrical power. That's today's Borg-Warner. Diversified for financial stability. A company worth watching. **BorgWarner**

Watch Borg-Warner

For an annual report write: Borg-Warner, Dept. 25, 200 South Michigan Avenue, Chicago, Illinois 60604.

Environmental concerns are the focus of new product development programs in many firms.

Courtesy Foote, Cone & Belding.

The Social Audit: How Do We Measure Up?

Corporate social audit
is a systematic assessment of and report on the social impact of a company's activities.[18]

Marketers should assess their strategies and their corporate social posture against the backdrop of societal expectations and the effects of their practices on the quality of life. Companies can undertake a **social audit** to assess the effects of their activities on society and to measure, somewhat as financial statements measure financial progress, the degree to which they have met social goals. Unless attention is given to measuring corporate social progress, the concept of social responsibility remains nebulous and impossible to implement.

Social audits are still at the experimental stage, so we can only address the marketing elements of a social audit. These steps are taken in a social audit:

- Identify the positive and negative social impacts of the firm's marketing activity on the quality of life of the firm's constituencies.

- Develop measures of those impacts.

■ Evaluate the impacts, and draw implications for management.

Three types of evaluations are used.[19] The first is an annual survey in which customers, suppliers, employees, and others complete a questionnaire on how well or badly a business satisfies its constituencies. The second is a social responsibility annual report prepared by management that inventories, explains, and evaluates the company's social contribution. The third is a socioeconomic operating statement in which management estimates social costs and benefits. These costs and benefits are attached to three areas of company impact: the physical environment, customers, and employees. Major accounting associations have been analyzing the issues and developing methodologies for social audits in recent years. However, the measurement problems are immense.

A number of firms have attempted to find a common denominator, such as dollars, for measuring social effects, but only a few have attempted to develop a social balance sheet. Dayton Hudson Corporation, a diversified retail organization headquartered in Minneapolis, attempted to define and measure social impacts relevant to the entire industry, but it soon found the task overwhelming. It then formed task forces on consumerism, human resources, environmental impact, and community development. Instead of precisely measuring social impacts, these task forces helped the company respond to areas of social need. However, measuring such impacts would enable companies to defuse social issues in their early stages.

Ethics and Marketing

Marketing ethics are culturally based standards that guide individual and organizational conduct.	A final social issue concerns the general area of **marketing ethics**—moral judgments and standards of conduct. Ethics tend to be an outgrowth of a culture and of its related customs and mores. But in the final analysis, ethics in marketing become an organizational and individual matter. Ethics within the corporate culture, as well as the actions of individuals, should be evaluated.

How morally right or wrong a decision is usually depends in part on the circumstances. Company ethical customs and precedents influence the decisions made, and judgments as to the rightfulness or wrongfulness of decisions are influenced by the organizational culture.

The minimum standards of ethical conduct are set by laws, but even these standards are sometimes violated. Laws in a democracy are a set of codified standards that reflect the values of the society and by the time the standards become law they usually have the support of the citizenry. Laws set standards for *social* responsibility; they are designed to protect the community or society as a whole. Ethics, however, become operational at the level of *individual* actions.

The 18th-century philosopher Immanuel Kant held that rules of conduct are to be applied universally and without exception.[20] Kant's categorical imperative admonishes that an action is appropriate only if we can say we would be pleased if everyone engaged in it. The problem is that few universal rules of conduct can be applied without exception (even "thou shalt not kill"). The antithesis of the imperative is situational ethics which admonishes us to engage in an action only if the resultant good exceeds the resultant evil. This is the model with which the ends are sometimes used to justify the means. If imperative and situational ethics represent the polar extremes of ethical posture, the reality of marketing usually places us somewhere between the two.

Although professional standards of conduct are imperative, most marketing decisions require a qualitative balancing of situational right and wrong. However, there are some generally accepted standards of business conduct. The American Marketing Association, for example, has a code of ethics for marketing researchers, and the American Institute for Certified Public Accountants has a much stronger code, as well as enforcement mechanisms for its membership. A certifying system has also been discussed for marketing professionals.

Specific ethical issues in marketing usually involve consumer and environmental matters. The following situations highlight the kinds of ethical issues that are encountered.

■ An advertising agency proposes that its client's ads for a new space-walk children's toy include actual space-walk footage. This conveys the concept in an exciting way, but it conveys unrealistic notions of the toy's actual capability. Should the idea be given a green light?

■ A salesperson is faced with a projected shortage of the company's hot selling semiconductor product. There is better than a 50-50 chance that production will be increased enough to cover new orders. The entire industry is facing excess demand. Should the salesperson describe the situation to customers before accepting orders for the product or wait two or three weeks until more is known?

■ An independent marketing researcher has been offered a research project that would involve secretly videotaping salesperson/customer negotiations in the firm's sales offices. It could also involve inadvertently taping private customer discussions when the salesperson steps out of the office. The results of the research project will be used to determine the product attributes of most importance to customers. Should the researcher accept the project?

■ A key competitor has increased its package size by one ounce and has increased its price by the equivalent of two ounces. Due to limited competition in your market area, you could make a similar move and customers would probably not detect what you had done. Should you do it?

Since marketing is heavily involved with persuasive verbal communication, marketers may have more temptation and freedom to err than do people in other business areas. Job performance in other business areas tends to be more specific and measurable than job performance in marketing, so marketers have both greater latitude and a greater responsibility to exercise restraint.[21] In an age of intense competition described by such expressions as "market *warfare*," "*target* market," and "*fighting* for market share," it is important for the marketing manager to occasionally step back from the firing line and inspect his or her ethical philosophy. Each manager must decide how moral to be.

Top level ethical leadership within the company and the marketing unit is also important. The company should:

■ Put into writing its ethical and social philosophy, and be certain that this material is effectively communicated to all employees.

■ Set a good example at the top. The marketing vice president and other key executives set the tone. Many of the problems involving ethical considerations are dealt with at internal planning meetings, where the gray area is often confronted. The corporate culture should reflect an ethical viewpoint in action as well as in writing.

■ Establish incentives to reward employees who engage in activities that bring the company credit in the larger community, and provide disincentives for employees who drift into unethical conduct.

■ Control ethics as part of the overall marketing control function. Watch for smoke in time to avoid major fires, and explicitly monitor this dimension of marketing performance.

Contemporary Legal Issues

Social and ethical concerns often lead to legislation and regulation that define the straight and narrow path for marketers. The laws cited in Chapter 3 have numerous implications for marketing management as they affect pricing, distribution, products, promotion, and marketing research. Large companies usually have in-house legal counsel, but management must be sufficiently aware of possible legal problems to know when to seek counsel. In today's environment, in-house legal awareness programs are directed at all levels of management, from the salesperson to the chief executive officer. Up to the mid-1980s, however, the trend was toward private litigation, because of a federal policy of minimal intervention by the regulatory agencies.[22]

Pricing Decisions

Pricing has probably involved more legal action than any other marketing area. Circumscribed practices include:

- Horizontal price-fixing (price collusion between competitors).
- Price discrimination (charging different customers different prices).
- Vertical price-fixing (specifying distributor's prices).
- The form and availability of price information for consumers.

Horizontal Price-Fixing. Joint or collusive price-setting between competitors at a given level of distribution, whether at the manufacturer, wholesaler, or retailer level, is illegal per se. Under the Sherman and FTC acts, attempts "to monopolize" or to "substantially lessen competition" are prohibited.

Pricing developments in recent years include FTC decisions to discourage price-fixing and restrictions on price advertising by medical associations, attorneys, pharmacists, and optometrists. Professional associations have long been known to foster price-fixing by establishing standard fees and banning advertising. The FTC decisions are oriented toward increasing competition and reliance on free market forces among professionals. Also in the 1980s, the Court reached several decisions that reduced the previous exemption of nonprofit organizations and municipal governments.

Price Discrimination. In the 1930s, large grocery chains, capitalizing on scale economies and special discounts from suppliers, offered consumers low prices and were viewed as a threat to smaller grocery stores. As a result, because the Clayton Act required that a firm be proven to have "substantially" lessened competition, the Robinson-Patman Act was passed to outlaw price discrimination that only "injured" competition. The courts have interpreted the Robinson-Patman Act largely in terms of injury to "competitors" (e.g., small grocers) rather than injury to "competition," contributing to a continual debate over whether the act does more good than harm. The act may actually restrict price competition and protect inefficient firms from head-on price competition.

Not all price discrimination is illegal under the Robinson-Patman Act. The main defense for charging different customers different prices for goods of "like grade and quality" is cost-based. If the costs for serving one group of customers can be shown to be lower than the costs of serving another group, then price differences (e.g., quantity discounts) are usually legal.

The Robinson-Patman Act also prohibits giving specific customers special advertising allowances and support services unless this is done in a good faith effort to match competitors.

If it can be shown that a company is meeting (but not exceeding) competitor price cuts in good faith or if merchandise is sold under distress sale circumstances, different prices may be allowed. Indeed, Supreme Court decisions at the end of the 1970s and in the 1980s greatly expanded the "meeting competitors' price cuts in good faith" defense.

A price difference is usually *not* illegal if:

■ It is based on actual cost differences in serving particular types of customers.

■ It did not harm competition.

■ The price was set in good faith to meet a competitor's price or to sell merchandise under distress conditions.

■ The goods sold to different customers are not of "like grade and quality."

Resale Price Maintenance.   In the mid-1970s, all interstate use of resale price maintenance was ended by the Consumer Goods Pricing Act, which put vertical price-fixing under the jurisdiction of the antitrust laws. Although it was never effectively demonstrated that the fair trade laws benefited small businesses or the consumer,[23] the issue continued to be debated well into the 1980s, with the Justice Department arguing that vertical price-fixing should be judged on whether it would unreasonably restrict competition. In recent years, the Justice Department's antitrust chief made it clear that he did not expect to prosecute such cases, despite objections from Congress.[24]

Consumer Information.   Other legal pricing issues have included unit pricing. Unit pricing provides consumers with a price per unit (per fluid ounce, per pound) on grocery items to facilitate price comparisons between brands. Certain states now require this information in grocery stores, although no federal statute has been enacted.

Channel Decisions

When manufacturers deal with members in their distribution channel, such as wholesalers or retailers, legal questions sometimes arise. Channel decisions on prices may raise legal questions; other channel decisions that raise legal questions include refusals to deal, exclusive dealing, tying contracts, and exclusive territories. In the mid-1980s, the Justice Department issued guidelines supporting the legality of most of the marketing restrictions that producers routinely impose on distributors, but not the following.[25]

Refusals to Deal.   According to the *Colgate doctrine* put forth by the Supreme Court in 1919, a trader or a manufacturer may exercise his "independent discretion as to parties with whom he will deal" as long as no intent exists to create or maintain a monopoly. More scrutiny, however, is usually directed at plans to drop distributors than at refusals to add new ones. Manufacturers and distributors must act in good faith in terminating a dealer and, specifically, cannot cut off dealers that refuse to engage in questionable arrangements, such as exclusive dealing or tying contracts.

Exclusive Dealing. This refers to a seller that requires its distributors to carry only its products and not to handle competitors' products. This goes beyond exclusive distribution, in which a distributor is given exclusive rights to sell a manufacturer's products but is allowed to sell other brands. **Exclusive dealing** is not illegal per se, but Section 3 of the Clayton Act outlaws it where its effect is to *substantially* lessen competition. Exclusive dealing arrangements may be mutually beneficial: beneficial to the manufacturer because the dealer concentrates sales efforts solely on its brands and beneficial to the dealer because the manufacturer usually assures the dealer of a source of supply and often gives the dealer exclusive rights to handle its brands in a given market area. Yet because such arrangements exclude competitive brands from the dealer's assortment, they may also serve to lessen competition. A major question is where the courts and the FTC should draw the line between "lessening" and "substantially lessening" competition. Franchise contracts that require the franchisee to purchase all products and supplies from the franchisor are considered suspect. Generally, if a manufacturer holds a dominant share of the market (and therefore may foreclose market entry and holds considerable power over distributors), exclusive dealing will be considered illegal.

Exclusive dealing is a seller requirement that the buyer carry only the seller's products.

Tying Contracts. Under Section 3 of the Clayton Act, **tying contracts** are illegal. Periods of shortages increase customer dependence and the potential for illegal tying contracts. Unless a tying device is being used by a small firm to break into a market, it is likely to be declared illegal.

Fast-food franchisees have faced **full-line forcing** in years past. A firm must usually possess considerable power over a dependent customer for this to occur.

Tying contracts require buyers to purchase products not wanted as a condition for obtaining desired products.

Full-line forcing requires buyers to purchase a full product line when only part of one is wanted.

Exclusive Territories. Franchisees and exclusive distributors are usually given a specified territory in which to distribute a manufacturer's brand. Until recently, however, cases indicated that the Supreme Court expected not only *inter*brand competition to be maintained (between different manufacturer's brands), but also *intra*brand competition (between the distributors of the same brand).[26] Consequently, the Court indicated that actual ownership of the distribution system, or at least consignment selling (in which the producer retains ownership of the products), is necessary if exclusive territories are allocated and intrabrand competition is restricted among the outlets in a given market. An early case (*Arnold Schwinn & Co.*) made the vertical control of consignees subject to the **rule of reason,** but attempts by producers to control distributors that took title to the goods were illegal per se.

The *GTE Sylvania* case (1977) changed this interpretation. For years, Sylvania maintained a policy of selective distribution for its television sets by including in the franchise agreement a clause that required retailers to obtain permission to change their location. A Sylvania dealer claimed violation of

Rule of reason required that each case be evaluated to decide whether it represented an unreasonable restraint of trade.

the Sherman Act, and in the *GTE Sylvania* case the Supreme Court ruled that a manufacturer's efforts to control its distributors on nonprice matters (e.g., where to locate and sell) would not be considered automatically illegal under the per se rule but that the legality of such efforts would be determined under the rule of reason.

The Court upheld GTE Sylvania's position that even though its franchise terms reduced the amount of intrabrand competition for Sylvania color television sets, the arrangement increased Sylvania's ability to engage in interbrand competition with other companies. The net result, reasoned the Court, was an increased market share (1 percent to 5 percent) for Sylvania and a generally more competitive marketplace.

Franchisors may use location clauses and, it appears, other vertical restrictions that are not "manifestly anticompetitive." This reversal of the per se rule drastically increases management flexibility and allows greater control over distribution channels. Application of the rule of reason, however, increases legal uncertainties with regard to potentially anticompetitive channel decisions. In fact, the first major case after *Sylvania* resulted in a decision that seemed at odds with the view in the *Sylvania* decision.[27]

Product Decisions

Governmental influence in product and packaging practices has grown significantly over the past two decades. Expanding product lines by mergers and acquisitions may be subject to government scrutiny. Additional management attention should be given to patents and trademarks, product labeling, product safety, and product liability.

Patents and Trademarks.   Under U.S. patent laws, a company may gain a monopoly over the production and marketing of a specific product or process for a 17-year period. Polaroid cameras were protected from direct competition for many years, giving Polaroid's marketing people added flexibility in pricing and other decisions. Eastman Kodak Company then entered the marketplace with its instant cameras, but in the mid-1980s, after a nine-year patent battle, Kodak was forced to cease marketing its instant cameras and film and to withdraw them from the marketplace. Patents are a legal exception that grant monopoly power in order to encourage invention by giving inventors protection from competitive infringement on potential profits. The patent gives its holder power to prevent others from offering an identical product unless the holder chooses to sell the patent or license its use by others. Restrictive licenses, however (requiring a licensee to sell the product for a specified price), are illegal under the Sherman Act because of their price-fixing and restraint-of-trade ramifications. Also, patent holders are not allowed to harass potential or existing competitors with the threat of a patent infringement suit. The net effects of patent policy on the public good are often debated—but with no change or resolution.

Trademarks, like patents, allow the owner to file suits against unauthorized users. Trademarks or trade names may be registered with the U.S. Patent Office to establish evidence of ownership (Lanham Act, 1946). Trademarks are often a key part of product differentiation and brand image, and they are registered for 20 years, with renewal possible. If the trade name becomes the generic term for the product, however, it may become available for general use, so a company may wish to avoid having a trade name (such as Xerox) become that well accepted.

Product Labeling. Labeling information requirements under the Food, Drug, and Cosmetics Act is highly related to product safety since:

■ Labeling may include warnings against product misuse and hazards.

■ Required safety labeling statements, to be factual and therefore legal, in effect compel products to measure up to the stated safety standards.

In addition to its safety-related role, labeling information may assist consumers in evaluating alternative products (e.g., information on weight, grade, nutritional content, and ingredients). Such information is usually required by the Fair Packaging and Labeling Act, though the Food, Drug, and Cosmetics Act also led to FDA regulations requiring nutritional information on packages and dictating the location and the size of labels.

At the state and local level, numerous labeling laws conflict with one another and with federal legislation. Since there are 87,000 local governments, this lack of uniformity can create havoc for national distributors.

Product Safety. The Consumer Product Safety Act (1972) established the powerful Consumer Product Safety Commission, which administers the Federal Hazardous Substances Act (as amended), the Poison Prevention Packaging Act, the Flammable Fabrics Act (and its 1967 amendment), the Refrigerator Door Safety Act, and the Toy Safety Act, all of which are intended to reduce injuries related to consumer products. The Consumer Product Safety Commission (CPSC) has jurisdiction over an estimated 43,000 products.

The Federal Hazardous Substances Act was designed to ensure that labeling information (such as the above-cited cautionary statements, instructions for safe use, and first-aid instructions) is provided, but the act may also be used to ban some substances entirely. The Flammable Fabrics Act and the Poison Prevention Packaging Act (PPPA) deal primarily with product safety standards rather than labeling. They were applied to raise standards concerning the flammability of children's sleepwear and childproof packages for toxic or harmful substances. Aspirin bottles and thousands of drugs and household substances (e.g., furniture polish) were affected.

The Consumer Product Safety Act requires that manufacturers have a "reasonable" product safety testing program, and it can require manufacturers to notify purchasers if a product is found to be defective. Reasonable safety standards may be set (such as for bicycles), or products may be banned or recalled and public warnings and refunds required.

A Consumer Product Safety Commission telephone hot line encourages consumer reports of product-related accidents, and a National Electronic Injury Surveillance System (NEISS) monitors product-related consumer injuries. Manufacturers, importers, distributors, and retailers must notify the commission within 24 hours of learning that a product defect could create a "substantial risk of injury to consumers."

Product liability is the legal liability of manufacturers, retailers, and other distributors that produce or distribute defective or unsuitable merchandise that causes injury to consumers.

Product Liability.   Sellers may incur **product liability** because of negligence, breach of either an express or implied warranty, fraudulent misrepresentation of the product, or, more recently, selling a defective product that is unreasonably dangerous to the user or consumer. This last concept of strict liability does not require proof of negligence, warranty, or misrepresentation.

A manufacturer can be held liable for consumer injuries due to negligence in producing a product. Until recently, however, in the case of an "implied warranty" the manufacturer was usually *not* held liable, but the retailer could be held liable. The increasing acceptance of the concept of strict liability makes it possible for a seller (including the manufacturer) to be held responsible for an injury caused by a defective product even if due care was exercised in its preparation and sale. Distributors that brand products as their own are treated as manufacturers, thereby exposing themselves to manufacturer's liability. The FTC can also set rules to guide manufacturers in disclosing the terms and conditions of express warranties (voluntarily given on products costing more than $15). Firms have been advised to take defensive actions against the possible application of a concept of "absolute liability" (liability imposed on a producer of goods irrespective not only of the standard of care used but also of proof that the defect exists) by:

- Improving quality control.
- Emphasizing safety in product design.
- Keeping accurate records.
- Increasing insurance protection.
- Adding to legal capacity.[28]

By the mid-1980s, however, the sentiment in Congress had shifted in favor of a bill that would limit the legal liability of manufacturers. Before a company would be considered liable, a consumer would have to prove negligence, in addition to proving that the product caused harm, and only the first person to bring such a case could win punitive damages.[29]

Promotion Decisions

Promotion activities are by definition very visible and subject to consumer criticism.

False, Deceptive, and Unfair Advertising.   Because misleading advertising hinders the functioning of the market system, the authority of the Federal Trade Commission Act was extended over the false advertising of foods, drugs, cosmetics, and therapeutic devices. The FTC is responsible for pursuing violations of the Wheeler-Lea Act in all media and for nearly all products and services except prescription drugs. The Federal Communications Commission (FCC) works to encourage responsible advertising in the broadcast media.

FTC interpretations and court decisions have broadened the term *false* to mean "deceptive" and even "unfair." The word *deceptive* has been most commonly defined in legal terminology as "having the capacity or tendency to deceive." Some analysts have pointed out that deception, to be sufficiently understood, requires attention to the characteristics of the customers involved and how the ads actually affect them.[30] "Unfairness" is an evolving concept, and future FTC actions will help clarify its applications to advertising regulation.[31] The FTC has focused primarily on the claims or representations made in advertisements. But in the mid-1980s it enacted a new enforcement policy in which the deception criterion used was whether or not a "reasonable" consumer would be injured by the advertising.[32] This represented a shift from a policy in which such groups as children and the elderly were regarded as deserving of special consideration. Under its new policy, the FTC will find fewer advertising practices to be illegal.

Major attention to advertising really began in the 1970s, with the creation of a Bureau of Consumer Protection in the FTC. The bureau was established to collect and interpret information concerning consumer problems. Its actions, with reinforcement from the courts, have had a major impact on corporate advertisers and advertising agencies.

Advertising Substantiation.   There was a time when shaving cream commercials shaved "sandpaper" that was really Plexiglas and loose sand and a soup company used marbles in its soup commercial to push the vegetables visibly to the top. Today, such clearly false advertisements are less of a problem than is advertising that falls into the changing gray area of acceptability.

The current scarcity of clearly false advertising is at least partly due to the existence of the FTC's advertising substantiation program. Thousands of companies have been required to provide data to support their advertised claims. The definition of "deceptive and unfair" that is used in evaluating a company's substantiation data is determined by the FTC's reasonable basis standard.

If "performance claims" are even implied in an advertisement, a company should have substantiating data that, if possible, are derived from testing procedures with scientific underpinnings and provide extensive and well-documented support.[33] The test requirement may also be applied to "uniqueness claims"; the FTC has challenged such purported brand differences as "accu-color," "instamatic," and "total automatic color" as well as the uniqueness of Crisco cooking oil in creating food that tastes "less greasy." Subjective claims pertaining to performance or uniqueness are difficult to substantiate, especially claims regarding matters which consumers can verify only by means of subjective indicators. Profile bread had its name reviewed (but not changed) because it was not lower in calories than other breads; and Mattel race cars endorsed by famous race-car drivers were questioned because of the drivers' lack of actual toy expertise. Each case provided a potentially misleading "surrogate indicator" to consumers.[34]

Other Deception.   The FTC is also charged with prohibiting deceptive practices such as bait and switch advertising, fictitious bargains, and the "you have been especially selected" tactic. Bait and switch refers to the practice of "baiting" consumers with a tempting advertised price and then encouraging them to trade up (switch) to a more expensive model once they arrive at the store. Fictitious bargains may be prices that are ostensibly, but not actually, reduced. The "especially selected" ploy uses flattery and the presentation of a unique opportunity to con consumers into buying merchandise that is actually available to anyone for as good a price. Deceptively large packages and misleading guarantees are other examples of deceptive practices that are subject to FTC action.

Personal Selling.   Deceptive personal selling practices are also subject to prosecution, although there has been little FTC action to date. Exceptions include a move against encyclopedia companies that required salespersons to state their actual selling intent to consumers instead of using a misleading sales approach. Also, a "cooling-off period" for door-to-door sales was enacted that gives a buyer the right to cancel a purchase from a door-to-door salesperson anytime prior to midnight of the third business day after the date of the transaction (if the purchase price is $25 or more).

FTC Procedures and Remedial Actions.   The mechanisms that the FTC can use against companies suspected of deceptive or anticompetitive practices are shown in Exhibit 24–3.[35] A firm may voluntarily acquiesce to an FTC action through a consent order. A *consent order* is an agreement between respondents and the FTC that they will refrain from engaging in the practices to which the commission objects, but it is not an admission of prior wrongdoing. The terms of the proposed consent order are then put on the public record for comment by any interested persons for 60 days, after which the order may be modified to reflect public comment or remain unchanged.[36] A firm may also fight an FTC action. If a firm fights and an administrative judge then rules against it, the firm may appeal through a circuit court of appeals and the Supreme Court, though most such appeals have not proved fruitful.

Voluntary compliance so as to avoid the complaint stage may be facilitated by a Trade Practice Conference (TPC), in which an *industry* seeks inter-

EXHIBIT 24–3 Settlement Mechanisms of the Federal Trade Commission

Remedy	Procedure	Remedy	Procedure
Consent order	Business ordered to consent to stop the questionable practice without admitting illegality	*Restitution*	Requires refunds or other restitution to consumers misled by deceptive advertising
Affirmative disclosure	Requires advertiser to provide additional information about products in its advertisements	*Counteradvertising*	Permits competitor advertisements in broadcast media to counteract advertising claims (also proviso for free time under certain conditions)
Corrective advertising	Requires company advertising to correct the past effects of misleading advertising (e.g., 25 percent of the media budget to FTC-approved advertisements of FTC-specified messages)	*Cease and desist order*	A final FTC order to cease an illegal practice—often challenged in the courts

Sources: William L. Wilkie, Dennis L. McNeill, and Michael B. Mazis, "Marketing's 'Scarlet Letter': The Theory and Practice of Corrective Advertising," *Journal of Marketing* 48 (Spring 1984), pp. 11–31; Robert E. Wilkes and James B. Wilcox, "Recent FTC Actions: Implications for the Advertising Strategist," *Journal of Marketing* 38 (January 1974), pp. 58–60; and Dorothy Cohen, "Court Decisions Weaken FTC's Public Interest Power," *Marketing News*, February 14, 1975, p. 4. Published by the American Marketing Association.

pretative rules regarding its practices from the FTC. Industry members may discuss and propose needed rules. In this case, the FTC staff obtains preliminary approval of the rules from the five-member commission and releases the rules for a public hearing. After the hearing, the commission issues the rules. *Industry guides*, limited to a particular problem practice, are sometimes issued, and these may involve more than a single industry. *Advisory opinions*, issued at the request of individual companies, also provide helpful guidelines. A firm might submit proposed advertising copy to the commission for approval, and the advisory opinion effectively provides an advance evaluation. Finally, *trade regulation rules* are conclusions of the commission as to the legality of specific practices. Once a final ruling has been issued, the FTC relies on the ruling to resolve issues in future adjudicative proceedings.

As for remedies, the FTC has historically issued *cease and desist* orders. If cases involving such orders are not settled by negotiation, they are pursued at length in the courts. Because of lengthy appeal problems associated with the cease and desist order, the commission has increasingly used other remedies, listed in Exhibit 24–3.

The FTC Improvement Act (1977) gave the FTC authority to "redress past wrongs and to remove the economic incentive" to commit unfair and deceptive acts or practices in or affecting commerce. Allowable remedies include the rescission or reformation of contracts, the refund of money or the return of property, compensatory damages, and public notification. Punitive damages were not provided for, and there is a three-year statute of limitations.

Some of the most effective efforts to ensure appropriate advertising have been through *self*-regulation, such as the efforts of the National Advertising Review Board.

Marketing Research Decisions

Marketing research activities have expanded in recent decades, and accompanying this growth has been attention to related ethical issues. These include consumer irritation over such practices as:

- Pressure to obtain interviews.
- Deceptive methods, such as using one-way mirrors or disguising study objectives.
- Invasion of privacy, particularly as it relates to the confidentiality of the respondents' answers in interviews.[37]

Although the above are ethical rather than legal issues, attention has also been given to the law of privacy. Four types of tort action (a civil wrong that will support an action for damages) include:

- Intrusion (intruding on an individual's private affairs, solitude, or seclusion).
- Disclosure (making public embarrassing private facts about an individual).
- False light (publicizing misrepresentative statements about an individual).
- Appropriation (using an individual's name or likeness for the appropriator's advantage).[38]

As long as no *individual* data are released and publicized, the last three types of tort should not pose a significant threat to marketing researchers. However, a future threat could come under the "intrusion" tort, if research were ever defined to encompass "mental or psychological" intrusion. Even here, a respondent's right is waived by consent, but it is not clear whether this would include consenting to be interviewed if disguised questioning were then used.[39] In these instances, the law of misrepresentation could also apply.

If consumers were to become generally offended by marketing research activities, the potential for new legislation would increase accordingly. Paradoxically, understanding consumer needs and implementing a customer orientation are largely dependent on information obtained from research. But it is clear that individual data should be guarded jealously and good taste should be exercised to avoid legal issues.

Application

Defending Comparative Advertisements[40]

Is Eastern Airlines truly "America's favorite way to fly"? Does Ford Motor Company make "the best-built American cars and trucks"? And how does Carnation Company know for sure that "three out of four" canines really prefer its New Breed dog food to all other brands? Texas Instruments used comparative advertising very effectively to position its product against the IBM personal computer (Exhibit 24–A).

While surveys have shown that some people are likely to dismiss such claims, to at least one audience they are a matter of great concern: the competition. And whether out of pride or genuine business interest, more companies are striking back when they think competitors have gone too far.

Challenges against comparative advertising have increased in the courts, before the Federal Trade Commission, and through a variety of private channels. Chesebrough-Pond's, Inc. sued Procter & Gamble Company and ad agency Benton & Bowles in federal court, charging that P&G used flawed scientific data to support a claim for its Wondra skin lotion. P&G responded by filing a suit against Chesebrough-Pond's, asserting that advertising for its Vaseline Intensive Care skin lotion was misleading. Both companies claim that their products are the best.

"We've seen a definite jump in cases in recent years," said Ronald H. Smithies, who headed a division of the Council of Better Business Bureaus that arbitrates advertising disputes between competitors. National Broadcasting Company, which runs a similar program for ads that appear on the network, said it settled 83 challenges in one year. "Ten years ago, you could have counted the number on one hand," says Richard Gitter, NBC's vice president of broadcast standards.

The weapons used in such battles are getting more sophisticated as well. To back assertions that competitors' advertising is misleading or

EXHIBIT 24–A

Texas Instruments uses comparative advertising to highlight its product advantages.

Courtesy McCann-Erickson/Houston.

inaccurate, companies are increasingly turning to elaborate scientific tests and consumer surveys. Competitive fervor between companies, combined with increased private litigation, promises to further complicate the legal environment for marketers ∎

Summary

Contemporary social and legal issues provide important guidelines for marketing management. The societal justification for marketing is to enhance the quality of life. The quality of life is affected by the way in which marketing relates to customers and other constituencies.

Gaps between societal standards and perceptions of marketing performance can raise consumerism and environmental issues. First, the advantages of the profit motive were shown. Then, consumerism was discussed—a social force from the environment that aids and protects consumers through the exertion of legal, moral, and economic pressure on business.

Corporate social progress is measured by means of a social audit, a systematic assessment of and report on company activities that have a social impact. Accountants and others continue to struggle with the issue of how to best devise a socioeconomic operating statement.

Marketing choices are often guided by ethical considerations. Ethics determine how the individual in the marketing organization distinguishes between right and wrong. Imperative ethics, adhering to universal rules of conduct, and situational ethics, in which circumstances dictate the propriety of an action, provide the polar extremes for making ethical decisions. Marketing managers usually blend the two viewpoints. A company should put its ethical philosophy into writing and communicate it to employees, set a good example at the top, establish incentives for good social as well as economic performance, and monitor for ethical problems as part of the control function.

Legal considerations also affect marketing. Management must be sufficiently aware of possible legal issues so as to know when to seek legal counsel. Pricing practices that may raise legal questions include price collusion, charging different customers different prices, and setting prices for distributors. Channel practices that may have legal ramifications include refusal to do business with another party, preventing a distributor from handling competitors' products, requiring customers to purchase unwanted products as a condition for obtaining desired products, and granting exclusive territories. Product-related legal issues arise concerning patents and trademarks, labeling, safety, and liability. Promotion decisions that are legally sensitive include false, deceptive, and unfair advertising; substantiation of advertising claims; and other deceptive advertising and personal selling practices. The Federal Trade Commission, Consumer Product Safety Commission, Food and Drug Administration, and other regulatory agencies play a critically important role in interpreting and enforcing the laws. The first half of the 1980s evidenced more conservative appointments to these bodies and, in general, less aggressive enforcement of existing laws and regulations. During this period, however, a Supreme Court decision overruled veto provisions established (and exercised) by Congress over administrative agencies. Thus, the 1980s are ending with a more conservative but more powerful role for regulatory bodies. With five justices of the Supreme Court over age 75, the winds of change may alter this body as well.

Exercises for Review and Discussion

1. Pickets are lining the street to protest your cereal company's use of plastic, nonbiodegradable packaging as environmentally irresponsible. Study the components of Exhibit 24–1, and identify for each a related possible explanation for the picketing and a possible solution.

2. Attention to the quality of life has increased greatly in the past few years. Interest has also grown in attempts to measure "consumer satisfaction." Although the marketing concept (Chapter 1) is two decades old, little need was seen until recently to go beyond the most general measures of satisfaction. This is a simple task on the surface, but limited analysis demonstrates its complexity. You are employed by a sporting goods company and charged with developing a set of measures for this purpose. Outline the major issues that you must face, make any necessary assumptions, and suggest possible measures.

3. Numerous social issues are encompassed under the consumerism umbrella. These include truthful advertising, product safety, unfair pricing methods, and personal selling tactics. Select

one such issue and analyze the pros and cons' for society and for management, of practices related to that issue (a limited library search would aid in the task).

4. Some ethical abuse in the marketing area has surfaced in the Mobil Oil Company. You are the CEO. How can you reduce the odds of such occurrences and adverse publicity in the future?

5. ABC Company manufactures small electrical appliances for a 10-state area. An employee in the quality control department informs her supervisor that uninsulated wire was inadvertently included in the assembly of several hundred hair dryers. The product case is plastic, and it is unlikely that users would suffer an electric shock if the hair dryer were in normal use. It is conceivable, however, that severe shock or even death could result if the wire slipped down to the inside of the metal switch plate. For this to happen, the product would probably have to be dropped or severely jolted several times.

High-level executives in the company are informed of this development at a hastily called meeting. You are present at this meeting as vice president of marketing for ABC. First, what is your considered opinion as to the appropriate action to take, if any? (Carefully detail potential legal violations as well as possible consequences.) Second, how would the actions taken differ if the case were evaluated from an ethical as opposed to a legal viewpoint?

6. XYZ Company has for years sold merchandise to CBA Retailing Company. CBA Retailing orders on a regular basis and continues to be one of XYZ Company's largest customers. Because of this relationship, CBA Retailing is given a special 7 percent discount. Exactly what would you need to know to determine whether this practice is legal?

7. A television advertisement for electric shavers includes a statement that the shaver is the "finest available." In fact, the manufacturer has no data to back this up. Is this misleading advertising? Why or why not? Should the practice be dropped?

8. Douglas-Myron, Inc., a small computer firm, is currently charging its corporate customers higher prices than it charges its wholesalers (who sell the same small computers through retailers for "hobby" use). The company has found competition in the hobby market to be extremely keen and growing. Competitors from Japan continue to lower their prices. Is the company nonetheless guilty of price discrimination? Explain.

9. Renee Parfum Company, a cosmetics firm, refused to continue to sell its products to Michele Department Stores in San Antonio because Renee Parfum Company has been given very poor display space in the stores in recent months. Can Renee Parfum Company do this under certain conditions? If so, what are the conditions?

10. Renee Parfum Company (see Exercise 9) is sending frequent notices to its retailers asking that they follow specific promotional policies and tactics. Is this legal? If so, under what conditions?

Notes

1. Adapted from Dan R. Dalton and Richard A. Cosier, "The Four Faces of Social Responsibility," *Business Horizons*, May–June 1982, p. 19. Copyright, 1982, by the Foundation for the School of Business at Indiana University. Reprinted by permission.

2. The reader would benefit from reviewing Chapter 3 as background for this chapter.

3. Angus Campbell, "Subjective Measures of Well-Being," *American Psychologist* 30 (February 1976), p. 118. See also David W. Cravens and Gerald E. Hills,

"Measurement Issues in Studying Marketing and the Quality of Life," in *Marketing and the Quality of Life*, ed. F. Reynolds and H. Barksdale (Chicago: American Marketing Association, 1978).

4. Peter House, Robert C. Livington, and Carol D. Swinburn, "Monitoring Mankind: The Search for Quality," *Behavior Science* 20 (January 1975), p. 58.

5. David A. Aaker and George S. Day, "A Guide to Consumerism," in *Consumerism: Search for the Consumer Interest*, ed. David A. Aaker and George S. Day (New York: Free Press, 1982), pp. 10–11.

6. David A. Aaker, "Developing Corporate Consumer Information Programs," *Business Horizons*, November 1981, p. 23.

7. Adapted from Lawrence Ingrassia, "Seeking to Aid Society, Control Data Takes On Many Novel Ventures," *The Wall Street Journal*, December 22, 1982, pp. 1, 10. Reprinted by permission of *The Wall Street Journal*, © Dow Jones & Company, Inc., 1982. All rights reserved.

8. Frederick D. Sturdivant, ed., *The Ghetto Marketplace* (New York: Free Press, 1969). See also Alan R. Andreason, ed., *Improving Inner-City Marketing* (Chicago: American Marketing Association, 1972); and Alan R. Andreason, *The Disadvantaged Consumer* (New York: Free Press, 1975).

9. Frederick D. Sturdivant, "Distribution in American Society: Some Questions of Efficiency and Relevance," in *Vertical Marketing Systems*, ed. Louis P. Bucklin (Glenview, Ill.: Scott, Foresman, 1970), pp. 94–115.

10. Fred I. Kent, "What Is Profit?" pp. 95–97. Reprinted with permission from the June 1961 *Reader's Digest*. Condensed from a publication of the New York State Economic Council. Copyright 1943, 1961, by The Reader's Digest Association, Inc.

11. Ibid., p. 97.

12. David W. Cravens and Gerald E. Hills, "Consumerism: A Perspective for Business," *Business Horizons*, August 1970, pp. 21–28.

13. Aaker and Day, "Guide to Consumerism," pp. 17–18; and Stephen Brobeck, "The Consumer Movement: An Assessment," in *At Home with Consumers* (Washington, D.C.: Direct Selling Foundation, 1984), p. 2.

14. Phillip T. Drotning, "Organizing the Company for Social Action," in *The Unstable Ground: Corporate Social Policy in a Dynamic Society*, ed. S. Prakash Sethi (Los Angeles: Melville, 1974), p. 259.

15. George Fisk, *Marketing and the Ecological Crisis* (New York: Harper & Row, 1974), pp. 1–19; and Karl E. Henion II, *Ecological Marketing* (Columbus, Ohio: Grid, 1976), pp. 19–30.

16. William G. Zikmund and William J. Stanton, "Recycling Solid Wastes: A Channels-of-Distribution Problem," *Journal of Marketing* 35 (July 1971), pp. 34–39.

17. Adapted from William M. Bulkeley, "After Costly Mistakes in '70's, Trash Processing Is Reviving," *The Wall Street Journal*, February 24, 1984, p. 25. Reprinted by permission of *The Wall Street Journal*, © Dow Jones & Company, Inc., 1984. All rights reserved.

18. Raymond A. Bauer and Dan H. Fenn, Jr., "What Is a Corporate Social Audit?" *Harvard Business Review*, January–February 1973, pp. 37–48.

19. Robert D. Hays and Edmund R. Gray, eds., *Business and Society* (Cincinnati: South-Western Publishing, 1981), pp. 384–85.

20. Paragraph based on Kenneth C. Schneider, "Marketing Research Industry Isn't Moving Toward Professionalism," *Marketing Educator* 3 (Winter 1984), p. 1, 6.

21. Franklin B. Krohn, "Four Difficult Ethical Problems and Ways for Professors to Overcome Them," *Marketing Educator*, Winter 1984, p. 3.

22. Ray O. Werner, "Marketing and the Supreme Court in Transition, 1982-1984," *Journal of Marketing* 49 (Summer 1985), p. 97.

23. For a discussion of this issue, see L. Louise Luchsinger and Patrick M. Dunne, "Fair Trade Laws— How Fair?" *Journal of Marketing* 42 (October 1978), pp. 50–53.

24. Robert E. Taylor, "Congress Objects as Administration Seeks Relaxing of 'Vertical Price-Fixing' Ban," *The Wall Street Journal*, May 16, 1983, p. 14.

25. Andy Pasztor, "Justice Department Guidelines Support Most Marketing Restrictions by Makers," *The Wall Street Journal*, January 24, 1985, p. 10.

26. Louis W. Stern and John R. Grabner, Jr., *Competition in the Marketplace* (Glenview, Ill.: Scott, Foresman, 1970), p. 135; also see Louis W. Stern and Thomas L. Eovaldi, *Legal Aspects of Marketing Strategy: Antitrust and Consumer Protection Issues* (Englewood Cliffs, N.J.: Prentice-Hall, 1984).

27. For an excellent analysis of the issues, see John F. Cady, "Reasonable Rules and Rules of Reason: Vertical Restrictions on Distributors," *Journal of Marketing* 46 (Summer 1982), pp. 27–37; also see Saul Sands and Robert J. Posch, Jr., "A Checklist of Questions for Firms Considering a Vertical Territorial Distribution Plan," *Journal of Marketing* 46 (Summer 1982), pp. 38–43.

28. Fred W. Morgan, "Marketing and Product Liability: A Review and Update," *Journal of Marketing* 46 (Summer 1982), pp. 64, 76.

29. Jeanne Saddler, "Bill Limiting Firms' Liability Gains in Senate," *The Wall Street Journal*, March 28, 1984, p. 2; and "U.S. Aims to Stem Tide of Product Liability Suits," *Chicago Tribune*, April 21, 1986, p. 9.

30. David M. Gardner, "Deception in Advertising: A Conceptual Approach," *Journal of Marketing* 39 (January 1975), pp. 40–46.

31. Dorothy Cohen, "Unfairness in Advertising Revisited," *Journal of Marketing* 46 (Winter 1982), p. 78.

32. Jeanne Saddler, "FTC's New Policy on Ads Triggering Protest in Congress," *The Wall Street Journal*, October 24, 1983, p. 31.

33. Robert E. Wilkes and James B. Wilcox, "Recent FTC Actions: Implications for the Advertising Strategist," *Journal of Marketing* 38 (January 1974), p. 56.

34. Dorothy Cohen, "Surrogate Indicators and Deception in Advertising," *Journal of Marketing* 36 (July 1972), pp. 10–15.

35. Abstracted from "FTC Adopts Two Rules to Speed Up Cases on Unfair Practices," *The Wall Street Journal*, February 21, 1975, p. 6. Reprinted by permission of *The Wall Street Journal*, © Dow Jones & Company, Inc., 1975. All rights reserved.

36. Laurence P. Feldman, *Consumer Protection: Problems and Prospects* (St. Paul, Minn: West Publishing, 1980), p. 49.

37. For related discussion, see Alice M. Tybout and Gerald Zaltman, "Ethics in Marketing Research: Their Practical Relevance," *Journal of Marketing Research* 38 (November 1974), p. 359.

38. Charles S. Mayer and Charles H. White, Jr., "The Law of Privacy and Marketing Research," *Journal of Marketing* 43 (April 1979), pp. 1–4.

39. Ibid., pp. 3–4.

40. Adapted from John Koten, "More Firms File Challenges to Rivals' Comparative Ads," *The Wall Street Journal*, January 12, 1984, p. 21. Reprinted by permission of *The Wall Street Journal* © Dow Jones & Company, Inc., 1984. All rights reserved.

Index

*This book has been set Linotron 202 in 10 and 9 point
Century Book, leaded 2 points. Part numbers are 33 and
34 Century Bold; chapter numbers are 16 point Century
Bold and chapter titles are 24 point Century Bold. The
size of the type area is 37 by 45 picas.*